PENGUIN BOOKS

THE COMPLETE GUIDE
TO AMERICAN FILM SCHOOLS

An Academy Award winner for *The Critic*, Ernest Pintoff is a former animator and film director in motion pictures and television. He is the author of a novel, *Zachary*, and of *Bolt from the Blue*, an autobiographical account. Pintoff is a professor of film at the University of Southern California, and lives in Hollywood with his wife, Caroline.

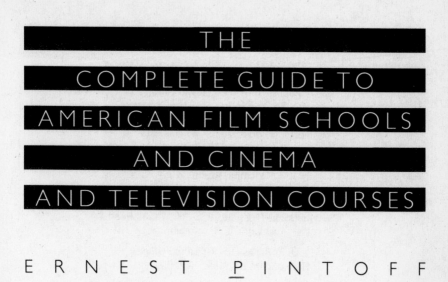

THE COMPLETE GUIDE TO AMERICAN FILM SCHOOLS AND CINEMA AND TELEVISION COURSES

ERNEST PINTOFF

PENGUIN BOOKS

PENGUIN BOOKS

Published by the Penguin Group
Penguin Books USA Inc., 375 Hudson Street,
New York, New York 10014, U.S.A.
Penguin Books Ltd, 27 Wrights Lane,
London W8 5TZ, England
Penguin Books Australia Ltd, Ringwood,
Victoria, Australia
Penguin Books Canada Ltd, 10 Alcorn Avenue,
Toronto, Ontario, Canada M4V 3B2
Penguin Books (N.Z.) Ltd, 182–190 Wairau Road,
Auckland 10, New Zealand

Penguin Books Ltd, Registered Offices:
Harmondsworth, Middlesex, England

First published in Penguin Books 1994

1   3   5   7   9   10   8   6   4   2

LIBRARY OF CONGRESS CATALOGING IN PUBLICATION DATA
Pintoff, Ernest.
The complete guide to American film schools and cinema and
television courses/ Ernest Pintoff.
p.   cm.
Includes indexes.
ISBN 0 14 01.7226 2
1. Motion pictures—Study and teaching—United States—
Directories.   2. Television broadcasting—Studying and teaching—
United States—Directories.   I. Title.
PN1993.8.U5P56   1994
778.5'071'173—dc20   93–30073

Printed in the United States of America
Set in Cheltenham Light
Designed by Katy Riegel

"The most important purpose of a film school should be to inspire. Whatever you learn there about the actual film-making is just a bonus."

—Milos Forman

CONTENTS

For all those seeking a career in cinema, television, or video, this guide provides a listing of programs offered throughout America, categorized by state. My intention with this book is to present the most complete reference source of such information.

Although I attended a liberal arts university, I majored in graphics and received a master's degree in art history. At the time, art was my passion. Now I wish I had pursued a broader liberal arts education, perhaps concentrating on literature. As you will glean from several of the articles interspersed throughout this book, the value of a broad-based background is shared by many filmmakers. Elia Kazan said: "A film director is better equipped if he's well-read. He should study the classics for construction, exposition of theme, the means of characterization, and for dramatic poetry."

My own hands-on introduction to film began as an apprentice animator at UPA in California. Then in 1963 I founded my own commercial studio in New York City and began producing ads as well as animated and live-action shorts. That led to an active period of directing numerous dramatic television films and a few theatrical movies. Since 1973 I have lectured and taught film directing and writing at the School of Visual Arts in New York, the USC School of Cinema and Television, UCLA Extension, and the American Film Institute. This book was written in the hope that the sum total of my professional experience will enable me to contribute to the needs of today's potential cinema and television students. To offer multiple perspectives, I have invited a number of former and current students to express their views. I have also solicited comments from film school graduates and from accomplished professionals who evaluate their scholastic experiences and present their own advice.

Choosing the right school for film or television studies is a challenge. Among other things, you will be evaluating each school's cost of tuition, location, size, academic opportunities, access to equipment, curriculum, general philosophy, and reputation. Depending on your goals, previous exposure, and available time and resources, you might consider practical alternatives such as seminars, workshops, and continuing-education programs. Institutions featuring seminars and workshops tend to offer a varied and changing curriculum, while continuing-education programs generally provide a more structured sequence of studies, often leading to a certificate in film or video.

As an undergraduate, by all means do not overlook the value of studying the humanities and social sciences. Absorbing technical and production knowledge should be only part of your education. Read and write as much as possible. Sensitivity to people and awareness of society is essential. A career in film or television can be extremely rewarding, both creatively and financially. Getting the right foundation is half the battle.

After you have completed your education, there are a number of ways to get started. There are no rules. You could write a screenplay or teleplay and submit it to an agent, producer, or bankable film or television performer. Studios and networks usually turn away unagented scripts, mainly to avoid litigation should they be developing a property along similar lines. Sometimes, however, a producer will consider an unsolicited piece, because the quest for good material is always paramount. Fortunately, paper is relatively inexpensive, so you can continue writing during your struggle to get established.

As for directing, a sample "director's reel" that shows your skill in handling film or videotape is basically what those in hiring positions look for. Another route to take would be to direct an original work and arrange for its distribution yourself. In any case, I recommend that all aspiring writers and directors learn about the business aspects of movies and television. To expect to be presented with a plush assignment, no matter how talented you are, is naive in the media arts. The competition is fierce—I can attest to that.

I wish to thank my colleagues as well as students and graduates whose remarks are quoted throughout this book. I also thank my agent, Jane Dystel, and Caroline White, my editor at Viking Penguin, both of whom encouraged and guided me. I am especially grateful to Patricia Capetola for her fine research and editing. Joseph Manduke, Ray Greene, and Kevin Gorman were also of valuable assistance, as was Oscar Dystel for his good ideas and advice. Finally, I want to thank my wife, Caroline Pintoff, for her support, affection, and numerous contributions.

Usually a renowned filmmaker might introduce a book such as this to readers. But in this case I asked Scott Browning, a former student, to write about his experience at film school. To me, Scott's attitude epitomizes the zeal with which most aspiring filmmakers approach their work.

FOREWORD

by Scott Browning

Since I am aware from personal experience that most film students want to become directors, the best knowledge I can share is that an effective director is first and foremost a good storyteller. And any good storyteller needs an understanding of the world around him: a broad exposure to different ideas, cultures, and modes of thought. However, many film schools—at least at the graduate level—are in fact "vocational schools." They teach technique, and, while important, technique without substance is hollow. That is why I believe you should first major in the humanities, such as history or literature, and then study film. Or you could choose an undergraduate program that blends production training with a strong liberal arts curriculum. Spending a bit of time working after completing your undergraduate degree and before going on to graduate school in film usually proves valuable as well, not just financially but in terms of life experiences.

Despite the often competitive atmosphere, do not set an agenda for yourself at film school: e.g., "I have to direct a great twenty-minute flick," or "I have to get out of here with a hot screenplay." This kind of thinking will paralyze you creatively. Instead, search out those projects and individuals that truly interest you. You'll be amazed to discover how chance and opportunity unfold. And when you do make your student films, inject them with something vital about yourself and your deepest passions. Forget about simply trying to make a slick feature. With a student crew and little money, it probably won't happen anyway. Better your work be technically flawed with originality than a pale imitation of big-budget Hollywood fare. Your audience will be able to tell the difference.

On the practical side, think about getting an internship or part-time job with a film company while in school. This could mean a real time crunch, but the contacts do pay off. Contacts are important in this field. In fact, probably the best thing about film school for me was the network of people with whom I have become friends, people whom I like and respect. Hopefully, most of them will be working in the industry someday. And they can be a great source of support—both morally and in more practical ways.

When considering film studies, you obviously should research schools you may wish to attend and that are most practical. Many new programs are springing up in specialized areas, while the older institutions offer a variety of emphases and philosophies. For example, some schools have an arts emphasis, and some are film industry oriented; others concentrate on television production, while some of the newest programs focus on the latest video technologies.

Some film programs (usually with origins in the humanities departments) and television programs (with origins in the social science departments) are now merging so their curriculums can be studied together. *The Complete Guide to American Film Schools* will help you sort out the information you need from this plethora of available programs, while providing a helpful reference source, whether you are considering undergraduate or graduate studies, general or intensive media programs. Use this book to help determine which program is right for you.

After you've pared down your list to a manageable selection of schools you are considering, be sure to send for each school's catalog as well as any supplemental information you can gather about particular programs. If at all possible, try to visit a prospective campus to get a general feel for the school and talk to faculty and students. Ask questions: for example, What are their alumni doing now? This will give you an idea about the kind of orientation the program has, and if it does in fact suit your goals.

While examining various programs, you may be heartened to find that some film and television departments allocate money for advanced student productions. But beware: In many such cases, only projects approved by committee get the nod. This may prove too restrictive for some people. Others may welcome the chance to make a student film without going into hock. It's also probably a good idea to find out what the school's policy is regarding the rights of the filmmaker: Does the school you're considering retain the rights to student productions, do such rights revert to the artist, or is there co-ownership of production projects?

As an aside, I realize it's tempting to concentrate on schools in Los Angeles or New York. Don't. There are plenty of programs between the coasts that deserve a serious look. And many of those schools offer a variety of summer internships both in New York and Los Angeles.

On a personal note, I received my B.A. in history from Northwestern University, then worked as a journalist on several metropolitan newspapers before enrolling in graduate film school. While earning my M.F.A. in cinema and television at USC, I did freelance story analysis for Dino De Laurentiis Productions. Since graduating, I have been employed there full-time. During my spare moments I'm either working on a screenplay or looking for the right opportunity to direct.

As a final word, sticking with your goals in this field will take perseverance. Filmmaking is not an occupation for the easily daunted. To me, it's been worth the struggles so far, because there's nothing else I'd rather be doing. If you feel the same way—and are willing to work hard, hard, hard—then film school is for you.

Each school entry that follows includes the name, address, and phone number of the institution and describes size, location, and academic calendar. In addition to indicating relevant degrees offered, information is provided concerning entrance requirements, curricular emphasis, facilities, and equipment. The alumni category, when given, lists some former students' areas of expertise in film, television, or both. This may help you determine the special interests and strengths of a particular department. The *Guide POV*—borrowed from the term "point of view," which refers to a director's choice of camera angle—provides a condensed overview of the program being examined and includes additional information about each school as well as its special offerings. The POV is designed to present a subjective analysis of each program based on research from departmental questionnaires, catalogs, student comments, and a variety of source materials.

Information for the Guide was compiled right up to publication. And while attempts were made to ensure that the information presented be current, it is inevitable that changes will have occurred. You should of course contact any schools you might be interested in for the most up-to-date information. Also, it is important to check application deadlines in order to complete the entire application process in time. If a school has a rolling admissions policy, you are encouraged to apply throughout the school year, as it may be possible to begin studies during the same academic year.

The "percent of acceptances" figure refers to the percentage of applicants admitted to the school in general and not to a specific program, unless otherwise indicated. This information is useful in order to help gauge your chances of admission, but such tallies may fluctuate.

To ensure fairness in the selection process, schools use a variety of criteria to screen applicants. An admissions department will rarely use an ACT or SAT score or grade-point average as an absolute measure. Such criteria are usually considered together with high school class standing, recommendations, and creative writing samples for a thorough evaluation of a student's potential. This process often allows admissions officers the latitude to extend offers to those individuals who otherwise might not have opportunities in higher education.

Finally, please note that although department chairs, deans, and/or heads are identified herein, it is recommended that general inquiries be directed to the department contact when listed.

THE
COMPLETE GUIDE TO
AMERICAN FILM SCHOOLS
AND CINEMA
AND TELEVISION COURSES

AUBURN UNIVERSITY

Auburn, AL 36849
(205)844–4000

State four-year comprehensive institution. Coed, small-town location. Undergraduate enrollment: 21,500. Graduate enrollment: 3,000.

DEPARTMENT OF COMMUNICATION

Chair/Contact: Dr. Margaret Fitch-Hauser, Chair
Calendar: Quarters
Degrees Offered: B.A., M.A.
Departmental Majors:
Undergraduate: 525 students. Graduate: 48 students
Entrance Requirements:
Undergraduate: ACT or SAT scores. Graduate: GRE scores; competitive undergraduate grade-point average; recommendations. Undergraduate and graduate application deadline: rolling. Percent of acceptances: Undergraduate: 89%. Graduate: 80%
Curricular Emphasis: Electronic media theory and culture; media writing; television production and programming; media law and management; additional media programs stress public relations; general communications
Special Activities: Film: international film series
Facilities: Television: studio; control room

Equipment: Television: ¾" studio and ½" location
Alumni: Lee Gaither, screenwriter; Macadore Lipscomb, broadcasting executive; M. Pritchett, TV promotional director

GUIDE POV: Auburn University offers communication studies as well as training in broadcast management and production; study abroad in five countries; selective entry; internship opportunities in television and radio production

SPRING HILL COLLEGE

4000 Dauphin St.,
Mobile, AL 36608
(205)460–2011

Private four-year comprehensive institution. Coed, suburban location. Undergraduate enrollment: 1,000. Graduate enrollment: 200.

COMMUNICATION ARTS DEPARTMENT

Chair/Contact: Thomas J. Loehr
Calendar: Semesters
Degrees Offered: B.A., communication arts (concentration in radio/TV/film)
Departmental Majors:
Undergraduate: 25–50 students
Entrance Requirements:
Undergraduate: 2.0 grade-point average; ACT or SAT scores;

recommendation from high school counselor. Undergraduate application deadline: August 15. Percent of acceptances: 80%

Curricular Emphasis: Historical and cultural foundations of mass communication; critical studies in film; media writing; television production; basic film production; media management; media law and ethics; mass communication theory and research

Special Activities: Television: program material produced for on-campus closed-circuit television

Facilities: Film: screening room; editing suite. Television: studio; audio bay; control room; editing suites

Equipment: Film: complete 16mm; Super-8 cameras; editing equipment; lighting; color film stock; projectors. Television/Video: complete ¾" studio; fixed and portable cameras

Alumni: Winn LeVert, film editor; Bob Monti, TV news director; Steve Gallien, TV news producer; Taylor Henry, TV news reporter

GUIDE POV: Founded in 1830 by a Jesuit bishop, this is the oldest four-year college in Alabama; program provides television production training with an emphasis on broadcast journalism; focus on ethics and society; basic course in single-camera film production; accelerated degree program; study abroad; media internship opportunities

Undergraduate enrollment: 4,000.
Graduate enrollment: 200.

HALL SCHOOL OF JOURNALISM

Chair/Contact: Merrill Bankester, Chair
Calendar: Quarters
Degrees Offered: B.A., B.S., broadcast journalism
Departmental Majors: Undergraduate television: 160 students
Entrance Requirements: Undergraduate: 2.0 grade-point average; minimum of 15 Carnegie units required; ACT or SAT scores required for students under 21 years of age; interview recommended. Undergraduate application deadline: rolling. Percent of acceptances: 70%
Curricular Emphasis: Broadcast television production; media writing
Special Activities: Television: program material produced for cable television; yearly journalism symposium
Facilities: Television: studio
Equipment: Television/Video: complete ¾" studio and location
Alumni: Tom Foreman, ABC/TV correspondent; Dale Owens, videographer

GUIDE POV: Students majoring in broadcast journalism at this state university receive hands-on training in broadcast techniques and news writing; required practice; study abroad in two countries; internship opportunities in television production

TROY STATE UNIVERSITY

Troy, AL 36082
(205)670-3100

State four-year comprehensive institution. Coed, rural location.

UNIVERSITY OF ALABAMA

Tuscaloosa, AL 35487-0152
(205)348-6010

State four-year comprehensive institution. Coed, rural location.

Undergraduate enrollment: 15,000.
Graduate enrollment: 3,000.

TELECOMMUNICATION AND FILM DEPARTMENT

Chair/Contact: Gary Copeland
Calendar: Semesters
Degrees Offered: B.A., M.A., communication (with emphasis in broadcasting or film); Ph.D., communication
Departmental Majors: Undergraduate: 400 students; Graduate: 15 students
Entrance Requirements: Undergraduate: 2.5 grade-point average; ACT or SAT scores; GED accepted; AP and CLEP credit accepted. Graduate: 3.0 grade-point average; transcripts; GRE or MAT scores. Undergraduate application deadline: April 15. Graduate application deadline: April 1. Percent of acceptances: 80%
Curricular Emphasis: Concentrations in film, broadcast production, broadcast news, management and policy, and new electronics technology
Special Activities: Film: film societies. Television: program material produced for cable television
Facilities: Film: screening room; editing suite. Television: two studios; audio bays; control rooms
Equipment: Film: complete Super-8 and 16mm. Television/Video: complete ½" studio and location
Alumni: Tom Cherones, NBC executive producer/director; Jon Petrovich, CNN executive vice-president; John Cochran, NBC-TV news correspondent; Chuck Gordon, film producer; Mel Allen, radio sports broadcaster

GUIDE POV: Students are offered concentrations in both film and television production; cross-registration with Stillman College; study abroad in Russia, Korea, and other countries; local and national media internships available

---

UNIVERSITY OF MONTEVALLO

Montevallo, AL 35115
(205)665–6000

State four-year comprehensive institution. Coed, rural location. Undergraduate enrollment: 2,400. Graduate enrollment: 300.

COMMUNICATION ARTS DEPARTMENT

Chair/Contact: Charles Harbour, Chair
Calendar: Semesters
Degrees Offered: B.A., B.S., communication arts
Departmental Majors: Undergraduate: 100 students
Entrance Requirements: Undergraduate: 2.4 grade-point average; ACT or SAT scores; interview; recommendations. Undergraduate application deadline: August 1. Percent of acceptances: 80%
Curricular Emphasis: News gathering and reporting; television production; computer graphics; special topics in film criticism and history; television documentary production; sports production; media management; mass communications law; copywriting for the electronic media
Special Activities: Television: program material, including weekly newscast, produced for cable television
Facilities: Television: studio; audio bay; control room; editing suites
Equipment: Television/Video:

complete 1" and ¾" studio; complete ¾" and ½" location
Alumni: Price Hicks, TV director/producer; Polly Holliday, TV/film actress

GUIDE POV: A comprehensive communications major featuring modern facilities and a large variety of broadcast course listings is available to students at this competitive public university; International Summer School provides study/travel opportunities; accelerated degree program; internship opportunities in television production

UNIVERSITY OF NORTH ALABAMA

Florence, AL 35632
(205)760–4100

State four-year comprehensive institution. Coed, urban location. Undergraduate enrollment: 5,600. Graduate enrollment: 200.

COMMUNICATIONS AND THEATRE DEPARTMENT

Chair/Contact: Dr. Eugene Balof
Calendar: Semesters
Degrees Offered: B.A., B.S.
Departmental Majors:
Undergraduate: 110 students
Entrance Requirements:
Undergraduate: high school diploma or GED; minimum ACT or SAT and high school rank standards; placement exams. Undergraduate application deadline: two weeks before registration
Curricular Emphasis: Film: history; Super-8 production. Television: program research; television criticism; regulation and management; broadcast production
Special Activities: Film: film and

video societies. Television: program material produced for cable television
Facilities: Film: screening room; editing suite; sound mixing room; sound stage; film library. Television: studio; audio bay; control room
Equipment: Film: complete Super-8. Television: complete ¾" studio and location; ½" (VHS) location; computer graphics
Alumni: Helen Howard Carroll, TV newsroom manager; Gus Hergert, TV newscaster

GUIDE POV: Offering electronic media production training as well as studies in management and criticism, this school provides practicum opportunities and summer study in Europe; newly redesigned facilities.

UNIVERSITY OF SOUTH ALABAMA

AD 182,
Mobile, AL 36688–0002
(205)460–6101

State four-year comprehensive institution. Coed, urban location. Undergraduate enrollment: 9,000. Graduate enrollment: 2,000.

DEPARTMENT OF COMMUNICATION

Chair/Contacts: Gerald L. Wilson, Acting Chair
Calendar: Quarters
Degrees Offered: B.A., B.S., communication (track in radio/TV/film)
Entrance Requirements:
Undergraduate: ACT required, with a minimum composite score of 16. Undergraduate application deadline: September 10. Percent of acceptances: 90%
Curricular Emphasis: The radio/TV/film track emphasizes television and

radio production; film studies; basic film production; writing for media; radio and television performance; broadcast news

Facilities/Equipment: Film: complete Super-8. Television/video: studio; location equipment

Alumni: Wendy Hogan, TV producer; Keith Tippitt, video executive

GUIDE POV: Students here may explore all aspects of mass communication with an emphasis on television production; film history, theory, and criticism; study-abroad program

The closest I came to film school was taking two extension courses: one in film editing and one in cinematography. The editing course was extremely valuable. It was very basic. As I recall, we were all assigned a scene from "Gunsmoke" and another piece of film about a student trying to park a car.

If you want to direct film, editing is probably the best teacher because you get a clear understanding of the dimension of cinema, the power of cuts.

I have lectured at USC, UCLA, NYU, Boston College, the AFI, and they all seemed formidable to me. My only concern for would-be filmmakers is when they go right to film school. More important, I would urge the study of art, literature, history, psychology, philosophy, maybe even cooking. It is vital that people in cinema have a humanistic background before they leap into film.

UNIVERSITY OF ALASKA— ANCHORAGE

3211 Providence Dr.,
Anchorage, AK 99508
(907)786–1800

State four-year comprehensive institution. Coed, urban location. Undergraduate enrollment: 15,000.

JOURNALISM AND PUBLIC COMMUNICATIONS DEPARTMENT

Chair/Contact: Linda Berg Smith, Associate Vice Chancellor of Student Services; Frank Schlehofer, Admissions Counselor
Calendar: Semesters
Degrees Offered: B.A., journalism and public communications (telecommunication/film option)
Departmental Majors: 100–200 students
Entrance Requirements: 2.5 grade-point average; ACT or SAT scores. Application deadline: April 1 for early admissions; July 1 for fall semester; November 1 for spring semester; April 1 for summer session. Percent of acceptances: 82%
Curricular Emphasis: Producing, writing, and directing for film and television; broadcast journalism production; film history; history of mass communications; audio production
Special Activities: Television: program material produced for on-campus closed-circuit television

Facilities: Television: studio; audio bay; control room
Equipment: Television/Video: complete ¾" studio and location
Alumni: J. D. Dolick, TV assistant producer; Patti Nathanson, TV newscaster

GUIDE POV: Students choosing the telecommunication and film option at this competitive state university receive comprehensive training in producing and writing for film and television; student-run television facilities; core curriculum emphasizes mass-media studies and broadcast journalism; study abroad in London; graduate creative-writing program; cross-registration through National Student Exchange Program; internship opportunities in television production

UNIVERSITY OF ALASKA— FAIRBANKS

Fairbanks, AK 99775
(907)474–7211

State four-year comprehensive institution. Coed, rural location. Undergraduate enrollment: 6,500. Graduate enrollment: 700.

DEPARTMENT OF JOURNALISM AND BROADCASTING

Chair/Contact: Television: Claudia Clark
Calendar: Semesters
Degrees Offered: B.A., broadcasting

Departmental Majors: Undergraduate television: 80 students

Entrance Requirements: Undergraduate: 2.0 grade-point average; 2.5 grade-point average in college preparation courses; ACT or SAT scores; AP and CLEP credit accepted. Undergraduate application deadline: August 1. Percent of acceptances: 84%

Curricular Emphasis: Electronic journalism; media management

Special Activities: Film: student publications. Television: program material produced for on-campus closed-circuit television and for public television

Facilities: Television: studio; audio bay; control room; editing suites; satellite telecommunications

Equipment: Television/Video: complete 1" and ¾" studio (campus public television facility); complete ¾" and ½" location

Alumni: Holly Zachman, TV producer; Ken Jernstrom, TV news reporter; Brent Butler, TV general manager

GUIDE POV: The University of Alaska at Fairbanks offers a small, well-equipped program emphasizing news and documentary video production; study abroad in eleven countries including Russia, England, France, Germany, and Italy; the university's College of Rural Alaska offers education programs to residents at rural sites via satellite telecommunications; internship opportunities in television production

My interest in show business began when I first saw Martin and Lewis in *The Caddy*. Since then I never wanted to do anything else. So after high school I went to New York in hopes of becoming an actor and playwright. As an actor I performed On, Off, and Off-Off Broadway, and in touring companies, summer stock, and films. For the past several years I have written numerous screenplays on speculation, most notably *Throw Momma from the Train*. I also wrote an Ace Award-winning sketch for Billy Crystal and Whoopi Goldberg, "Comic Relief."

Everything I have done in preparation for my present career has been invaluable: acting, waiting tables, everything. Although the only formal film class I ever took was an extension course in directing at UCLA, that, too, has proven to be productive and enlightening.

ARIZONA STATE UNIVERSITY

Tempe, AZ 85287–1305
(602)965–9011

*State four-year comprehensive
institution. Coed, suburban location.
Undergraduate enrollment: 32,000.
Graduate enrollment: 11,000.*

INTERDISCIPLINARY FILM STUDIES

Chair/Contact: Jay Boyer

WALTER CRONKITE SCHOOL OF JOURNALISM AND TELECOMMUNICATION

Chair/Contact: Frederic A. Leigh
Calendar: Semesters
Degrees Offered: Minor in film; B.A.,
journalism; B.A., broadcasting; M.A.,
mass communication
Departmental Majors: Undergraduate
television: 1,192 students. Graduate
television: 57 students
Entrance Requirements:
Undergraduate: 3.0 grade-point
average; competitive ACT or SAT
scores. Graduate: 3.0 grade-point
average; competitive GRE scores;
recommendations; written statement of
purpose. Undergraduate application
deadline: April 15 for fall admission;
November 15 for spring admission.
Graduate application deadline: April
15 for fall admission; October 15 for
spring admission. Percent of
acceptances: Undergraduate: 77%.
Graduate: 60%
Curricular Emphasis: Film minor:
criticism, history, and theory.
Journalism and Telecommunication:
broadcast news; electronic media
theory and culture; media writing;
television production; media
management
Special Activities: Television: wide
variety of program material produced
for KAET-TV, the university's public
television station
Facilities: Television: studio; audio
bay; control room
Equipment: Television/Video:
complete ¾" studio; complete ¾" and
½" location
Alumni: Mike Arnold, director, TV
network sports; Bill Redeker, TV
network news reporter; Al Michaels,
TV network sports reporter; Bob Petty,
TV news anchor

GUIDE POV: Arizona State University
offers varied course listings in film
criticism; the Cronkite School offers
competitive, comprehensive
undergraduate and graduate
production training with an emphasis
on broadcast news; study abroad;
internship opportunities in television
production

COCHISE COLLEGE

Douglas, AZ 85607
(602)364–7943

*State two-year institution. Coed, rural
location. Enrollment: 2,800.*

MEDIA COMMUNICATIONS PROGRAM

Chair/Contact: Janet Martinez Bernal
Calendar: Semesters
Degrees Offered: A.A., A.S., A.G.S., A.A.S., communications; certificate in media communications
Entrance Requirements: Open-door policy; high school diploma or equivalent; required placement testing. Application deadline: rolling
Curricular Emphasis: Critical studies in film; television production (instructional/industrial); video art; print media (desktop publishing)
Special Activities: Film: film series/ festivals; award-winning literary magazine. Television: program material produced for local public television station; career placement center
Facilities: Video studio
Equipment: Super-8 and 16 mm projectors; cameras; screens; video cameras
Alumni: Gabe Hoyos, scriptwriter

GUIDE POV: This growing program provides two-year communication studies; some equipment available for basic film and video production; transfer and certificate programs; internships available for academic credit

MESA COMMUNITY COLLEGE

1833 W. Southern Ave.,
Mesa, AZ 85202
(602)461–7000

District two-year institution. Coed, urban location. Enrollment: 18,700.

COMMUNICATIONS DEPARTMENT

Chair/Contact: Dr. Ron L. McIntyre
Calendar: Semesters
Degrees Offered: A.A., telecommunications

Departmental Majors: 40 students
Entrance Requirements: High school diploma or GED scores. Application deadline: rolling. Percent of acceptances: 100%
Curricular Emphasis: Broadcast journalism
Facilities: Television: studio; control room
Equipment: Television/Video: studio and complete ½" location
Alumni: Carl Helm, TV sports producer; Kurt Bailey, TV sports editor; Chris Pace, TV editor

GUIDE POV: This district community college provides hands-on training in announcing and broadcast journalism; good student-faculty ratio; attention to individual projects; transfer program; some media internships available

NORTHERN ARIZONA UNIVERSITY

Box 5619,
Flagstaff, AZ 86011–5619
(602)523–9011

State four-year comprehensive institution. Coed, urban location. Undergraduate enrollment: 13,000. Graduate enrollment: 2,000.

SCHOOL OF COMMUNICATION

Chair/Contact: Dr. Tony Parker, Chair
Calendar: Semesters
Degrees Offered: B.A., B.S., communication
Departmental Majors: Undergraduate radio-TV: 275 students
Entrance Requirements: Undergraduate: 2.25 grade-point average; ACT or SAT scores; required composite SAT scores are 930 for residents and 1010 for nonresidents; required composite ACT scores are 21 for residents and 23 for nonresidents.

Undergraduate application deadline: rolling. Percent of acceptances: 60%
Curricular Emphasis: Broadcast journalism, management
Special Activities: Television: program material produced for on-campus closed-circuit television and for student-run cable television
Facilities: Television: studio; audio bay; control room; A/B roll editing suite
Equipment: Film: various cameras, projectors, and editors. Television/Video: complete ¾" studio; complete ¾" and ½" location
Alumni: Heidi Foglesong, TV news anchor; Cynthia Santana, TV news producer; Jerre Parkhurst, TV research associate

GUIDE POV: Broadcast journalism, management, and production courses are offered to students seeking practical training for careers in television; intensive film production class offered during summer; cross-registration with many schools through the Western Interstate Commission for Higher Education and the National Student Exchange; study abroad in Mexico, England, Germany, China, and Japan; internship opportunities in television production

---

UNIVERSITY OF ARIZONA

Tucson, AZ 85723
(602)621–2211

State four-year comprehensive institution. Coed, urban location. Undergraduate enrollment: 26,000. Graduate enrollment: 7,500.

MEDIA ARTS DEPARTMENT

Chair/Contact: Dr. Caren J. Deming, Chair

Calendar: Semesters
Degrees Offered: B.A., B.F.A., M.A.
Departmental Majors: Media arts: 300 students in B.A. program; 500 students in B.F.A. program; 18 students in M.A. program
Entrance Requirements:
Undergraduate residents: 1000 SAT or 22 ACT score; 2.5 GPA or upper 50% of high school class. Undergraduate nonresidents: 1010 SAT or 24 ACT score; 3.0 grade-point average or upper 25% of high school class. Graduate: 3.0 grade-point average; transcripts; two-page essay; writing sample from undergraduate course; three letters of recommendation. Undergraduate and graduate application deadline: April 1
Curricular Emphasis: Film: theory and history; 16mm production. Television/Video: electronic media theory and culture; studio and field production; media management
Special Activities: Film: film series/festivals. Television: news production for local cable origination channel; management training
Facilities: Film: Super-8 and 16mm editing; audio facilities. Television: studio; audio studio; control room
Equipment: Film: Super-8 and 16mm cameras and editing. Television/Video: complete ¾" studio and location
Alumni: Gilbert Grant, screenwriter; Kevin Inch, TV producer; Jeff Benson, casting director

GUIDE POV: Critical and management studies as well as production training in film and video are offered through this selective Media Arts program; diverse course listings; study abroad; undergraduate internship program

First, let me say that I do not feel that a formal film education is a requirement for aspiring professionals. On the other hand, I went to NYU Graduate Film School and found it to be very helpful. I think the best way to learn to become a director is through hands-on experience, and film school gave me the opportunity to make several short films. It also provided me with access to the equipment I needed, a crew made up of fellow classmates, and teachers who could critique my work. In essence, film school gave me a structure and an atmosphere that was conducive to making films. The first low-budget "professional" feature film that I directed, *Smithereens*, was a natural outgrowth of my film school experience, since many of the crew members were my former classmates. And it was because of the success of that movie that I got the opportunity to direct *Desperately Seeking Susan*.

I believe the biggest problem with student films is that the director tries to do too much. The students often write, direct, produce, and edit their own films. This makes for a great learning experience but not always a great film. Many student films are well directed but not well written—or a film may contain a good story idea that is not well executed. It is important for a director to know his or her strengths and limitations. If you are potentially a good director but not a good writer, then collaborate with someone who is. It only helps your film to work with people you trust, who also have a critical eye. No one can be great at everything. Directing is a big job.

ARKANSAS STATE UNIVERSITY

P.O. Drawer 2160
State University, AR 72467
(501)972-2100

*State four-year comprehensive
institution. Coed, rural location.
Undergraduate enrollment: 9,500.
Graduate enrollment: 1,000.*

DEPARTMENT OF RADIO-TELEVISION

Chair/Contact: Richard Carvell, Chair
Calendar: Semesters
Degrees Offered: B.S., radio-
television; M.S.M.C., radio-television
Departmental Majors:
Undergraduate: 250 students. Graduate:
15 students
Entrance Requirements:
Undergraduate: 2.0 grade-point
average; ACT scores. Graduate: 3.0
grade-point average on last 60 hours or
2.75 overall; recommendations.
Undergraduate and graduate
application deadline: rolling
Curricular Emphasis: News
production; media management; sales;
cable television; corporate video;
telecommunications research
Special Activities: Television:
program material produced for city
cable television system, as well as for
local public and commercial television
stations; vocational placement service;
telecommunications research; AERho
and WICI chapters

Facilities: Television: studios; audio
bays; control rooms
Equipment: Television/Video: two
complete ¾" studios and ¾" location
including Sony ENG video edit suites;
½", ¾", and 2" videotape equipment;
chromakey capability; special effects
and other graphics potential; KASU
public radio located on campus
features compact disc technology and
satellite down-linking capability
Alumni: Roger Bumpass, screenwriter;
Ken Simington, TV producer/director;
Gary Jones, TV/film producer; Barbara
Nellis, electronic graphics editor; Mike
Roy, TV producer

GUIDE POV: Students who choose the
Radio-Television major at this well-
equipped state university will gather
hands-on experience producing a
variety of telecasts, news videos, and
radio programs; faculty of recognized
professionals and scholars; core theory
courses prepare students for graduate
work; summer media internship
opportunities

HARDING UNIVERSITY

Searcy, AR 72143
(501)279-4000

*Private four-year comprehensive
institution. Coed, small town location.
Undergraduate enrollment: 4,000.*

DEPARTMENT OF COMMUNICATION

Chair/Contact: Dr. John H. Ryan, Chair
Calendar: Semesters
Degrees Offered: B.A., mass communication (students may select emphasis in broadcast journalism)
Departmental Majors: Radio and television: 83 students
Entrance Requirements: Minimum *B* high school grade point average; minimum 19 on ACT or 780 on SAT; interview highly recommended; AP and CLEP credits accepted. Application deadline: November 30. Percent of acceptances: 64%
Curricular Emphasis: Electronic media theory and culture; news and documentary production; media management; corporate video; sports journalism
Special Activities: Television/Radio: Cable Channel 19 located on campus is a training laboratory for students enrolled in television courses; student-operated radio station KHCA provides variety of programming.
Facilities: Television/Radio: studio; audio bay; control room; two video-editing suites; computer graphics lab; Video Toaster; radio station and production facilities
Equipment: Television/Video: complete ¾" studio and location including S-VHS editing and camcorders
Alumni: Greg Hurst, TV news anchor; Lorie Johnson, TV news reporter; Michael Murrie, media teacher

GUIDE POV: Harding University offers complete training in broadcast production, writing, management, and sales; emphasis on news journalism as well as modern media technologies; selective admissions; study abroad at Harding campus in Florence, Italy; honors program; media internships available

OUACHITA BAPTIST UNIVERSITY

410 Ouachita,
Arkadelphia, AR 71998–0001
(501)245–5000

Private four-year comprehensive institution. Coed, rural location. Undergraduate enrollment: 1,400.

COMMUNICATIONS DEPARTMENT

Chair/Contact: Dr. William D. Downs, Chair
Calendar: Semesters
Degrees Offered: B.A., B.S.E.
Departmental Majors: 100 students
Entrance Requirements: 2.0 grade-point average; transcripts; minimum enhanced ACT score of 19. Application deadline: rolling. Percent of acceptances: 80%
Curricular Emphasis: Communications theory; video production; video art; broadcast journalism; motion picture production course; print journalism; photography
Special Activities: Television: program material produced for cable television yearbook; newspaper
Facilities: Television: studio; audio bay; control room
Equipment: Television/Video: complete ¾" studio and ½" location
Alumni: Kevin Story, TV cameraman; Melinda Dunston, TV news anchor; Darrel Potts, media designer

GUIDE POV: This Baptist university offers courses in both print journalism and video technology with an emphasis on broadcast television production; international study program; media internships available

UNIVERSITY OF ARKANSAS— FAYETTEVILLE

Fayetteville, AR 72701
(501)575–2000

State four-year comprehensive institution. Coed, rural location. Undergraduate enrollment: 14,000.

DEPARTMENT OF COMMUNICATION

Chair/Contact: Jimmie N. Rogers, Chair
Calendar: Semesters
Degrees Offered: B.A., M.A., communication (students may select emphasis in mass communication)
Departmental Majors:
Undergraduate: 200 students. Graduate: 50 students
Entrance Requirements:
Undergraduate: 2.5 grade-point average; 20 enhanced ACT score or 780 SAT score. Undergraduate application deadline: August 15 for fall admission; January 1 for spring admission. Percent of acceptances: 95%
Curricular Emphasis:
Communication theory; critical studies; media writing; broadcast production
Special Activities: Television: program material produced for cable television
Facilities: Television: studio
Equipment: Television/Video: complete ½" location
Alumni: Daniel Boyd, filmmaker; Ken Teutsch, TV producer; Steve Gilliland, set designer; Steve Voorhies, TV news reporter

GUIDE POV: The University of Arkansas at Fayetteville serves as the primary land-grant campus in the state; communication program emphasizes media theory and research methodology with basic production training; extensive study abroad programs in Costa Rica, Italy, Japan, and other countries; internship opportunities in television production

UNIVERSITY OF ARKANSAS— LITTLE ROCK

2801 S. University,
Little Rock, AR 72204
(501)569–3000

State four-year comprehensive institution. Coed, urban location. Undergraduate enrollment: 10,141. Graduate enrollment: 1,500.

RADIO/TELEVISION/FILM DEPARTMENT

Chair/Contact: Dr. Lynn E. Wilson
Calendar: Semesters
Degrees Offered: B.A., Radio-TV-Film
Departmental Majors:
Undergraduate: 150 students
Entrance Requirements:
Undergraduate: 2.5 grade-point average; composite scores of 19 ACT or 750 SAT. Undergraduate application deadline: August 1. Percent of acceptances: 95%
Curricular Emphasis: Radio and television production; film history and criticism; communication theory; television performance; broadcast journalism; media sales, programming, and management
Special Activities: Television/Radio: program material produced for Cable TV Channel 29, the University Access Channel; radio news programs produced for public radio station KUAR
Facilities: Television: studio; audio bay; control room

Equipment: Television/Video: complete ¾" studio and location; S-VHS cameras and editing; audio and performance labs; radio/TV newsroom
Alumni: John LaRue, TV director; Sandy Finkbeiner, TV news reporter/ producer; Ben Fry, TV news information director

GUIDE POV: Designed to prepare students for graduate studies as well as entry-level positions in tele-communications, this professional program has a special broadcast news track; summer study in France, Spain, and Austria available; internship opportunities in all electronic media-related fields

Special Activities: Film: film series. Television: program material produced for local cable television
Facilities: Film: screening room. Television/Video: studio; video editing suites
Equipment: Television/Video: complete ½" location
Alumni: Reginald Hamleth, TV producer; Stephanie Calhoun, radio personality

GUIDE POV: This campus of the University of Arkansas system offers comprehensive training in television production with an emphasis on news journalism; study abroad; internship opportunities in television production

UNIVERSITY OF ARKANSAS —PINE BLUFF

University Ave., Pine Bluff, AR 71601 (501)543–8000

State four-year comprehensive institution. Coed, small town location. Undergraduate enrollment: 3,500.

SPEECH AND DRAMATIC ARTS DEPARTMENT

Chair/Contact: King D. Godwin, Chair
Calendar: Semesters
Degrees Offered: B.A., journalism
Departmental Majors: Undergraduate television: 50 students
Entrance Requirements: Undergraduate: 2.0 grade-point average; ACT or SAT scores; the ACT, with a minimum composite score of 15, is preferred. Undergraduate application deadline: rolling. Percent of acceptances: 96%
Curricular Emphasis: Media writing; television production; media management

UNIVERSITY OF CENTRAL ARKANSAS

Conway, AR 72035 (501)450–3128

State four-year comprehensive institution. Coed, small town location. Undergraduate enrollment: 7,500. Graduate enrollment: 1,000.

DEPARTMENT OF ENGLISH

Chair/Contact: Dr. Robert Willenbrink, Chair
Calendar: Semesters
Degrees Offered: B.A., journalism (emphasis in mass communication)
Departmental Majors: Undergraduate radio and television: 125 students
Entrance Requirements: Undergraduate: ACT or SAT scores; for unconditional admission, a minimum GPA of 2.5 and an ACT score of 19 are necessary; GED is accepted; AP and CLEP credits accepted. Undergraduate application deadline: rolling. Percent of acceptances: 87%

Curricular Emphasis: Broadcast history; writing continuity news and dramatic material for television and radio; television production; radio production; broadcast announcing; broadcast management; broadcasting and the law

Special Activities: Television: program material produced for on-campus closed-circuit Channel 6 TV. Radio: student-operated KUCA-FM

Facilities: Film: screening room. Television/Video: studio; audio bay; control room; video-editing suites

Equipment: Television/Video: complete ¾" studio and location

Alumni: Lucy Himstedt, TV news producer; Tom Bonner, TV meteorologist/executive; Steve Barnes, TV news anchor

GUIDE POV: This large public university offers comprehensive studies in broadcast production; hands-on experience; emphasis on dramatic writing as well as news and sports journalism; study abroad; media internships available

EDWARD DMYTRYK, TEACHER, WRITER

The somewhat unusual circumstances of my life and career permit me to discuss film education only from a teacher's point of view. I have never been a film student in the narrow sense of the term. I invaded the academic field rather later in life because, as far as I know, there were no film schools in 1923. And that requires a brief explanation.

The year I started working as a messenger boy at Famous Players Lasky, which, as we both grew older, became Paramount Pictures, was 1923. At the age of fourteen, I had left home and was working my way through high school. By the summer of that year, I had wormed my way into the projection rooms, and after school on weekdays, on weekends, and full-time through the summer holidays, I was a studio projectionist.

Despite several years of acclimation, I had no intention of making film my career. I was a mathematician, and a scholarship allowed me to enroll at Cal-Tech, where I planned to major in mathematical physics. But I continued working at Paramount on weekends and holidays, and by the end of my first year decided to make motion pictures my life's work. What changed my mind was a perception that the directors, producers, actors, et al. whom I had met as a projectionist were much more interesting than those people I had associated with outside the studio environment. The imminent arrival of *sound* may have been another incentive.

From June 1927 I worked full-time in the projection booths, but when *talkies* became a part of the film scene, I negotiated a transfer to the editorial department. Within a few months I became a full-time film editor (there was no union to monitor my advancement). After ten years of editing for directors like Leo McCarey and George Cukor, I was asked to take over the direction of a B picture. From 1939 to my semi-retirement in 1978 I directed (and occasionally produced) 57 features, 17 of which were Bs, the rest As.

In addition to writing six technical books on film, my directing credits include: *Hitler's Children; Murder, My Sweet; Till the End of Time; Crossfire; Christ in Concrete; The Caine Mutiny; Broken Lance; The End of the Affair; Raintree County; The Young Lions; Warlock; A Walk on the Wild Side; The Carpet Baggers;* and *Mirage.*

In 1978, I started teaching, first at the University of Texas at Austin. Then in 1981 I came to USC, where I am still teaching a full schedule.

It may seem odd that I was not *hooked* on films during my first four years at the studio, or that when I finally chose filmmaking as a career, I had no *vision*, no dream, no real idea of exactly what I wanted to do. I had only a highly competitive nature, a desire to excel at anything I did, and an unusual but well-rounded education. I was an autodidact, with a catholic interest in the human condition.

Although I became a director by accident, I realized long ago that I had the best possible preparation for the job—internship with great directors. The only thing in question was the presence of the special talent required, and there was no way to test that except in the fire. It follows naturally that I consider apprenticeship the best way to learn not only the fundamentals but especially the esoterica of any art. Today, of course, such opportunities are rare if they exist at all. So with no *air-lock* to monitor their passage, thousands of aspiring young visionaries matriculate at hundreds of colleges and universities to learn all there is to know about filmmaking—except those intangible things a good filmmaker must know.

I sometimes mystify my students by admitting I don't know how to load a camera or set a light. I never had to do either of those things. Skilled experts in those fields did them for me. Technique and mechanical expertise are not the secrets of good filmmaking, but a proper education is. A number of men and women, more interested in education than I, have said that few of today's university students are truly educated. Of college students, Norman Cousins wrote, "They are beautifully skilled but intellectually underdeveloped. They know everything there is to know about the functional requirements of their trade but little about the human situation that serves as the context for their work." And the great ballet artist Baryshnikov said, "We are a lost generation, a lot of people who are aggressive and virtuosic but who have little inside." Very few of those whose hearts are set on the movies recognize that creative filmmaking requires the study of many disciplines that have nothing to do with films directly. These disciplines concern human belief, human history, human behavior, human character, and human intercommunication. In short, all aspects of human nature. And none of these has anything to do with the mechanics of filmmaking.

Of course, the more skillful the techniques the better the presentation, and these are well taught at most film schools. But if such skills were indispensable, some of our greatest filmmakers would never have been allowed to expose a foot of film. And if the characters and the contexts of their work had been shallow, all the techniques available would not have made their films live. Only a deep understanding of life could do that, and it seems a mere handful of students seek the real sources of such understanding.

The student must realize that although he can learn the basic techniques of filmmaking in a few months, he cannot learn all he should know about the characters who inhabit his films and the problems that beset them in a hundred years. But by God, he should try.

ALLAN HANCOCK COLLEGE

800 S. College,
Santa Maria, CA 93454
(805)922–6966

*District/state two-year institution. Coed,
suburban location. Undergraduate
enrollment: 3,000.*

FINE ARTS DEPARTMENT

Chair/Contact: Casey Case
Calendar: Semesters
Degrees Offered: A.S., applied
design/media; certificate in video
production
Departmental Majors: Approximately
20 students are production majors.
Entrance Requirements: Open-door
policy with placement testing.
Undergraduate application deadline:
rolling
Curricular Emphasis: Hands-on
television/video production
Special Activities: Students write,
produce, direct, and crew four 30-
minute dramas for KCOY-TV, local CBS
affiliate
Facilities: Film: lecture hall with
16mm projection; sound mixing room;
screening room; editing room;
animation stand; film library; lighting
studio. Television/Video: S-VHS/VHS
and laser disc projection; production
classroom and postproduction editing
facilities
Equipment: Film: complete Super-8.
Television: complete VHS/S-VHS

location and editing; ¾" video
animation
Alumni: R. Timothy Kring,
screenwriter; Phillip Norwood,
designer/storyboard artist; Winnifred
Hervey, TV executive producer

GUIDE POV: A two-year film and
television production program is
offered at Allan Hancock College;
transfer program; media internships
available

THE AMERICAN FILM INSTITUTE

2021 N. Western Ave.,
Los Angeles, CA 90027
(213)856–7600

*Private two-year graduate institution.
Coed, urban location. Graduate
enrollment: 196.*

CENTER FOR ADVANCED FILM AND TELEVISION STUDIES

Chair/Contact: Admissions office
Calendar: Enrollment is for the entire
academic year
Degrees Offered: M.F.A.; advanced
certificates
Departmental Majors: Graduate
film and television: 28 directing; 28
producing; 28 screenwriting; 28
cinematography; 14 editing; 12
production design
Entrance Requirements: Graduate:
transcripts; creative portfolio;
summarization of prior filmmaking

experience; personal essay. Graduate application deadline: February 1. Percent of acceptances: 20%
Curricular Emphasis: Advanced courses in film and video producing, directing, editing, cinematography, screenwriting, and production design
Special Activities: Film: film series/ festivals; visiting lecturers. Television: American Video Conference; National Video Festival
Facilities: Film: 35mm, 16mm, and video-screening rooms; 16mm editing suites; sound stage; film library; film research library. Television/Video: editing rooms
Equipment: Film: complete 16mm. Television/Video: ¾" VTR; portable lighting packages; ¾" cassette recorders; portable cameras; monitors; sound recording and editing equipment; audio mixers
Alumni: David Lynch, film/TV director/writer/producer; Terrence Malick, film director; Jeremy Paul Kagan, TV/film director; Paul Schrader, screenwriter/film director; Amy Heckerling, film director; Tim Hunter, film director; Caleb Deschanel, cinematographer; Tom Rickman, film director/screenwriter; Ed Zwick, film/ TV writer/director/producer; Jonathan Avnet, film/TV producer; Marty Brest, film director

GUIDE POV: This highly professional, selective conservatory-style school offers a one-year structured curriculum providing advanced training to Fellows who have chosen an area of specialization; second-year Fellows are chosen from first-year class; extensive internship opportunities in film and television production

ART CENTER COLLEGE OF DESIGN

1700 Lida St.,
Pasadena, CA 91103
(818)584–5000

Private four-year comprehensive arts institution. Coed, urban location. Undergraduate enrollment: 1,200. Graduate enrollment: 25.

FILM DEPARTMENT

Chair/Contact: Film: Bob Petersen, Chair
Calendar: Trimesters
Degrees Offered: B.F.A., film
Departmental Majors: Undergraduate film: 50 students
Entrance Requirements: Undergraduate: 2.5 grade-point average; ACT or SAT scores; official transcripts; portfolio required; interview recommended. Undergraduate application deadline: March 1. Percent of acceptances: 60%
Curricular Emphasis: Film and video production with courses in cinematography, lighting, production design, directing, editing, and writing; all forms explored, including documentary, television, commercials, music videos, industrials, sales films, cel and computer animation, and feature films
Special Activities: Los Angeles film and television industry offers sponsored assignments; vocational placement service
Facilities: Film: 35mm screening facilities; screening room; editing suite; sound mixing room; animation stand; permanent film library
Equipment: Film: complete Super-8 and 16mm; 35mm editing equipment. Television/Video: ¾" VTR; portable lighting packages; ½" and ¾" cassette recorders; portable cameras; monitors;

sound recording equipment; audio mixers; ¾" editing
Alumni: Irvin Kershner, film director; Ron Osborn, film/TV writer; Doug Claybourne, film producer; Ralph McQuarrie, special effects artist; Steven Poster, cinematographer

GUIDE POV: Students attending the Art Center are offered a well-equipped, professional program in film/video with training in narrative, experimental, and animated forms; many entering students have transferred from another college; graduates are placed in production, writing, and conceptual design areas of film/video industry; faculty of practicing artists and designers; Art Center affiliate campus in La-Tour-de-Peilz, Switzerland; extensive Los Angeles internship opportunities in film and television production

BIOLA UNIVERSITY

13800 Biola Ave.,
La Mirada, CA 90639
(310)930–6000

Private four-year interdenominational Christian college. Coed, suburban location. Undergraduate enrollment: 1,800. Graduate enrollment: 700.

COMMUNICATIONS DEPARTMENT

Chair/Contact: Dr. Tom Nash
Calendar: Semesters
Degrees Offered: B.A., communication
Departmental Majors: Undergraduate film: 20 students. Undergraduate television: 30 students
Entrance Requirements: Undergraduate: 2.7 grade-point average; ACT or SAT scores.

Undergraduate deadline: rolling.
Percent of acceptances: 60%
Curricular Emphasis: Four-course sequence in film production; comprehensive television and radio production
Special Activities: Film: production of dramatic motion pictures for religious market
Facilities: Film: sound studio including 8-track recorder. Television: studio; system including S-VHS and U-Matic time code, A/B rolls editing; portable cameras
Equipment: Film: complete 16mm film production setup including Cinema Products GSMO; Arri BL; Moviola flatbed
Alumni: Duncan Dodds, film producer/director; Bob Vernon, film producer/director

GUIDE POV: Located near Hollywood, Biola University offers a small, selective program with hands-on film and video production training; material produced for religious markets; study abroad in Israel and Central America; media internship opportunities

BROOKS INSTITUTE OF PHOTOGRAPHY

801 Alston Rd.,
Santa Barbara, CA 93108
(805)966–3888

Private three-year professional institution. Coed, suburban location. Undergraduate enrollment: 500.

MOTION PICTURE/VIDEO DEPARTMENT

Chair/Contact: Shirley Conley, Director of Admissions
Calendar: Six 7-week sessions per year

Degrees Offered: B.A., M.S., film/video

Departmental Majors:
Undergraduate: 100 students

Entrance Requirements:
Undergraduate: high school and college transcripts; written statement of purpose; 15 semester college credits in general education.
Undergraduate application deadline: rolling

Curricular Emphasis: Film and video production; technical emphases include proposals, scripting, editing, and budgeting

Special Activities: Film: annual international film festival

Facilities: Film: two shooting stages with full lighting and grip equipment; 35mm screening facilities; screening room; editing suite; sound mixing room; animation stand. Television: studio; audio bay; control room; Bates computer editing

Equipment: Film: complete 16mm including flatbed and moviola editing. Television/Video: complete ½" location; VHS offline and Betacam on-line editing

Alumni: Isidore Mankofsky, cinematographer; Mark Stouffer, film producer/director; Dominic Palmieri, cinematographer

GUIDE POV: Students attending this professional arts institute concentrate on developing technical and creative production skills in both film and video; media internships available

---

BUTTE COMMUNITY COLLEGE

3536 Butte Campus Dr.,
Oroville, CA 95956
(916)895–2511

Two-year comprehensive institution. Coed, rural location. Undergraduate enrollment: 9,300.

COMMUNICATION ARTS AND TECHNOLOGY PROGRAM

Chair/Contact: Mark Hall

Calendar: Semesters

Degrees Offered: A.S., communication arts and technology; certificates of achievement in video technology; sports video production; TV computer graphics; video production; remote video production; media sales and management; desktop video production; videography/editing; master control operations

Departmental Majors: Undergraduate television: 250 students

Entrance Requirements:
Undergraduate: open-door policy; high school diploma or GED.
Undergraduate application deadline: August 20

Curricular Emphasis: Television production; television computer graphic design; corporate/agricultural advertising; television sports production; broadcast sales and management; media performance

Special Activities: Television: program material produced for community access cable television and college cable station

Facilities: Television: studio; audio bay; control room; five-camera remote van

Equipment: Television/Video: complete ¾" studio and ½" location; six ½" VHS editors; 15 computer graphics systems

Alumni: Luchia Hansen, TV news director; Millicent Hernandez, TV news producer; Tim Steffens, camera operator; Carl Galagher, videographer

GUIDE POV: For students seeking hands-on video and audio production training, this community college provides a diversified program with modern equipment; transfer program or variety of certificate options available; emphasis on new technologies; internship opportunities in television/video production

CALIFORNIA COLLEGE OF ARTS AND CRAFTS

5212 Broadway, Oakland, CA 94618–1487 (510)653–8118

Private four-year professional arts college. Coed, urban location. Undergraduate enrollment: 1,100. Graduate enrollment: 70.

FILM/VIDEO/PERFORMANCE DEPARTMENT

Chair/Contact: Jeanne C. Finley
Calendar: Semesters
Degrees Offered: B.A., M.F.A., fine arts
Departmental Majors: Undergraduate: 40 students. Graduate: 10 students
Entrance Requirements: Undergraduate: portfolio; personal essay; high school/college transcripts; recommendations. Graduate: film reel/videotape; transcripts; essay; recommendations. Undergraduate and graduate application deadline: rolling. Percent of acceptances: Undergraduate: 67%. Graduate: 18%
Curricular Emphasis: Fine arts curriculum emphasizing independent production and experimental media
Special Activities: Film: film series/festival; film society. Television: program material produced for cable television

Equipment: 16mm film production and postproduction; HI-8 and ¾" video production and postproduction
Alumni: Phil Elie, TV/film producer/director

GUIDE POV: This highly selective arts college places strong emphasis on independent film and video projects; cross-registration with Mills College and Holy Names College; media internships available

CALIFORNIA INSTITUTE OF THE ARTS

24700 McBean Pkwy., Valencia, CA 91355 (805)255–1050

Private four-year comprehensive arts institution. Coed, suburban location. Undergraduate enrollment: 670. Graduate enrollment: 300.

SCHOOL OF FILM/VIDEO

Chair/Contact: Larry Coleman, Film/Video Counselor
Calendar: Semesters
Degrees Offered: B.F.A., M.F.A.
Departmental Majors: Undergraduate live action 29; experimental animation 23; character animation 159; Interschool (includes directing for theatre and cinema) 3 students. Graduate live action 50; experimental animation 40; interschool 27 students
Entrance Requirements: Undergraduate: portfolio; written statement of purpose. Graduate: B.F.A. degree; written statement of purpose; portfolio; production credits. Undergraduate application deadline: February 1. Graduate application deadline: February 1. Percent of acceptances: Undergraduate: 21%. Graduate: 41%

Curricular Emphasis: Production of innovative films and videos; separate programs in experimental animation, character animation, and live action; film history, theory, and aesthetics

Special Activities: Film: visiting artists program; student film festival. Television/Video: program material produced for on-campus closed-circuit television and for cable television

Facilities: Film: screening room; editing suite; sound mixing room; sound stage; computer animation laboratories; motion control camera; optical printer; animation stand; film library. Television: video studio with CMX; audio studio; control room

Equipment: Film: complete Super-8 and 16mm. Video: complete 1" and ¾" studio; ¾", 8, and Hi-8 location; video synthesizer

Alumni: Tim Burton, film director; John Lassiter, director/animator; Michael Pressman, film/TV director; Robert Blalack, special effects designer; Michael Patterson, music video director/writer

GUIDE POV: Founded in 1961 by Walt Disney, Cal Arts offers degree programs in film and video production; emphasis on individualized course of studies; school specializes in study of both character and experimental animation; faculty of practicing visual and performing artists; extensive media internship opportunities

---

CALIFORNIA STATE POLYTECHNIC UNIVERSITY—POMONA

3801 West Temple Ave.,
Pomona, CA 91768
(909)869–7659

State four-year occupationally-oriented institution. Coed, suburban location. Undergraduate enrollment: 17,000.

COMMUNICATION DEPARTMENT

Chair/Contact: Professor Al Sheldon, Chair; Prudence Faxon; B. J. Anderson

Calendar: Quarters

Degrees Offered: B.S., telecommunications

Departmental Majors: Undergraduate: 200 students

Entrance Requirements: Undergraduate: 2.0 grade-point average; ACT or SAT scores. Undergraduate application deadline: November 1. Percent of acceptances: 58%

Curricular Emphasis: Television and video production; film theory

Special Activities: Film: film series. Television: program material produced for cable television; student publications

Facilities: Television: studio; audio bay; control room

Equipment: Television/Video: complete ½" studio and location

Alumni: Ernest Rose, media teacher; Jan Ostrom, TV director/media teacher; Mary Kay Switzer, telecommunications specialist/teacher

GUIDE POV: The telecommunications option within this communications major is designed for students planning careers in television, radio, or cable professions; cross-registration with any California state university school; internship opportunities in television production

---

CALIFORNIA STATE UNIVERSITY—CHICO

Chico, CA 95929–0504
(916)898–6116

State four-year comprehensive institution. Coed, suburban location. Undergraduate enrollment: 14,000.

COMMUNICATION DESIGN/MEDIA ARTS

Chair/Contact: Dr. Robert Braden, Chair
Calendar: Semesters
Degrees Offered: B.A., information studies; B.S., M.A., instructional technology
Departmental Majors: Undergraduate television: 300 students. Graduate television: 45 students
Entrance Requirements: Undergraduate: academic rank within top third of high school graduating class; 2.5 grade-point average; ACT or SAT testing, with minimum scores of 20 or 800 respectively. Graduate: GRE scores; recommendations. Undergraduate application deadline: rolling; November 1–30 for priority filing. Graduate application deadline: April 5. Percent of acceptances: 89%
Curricular Emphasis: Media arts; graphic design; graphic arts; information systems; instructional technology
Special Activities: Television: program material produced for local public television station; grant contracts; interactive multimedia long-distance learning project (INTERACT) run by students with supervision of professors and support from industry
Facilities: Television: studio; audio bay; control room; computer writing and design labs
Equipment: Television: complete ¾" studio; complete ½" location; interactive video equipment
Alumni: Russ Woody, TV writer; Geraud Moncure, TV sports anchor

GUIDE POV: This state university offers a comprehensive commercial/industrial video training program; emphasis on new technologies and information systems; modern graphic arts facilities; co-op programs and cross-registration available; member of National Student Exchange; study abroad; internship opportunities in television and video production

---

CALIFORNIA STATE UNIVERSITY—DOMINGUEZ HILLS

1000 E. Victoria Blvd.,
Carson, CA 90747
(301)516–3696

State four-year comprehensive institution. Coed, suburban location. Undergraduate enrollment: 6,000. Graduate enrollment: 2,000.

COMMUNICATIONS (TELEVISION PRODUCTION)

Chair/Contact: Dr. George Vinovich
Calendar: Semesters
Degrees Offered: B.A., communications (television studies option); certificate in television production
Departmental Majors: Undergraduate: 45 students
Entrance Requirements: Undergraduate: 2.0 grade-point average; ACT or SAT scores; interview; teachers' recommendations. Undergraduate application deadline: June 1. Percent of acceptances: 80%
Curricular Emphasis: Electronic media theory and culture; media writing; producing and directing multi-camera studio productions; ENG field production; on-line video editing; media management
Special Activities: Film: film series/festivals. Television: program material produced for local public television station and for cable television

Facilities: Television: studio; audio bay; control room
Equipment: Television/Video: complete ¾" studio and location
Alumni: Jason Anderson, video field reporter; Vanessa Cisneros, TV news editor; Joe Lewis, video editor; Joe Pena, TV network producer; Brian Denny, video editor; Alicia DeSantis-Martin, TV associate producer

GUIDE POV: A specialization in television production is offered to communication students at this state university; variety of course listings; certificate and transfer programs; cross-registration with seven other California state university schools; study abroad in 15 countries; media internship opportunities

CALIFORNIA STATE UNIVERSITY—FRESNO

Fresno, CA 93740–0046
(209)278–4240

State four-year comprehensive institution. Coed, urban location. Undergraduate enrollment: 15,600. Graduate enrollment: 3,500.

DEPARTMENT OF TELECOMMUNICATIONS

Chair/Contact: R. C. Adams, Chair
Calendar: Semesters
Degrees Offered: B.A., tele-communications; M.A., mass communications (offered jointly with journalism department)
Departmental Majors: Undergraduate telecommunications: 27 creative; 29 management; 71 news/public affairs; 109 production students. Graduate mass communications: 20 students
Entrance Requirements:
Undergraduate: 3.0 grade-point average; ACT or SAT scores. Graduate:

transcripts; GRE scores; interview. Undergraduate and graduate application deadline: December 9. Percent of acceptances: 85%
Curricular Emphasis: Television and radio production
Special Activities: Television: student production company provides program material for on-campus closed-circuit television, local public television, and cable television; competitions; member of AERho (National Broadcasting Honorary)
Facilities: Television: studio; audio studio; control room; announce booths; editing suites
Equipment: Film: Super-8. Television/Video: complete ¾" studio; complete ¾" and ½" location
Alumni: Vivienne Radkoff, screenwriter; James Mowery, TV operations director; Mike Gavaldon, TV editor/associate producer

GUIDE POV: This selective state university offers intensive training in television production with an emphasis on broadcast journalism; London, China, and South Pacific semesters abroad; media internship opportunities

CALIFORNIA STATE UNIVERSITY—FULLERTON

Fullerton, CA 92634
(714)773–2011

State four-year comprehensive institution. Coed, urban location. Undergraduate enrollment: 22,000. Graduate enrollment: 4,000.

DEPARTMENT OF COMMUNICATIONS

Chair/Contact: Terry Hynes, Chair; Larry Ward, Radio/TV/Film Sequence Coordinator

Calendar: Semesters
Degrees Offered: B.A., M.A.,
communications (students may select
emphasis in radio/television/film)
Departmental Majors: Undergraduate
film, radio, and television: 500
students. Graduate: 20 students
Entrance Requirements:
Undergraduate: academic rank within
top one-third of high school graduating
class; 2.0 grade-point average; ACT or
SAT scores. Graduate: GRE scores;
recommendations; personal statement.
Undergraduate application deadline:
March 31. Graduate application
deadlines: May 1; December 1. Percent
of acceptances: Undergraduate: 75%.
Graduate: 68%
Curricular Emphasis: Film and
television studio and field production;
film history and aesthetics; media
management; broadcast journalism;
documentary production
Special Activities: Film: film series/
festivals. Television: program material
produced for cable television as well
as for local public and commercial
television stations
Facilities: Film: editing suite; sound
mixing room. Television: studio; audio
bay; control room; video editing suites
Equipment: Film: complete 16mm.
Television/Video: complete ¾" studio;
complete ¾" and ½" location
Alumni: Terry Rossio, screenwriter;
Vikki Vargas, TV news reporter;
Helene Lynne, TV development
executive

GUIDE POV: Communication students
may participate in sequential hands-on
training programs that provide
preparation for entry-level positions in
the broadcasting, cable, and film
industries; cross-registration with other
schools in the California state
university system; study abroad;

internship opportunities in film and
television production

CALIFORNIA STATE UNIVERSITY—LONG BEACH

1250 Bellflower Blvd.,
Long Beach, CA 90840–2803
(310)985–4111

*State four-year comprehensive
institution. Coed, suburban location.
Undergraduate enrollment: 26,000.
Graduate enrollment: 7,000.*

RADIO, TELEVISION, AND FILM DEPARTMENT

Chair/Contact: Dr. Robert G. Finney,
Chair
Calendar: Semesters
Degrees Offered: B.A., radio,
television, and film
Departmental Majors: Undergraduate
radio, television and film: 225 students
Entrance Requirements:
Undergraduate: 2.7 grade-point
average; ACT or SAT scores; interview;
portfolio. Undergraduate application
deadline: November 30. Percent of
acceptances: Undergraduate: 91%.
Radio, Television, and Film
Department: 50%
Curricular Emphasis: Electronic
media theory and culture; critical film
studies; media writing; audio-video-film
production; media management
Special Activities: Film: film series/
festival; film society; guest speakers.
Television: program material produced
for cable television; guest speakers
Facilities: Film: 35mm screening
facilities; screening room; editing
room; sound mixing room; animation
stand. Television: studio; audio studio;
control room
Equipment: Film: complete Super-8
and 16mm including CMX 6000,

Callaway/Grass Valley Computerized A/B Roll; Flatbed editor (16mm); five film-cutting rooms; Aaton and Arri 16mm cameras. Television/Video: complete ¾" studio and location including three cuts-only video editing rooms; five audio production suites; small format video studio; four video portapaks

Alumni: Steven Spielberg, film/TV director/producer; Steve Martin, film actor/screenwriter; Jonathan Lawton, screenwriter/film director; David Twohy, screenwriter

GUIDE POV: The California state university system has declared this quality program "impacted," meaning limited admission to department is possible only to students enrolled at CSULB; modest budget available for student projects; department is markedly well equipped; study abroad in London; extensive internship opportunities in film, video, and television production

CALIFORNIA STATE UNIVERSITY—LOS ANGELES

5151 State University Dr.,
Los Angeles, CA 90032
(213)343–3000

State four-year comprehensive institution. Coed, urban location. Undergraduate enrollment: 15,200. Graduate enrollment: 5,900.

DEPARTMENT OF TELEVISION AND FILM

Chair/Contact: Dr. Robert Vianello
Calendar: Quarters
Degrees Offered: B.A., radio and TV broadcasting (options in telecommunications and film, advertising, broadcast journalism, and mass communication theory)

Departmental Majors:
Undergraduate: 350 students
Entrance Requirements:
Undergraduate: high school diploma or GED certificate; ACT or SAT scores; AP and CLEP credit accepted. Undergraduate application deadline: August 7. Percent of acceptances: 55%
Curricular Emphasis: Media writing; television production; media law and management
Special Activities: Film: film series/festivals. Television: program material produced for on-campus closed-circuit television and for cable television
Facilities: Film: screening room; editing suite; film library. Television: two three-camera studios; audio bays; control rooms
Equipment: Film: Super-8 cameras; editing equipment; lighting; projectors. Television/Video: complete ¾" studio and location
Alumni: Fernando Lopez, TV news director; Florina Roberts-Kendrick, TV/film actress; Erin Baxter, cinematographer; Clark Moffat, talent agent

GUIDE POV: Designed to meet the needs of both career-oriented students and those planning to pursue academic graduate studies, this multidisciplinary degree program offers courses in production, management, writing, history, theory, and research; cross-registration with other California state university schools; admission to program is competitive; study abroad; extensive internship opportunities at Los Angeles television and radio stations, film studios, and other media firms

CALIFORNIA STATE UNIVERSITY—NORTHRIDGE

18111 Nordhoff St.,
Northridge, CA 91330
(818)885-1200

State four-year comprehensive institution. Coed, suburban location. Undergraduate enrollment: 26,000. Graduate enrollment: 6,100.

RADIO-TELEVISION-FILM DEPARTMENT

Chair/Contact: Dr. Judith Marlane, Chair
Calendar: Semesters
Degrees Offered: B.A., radio-television-film; M.A., mass communications (students may select radio-television-film option)
Departmental Majors: Undergraduate radio-television-film: 750 students. Graduate radio-television-film: 30 students
Entrance Requirements: Undergraduate: high school diploma; average of *C* or better in college preparatory classes. Graduate: transcripts; 2.5 GPA in last 60 units attempted; recommendations. Undergraduate and graduate application deadline: rolling. Percent of acceptances: Undergraduate: 50%. Graduate: 75%
Curricular Emphasis: Media theory and criticism; writing for television and film; radio-TV production; film production; television directing; corporate and educational media; media management
Special Activities: Film: film societies; annual screening of outstanding student films at Directors Guild of America; film publication
Facilities: Film: sound mixing room; screening room; editing rooms; film library. Television: studio; audio bay; control room
Equipment: Film: complete 16mm; Nagra sound; flatbed editing; mixing. Television: complete ¾" studio and ½" location
Alumni: Kathy McWorter, screenwriter; Lance Taylor, broadcasting/film executive; Paul Sumi, broadcasting executive

GUIDE POV: This well-equipped program offers intensive undergraduate training in film and television writing, production, and theory/criticism; upper-division students select area of emphasis; graduate specialties in screenwriting and theory/criticism; faculty of working professionals; cross-registration offered through the Intra System Visitor Program; study abroad in 16 countries; London semester; extensive film and television production internship opportunities in Los Angeles

CALIFORNIA STATE UNIVERSITY—SAN BERNARDINO

5500 University Pkwy.,
San Bernardino, CA 92407
(714)880-5000

State four-year comprehensive institution. Coed, urban location. Undergraduate enrollment: 10,000. Graduate enrollment: 4,000.

COMMUNICATION STUDIES DEPARTMENT

Chair/Contact: Catherine Gannon, Acting Chair
Calendar: Quarters
Degrees Offered: B.A., communication (students may select emphasis in media); M.A., communication (1995)

Departmental Majors:
Undergraduate: over 300 students
Entrance Requirements:
Undergraduate: 2.0 grade-point
average; ACT or SAT scores. Graduate:
GRE scores; recommendations.
Undergraduate application deadline:
November 30. Graduate application
deadline: rolling. Percent of
acceptances: 95%
Curricular Emphasis:
Communication studies; television and
radio production; print journalism;
public relations; critical studies in film
Special Activities: Film: film series/
festivals. Television: program material
produced for cable television
Facilities: Film: film library.
Television: studio; audio bay; control
room; journalism laboratory
Equipment: Film: 16mm projectors.
Television/Video: complete ¾" studio;
complete ¾" and ½" location
Alumni: Dan Bilson, TV writer/
producer; Paul DeMeo, TV writer/
producer; Robert Diaz Leroy,
documentary filmmaker

GUIDE POV: Offering a concentration
in media production that includes
practical broadcast training in radio
and television, this Communication
Department has recently expanded;
professional writing program; cross-
registration with other CSU campuses
and with Loma Linda University; study
abroad through the National and
International Student Exchange;
internship opportunities in television
production

CHAPMAN UNIVERSITY

333 N. Glassell St.,
Orange, CA 92666
(714)997–6815

*Private four-year comprehensive
institution. Coed, urban location.
Undergraduate enrollment: 2,000.
Graduate enrollment: 300.*

FILM AND TELEVISION DEPARTMENT

Chair/Contact: Robert Bassett, Chair
Calendar: Semesters
Degrees Offered: B.F.A.,
communication (students may select
emphasis in film and television
production); B.A., communication
(emphasis in broadcast journalism or
film and television studies); M.A.,
communication (concentration in film
studies); M.F.A., film and television
production
Departmental Majors:
Undergraduate: 250 students. Graduate:
10 students
Entrance Requirements:
Undergraduate: 2.5 grade-point
average; ACT or SAT scores; essay.
Graduate: transcripts; 3.0 grade-point
average; GRE scores. Undergraduate
and graduate application deadline:
August 1. Percent of acceptances:
Undergraduate: 86%. Graduate: 75%
Curricular Emphasis: Comprehensive
undergraduate and graduate film and
television production; critical studies;
writing
Special Activities: Film: film series/
festivals. Television: community news
and feature programming produced
for Time/Warner cable station located
on campus; department offers talent
awards
Facilities: Film: 16mm screening
facilities; screening room; editing suite;
sound mixing room. Television: studio;
audio bay; control room;
postproduction suites
Equipment: Film: complete 16mm.
Television/Video: complete ¾"
Betacam and Hi-8 studio and location
Alumni: Debbie Stanley, TV news

director; Connie Johnson, TV producer; Carolyn Inman-Johnson, TV editor

GUIDE POV: Chapman University offers a small, supportive community for the production-oriented student; highly diverse curriculum; international locations on inter-term film projects; television pilot developmental program; master's program in media writing offered through English Department; study abroad; media internships available

CITY COLLEGE OF SAN FRANCISCO

50 Phelan Ave.,
San Francisco, CA 94112
(415)239–3000

City and country two-year institution. Coed, urban location. Undergraduate enrollment: 33,000.

PHOTOGRAPHY/FILM PRODUCTION

Chair/Contact: Dick Ham

BROADCASTING DEPARTMENT

Chair/Contact: Phillip Brown
Calendar: Semesters
Degrees Offered: A.S., film production; A.A., general degree (television emphasis)
Departmental Majors: Undergraduate film: 50 students. Undergraduate television: 200 students
Admission Requirements: Undergraduate: open-door policy; high school diploma or equivalent. Undergraduate application deadline: start of semester
Curricular Emphasis: Film, television, and radio production
Special Activities: Film: film series and festivals. Television: program

material produced for on-campus closed-circuit television and for cable television
Facilities: Film: sound mixing room; screening room; editing room; animation stand; film library. Television: studio; two audio studios; three audio booths; one air audio booth for campus radio station; two student editing suites; one multitrack studio; cable head and video master
Equipment: Film: complete Super-8 and 16mm including Eclair, Arriflex, Scoopic, Beaulieu; three-channel mixing; flatbed editing and upright moviolas; Nagras; optical printer. Television/Video: complete ¾" studio and location; S-VHS to ¾" editing; Beta to 1" editing; optical printer
Alumni: Rosie Cheus, TV producer; Nick Daluca, TV public affairs director; Carter B. Smith, radio announcer/personality

GUIDE POV: Separate comprehensive departments exist for film and television production at this well-equipped two-year college; all students receive hands-on training in a variety of productions; extensive internship opportunities in film and television production

CLAREMONT McKENNA COLLEGE

890 Columbia Ave.,
Claremont, CA 91711–6400
(909)621–8000

Private four-year comprehensive institution. Coed, suburban location. Undergraduate enrollment: 1,000.

FILM STUDIES PROGRAM

Chair/Contact: Michael M. Riley, Chair
Calendar: Semesters

Degrees Offered: B.A.
Departmental Majors: Undergraduate film: 20–40 students
Entrance Requirements: Undergraduate: transcripts; recommendations; ACT or SAT scores; average freshmen has combined SAT scores of 1200 or better; personal statement required; interview recommended. Undergraduate application deadline: February 1; early decision December 1. Percent of acceptances: 37%
Curricular Emphasis: History, theory, and critical assessment of film in terms of its impact upon, and reflection of, contemporary society
Special Activities: Film: distinguished guest speaker series/film festivals
Alumni: Paul Brickman, director/screenwriter; John Kander, film producer; Dan Filie, TV drama executive

GUIDE POV: Students in this small Film Studies program are provided with an opportunity to pursue an interdisciplinary course of critical studies; all students must take an introductory course in film and video production; selective admissions; cross-registration and dual majors with the four other Claremont colleges; exchange programs with Colby College and Haverford College; study abroad in Latin America, Europe, or Asia

COLLEGE OF MARIN

Kentfield, CA 94904
(415)457–8811

State two-year institution. Coed, suburban location. Undergraduate enrollment: 10,000.

COMMUNICATIONS DEPARTMENT

Chair/Contact: Sandra Douglas, Chair
Calendar: Semesters
Degrees Offered: A.A., communications (with emphasis in film production, television production, screenwriting, or mass media)
Departmental Majors: Undergraduate film: 60 students. Undergraduate television: 60 students
Entrance Requirements: Undergraduate: open-door policy; 2.0 grade-point average; ACT or SAT scores. Undergraduate application deadline: rolling. Percent of acceptances: 95%
Curricular Emphasis: Media writing; audio-film-video production; media management
Special Activities: Film: film series/festivals. Television: program material produced for on-campus closed-circuit television, for cable television, and for local public television station
Facilities: Film: sound stage; screening room; editing suite; sound mixing room; film library. Television: studio; audio bay; control room
Equipment: Film: complete Super-8 and 16mm. Television/Video: complete ¾" studio and location
Alumni: Stewart Barbee, cinematographer; Keri Kimbrell, film/TV editor; Duncan Sutherland, cinematographer

GUIDE POV: Offering comprehensive studies in both film and television production, this two-year community college provides career and transfer tracks; media program also offered through Indian Valley campus; internship opportunities in film and television production

COLLEGE OF SAN MATEO

1700 W. Hillsdale Blvd.,
San Mateo, CA 94402
(415)574–6444

*State four-year comprehensive
institution. Coed, suburban location.
Undergraduate enrollment: 14,000.*

FILM/BROADCASTING ARTS DEPARTMENT

Chair/Contact: Joe Price, film; George Mangan, broadcasting arts
Calendar: Semesters
Degrees Offered: A.A., film; A.A., broadcasting (production, engineering, or operations)
Departmental Majors: Undergraduate film: 57 students. Broadcasting arts: 157 students
Entrance Requirements: Undergraduates: open-door policy; placement testing. Application deadline: February 1
Curricular Emphasis: Hands-on film and television production experience as well as critical studies; utilization of KCSM-TV facilities; PBS station on campus
Special Activities: Film: film series/festivals. Television: program material produced for college-operated public television station
Facilities: Film: sound mixing room; screening room; editing room; sound stage; permanent library. Television: operating on-campus station KCSM-TV
Equipment: Film: complete Super-8. Television: complete ¾" studio; complete ¾" and ½" location
Alumni: Richard Lehman, camera operator/animator; Laura Louis, sound editor; Bob Carmody, assistant camera operator; Troy Harris, TV/film production assistant

GUIDE POV: Theory and training in both film and broadcast production are provided at this low-cost community college whose core curriculum prepares students for transfer to a four-year university; study abroad; media internship opportunities

COLLEGE OF THE SEQUOIAS

915 S. Mooney Blvd.,
Visalia, CA 93277
(209)730–3700

District/state four-year comprehensive institution. Coed, rural location. Undergraduate enrollment: 8,000.

CINEMA ARTS DEPARTMENT, FINE ARTS DIVISION

Chair/Contact: Noble K. Johnson, Jr.
Calendar: Semesters
Entrance Requirements: Undergraduate: ACT or SAT scores. Undergraduate application deadline: rolling. Percent of acceptances: 99%
Curricular Emphasis: Film program emphasizes history, theory/aesthetics, and criticism
Special Activities: Film: film series/festivals
Alumni: Jerri Fiala, TV news anchor

GUIDE POV: Students in this small program receive instruction in the theoretical and critical aspects of film before transferring to four-year schools

COLUMBIA COLLEGE— HOLLYWOOD

925 N. La Brea Ave.,
Hollywood, CA 90038
(213)851–0550

Private four-year comprehensive institution. Coed, urban location. Undergraduates: 275 students.

MEDIA ARTS DEPARTMENT

Chair/Contact: Frank Zuniga; Kurt Wolfe
Calendar: Quarters
Degrees Offered: A.A., television production; B.A., cinema or television production
Departmental Majors: Television: 47 students. Cinema: 149 students
Entrance Requirements: Undergraduate: 2.0 grade-point average; high school graduate or equivalent; interview; two letters of reference; 250-word essay. Application deadline: rolling. Percent of acceptances: 78%
Curricular Emphasis: Hands-on production skills taught by area professionals
Special Activities: Industry seminars
Facilities: Complete TV studio; complete mixing room; sound transfer room; extensive sound effects and music library; two sound stages; extensive scene dock with variety of flats; 1,700-work screenplay library
Equipment: Film: complete 16mm including Arriflex S; Eclair NPR; Bolex; moviolas. Television: complete ¾" studio; complete ¾" and ½" location including convergence and Abner videotape editing systems; Grass Valley switcher; three Sony CCD chip cameras on professional pedestals; portable ENG package; full lighting package
Alumni: Sam Firstenberg, film director; Jamie Farr, actor; Bob Ferretti, film editor

GUIDE POV: Intensive professional training in film and television production is offered from faculty of working professionals who teach evenings; extensive Los Angeles internship opportunities

COSUMNES RIVER COLLEGE

8401 Center Pkwy.,
Sacramento, CA 95823
(916)688-7200

County two-year comprehensive institution. Coed, suburban location. Undergraduate enrollment: 7,000.

COMMUNICATIONS MEDIA DEPARTMENT

Chair/Contact: Doree Steinmann
Calendar: Semesters
Degrees Offered: A.A., communications media (with emphasis in television, radio, or broadcast journalism)
Departmental Majors: Communications media: 200 students
Entrance Requirements: Undergraduate: open-door policy; high school diploma or equivalent. Undergraduate application deadline: rolling
Curricular Emphasis: Two-year program leading to A.A. degree transferable to a California state university
Special Activities: Students produce a weekly news and entertainment program for local cable outlet as well as several original television plays each year; broadcast sports interns shoot and provide live television coverage of local games on cable; apprenticeships; vocational placement service
Facilities: TV studio; two editing rooms, Amiga graphics
Equipment: Three color Panasonic 3 chip cameras; Grass Valley switcher, Amiga teleprompter; Mircogen CG; Spartan audio board; four portable cameras/recorders, Sony 3000 portable camera/recorder
Alumni: Frank Luna, TV director;

Martha Weiler, TV news assignment editor; Colleen Jackson, TV copywriter

GUIDE POV: Hands-on training is offered in broadcast production at this two-year college; school works closely with local cable station; production internships available

DE ANZA COLLEGE

21250 Stevens Creek Blvd.,
Cupertino, CA 95014
(408)864–5678

District two-year institution. Coed, suburban location. Undergraduate enrollment: 25,000.

CREATIVE ARTS DIVISION, FILM/TELEVISION

Chair/Contact: Zaki Lisha
Calendar: Quarters
Degrees Offered: A.A., film/television production
Departmental Majors: Undergraduate film/television: 200 students
Entrance Requirements: Undergraduate: open-door policy; high school diploma or equivalent. Undergraduate application deadline: rolling
Curricular Emphasis: Film and television production; live-action narrative and animation
Special Activities: Film: film societies. Television: program material produced for on-campus closed-circuit television and cable television
Facilities: Film: sound mixing room; screening room; editing room; animation stand. Television: complete studio; audio studio; control room
Equipment: Film: Super-8 and 16mm with flatbed editors. Television: ¾" studio equipment; ¾" and ½" location

Alumni: Eric Luke, film director; David Casci, screenwriter; Joe Murray, animator; Vance Piper, cinematographer; Doreen Berman, TV/film production manager; Karl Cohen, writer/filmmaker

GUIDE POV: Both film and television production tracks are available at this highly regarded community college; media internship opportunities

DIABLO VALLEY COLLEGE

321 Golf Club Rd.,
Pleasant Hill, CA 94523
(510)685–1230

District two-year institution. Coed, suburban location. Undergraduate enrollment: 20,000.

COMMUNICATIONS DEPARTMENT

Chair/Contact: Michael D. Lee, Chairman, television arts certificate program
Calendar: Semesters
Degrees Offered: A.A., communications; certificate in television arts
Departmental Majors: Undergraduate television: 300 students
Entrance Requirements: Undergraduate: high school diploma or qualification for GED. Undergraduate application deadline: rolling. Percent of acceptances: 90%
Curricular Emphasis: Preparing students for immediate employment in the television or film industries; courses include those in film and TV scriptwriting; studio and field production; and music video production
Facilities: Fully equipped television studio, several theatre facilities

Equipment: Three broadcast-quality television studio cameras; video switcher; audio board; ¾" and ½" editing; field production equipment; computer graphics
Alumni: Jim Haman, TV director; James Allen, sound designer; Khash Naraghi, TV engineer; Christine Hansen, TV engineer

GUIDE POV: The television arts certificate program at this two-year college offers practical training that focuses on preparing students for immediate employment in the broadcast industry; core curriculum provides requirements for transfer to four-year university; music video production

FOOTHILL COLLEGE

12345 El Monte Rd.,
Los Altos Hills, CA 94022
(415)949-7777

State two-year comprehensive institution. Coed, suburban location. Undergraduate enrollment: 17,000.

FINE ARTS AND COMMUNICATIONS DIVISION

Chair/Contact: Stuart Roe
Calendar: Quarters
Degrees Offered: A.A. film/television
Departmental Majors: Undergraduate film/television: 125 students
Entrance Requirements: Undergraduate: open-door policy. Undergraduate application deadline: rolling
Curricular Emphasis: Television production; media writing; film theory; animation; computer graphics; radio broadcasting
Special Activities: Television: program material produced for cable

television as well as on-campus closed-circuit television
Facilities: Television studio; editing stations; control room
Equipment: Television/Video: complete three-camera advanced studio equipment and field production units
Alumni: Wayne Wang, film director/producer; John Armstrong, corporate film producer/director; Tom Fraser, corporate film producer/director

GUIDE POV: Foothill College provides training in television production as well as basic courses in film production, writing, and theory; computer animation workshops; media internship opportunities throughout northwest California including San Francisco

GROSSMONT COLLEGE

8800 Grossmont College Dr.,
El Cajun, CA 92020
(619)465-1700

State two-year comprehensive institution. Coed, suburban location. Undergraduate enrollment: 16,000.

TELECOMMUNICATIONS DEPARTMENT

Chair/Contact: Gay Russell, Chair
Calendar: Semesters
Degrees Offered: A.A.
Departmental Majors: Telecommunications: 150 students
Entrance Requirements: Undergraduate: high school diploma or 18 years of age
Curricular Emphasis: Audio and video production training, including media management; video conference classes; video art
Special Activities: Campus radio station and satellite teleconferencing

Facilities: Television/Video: studio; audio bay; control room; video editing labs
Equipment: Television/Video: three-camera studio equipment with ¾", S-VHS, and VHS; field production and editing equipment format (VHS and S-VHS); satellite downlink
Alumni: Steve Buss, screenwriter; Mark Greenburg, TV producer; Kimberly Montour, broadcasting executive; John Silva, TV engineer; Roma Robbins, TV technical director

GUIDE POV: The diverse telecommunications program at Grossmont College is designed to help students meet transfer requirements as well as to develop skills for immediate job placement in both broadcast and non-broadcast industries; students have opportunity to crew live satellite teleconferences; media internship opportunities

HUMBOLDT STATE UNIVERSITY

Arcata, CA 95521
(707)826–3011

State four-year comprehensive institution. Coed, rural location. Undergraduate enrollment: 6,500. Graduate enrollment: 500.

THEATRE ARTS DEPARTMENT

Chair/Contact: Ivan E. Hess, Chair
Calendar: Semesters
Degrees Offered: B.A., M.A., M.F.A.
Departmental Majors:
Undergraduate: 115 students. Graduate: 35 students
Entrance Requirements:
Undergraduate: academic rank within top 33% of graduating class; 2.0 grade-point average; ACT or SAT scores. Graduate: 3.0 grade-point average;

transcripts; GRE scores. Undergraduate application deadline: May 1. Graduate application deadline: apply at least one month prior to registration. Percent of acceptances: undergraduate and graduate: 77%
Curricular Emphasis: Film production including documentary, experimental, and animated
Special Activities: Film: film series/ festivals; film societies
Facilities: Film: studio; audio bay; screening room; editing suite; sound mixing room; animation stand; computer graphics; film library
Equipment: Film: complete Super-8 and 16mm. Television/Video: ½" cassette recorders; portable cameras; sound recording equipment; audio mixers
Alumni: Dan Curry, art director/ producer; Michael Mills, TV/film makeup artist

GUIDE POV: Humboldt State University provides comprehensive training in film with an emphasis on independent and documentary production; interdisciplinary arts program involves theatre, film, and dance; media internship opportunities

LA SIERRA UNIVERSITY

4700 Pierce St.,
Riverside, CA 92515–8247
(909)785–2000

Private four-year comprehensive institution. Coed, small city location. Undergraduate enrollment: 14,000. Graduate enrollment: 300.

COMMUNICATION DEPARTMENT

Chair/Contact: Martie Erne, Chair; Larry Arany, Adviser
Calendar: Quarters

Degrees Offered: B.A.
communication (concentration in
radio, television and film)
Entrance Requirements:
Undergraduate: transcripts; 2.0 grade-
point average; ACT or SAT scores;
recommendations. Undergraduate
application deadline: rolling. Percent
of acceptances: 80%
Curricular Emphasis: Television
production; film production; broadcast
journalism; screenwriting;
communication law; media
management
Special Activities: Film: film series/
festivals. Television: program material
produced for cable television
Facilities: Film: screening room;
editing suite; sound mixing room.
Television: studio; audio bay; control
room
Equipment: Film: complete Super-8
and 16mm. Television/Video: complete
¾" studio and location
Alumni: Izear Feagins, TV journalist

GUIDE POV: Affiliated with the
Seventh-day Adventist Church, La
Sierra University offers a program
combining courses in writing,
business, and liberal arts with practical
training in film and television
production; internship opportunities in
film and television

LOS ANGELES CITY COLLEGE

855 N. Vermont Ave.,
Los Angeles, CA 90029
(213)953–4000

*City two-year institution. Coed, urban
location. Enrollment: 15,000.*

**RADIO, TELEVISION AND
FILM DEPARTMENT**

Chair/Contact: Dr. Robert Stahley
Calendar: Semesters
Degrees Offered: A.A., radio-
television-film department; production
certificates in film, television, film/
video, and recording arts and sciences
Departmental Majors: Film, radio
and television: 650 students
Entrance Requirements: High school
graduate or 18 years of age.
Application deadline: rolling. Percent
of acceptances: 100%
Curricular Emphasis: Television and
film production; film writing
Special Activities: Film festival at
Directors Guild of America. Television/
Video: program material produced for
cable television
Facilities: Film: sound stage; 26
editing rooms; three screening rooms;
35mm screening room; sound mixing
rooms; Oxberry animation stand;
permanent library. Television: two full-
color studios; off-line video editing
suites; control room; audio studio with
8-track and 16-track recording
Equipment: Film: complete Super-8
and 16mm. Television: complete 1"
and ¾" studio; complete ¾" and ½"
location; animation and recording
Alumni: Alan Arkin, film actor;
Morgan Freeman, film actor/director;
Albert Brooks, film director/actor;
Tamra Davis, film director; Chris
Walas, film director; Jim Whittaker,
screenwriter; Chuck Vinson, TV
director; Mimi Cederer, TV director;
Kasey Arnold Ince, TV writer; David
Vassar, TV producer/writer

GUIDE POV: This well-equipped,
affordable two-year program in the
heart of Los Angeles is taught by
active film and television professionals;
complete training in both film and

television production, including animation; transfer or certificate options; extensive internship opportunities

LOS ANGELES HARBOR COLLEGE

1111 Figueroa Place,
Wilmington, CA 90744
(310)522–8200

City two-year institution. Coed, suburban location. Enrollment: 10,000.

ENGLISH DEPARTMENT

Chair/Contact: John Corbally
Calendar: Semesters
Degrees Offered: no degrees offered in film or television
Entrance Requirements: Open-door policy. Application deadline: rolling
Curricular Emphasis: The English Department offers several theory courses in film, with an emphasis on comparative media
Alumni: Randy Shanofsky, TV cameraman; John Bruce, TV art director

GUIDE POV: Los Angeles Harbor College offers several theory courses in film that fulfill part of the requirements for liberal arts and fine arts majors transferring to four-year universities; open enrollment to state residents.

LOS ANGELES VALLEY COLLEGE

5800 Fulton Ave.,
Van Nuys, CA 91401
(818)782–5539

City two-year institution. Coed, urban location. Enrollment: 21,000.

DEPARTMENT OF THEATRE AND CINEMA ARTS

Chair/Contact: Joseph A. Daccurso, Chair
Calendar: Semesters
Degrees Offered: A.A., theatre/cinema arts; occupational certificate, motion picture production technician
Departmental Majors: 100 students
Entrance Requirements: Open-door policy as space allows. Application deadline: rolling
Curricular Emphasis: Film writing and production; visual, multimedia approach; extensive screenings; hands-on training. Video: adjunct program in video production; television broadcasting; radio broadcasting
Special Activities: Film: film series/festivals; guest speakers. Television: program material produced for on-campus closed-circuit television and for cable television
Facilities: Film: screening room; editing suite; sound mixing room; animation stand; optical printer; SPFX screen
Equipment: Film: complete Super-8 and 16mm. Video: state-of-the-art video projection system
Alumni: Ed Begley, Jr., film/TV actor; Richard Bennett, special effects supervisor; Dave Diano, cinematographer; Jerry Immel, TV/film composer; Bill Munns, film/TV makeup artist; Ebbe Roe Smith, scriptwriter; Jan Yarbrough, video executive

GUIDE POV: This two-year film program offers practical training "from script to screen," focusing on theory and its practical application, and providing students with a basis in visual literacy; day and evening classes; extensive media internship opportunities

LOYOLA MARYMOUNT UNIVERSITY

Loyola Blvd. at West 80th St.,
Los Angeles, CA 90045
(310)338–2977

Private four-year comprehensive
institution. Coed, urban location.
Undergraduate enrollment: 4,000.
Graduate enrollment: 1,000.

COMMUNICATION ARTS DEPARTMENT

Chair/Contact: Patricia Oliver, Chair
Calendar: Semesters
Degrees Offered: B.A., M.A., writing
for film and TV; B.A., M.A., film
production; B.A., M.A., television
production; B.A., recording arts; B.A.,
communication studies
Departmental Majors: Undergraduate
and graduate: 450 students
Entrance Requirements:
Undergraduate: 3.0 grade-point
average; ACT or SAT scores; essay;
recommendation by school counselor
or teacher. Graduate: 3.0 grade-point
average; GRE scores; minimum of 600
on TOEFL for foreign applicants;
written statement of purpose;
professional recommendations.
Undergraduate application deadline:
February 1; transfer and international
students, July 1. Graduate application
deadline: March 15
Curricular Emphasis: Undergraduate
and graduate film and television
production and writing, including
narrative, documentary, experimental,
and animation
Special Activities: Film: film series/
festivals; guest lecturers; screenings.
Television: program material produced
for cable television
Facilities: Film: 60' by 90' sound
stage; 16mm and 35mm screening
facilities; screening room; editing

suites; sound mixing rooms; Oxberry
animation stand; film library.
Television: 30' by 60' studio; audio
bay; control room; four editing suites.
Recording arts: four sound recording
studios
Equipment: Film: complete Super-8
and 16mm; including cameras, lights,
and grip equipment. Television/Video:
complete ¾" studio and location
Alumni: Jack Haley, Jr., TV/film
producer; Brian Helgeland,
screenwriter; John Cosgrove, TV
producer; Allen Daviau,
cinematographer; Winnie Hervey, TV
producer/writer; Terry Dunn Meurer,
TV producer

GUIDE POV: Affiliated with the Roman
Catholic Church, this selective private
university offers a production-oriented
communications program with
specializations in film and television as
well as screenwriting; production
facilities open to all student levels;
graduate work culminates in thesis
project; extensive internship
opportunities in film and television
production

MOORPARK COLLEGE

7075 Campus Rd.,
Moorpark, CA 93021
(805)378–1400

County two-year institution. Coed,
suburban location. Enrollment: 12,000.

RADIO/TELEVISION DEPARTMENT

Chair/Contact: Sidney Adler, Chair,
humanities division
Calendar: Semesters
Degrees Offered: A.S., radio and
television
Departmental Majors: Television: 300
students

Entrance Requirements: Open-door policy. Application deadline: beginning of semesters
Curricular Emphasis: Audio-video production; broadcast journalism
Special Activities: Television: program material produced for cable television
Facilities: Television: studio; audio bay; control room; editing suites
Equipment: Television/Video: complete ¾" studio; S-VHS location; editing equipment
Alumni: Matt Mahurin, music video director; Terry Szostek, film editor; Peter Macrae, music and corporate video director

GUIDE POV: A varied curriculum introducing students to both radio and television broadcasting is offered at this two-year college; recently completed modern facilities; practical emphasis on career training for technical support positions; students involved in both creative and technical aspects of studio and remote productions; internship opportunities in television production

NAPA VALLEY COLLEGE

2277 Napa–Vallejo Hwy.,
Napa, CA 94558
(707)253–3000

District two-year institution. Coed, rural location. Enrollment: 11,000.

TELECOMMUNICATIONS TECHNOLOGY

Chair/Contact: Gary P. Vann, Television Coordinator; Joe Monaghan
Calendar: Semesters
Degrees Offered: A.S., telecommunications technology
Departmental Majors: Television: 70 students

Entrance Requirements: Open-door policy; official transcripts required; high school diploma or equivalent; interview recommended. Application deadline: two months prior to start of semester
Curricular Emphasis: Training for technical support positions in television/video; electronics; maintenance
Special Activities: Television: program material produced for various outlets; SMPTE chapter; S.B.E. certification
Facilities: Television: studio; control room; equipment maintenance lab
Equipment: Television/Video: complete 1" and ¾" studio; ½" components; complete ¾" location
Alumni: Lea Blicker, producer/director; Reys Ludlow, producer/director; Bob Griffin, video engineer; Tommy Tucker, TV camera operator; David Webb, video engineer

GUIDE POV: Students seeking technical training in television may choose this two-year vocational program that gears graduates for immediate employment as studio and field technicians/engineers; emphasis on new technologies; media internship opportunities

NEW COLLEGE OF CALIFORNIA

766 Valencia St.,
San Francisco, CA 94110
(415)241–1300

Private four-year institution. Coed, urban location. Undergraduate enrollment: 150. Graduate enrollment: 300.

VIDEO ARTS DEPARTMENT

Chair/Contact: Maria Luisa Mendonca
Calendar: Trimesters

Degrees Offered: B.A., humanities
Departmental Majors: Undergraduate
media arts: 20 students
Entrance Requirements:
Undergraduate: graduation from
accredited secondary school or GED;
essay. Application deadline:
September 21
Curricular Emphasis: Independent
video production and criticism;
combines video production with
topics in social sciences, education,
and politics; media literacy
Special Activities: Monthly program
showcasing student videos on local
public access channel
Equipment: Three HI-8 cameras; ½"
dubbing deck; HI-8 to ¾" U-matic
editing suite; audiovisual switches
Alumni: Jennifer Maytorena Taylor,
film executive; Chris Atkins, TV co-
director

GUIDE POV: Interdisciplinary studies
are offered by professionally active
faculty; experimental and
documentary video production stresses
social, cultural, and political issues

OCCIDENTAL COLLEGE

1600 Campus Rd.,
Los Angeles, CA 90041
(213)259–2500

*Private four-year comprehensive
institution. Coed, urban location.
Enrollment: 17,000.*

ART DEPARTMENT

Chair/Contact: Chick Strand
Calendar: Quarters
Degrees Offered: B.A., art
Departmental Majors: Film and
television: 38 students
Entrance Requirements: Academic
rank within top 10% of high school

graduating class; competitive SAT
scores. Application deadline: February
1; April 1 for transfer students. Percent
of acceptances: 25%
Curricular Emphasis: Film study as a
personal art form with experimental
courses in Super-8, 16mm, and ½"
video; documentary; narrative; critical
studies; international cinema
Special Activities: Film: film series/
festivals; film societies. Television:
program material produced for on-
campus closed-circuit television, local
public television station and local
commercial television station
Facilities: Film: sound mixing room;
screening room; editing room; sound
stage; permanent library. Television:
studio; audio studio; editing rooms
Equipment: Film: complete 16mm
and Super-8; Television: complete ½"
location
Alumni: Marcel Ophuls, filmmaker;
Terry Gilliam, film director; George
Stevens, Jr., film producer; Steve de
Jarnett, film director/writer; Ken
Wheat, film director; Tom Thayer,
studio executive

GUIDE POV: This is a highly selective,
individualized program in film and
television production stressing artistic
and creative freedom; personal
exploration of cinematic/video forms
of expression; solid liberal arts
program; faculty of working media
artists; cross-registration with California
Institute of Technology and Art Center
College of Design; cooperative
programs available with Columbia
University; study abroad in Europe,
Asia, and Latin America; Los Angeles
media internships available for credit

ORANGE COAST COLLEGE

2701 Fairview Rd.,
P.O. Box 5005,
Costa Mesa, CA 92628
(714)432–0202

District two-year institution. Coed,
suburban location. Enrollment: 23,000.

FILM/VIDEO DEPARTMENT

Chair/Contact: Brian Lewis; William
Hall
Calendar: Semesters
Degrees Offered: A.A., film/video
Departmental Majors: Film/television:
800 students
Entrance Requirements: High school
diploma or equivalent; 18 years or
older. Application deadline: rolling.
Percent of acceptances: 90%
Curricular Emphasis: Film/video and
television production; computer
graphics; additional offerings in critical
studies
Special Activities: Film: film/video
festival; film society. Television:
program material produced for cable
television as well as for local public
and commercial stations
Facilities: Film: sound stage;
screening room; editing room; sound
mixing room; animation stand.
Television: broadcast full-color studio;
audio studio; control room
Equipment: Film: Super-8 and 16mm.
Television/Video: ¾" studio and ½"
location; off-line and on-line editing
Alumni: Alan Ruffier, film director/
producer; Kurt Bennett, recording
artist/sound engineer; William Mings,
TV/film executive; Rick Carter, special
effects artist

GUIDE POV: Professional, intensive
two-year film and television
production training is offered at
Orange Coast College; diverse course
listings; film animation and computer
graphics; media internship
opportunities

OXNARD COLLEGE

4000 S. Rose Ave.,
Oxnard, CA 93033
(805)986–5800

State two-year institution. Coed,
suburban location. Enrollment: 6,000.

TELECOMMUNICATIONS PROGRAM

Chair/Contact: Kitty Merrill; Leroy
Robinson
Calendar: Semesters
Degrees Offered: A.A.,
telecommunications
Departmental Majors: Television: 30
students
Entrance Requirements: Open-door
policy; high school diploma or
equivalent. Application deadline:
rolling
Curricular Emphasis: Broadcast
studio operation; television
production; directing; editing; film and
television criticism; broadcast
journalism
Special Activities: Television: variety
of program material produced for
Oxnard College Television seen
throughout the community, for
Ventura County Cablevision, and
for educational channel Jones
Intercable 52
Facilities: Television: studio; master
control room
Equipment: Television/Video:
complete ¾" studio; complete ¾" and
½" location
Alumni: Lorraine Kernagis, associate
producer/video editor; George Sylva,
cinematographer; Julie Moye, video
editor

GUIDE POV: Students enrolled in this small hands-on program will produce diverse program material for a variety of local public television and cable outlets; internship opportunities in television production

PALOMAR COMMUNITY COLLEGE

1140 W. Mission Rd.,
San Marcos, CA 92069
(619)744–1150

State two-year institution. Coed, suburban location. Enrollment: 21,000.

COMMUNICATIONS DEPARTMENT

Chair/Contact: Richard Peacock
Calendar: Semesters
Degrees Offered: A.A., communications
Departmental Majors: Film: 75 students. Television: 300 students
Entrance Requirements: Open-door policy. Application deadline: rolling
Curricular Emphasis: Film: history and aesthetics; nonfiction; experimental forms; special subjects. Television: broadcast journalism; fiction; instructional/industrial
Special Activities: Film: film series and festivals. Television: program material produced for on-campus closed-circuit television, for local public television station, and for cable television; students compete for local awards; vocational placement service
Facilities: Film: screening room; editing suites; film library. Television: complete 1" and ¾" studio; complete ¾" location
Equipment: Television: ¾" and ½" cameras. Film: Super-8 cameras
Alumni: Jeff House, screenwriter; Phil Tippet, special effects artist; David Hines, screenwriter

GUIDE POV: Palomar Community College offers a two-year program with some film production classes as well as studies in television broadcast production and writing; media internship opportunities

PEPPERDINE UNIVERSITY

24255 Pacific Coast Hwy.,
Malibu, CA 90263
(310)456–4000

Private four-year comprehensive institution. Coed, suburban location. Undergraduate enrollment: 2,600. Graduate enrollment: 5,600.

COMMUNICATION DIVISION

Chair/Contact: Dr. Donald L. Shores, Chair
Calendar: Semesters
Degrees Offered: B.A., communication (students may select emphasis in telecommunications); M.A., communication (students may select emphasis in broadcasting)
Departmental Majors: Undergraduate television: 135 students. Graduate: 8 students
Entrance Requirements: Undergraduate: 2.9 grade-point average; ACT score (minimum 21) or SAT score (minimum 1000); essay required; interview recommended; recommendations. Graduate: GRE scores, with above median level on verbal portion; 3.0 grade-point average; recommendations. Undergraduate application deadline: January 1. Graduate application deadline: May 1; March 1 for students requesting financial aid. Percent of acceptances: 65%
Curricular Emphasis: Electronic media theory and culture; media

writing; television/video production; news/documentary; media management

Special Activities: Film: student publications; screenings. Television: program material produced for on-campus closed-circuit television and for cable television

Facilities: Television: studio; audio bay; control room

Equipment: Television/Video: complete ¾" studio and location

Alumni: Ann Lanker, TV news anchor; Stephanie Summerhill, TV news anchor; Scott Swan, entertainment executive; Stephanie Riggs, TV news anchor

GUIDE POV: This competitive, nonsectarian private university offers undergraduate specializations in broadcast journalism, production, or management; graduate work emphasizes advanced communication theory and media projects; study abroad in three countries; internship opportunities in television production

PITZER COLLEGE

1050 N. Mills Ave.,
Claremont, CA 91711–6110
(909)621–8129

Private four-year comprehensive institution. Coed, urban location. Enrollment: 750.

FILM AND VIDEO STUDIES

Chair/Contact: Dawn Wiedemann
Calendar: Semesters
Degrees Offered: B.A.
Departmental Majors: 45–60 students
Entrance Requirements: ACT or SAT scores; AT scores in English, Math, and one other subject; teachers'

recommendations; written statement of purpose. Application deadline: February 1. Percent of acceptances: 40%

Curricular Emphasis: Experimental narrative and documentary production; interdisciplinary theoretical and critical analysis

Special Activities: Film: film series/ festivals

Facilities: Film: screening rooms; Super-8 and 16mm editing suites; film library. Television: studio

Equipment: Film: complete Super-8; 16mm cameras and projectors. Video: S-VHS camcorders; V8mm camcorders; ½" cassette recorders; S-VHS camcorders; portable lighting packages; monitors; sound recording equipment; ½" VHS on-line editing system

Alumni: Margaret Adachi, film editor; David Burkett, TV production coordinator; James Hightower, TV production assistant

GUIDE POV: This small, selective school offers an interdisciplinary liberal arts education emphasizing experimental and documentary forms in film and video; cross-registration with any of the other Claremont colleges; extensive study abroad programs in Africa, Asia, Europe, Latin America, North America, and Oceania; local and area media internship opportunities

POMONA COLLEGE

Claremont, CA 91711
(909)621–8134

Private four-year comprehensive institution. Coed, suburban location. Enrollment: 1,380.

MEDIA STUDIES DEPARTMENT

Chair/Contact: Brian Stonehill
Calendar: Semesters
Degrees Offered: B.A. in media studies
Departmental Majors: Media studies: 15 students
Entrance Requirements: High school transcripts; SAT or ACT scores; personal essay; recommendations. Application deadline: January 15. Percent of acceptances: 10%
Curricular Emphasis: Visual literacy
Special Activities: Film series and live theatre
Facilities: Film: production available at nearby institutions
Equipment: Film: editing facilities available through the Claremont colleges; laser disc to VCR carrels for screening
Alumni: Robert Towne, screenwriter/film director; David Ward, film director; Richard Chamberlain, TV/film actor; Twyla Tharp, TV/film choreographer; Kris Kristofferson, film actor; Frank Wells, studio executive

GUIDE POV: This selective liberal arts college offers a comprehensive program with studies in film scholarship; high percentage of placing undergraduates in major graduate film schools; cross-registration at any of the Claremont colleges; study abroad in 18 countries; internship opportunities locally and in neighboring Los Angeles

TV/VIDEO COMMUNICATIONS DEPARTMENT

Chair/Contact: Terry Bales, Chair
Calendar: Semesters
Degrees Offered: A.A., television production, broadcast news; certificate, television scriptwriting, television production, broadcast news
Departmental Majors: 250 students
Entrance Requirements: Open-door policy; ACT or SAT scores. Application deadline: rolling. Percent of acceptances: 95%
Curricular Emphasis: Broadcast journalism; television scriptwriting; television production; corporate video; television graphics
Special Activities: Television: student-run cable station produces weekly newscast as well as various remote productions; vocational placement service
Facilities: Television: studio; audio bay; control room
Equipment: Television/Video: complete ¾" studio; complete ¾" and ½" location
Alumni: Rhoshav Amir, TV producer

GUIDE POV: This well-equipped TV/Video program at this two-year college provides hands-on training for those students wishing to pursue careers in broadcast production; easy admissions standards; faculty of working professionals; media internship opportunities

RANCHO SANTIAGO COLLEGE

17th at Bristol St.,
Santa Ana, CA 92701
(714)564-6000

District two-year institution. Coed, suburban location. Enrollment: 26,000.

RIO HONDO COLLEGE

3600 Workman Mill Rd.,
Whittier, CA 90601-1699
(310)692-0921

State two-year institution. Coed, urban location. Enrollment: 10,000.

MASS COMMUNICATIONS/TELEVISION

Chair/Contact: Film: Jerry Lenington.
Television: Larry Scher
Calendar: Semesters
Degrees Offered: A.S., mass
communication
Departmental Majors: 30 students
Entrance Requirements: Portfolio;
recommendations; interview required;
assessment testing. Application
deadline: July 10
Curricular Emphasis: Electronic
media theory and culture; critical
studies in film; media writing; film
production; television/video
production
Special Activities: Television:
program material produced for local
public television station and for cable
television
Facilities: Film: film library.
Television: studio
Equipment: Film: Super-8 and 16mm
cameras; sound recording equipment;
projectors. Television/Video: complete
¾" studio and ½" location
Alumni: Alex Morales, TV director;
Mark Zarate, commercial director/
special effects editor; John Olson,
video producer; Nazir Raslan,
postproduction executive; Brent
Armenta, video producer

GUIDE POV: Rio Hondo College offers
mass communication majors a
practical two-year program with
special attention to film theory and
television production; emphasis on
broadcast journalism and video
editing techniques; internship
opportunities in both film and
television production

SAN DIEGO STATE UNIVERSITY

San Diego, CA 92182
(619)594–5200

*State four-year comprehensive
institution. Coed, urban location.
Undergraduate enrollment: 33,000.
Graduate enrollment: 7,000*

TELECOMMUNICATIONS AND FILM DEPARTMENT

Chair/Contact: Hayes Anderson
Calendar: Semesters
Degrees Offered: B.S., television-film
production; B.A., M.A.,
telecommunications
Departmental Majors:
Undergraduate: 250 students. Graduate:
40 students
Entrance Requirements:
Undergraduate: 3.0 grade-point
average; ACT or SAT scores; written
statement of purpose; letters of
recommendation. Graduate: 3.0 grade-
point average in last sixty credits;
minimum scores on GRE of 500 Verbal
and 550 Quantitative; teachers'
recommendations; written statement of
purpose; professional
recommendations. Undergraduate and
graduate application deadline:
March 1
Curricular Emphasis: All aspects of
film, radio, and television production;
screenwriting; telecommunications
technology; media management;
communication theory and research
Special Activities: Film/Video: film
and video series/festivals/competitions;
extensive on-campus film/video
archives. Television: program material
produced for on-campus closed-circuit
television and cable television
Facilities: Film: 35mm screening
facilities; screening room; editing
room; sound mixing room; animation

stand. Television: studio; audio studio; control room

Equipment: Film: complete Super-8 and 16mm. Television/Video: complete ¾" studio; complete ¾" and ½" location

Alumni: Kathleen Kennedy, film producer; Gary David Goldberg, TV producer; Sal Sardo, TV executive; Bud Carey, TV executive; Wally Schlotter, film executive; Bob Badimi, music editor

GUIDE POV: This well-equipped, diverse program features a comprehensive curriculum in both film and television production and criticism; selective admissions; graduate program offers full creative specialization with advanced work in screenwriting and film/telecommunications production; study abroad in London; extensive local and area media internship opportunities

---

SAN FRANCISCO ART INSTITUTE

800 Chestnut St.,
San Francisco, CA 94133
(415)771–7020

Private four-year professional arts institution. Coed, urban location. Undergraduate enrollment: 450. Graduate enrollment: 250. Undergraduate and graduate tuition: $11,350 per academic year.

FILMMAKING DEPARTMENT

Chair/Contact: Ernie Gehr
Calendar: Semesters
Degrees Offered: B.F.A., M.F.A.
Departmental Majors:
Undergraduate: 60 students. Graduate: 18 students

Entrance Requirements:
Undergraduate: transcripts; ACT or SAT scores; essay; portfolio; interview. Graduate: transcripts; statement of purpose; film portfolio. Undergraduate application deadline: rolling. Graduate application deadline: March 23. Percent of acceptances: undergraduate and graduate: 80%

Curricular Emphasis: Filmmaking is taught in a fine arts context, where the expressive intent of the maker is emphasized; intermedia courses offered combining film with other art disciplines; studio courses in video explore video sculpture; narrative video; tele-performance; installation; computer-based interactive forms; forms based on virtual reality; screen-mediated images; site-sensitive approaches related to architecture, and other approaches

Special Activities: Film/Video: visiting lecturers; San Francisco Cinematheque screenings; showcases of independent and personal cinema; annual international film festival

Facilities: Film: screening room; editing suite; sound stage; sound mixing and recording studio; two animation stands, one with tracking camera mount and rotoscope capabilities; two pin-registration optical printers; flatbed editing tables; film library

Equipment: Film: complete Super-8 and 16mm; 16mm processing lab; hand-processing equipment for Super-8

Alumni: Lynne Sachs, filmmaker; Janis Crystal Lipzin, film teacher; Alan Mukamal, filmmaker; Al Wong, film teacher

GUIDE POV: Established in 1871, this is one of the oldest colleges of art in the United States; highly selective, professionally equipped fine arts program for filmmakers; supportive artist-based community; 24-hour access to facilities; faculty of practicing media artists; study abroad in nine countries; local and area media internships available

SAN FRANCISCO STATE UNIVERSITY

1600 Holloway Ave.,
San Francisco, CA 94132
(415)338-1111

State four-year comprehensive institution. Coed, urban location. Undergraduate enrollment: 25,000. Graduate enrollment: 4,000.

CINEMA DEPARTMENT/BROADCAST COMMUNICATION ARTS

Chair/Contact: Film: Steve Kovacs, Chair; Broadcast Communication Arts; Dr. Ronald J. Compesi
Calendar: Semesters
Degrees Offered: B.A., film; B.A., radio/television; M.A., film studies; M.A., radio/television; M.F.A., film production
Departmental Majors: Undergraduate film: 500 students. Graduate: 90. Undergraduate television: 900 students; Graduate: 100
Entrance Requirements: Undergraduate: 2.0 grade-point average; SAT or ACT scores. Graduate: 3.0 grade-point average; written portfolio; recommendations; essay. Undergraduate deadline: November for fall admission; August for spring admission. Graduate deadline: March 16
Curricular Emphasis: Specialized undergraduate and graduate programs in film and television with full production training and studies in criticism
Special Activities: Film: film series/festivals; guest lecturers; special screenings. Television: program material produced for both on-campus closed-circuit and cable television; vocational placement service
Facilities: Film: 35mm screening facilities; screening room; editing room; sound mixing room; animation stand; film library. Television: three full-color TV studios with control rooms; on-line and off-line videotape editing lab; radio station; 24-track audio recording studio; audio practice labs; computer graphics/writing labs
Equipment: Film: eight Sync-Sound 16mm cameras; some video. Television/Video: complete ¾" studio; complete ¾" and ½" location including three VHS one-chip, three Super VHS one-chip, and two Super VHS three-chip video cameras; eight crystal sync tape recorders; seven cassette recorders; microphones; open-faced, Fresnel and soft lights.
Alumni: Brian Frankish, film producer; Meg Partridge, filmmaker; Patricia Amlin, animator; Steve Okasaki, film director; Arthur Dong, filmmaker; Emiko Omori, cinematographer; Ellen Osborne, filmmaker

GUIDE POV: Separate sequential programs in film and television are provided at this professionally equipped state college; undergraduate programs offer diverse course listings; highly selective Cinema Department graduate program dedicated to training students in an independent cinema; separate major for graduate film studies; graduate program in radio and television offers curriculum blending theory and practice; cross-registration with area colleges; study abroad programs; internship opportunities in film and television production

SAN JOSE STATE UNIVERSITY

One Washington Square,
San Jose, CA 95192–0098
(408)924–1000

State four-year comprehensive institution. Coed, urban location. Undergraduate enrollment: 26,500. Graduate enrollment: 5,000.

DEPARTMENT OF THEATRE ARTS/RADIO-TELEVISION-VIDEO-FILM

Chair/Contact: Charles L. Chess
Calendar: Semesters
Degrees Offered: B.A., radio-television; B.A., radio and television (concentration in film)
Departmental Majors:
Undergraduate: 375–400 students
Entrance Requirements:
Undergraduate: ACT or SAT scores. Undergraduate application deadline: November 1. Percent of acceptances: 88%
Curricular Emphasis: Film production; media writing; television production; video art; screenwriting; communications theory; media management
Special Activities: Film: film series/ festivals; film societies. Television/ Radio: guest professors; program material produced for on-campus closed-circuit television, and for local public and commercial television stations; KSJS-FM is the nation's top-rated college radio station
Facilities: Film: screening room; editing suite; sound mixing room; sound stage. Television: studio; audio bay; control room; 24-hour FM radio station
Equipment: Film: complete 16mm; optical printers; sound mixers. Television/Video: complete ¾" studio; complete ½" location
Alumni: Bill Craig, film director/ producer; Ralph Gerard, TV head of production; Steven Flick, film production specialist

GUIDE POV: This professional program provides comprehensive production training in both film and television; diverse curriculum; broadcast and nonbroadcast television; film/TV projects in fiction and nonfiction; competitive admissions standards; study abroad in 16 countries; honors program in Theatre Arts; media internship opportunities locally and throughout the Silicon Valley area

SANTA CLARA UNIVERSITY

Santa Clara, CA 95053–2999
(408)554–4000

Private four-year comprehensive institution. Coed, suburban location. Undergraduate enrollment: 4,000. Graduate enrollment: 4,000.

COMMUNICATION DEPARTMENT

Chair/Contact: Rev. Paul Soukup, Chair; Shelly Irvine; Steven Lee
Calendar: Quarters
Degrees Offered: B.A., communication (students may select emphasis in television)
Departmental Majors:
Undergraduate: 225 students
Entrance Requirements:
Undergraduate: competitive grade-point average; SAT scores; GED not accepted; AP credit accepted; essay required; recommendations.

Undergraduate application deadline: February 1. Percent of acceptances: 65%
Curricular Emphasis: Communication theory; media writing; television production; media ethics
Special Activities: Television: program material produced for local cable television
Facilities: Television: classroom studio
Equipment: Television/Video: classroom studio; complete ½" location
Alumni: Andy Ackerman, TV producer/director; Bud Nameck, TV sports director/anchor; Sean Bobbitt, cinematographer; Leo Clarke, TV producer; Julie Jorgensen, TV producer/reporter

GUIDE POV: Highly selective, this private Jesuit university instituted its radio and print journalism program in the early 1900s; television production sequence provides practical training with an emphasis on broadcast journalism; media ethics; study abroad in Rome, Paris, Madrid, Hong Kong, Tokyo, and other cities; internship opportunities for credit in television production

SANTA MONICA COLLEGE

1900 Pico Blvd.,
Santa Monica, CA 90405
(310)450–5150

District two-year institution. Coed, suburban location. Enrollment: 22,000.

GRAPHIC ARTS DEPARTMENT

Chair/Contact: Robert L. Jones, Chair
Calendar: Semesters
Degrees Offered: A.A.
Entrance Requirements: Open-door

policy. Undergraduate application deadline: rolling
Curricular Emphasis: The graphic arts program offers one basic film production class; several courses in film theory and genre through cinema program; mass media criticism and theory courses through communication program; scriptwriting program offers two courses in writing for film, television, and theatre
Special Activities: Radio: KCRW, major NPR affiliate, located on campus. General: Emeritus College designed to serve needs of adult students 55 and over
Alumni: James Dean, film actor; Dustin Hoffman, film actor; Sean Penn, film actor; Arnold Schwarzenegger, film actor

GUIDE POV: Limited film production coursework is offered at this community college; theory courses through cinema and communication programs; transfer program to all area universities

SANTA ROSA JUNIOR COLLEGE

1501 Mendocino Ave.,
Santa Rosa, CA 95401–4395
(707)546–3485

District two-year institution. Coed, suburban location. Enrollment: 6,000.

COMMUNICATION STUDIES DEPARTMENT

Chair/Contact: Walter McCallum, Instructor, media program
Calendar: Semesters
Degrees Offered: Certificate of completion in media
Departmental Majors: 60 students
Entrance Requirements: Open-door policy. Application deadline: rolling
Curricular Emphasis: Film and

television production and critical studies

Special Activities: Film: film series/ festivals. Television: program material produced for cable television

Facilities: Film: screening room; editing suite; sound mixing room; film library. Television: studio; audio bay; control room

Equipment: Film: complete Super-8. Television/Video: complete ¾" studio; complete ¾" and ½" location

Alumni: Richard Gentner, film director; Tom Bianco, screenwriter; Debbie Swearingen, TV news anchor; Lorne Morse, TV/film editor

GUIDE POV: Through the media program, students have an opportunity to learn the basics of both film and television production before transferring to a four-year university program; internship opportunities in television production

---

SHASTA COLLEGE

P.O. Box 6006,
Redding, CA 96099–6006
(916)225–4600

State two-year institution. Coed, rural location. Enrollment: 6,000.

COMMUNICATION ARTS DEPARTMENT

Chair/Contact: Jean L. Carpenter
Calendar: Semesters
Degrees Offered: A.A., humanities (concentration in communication arts)
Entrance Requirements: Open-door policy. Application deadline: rolling
Curricular Emphasis: Electronic media theory and culture; basic television production
Special Activities: Television: program material produced for local public television station

Facilities and Equipment: Production classes taught at local PBS station

Alumni: Clyde Powell, TV camera operator; Dennis Kennedy, radio disc jockey

GUIDE POV: Shasta College offers students a broad liberal arts program stressing communication theory and providing basic television production training; transfer program

---

SIERRA COLLEGE

5000 Rocklin Rd.,
Rocklin, CA 95677
(916)624–3333

State two-year institution. Coed, suburban location. Enrollment: 13,000.

HUMANITIES/FINE ARTS DIVISION

Chair/Contact: Michael Hunter, Communication Studies
Calendar: Semesters
Degrees Offered: A.A.
Departmental Majors: 45 students
Entrance Requirements: ACT or SAT scores. Application deadline: rolling
Curricular Emphasis: Electronic media theory and culture; critical studies in film; video and television production; writing for mass media
Special Activities: Film: film-lecture series. Television: program material produced for on-campus closed-circuit television, for local public and commercial television, and for cable television
Facilities: Film: screening room; editing suite; film library. Television: studio; audio bay; control room; editing suites
Equipment: Film: complete Super-8. Television/Video: complete 1" and ¾" studio; complete ¾" and ½" location

Alumni: Doug Richardson, screenwriter; David DiFrancesco, TV/ film actor

GUIDE POV: Offering students modern television facilities, this small two-year communication studies program features practical training in video production with special attention to stylistic differences between film and video forms; critical film theory and genre study offered through English Department; vocational work experience for credit

SOLANO COMMUNITY COLLEGE

4000 Suisun Valley Rd.,
Suisun City, CA 94585
(707)864–7000

State two-year institution. Coed, suburban location. Enrollment: 10,000.

TV AND FILM DEPARTMENT, TELECOMMUNICATIONS

Chair/Contact: Maile Ornellas
Calendar: Semesters
Degrees Offered: A.A., telecommunications
Departmental Majors: 40 students
Entrance Requirements: 2.0 grade-point average. Application deadline: first week of classes
Curricular Emphasis: applied production program in film and video including course in film aesthetics/ history and a multi-cultural film course; production courses include computer art; television and film writing; special topics
Special Activities: Film: film societies; Solano student film awards; screenings of student film projects. Television: students produce weekly public affairs program that airs in prime time on local cable channels

Facilities: Film: screening room; editing suite; animation stand; film library. Television: studio; audio bay; control room
Equipment: Film: complete Super-8; 16mm cameras; editing equipment; lighting; projectors. Television/Video: complete ¾" studio and ½" location including Grass Valley switcher; audio mixing board
Alumni: John Duncan, TV news director; Joe Martinez, special effects artist

GUIDE POV: Offering students a two-year program with class projects to suit a variety of interests, Solano Community College provides film and television production training with special attention to public affairs programming, music videos, experimental cinema, and animation; small classes; transfer program; internship opportunities in film and television production

SOUTHERN CALIFORNIA COLLEGE

55 Fair Dr.,
Costa Mesa, CA 92626–6597
(714)556–3610

Private four-year comprehensive institution. Coed, suburban location. Enrollment: 1,000.

COMMUNICATION DEPARTMENT

Chair/Contact: Gerald Fisher
Calendar: Semesters
Degrees Offered: B.A., communication (with emphasis in television production, broadcast journalism, or production management)
Departmental Majors: Television: 60 students
Entrance Requirements: 2.5 grade-

point average; ACT or SAT scores; written statement of purpose. Application deadline: March. Percent of acceptances: 83%

Curricular Emphasis: Electronic media theory and culture; media writing; television production; media management

Special Activities: Television: program material produced for cable television

Facilities: Television: studio; audio bay; control room

Equipment: Television/Video: complete ¾" studio and location

Alumni: John Boxley, TV sports director; Debra Galloway, TV producer; Djordje Gvozdic, TV producer/director

GUIDE POV: Affiliated with the Assemblies of God, Southern California College seeks to provide a thorough Christian liberal arts education; communication majors are offered professional training in all aspects of television production and management; internship opportunities in television production

SOUTHWESTERN COLLEGE

900 Otay Lakes Rd., Chula Vista, CA 92010 (619)421–6700

State two-year comprehensive institution. Coed, suburban location. Enrollment: 14,000.

TELEMEDIA DEPARTMENT

Chair/Contact: Robert Schneider; John Newhouse
Calendar: Semesters
Degrees Offered: A.A., telemedia

(transfer program); A.S., telemedia specialist; A.S., television engineering

Departmental Majors: 45 students, telemedia program; 15 students, telemedia specialist program

Entrance Requirements: Open-door policy; high school diploma, GED certificate, or 21 years of age. Application deadline: rolling

Curricular Emphasis: Combines foundation in theory and aesthetics with hands-on practice in film and television production

Special Activities: Television: program material produced for on-campus closed-circuit television and for cable television

Facilities: Film: screening room; editing suite; sound mixing room; animation stand; film library. Television: studio; audio bay; control room; computer graphics lab

Equipment: Film: complete Super-8 and 16mm. Television/Video: complete ¾" studio and ½" location; computer graphics with paint, video, and animation

Alumni: Gustavo Vasquez, documentary film director; Issac Artenstein, film director/writer; Jud Pauline Eberhard, film producer; Marian Inova, TV production supervisor

GUIDE POV: This two-year program offers production training in both film and television; students may choose transfer or career tracks; practical emphasis; media internship opportunities

STANFORD UNIVERSITY

Stanford, CA 94305–2050 (415)723–2300

Private four-year comprehensive institution. Coed, suburban location. Undergraduate enrollment: 6,700. Graduate enrollment: 6,850.

COMMUNICATION DEPARTMENT

Chair/Contact: Henry Breitrose
Calendar: Quarters
Degrees Offered: B.A., communication; M.A., documentary film and video, journalism, media studies; Ph.D., communication research
Departmental Majors: Undergraduate communication: 100 students. Graduate: 60 students
Entrance Requirements: Undergraduate: high SAT scores; high grade-point average; record of personal accomplishment. Graduate: high academic record; good GRE scores; desire to work in documentaries. Application deadline: December 31. Percent of acceptances: 10–15%
Curricular Emphasis: Documentary film and video production; film and television theory/aesthetics and criticism
Special Activities: Film: film series; festivals; film societies. Television: program material produced for on-campus closed-circuit television, cable television and public television station; teacher training
Facilities: Film: screening room; editing room; sound mixing room; sound stage; film library. Television: studio; audio studio; control room
Equipment: Film: complete Super-8 and 16mm. Television/Video: complete ¾" studio and location
Alumni: Roger Corman, film producer/director; Paul Cowan, TV/film director; Michael Rubbo, TV/film director; Bonnie Klein, documentary film director; Lauren Lazin, TV producer; Michael Chandler, TV/film editor

GUIDE POV: This most selective program features intensive training in documentary filmmaking; undergraduate program emphasizes communication, film, and video studies within a comprehensive liberal arts context; internship opportunities

---

UNIVERSITY OF CALIFORNIA— BERKELEY

Berkeley, CA 94720
(510)642–6000

State four-year comprehensive institution. Coed, urban location. Undergraduate enrollment: 21,000. Graduate enrollment: 9,000.

GROUP MAJOR IN FILM

Chair/Contact: Marty Gaetjens

GRADUATE SCHOOL OF JOURNALISM

Chair/Contact: Andrew Stern
Calendar: Semesters
Degrees Offered: B.A., film; M.A., journalism
Departmental Majors: Undergraduate film: 75 students. Graduate television: 15 students
Entrance Requirements: Undergraduate: 3.0 grade-point average for CA state residents; slightly higher for nonresidents; transcripts; SAT or ACT scores; three ATs; recommendations; essay. Graduate: 3.0 grade-point average; GRE scores; recommendations; written statement of purpose. Application deadline: Undergraduate: rolling; Graduate: January 5. Percent of acceptances: undergraduate: 40%. Graduate: 35%

Curricular Emphasis: Film: theory/. aesthetics; criticism; genre study; related courses in comparative literature and philosophy. Television: media studies and production with emphasis on broadcast journalism

Special Activities: Film: film series/ festivals; film societies; Pacific Film Archive. Television: program material produced for national PBS as well as local cable and broadcast outlets

Facilities: Film: screening room; permanent library of student and commercial/professional films. Television: studio; control room; newsroom

Equipment: Film: 16mm cameras; lighting and projectors. Television/ Video: complete 1" studio and ½" location (professional Betacam); Macintosh computers with graphics interface; portable cameras and lighting packages; monitors and editing equipment

Alumni: Gregory Peck, film actor; Peter Chernin, film executive; Ralph Edwards, TV personality; Joe Spano, TV/film actor; Bill Bixby, TV actor/ director

GUIDE POV: This highly selective school offers a film major stressing critical studies; television production under auspices of Graduate School of Journalism; limited internship opportunities

UNIVERSITY OF CALIFORNIA— IRVINE

Irvine, CA 92717–2435
(714)856–5011

State four-year comprehensive institution. Coed, urban location. Undergraduate enrollment: 13,000. Graduate enrollment: 3,000.

PROGRAM IN FILM STUDIES

Chair/Contact: Eric Rentschler, Chair
Calendar: Quarters
Degrees Offered: B.A., film studies
Departmental Majors:
Undergraduate: 80 students
Entrance Requirements:
Undergraduate: academic rank within top 12.5% of graduating class or 3.30 grade-point average; ACT or SAT scores; essay; achievement test scores in English composition, math, and a third subject. Undergraduate application deadline: November 1. Percent of acceptances: 59%

Curricular Emphasis: History, theory, and aesthetics of cinema, television, and video; two courses in basic video production; three upper-division screenwriting courses

Special Activities: Film: study abroad program features film theory courses in Paris at the Critical Studies Institute; visiting lecturers have included Spike Lee, Percy Adlon, Laura Mulvey, and Wolfgang Kohlhasse; student film society, 24 Frames per Second, presents weekly program of alternative, experimental, and art films to local community

Facilities: Film: screening room; editing suite; sound mixing room; film library

Equipment: Film: complete Super-8; 16mm cameras; lighting; projectors. Television/Video: VHS video; monitors

Alumni: Rebecca Swett, TV executive; Diane Max, media executive

GUIDE POV: Highly selective, this university offers a comprehensive critical studies program in cinema; internship opportunities in research, criticism, and production; practical student-faculty ratio; production classes currently use video equipment exclusively

UNIVERSITY OF CALIFORNIA— LOS ANGELES

405 Hilgard Ave.,
Los Angeles, CA 90024
(310)825–4321

*State four-year comprehensive
institution. Coed, urban location.
Undergraduate enrollment: 23,000.
Graduate enrollment: 12,000.*

SCHOOL OF THEATER, FILM, AND TELEVISION

Chair/Contact: Gilbert Cates, Dean;
Steven Moore, Counselor
Calendar: Quarters
Degrees Offered: B.A., film and
television; M.F.A., film/television
production; screenwriting; animation;
producers program; M.A., Ph.D.,
critical studies
Departmental Majors: Undergraduate
film and television: 60 students.
Graduate film and television: 250
students
Entrance Requirements:
Undergraduate: academic rank within
top 12.5% of high school graduating
class; 3.0 grade-point average;
competitive ACT or SAT scores; ATs in
English composition, mathematics, and
one additional subject required;
written portfolio. Graduate: 3.0 grade-
point average; GRE scores; personal
statement; teachers' and professional
recommendations; supporting
materials. Undergraduate application
deadline: November 30. Graduate
application deadline: November 1.
Percent of acceptances: undergraduate
and graduate: 5–15%
Curricular Emphasis: Film: criticism;
screenwriting; production; animation.
Television/Video: criticism; writing;
production; video art. Graduate:
programs in film and television

production; screenwriting; animation;
critical studies; producers program
Special Activities: Film: screenings;
visiting lecturers. Television: program
material produced for on-campus
closed-circuit television; cable
television; the UCLA Film and
Television Archive is the largest
collection of film and video holdings
in the United States outside of the
Library of Congress
Facilities: Film: three sound stages;
screening rooms; editing suites; sound
mixing rooms; animation studio; film
library; film archive. Television/Video:
three studios; editing rooms; master
control room; video archive
Equipment: Film: complete 16mm.
Television/Video: complete ¾" studio;
complete ¾" and ½" location
Alumni: Francis Ford Coppola,
director/screenwriter/producer; Danny
DeVito, director/actor; Tim Robbins,
director/actor; Paul Schrader,
screenwriter/director; Penelope
Spheeris, director; Neil Jimenez,
screenwriter; Alex Cox, film director;
Joanna Gleason, film director; Jeff
Margolis, screenwriter

GUIDE POV: Students in this selective
and well-equipped Department of Film
and Television learn history and theory
as well as the creative and
technological aspects of both film and
television; animation workshop
program provides intensive training; all
films and videos made in the
department are the property of the
students who have created them; study
abroad in 33 countries; extensive area
internship opportunities in film and
television production

UNIVERSITY OF CALIFORNIA— SAN DIEGO

9500 Gilman Drive,
La Jolla, CA 92093
(619)534-2230

*State four-year comprehensive
institution. Coed, suburban location.
Undergraduate enrollment: 15,000.
Graduate enrollment: 3,000.*

VISUAL ARTS DEPARTMENT

Chair/Contact: Jerome Rothenberg,
Chair; Caron Coke, undergraduate
studies; B.J. Barclay, graduate studies

DEPARTMENT OF COMMUNICATION

Chair/Contact: Robert Horwitz, Chair
Calendar: Quarters
Degrees Offered: B.A., M.F.A., visual
arts; B.A., Ph.D., communication
Departmental Majors: Undergraduate
visual arts: 360 students (65 art history/
criticism; 174 media; 121 studio).
Graduate visual arts: 42 students.
Undergraduate communication (film
and television): 125 students. Graduate
communication (film and television):
10 students
Entrance Requirements:
Undergraduate: contact admissions
office; UCSD consists of five colleges;
the student must choose a college
when admitted to UCSD and each
college has different requirements.
Undergraduate application deadline:
apply between November 1 and
November 30. Graduate: for Visual Arts
Department, emphasis placed on
portfolio and statement of purpose; for
Department of Communication,
emphasis is placed on GRE scores and
teachers' recommendations. Graduate
application deadline: January 15
Curricular Emphasis: Visual Arts

Department: theoretical/conceptual
program emphasizing avant-garde
production including studies in film,
video, computer media, environmental
art, and performance as well as critical
theory. Department of Communication:
Critical survey of electronic media
culture and criticism; studio and field
production with an emphasis on
broadcast journalism
Special Activities: Visual Arts
Department: Annually held
Undergraduate Arts Festival showcases
student work in film and video;
foundation grants; film series; film
societies; student publications.
Department of Communication:
television program material produced
for on-campus closed-circuit television
and for cable television
Facilities: Film/Video: 35mm
screening facilities; screening room;
editing suite; sound mixing studio with
16mm, ¾", and VHS video; 16mm
Interlock mixing studio; sound studio
for CD sound effects; format
conversion room; animation stand and
optical printer; film library. Television:
studios; audio bays; control rooms;
screening rooms; video editing rooms
Equipment: Film: complete 16mm.
Television/Video: two complete ¾"
studios and ¾" location; A/B roll with
toaster
Alumni: Rico Martinez, filmmaker;
Jayce Salloum, video artist; Kip
Fulbeck, video artist

GUIDE POV: UC San Diego offers
independent film and video studies
through the Visual Arts Department
with an emphasis on avant-garde
production; comprehensive program in
broadcast journalism is offered
through the Department of
Communication; admission to both

programs is selective; area internship opportunities in film and television production

UNIVERSITY OF CALIFORNIA— SANTA BARBARA

Santa Barbara, CA 93106–4010
(805)893–8000

State four-year comprehensive university. Coed, suburban location. Undergraduate enrollment: 16,500. Graduate enrollment: 2,100.

FILM STUDIES PROGRAM

Chair/Contact: Marti Mangan
Calendar: Quarters
Degrees Offered: B.A., film studies
Departmental Majors: Undergraduate film studies: 260 students
Entrance Requirements:
Undergraduate: 2.78–3.30 grade-point average; ACT or SAT scores.
Undergraduate application deadline: November 30
Curricular Emphasis: Film studies: history; analysis; theory; criticism. Film production: narrative; animation; documentary; experimental
Special Activities: Film: Annual film journal; quarterly alumni newsletter
Facilities: Film: 16 and 35mm screening rooms; editing rooms; library
Equipment: Film: 16mm cameras; 16mm editing; animation stand
Alumni: Scott Frank, screenwriter; Daniel Stewart, film producer; Karyn Foster, sound editor; Dana Bartz, editor; Tony Safford, studio executive

GUIDE POV: This competitive university offers a foundation in critical film studies with an introduction to 16mm production;

study abroad in 33 countries; media internship opportunities

UNIVERSITY OF CALIFORNIA— SANTA CRUZ

Santa Cruz, CA 95064
(408)459–0111

Public four-year comprehensive institution. Coed, urban location. Undergraduate enrollment: 9,400. Graduate enrollment: 1,000.

THEATRE ARTS DEPARTMENT

Chair/Contact: Mary Hiatt; Eli Hollander
Calendar: Quarters
Degrees Offered: B.A., theatre arts (concentration in film/video)
Departmental Majors:
Undergraduate: 100 students
Entrance Requirements:
Undergraduate: SAT or ACT scores; three ATs required; essay; interview; teachers' recommendations; portfolio.
Undergraduate application deadline: November 30. Percent of acceptances: 65%
Curricular Emphasis: Integration of film and video/television production work; parallel paths in production and critical studies
Special Activities: Film: film series/festivals
Facilities: Film/Video: complete postproduction for film and video including editing suites; sound mixing rooms; screening rooms
Equipment: Film/Video: complete Super-8 and 16mm; ¾", ½" Betacam, VHS, and S-VHS video
Alumni: Brannon Braga, TV writer/producer; Harrod Blank, film director/producer; Juliet Bashore, documentary film and video director/producer

GUIDE POV: Production students in this competitive program work in both cinema and video, although film techniques are emphasized; separate track in critical studies; cross-registration with other University of California campuses and with Hampshire College; innovative educational philosophy includes optional grades; local and area media internships available

UNIVERSITY OF THE PACIFIC

Stockton, CA 95211
(209)946–2011

Private four-year comprehensive institution. Coed, urban location. Undergraduate enrollment: 3,600. Graduate enrollment: 1,000.

DEPARTMENT OF ENGLISH

Chair/Contact: John D. Smith, Chair; Diane Borden
Calendar: Semesters
Degrees Offered: B.A., English (students may select emphasis in film); M.A., English (students may select emphasis in film aesthetics)
Departmental Majors: Undergraduate: 90 students. Graduate: 12 students
Entrance Requirements: Each student considered individually. Percent of acceptances: 60–70%
Curricular Emphasis: Critical analysis from varied theoretical perspectives; course listings include aesthetics of film; major filmmakers; and film, literature, and the arts
Special Activities: Film: each summer the university offers special topics in film, emphasizing close critical analysis
Alumni: Janet Leigh, film actress; David Jansen, TV actor; Jay Hammer,

TV/film producer; Robert Culp, TV actor; Darren McGavin, TV actor; Ken Kercheval, TV actor

GUIDE POV: University of the Pacific offers critical studies in film through the English Department; small, seminar-style classes; study abroad in over 50 countries

UNIVERSITY OF SAN FRANCISCO

2130 Fulton St.,
San Francisco, CA 94117–1080
(415)666–6886

Private four-year comprehensive institution. Coed, urban location. Undergraduate enrollment: 4,500. Graduate enrollment: 1,500.

MASS MEDIA STUDIES PROGRAM

Chair/Contact: Steven C. Runyon, Chair
Calendar: Semesters
Degrees Offered: B.A.
Departmental Majors: Undergraduate television: 140 students
Entrance Requirements:
Undergraduate: written statement of purpose; SAT scores recommended; ACT scores accepted. Undergraduate application deadline: rolling. Percent of acceptances: 77%
Curricular Emphasis: Electronic media theory and culture; media writing; television/video production; media management
Special Activities: Film: film series/festivals. Television: program material produced for on-campus closed-circuit television and for cable television
Facilities: Television: studio; audio bay; control room
Equipment: Television/Video: complete ¾" studio; complete ¾" and ½" location

Alumni: Pierre Salinger, Pulitzer prize-winning journalist; Elizabeth Gonzales, TV news anchor; "Big" Rick Stewart, radio personality

GUIDE POV: Affiliated with the Roman Catholic Church and run by the Jesuit Fathers, this competitive private university provides students with television production training along with a comprehensive liberal arts foundation; study abroad in Japan and Europe; required senior internship in San Francisco Bay area

UNIVERSITY OF SOUTHERN CALIFORNIA

University Park,
Los Angeles, CA 90089–2111
(213)740–2311

Private four-year comprehensive institution. Coed, urban location. Undergraduate enrollment: 16,000. Graduate enrollment: 12,000.

SCHOOL OF CINEMA-TELEVISION

Chair/Contact: USC Cinema-Television Student Affairs Office
Calendar: Semesters
Degrees Offered: B.A., film/video production, critical studies, still photography; B.F.A., filmic writing; M.A., film/video production, critical studies; M.F.A., Peter Stark motion picture producing program, graduate screenwriting; film/video production; Ph.D., critical studies, film and literature
Departmental Majors:
Undergraduate: 400 students. Graduate: 400 students
Entrance Requirements:
Undergraduate: 3.0 grade-point average; ACT or SAT scores; three letters of recommendation; written statement of purpose; contact Student Affairs Office for additional departmental requirements. Graduate: 3.0 grade-point average; GRE scores; three letters of recommendation; written statement of purpose; contact Student Affairs Office for additional departmental requirements. Undergraduate application deadline: February 1. Graduate application deadline: December 10. Percent of acceptances: Production: 10%; graduate production: 9%; filmic writing: 15%; Peter Stark M.F.A.: 15%; graduate screenwriting: 20%; critical studies: 30%; graduate critical studies: 19%
Curricular Emphasis: Extensive liberal arts education encompassing cinema and video history/theory with hands-on training in all areas of production; Ph.D. program in critical studies; B.A., M.A. in broadcast journalism offered through School of Journalism
Special Activities: Film: series of guest speakers; special film and video screenings and retrospectives; film societies; film journals; postgraduate writing workshops
Facilities: Film: 35mm and 70mm screening facilities; screening rooms; editing suites; sound mixing room; complete animation studio; computer animation laboratory; music scoring studio; permanent video cassette/laser disc library. Television/Video: studio; sound stage; control room; editing suites
Equipment: Film: complete 16mm; complete 8mm location. Television/Video: complete ¾" studio; complete ¾" and ½" location; computer graphics
Alumni: George Lucas, director/screenwriter/producer; Irvin Kershner, film director; John Milius, film director;

Robert Zemekis, film director/writer; Randall Kleiser, film director; Les Blank, documentary film director; Laura Ziskin, film producer; William Fraker, cinematographer; Caleb Deschanel, cinematographer; Ron Howard, film director/producer; John Singleton, screenwriter/director; Dan O'Bannon, screenwriter/director

GUIDE POV: This prestigious School of Cinema-Television, founded in 1929 and the nation's first film school, offers professional undergraduate and graduate training in all aspects of cinema and television production, writing, and criticism; undergraduate and graduate admissions are highly selective; the department funds selected advanced projects; extensive area internship opportunities in film and television production

---

YUBA COLLEGE

N. Beale Rd.,
Marysville, CA 95901
(916)741–6700

State two-year institution. Coed, suburban location. Enrollment: 5,000.

MASS COMMUNICATION DEPARTMENT

Chair/Contact: Stephen Cato
Calendar: Semesters

Degrees Offered: A.S., mass communication; certificate of training
Departmental Majors: 100 students
Entrance Requirements: Open-door policy; high school diploma or GED scores; 18 years of age. Application deadline: rolling
Curricular Emphasis: Electronic movie-making; state-of-the-art computer effects and editing
Special Activities: Film: film societies. Television: program material produced for on-campus closed-circuit television, local public television station, and cable television; vocational placement service
Facilities: Film: editing suite; sound mixing room; sound stage; animation stand; film library. Television: studio; audio bay; control room; editing facility
Equipment: Film: complete Super-8 and 16mm. Television/Video: complete ¾" studio; complete ¾" and ½" location; postproduction includes A/B roll with Toaster EFX.
Alumni: Mark Swain, animator; Jean Pomeroy, videographer; Bill Dion, video producer; Julie Duane, videographer

GUIDE POV: This well-equipped two-year program allows students to, in the words of Professor Cato, "produce, produce, produce."

For me, coming directly from Sullivan North High School in Kingsport, Tennessee, to film school meant that I was still very young, not even close to maturity. I knew I wanted to "make films." I had been making movies since I was ten, and that was about all I knew I wanted.

It is difficult for me to talk about film school because I have very mixed feelings about it. I'm glad I had to take two years of liberal arts before entering production classes—though at the time I hated it. I've also had the benefit of meeting many fascinating people with whom I still keep in close contact. And from a program designed to cover every aspect of film, my technical grasp on how films are made increased tremendously. A lot of good came out of it. However, there was a price.

At the time, my self-esteem was not very high. I considered it arrogant to question the opinions of my teachers or sometimes even fellow students when it seemed they knew more than I. The result was a disaster in regard to my personal growth and filmmaking style. By my senior year I decided not to even try to direct a special student project with dialogue, because I knew I would allow what I intended to do to be warped by others.

I would like to emphasize that it is very important for young students, especially undergrads, to realize that teachers do not have all the answers on the "right way" to make a film. Students have to be open to suggestions, but at the same time realize that their ideas are still *their ideas*. It's a fine line, but a critical one when you are dealing with those professors who want to make your films *their* films.

There are a few more things to remember: First, don't expect film school to make you into that creative individual or "perfect" director, writer, editor, cinematographer, etcetera. School gives you some of the basics, but it is up to you to expand on these, and it takes a lot more time than just two years to do so. Second, don't expect to land a job immediately after graduating or to be "discovered." If it happens, great, but don't count on it. Third, you don't *need* film school to make a movie. As I write this, I have just finished school and I am working on my own privately financed feature-length, low-budget (*real* low budget), 16mm film, with several other film grads. So far it has been the most educational and rewarding experience I have ever participated in—partly because of the knowledge I have obtained from film school, and partly because I am no longer in the confines of a formal institution. Now working in an environment of more creative freedom, I have finally begun to believe in myself.

AIMS COMMUNITY COLLEGE

P.O. Box 69,
Greeley, CO 80632
(303)330–8008

*District two-year institution. Coed,
suburban location. Enrollment: 15,000.*

COMMUNICATIONS MEDIA DEPARTMENT

Chair/Contact: Kenneth F. Sauer,
Chair
Calendar: Quarters
Degrees Offered: A.A., liberal arts
(students may select emphasis in
communications media)
Departmental Majors:
Communications media: 70 students
Entrance Requirements: Open-door
policy; high school diploma or GED
certificate. Application deadline:
rolling
Curricular Emphasis: Television and
radio broadcasting and production
including offerings in computer
graphics and electronic theory
Special Activities: Television program
material produced for on-campus
closed-circuit television and cable
television; media club
Facilities: Television: two studios; two
audio studios; one cuts-only control
room/editing system; ¾", S-VHS, and
VHS A/B roll postproduction editing
suites; audio mixing suite and radio
station mock-up
Equipment: Television/Video:
complete ¾" and ½" studio and EFP
configurations

Alumni: Carson Hamlin, TV producer/
technical director; Mario Caballero,
TV technical director; Mark Anderson,
TV technical director

GUIDE POV: This hands-on program
offers technical training in
video and audio production; media
internship opportunities

COLORADO MOUNTAIN COLLEGE

P.O. Box 775288,
Steamboat Springs, CO 80477
(303)870–4444

*District two-year institution. Coed, rural
location. Enrollment: 1,500.*

HUMANITIES DEPARTMENT

Chair/Contact: Bob Baker, Chair
Calendar: Semesters
Degrees Offered: None
Entrance Requirements: ACT or SAT
scores. Application deadline: rolling
Curricular Emphasis: Film studies
including theory/aesthetics; history;
criticism
Alumni: Brant Brantman,
videographer; Ward Holmes, radio
broadcaster

GUIDE POV: Colorado Mountain
College is a small two-year district
institution providing students with
theory courses in film through the
Humanities Department; core
curriculum fulfills transfer
requirements to four-year universities;
residential campuses in Steamboat

Springs, Glenwood Springs, and
Leadville

COLORADO STATE UNIVERSITY

Fort Collins, CO 80523
(303)491–1101

*State four-year comprehensive
institution. Coed, suburban location.
Undergraduate enrollment: 18,000.
Graduate enrollment: 4,000.*

DEPARTMENT OF TECHNICAL JOURNALISM

Chair/Contact: Fred Shook; Greg Luft
Calendar: Semesters
Degrees Offered: B.A., technical
journalism; M.S., technical
communication
Departmental Majors: Undergraduate
television: 60 students
Entrance Requirements:
Undergraduate: ACT (minimum 22) or
SAT (minimum 467 verbal; 525 math)
scores. Graduate: GRE scores;
interview; recommendations; written
statement of purpose. Undergraduate
application deadline: March 1.
Graduate application deadline: rolling.
Percent of acceptances: undergraduate
and graduate: 59%
Curricular Emphasis: Electronic
media theory and culture; media
writing; television production; news/
documentary
Special Activities: Film: film series/
festivals. Television: program material
produced for on-campus closed-circuit
television and for cable television
Facilities: Television: studio; video
editing suites
Equipment: Television/Video:
complete ¾" studio and location
Alumni: Roy Brunett, TV executive;
Jim Bienemann, TV news anchor;
Mike Jensen, TV photojournalist; John

Fosholt, TV producer/reporter; Kim
Katchur, TV photojournalist

GUIDE POV: Comprehensive television
production and theoretical studies are
taught at this highly selective state
university as part of a comprehensive
technical journalism curriculum; co-op
programs with Metropolitan State
College and Universidad Autonoma in
Mexico; participation in National
Student Exchange; cross-registration
with Aims Community College and
Front Range Community College;
semester-at-sea program; study abroad;
internship opportunities in television
production

FORT LEWIS COLLEGE

1000 Rim Dr.,
Durango, CO 81301–3999
(303)247–7010

*State four-year comprehensive
institution. Coed, rural location.
Enrollment: 4,100.*

ENGLISH/THEATRE DEPARTMENTS

Chair/Contact: Television: Dinah
Leavitt
Calendar: Trimesters
Degrees Offered: B.A., English
(communications option)
Entrance Requirements: Academic
rank within top third of high school
graduating class; 2.0 grade-point
average; ACT (minimum 17 or 20
enhanced) or SAT (minimum 800)
scores; interview recommended; GED
accepted. Application deadline:
August 1 or at least one month
prior to registration. Percent of
acceptances: 90%
Curricular Emphasis: Television and
radio production featuring news/

documentary; small-format video production; media writing; video art
Special Activities: Film: film societies. Television: program material produced for local commercial television station or for FLC News
Facilities: Television: studio
Equipment: Television/Video: complete ¾" studio; complete ¾" and ½" location
Alumni: Christopher Schauble, TV news anchor; Susan Witkin, radio announcer

GUIDE POV: Fort Lewis College offers hands-on television and video production training through both its English and Theatre departments; Native American students offered full-tuition scholarships; students produce news and documentary programs; training offered in video art; study abroad; internship opportunities in television production

METROPOLITAN STATE COLLEGE OF DENVER

Campus Box 16,
P.O. Box 173362,
Denver, CO 80204
(303)556–2400

State four-year comprehensive institution. Coed, urban location. Enrollment: 17,800.

BROADCASTING/TELECOMMUNICATION

Chair/Contact: Television: James R. Craig
Calendar: Semesters
Degrees Offered: B.A., communications (multi-major broadcasting)
Entrance Requirements: Must meet minimum Standard Index Score of 76; submission of high school grade-

point average; ACT or SAT scores. Application deadline: July 31. Percent of acceptances: 97%
Curricular Emphasis: Television/video production; computer graphics; video art; instructional/industrial
Special Activities: Television: program material produced for local cable, public, and commercial television stations and for on-campus closed-circuit television
Facilities: Television: studio; audio bay; control room
Equipment: Television/Video: complete Beta, ½" and ¾" studio; complete Beta, ½" and ¾" location; Beta, ½" and ¾" editing equipment
Alumni: Molly Archibold, videographer

GUIDE POV: Students attending this state college—which is the largest urban, nonresidential four-year college in the United States—learn all aspects of broadcasting while working on a variety of projects; over 100 outside internship opportunities in television production

UNIVERSITY OF COLORADO— BOULDER

Boulder, CO 80309–0316
(303)492–1411

State four-year comprehensive institution. Coed, urban location. Undergraduate enrollment: 20,000. Graduate enrollment: 4,000.

FILM STUDIES DEPARTMENT

Chair/Contact: Virgil Grillo, Chair

SCHOOL OF JOURNALISM AND MASS COMMUNICATION

Chair/Contact: Stephen B. Jones
Calendar: Semesters

Degrees Offered: B.A., film; B.F.A., film production; B.S., journalism and mass communication; M.A., journalism and mass communication; Ph.D., communication
Departmental Majors:
Undergraduate: 50 critical film studies; 50 film production; 108 television. Graduate: 10 television
Entrance Requirements:
Undergraduate: 2.5 grade-point average; ACT or SAT scores; interview; portfolio. Graduate: 3.0 grade-point average; GRE scores; recommendations. Undergraduate and graduate application deadline: rolling
Curricular Emphasis: Film: critical studies and 16mm independent production. Television: production with stress on broadcast journalism
Special Activities: Film: film series/ festivals; film societies. Television: program material produced for on-campus closed-circuit television and local commercial television station
Facilities: Film: 35mm screening facilities; 16mm, video, and Super-8 editing rooms; animation stands; film library. Television: studio; audio bay; control room
Equipment: Film: Super-8 and 16mm; 16mm flatbed editors. Television: complete ¾" studio; complete ¾" and ½" location; VHS editing; video toaster; optical printer
Alumni: Ted Rose, film editor

GUIDE POV: This selective, professionally equipped university offers separate, comprehensive programs in both film and television; critical studies along with commercial and independent production training; summer session includes a creative arts festival; study abroad; internship opportunities in film and television

UNIVERSITY OF COLORADO— COLORADO SPRINGS

1420 Austin Bluffs Pkwy.,
P.O. 7150,
Colorado Springs, CO 80933
(719)593-3000

State four-year comprehensive institution. Coed, urban location. Undergraduate enrollment: 5,000. Graduate enrollment: 600.

COMMUNICATION DEPARTMENT

Chair/Contact: Kim Walker
Calendar: Semesters
Degrees Offered: B.A., communication (students may select emphasis in industrial media management); M.A., communication (students may select emphasis in organizational communication)
Departmental Majors:
Undergraduate: 365 students. Graduate: 25 students
Entrance Requirements:
Undergraduate: 2.6 grade-point average; ACT or SAT scores; teachers' recommendations. Graduate: transcripts; GRE scores; professional recommendations; teachers' recommendations; written statement of purpose. Undergraduate and graduate application deadline: rolling. Percent of acceptances: 73%
Curricular Emphasis: Electronic media theory and culture; media writing; television production; media management
Special Activities: Television: program material produced for on-campus closed-circuit television, for local public and commercial television stations, and for cable television
Facilities: Television: studio; audio bay; control room; three editing suites
Equipment: Television/Video:

complete 1" and ¾" studio; complete ¾" and ½" location

Alumni: Mitch Riley, filmmaker; Jim Arthurs, filmmaker; Janet Alexander, animator/filmmaker

GUIDE POV: Professionally equipped, this competitive program provides comprehensive training in all aspects of broadcast and nonbroadcast television production; media writing; programming, sales, and management training; local and area media internship opportunities

---

UNIVERSITY OF DENVER

2490 S. Gaylord St.,
Denver, CO 80208
(303)871–2000

Private four-year comprehensive institution. Coed, urban location. Undergraduate enrollment: 3,000. Graduate enrollment: 3,000.

MASS COMMUNICATIONS AND JOURNALISM STUDIES

Chair/Contact: Phil Stephens
Calendar: Quarters
Degrees Offered: B.A., mass communications (students may select emphasis in television); M.A., mass communications
Departmental Majors:
Undergraduate: 200 students. Graduate: 13 students
Entrance Requirements:
Undergraduate: transcripts; 2.0 grade-point average; ACT or SAT scores; essay; teachers' recommendations. Graduate: transcripts; 3.0 grade-point average; GRE scores; three letters of recommendation. Undergraduate and graduate application deadline: March 1. Percent of acceptances: 70%

Curricular Emphasis: Film criticism; video production; documentary production; video art; media writing; media law
Special Activities: Television: program material produced for cable television; travel classes to Hollywood; travel classes in documentary production to South and Central America; Institute for Documentary Studies
Facilities: Television: studio; audio bay; control room
Equipment: Television: complete ¾" studio and location
Alumni: Mel Damski, TV/film director; Tim Wurtz, TV/film writer; Don Levy, studio executive

GUIDE POV: This private university offers a production-based video program with special attention to documentary forms; small classes with attention to individual projects; study abroad and extensive area internship opportunities

---

UNIVERSITY OF NORTHERN COLORADO

Greeley, CO 80639
(303)351–1890

State four-year comprehensive institution. Coed, small city location. Undergraduate enrollment: 7,500. Graduate enrollment: 1,500.

JOURNALISM AND MASS COMMUNICATIONS

Chair/Contact: Charles H. Ingold; Petie Vonk
Calendar: Semesters
Degrees Offered: B.A.
Departmental Majors: Undergraduate journalism and mass communications: 360 students

Entrance Requirements:
Undergraduate: high school diploma
or GED certificate; transcripts;
academic rank within top half of
graduating class; SAT or ACT scores; 2.3
undergraduate grade-point average for
admission to program. Undergraduate
application deadline: at least one
month prior to start of semester;
students wishing to become majors in
journalism and mass communications
must submit all documents by
February 15 for fall semester; October
15 for spring semester. Percent of
acceptances: 75–80%
Curricular Emphasis: Liberal arts
studies combined with practical audio
and video training
Special Activities: Television:
program material produced for local
cable television
Facilities: Television: three-camera
full-color studio; control room; editing
room
Equipment: Television/Video:
cameras for studio and location;
single-source editing in Beta, VHS, and
¾"; VHS camcorders; Beta EFP gear
Alumni: Mary Liggett, TV news
anchor; Tony Lamb, TV assignment
editor; Anna Osborn, TV news
reporter; Andrew Findlay, TV technical
director; Jim Blaney, TV sportscaster

GUIDE POV: Undergraduates enrolled
in this competitive television
production program are offered
practical training with an emphasis on
broadcast journalism; internship
opportunities in television production

UNIVERSITY OF SOUTHERN COLORADO

2200 Bonforte Blvd.,
Pueblo, CO 81001
(719)549–2100

*State four-year comprehensive
institution. Coed, urban location.
Enrollment: 6,000.*

MASS COMMUNICATIONS DEPARTMENT

Chair/Contact: Patricia Orman, Chair
Calendar: Semesters
Degrees Offered: B.A., B.S.C., mass
communication (students may select
emphasis in telecommunications)
Departmental Majors: Television: 65
students
Entrance Requirements: 2.0 grade-
point average; ACT or SAT scores;
creative portfolio. Application
deadline: April 15. Percent of
acceptances: 90%
Curricular Emphasis: Mass
communication theory; critical studies
in film; media writing; broadcast
journalism
Special Activities: Film: student
publications. Television: USC's PBS
affiliate, KTSC-TV, provides laboratory
training and on-campus jobs for
television students
Facilities: Television: two studios;
audio bays; control rooms
Equipment: Television/Video:
complete 1" and ¾" studio; S-VHS
location
Alumni: J. Ralph Carter, TV broadcast
consultant; Sandra Mann, TV news
anchor

GUIDE POV: This well-equipped state
university offers students ample
television production experience;
broadcast journalism emphasis; theory
courses in film; study abroad; member
of the National Student Exchange;
internship opportunities in television
production

I come to the following viewpoint from various perspectives. Having been a student in film production at a number of schools, I acquired substantial credentials: a B.A. from NYU, an M.A. from the University of Southern California, and additional advanced studies from AFI. After completing my education, I spent several years working on features, documentaries, industrials, educational films, and videos.

Recently I returned to academia, and am now a tenure track professor in production at USC. Most of my outside work involves teaching video programming in developing countries—primarily in Africa—around aspects of social change, such as family planning, teenage pregnancy, AIDS information, environmental and women's issues.

It is clear that film schools throughout the country—including my own— suffer from small female enrollments. Currently, women represent less than 30% of the students in our production program. Approximately 25% of those who originally apply are women. So we accept a higher percentage than our application pool. As head of my school's Committee for a More Diverse Student Body, I need to ask myself why this is. One answer is that women get the message both in the real world and from movies that there are few places for them behind the camera. There may be some superstars like Barbra Streisand and Penny Marshall who have made it as directors, but one still finds a dearth of female names. Sexism is rampant in the film and television business. Witness how few women are teaching production, or function as role models in our training institutions.

For those of us sickened by the portrayal of violence, guns, and the treatment of women and minorities, there is a chance to effect change. As educators, we have an obligation to offer options. We need to encourage students—both men and women—to question society, not just to repeat the old values we grew up with. We need to provide alternative styles and points of view. And we need to understand that power is not enough. We must encourage creativity and individuality, and provide a climate where students can question and articulate ethical issues in the classroom. There is not only one way to tell a story, and it is our job to help students tell their stories in the most compelling ways possible. Although we teach technical and production skills, a university is more than a trade school. The healthier and safer a climate is for students to express themselves, the better chance we have of affecting society once they graduate.

MANCHESTER COMMUNITY COLLEGE

60 Bidwell St.,
Manchester, CT 06040
(203)646–4900

State two-year comprehensive institution. Coed, suburban location. Enrollment: 6,500.

MEDIA STUDIES DEPARTMENT

Chair/Contact: Robert Kagan, Coordinator
Calendar: Semesters
Degrees Offered: A.S.
Departmental Majors: Media: 90 students
Entrance Requirements: Open-door policy; ACT or SAT scores. Application deadline: rolling. Percent of acceptances: 95%
Curricular Emphasis: Electronic media theory and culture; film appreciation; media writing; audio-video production
Special Activities: Television: program material produced for on-campus closed-circuit television and for cable television
Facilities: Video: screening room; editing suite. Television: studio; control room; audio booth
Equipment: Television/Video: complete ¾" studio; extensive ¾" and ½" portable equipment
Alumni: Janet Sombric, video producer; Amaral Santos, cable TV coordinator; Paul Smith, video producer

GUIDE POV: Manchester Community College offers practical media training for those students seeking technical support positions after graduation; core curriculum fulfills transfer requirements to four-year universities; strong internship program with surrounding media outlets

MIDDLESEX COMMUNITY COLLEGE

100 Training Hill Rd.,
Middletown, CT 06457
(203)343–5800

State two-year comprehensive institution. Coed, suburban location. Enrollment: 3,000.

BROADCAST COMMUNICATIONS DEPARTMENT

Chair/Contact: John Shafer, Chair
Calendar: Semesters
Degrees Offered: A.A.
Departmental Majors: 65 students
Entrance Requirements: Open-door policy; high school diploma or GED scores. Application deadline: rolling
Curricular Emphasis: Television production
Special Activities: Television: weekly program material produced for cable television; student involvement in production of corporate/educational videos

Facilities: Film: screening room; editing room; film library. Television: studio; audio bay; control room

Equipment: Film: 16mm cameras; flatbed editing equipment; lighting; black-and-white film stock; color film stock. Television/Video: complete ¾" studio; complete ¾" and S-VHS location with three-chip cameras; computer graphics

Alumni: Victor Gonzalez, TV/film director; Johna Guild, TV program director; David Flood, TV assignment director

GUIDE POV: Middlesex Community College offers an affordable, well-equipped broadcast production program; students may also work in 16mm film; balance of academic studies with practical training; high job placement and transfer rates; variety of internship opportunities in television/video production

QUINNIPIAC COLLEGE

Mount Carmel Ave.,
Hamden, CT 06518
(203)288–5251

Private four-year comprehensive institution. Coed, suburban location. Enrollment: 2,500.

MASS COMMUNICATIONS DEPARTMENT

Chair/Contact: John Gourlie
Calendar: Semesters
Degrees Offered: B.A.
Departmental Majors: Television: 100 students
Entrance Requirements: Academic rank within top half of high school graduating class; ACT (minimum 20) or SAT (minimum composite 950) scores; recommendations. Application

deadline: rolling. Percent of students accepted: 93%

Curricular Emphasis: Electronic media theory and culture; critical studies in film; media writing; film and television production

Special Activities: Film: film series/festival. Television: program material produced for on-campus closed-circuit television

Facilities: Film: film library. Television: studio; audio bay; control room

Equipment: Film: complete Super-8. Television/Video: complete ¾" studio; complete ¾" and ½" location

Alumni: Albert Magnoli, film director; Jeffrey Chernov, film producer; Michael Baker, film director

GUIDE POV: This small private college offers a diversified program with production and writing studies in both film and television; course listings in film and electronic media theory, history, and criticism; cross-registration with the University of New Haven and Albertus Magnus College; study abroad in China, Japan, Greece, Italy, and the West Indies; internship opportunities in television production

SACRED HEART UNIVERSITY

Fairfield, CT 06432–1000
(203)371–7999

Private four-year comprehensive institution. Coed, suburban location. Enrollment: 6,000.

MEDIA STUDIES DEPARTMENT

Chair/Contact: Rebecca L. Abbott, Associate Professor
Calendar: Semesters
Degrees Offered: B.A., B.S., media studies

Entrance Requirements: 2.75 grade-point average; SAT required; ATs in English, mathematics, and language recommended; essay required; portfolio recommended; interview recommended. Application deadline: rolling. Percent of acceptances: 70%

Curricular Emphasis: Study of communications theory and technology combined with liberal arts; sequential courses in video and film production

Special Activities: Film: student publications. Television: program material produced for local public access television

Facilities: Film: screening room; editing suite. Television: studio; audio bay; control room

Equipment: Film: complete Super-8 and 16mm projectors. Television/Video: complete ¾" studio; complete ¾" and ½" location

Alumni: R. Stacy Ratliff, cinematographer/videographer; Melany Secrist, corporate film executive; Jan Moody, script supervisor

GUIDE POV: The media studies program at Sacred Heart University offers a major that equally stresses formal studies in communication theory and practical production workshops; co-operative programs; cross-registration with Fairfield University; study abroad in Europe and Japan; extensive paid and unpaid area media internship opportunities

---

UNIVERSITY OF HARTFORD

200 Bloomfield Ave.,
West Hartford, CT 06117
(203)768–4100

Private four-year comprehensive institution. Coed, suburban location.

Undergraduate enrollment: 5,000. Graduate enrollment: 300.

ENGLISH DEPARTMENT

Chair/Contact: Michael Walsh
Degrees Offered: B.A., English (concentration in film criticism)

COMMUNICATION DEPARTMENT

Chair/Contact: Harvey Jassem, Chair
Degrees Offered: B.A., M.A., communication (emphasis offered in mass communication)

Calendar: Semesters

Departmental Majors: Undergraduate English: 138 students. Undergraduate communication: 450 students. Graduate communication: 50 students

Entrance Requirements: Undergraduate: high school diploma or GED certificate; SAT scores; essay required; AT recommended in English composition; interview recommended. Graduate: transcripts; *B* average in undergraduate class work relating to major; GRE scores. Undergraduate and graduate application deadline: February 1. Percent of acceptances: 79%

Curricular Emphasis: Concentration in film history, theory, and aesthetics is offered through the English Department; concentrated work in television production offered through Communication Department

Special Activities: Film: film series/festivals; student publications; teacher training. Television/Video: program material produced for various media outlets; corporate video projects

Facilities: Film: screening room; editing suite; film library. Television: studio; audio bay; control room

Equipment: Film: 16mm projector. Television/Video: complete ¾" studio and location

Alumni: Michael Mongillo, filmmaker

GUIDE POV: Communication majors at the University of Hartford develop skills in broadcast television and corporate video production; there is a minor and special internship in sports journalism; English majors may elect a concentration in film theory, history, and aesthetics; cross-registration with the Greater Hartford Consortium; study abroad; internship opportunities in television production

WESLEYAN UNIVERSITY

Middletown, CT 06457
(203)347–9411

Private four-year comprehensive institution. Coed, rural location. Undergraduate enrollment: 2,600. Graduate enrollment: 500.

FILM PROGRAM

Chair/Contact: Jeanine Basinger
Calendar: Semesters
Degrees Offered: B.A.
Departmental Majors:
Undergraduate: 40–50 students. Graduate: a master's degree with a concentration in film may be pursued by special arrangement only
Entrance Requirements:
Undergraduate: transcripts; SAT scores of approximately 1300; three achievement test scores; English composition test scores; ACT accepted; interview; essay; recommendations; AP credit accepted. Graduate: transcripts; GRE scores; interview; essay; recommendations. Undergraduate application deadline: November 15 for early decision option I; January 15 for early decision option II; February 1 final deadline. Graduate application deadline: March 15. Percent of acceptances: 36%
Curricular Emphasis: Students complete both film theory and production courses as part of unified program; students are encouraged to take full liberal arts program in addition to film
Special Activities: Film: university film series; film societies; student screenings; cinema archives; alumni employment service
Facilities: Film: 35mm screening facilities; screening room; editing suite; sound mixing room; animation stand; film library
Equipment: Film: complete Super-8 and 16mm; 35mm projectors. Video: complete ½" location
Alumni: Elia Kazan, film director; Paul Schiff, film producer; Joss Whedon, screenwriter; Jeffrey Lane, screenwriter; Laurence Mark, film producer; David Kendall, TV writer/producer; Michael Fields, film director; Strauss Zelnick, film executive

GUIDE POV: This prestigious school offers an interdisciplinary critical studies program in film with required core offerings in production; practical student-faculty ratios in all production courses; attention to independent projects; cross-registration with 11 area colleges; study abroad in 10 countries; local and area film internships available

YALE UNIVERSITY

New Haven, CT 06520
(203)432–4771

Private four-year comprehensive institution. Coed, urban location. Undergraduate enrollment: 5,000. Graduate enrollment: 2,500.

FILM STUDIES PROGRAM

Chair/Contact: Charles Musser; David Rodowick
Calendar: Semesters
Degrees Offered: B.A., film studies
Departmental Majors: Undergraduate film: 25 students
Entrance Requirements:
Undergraduate: competitive grade-point average; applicants must take either the SAT and any three ATs, or the ACT; interview recommended; essay required. Undergraduate application deadline: December 31. Percent of acceptances: 18%
Curricular Emphasis: History, criticism, and aesthetics of cinema as well as the study of film in relation to national cultures
Special Activities: Film: film societies

Facilities: Yale Film Study Center maintains research facilities; archive of 2,000 classic films and other materials
Alumni: Brandon Tartikoff, media executive; Don Pennebaker, documentary filmmaker; Jodie Foster, film actress/director; Larry Lasker, film writer/producer; Jennie Livingston, documentary filmmaker

GUIDE POV: Founded in 1701, Yale University offers an interdisciplinary film studies program that draws on the study of art history, national cultures and literatures, philosophy, literary theory, sociology, and other tracts; students may define area of concentration; production classes in small-format video; senior seminar essay required; screenwriting courses offered through School of Drama

In 1937, America was captivated by a timeless story brought to the screen in a new way. It was *Snow White and the Seven Dwarfs*, the first animated full-length feature film—the culmination of the dreams and vision of Walt Disney. Vast numbers of artists have contributed their talents and imagination to the production of classics like this. Today, a new generation of artists continues to expand animation's limitless possibilities.

My own career in animation started with Disney more than 35 years ago, working on *Sleeping Beauty* as well as the original "Mickey Mouse Club" and "Disneyland" television series. During the sixties, I worked in the animation department for NASA's Jet Propulsion Laboratory in Pasadena, California. Later, I helped start up North America's first Disney-influenced professional animation program at Sheridan College in Ontario, Canada. Returning to Hollywood in 1979, I worked at Hanna-Barbera and Filmation Studios. I was subsequently invited back by Disney Studios to set up a comprehensive training program for Feature Animation to scout artistic talent that enables me to function as a liaison with the educational establishment.

Many young artists grow up with hopes of becoming professional animators. But it takes more than mere dreaming. Preparation for a career as an animation artist requires the discipline of appropriate training. Talent must be nourished and guided by professionals through academic study and, when possible, through internships. The opportunities for artistic careers in animation production at major studios—in addition to that of the animator—include positions in such departments as story sketch, visual development, layout, background painting, computer animation, and special effects animation.

Disney Feature Animation offers internship programs of approximately three months' duration each. Generally, applicants are qualified students in their senior year of art training, or fairly recent graduates. The selection process for the limited number of openings for each program is through a portfolio competition. So if your plan is to create exciting animation, select a school, commit yourself to a solid program of training, then assemble a professional-looking portfolio. We'll want to take a look at it.

UNIVERSITY OF DELAWARE

Newark, DE 19716
(302)831–2000

Independent, public-supported four-year comprehensive institution. Coed, suburban location. Undergraduate enrollment: 15,200. Graduate enrollment: 2,500.

COMMUNICATION DEPARTMENT

Chair/Contact: Television: John Courtright, Chair
Calendar: Semesters
Degrees Offered: B.A., M.A., communication
Entrance Requirements: Undergraduate: academic rank within top half of high school graduating class; SAT required; scores from advanced placement tests or CEEB achievement tests recommended; essay required for honors consideration. Graduate: GRE scores; competitive undergraduate grade-point average. Undergraduate and graduate application deadline: March 1; however, to be assured full consideration for academic scholarships and first choice of major, recommended deadline is January 1. Percent of acceptances: 53%
Curricular Emphasis: Media writing; broadcast and field production
Special Activities: Film: film series/ festivals. Television: program material produced for various outlets

Facilities: Television: studio; control room
Equipment: Television/Video: complete ¾" studio and location
Alumni: Nancy Karibjanean, TV news anchor; Renee Schuman, TV producer; Bob Russell, video producer; John Rusk, assistant director

GUIDE POV: Founded in 1743 and chartered in 1833, this privately controlled land-grant institution offers a growing communication program with a theoretical emphasis on the social and behavioral sciences; practical training in broadcast journalism; study abroad; internship opportunities in television production

WESLEY COLLEGE

120 N. State St.,
Dover, DE 19901
(302)736–2300

Private four-year comprehensive institution. Coed, urban location. Enrollment: 850.

COMMUNICATION DEPARTMENT

Chair/Contact: Dr. Mike Nielsen
Calendar: Semesters
Degrees Offered: B.A.
Departmental Majors: 45 students
Entrance Requirements: Open-door policy; high school diploma or GED certificate; ACT or SAT scores. Application deadline: rolling

Curricular Emphasis: Media writing; video production; integration of computers, video, audio, and print

Special Activities: Television: program material produced for cable television

Facilities: Television: studio; audio bay; control room

Equipment: Television/Video: complete ¾" studio; editing suite with Amiga video graphics

Alumni: Andrea Di Rocco, videographer

GUIDE POV: This growing program provides comprehensive training in television/video production with an emphasis on technical skills; focus on creating original video programs; media internship opportunities

Both an advantage and drawback to attending film school in Los Angeles is that you are so close to the epicenter of the most thriving film culture on the planet, it's almost too easy to imagine being a part of it. In Hollywood, gossip tends to work its way into casual conversation even among people whose interest in movies doesn't extend much further than a line at the local theatre. In an L.A. film school, where celebrities routinely accompany their latest projects to student screenings, it can become difficult to remember that while the commercial Hollywood approach to film is perfectly legitimate, it is far from the only way of working in what may be the most exciting and versatile artistic medium yet created.

The L.A.-based film schools themselves often mold the students entrusted to them toward a system of aesthetics based primarily on turning a profit, at a point in their careers when that could easily afford to be the last thing on their eager young minds. That problem is especially acute at two of the better-known L.A. film programs: UCLA and my alma mater, USC.

While I enjoyed my time there and would heartily recommend USC to a student interested in mastering filmmaking as a craft, I might steer those interested in making personal or unconventional statements on film away from the program—unless sure they would arrive in Los Angeles with their sense of artistic purpose armed and ready for battle.

USC certainly has one of the best physical plants of any film school, thanks to liberal donations from alum George Lucas and his equally illustrious pals. Steven Spielberg has also been a generous patron, despite the fact that he never officially attended the school. (In a delicious historical irony, it is rumored he was repeatedly turned down for admission.) Fully equipped sound stages, an ever-expanding computer graphics curriculum, on- and off-line video editing gear, and state-of-the-art music recording facilities exist beside time-honored dinosaurs like moviola and flatbed editing systems, and some battle-scarred 16mm movie cameras dating back to WWII. There are also numerous projection rooms available to students shooting on 16mm, as well as all the camera, lighting, and sound tools necessary for advanced synch-sound movie-making.

I now realize that loving movies is equal parts euphoria and despair. But I would say to the filmmaker willing to tough it out that the commercial pressures of Hollywood will come soon enough, while the chance to find a unique way of seeing and commenting on the great wide world is rare outside the protected environment of film school. It should be cherished.

THE AMERICAN UNIVERSITY

4400 Massachusetts Ave.
NW, Washington, DC 20016
(202)885–1000

*Private four-year comprehensive
institution. Coed, urban location.
Undergraduate enrollment: 5,000.
Graduate enrollment: 4,000.*

**VISUAL MEDIA/GRADUATE FILM
AND VIDEO**

Chair/Contact: Glenn Harnden; John
Douglass
Calendar: Semesters
Degrees Offered: B.A., M.A.
Departmental Majors:
Undergraduate: 135 students. Graduate:
90 students
Entrance Requirements:
Undergraduate: transcripts; ACT or SAT
scores; average SAT approximately
1100. Graduate: minimum 3.0 grade-
point average; GRE scores; 1,000 word
statement of purpose; two letters of
recommendation; TOEFL scores
required of foreign students.
Undergraduate and graduate
application deadline: February 15.
Percent of acceptances: 50%
Curricular Emphasis: Film studies:
criticism, theory, aesthetics.
Scriptwriting: feature, documentary,
television comedy. Production:
documentary, narrative, instructional/
educational in 16mm film and various
video formats, and broadcast
television
Special Activities: Film: film series/
festivals; guest speakers and
screenings. Television: program
material produced for on-campus
closed-circuit television
Facilities: Film: 35mm screening
facilities; screening room; editing suite;
film library. Television: studio; control
room
Equipment: Film: complete Super-8
and 16mm. Television/Video: complete
¾" studio; complete ¾" and S-VHS
location
Alumni: Joe Becker, film/TV director;
Anne Bohlen, film documentarian;
Bob Kanter, TV executive; Desson
Howe, film critic; Alison Abelson,
video producer; Cecilia Domeyko, TV
producer/executive

GUIDE POV: This professionally
oriented program provides
comprehensive training in all aspects
of film and television production;
graduate students choose
specialization in film production,
video production, scriptwriting, or
criticism; extensive internship
opportunities in film and television

GALLAUDET UNIVERSITY

800 Florida Ave. NE,
Washington, DC 20002–3695
(202)651–5000

Private four-year comprehensive institution. Coed, urban location. Enrollment: 2,000.

DEPARTMENT OF TELEVISION, FILM, AND PHOTOGRAPHY

Chair/Contact: Don Bangs; Donna C. Maclean
Calendar: Semesters
Degrees Offered: B.A.
Departmental Majors: 15 students
Entrance Requirements: Transcripts, recommendations, and interview required; results of eighth or seventh edition of the Stanford Achievement Test; knowledge and understanding of American Sign Language; recent audiogram; university essay test. Application deadline: April 15. Percent of acceptances: 65%
Curricular Emphasis: Electronic media theory and culture; critical studies in film; media writing; audio-film-video production; media management; evolving technologies; still photography
Special Activities: Television: program material produced for on-campus closed-circuit television, for local public television, and for cable television
Facilities: Film: screening room; editing suite; sound mixing room; animation stand; film library. Television/Video: studio; audio bay; control room; video toaster/editing
Equipment: Film: complete 16mm. Television/Video: complete 1" and ¾" studio; complete ¾" and ½" location
Alumni: Barry White, TV production specialist; Laura Harvey, TV production assistant; Johnston Grindstaff, photography teacher; Yoon Lee, TV production assistant

GUIDE POV: Established in 1864, this competitive private college is the only four-year liberal arts university in the world designed exclusively for deaf and hard of hearing students; all instructors teach using sign language; students may pursue both film and television studies; modern facilities; balanced offering of theory and practice; film animation and video art; internship opportunities in television production

---

GEORGE WASHINGTON UNIVERSITY

Washington, DC 20052
(202)994–1000

Private four-year comprehensive institution. Coed, urban location. Undergraduate enrollment: 6,000. Graduate enrollment: 10,000.

RADIO AND TELEVISION PROGRAM

Chair/Contact: Joan Thiel; Marie Travis
Calendar: Semesters
Degrees Offered: B.A., radio and television
Departmental Majors: Undergraduate radio and television: 75 students
Entrance Requirements: Undergraduate: 2.75 grade-point average; ACT (minimum 23) or SAT (minimum composite 1000) scores; teachers' recommendations; written statement of purpose; three ATs recommended. Undergraduate application deadline: February 1. Percent of acceptances: 79%
Curricular Emphasis: Electronic media theory and culture; critical studies in film; media writing; audio-video production
Special Activities: Film: film series/festivals; student publication. Television: guest speakers; program material produced for various outlets

Facilities: Film: screening room; editing suite; sound mixing room; film library. Television: studios; audio bays; control rooms; multi-camera mobile unit; CMX editors; video teleconferencing center

Equipment: Film: complete Super-8. Television/Video: complete ¾" studio; ¾" location and editing

Alumni: Larry King, TV broadcaster; Alec Baldwin, film actor; Molly Boyle, CNN-TV director of human resources; Lynn Neufer, ABC-TV network producer; Graham Marshall, cinematographer

GUIDE POV: Communication majors at this selective private university are offered comprehensive television production training as well as studies in mass communication theory; cross-registration with area universities; study abroad; faculty of working professionals; extensive internship opportunities in television production available

---

HOWARD UNIVERSITY

525 Bryant St. NW,
Washington, DC 20059
(202)806–6100

Private four-year comprehensive institution. Coed, urban location. Undergraduate enrollment: 7,000. Graduate enrollment: 4,000.

RADIO, TELEVISION, AND FILM DEPARTMENT

Chair/Contact: Dr. Bishetta D. Merritt, Chair
Calendar: Semesters
Degrees Offered: B.A., radio-television-film; M.F.A., film
Departmental Majors: Undergraduate and graduate combined: 1,000 students

Entrance Requirements:
Undergraduate: academic rank within top half of graduating class; 2.5 grade-point average; ACT (minimum 18) or SAT (minimum composite 800) scores; AP credit accepted. Graduate: transcripts; statement of purpose; sample of work; GRE scores; 3.0 grade-point average; recommendations. Undergraduate and graduate application deadline: April 1. Percent of acceptances: 47%

Curricular Emphasis: Film, television, and radio production; telecommunications management

Special Activities: Film: film series/festivals. Television: program material produced for cable television, for local public and commercial television stations, and for school's on-campus closed-circuit television station WHMM; Society of Professional Journalists

Facilities: Film: 35mm screening facilities; screening rooms; editing suite; 24-track sound mixing room; animation stand. Television and Video: two studios; audio bays; control rooms

Equipment: Film: complete Super-8 and 16mm. Television/Video: complete ¾" studio and location; VHS and Betacam equipment

Alumni: Debbie Allen, TV director/choreographer; Patricia Hilliard, filmmaker; Bobby Crawford, screenwriter; A. J. Fielder, cinematographer

GUIDE POV: Howard University offers its students both film and television production tracks in a competitive atmosphere; practical faculty to student ratio; cross-registration with the Consortium of Universities in the Washington metropolitan area; study abroad in Europe and Africa; extensive internship opportunities in film and television production

UNIVERSITY OF THE DISTRICT OF COLUMBIA

4200 Connecticut Ave. NW, Washington, DC 20008 (202)282-7300

Publicly funded land-grant four-year comprehensive institution. Coed, urban location. Enrollment: 4,000.

DEPARTMENT OF MASS MEDIA AND PERFORMING ARTS

Chair/Contact: Amelia C. Gray, Chair
Calendar: Semesters
Degrees Offered: B.A., mass media (with emphasis in film or television)
Entrance Requirements: Open-door policy. Application deadline: rolling; April 8–19 advance registration for fall
Curricular Emphasis: Mass media studies; film production and cinematography; studio and remote television production; documentary film; broadcast journalism
Special Activities: Film: film series/ festivals. Television: program material produced for cable television
Facilities: Film: screening room; editing suite; sound mixing room. Television: studio; audio bay; control room; video editing suites
Equipment: Film: complete 16mm. Television/Video: complete ¾" studio and location
Alumni: Cheryl Lewis, TV program manager; Juanita "Nikki" Jeter, media public relations director; Peter Woolfolk, government press secretary

GUIDE POV: Students in this mass media program may concentrate in either film or television studies; comprehensive, sequential production programs in both areas; cross-registration with local universities; hands-on training coupled with studies in communication theory; study abroad opportunities; internships available in television production

You have to start somewhere, and graduate students at the Big Five film schools (USC, UCLA, NYU, AFI, and Columbia) start their education just about every-where—in journalism, poetry, chemistry, law, and so on. One graduate student emigrated from the priesthood, several others from motherhood.

I suppose I took the obvious route, earning my bachelor of arts in telecom-munications (video production emphasis) at Indiana University. The campus was beautiful, the production facilities reflected industry standards, and the faculty, for the most part, brought a wealth of experience and expertise to the classroom.

But Bloomington was a long way from Hollywood, and while the hands-on instruction from field and studio production courses provided me with a nuts-and-bolts understanding of TV, I soon realized this was not to be the final step toward a creative career in film or network television. The magazine subscrip-tion recommended by the telecom faculty was not *Variety* but *Broadcasting*, with the department gearing its production students toward entry-level positions at local TV/cable stations or ad houses in Indianapolis and Chicago.

All of that was understandable considering the location of the school; still, I benefited tremendously by supplementing my B.A. with a certificate in Film Studies. I learned the history of film theory and studied Chaplin, Welles, and Hitchcock (among others) with authoritative Chaplin, Welles, and Hitchcock scholars—all the while flexing my critical muscles and absorbing, mostly by osmosis, the nuances of film language. It should also be noted that Bloomington is very film culture savvy; bookings at local chain theaters are mostly above the schlock line, and fine film series bring the latest independent and foreign films to town.

The two courses of study worked wonderfully in tandem, with film studies teaching me *where* to set up the camera, and telecom teaching me *how* to set it up. Both departments were very good at what they did, and although neither was particularly revered by movie moguls, together they made my experience at IU an excellent primer for graduate-level film school.

BARRY UNIVERSITY

11300 NE Second Ave.,
Miami Shores, FL 33161
(305)899–3000

*Private four-year comprehensive
institution. Coed, urban location.
Undergraduate enrollment: 4,000.
Graduate enrollment: 1,200.*

DEPARTMENT OF COMMUNICATION

Chair/Contact: Dr. Kathy Wahlers,
Chair
Calendar: Semesters
Degrees Offered: B.A., M.A., M.S.
Departmental Majors:
Undergraduate: 75 students. Graduate:
50 students
Entrance Requirements:
Undergraduate: 2.0 grade-point
average; ACT or SAT scores;
recommendations; essay; interview
recommended. Graduate: 3.0 grade-
point average; GRE score, with a
minimum composite of 1000;
MAT minimum score 40;
recommendations; written statement
of purpose. Undergraduate and
graduate application deadline:
May 1
Curricular Emphasis: Electronic
media theory and culture; media
writing; broadcast production; media
management
Special Activities: Television:
program material produced for on-
campus closed-circuit television, for
cable television, and for local and
commercial television stations
Facilities: Television: studio; audio
bay; control room
Equipment: Television/Video:
complete ¾" studio and location;
satellite uplink capability for
teleconferencing
Alumni: Estella Garcia, TV director;
Jeannie Kelly, TV producer; Ron
Kovak, media production executive;
Adrienne Kennedy, TV producer/
director; Roxanne Garcia, TV news
editor

GUIDE POV: Affiliated with the Roman
Catholic Church, this private liberal
arts institution offers both
undergraduate and graduate
communication studies; study abroad
in five European countries; special
programs for adult students; internship
opportunities in television production

FLORIDA ATLANTIC UNIVERSITY

P.O. Box 3091,
Boca Raton, FL 33431–0991
(407)367–3000

*State four-year comprehensive
institution. Coed, urban location.
Undergraduate enrollment: 11,000.
Graduate enrollment: 4,000.*

DEPARTMENT OF COMMUNICATION

Chair/Contact: Dr. Mike Budd
Calendar: Semesters

Degrees Offered: B.A.,
communication (students may select
emphasis in film and television); M.A.,
communication (students may select
emphasis in film and television)
Departmental Majors:
Undergraduate: 450 students. Graduate:
25 students
Entrance Requirements:
Undergraduate freshmen: 3.0 grade-
point average; ACT (minimum 23) or
SAT (minimum composite 1000)
scores. Undergraduate transfer
students: A.A. or A.S. degree.
Graduate: GRE scores (minimum
composite 1000); minimum 3.0 grade-
point average in last 60 hours of
undergraduate work. Undergraduate
application deadline: May 31.
Graduate and transfer application
deadline: July 5. Percent of
acceptances: undergraduate: 29%
Curricular Emphasis: Critical and
cultural studies of media; media
writing; video production
Facilities: Television: studio; control
room; editing suite
Equipment: Television/Video: ½"
studio and location
Alumni: Greg Nye, film director; Al
Berman, TV producer; Tim Dee, film
director

GUIDE POV: Critical and cultural
analysis make up the major thrust of
Florida Atlantic's film and television
program; video production treated as
part of media studies curriculum;
cross-registration with all Florida state
universities; study abroad through all
state university system programs;
extensive media internship and career
opportunities in south Florida

FLORIDA COMMUNITY COLLEGE AT JACKSONVILLE

South Campus,
11901 Beach Blvd.,
Jacksonville, FL 32216–6624
(904)633–8100

*State two-year comprehensive
institution. Coed, urban location.
Enrollment: 20,000.*

DEPARTMENT OF HUMANITIES AND ARTS

Chair/Contact: Julian Earl Farris,
Assistant Dean
Calendar: Semesters
Degrees Offered: A.A., A.S., radio
and television broadcast programming
Departmental Majors: 150 students
Entrance Requirements: Open-door
policy; high school diploma or GED
scores; placement tests. Undergraduate
application deadline: rolling
Curricular Emphasis: The A.A.
degree program is designed for
students transferring to four-year
universities with majors in film and
television; the A.S. degree program
prepares students for technical support
positions
Special Activities: Film: film series/
festivals; film societies. Television:
program material produced for cable
television
Facilities: Television: studio; 16-track
audio studio; control room
Equipment: Television/Video:
complete ¾" studio and ½" location
Alumni: Marion Stratford, TV
producer; Alan Neugent, TV studio
supervisor; Gary Rogers, TV/film
assistant director; Margaret Grimes,
film editor; Saul Lucio, stage manager

GUIDE POV: This two-year college
provides comprehensive studies and
practical training in film and

television; computer-based audio and video equipment; diverse course listings; internship opportunities in television production

FLORIDA STATE UNIVERSITY

Undergraduate: R-42,
Tallahassee, FL 32306–4021
(904)644–2525

Graduate: Asolo Center,
5555 N. Tamiami Tr.,
Sarasota, FL 34243
(813)355–6611

State four-year comprehensive institution. Coed, urban location. Undergraduate enrollment: 19,000. Graduate enrollment: 8,000.

SCHOOL OF MOTION PICTURE, TELEVISION, AND RECORDING ARTS

Chair/Contact: Undergraduate: Peter Stowell. Graduate: Stuart Kaminsky
Calendar: Semesters
Degrees Offered: B.F.A., M.F.A., motion picture, television and recording arts
Departmental Majors: Undergraduate motion picture, television and recording arts: 120 students (maximum). Graduate motion picture, television and recording arts: 48 students (maximum)
Entrance Requirements:
Undergraduate: SAT or ACT scores; competitive grade-point average; teachers' recommendations; 500–1,000-word statement of purpose. Graduate: competitive grade-point average; GRE scores; professional résumé; 500–1,000-word statement of purpose; three letters of recommendation. Application deadline: February 1. Percent of acceptances: 15%
Curricular Emphasis: B.F.A.: film

production skills with an emphasis on fictional narrative, screenwriting, management techniques, and interpretive analysis. M.F.A.: specialized advanced training in screenwriting, producing, directing, cinematography, sound, and editing; program culminates in selected theses projects paid for with departmental funds
Special Activities: Film: London workshop for sophomores each summer session; production workshop for freshmen students and first-year graduate students at Disney/MGM and Universal Studios in Orlando; film series/festivals; literature/film conference; teacher training. Television: program material produced for cable television
Facilities: Film: sound stage; screening room; editing room; sound mixing room; 35mm screening facilities; film library. Television: studio; audio studio; control room; editing suite
Equipment: Film: complete 16mm; 35mm equipment available on rental basis; limited digital audio editing. Television/Video: complete 1" and ¾" studio; complete ¾" and ½" location
Alumni: Jonathan Demme, film director; Burt Reynolds, film/TV actor/producer; Christine Lahti, film actress; Donna Wheeler, video director; Ronald Braddock, cinematographer; Jordan Freid, assistant editor

GUIDE POV: This unusually well-equipped, rapidly expanding program provides professional production training in film and video; the film school pays all production expenses for workshop and theses productions on both the graduate and undergraduate levels; graduate program located in Sarasota; limited enrollments; very selective admissions; extensive internship opportunities in film and television production

MIAMI-DADE COMMUNITY COLLEGE

North Campus,
11380 NW 27 Ave.,
Miami, FL 33167
(305)237–1000

State two-year comprehensive institution. Coed, urban location. Enrollment: 50,000.

FLORIDA CENTER OF EXCELLENCE IN FILM AND VIDEO

Chair/Contact: John Kern, Chair
Calendar: Semesters
Degrees Offered: A.S., film production technology; A.S., radio/television broadcasting; A.A., broadcasting
Departmental Majors: 120 students
Entrance Requirements: Open-door policy; high school diploma or GED certificate; MAPS test scores. Application deadline: rolling
Curricular Emphasis: Media writing; film and video production; computer graphics; animation; postproduction techniques; programming and management
Special Activities: Film: film series/festivals. Television: program material produced for on-campus closed-circuit television
Facilities: Film: studio; screening room; editing suite; sound mixing room; animation stand; large set construction and storage room with loading dock. Television: studio; audio bay; master control center; on-line control room with digital video effects; computer video graphics and special effects studio; grip truck; audio production studio; off-line video editing suite
Equipment: Film: complete 16mm. Television/Video: complete Betacam SP and Hi-8 studio and editing equipment; computer video graphics
Alumni: Carlos Colina, TV cameraman/producer; Jose Menendez, TV production assistant; Juan Urbano, TV/film editor; Jose Guzman, cinematographer

GUIDE POV: Enjoying new facilities, this rapidly growing production-oriented program provides comprehensive film, video, and audio training; diverse course listings; certificate and transfer programs available; extensive internship opportunities in film and television production

ORLANDO COLLEGE

North Campus: 5500 Diplomat Circle, Orlando, FL 32810
(407)628–5870

South Campus: 925 South Orange Ave., Orlando, FL 32806

Private two-year commuter institution. Coed, urban location. Enrollment: 5,000.

VIDEO ARTS AND SCIENCES

Chair/Contact: Brent Pirie, Chair
Calendar: Quarters
Degrees Offered: A.A., video arts and sciences
Entrance Requirements: High school diploma or equivalent; assessment testing. Application deadline: rolling
Curricular Emphasis: All aspects of video production including both

broadcast and nonbroadcast; computer graphics

Special Activities: Television/Video: material produced for various outlets; sponsored projects

Facilities: Television: studio; audio bay; control room; video editing suites; computer graphics labs

Equipment: Television/Video: complete S-VHS studio and location; S-VHS editing; ¾" dubbing capability; computer graphics equipment includes Amiga system

Alumni: Michelle Ruscoe, TV studio technician; James Evans, TV production manager; Donald Jackson, audio/video technician

GUIDE POV: With an emphasis on video technology and television production, this practical two-year program is designed to prepare students for employment in both broadcast and nonbroadcast industries; script development to postproduction training in varied genres including broadcast news, music videos, documentaries, and commercials; concentration in computer animation; internship opportunities in television/video production

PALM BEACH ATLANTIC COLLEGE

901 S. Flagler, Box 24708,
West Palm Beach, FL 33416–4708
(407)650–7700

Private four-year comprehensive institution. Coed, urban location. Enrollment: 1,100.

COMMUNICATION AND THEATRE ARTS

Chair/Contact: Charles Lester
Calendar: Semesters

Degrees Offered: B.A., communication arts

Departmental Majors: Theatre arts: 30 students. Communication: 30 students

Entrance Requirements: 2.0 grade-point average; ACT (minimum 18) or SAT (minimum 800) scores; essay; interview; GED accepted; portfolio recommended. Application deadline: June 1. Percent of acceptances: 65%

Curricular Emphasis: Film and media studies; liberal arts foundation

Special Activities: Film: students spend one semester in Hollywood at the Christian College Coalition's LA Film Studies Center to study production and to intern at a film studio

Facilities: Local broadcast and production companies cooperate with the school for use of facilities

Alumni: Mike Bingham, radio station manager; Bruce Cambell, music recording producer; Julie Seckman, media specialist; Janie Gavin, film actress; Dan Hurst, TV sports announcer

GUIDE POV: This small Christian college offers its undergraduates a thorough foundation in film and television studies within a broad liberal arts curriculum; interdisciplinary honors program; internships locally and in Los Angeles for film students

ST. THOMAS UNIVERSITY

16400 NW 32nd Ave.,
Miami, FL 33054
(305)625–6000

Private four-year comprehensive institution. Coed, urban location.

Undergraduate enrollment: 1,500.
Graduate enrollment: 1,000.

COMMUNICATION ARTS PROGRAM

Chair/Contact: Dr. Philip Shepardson
Calendar: Semesters
Degrees Offered: B.A.,
communication arts (with emphasis in
production, written, oral, or critical
communication)
Departmental Majors:
Undergraduate: 100 students
Entrance Requirements:
Undergraduate: 2.5 grade-point
average; ACT or SAT scores.
Undergraduate application deadline:
rolling. Percent of acceptances: 67%
Curricular Emphasis: Electronic
media theory and culture; critical
studies in film; media writing;
television production; public and
personal communications studies
Special Activities: Film: film series/
festivals; Media Center Archival
Collection. Television: program
material produced for instructional
television
Facilities: Film: screening room;
editing suite; film library. Television:
studio; control room
Equipment: Film: complete Super-8
and 16mm. Television/Video: complete
¾" studio and ½" location
Alumni: John Zarella, CNN bureau
chief; Pablo Perdomo, TV writer;
Jessica Benitez, TV producer

GUIDE POV: St. Thomas University
offers a communications program
emphasizing television journalism as
well as the development of writing,
speaking, and critical skills; practical
studies combined with liberal arts
curriculum; study abroad in Italy and
Spain; internship opportunities in
television production

UNIVERSITY OF CENTRAL FLORIDA

P.O. Box 25000,
Orlando, FL 23816
(407)823–2000

State four-year comprehensive
institution. Coed, urban location.
Undergraduate enrollment: 21,000.
Graduate enrollment: 3,000.

SCHOOL OF COMMUNICATION

Chair/Contact: Motion picture
division: Dr. James Welke; Radio/TV
division: Dr. Milan Meeske.
Calendar: Semesters
Degrees Offered: B.A.,
communication (radio/TV or film)
Departmental Majors: Undergraduate
motion picture technology: 60
students. Undergraduate radio/TV: 210
students
Entrance Requirements:
Undergraduate: grade-point average of
3.0 for motion picture division; 2.80 for
radio/TV division; ACT or SAT scores;
production credits; portfolio; written
statement of purpose; grammar
proficiency exam; typing test for radio/
TV division. Undergraduate application
deadline: rolling. Percent of
acceptances: motion picture division:
15%; radio/TV division: 50%
Curricular Emphasis: Motion picture
division: Students select the
production and screenwriting track or
the animation track; blend of practice
and theory. Radio/TV division: radio
and television broadcast production
Special Activities: Film: film societies;
classes and student productions have
frequent access to nearby studios.
Television: program material produced
for on-campus closed-circuit television
and local cable television
Facilities: Film: 35mm screening
facilities; screening room; 16mm

editing suite; sound mixing room; animation stand. Television: studio; audio studio; control room

Equipment: Film: complete 16mm cameras; complete postproduction; cel animation; computer animation. Television/Video: complete 1" and ¾" studio; complete ¾" location

Alumni: Ben Herschleder, film director/producer; Roger Donnell, film writer/producer; Jenni Gold, film producer

GUIDE POV: Complete production training in both film and television is offered through this rapidly expanding department; limited enrollment; state-of-the-art facilities in film, animation, television, and video; some production access to area studio facilities; extensive internship opportunities in film and television production

UNIVERSITY OF FLORIDA

Gainesville, FL 32611
(904)392–3261

State four-year comprehensive institution. Coed, urban location. Undergraduate enrollment: 30,000. Graduate enrollment: 5,000.

INTERDISCIPLINARY STUDIES

Chair/Contact: Robert Ray, Director of Film and Media Studies
Calendar: Semesters
Degrees Offered: B.A., film studies; Ph.D., cultural studies
Departmental Majors: Undergraduate film: 40 students. Graduate film: 7 students
Entrance Requirements: Undergraduate competitive grade-point average; ACT or SAT scores; essay; recommendations. Graduate: 3.0 grade-point average; GRE scores;

recommendations. Undergraduate and graduate application deadline: February 1. Percent of acceptances: 70%

Curricular Emphasis: Film history and theory; electronic arts; video as architecture; video as theory; visual and cognitive anthropology; social and cognitive psychology; photography; educational media; 16mm film production; varied electives provide supplementary focus on media history, theory, and criticism

Special Activities: Film: film series/festivals; film societies; student film/video competition. Television: program material produced for on-campus closed-circuit television

Facilities: Film: 35mm screening facilities; screening room; editing suite; sound mixing room; animation stand. Television: studio; audio bay; control room

Equipment: Film: complete 16mm. Television/Video: complete ¾" studio and ½" location

Alumni: Tom Kennington, entertainment executive; Tom Sheddan, cable TV

GUIDE POV: Students in this growing interdisciplinary program work in both film and video while exploring varied genres; admission to program is highly selective; study abroad in 32 countries; internship opportunities in film and television production

UNIVERSITY OF MIAMI SCHOOL OF COMMUNICATION

P.O. Box 248127,
Coral Gables, FL 33124
(305)284–2265

Private four-year comprehensive institution. Coed, suburban location.

Undergraduate enrollment: 8,000.
Graduate enrollment: 5,000.

MOTION PICTURES DEPARTMENT

Chair/Contact: Dr. Paul N. Lazarus, III
Calendar: Semesters
Degrees Offered: B.S., motion pictures or video-film; B.F.A., communications; M.A., film studies; M.F.A., motion pictures (tracks in production and screenwriting)
Departmental Majors:
Undergraduate: 280 students. Graduate: 50 students
Entrance Requirements:
Undergraduate: competitive grade-point average; SAT or ACT scores. Graduate: GRE scores; recommendations. Undergraduate application deadline: May 1. Graduate application deadline: April 1
Curricular Emphasis: The motion picture major offers tracks in producing, writing, business, or film studies; there is a video-film major with diverse curriculum; double major in College of Arts and Sciences required; most often selected second major is theatre arts; graduate programs in production, screenwriting, and critical studies
Special Activities: Film: student involvement with Miami Film Festival; L.A. Spring Break Trip; Visiting Filmmaker Program; summer program at the State Film School of Performing Arts in Prague, Czechoslovakia
Facilities: Film: sound stage; editing suites; mixing theatre; 35mm/16mm 280-seat theatre. Video: studio; audio bay; control room; editing suites
Equipment: Film: complete 16mm and 8mm; flatbed editing; mixing theatre; Oxberry animation stand. Video: complete ¾" and ½" studio and location
Alumni: Cynthia Cidre, screenwriter; Florie Brizel, TV/film producer; John Pike, studio TV executive; David Isaacs, film/TV writer/producer; Andy Kuehn, media executive

GUIDE POV: Motion Picture majors in this highly selective program are offered comprehensive training in 16mm and 8mm film production as well as background studies in film theory and history; separate major in video-film combines curricula from motion pictures and broadcasting; faculty possesses both academic and professional experience; graduate production, screenwriting, and critical studies; study abroad in 18 countries; extensive internship opportunities in film and video production

UNIVERSITY OF SOUTH FLORIDA

4202 Fowler Ave.,
Tampa, FL 33620–7720
(813)974–2011

State four-year comprehensive institution. Coed, urban location. Undergraduate enrollment: 32,000. Graduate enrollment: 9,000.

SCHOOL OF MASS COMMUNICATIONS

Chair/Contact: Donna L. Dickerson
Calendar: Semesters
Degrees Offered: B.A., broadcast news; B.A., broadcast programming and production; M.A., mass communications (students may select emphasis in broadcasting)
Departmental Majors:
Undergraduate: 150 students. Graduate: 4 students
Entrance Requirements:
Undergraduate: 2.7 grade-point average; ACT or SAT scores. Graduate: 3.0 grade-point average; GRE scores; interview; written statement of

purpose. Undergraduate and graduate application deadline: rolling. Percent of acceptances: undergraduate: 60%. Graduate: 55%

Curricular Emphasis: Broadcast journalism; media management; video and film production
Special Activities: Film: screenings. Television: program material produced for various outlets
Facilities: Film: screening room; editing suites. Television: studio and control room; three audio bays; five editing suites
Equipment: Film: complete 8mm and 16mm. Television/Video: complete ¾" studio; complete ¾" and ½" location
Alumni: Mark Garbarino, film special effects artist; Donald Hogestyn, TV actor

GUIDE POV: Specializing in preparing students for career positions in television broadcasting, this program develops oral and written communication as well as technical skills; opportunity to work in film as well as video; in addition, experimental and animated filmmaking offered through Fine Arts Department; co-op and cross registration available; study abroad; internship opportunities in television and film production

---

VALENCIA COMMUNITY COLLEGE

7701 N. Econlockhatchee Trail, Orlando, FL 32802
(407)299–5000

State two-year comprehensive institution. Coed, urban location. Enrollment: 15,000.

FILM PRODUCTION TECHNOLOGY

Chair/Contact: J. Anthony Walsh, Director, Institute of Entertainment Technologies
Calendar: Semesters
Degrees Offered: A.S., film production technology
Departmental Majors: 50 students
Entrance Requirements: Demonstrated technical proficiency or industry related experience. Application deadline: rolling
Curricular Emphasis: Training for entry-level positions in film production, covering camera, editing, lighting, gripping, and sound
Special Activities: Film: filmmaker-in-residence program; successful career placement program
Facilities: Film: sound stage; screening; editing and mixing studio with Sound Tools, audio package includes Nagra IV-STC, Coopersound mixer
Equipment: Film/Video: complete 16mm; five-ton grip truck; camera truck; Video F/X system
Alumni: Sean Torge, film/TV producer; R. J. Istavan, film/TV producer; Jaime Marlow, camera assistant; Katherine Moore, animation editor; David Brame, videographer; Tim Whitall, production assistant; Kory Bessinger, videographer

GUIDE POV: This two-year program offers extensive technical training to students planning careers in film production; limited enrollment for master classes during second year program; most students are employed within the industry upon graduation; extensive internship opportunities at nearby Disney, MGM, and Universal studios, among others

When I was a child, from time to time my mother and father could not afford to pay the ticket price of the local movie theatre in Poughkeepsie, New York, where I was born. So as a substitute to soothe my sister's and my persistent whining, my parents would pop a bag of popcorn on Saturday afternoon, park our car on the homespun main street, and comment on strangers as they passed our sagging car. My father and mother would quiz my sister and me on what we felt about these people. Between popcorn crunchings my father and mother would ask, "What do you think he or she does for a living?" "How old do you think he or she is?" or "Where do you think he or she is going to or coming from?" Our answers were based totally upon our observations and the attention that we paid to details of overrun shoes, too tight-fitting suits, the quality of clothing, or how a person stood or walked and the urgency with which they moved.

Although we may have disagreed, my parents always emphasized there were never any wrong answers to their questions. But the essential lesson we learned, and would be able to apply later on in our lives, was that it was important to have a point of view, and that our point of view was as valid as theirs or anyone else's. In this regard, filmmaking imitates life. It is not an empirical response to life but a visceral one—visceral in the sense that it calls upon the complete commitment and involvement of our intellect, observation, instinct, senses, compassion, passion, and heart. I do not believe that you can teach anyone how to become a filmmaker. It is something that you are born with or not.

What must be given to an aspiring filmmaker is an environment in which he or she has the opportunity to fail. Fail in the attempt to realize his or her vision through the tools that create film language. I say fail because success is merely an accident or a confirmation of what's already known. But failing is that process that pushes us further and further toward the abyss of our ignorance, and only by confronting our ignorance can we grow. Academic institutions that create such opportunities provide an important service, particularly to minorities and the underprivileged in our society.

Film shapes our perception of ourselves and the world around us; it is probably the second most influential factor in our lives, after our parents. Film instills within us the very mores and ethics of our culture. If the voiceless who stand outside the walls of opportunity, if the desperate that scream to us through acts of violence, find in our vision of the world their images reflected in a fair manner, that depicts their humanity as well as their dismay, we then may be able to help diffuse man's problems.

My sister and I viewed the world through the cracked and stained windows of my father's car. It reflected the innocence of that time, a time before television, the fax machine, telecommunication systems, personal computers, morphing, and computer graphics.

Today this inventiveness can be either misused as an encumbrance to true communication, or used as a tool that enables us to realize a world where all dreams are valid and all points of view have a voice. I believe that cinema studies provide an opportunity to make a difference in the way we perceive ourselves and the world around us by reaching out to those who have been forgotten or written off. There are people in areas surrounding our relatively safe academic communities whose frustration and despair can be turned into yet unthought-of visions that can help bridge the gap that separates us all on this cold and vacant winter of our nights.

Having received my M.F.A. at NYU and master's degree from AFI, I subsequently directed several off-Broadway plays; as a filmmaker, I directed *A Rage in Harlem*, *Deep Cover*, and, more recently, *Cemetery Club*.

ATLANTA COLLEGE OF ART

Atlanta, GA 30309
(404)898-1164

Private four-year professional institution. Coed, urban location. Enrollment: 350.

ELECTRONIC ARTS, COMPUTER, VIDEO, AND SOUND DEPARTMENT

Chair/Contact: Scott Vogel; Evelyn Hirata
Calendar: Semesters
Degrees Offered: B.F.A., video
Departmental Majors: Video: 35 students
Entrance Requirements: Portfolio and essay required; ACT or SAT scores; interview recommended. Application deadline: rolling. Percent of acceptances: 65%
Curricular Emphasis: Electronic media theory and culture; video production within a media arts context; electronic arts
Special Activities: Film/Video: student screenings; exhibitions; film and video series/festivals; guest lecturers. Television: program material produced for local cable television
Facilities: Video: video editing suites; computer graphics lab
Equipment: Video: complete ¾" location
Alumni: Susan Strathman, video graphics artist; Jim Chappell, video graphics artist; Anthony Grillo, video production assistant

GUIDE POV: A full video major is offered at this prestigious college of art; cross-registration with the colleges of the University Center in Georgia; member of the East Coast Consortium of Art Colleges and the Art College Exchange; supervised fine/media arts internships encouraged

AUGUSTA COLLEGE

2500 Walton Way,
Augusta, GA 30910
(706)737-1400

State four-year comprehensive institution. Coed, urban location. Undergraduate enrollment: 4,600. Graduate enrollment: 400.

DEPARTMENT OF LANGUAGES AND LITERATURE

Chair/Contact: Fred Wharton, Chair
Calendar: Quarters
Degrees Offered: B.A., communications (concentration in broadcasting/film)
Departmental Majors: Undergraduate: 32 students
Entrance Requirements: Undergraduate: 2.0 grade-point average; ACT (minimum score 14) or SAT (minimum score 350 on both verbal and math sections). Graduate: transcripts; GRE scores; 2.5 grade-point average; GMAT (minimum score 450). Undergraduate application deadline: at

least 30 days before start of quarter.
Percent of acceptances: 87%
Curricular Emphasis: Electronic
media theory and culture; critical
studies in film; media writing; film-
audio-video production; corporate uses
of media; media management
Special Activities: Film: film series/
festivals. Television: program material
produced for cable television;
vocational placement service
Facilities: Film: editing suite; sound
mixing room. Television: studio; audio
bay; control room. Radio: studio
Equipment: Film: complete Super-8
and 16mm. Television/Video: complete
¾" studio; complete ¾" and ½"
location; ENG cameras; computer
graphics palette
Alumni: Gershon Ginsburg, film/TV art
director; Anita Wiggins, TV newscaster;
Richard Nohe, communications
specialist

GUIDE POV: Communication students
at this well-equipped commuter
college are offered a concentration in
varied aspects of broadcasting and
video production; cross-registration
with Paine College; study abroad;
internship opportunities in film and
television production

CLARK ATLANTA UNIVERSITY

240 James P. Brawley Dr. SW,
Atlanta, GA 30314
(404)880–8000

*Private four-year comprehensive
institution. Coed, urban location.
Enrollment: 2,000.*

MASS COMMUNICATIONS DEPARTMENT

Chair/Contact: James D. McJunkins,
Chair
Calendar: Semesters

Degrees Offered: B.A.
Departmental Majors: Film: 20
students. Undergraduate television: 40
students
Entrance Requirements: 2.0 grade-
point average; ACT or SAT scores.
Application deadline: March 1. Percent
of acceptances: 68%
Curricular Emphasis: Electronic
media theory and culture; critical
studies in film; media writing; film,
television, and radio production;
media management
Special Activities: Film: film series/
festivals. Television: program material
produced for cable television and for
local commercial television station
Facilities: Film: screening room;
editing suite; sound mixing room; film
library. Television: studio; audio bay;
control room
Equipment: Film: complete Super-8
and 16mm. Television/Video: complete
¾" studio; complete ¾" and ½"
location
Alumni: Monty Ross, film company
executive; Amanda Davis, TV news
anchor

GUIDE POV: Featuring a concentration
in radio-television-film, this mass
communication program offers
undergraduates comprehensive
training in media criticism,
writing, and production; student
body from more than 40 states and 50
foreign countries; internship
opportunities in film and television
production

COLUMBUS COLLEGE

Columbus, GA 31995
(706)568–2035

*State four-year comprehensive
institution. Coed, urban location.*

Undergraduate enrollment: 3,800.
Graduate enrollment: 500.

LANGUAGE AND LITERATURE DEPARTMENT

Chair/Contact: Film: Dr. Joseph Francavilla

SPEECH/THEATRE DEPARTMENT

Chair/Contact: William P. Crowell
Calendar: Quarters
Degrees Offered: B.A., English, speech/theater
Entrance Requirements:
Undergraduate: minimum 1.8 grade-point average; ACT or SAT scores; high school diploma or GED certificate. Undergraduate application deadline: August 25 for fall entry; December 6 for winter entry; March 9 for spring entry; June 2 for summer entry. Percent of acceptances: 80%
Curricular Emphasis: Film history and aesthetics; television production emphasizing news/documentary
Special Activities: Film: film series/festival. Television: program material produced for on-campus closed-circuit television and local commercial television station
Facilities: Television: studio and control room
Equipment: Film: 16mm projectors. Television/Video: complete ¾" studio and ½" location; lighting packages; monitors; switcher; sound recording equipment; audio mixers
Alumni: Dick McMichael, TV news anchor; Todd McDurmont, TV actor

GUIDE POV: Several courses in basic broadcast production and film theory are offered at Columbus College as part of a general liberal arts curriculum; study abroad in France; internship opportunities in television production

DEKALB COLLEGE

555 N. Indian Creek Dr.,
Clarkston, GA 30021
(404)299–4000

State two-year institution. Coed, suburban location. Enrollment: 16,000.

FINE ARTS DEPARTMENT

Chair/Contact: Jon F. Downs; Lane Wells
Calendar: Quarters
Degrees Offered: A.A., radio/TV broadcasting
Entrance Requirements: Open-door policy; high school diploma or equivalent; ACT or SAT scores. Undergraduate application deadline: August 28
Curricular Emphasis: Emphasis on television/video production training; film studies
Special Activities: Film: film series/festivals. Television: program material produced for on-campus closed-circuit television
Facilities: Film: 35mm screening facilities; screening room; film library. Television: studio; control room
Equipment: Television: complete studio equipment for closed-circuit television production
Alumni: Jim Whaley, TV personality/producer; Spencer Thornton, TV announcer; Paul Burke, TV actor/announcer; Kathy Simmons, radio production staff; Judy Tatum, film actress; Pam Pruitt, TV performer

GUIDE POV: DeKalb College offers media studies featuring radio/television production training; transfer program to four-year universities; weekend college program for those working full-time; internship opportunities in television production

FORT VALLEY STATE COLLEGE

1005 State College Dr.,
Fort Valley, GA 31030
(912)825–6211

*State four-year comprehensive
institution. Coed, rural location.
Undergraduate enrollment: 2,400.
Graduate enrollment: 200.*

MASS COMMUNICATIONS PROGRAM

Chair/Contact: Anna R. Holloway
Calendar: Quarters
Degrees Offered: B.A., mass
communications
Departmental Majors:
Undergraduate: 30 students
Entrance Requirements:
Undergraduate: 2.0 grade-point
average; ACT or SAT scores; AP and
CLEP credit accepted. Undergraduate
application deadline: rolling. Percent
of acceptances: 71%
Curricular Emphasis: Public
relations; broadcast production; print
and graphics
Special Activities: Television:
program material produced for local
public access television
Facilities: Television: studio; audio
bay; control room
Equipment: Television/Video:
complete ¾" studio; complete ¾" and
½" location
Alumni: Kevin Stanley, TV reporter;
Angela McKinney, TV news anchor;
Ron Hatcher, videographer; Tshimpole
Mukenge, TV technical assistant

GUIDE POV: Students in this mass
communications program are
instructed in media theory, television
production, and management; student
participation in a variety of
broadcast productions; effective
student-faculty ratio; study abroad;
internship opportunities in television
production

GEORGIA SOUTHERN UNIVERSITY

Landrum Box 8091,
Statesboro, GA 30460–8091
(912)681–5611

*State four-year comprehensive
institution. Coed, rural location.
Undergraduate enrollment: 12,300.
Graduate enrollment: 1,500.*

DEPARTMENT OF COMMUNICATION ARTS

Chair/Contact: Dr. David Addington,
Chair; broadcasting: Kent Murray; film:
Ernest Wyatt
Calendar: Quarters
Degrees Offered: B.S., broadcasting,
communication arts (film emphasis)
Departmental Majors: Undergraduate
communication arts: 660 students
Entrance Requirements:
Undergraduate: SAT scores (minimum
370 verbal and 380 math); ACT scores
accepted; high school diploma or
equivalent; interview recommended.
Undergraduate application deadline:
September 1. Percent of
acceptances: 85%
Curricular Emphasis: Television
broadcasting; film history and criticism
Special Activities/Offerings:
Television program material produced
for news/documentary; vocational
placement assistance
Facilities: Television: ¾" studio; audio
studio; control room; editing room
Equipment: Television/Video:
complete ¾" studio and location
Alumni: Jeff Dudley, media promotion
director; Delano Little, TV sportscaster;
Mike Daley, news reporter/
photographer; Natalie Hendrix, TV
news anchor; Steve Vance, TV news
anchor/reporter; Missie Kitchens, TV

news editor; Ben Roberts, TV news reporter

GUIDE POV: Production emphasis at this state university is in broadcast journalism; basic studies in use of the video medium for dramatic purposes; foundation work offered in critical film theory; study abroad in Europe; internship opportunities in television production

GEORGIA STATE UNIVERSITY

1 Park Place S.,
Atlanta, GA 30303–3085
(404)651–2000

State four-year comprehensive institution. Coed, urban location. Undergraduate enrollment: 23,000. Graduate enrollment: 7,000.

DEPARTMENT OF COMMUNICATION

Chair/Contact: Dr. Frank P. Tomasulo, Chair; Dr. Jack Boozer; Dr. Kay Beck; Gary Moss; Dr. R. Barton Palmer
Calendar: Quarters
Degrees Offered: B.A., film and video; M.A., communication (concentration in film and video)
Departmental Majors:
Undergraduate: 160 students. Graduate: 20 students
Entrance Requirements:
Undergraduate: 2.5 grade-point average; SAT required (minimum scores 400 verbal, 400 math); Department of Communication requirements are slightly higher (3.0 grade-point average and score of 500 minimum verbal SAT). Graduate: GRE required (minimum score 500 verbal); 2.8 minimum grade-point average; two letters of reference; Department of Communication requirements are

slightly higher. Undergraduate application deadline: rolling. Graduate application deadline: March 1. Percent of acceptances: 89% of university applicants; 45% of students applying to Department of Communication
Curricular Emphasis: Film history, theory and criticism; media management; screenwriting; film and television production
Special Activities: Film: Cinefest, a program of daily screenings; guest speakers; annual film festival; film societies; home of *Journal of Film and Video*. Television: program material produced for on-campus closed-circuit television, for local public and commercial television stations, and for cable television
Facilities: Film: screening room; editing suites; film/video library; animation stand; film/video library. Television: ¾" and ½" studios; audio bays; control rooms; editing suites
Equipment: Film: complete Super-8 and 16mm. Television/Video: complete studio and location; off-line and on-line video editing
Alumni: Roy Johansen, screenwriter; Ruth L. Otte, TV executive

GUIDE POV: This state university offers students a full major in film and video; entry to program is competitive; limited enrollment maintained in production classes; thorough critical film studies curriculum; expanding graduate program; cross-registration with the University Center in Georgia; study abroad in Russia, Canada, Mexico, Israel, and Western Europe; extensive internships available for undergraduates and graduates in film and television production

MERCER UNIVERSITY

1400 Coleman Ave.,
Macon, GA 31207–0001
(912)752–2900

*Private four-year comprehensive
institution. Coed, urban location.
Enrollment: 2,400.*

COMMUNICATION AND THEATRE ARTS DEPARTMENT

Chair/Contact: Dr. John J. Chalfa, Jr., Chair
Calendar: Quarters
Degrees Offered: B.A.,
communication, theatre arts
Departmental Majors:
Communication and theatre arts: 100
Entrance Requirements: 2.0
minimum grade-point average; ACT or
SAT scores. Application deadline:
March 1
Curricular Emphasis: Video
production; film theory and history;
writing for video and film
Special Activities: Intermedia arts
activities with theatre program
Facilities: Film: screening room.
Television: studio; control room;
editing bay
Equipment: Television: complete ¾"
studio; complete ¾" and ½" location
Alumni: Rhonda Green, TV news
editor; Jerry Bridges, radio broadcaster

GUIDE POV: Founded in 1833, this
competitive private university offers its
students a communications major
combining practical training with a
comprehensive liberal arts foundation;
intermedia arts; study abroad in Spain,
France, and Great Britain; internship
opportunities in television production

SAVANNAH COLLEGE OF ART AND DESIGN

P.O. Box 3146,
Savannah, GA 31401–3146
(912)238–2400

*Private four-year comprehensive
institution. Coed, urban location.
Undergraduate enrollment: 1,700.
Graduate enrollment: 300.*

VIDEO PRODUCTION DEPARTMENT

Chair/Contact: John Drop, Chair
Calendar: Quarters
Degrees Offered: B.A., M.F.A., video
production
Departmental Majors:
Undergraduate: 149 students. Graduate:
22 students.
Entrance Requirements:
Undergraduate: SAT or ACT scores;
transcripts; letters of recommendation;
portfolio presentation and interview
are encouraged but not required.
Graduate: transcripts; portfolio;
interview (may be waived due to
distance); letters of recommendation.
Undergraduate and graduate
application deadline: rolling. Percent
of acceptances: 48%
Curricular Emphasis: Video
production; video art; traditional
continuity narrative; documentary;
music video; commercial/industrial;
sound design; interactive laser
disc
Special Activities: Television:
program material produced for cable
television as well as for local
commercial stations
Facilities: Video/Audio: 40' × 90'
sound stage; two 30' × 30' sound
stages; blue screen studio with hard
cyc; 30' × 35' audio recording studio;
mix down suite; foley facilities;
screening room; voiceover studio;

video wall and gallery; film/video library

Equipment: Video/Audio: Five CMX-clone on-line editing suites with variable speeds; eight cuts-only suites; eight component MII camcorders; Steadicam EFP; complete Super Panther production dolly system; Probe lens system; lights and grip equipment; ten LX100 HI-8 camcorders; ten HI-8 cuts-only suites; digital audio workstation with Pro Tools and Pro Store; Midi stereo digital sampler; Tascam MidiStudio 688; studio DAT recorder; field DAT recorder; seven video toasters; two rendering workstations with single frame controllers; chroma-key

Alumni: David Cann, TV producer/director; Ferre Dollar, TV editor; Katherine He, TV editor; Jason Talbert, TV production assistant

GUIDE POV: Recently provided with new facilities, this quality-oriented school offers a comprehensive hands-on video program emphasizing both the technical and artistic aspects of production; narrative, experimental, and industrial film studies offered; special interest in new technologies; highly selective admissions; media internship opportunities

---

UNIVERSITY OF GEORGIA

Athens, GA 30602
(706)542–3000

State four-year comprehensive institution. Coed, rural location. Undergraduate enrollment: 22,000. Graduate enrollment: 6,000.

COLLEGE OF JOURNALISM AND MASS COMMUNICATION

Chair/Contact: Dr. Alison Alexander
Calendar: Quarters
Degrees Offered: A.B.J., M.A., M.M.C., Ph.D.
Departmental Majors:
Undergraduate: 177 students. Graduate: 27 students
Entrance Requirements:
Undergraduate: 2.5 grade-point average; SAT (minimum 900) or ACT scores. Graduate: 3.0 grade-point average; GRE scores; written statement of purpose; teachers' recommendations. Undergraduate application deadline: February 1. Graduate application deadline: rolling. Percent of acceptances: Undergraduate: 69%. Graduate: 65%
Curricular Emphasis: Electronic media theory and culture; media writing; audio-film-video production; media management
Special Activities: Film: film series/festivals; film societies; student publications. Television: program material produced for on-campus closed-circuit television, for local public television station, for local commercial television, and for cable television; the college is home and administrator of the Peabody Awards; Dowden Center for Telecommunication Studies; Himan Brown Audio Production Center; Cox International Center
Facilities: Film: screening room; editing suite; animation stand. Television/Video: studios; audio bays; control rooms; video editing suites; computerized newsroom
Equipment: Film: complete 16mm; editing equipment. Television/Video: two complete ¾" studios; complete ¾", ½", and High 8 camera and

editing equipment; 10 ENG cameras; satellite technology

Alumni: W. Thomas Johnson, CNN president; Deborah Norville, TV network news anchor; John Holliman, TV reporter; Deborah Roberts, TV network correspondent

GUIDE POV: Chartered in 1785, this comprehensive land-grant institution offers a highly regarded communications program that focuses on broadcast journalism; cross-registration through the Southern Regional Education Board; admission to program is selective; study abroad; internship opportunities in television production

---

VALDOSTA STATE COLLEGE

Valdosta, GA 31698
(912)333–5800

State four-year comprehensive institution. Coed, small city location. Undergraduate enrollment: 5,000. Graduate enrollment: 2,500.

COMMUNICATION ARTS DEPARTMENT

Chair/Contact: Dr. John Gaston
Calendar: Quarters
Degrees Offered: B.F.A., theatre (students may select emphasis in telecommunication)
Departmental Majors: Undergraduate telecommunications: 60 students
Entrance Requirements: Undergraduate: transcripts; ACT or SAT scores. Undergraduate application deadline: rolling. Percent of acceptances: 92%
Curricular Emphasis: Television, video, and radio production; media management
Special Activities: Film: film series/festivals. Television/Radio: program

material produced for cable television; FM radio station

Facilities: Television: studio; audio bay; control room; radio station; remote van
Equipment: Television/Video: complete ¾" studio and location including Ikigami cameras; Sony VCRs; Sony 910 editing; and ENG equipment
Alumni: Deanna Fenee, radio/TV news anchor; Krista Kinert, TV news reporter; Leland Lyle, TV production manager; Rick Strickland, media attorney

GUIDE POV: Valdosta State College provides a high degree of experiential television and video production training in a supportive atmosphere; small production classes; graduates have high job placement rate in areas of interest; study abroad; local and area media internship opportunities

---

WEST GEORGIA COLLEGE

Maple St.,
Carrollton, GA 30118
(404)836–6500

State four-year comprehensive institution. Coed, rural location. Undergraduate enrollment: 6,200. Graduate enrollment: 500.

MASS COMMUNICATION AND THEATRE ARTS DEPARTMENT

Chair/Contact: Dr. Chester Gibson, Chair
Calendar: Quarters
Degrees Offered: B.A., mass communications (students may select emphasis in electronic media)
Departmental Majors: Undergraduate television: 200 students
Entrance Requirements: Undergraduate: 2.5 grade-point

average; ACT or SAT scores.
Undergraduate application deadline:
April 1. Percent of acceptances: 78%
Curricular Emphasis: Mass
communication theory; television
studio production; small format video
production; critical studies in film;
broadcast journalism; writing for radio
and television; radio and television
announcing; mass communications
law; effects and uses of mass
communications
Special Activities: Film: film series/
festivals; film society. Television:
program material produced for cable
television
Facilities: Film: sound stage;
screening room; editing suite; film
library. Television: studio; audio bay;
control room

Equipment: Film: complete 16mm.
Television/Video: complete ¾" studio;
complete ¾" and ½" location
Alumni: Shelby Hofer, TV/film actress;
Kimberly Thompson, TV promotion
assistant; Caroline Beasley, TV
meteorologist

GUIDE POV: Mass communications
students at this state college
concentrate on all aspects of
television production, including public
affairs and news writing, but may
also work in 16mm film; effective
student-faculty ratio; study abroad in
Europe, Canada, and Taiwan;
internships available in television
production

I have always been a believer in formal education as a way to research and develop a background philosophy in any given subject. With a master's degree from Harvard and a bachelor's degree from UC Berkeley, I practiced landscape architecture and planning for more than ten years. Simultaneously, I enjoyed a career in community relations and politics, including one term as mayor of my hometown in Marin County. But the more immersed I became in bureaucracy, the more I longed for personal creative expression. So when the opportunity arose for me to make a career break, I moved to L.A., prepared to "eat, sleep, and drink film."

Ultimately, I wanted to produce epics like *Out of Africa*, an expression, I imagine, of my love for large, sweeping landscapes. But with some experience in writing—I'd written a spec teleplay for "L.A. Law"—and an interest in character pieces like *Raging Bull*, I remained a hopeless generalist—probably ripe for studio bureaucracy.

Fortunately, I was accepted at the American Film Institute, which provided a setting most appropriate for students with some life experience. And AFI gave me an opportunity to meet other filmmakers, as I was one of 128 writers, directors, cinematographers, and producers. The institute helped me in two important ways. First, the emphasis in the program on story, narrative filmmaking, and film analysis provided the background I was looking for. At the same time—while coordinating three film projects—I gained practical know-how in the mechanics of film production. We dealt with such problems as selecting material, putting a crew together, acquiring equipment, obtaining permits, etc.

In the end, a film school experience in L.A. makes all the difference if you want to work in the industry. Here you can make real contacts in the movie world while establishing a solid philosophical and technical background.

HONOLULU COMMUNITY COLLEGE

874 Dillingham Blvd.,
Honolulu, HI 96817
(808)845–9211

State two-year institution. Coed, urban location. Enrollment: 5,000.

HUMANITIES DEPARTMENT

Chair/Contact: Film: David Panisnick
Calendar: Semesters
Degrees Offered: A.A., humanities
Entrance Requirements: High school diploma or equivalent. Application deadline: rolling
Curricular Emphasis: Film theory, history, and aesthetics
Facilities: Film: film library
Alumni: Gail Oshita, TV technical director

GUIDE POV: A two-year humanities program is offered with courses in film theory, history, and criticism; transfer program to four-year institutions

LEEWARD COMMUNITY COLLEGE

96-045 Ala Ike,
Pearl City, HI 96782
(808)455–0011

State two-year institution. Coed, suburban location. Enrollment: 5,500.

TELEVISION PRODUCTION

Chair/Contact: Robert W. Hochstein
Calendar: Semesters
Degrees Offered: A.S., television production; certificate of achievement; certificate of completion, vocational/technical division
Departmental Majors: 40 students
Entrance Requirements: Open-door policy; high school diploma or GED certificate. Application deadline: July 31
Curricular Emphasis: Electronic media theory and practical application covering numerous phases of television production, i.e., graphics, audio, lighting, directing, editing, engineering, camera operation, location production
Special Activities: Film: film series/festivals. Television: program material produced for on-campus closed-circuit and statewide cable television; vocational placement assistance service
Facilities: Television: studio; audio bay; control room
Equipment: Television/Video: complete ¾" studio and Hi-8 location, including A/B roll suite with time code; three cuts-only editing suites; full audio; computer graphics; digital effects; computerized lighting board; AVID nonlinear editing
Alumni: Colleen McCabe, TV director; Jennifer Cravallho, TV director; Angela Angel, media center director

GUIDE POV: This two-year school offers a recently expanded production-oriented television program; practical training prepares students for immediate employment; high job placement rate; internship opportunities in television and video production

UNIVERSITY OF HAWAII AT HILO

Hilo, HI 96720–4091
(808)933–3311

State four-year comprehensive institution. Coed, urban location. Enrollment: 2,600.

SPEECH AND COMMUNICATION DEPARTMENT

Chair/Contact: Mass media: Steven Muira
Calendar: Semesters
Degrees Offered: B.A.
Entrance Requirements: 2.0 grade-point average; SAT scores. Application deadline: July 1. Percent of acceptances: 68%
Curricular Emphasis: Media analysis and criticism; critical studies in film; equipment and facilities not generally available to students but instead used primarily to support the delivery of telecourses to various islands through the Hawaii Interactive Television System
Special Activities: Film: film series/festivals
Facilities: Film: screening room; film library. Television: studio; audio bay; control room
Equipment: Television/Video: complete ¾" studio; ½" portable cameras
Alumni: Jeffrey Haun, TV producer

GUIDE POV: Theoretical studies in media analysis form the major thrust of this mass communications curriculum; broad-based liberal arts program prepares student for graduate research studies; limited access to facilities and equipment for student video production; periodic internship opportunities in radio production

UNIVERSITY OF HAWAII AT MANOA

2560 Campus Rd.,
Honolulu, HI 96822
(808)956–8111

State four-year comprehensive institution. Coed, urban location. Undergraduate enrollment: 12,000. Graduate enrollment: 6,000.

DEPARTMENT OF COMMUNICATION

Chair/Contact: Dr. Dan J. Wedemeyer, Chair
Calendar: Semesters
Degrees Offered: B.A., M.A., communication; Ph.D., communication and information services
Entrance Requirements: Undergraduate: 2.5 grade-point average; ACT or SAT scores. Graduate: statement of academic goals; three letters of recommendation. Undergraduate application deadline: June 15. Graduate application deadline: March 1; September 1. Percent of acceptances: 50%
Curricular Emphasis: Electronic media theory and culture; media writing; audio-video production; nonlinear editing; multimedia production; new technologies; media management
Special Activities: Television: program material produced for cable

television; multimedia/computer-based production

Facilities: Television: studio; audio bay; AVID nonlinear editing bay; control room

Equipment: Television/Video: complete Hi-8 and ¾" studio and location; AVID system

Alumni: Shawn Hiatt, TV camera operator; Robert Scott, TV/film assistant director; Kim Nakakura, TV/film assistant director; Richard Fewell, videographer; Jay Liu, media specialist/TV producer/director; Clifford Tom, TV production executive

GUIDE POV: This is the major research institution in the University of Hawaii system; communication students learn all aspects of studio and remote production in news, instructional, and dramatic formats; graduate program focuses on communication research and emerging technologies; internship opportunities in television production

Recently I read a screenplay by a fortyish but first-time writer. I was flabbergasted. The script had exciting characters, colorful dialogue, and imaginative plotting. The point being: the author had innate talent and worldliness, something I'm not quite sure one acquires in film school. As it happened, when I got my B.A. from Duke University in psychology, film studies were not widely offered.

After acquiring invaluable experience in the Marine Corps, I completed three novels—none of which by the way was published. I also drove tractor-trailers and taxicabs, worked on offshore oil rigs, picked fruit, taught school, and in general paid a few dues in the school of "real life." Finally I landed an assignment from Dino DeLaurentiis to write, in collaboration with Ron Shusett, *King Kong Lives*—not exactly a boffo hit. Nonetheless we went on to write *Above the Law*, followed by *Freejack*. And although I was uncredited, I had the opportunity to work on *Total Recall*. Now I am involved in a number of new projects. I believe that in order to become a skilled and successful screenwriter one needs to enrich one's life experience.

Film school can be extremely helpful, but there is always the danger of becoming too technical and insular. Concept, structure, and character are still what it's all about. By all means study film. But don't forget to absorb as much from life as possible.

BOISE STATE UNIVERSITY

1910 University Dr.,
Boise, ID 83725
(208)385–1011

State four-year comprehensive institution. Coed, urban location. Undergraduate enrollment: 12,054. Graduate enrollment: 5,995.

COMMUNICATION DEPARTMENT

Chair/Contact: Dr. Peter Lutze
Calendar: Semesters
Degrees Offered: B.A., M.A.
Departmental Majors:
Undergraduate: 420 students
Entrance Requirements:
Undergraduate: transcripts or GED certificate; ACT, or SAT scores. Graduate: GRE scores; recommendations. Undergraduate and graduate application deadline: August 1. Percent of acceptances: Undergraduate and graduate: 87%
Curricular Emphasis: Electronic media theory and culture; media writing; video production; media management
Special Activities: Television: program material produced for community access television and for local cable television
Facilities: Television: studio; audio bay; control room; three cuts-only S-VHS editing suites; 1 A/B editing suite with video toaster; remote switcher for live events

Equipment: Television/Video: complete S-VHS studio and location
Alumni: Brad Larrondo, TV news reporter; Robyn Jacobs, video producer; Jody Howard, video producer/editor

GUIDE POV: This growing department, which has recently instituted an M.A. program, places emphasis on critical understanding of media coupled with practical television production training; extensive media internships available with pay and credit

IDAHO STATE UNIVERSITY

741 South 7th Ave.,
Pocatello, ID 83209
(208)236–0211

State four-year comprehensive institution. Coed, urban location. Undergraduate enrollment: 6,000. Graduate enrollment: 1,000.

MASS COMMUNICATION DEPARTMENT

Chair/Contact: Mike Trinklein, Chair
Calendar: Semesters
Degrees Offered: B.A., mass communication (students may select emphasis in television)
Departmental Majors:
Undergraduate: 135 students
Entrance Requirements:
Undergraduate: high school diploma or GED certificate; 2.0 grade-point average; ACT, SAT, or WPCT scores;

AP and CLEP credit accepted.
Undergraduate application deadline:
rolling. Percent of acceptances:
almost 100%
Curricular Emphasis: Television
production including news
broadcasting, corporate videos,
graphic design, and media ethics
Special Activities: Television:
program material produced for cable
television
Facilities: Television: studio; audio
bay; control room
Equipment: Television/Video:
complete ¾" studio and location
Alumni: James R. Hall, TV news
photographer; Athena Vadnis, TV news
reporter

GUIDE POV: Idaho State University has
recently completed new television
studio facilities for its growing
program; cross-registration through the
Western Education Exchange; media
internship opportunities

UNIVERSITY OF IDAHO

Moscow, ID 83843
(208)885–6111

*State four-year comprehensive
institution. Coed, rural location.
Undergraduate enrollment: 7,000.
Graduate enrollment: 2,000.*

SCHOOL OF COMMUNICATION

Chair/Contact: Peter A. Haggart,
Chair

Calendar: Semesters
Degrees Offered: B.A., B.S.,
communication (students may select
emphasis in visual communication)
Departmental Majors: Undergraduate
visual communication: 100 students
Entrance Requirements:
Undergraduate: 2.0 grade-point
average; ACT or SAT scores.
Undergraduate application deadline:
August 1. Percent of acceptances: 95%
Curricular Emphasis: Film history;
television production
Special Activities: Film: film series/
festivals. Television: program material
produced for on-campus closed-circuit
television, and for local public and
cable television
Facilities: Television: studio; audio
bay; control room; remote van
Equipment: Television/Video:
complete 1" and ¾" studio; complete
¾" and ½" location
Alumni: Christian Nyby, TV director;
Bill Fagerbakker, TV actor

GUIDE POV: The School of
Communication at this competitive,
well-equipped state university offers
thorough television production
training; curriculum prepares student
for graduate study in communications
or employment in the field; cross-
registration with Washington State
University; study abroad; internship
opportunities in television
production

Throughout my college years, the study and making of films was of primary interest to me. At Harvard, my undergraduate thesis focused on the works of Sergei Eisenstein. I began making short films as a graduate student at New York University and The American Film Institute. Yet curiously, I had no formal plans to engage in a professional career as a filmmaker. I just wanted to make interesting films. But several of my student films won awards, and happily this led to professional opportunities.

I have always been interested in all aspects of filmmaking—writing, directing, and producing. And I choose to work in varied genres as well. Among my feature directing credits are *Heroes* and *The Big Fix*. I also directed *The Chosen*, whose screenplay I adapted from the novel by Chaim Potak. For Disney Productions I directed *The Journey of Natty Gann*. My latest theatrical feature, *By the Sword*, is now in post-production. I also enjoy working extensively in television, particularly when a project involves a feature-length dramatic presentation. Among many special projects, I wrote, directed, and produced "Conspiracy: The Trial of the Chicago 8" for HBO, which won an Ace Award. Currently, I have projects in development at ABC and HBO.

Had I not been given the chance to make films as a student, I believe I would not be directing, writing, and producing today. Film school is most valuable in that this is a craft learned by doing. It also helps to possess a measure of talent, perseverance, ambition, and luck. Above all, I would encourage today's student to use the time to study the films you love and to make the films your heart calls you to make.

AURORA UNIVERSITY

347 S. Gladstone,
Aurora, IL 60506
(708)892–6431

Private four-year comprehensive institution. Coed, suburban location. Enrollment: 1,800.

COMMUNICATION/MEDIA STUDIES DEPARTMENT

Chair/Contact: Laurel Church/John Bitterman
Calendar: Trimesters
Degrees Offered: B.A., communication (media studies concentration)
Departmental Majors: 75 students
Entrance Requirements: 2.0 grade-point average; ACT or SAT scores; interview. Application deadline: rolling. Percent of acceptances: 83%
Curricular Emphasis: Electronic media theory and culture; media writing; television production
Special Activities: Film: film series/festivals. Television: program material produced for local access studio and station for the city of Aurora
Facilities: Television: studio; audio bay; control room
Equipment: Television/Video: complete ¾" studio and location
Alumni: Steve Moga, TV producer/director; Lisa Aprati, TV sports producer/director

GUIDE POV: The media studies concentration offered by this interdisciplinary communications program prepares students for careers in television, radio, print journalism, or graduate study in communication; sequential program in television production and writing; cross-registration with North Central and Illinois Benedictine colleges; study abroad; internship opportunities in television production

BLACK HAWK COLLEGE

6600 34th Ave.,
Moline, IL 61265
(309)796–1311

State/district two-year comprehensive institution. Coed, urban location. Enrollment: 4,500.

CREATIVE ARTS DEPARTMENT

Chair/Contact: Dolores Hill
Calendar: Semesters
Degrees Offered: A.A., creative arts (students may select emphasis in television); A.A.S.
Departmental Majors: 20–40 students
Entrance Requirements: Open-door policy; applicants should present high school diploma or GED certificate; 18 years of age. Application deadline: rolling
Curricular Emphasis: Program offers A.A. degree for those planning transfer

to four-year institution, as well as A.A.S. degree for those seeking technical support positions in television production
Special Activities: Television: program material produced for public television station WQPT-TV located on campus
Facilities: Film: film library. Television: studio; control room
Equipment: Television/Video: complete ¾" studio and ½" location
Alumni: Patricia Dietz, TV director; Jerry Myers, TV programmer; Jim Albracht, radio producer

GUIDE POV: This affordable two-year program offers technical training in television production with both career and transfer options; emphasis on producing a variety of programming; internship opportunities in television production

BRADLEY UNIVERSITY

Bradley Ave.,
Peoria, IL 61625
(309)676–7611

Private four-year comprehensive institution. Coed, urban location. Enrollment: 5,000.

DIVISION OF COMMUNICATION

Chair/Contact: Professor Claussen, Acting Director
Calendar: Semesters
Degrees Offered: B.A., communication (concentrations in radio/video/photography, news production, speech, advertising, public relations)
Departmental Majors: 600 students
Entrance Requirements: 2.25 grade-point average; ACT or SAT required with recommended minimum scores

of 18 or 900, respectively. Application deadline: June 30. Percent of acceptances: 90%
Curricular Emphasis: Television production; news writing; emphasis on studio/field production; media management
Special Activities: Film: student publications. Television: program material produced for local commercial television station and for cable television
Facilities: Video: screening room; editing suite; sound mixing room; tape library. Television: studio; control room
Equipment: Film: complete Super-8. Television/Video: complete ¾" studio; complete ½" location
Alumni: David Horowitz, TV personality; Charles Steiner, TV sports broadcaster; Joel Okenin, TV producer

GUIDE POV: Communication majors here may choose a concentration in radio-video-photography or news production; variety of group assignments include studio and field feature presentations, newscasts, and television commercials; photo option includes exploration of both 35mm still photography and video as forms of personal expression; graphic design; study abroad; internship opportunities in television production

COLLEGE OF DUPAGE

22nd St. and Lambert Rd.,
Glen Ellyn, IL 60137–6599
(708)858–2800

County two-year institution. Coed, suburban location. Enrollment: 34,000.

COMMUNICATION ARTS AND SCIENCES PROGRAM

Chair/Contact: Tom Klodin; Claudine Jordan
Calendar: Quarters
Degrees Offered: A.A.S.
Departmental Majors: 60 students
Entrance Requirements: Open-door policy; transcripts; ACT testing recommended. Application deadline: rolling, but registration priority given to early applicants
Curricular Emphasis: Film and television production; writing for media; multi-image production; 2-D and 3-D computer animation
Special Activities: Television: program material produced for cable television
Facilities: Film: screening room; editing suite; sound mixing room; film library. Television: studio; audio bay; control room
Equipment: Film: complete Super-8 and 16mm. Television/Video: complete ¾" studio; complete ¾" and ½" location; 2-D and 3-D computer animation
Alumni: James Belushi, film actor; Millie Cave, film/TV producer; David Pierro, motion picture gaffer; Tim Throop, media executive; Jerry Robinson, TV production manager

GUIDE POV: With an unusually diverse program for a two-year county institution, this large college offers a communication program specializing in preparing students for employment in the fields of video, film, slide-tape, multi-image, and audio production; hands-on experience; several courses are transfer-oriented; study abroad in England, Scotland, and Austria; internship opportunities in television and video production

COLLEGE OF LAKE COUNTY

19351 W. Washington St.,
Grayslake, IL 60030
(708)223–6601

State two-year comprehensive institution. Coed, suburban location. Enrollment: 12,000.

DIVISION OF COMMUNICATION ARTS

Chair/Contact: Sandria Rodriguez
Calendar: Semesters
Degrees Offered: None in film or television
Entrance Requirements: ACT or SAT scores; teachers' recommendations. Application deadline: contact admissions
Curricular Emphasis: Introductory courses in film history, genre studies, screenwriting
Special Activities: Film: film series/festivals; film societies
Facilities: Film: permanent library of student films. Television: studio
Equipment: Television: ½" and ¾" cassette recorders; portable cameras
Alumni: Bob Jeffers, media executive

GUIDE POV: This two-year school provides introductory studies in film theory and technique, after which students may transfer to four-year institutions

COLUMBIA COLLEGE

600 S. Michigan Ave.,
Chicago, IL 60605–1996
(312)663–1600

Private four-year comprehensive institution. Coed, urban location. Undergraduate enrollment: 6,750. Graduate enrollment: 342.

FILM AND VIDEO DEPARTMENT

Chair/Contact: Chap Freeman;
Doreen Bartoni

TELEVISION DEPARTMENT

Chair/Contact: Edward L. Morris
Calendar: Semesters
Degrees Offered: B.A., M.F.A., film
and video; B.A., television, broadcast
journalism
Departmental Majors: Undergraduate
film and video: 908 students;
Undergraduate television: 488 students.
Graduate film & video: 120 students
Entrance Requirements:
Undergraduate: transcripts; high school
diploma or GED certificate. Graduate:
3.0 grade-point average; interview;
written statement of purpose; portfolio.
Undergraduate application deadline:
rolling. Graduate application deadline:
March 15 (fall admission only);
February 15 for international students
Curricular Emphasis: Intensive
production training with additional
offerings in critical studies,
screenwriting, and management
Special Activities: Film: film series/
festivals; student publications;
placement assistance. Television:
annual student exhibition; program
material produced for on-campus
closed-circuit television and for cable
television, including musical, dramatic,
and news programming; placement
assistance
Facilities: Film/Video: sound studio
for recording, mixing, and transfer
with timecode and sampling
capabilities; two screening rooms with
Cinemascope, laserdisc and tape
projection; 12 Steenbeck editing
rooms; six ¾" off-line systems;
animation studio with three Oxberry
cameras; 3,300-square-foot shooting
stage; film library. Television: two
color studios with three Sony BVP3A
cameras; two control rooms with
broadcast-style Grass Valley switchers
(1-200 model, 1-100 model); audio
equipment and playback for CD, tape,
or conventional recordings; Laird CG
and VTR recording facilities with TBC;
eight off-line and on-line suites with
timecode; one advanced editing
facility for AB roll editing
Equipment: Film/Video: 16mm, ¾"
and Hi-band camera packages; 16mm
and ¾" off-line editing. Television:
complete studio equipment; 24 mobile
field units including Sony DXC325 and
327 and Hi-band cameras with
docking capabilities; three-camera
remote truck for multiple camera field
shooting
Alumni: John McNaughton,
screenwriter/director; Buzz Hirsch, film
producer; Marcia Lamoureux,
animator/filmmaker; Bill Thinnes,
animator

GUIDE POV: Columbia College offers
its students separate majors in film and
video, television, or broadcast
journalism; numerous internship
opportunities in film, broadcasting,
cable, and postproduction

CONCORDIA UNIVERSITY

7400 Augusta,
River Forest, IL 60305
(708)771–8300

*Private four-year comprehensive
institution. Coed, suburban location.
Enrollment: 1,000.*

COMMUNICATION AND THEATRE DEPARTMENT

Chair/Contact: Film: Paul
Grotelueschen; Television: Richard
Richter

Calendar: Quarters
Degrees Offered: B.A.,
communication/theatre
Departmental Majors: Film, radio
and television: 10–30 students
Entrance Requirements: 2.0 grade-
point average; ACT required, with a
minimum score of 18;
recommendations. Application
deadline: rolling. Percent of
acceptances: 82%
Curricular Emphasis: Film and·
television production
Special Activities: Film: student
screenings. Television: program
material produced for various outlets
Facilities: Television: studio; audio
bay; control room
Equipment: Film: complete 16mm.
Television/Video: complete ¾" studio;
¾" and ½" location
Alumni: Paul Fries, TV production
coordinator

GUIDE POV: Concordia University
offers a small communications
program with personal attention to
student interests in film and television
production projects; core curriculum
focuses on liberal arts studies; cross-
registration with Rosary College and
the Chicago Consortium of Colleges;
study abroad in London; internship
opportunities in television production

DEPAUL UNIVERSITY

2323 N. Seminary,
Chicago, IL 60604
(312)362–8000

*Private four-year comprehensive
institution. Coed, urban location.
Undergraduate enrollment: 9,200.
Graduate enrollment: 6,000.*

COMMUNICATION DEPARTMENT

Chair/Contact: Film: Richard de
Cordova; Television: Kate Kane; Radio:
Sarah Wortman
Calendar: Quarters
Degrees Offered: B.A.,
communication
Departmental Majors: Undergraduate
film: 75 students. Undergraduate
television: 50 students
Entrance Requirements:
Undergraduate: ACT or SAT scores;
Graduate: transcripts; three letters of
recommendation. Undergraduate
application deadline: August 15.
Percent of acceptances: 65%
Curricular Emphasis: Program
emphasizes film and television critical
studies and video production; one
course in screenwriting offered
through English Department
Special Activities: Film: film series/
festivals. Television: off-campus
training in television production
Facilities: Television: small format
video lab. Radio: station and
production lab
Equipment: Television/Video: small
format video production
Alumni: Karl Malden, film actor; Joe
Mantegna, film actor; Linda Hunt, film
actress; Elizabeth Perkins, film/TV
actress

GUIDE POV: Mass media studies as
well as video/radio production training
are offered at this selective private
university; study abroad offered in 13
countries; numerous internship
opportunities in television and radio
production

ELGIN COMMUNITY COLLEGE

1700 Spartan Dr.,
Elgin, IL 60123
(708)697-1000

District two-year comprehensive institution. Coed, suburban location. Enrollment: 5,000.

SPEECH DEPARTMENT

Chair/Contact: Terry Domschke; Gail Shadwell
Calendar: Semesters
Degrees Offered: A.A.
Departmental Majors:
Undergraduate: 10–50 students
Entrance Requirements: High school diploma; 2.0 grade-point average. Application deadline: rolling
Curricular Emphasis: Electronic media theory and culture; critical studies in film; basic film and television production
Special Activities: Film: film series/ festivals. Television: program material produced for cable television
Facilities: Film: screening room; film library
Equipment: Television/Video: portable cameras; monitors; video editing equipment
Alumni: Phillip Ranstrom, film/TV/ video executive; Michael Prenevost, TV media teacher

GUIDE POV: Students study mass communication theory under the auspices of the Speech Department; basic field production equipment available; core program concentrates on preparation for transfer to four-year schools; media internships available

ILLINOIS STATE UNIVERSITY

Normal, IL 61761–6901
(309)438-2111

State four-year comprehensive institution. Coed, suburban location. Undergraduate enrollment: 20,000. Graduate enrollment: full-time 300; part-time 2,000.

THEATRE DEPARTMENT

Chair/Contact: Dr. Ron Mottram
Calendar: Semesters
Degrees Offered: B.A., B.S., theatre (minor in film studies)
Departmental Majors: Undergraduate film studies minor: 40
Entrance Requirements:
Undergraduate: high school diploma or GED certificate; class rank; SAT or ACT scores; AP and CLEP credit accepted. Application deadline: rolling
Curricular Emphasis: Critical studies in film within context of theatre arts and literature
Special Activities: Film: film series/ festivals; film societies; independent study
Facilities: Film: 35mm screening facilities; film library
Equipment: Film: 8mm cameras
Alumni: John Malkovich, film/TV actor/director; Rhonda Johnson, postproduction supervisor; Laurie Metcalf, TV/film actor; Dan Craft, film critic

GUIDE POV: A newly instituted film studies minor is now available through the Department of Theatre at this competitive state university; additional critical studies courses on literature and film are offered through the English Department; there exists one production course in film and video through the Art Department; qualifying juniors and seniors may study for up to one year at several hundred colleges throughout the country through the university's membership in the National Student Exchange

ILLINOIS VALLEY COMMUNITY COLLEGE

Route 1, Oglesby, IL 61348
(815)224–2720

State/district two-year institution. Coed, rural location. Enrollment: 4,000.

HUMANITIES AND FINE ARTS DIVISION/ SPEECH AND THEATRE STUDIES

Chair/Contact: Film: James C. Jewell; television: Samuel Rogal, Chair, Humanities and Fine Arts Division; theatre: Giacomo R. Leone
Calendar: Semesters
Degrees Offered: A.A.
Entrance Requirements: Open-door policy; high school graduate or equivalent. Application deadline: rolling
Curricular Emphasis: Critical studies in film; media writing; sequential course work in television and radio broadcast production; media sales and management
Special Activities: Film: film series/ festivals
Facilities: Film: film library; screening room. Television: studio; audio bay; control room
Equipment: Film: complete Super-8 and 16mm. Television/Video: complete ½" location; VHS editing
Alumni: Michael Krewer, filmmaker; Tim Filipiak, film critic; Lisa Visione, TV/film makeup artist

GUIDE POV: Students enrolled in this two-year community college may opt for studies in film theory as well as participate in practical hands-on broadcast production training that includes on-the-air techniques, media writing, and radio/television sales

LEWIS UNIVERSITY

Route 53, Romeoville, IL 60441–2298
(815)838–0500

Private four-year comprehensive institution. Coed, suburban location. Undergraduate enrollment: 3,300. Graduate enrollment: 400.

ELECTRONIC MEDIA

Chair/Contact: Television: John P. Carey
Calendar: Semesters
Degrees Offered: B.A., radio-TV broadcasting; B.A., communications/ speech; B.A., journalism
Departmental Majors: Undergraduate television: 60 students
Entrance Requirements: Undergraduate: 2.0 grade-point average; ACT or SAT scores; recommendations. Undergraduate application deadline: summer. Percent of acceptances: 77%
Curricular Emphasis: Television history and production; media administration
Special Activities: Television: program material produced for cable television and for on-campus closed-circuit television includes news programs, sports coverage, and special features
Facilities: Television: studio; audio bay; control room; animation facilities
Equipment: Television/Video: complete Betacam and ¾" studio; complete ¾" and ½" location
Alumni: John Strolia, TV director/ producer; Angelo Lazzara, associate

TV producer; Sandy O'Brien, TV news coordinator

GUIDE POV: This competitive private university prepares students for careers in commercial, educational, and industrial broadcasting; concentration in media management; variety of student production projects; internship opportunities in Chicago broadcast studios

LOYOLA UNIVERSITY OF CHICAGO

820 N. Michigan Ave.,
Chicago, IL 60611
(312)915–6000

Private four-year comprehensive institution. Coed, urban location. Undergraduate enrollment: 9,000. Graduate enrollment: 3,500.

COMMUNICATION DEPARTMENT

Chair/Contact: Film: Jeff Harder; television: Craig Kois
Calendar: Semesters
Degrees Offered: B.A., communication (students may select emphasis in radio/TV/film)
Departmental Majors: Undergraduate film, radio and television: 200 students
Entrance Requirements: Undergraduate: academic rank within top half of graduating class; ACT or SAT scores. Undergraduate application deadline: July 13. Percent of acceptances: 75%
Curricular Emphasis: Electronic media theory and culture; critical studies in film; media writing; audio-film-video production; media management
Special Activities: Film: film series/festivals. Television: program material produced for cable television
Facilities: Film: screening room;

editing suite. Television: studio; audio bay; control room
Equipment: Film: 16mm cameras. Television/Video: complete ¾" studio and location
Alumni: Jim Collins, TV production coordinator; Dianne Totura, TV production coordinator

GUIDE POV: This private Roman Catholic university offers a comprehensive degree program in both film and television production; study abroad in Rome; cross-registration with Mundelein College; internship opportunities in film and television production

MILLIKIN UNIVERSITY

1184 W. Main St.,
Decatur, IL 62522
(217)424–6211

Private four-year comprehensive institution. Coed, urban location. Enrollment: 1,800.

COMMUNICATIONS DEPARTMENT

Chair/Contact: Dr. Hazel Rozema
Calendar: Semesters
Degrees Offered: B.A., communication (mass media emphasis)
Departmental Majors: Television: 30 students
Entrance Requirements: Minimum ACT score 20; academic rank within top half of high school graduating class. Application deadline: rolling. Percent of acceptances: 80%
Curricular Emphasis: Television production
Special Activities: Program material produced for local commercial television station
Facilities: Television: music video

production studio; access to area broadcast facilities and equipment
Equipment: Television/Video: single-tube cameras; S-VHS format; PC-based editor
Alumni: Jodi Benson, film/TV actress; Joel Benson, video editor; Dwight Jordan, TV choreographer/director

GUIDE POV: This small private college offers television production training; study abroad in Europe, Mexico, Japan, and Singapore; internship opportunities in television production

MONMOUTH COLLEGE

700 E. Broadway,
Monmouth, IL 61462–9989
(309)457–2311

Private four-year comprehensive institution. Coed, rural location. Enrollment: 650.

DEPARTMENT OF SPEECH COMMUNICATION AND THEATRE ARTS

Chair/Contact: Television: Lee McGaan
Calendar: Semesters
Degrees Offered: B.A., speech communication (emphasis on mass communication)
Departmental Majors: Mass communication: 20 students
Entrance Requirements: 2.0 grade-point average; ACT, with a minimum score of 20, or SAT, with a minimum composite score of 1000; essay required. Application deadline: March 1. Percent of acceptances: 87%
Curricular Emphasis: Electronic media theory and culture; media writing; television production; media management; theatre
Special Activities: Film: series/festivals. Television: program material

produced for on-campus closed-circuit television
Facilities: Film: screening room; film library. Television: studio; audio bay; control room; editing suites
Equipment: Video: studio and editing equipment
Alumni: C. Edward Greene, TV news anchor; Bonnie B. Oliver, media consultant; Richard A. Hessel, technical operations director

GUIDE POV: This private liberal arts college offers a degree program with course listings in photography and video production; attention to experimental as well as mainstream forms of expression; internship opportunities in film and television production

NORTHERN ILLINOIS UNIVERSITY

DeKalb, IL 60115–2854
(815)753–1000

State four-year comprehensive institution. Coed, rural location. Undergraduate enrollment: 20,000. Graduate enrollment: 4,000.

DEPARTMENT OF COMMUNICATION STUDIES

Chair/Contact: Richard L. Johannesen, Chair; Dr. Martha Cooper, Graduate Director
Calendar: Semesters
Degrees Offered: B.A., M.A., communication studies (students may select emphasis in media studies)
Departmental Majors: Undergraduate film: 40 students. Undergraduate television: 90 students. Graduate media studies: 20 students
Entrance Requirements: Undergraduate: 2.40 grade-point average; ACT or SAT scores. Graduate:

3.0 grade-point average; GRE scores; recommendations; written statement of purpose. Undergraduate application deadline: August 1. Graduate application deadline: June 1. Percent of acceptances: 69%

Curricular Emphasis: Electronic media theory and culture; critical studies in film; media writing; film and video production including documentary production; media management

Special Activities: Film: film series/ festivals; film societies. Television: program material produced for cable television and for on-campus closed-circuit television include nightly newscasts, a magazine show, public service announcements, documentaries, and entertainment programs; corporate video projects

Facilities: Film: screening room; editing suite; animation stand; film library. Television: studio; three audio bays; control room; six VHS video editing stations

Equipment: Film: complete 16mm; video transfer equipment. Television/Video: complete ¾" studio; ¾" and ½" location

Alumni: Robert Zemekis, film/TV director/writer; Jamie Martellaro

GUIDE POV: The media studies program at this competitive state university encourages undergraduate concentrations in either critical studies or media production; film projects are shot and roughly edited; students produce a variety of broadcast material; graduate program offers concentration in media studies blending critical theory with advanced production projects; internship opportunities in film and television production

NORTHWESTERN UNIVERSITY

1905 N. Sheridan Rd.,
Evanston, IL 60208
(708)491–3741

Private four-year comprehensive institution. Coed, suburban location. Undergraduate enrollment: 7,500. Graduate enrollment: 2,500.

RADIO/TV/FILM DEPARTMENT

Chair/Contact: Undergraduate: Michelle Citron, Annette Barbier; graduate: Marjureth Perdekur.

Calendar: Quarters

Degrees Offered: B.S., M.A., Ph.D., radio/TV/film; M.F.A., writing, production

Departmental Majors: Undergraduate radio/TV/film: 300 students. Graduate: 50 students

Entrance Requirements: Undergraduate: SAT or ACT scores; transcripts; personal statement; teachers' recommendations; TOEFL for foreign students. Graduate: GRE scores; transcripts; statement of purpose; two letters of recommendation. Application deadline: January 15 to be considered for financial aid; otherwise April 15. Percent of acceptances: Graduate: 20–30%

Curricular Emphasis: Strong emphasis on a blend of theory and practice

Special Activities: Film: off-campus production training. Television: program material produced for cable television

Facilities: Film: screening room; editing suites; sound mixing room; film library. Television: sound stage; computer graphics facility; studio; audio bay; control room; editing and postproduction

Equipment: Film: 16 mm (Steenbeck flatbeds; Arri, Bolex, Eclair cameras). Television/Video: complete ¾" studio; complete ¾" and ½" location; Macintosh based computer animation; 3-D computer animation (Silicon Graphics/Wavefront Advanced Visualizer)

Alumni: Garry Marshall, TV/film writer/director/producer; Walter Mirisch, film producer; Ken Kwapis, film director; Stuart Hagmann, TV/film/commercials director; Mary Ann Childers, TV news anchor; Dermot Mulroney, TV/film actor; Howard Smith, film editor

GUIDE POV: This prestigious professional school offers students a program that integrates film and television production training with liberal arts studies; highly selective admissions; study abroad around the world; media internship opportunities in Chicago

ROSARY COLLEGE

7900 W. Division St.,
River Forest, IL 60305
(708)366-2490

Private four-year comprehensive institution. Coed, suburban location. Undergraduate enrollment: 950. Graduate enrollment: 800. Undergraduate tuition: $9,990 per academic year.

DEPARTMENT OF COMMUNICATION ARTS AND SCIENCES

Chair/Contact: Dr. Patricia Brett Erens
Calendar: Semesters
Degrees Offered: B.A., communication

Departmental Majors: Undergraduate film: 80 students
Entrance Requirements:
Undergraduate: academic rank within top half of high school graduating class; essay required; 2.5 grade-point average; ACT or SAT scores. Undergraduate application deadline: rolling. Percent of acceptances: 75%
Curricular Emphasis: Electronic media theory and culture; film history and criticism; basic video production
Facilities: Video: editing suites; screening room
Equipment: Television/Video: camcorders; ½" editing system; laserdisc; laser player
Alumni: Nicolette Ferri, TV producer; Catherine Watkins, radio programmer; Linda Adams, advertising executive; James Zbiron, video production executive

GUIDE POV: Students choosing this liberal arts program will study communication theory and media criticism while learning basic video production techniques; study abroad in Europe; cross-registration with Concordia College; internship opportunities in television production

SANGAMON STATE UNIVERSITY

Shepherd Rd.,
Springfield, IL 62794–9243
(217)786–6600

State four-year comprehensive institution. Coed, urban location. Undergraduate enrollment: 2,200. Graduate enrollment: 1,800.

COMMUNICATION DEPARTMENT

Chair/Contact: J. Michael Duvall
Calendar: Semesters

Degrees Offered: B.A., M.A., communication (students may select emphasis in mass media)

Departmental Majors: Undergraduate: 230 students. Graduate: 55 students

Entrance Requirements: Undergraduate: high school diploma or GED certificate; ACT or SAT scores. Graduate: transcripts; GRE scores; contact department for additional requirements. Undergraduate and graduate application deadline: August 15

Curricular Emphasis: Communication theory; news and documentary production; media management; film theory courses offered through literature program

Special Activities: Television: program material produced for on-campus public television station and community access television; vocational placement service; apprenticeships

Facilities: Television: two studios; audio bays; control rooms

Equipment: Television: complete ¾" studio; complete ¾" and ½" location; editing suites

Alumni: Jill Turek, film/TV director; Deb Smith, film/TV director; Mike Murphy, media specialist; Mike Madjic, corporate video manager

GUIDE POV: This is a practical career program that emphasizes business and corporate video production within a liberal arts structure; internship opportunities in television and corporate video production

SCHOOL OF THE ART INSTITUTE OF CHICAGO

280 S. Columbus,
Chicago, IL 60603
(312)899–5100

Private four-year professional arts institution. Coed, urban location. Undergraduate enrollment: 1,600. Graduate enrollment: 250.

FILM DEPARTMENT

Chair/Contact: Sharon Couzin, Chair

Calendar: Semesters

Degrees Offered: B.F.A., M.F.A.

Departmental Majors: Undergraduate film: 150 students. Graduate film: 25 students

Entrance Requirements: Undergraduate: ACT or SAT scores; written statement of purpose; art or film portfolio. Graduate: film portfolio; statement of purpose. Undergraduate application deadline: August 15. Percent of acceptances: 87%

Curricular Emphasis: Experimental, documentary, experimental narrative and animated film production

Special Activities: Film: film center; visiting video artists; multimedia and multi-arts performances; local exhibitions; apprenticeships offered abroad. Video: program material produced for local public television station

Facilities: Film: screening rooms; sound studio; editing suites; sound mixing rooms; transfer rooms; animation stand; film library. Television: studio

Equipment: Film: complete Super-8 and 16mm; Oxberry 1500 optical printer. Video: complete ¾" studio and location; video synthesis systems; color special effects generator; character generator; A/B roll editing; specially designed equipment to support electronic experimentation

Alumni: Tom Kalin, film/video producer; Yvonne Welbon, film/video producer/director; Sheri Wills, film producer

GUIDE POV: The School of the Art Institute is a studio fine arts institution that offers degree programs featuring animation, documentary and experimental film and video production; department encourages multidisciplinary arts interaction; personal exploration; internship opportunities in film and video production

---

SOUTHERN ILLINOIS UNIVERSITY AT CARBONDALE

Carbondale, IL 62901
(618)453–2121

State four-year comprehensive institution. Coed, rural location. Undergraduate enrollment: 20,000. Graduate enrollment: 4,000.

DEPARTMENT OF CINEMA AND PHOTOGRAPHY

Chair/Contact: Gary Kolb, Chair

DEPARTMENT OF RADIO AND TELEVISION

Chair/Contact: Joe Foote, Chair
Calendar: Semesters
Degrees Offered: B.A., M.F.A., cinema and photography; B.A., radio and television; M.A., telecommunications
Departmental Majors: Undergraduate cinema and photography: 305 students; Graduate: 30 students. Undergraduate television: 406 students; Graduate: 30 students
Entrance Requirements: Undergraduate: high school degree/

GED certificate; ACT score of 20 if in top quarter of high school graduating class or ACT score of 22 if in top half of graduating class; transfer credit *C* average. Graduate: transcripts; portfolio of films; recommendations. Undergraduate application deadline: April 1. Graduate application deadline: March 11; November 1

Curricular Emphasis: Department of Cinema and Photography: film and photography production, history, and criticism. Department of Radio-Television: broadcast journalism; corporate video; television production; broadcast meteorology; new technologies; audio production; media sales and management

Special Activities: Film: Big Muddy Film Festival; Photography: visiting artist lecture series. Television: program material produced for on-campus closed-circuit television, and for cable, public, and commercial television stations; member AERho, BICA, ITVA, Radio Active, WICI, SINBA, TELEPRO, WIDB

Facilities: Film: sound stage; screening rooms; editing rooms; sound mixing rooms; conforming rooms; animation stand; film/video library. Television: studio; audio studio; control room

Equipment: Film: complete 16mm. Television: complete 1" and ¾" studio; complete ¾" and ½" location

Alumni: Robert K. Weiss, film director/producer; Jim Crocker, screenwriter/producer; John Behnke, TV/film writer; Liz Ralston, special effects production; David Eubank, cinematographer

GUIDE POV: Southern Illinois University offers separate production majors for those choosing film or television; both departments are well equipped and provide comprehensive training; study abroad at over 100 sites in Europe, China, Africa, and Latin America; variety of internship opportunities in film and television production

UNIVERSITY OF CHICAGO

Chicago, IL 60637
(312)702–1234

Private four-year comprehensive institution. Coed, urban location. Undergraduate enrollment: 3,000. Graduate enrollment: 6,000.

FILM STUDIES PROGRAM

Chair/Contacts: Professors Miriam Hansen; James Lastra
Calendar: Quarters
Degrees Offered: B.A., M.A., Ph.D., cinema studies (interdisciplinary program)
Departmental Majors: Undergraduate: 5–10 students
Entrance Requirements: Undergraduate: ACT or SAT scores; interview recommended; essay required. Graduate: GRE scores; recommendations; essay required. Undergraduate and graduate application deadline: January 15. Percent of acceptances: 40%, undergraduate and graduate
Curricular Emphasis: Study of the moving image in various contexts and disciplines; film, video, and television textual analysis; theory and aesthetics; history; global culture, etc.
Special Activities: Film Studies Center hosts visiting filmmakers; screenings; workshops; special series; performances; Mass Culture Workshop holds regular meetings and screenings in Film Studies Center

Facilities: State-of-the-art projection for 16mm film, slides, laserdiscs, and variety of video formats; the Film Studies Center houses the University's Film Archive, which holds over 1,600 film, video, and laserdisc titles, including feature films, experimental cinema, silent films, classic Hollywood cinema, European art cinema, etc.
Alumni: Mike Nichols, film director; Phillip Kaufman, film writer/director; David Kehr, film critic; Wileen Dragovan, independent filmmaker

GUIDE POV: This selective private university provides a strong cinema studies program at both the undergraduate and graduate levels that draws upon the disciplines of art, world literature, theatre, and social/cultural history, among others; basic courses in video production offered through the Committee on Art and Design; study abroad in twelve countries

UNIVERSITY OF ILLINOIS

506 S. Wright St.,
Urbana, IL 61801
(217)333–1000

State four-year comprehensive institution. Coed, rural location. Undergraduate enrollment: 26,000. Graduate enrollment: 8,800.

DEPARTMENT OF JOURNALISM

Chair/Contact: Steven J. Helle

CINEMATOGRAPHY PROGRAM

Chair/Contact: Julius Rascheff

UNIT FOR CINEMA STUDIES

Chair/Contact: Edwin Jahiel
Calendar: Semesters
Degrees Offered: B.S., M.S.,

journalism; B.A., humanities (students may select emphasis in film studies), art (students may select emphasis in cinematography-production)
Departmental Majors: Undergraduate television: 50 students. Graduate television: 5 students. Undergraduate film studies: 30 students. Undergraduate film production: 80 students. Graduate film production: 15 students
Entrance Requirements: Undergraduate: transcripts; ACT or SAT scores; teachers' recommendations; AP and CLEP credit accepted. Graduate: transcripts; GRE scores; recommendations; interview; portfolio; written statement of purpose. Undergraduate application deadline: November 1. Graduate application deadline: February 15. Percent of acceptances: 65%
Curricular Emphasis: Film: complete program of study in cinematography through Art Department; complete undergraduate cinema studies program covering theory and criticism through Humanities Department. Television: broadcast journalism sequence; opportunities to produce both long- and short-form productions in broadcast journalism
Special Activities: Film: film series/festivals. Television: newscast and documentary material produced for cable television
Facilities: Film: 35mm screening facilities; sound mixing room; screening room; editing room; animation stand; computerized optical printing and SFX lab; video transfers; film library. Television: studio; audio bay; control room
Equipment: Film: complete Super-8 and 16mm. Television: matched studio cameras; ¾" VTR; telecine; ENG cameras; portable lighting packages;

¾" and ½" cassette recorders; switcher/special effects generator; portable cameras; Amiga desktop video system
Alumni: Roger Ebert, film critic; Dennis Swanson, TV network sports executive; Hal Bruno, TV network political analyst; Gene Shalit, film critic

GUIDE POV: The Art Department presents comprehensive studies in the craft of cinematography; separate degree program in film theory and criticism; the Journalism Department offers a highly professional television program emphasizing public affairs journalism; selective admissions; internships in film production; credit for summer internships in broadcast newsrooms

---

UNIVERSITY OF ILLINOIS—CHICAGO

850 S. Halstead,
Chicago, IL 60680
(312)996–7000

State four-year comprehensive institution. Coed, urban location. Undergraduate enrollment: 25,000. Graduate enrollment: 8,000.

COLLEGE OF ARCHITECTURE, ART, AND URBAN PLANNING

Chair/Contact: Judith Russi Kirshner, Director, art and design; Ellen Baird, Dean, College of Architecture, Art, and Urban Planning
Calendar: Semesters
Degrees Offered: B.F.A., M.F.A., photography/film/electronic media
Departmental Majors: Undergraduate film: 30 students. Graduate film: 11 students
Entrance Requirements: Undergraduate: 3.25 grade-point

average; ACT or SAT scores. Graduate: 4.0 grade point average (5.0 point scale); portfolio; short statement of purpose/goals. Undergraduate application deadline: February 28 priority deadline; June 25 final deadline. Graduate application deadline: March 1, with late extension if space permits up to June 25. Percent of acceptances: Undergraduate: 85%. Graduate: 25%

Curricular Emphasis: Film and electronic media production including narrative, experimental, and animated forms; graphic design program

Special Activities: Film: film series/festivals; film societies; student screenings. Television/Video: program material produced for cable television

Facilities: Film: screening room; sound synthesis, transfer and mixing room; Oxberry animation stand; film library. Video: computer animation facility; video editing, projection and studio space

Equipment: Film: complete 16mm. Television/Video: complete ¾" and ½" location including monitors; audio mixers; switcher/special effects generator; Eclair, Nagra, and CP16 double-system cameras; flatbed editing machines; optical printer; portapack video equipment

Alumni: Ed Coffey, special effects animator; Robert Ziembecky, film art director; Cheng-Fu Shen, film/video producer; Mehrnaz Saeed-Vafa, film/video teacher; Candice Reichner, music video producer

GUIDE POV: Students in this selective fine arts program explore the social, cultural, and ideological possibilities of film and electronic media including electronic visualization and computer graphics; separate concentration in graphic design utilizes contemporary technology in film, video, print, and digital computers; multimedia projects; study abroad; internship opportunities

---

WESTERN ILLINOIS UNIVERSITY

Macomb, IL 61455
(309)295–1414

State four-year comprehensive institution. Coed, rural location. Undergraduate enrollment: 10,000. Graduate enrollment: 2,300.

ENGLISH AND JOURNALISM DEPARTMENT

Chair/Contact: Janice Welsch; John Orlandello

COMMUNICATION ARTS AND SCIENCES

Chair/Contact: Sharon Evans, broadcasting
Calendar: Semesters
Degrees Offered: Interdisciplinary minor in film; B.A., M.A., broadcasting (students may select emphasis in television)
Entrance Requirements: Undergraduate: transcripts; academic rank within top half of high school graduating class; ACT (minimum score of 15) or SAT (minimum composite score of 700). Graduate: transcripts; GRE scores. Undergraduate and graduate application deadline: rolling
Curricular Emphasis: College of Arts and Sciences, Education, and Fine Arts: critical film studies; basic independent film production; animation. College of Communication Arts and Sciences: comprehensive broadcast production training
Special Activities: Film: cinema showcase; film society. Television: program material produced for on-campus closed-circuit television and for cable television
Facilities: Film: screening room;

editing suite; animation stand; studio; audio bay; control room
Equipment: Film: complete Super-8 and 16mm. Television: complete ¾" studio; ¾" and ½" location
Alumni: Michael Kelly, TV producer; Tom Boyd, TV program coordinator; Joe Dix, TV program coordinator

GUIDE POV: The interdisciplinary film program at this university focuses on criticism, alternative cinema, and animation production; there is a comprehensive major in broadcasting through the Communication Department emphasizing news journalism; study abroad in two countries; internship opportunities in film and television production

WHEATON COLLEGE

500 E. College Ave.
Wheaton, IL 60187–5593
(708)752–5000

Private four-year comprehensive institution. Coed, suburban location. Undergraduate enrollment: 2,000. Graduate enrollment: 350.

DEPARTMENT OF COMMUNICATIONS

Chair/Contact: Mark Fackler
Calendar: Semesters
Degrees Offered: B.A., communications (concentrations in public address, interpersonal, media, and theatre); M.A., communication (with emphasis in writing or marketing-management)

Departmental Majors: Undergraduate communications: 150 students. Graduate: 30 students
Entrance Requirements: Undergraduate: competitive grade-point average; ACT or SAT scores. Graduate: GRE scores; recommendations. Undergraduate application deadline: February 15. Graduate application deadline: June 1
Curricular Emphasis: Television/Video: communications major with an undergraduate concentration in media (other concentrations include public address, interpersonal, and theatre), and graduate emphases in writing and marketing-management
Special Activities: Television: program material produced for local cable and commercial television
Facilities: Film: screening room; editing room. Television: studio; audio studio; control room
Equipment: Film: complete 16mm. Television/Video: complete ¾" studio; complete ¾" and ½" location
Alumni: Roberta Rossi, TV producer; Ron Schnemer, TV research director; Lou Schierbeck, TV station manager

GUIDE POV: This selective private college offers an undergraduate degree program in television production; graduate program offers concentrations in writing for television and film, as well as media management; study abroad in six countries; internship opportunities in television production, marketing, and management

I obtained my undergraduate degree from Wellesley. After earning an M.F.A. at USC, I worked as a journalist and wrote TV documentaries. Film school gives you tools. What you build with them is up to you.

My own path has been single-minded: Since the age of six, I wanted to write for movies. So I chose cinema studies to gain a better understanding of directing, editing, sound, and cinematography, which I hoped would inform my screenwriting. But there is a downside to graduate film school. First, the cost is tremendous. I had to float several student loans, and the payments can be crippling. Second, the curriculum is purely vocational.

I would not recommend that anyone major in film as an undergraduate, especially not aspiring writers or directors. I would personally be lost without my liberal arts education as a foundation. Finally, don't expect much nurturing or artistic experimentation if you are studying in Los Angeles. At least while I was there, USC was based on the Hollywood studio system, and that's exactly how student films were selected and produced.

But among the high points for me at film school were the relationships I formed. I found most of my instructors qualified and caring individuals who went beyond the basic course requirements in terms of conveying the film-making craft. And with my peers I made enduring friendships. Intimacy happens quickly when you're baring your soul on screen. Personally and professionally, I have made close contacts that will last my lifetime.

Basically, if you want to tackle Hollywood—if you can afford it or you're a gambler, and if you have a strong sense of self and purpose—graduate film school can be marvelous. But don't get deluded. Try not to go bankrupt. And be aware of those people who come along to change your soul.

ANDERSON UNIVERSITY

1100 E. 5th St.,
Anderson, IN 46012
(317)649–9071

*Private four-year comprehensive
institution. Coed, urban location.
Enrollment: 1,800.*

RADIO, TELEVISION, AND FILM
DEPARTMENT

Chair/Contact: Donald Boggs
Calendar: Semesters
Degrees Offered: B.A., mass
communication (students may select
emphasis in broadcasting)
Departmental Majors: Television: 80
students
Entrance Requirements: 2.0 grade-
point average; academic rank within
top 60% of graduating class; ACT or
SAT scores. Application deadline:
August 1. Percent of acceptances: 77%
Curricular Emphasis: Media writing;
television production; media
management
Special Activities: Television:
Covenant Productions, the university
teleproduction facility, produces
family/religious programming for a
national market
Facilities: Television: 60' × 40' studio;
audio bay; control room
Equipment: Television/Video:
complete 1" VTR and Betacam SP
VTRS studio; complete ¾" and ½"
location; Grass Valley switcher; Chyron

Superscribe character generator; 24-
channel audio board; Pinnacle Prizm
Alumni: Mort Crim, TV news anchor;
Gery Gerould, TV sportscaster

GUIDE POV: This small liberal arts
college, affiliated with the Church of
God, offers a well-equipped television
production program that stresses
religious programming; co-op programs
with Purdue University; study abroad
in 25 countries through the
International Studies Program;
internship opportunities in television
production

BALL STATE UNIVERSITY

Muncie, IN 47306
(317)289–1241

*State four-year comprehensive
institution. Coed, small city location.
Undergraduate enrollment: 18,000.
Graduate enrollment: 2,000.*

TELECOMMUNICATIONS DEPARTMENT

Chair/Contact: Dr. J. Misiewicz, Chair
Calendar: Semesters
Degrees Offered: B.A.
telecommunications (options in
production; corporate media; news;
sales and management)
Departmental Majors: Undergraduate
film, radio, and television: 225 students
Entrance Requirements:
Undergraduate: academic rank within
top half of high school graduating

class; ACT or SAT scores, with a minimum score of 18 on the ACT or 800 on the SAT. Undergraduate application deadline: March 1. Percent of acceptances: 75%

Curricular Emphasis: Media writing; television production; broadcast journalism; media management and promotion; media analysis and criticism; Super-8 film production; video graphics technology; instructional video

Special Activities: Television: program material produced for on-campus closed-circuit television and for local public television station; AERho chapter

Facilities: Film: screening room; editing suite. Television: five production studios; audio bays; control rooms; video editing facilities

Equipment: Film: complete Super-8. Television/Video: complete ¾" studio and VHS location; computer graphics

Alumni: David Letterman, TV personality/writer/producer; Tom Watson, TV executive producer; Terry Lingner, TV producer; Phil Lengyel, film production executive

GUIDE POV: Students majoring in telecommunications will choose from a variety of production-oriented courses in television, film, radio, and corporate video; modern expanded television production facilities; emphasis on broadcast journalism; internship opportunities in television production

---

BUTLER UNIVERSITY

4600 Sunset Ave.,
Indianapolis, IN 46208
(317)283–8000

Private four-year comprehensive institution. Coed, urban location. Undergraduate enrollment: 2,100. Graduate enrollment: 1,300.

DEPARTMENT OF RADIO-TELEVISION

Chair/Contact: Dr. Kenneth Creech, Chair

Calendar: Semesters

Degrees Offered: B.S., M.S.

Departmental Majors: Undergraduate: 104 students. Graduate: 14 students

Entrance Requirements: Undergraduate: 2.0 grade-point average; ACT or SAT scores; recommendations. Graduate: transcripts; GRE scores; recommendations; 2.5 grade-point average; interview. Undergraduate and graduate application deadline: March 15. Percent of acceptances: undergraduate and graduate: 70–75%

Curricular Emphasis: Electronic journalism; audio-video production; management/administration

Special Activities: Film: film series/festivals. Television: program material produced for WTBU, the student-operated UHF television

Facilities: Television: studio; audio bay; control room

Equipment: Television/Video: complete ¾" studio and location

Alumni: Howard Caldwell, TV news anchor; Core McPherrin, TV sports anchor; Brian Hammons, TV sports anchor

GUIDE POV: Butler University offers professional undergraduate and graduate television studies and practical training within a strong liberal arts curriculum; selective admissions; cross-registration with the four other members of the Consortium for Urban Education; study abroad in six countries; internship opportunities in television production

GOSHEN COLLEGE

Goshen, IN 46526
(219)535–7000

Private four-year comprehensive institution. Coed, suburban location. Enrollment: 1,100.

DEPARTMENT OF COMMUNICATION

Chair/Contact: Stuart W. Showalter
Calendar: Trimester
Degrees Offered: B.A., communication, theatre
Departmental Majors: Communication: 65 students
Entrance Requirements: Academic rank within top half of graduating class; 800 minimum SAT. Application deadline: rolling. Percent of acceptances: 95%
Curricular Emphasis: Communication theory; television production with an emphasis on broadcasting
Special Activities: Television: student journal; program material produced for closed-circuit on-campus television
Facilities: Television: studio functions as classroom
Equipment: Television/Video: single-tube cameras, SVHS format, PC-based editor
Alumni: Joel Kauffmann, screenwriter; Les Miller, studio script analyst

GUIDE POV: This small college, founded in 1894 and affiliated with the Mennonite Church, offers students a theoretical foundation in communication theory and ethics with practical broadcast training; a year

abroad in the required Study Service Term is currently possible in China, Germany, the Dominican Republic, Guadeloupe, or Costa Rica; media internship opportunities

HANOVER COLLEGE

Hanover, IN 47243–0108
(812)866–7000

Private four-year comprehensive institution. Coed, rural location. Enrollment: 1,100.

COMMUNICATION DEPARTMENT

Chair/Contact: Barbara O. Garvey
Calendar: Terms
Degrees Offered: B.A., communication
Entrance Requirements: 2.5 grade-point average; ACT or SAT scores, with a minimum score of 22 on the ACT or 1000 composite on the SAT. Application deadline: March 15. Percent of acceptances: 60%
Curricular Emphasis: Electronic media theory and culture; media writing; audio and video production
Special Activities: Television: program material produced for local outlets
Facilities: Television/Video: studio; audio bay; control room
Equipment: Television/Video: complete studio and location
Alumni: Chris Field, TV news anchor; Anne Hittle, TV program coordinator; Tera Gottbrath, TV program coordinator

GUIDE POV: Founded in 1827, Hanover College is the oldest private college in Indiana; both studio and remote video production training offered within context of modern communication theory; emphasis on broadcast journalism; critical examination of mass media and society; focus on new technologies; cross-registration with area colleges and universities; study abroad; internship opportunities in television production

HUNTINGTON COLLEGE

2303 College Ave.,
Huntington, IN 46750
(219)356–6000

Private four-year comprehensive institution. Coed, suburban location. Undergraduate enrollment: 600. Graduate enrollment: 50. Undergraduate tuition: $8,480 per academic year.

SPEECH COMMUNICATION DEPARTMENT

Chair/Contact: William G. Covington, Jr.
Calendar: 4–1–4
Degrees Offered: B.A., mass communication (concentration in broadcasting)
Entrance Requirements: Undergraduate: 2.3 grade-point average; ACT or SAT scores. Undergraduate application deadline: August 31. Percent of acceptances: 79%
Curricular Emphasis: Electronic media theory and culture; television/video production; audio production
Facilities: Television: studio; audio bay; control room
Equipment: Television/Video: complete ¾" studio; ¾" and ½" location includes switcher/special effects generator
Alumni: Sandy Thompson, TV meteorologist; Burton Lange, radio broadcaster

GUIDE POV: At Huntington College, a private school affiliated with the Church of the United Brethren in Christ, undergraduates may pursue a practical degree program in audio and video broadcasting; study abroad in Costa Rica, Jamaica, and Israel; internship opportunities in television production

INDIANA—PURDUE UNIVERSITY

2101 Coliseum Blvd. E.,
Fort Wayne, IN 46805
(219)481–6100

State four-year comprehensive institution. Coed, urban location. Undergraduate enrollment: 10,000. Graduate enrollment: 1,100.

COMMUNICATION STUDIES/RADIO-TELEVISION

Chair/Contact: Film: Steven Phipps; television: James Smead
Calendar: Semesters
Degrees Offered: B.A., radio-television; M.A., professional communication (students may select emphasis in radio-television)
Departmental Majors: Undergraduate radio and television: 175 students. Graduate: 10 students
Entrance Requirements: Undergraduate: academic rank within upper 50% of graduating class; high school diploma or GED certificate; minimum composite 800 SAT score; AP credit accepted; interview recommended. Undergraduate application deadline: August 1
Curricular Emphasis: Critical studies in film; television production and critical studies
Special Activities: Television: program material produced for on-

campus closed-circuit and local cable television

Facilities: Television: studio; audio studio; control room; ¾" ENG setups; two Amiga computers with toasters
Equipment: Film: 16mm cameras; editing equipment; projectors. Television/Video: complete ¾" studio and location including on-line and off-line editing
Alumni: Julie Barr, TV actress; Dan Butler, film/TV actor; Valerie Karasek, film/TV actress; Sharon Gavet, film/TV actress

GUIDE POV: Comprehensive broadcast training within the context of mass media studies is offered at this state university; study abroad in four countries; internship opportunities in television production

INDIANA STATE UNIVERSITY

Terre Haute, IN 47809
(812)237–6311

State four-year comprehensive institution. Coed, rural location. Undergraduate enrollment: 25,000. Graduate enrollment: 7,500.

COMMUNICATION DEPARTMENT, RADIO/TV/FILM

Chair/Contact: Joe Tenerelli, Head of radio/TV/film
Calendar: Semesters
Degrees Offered: B.A., radio/TV/film
Departmental Majors: Undergraduate film, radio, and television: 250 students
Entrance Requirements: Undergraduate: 2.0 grade-point average; ACT or SAT scores. Undergraduate application deadline: August 15. Percent of acceptances: 90%
Curricular Emphasis: Critical theory;

audio-film-video production; media writing; corporate/private video; sports broadcasting; new technologies; media law
Special Activities: Television: program material produced for on-campus closed-circuit television; special corporate and video field projects
Facilities: Film: editing suite; sound mixing room; film library. Television: studio; audio bay; control room; video editing suites
Equipment: Film: complete Super-8. Television/Video: complete ¾" studio and ½" location
Alumni: Vince Clews, TV/film producer; Bill Wimsett, corporate video producer

GUIDE POV: This state university offers students a comprehensive communications major with production requirements in both film and video; students are encouraged to develop advanced independent projects; some paid internship opportunities in television production and related areas

INDIANA UNIVERSITY

Bloomington, IN 47405
(815)855–4848

State four-year comprehensive institution. Coed, small city location. Undergraduate enrollment: 25,000. Graduate enrollment: 7,500.

FILM STUDIES PROGRAM

Chair/Contact: James Naremore, Chair

DEPARTMENT OF TELECOMMUNICATIONS

Chair/Contact: Kathy A. Krendl, Chair
Calendar: Semesters

Degrees Offered: B.A., comparative literature (students may select emphasis in film, telecommunications); Ph.D. minor in film studies; M.S., media management; M.A., Ph.D., mass communications
Departmental Majors: Undergraduate film studies: 60 students. Graduate: 15 students (Ph.D. minor). Undergraduate telecommunications: 591 students. Graduate: 43 students
Entrance Requirements: Undergraduate: 2.5 grade-point average; ACT or SAT scores; written statement of purpose. Graduate: 3.0 grade-point average; GRE scores; written statement of purpose; teachers' recommendations; minimum 600 on TOEFL. Undergraduate and graduate application deadline: February 15. Percent of acceptances: Undergraduate: 75%. Graduate: 50%
Curricular Emphasis: Film: critical studies within liberal arts context. Television: critical studies; electronic media production; media management; electronic communications research
Special Activities: Film: film series/festival; film societies. Television: TELEPRO, a student-run production club, produces a variety of program material for local commercial station; ITVA chapter
Facilities: Film: sound mixing room; screening room; editing room; 35mm screening facilities; animation stand; Semiotics Research Institute; Black Film Study Center; extensive film and video library. Television: studios; audio studios; control rooms; Institute for Communication Research
Equipment: Film: complete 16mm; video translators. Television: two complete ¾" studios; complete ¾" and ½" location; interactive media equipment; computer-assisted laserdisc video
Alumni: John Rappaport, TV writer/producer; Joe Angotti, TV news executive; Jennifer Shull, casting director

GUIDE POV: The selective film studies program offered through the Comparative Literature Department focuses on film history, theory, and criticism while providing students with basic production experience; doctoral minor in film studies; university press specializes in film books; separate concentration in electronic media production, offered through the Telecommunications Department, prepares students for careers in broadcasting, cable, corporate, instructional, or management fields; internship opportunities in television production

INDIANA UNIVERSITY— INDIANAPOLIS

425 N. Agnes,
Indianapolis, IN 46202
(317)274-5555

State four-year comprehensive institution. Coed, urban location. Enrollment: 26,000.

TELECOMMUNICATIONS DEPARTMENT

Chair/Contact: Stan Denski
Calendar: Semesters
Degrees Offered: B.A., telecommunications
Departmental Majors: Telecommunications: 200 students
Entrance Requirements: 2.0 grade-point average; ACT or SAT scores. Application deadline: rolling. Percent of acceptances: 93%
Curricular Emphasis: Media

production including video, audio, graphics, sync slide tape
Facilities: Television: studio; audio studio; control room; video editing suites; computer graphics labs
Equipment: Television/Video: complete ¾" studio and location including cuts-only and A/B editing; TARGA computer graphics computer system
Alumni: Clair Staley, TV producer; Linda Kirby, TV public affairs director; Christina Melandro, TV actress

GUIDE POV: Students at this state university are offered a telecommunications major emphasizing new technologies; hands-on video production training; study abroad program; extensive internship opportunities in television production

INDIANA UNIVERSITY— SOUTH BEND

1700 Mishawaka Ave.,
P.O. Box 7111,
South Bend, IN 46634
(219)237–4111

State comprehensive institution. Coed, urban location. Undergraduate enrollment: 7,500. Graduate enrollment: 700.

COMMUNICATION ARTS

Chair/Contact: Paul Schaver, Chair
Calendar: Semesters
Degrees Offered: B.A., communication arts, minor in mass media, minor in film studies
Entrance Requirements: Undergraduate: ACT or SAT scores. Undergraduate application deadline: July 1
Curricular Emphasis: Mass communication studies; writing for

mass media; critical theory in film
Special Activities: Film: series/festivals.
Facilities: Film: screening room; editing room; film library
Equipment: Film: Super-8 and 16mm editing equipment; lighting; projectors; sound recording equipment. Television/Video: ¾" VTR; portable cameras and lighting packages
Alumni: Philip Patnaude, corporate film executive; J. Randall Colborn, media teacher

GUIDE POV: Students attending this commuter school of the state university system are offered a communication arts program emphasizing theory and writing for media; interdisciplinary film studies program emphasizes substantive and scholarly aspects of cinema; both programs provide students with critical foundation for later scholarship or graduate production training; study abroad; cross-registration with area schools

MANCHESTER COLLEGE

College Ave.,
North Manchester, IN 46962
(219)982–5000

Private four-year comprehensive institution. Coed, rural location. Enrollment: 1,000.

DEPARTMENT OF COMMUNICATION STUDIES

Chair/Contact: Dr. Scott K. Strode, Chair
Calendar: 4–1–4
Degrees Offered: B.S., B.A., communication studies
Departmental Majors: 40 students
Entrance Requirements: ACT or SAT

scores, with minimum of 18 on ACT and minimum composite 800 on SAT; interview recommended; ATs recommended. Application deadline: rolling. Percent of acceptances: 75%

Curricular Emphasis: Media studies; radio/television writing and production

Special Activities: Video: students produce independent work at modern campus postproduction video laboratory. Radio: associate NPR station on campus

Facilities: Television: postproduction laboratory; four editing bays

Equipment: Television/Video: complete ½" location; S-VHS; editing equipment; A/B roll, video toaster; Amiga computers

Alumni: David Sollenberger, video producer; Mike Emrick, sportscaster; Katherine Black Joyce, radio news director

GUIDE POV: Affiliated with the Church of the Brethren, this small private college offers a communication program focusing on applied media studies; study abroad through the Brethren Colleges program; co-op program with Goshen College; internship opportunities in radio and television production

---

PURDUE UNIVERSITY

West Lafayette, IN 47907
(317)494–4600

State four-year comprehensive institution. Coed, suburban location. Undergraduate enrollment: 30,000. Graduate enrollment: 6,000.

DEPARTMENT OF COMMUNICATION, TELECOMMUNICATION STUDIES

Chair/Contact: Charles Stewart, Head, Department of Communication

Calendar: Semesters

Degrees Offered: B.A., communication (concentration in telecommunications); M.A., M.S., Ph.D., communication (concentration in mass communication theory and research)

Departmental Majors: Undergraduate television: 275 students. Graduate: 4 students

Entrance Requirements: Undergraduate: 4.8 on a 6.0 grade-point average; interview required; recommendations. Graduate: GRE scores; recommendations. Undergraduate and graduate application deadline: rolling

Curricular Emphasis: Television/ video production and critical studies

Special Activities: Television: program training for on-campus closed-circuit television, cable television, and local commercial television station

Facilities: Television: studio; audio bay; control room

Equipment: Television/Video: complete ¾" studio and location

Alumni: Brian Lamb, C-SPAN executive/broadcaster; Julian Phillips, TV news reporter; Michael Sanders, video production executive

GUIDE POV: Telecommunication majors at this school, founded in 1869 and now among the largest universities in the nation, concentrate on broadcast production techniques and theory; graduate mass communication program emphasizes theory and research; selective admissions; various study abroad and co-op programs; internship opportunities in television production

PURDUE UNIVERSITY—CALUMET

Hammond, IN 46323–2094
(219)989–2993

*State four-year comprehensive
institution. Coed, urban location.
Undergraduate enrollment: 8,500.
Graduate enrollment: 1,000.*

COMMUNICATION AND CREATIVE ARTS

Chair/Contact: Dr. Yahya R.
Kamalipour
Calendar: Semesters
Degrees Offered: B.A., radio-
television; M.A., telecommunications
Departmental Majors:
Undergraduate: 160 students. Graduate:
65 students
Entrance Requirements:
Undergraduate: high school diploma
or GED certificate; ACT or SAT scores;
placement examinations. Graduate:
transcripts; 3.0 grade-point average;
GRE scores; three letters of
recommendation; interview; personal
statement of goals. Undergraduate
application deadline: rolling. Graduate
application deadline: April 15. Percent
of acceptances: Undergraduate: 94%.
Graduate: 85%
Curricular Emphasis: Broadcast
production; broadcast management;
telecommunications
Special Activities: Television:
program material produced for cable
television and for local public
television station; teacher training
Facilities: Television: studio; audio
bay; control room
Equipment: Television/Video:
complete ¾" studio; complete ¾" and
½" location; ENG/EFP equipment
Alumni: Carolyn L. Moore, media
executive; Kelly McCay, TV production
manager; Linda Nejak, TV production
assistant

GUIDE POV: This commuter university
offers a comprehensive television
production program; M.A. program
focuses on documentary production
and communication theory; internship
and practicum opportunities

UNIVERSITY OF NOTRE DAME

Notre Dame, IN 46556
(219)631–5000

*Private four-year comprehensive
institution. Coed, urban location.
Undergraduate enrollment: 7,000.
Graduate enrollment: 3,000.*

DEPARTMENT OF COMMUNICATION AND THEATRE

Chair/Contact: Mark C. Pilkinton,
Chair
Calendar: Semesters
Degrees Offered: B.A.,
communication and theatre
(communication concentration
with emphasis on critical studies,
film and video production, or
telecommunications)
Departmental Majors: Undergraduate
communication: 100 students.
Undergraduate theatre: 25 students
Entrance Requirements:
Undergraduate: competitive grade-
point average; SAT scores required;
essay required; AT in a foreign
language recommended.
Undergraduate application deadline:
November 1 for early decision;
January 10 final deadline. Percent of
acceptances: 30%
Curricular Emphasis: Electronic
media theory and culture; critical
studies in film; media writing; film/
video production; broadcast television
production
Special Activities: Film: film series/
festivals. Television: program material

produced for various outlets including university-owned WNDU-TV, an NBC affiliate

Facilities: Film: screening room; editing suite; film library. Television: studio; control room

Equipment: Film: complete Super-8 and 16mm. Television/Video: complete ¾" studio; complete ¾" and ½" location

Alumni: Phil Donahue, TV personality/producer; Regis Philbin, TV personality; Catherine Hicks, TV/film actress; Tony Bill, film director/producer/actor; John Dardis, TV/film producer; Bill Donarumma, TV/film producer

GUIDE POV: Founded in 1842, this highly selective liberal arts university offers a communications program blending critical media studies with intensive production activity; students may choose concentration in either film/video or telecommunications; small classes; diverse course listings; internship opportunities in television production

---

UNIVERSITY OF SOUTHERN INDIANA

8600 University Blvd.,
Evansville, IN 47712
(812)464–8600

State four-year comprehensive institution. Coed, suburban location. Enrollment: 5,200.

DEPARTMENT OF COMMUNICATIONS

Chair/Contact: Dr. Dal M. Herring, Chair
Calendar: Semesters
Degrees Offered: B.A., B.S., communications (with emphasis in radio-television production or broadcast journalism)

Departmental Majors: Television: 100 students

Entrance Requirements: 2.0 grade-point average; ACT or SAT scores. Application deadline: August 15. Percent of acceptances: 95%

Curricular Emphasis: Radio and television production including writing for media; broadcast management

Special Activities: Television: program material produced for cable television as well as for local television stations

Facilities: Television: studio; audio bay; control room; editing suites

Equipment: Film: complete Super-8 and 16mm. Television/Video: complete ¾" studio and ½" location; VHS editing equipment

Alumni: David Sauls, TV assistant photographer; Ann Komis, TV news anchor; Rick Notter, media publishing editor

GUIDE POV: The radio and television concentration at this state university offers communication majors thorough studio and field production experience combined with writing and management studies; small classes; internship opportunities in television production at five local television stations

---

VALPARAISO UNIVERSITY

Valparaiso, IN 46382
(219)464–5000

Private four-year comprehensive institution. Coed, urban location. Undergraduate enrollment: 3,000. Graduate enrollment: 300.

FILM STUDIES/ENGLISH DEPARTMENT

Chair/Contact: Richard Maxwell; Doug Kocher
Calendar: Semesters
Degrees Offered: Film studies minor
Departmental Majors:
Undergraduate: 15 students
Entrance Requirements:
Undergraduate: high school diploma or GED certificate; essay; interview recommended; ACT (minimum score 25) or SAT (minimum score 510 verbal and 570 math). Undergraduate application deadline: rolling. Percent of acceptances: 92%
Curricular Emphasis: Film theory, history, and criticism

Special Activities: Film: film series/festivals
Facilities: Film: screening room; film library
Equipment: Film: Super-8 editing equipment and projectors
Alumni: Sarah Churness, TV producer; Erin Schneeberger, TV news reporter

GUIDE POV: Affiliated with the Lutheran Church, this private university offers a film studies minor as part of a comprehensive liberal arts curriculum; co-op programs; study abroad in England, Germany, Mexico, France, Japan, and China

What does it take to make it in the film business? I rack my brain over that question every day. Besides an endless supply of self-esteem, a good education is your best bet toward realizing your dream. For my money, though, a film school education is by no means a first-class ticket to the top of the Hollywood heap. In fact, if I were starting all over again, I would take the same basic collegiate route: straight through the English major.

Years ago I enrolled at UCLA with every intention of declaring motion pictures/television as my major come my junior year. While waiting, I ambled through a core curriculum consisting mostly of liberal arts courses. To be honest, I remember little from my freshman and sophomore years because my focus was on the greener pastures ahead: film school.

I had my future already scripted. Surely my thesis film would land me a writing/directing job at one of the major studios. I could take my pick. After that—with a few top-grossing flicks tucked modestly under my belt—I would rediscover my artistic integrity and make a small but arty film. One that would certainly garner a few Oscar nominations. Now that I think about it, I believe I still have my acceptance speech lying around somewhere. You can imagine my horror then upon learning I was not accepted into the M.P./T.V. program.

Ruling out suicide, I moped into the English Department and begrudgingly signed up for two more tedious years of reading and analyzing, of all things, "literature." As it turned out, that was the smartest move I ever made. Here's why: The fundamental element of good filmmaking is good storytelling. And where better to learn the art of storytelling than the annals of classic literature?

It goes without saying that your term papers on Shakespeare and Dickens will not land you a three-picture deal at Paramount, but never discount the importance of a literary background, especially when trying to separate yourself from the droves of other screenwriters out there. All those great high-concept story ideas you have brewing are nothing more than ideas until they are artfully translated into a literate medium. To paraphrase one renowned movie mogul: "If it ain't on the page, I can't see it."

None of this is to knock film school. Quite the contrary. I did manage to audit a number of cinema studies classes, screenwriting seminars, and television production courses. I saw countless films and developed a new lexicon of industry terminology. But the knowledge I apply to my writing career every day was culled primarily from my English and creative writing classes. While still at college I sold my first screenplay, *Evil Altar*. Since then I have had a one-act play produced as well as nine feature films, ranging from my H.P. Lovecraft adaptation *The Resurrected* to a children's comedy collaboration called *Pet Shop*.

So even if you take the film school route, I would strongly recommend supplementing your education with as many literature classes as you can cram into your schedule. And don't make the same mistake I did my first two years. Listen and learn. Retain everything. Because no matter what your goal in the film industry, if you can't tell a good story, nobody is going to listen.

In the end there is no simple answer, but over the years I have discovered that there are three keys to success: direction, dedication, and discipline. You must know what you want—a star on the Hollywood Walk of Fame is a little too vague. You must be prepared to make sacrifices—usually in your social life. Finally, you must never stop, even when your eyes start to crust over and your head feels like a dry sponge. You must keep plugging away. And if, like me, you venture forward without benefit of a formal film school education, keep educating yourself: read produced screenplays and watch movies religiously. You'll have to work that much harder. But you'll be wiser for the wear.

BRIAR CLIFF COLLEGE

3303 Rebecca St.,
Sioux City, IA 51104–2100
(712)279–5321

*Private four-year comprehensive
institution. Coed, rural location.
Enrollment: 1,200.*

DEPARTMENT OF MASS COMMUNICATIONS

Chair/Contact: Ralph Swain
Calendar: Three 10-week terms
Degrees Offered: B.A., mass
communications
Departmental Majors: Television: 50
students
Entrance Requirements: High school
diploma or GED; ACT or SAT scores.
Application deadline: rolling. Percent
of acceptances: 80%
Curricular Emphasis: Media studies;
radio and television production;
photography; print journalism;
advertising; public relations
Special Activities: Television/Video:
program material produced for cable
television, local public and
commercial television stations, public
service agencies and corporate video
usage
Facilities: Television: studio; audio
bay; control room; editing suites; cable
origination head end; satellite
downlink facility
Equipment: Television/Video:
complete ¾" video studio and

location; two editing suites; Chyron
graphics; electronic paint box
Alumni: Mike Wankum, TV
meteorologist; Ron Demers, TV
reporter; Elizabeth Wold, media
promotions director; Susan Finzen, TV
news anchor

GUIDE POV: This is a small, well-
equipped school, aiming to provide
students with career opportunities in
television and corporate video
production and management;
emphasis on new technologies

BUENA VISTA COLLEGE

4th and College,
Storm Lake, IA 50588
(712)749–2351

*Private four-year comprehensive
institution. Coed, rural location.
Enrollment: 1,000.*

MASS COMMUNICATION DEPARTMENT

Chair/Contact: Paul Bowers
Calendar: Semesters
Degrees Offered: B.A., mass
communication
Departmental Majors: Television: 30
students
Entrance Requirements: 2.5 grade-
point average; ACT or SAT scores;
interview; teachers' recommendations;
essay. Application deadline: May 1.
Percent of acceptances: 78%
Curricular Emphasis: Electronic

media theory and culture; television/ video production; media management
Special Activities: Television: program material produced for cable television as well as for local public and commercial television stations
Facilities: Television: studio; audio bay; control room
Equipment: Television/Video: complete ¾" studio and location
Alumni: Mark Huegerich, TV director/ editor; Robert Fiorendino, Jr., videographer/editor; Geri Laflin, videographer/editor; Paul Fredrickson, TV executive

GUIDE POV: This small liberal arts college offers students a competitive media program preparing students for careers in the television and video industries; curriculum combines theory and media practice; internship opportunities in television production

DRAKE UNIVERSITY

Des Moines, IA 50311–4505
(515)271–2011

Private four-year comprehensive institution. Coed, urban location. Enrollment: 4,500.

SCHOOL OF JOURNALISM AND MASS COMMUNICATION

Chair/Contact: Television: Michael Cheney
Calendar: Semesters
Degrees Offered: B.A., journalism and mass communication (students may select emphasis in radio-television with separate tracks in production and management)
Departmental Majors: Television: 110 students
Entrance Requirements: Competitive grade-point average; ACT or SAT

scores; written statement of purpose. Application deadline: February 15 for priority consideration; August 1 final deadline. Percent of acceptances: 85%
Curricular Emphasis: Television and video production training; media sales and management; separate sequence in broadcast journalism; film studies offered through English Department
Special Activities: Television: program material produced for on-campus closed-circuit television and for cable television
Facilities: Television: studio; audio bay; control room; editing suites
Equipment: Television/Video: complete ¾" studio and location; editing and video toaster
Alumni: Arne Harris, TV producer/ director; Bob Smith, senior TV producer/director; Steve Oswalt, TV investigative reporter/anchor

GUIDE POV: Journalism and mass communication majors may choose an intensive radio-television production program preparing them for careers in traditional broadcasting, corporate video, and cable television; separate track in broadcast management; separate program in broadcast news; internship opportunities in television production

IOWA STATE UNIVERSITY

Ames, IA 50011–2090
(515)294–4111

State four-year comprehensive institution. Coed, rural location. Undergraduate enrollment: 21,500. Graduate enrollment: 4,000.

DEPARTMENT OF JOURNALISM AND MASS COMMUNICATION

Chair/Contact: Steve Coon
Calendar: Semesters
Degrees Offered: B.A., B.S.
Departmental Majors: Undergraduate journalism and mass communication: 80 students
Entrance Requirements: Undergraduate: ACT or SAT scores; upper 50% of graduating class; transcripts; GED accepted. Undergraduate application deadline: August 24. Percent of acceptances: 85%
Curricular Emphasis: Television: electronic media studies; broadcast journalism
Special Activities: Television: program material produced for cable television and local commercial television station
Facilities: Film: screening room; editing suite; sound mixing room; animation stand. Television: studio; audio bay; control room
Equipment: Film: complete 16mm. Television: complete ¾" studio and location
Alumni: Ed Rearick, TV/film director; Ron Bernnel, media production executive; Mike Shetter, TV operations manager

GUIDE POV: This lively, production-oriented program offers intensive television broadcasting experience along with formal media studies; cross-registration with the universities of Iowa and Northern Iowa; university offers study abroad in 70 countries; local and area media internship opportunities

KIRKWOOD COMMUNITY COLLEGE

6301 Kirkwood Blvd. SW,
Cedar Rapids, IA 52406–2068
(319)398–5411

District two-year institution. Coed, suburban location. Enrollment: 9,234.

COMMUNICATION MEDIA DEPARTMENT

Chair/Contact: Television: Rose K. Kodet
Calendar: Semesters
Degrees Offered: A.A., A.S. (students may select emphasis in career options-media)
Entrance Requirements: ACT or SAT scores. Application deadline: rolling
Curricular Emphasis: Media writing; television production; video art; theory courses in film
Special Activities: Television: program material produced for on-campus closed-circuit television, for local public and commercial television stations, and for cable television
Facilities: Television: studio; audio bay; control room
Equipment: Television/Video: complete ¾" studio
Alumni: Allen Schmidt, TV producer; Bob Reynolds, audio/video specialist; Ken Rinehart, radio producer

GUIDE POV: Students at this district community college may take production and theory courses in television before transferring to four-year schools

LORAS COLLEGE

1450 Alta Vista,
Dubuque, IA 52001
(319)588–7100

Private four-year comprehensive institution. Coed, urban location. Enrollment: 2,000.

SPEECH COMMUNICATION

Chair/Contact: Dr. Dennis Corso
Calendar: Semesters
Degrees Offered: B.A. media (radio-television)
Departmental Majors: Radio and television: 32 students
Entrance Requirements: Upper half of high school class; 2.0 grade-point average; SAT or ACT; personal recommendations; essay; interview. Application deadline: rolling. Percent of acceptances: 85%
Curricular Emphasis: Television studies: history and aesthetics. Television production: instructional and industrial
Special Activities: Film: student publication. Television: program material produced for cable television; independent study
Facilities: Television: studio; campus cable system; control room; editing suite; campus radio station
Equipment: Television/Video: complete ¾" studio and location
Alumni: David Rabe, writer; Don Ameche, film actor; Greg Gumbel, TV sports anchor

GUIDE POV: Hands-on training in broadcast writing and production is offered at this competitive private college, founded in 1839; internship opportunities in television production

---

UNIVERSITY OF IOWA

Iowa City, IA 52242
(319)335–3500

State four-year comprehensive institution. Coed, rural location.
Undergraduate enrollment: 19,110. Graduate enrollment: 8,935.

DEPARTMENT OF COMMUNICATION STUDIES

Chair/Contact: John Lyne, Chair; film: Dudley Andrew
Calendar: Semesters
Degrees Offered: B.A., broadcasting and film; M.A., film studies, media/broadcast studies, production studies; Ph.D., film studies, broadcasting studies
Departmental Majors: Communication studies with undergraduate film emphasis: 350 students; undergraduate television emphasis: 150 students. Graduate film: 30 students. Graduate television: 20 students
Entrance Requirements: Undergraduate: 2.5 grade-point average; academic rank within upper half of high school graduating class; ACT or SAT scores; statement of purpose; minimum test score and high school rank requirements are higher for out-of-state applicants. Graduate: highly competitive GRE scores; recommendations; written statement of purpose. Undergraduate and graduate application deadline: May 15. Percent of undergraduate acceptances: 80%
Curricular Emphasis: Comprehensive film and television criticism and production including animation and video art
Special Activities: Film: film series/festivals; film societies; student-run Bijou Theatre. Television: program material produced for cable television and for local public and commercial television stations; student-conducted computer graphics and animation demonstrations
Facilities: Film: 35mm screening facilities; screening room; editing suite;

sound mixing room; animation stand; film library. Television: studio; audio bay; control room; video editing suites **Equipment:** Film: complete Super-8 and 16mm. Television/Video: complete 1" and ¾" studio; complete ¾" location **Alumni:** Nicholas Meyer, film director; Gene Wilder, film director/actor; Mark Johnson, film producer/director; Mary Beth Hurt, film actress

GUIDE POV: Founded in 1847, this public university presents a comprehensive film and electronic media curriculum; undergraduate students offered production experience coupled with studies in media theory and criticism; separate graduate concentrations in production and critical studies; graduate program is highly selective; students enjoy professional studio facilities; study abroad programs in 30 countries; internship opportunities in film and television production

---

UNIVERSITY OF NORTHERN IOWA

Cedar Falls, IA 50614–0139
(319)273–2311

State four-year comprehensive institution. Coed, rural location. Undergraduate enrollment: 11,500. Graduate enrollment: 2,000.

DEPARTMENT OF COMMUNICATION STUDIES

Chair/Contact: Television: Dr. J. C. Turner, Coordinator, broadcasting division

Calendar: Semesters
Degrees Offered: B.A., broadcasting (options in production/performance/ writing; broadcast journalism; broadcast business)
Departmental Majors: Undergraduate Television: 150 students
Entrance Requirements: Undergraduate: academic rank within upper half of high school graduating class; 2.5 grade-point average; ACT or SAT scores. Undergraduate application deadline: rolling. Percent of acceptances: 83%
Curricular Emphasis: Electronic media theory and culture; critical film studies; media writing; television production; media management
Special Activities: Television/Video: program material produced for cable television; student-managed and operated production house
Facilities: Television: two studios; audio bays; control rooms; three edit stations; three Amiga stations; four remote video units
Equipment: Television/Video: complete ¾" studio; complete ¾" and ½" location
Alumni: Carol LeBeau, TV news anchor; David Oman, TV executive; Tom Pettit

GUIDE POV: Communication students attending this competitive state university are offered a choice of separate concentrations in either production/performance/ writing, broadcast journalism, or media management; study abroad; internship opportunities in television production

I received my B.A. from Colgate University with a major in psychology and a minor in German. My desire at the time was to follow the path of Sigmund Freud to the University of Vienna Medical School, where I would study psychoanalysis while supporting myself as a musician. But I returned to New York for some "real world" experience, and my career direction changed altogether on a trip to Los Angeles to see my cousin, Ira Gershwin. While there, I visited Universal Studios and got hooked—so I happily announced at dinner: "I want to be a tour guide at Universal." This was followed by a couple of pronouncements from Ira's wife, including, "Not with your name you won't." However, when I returned to New York I set my sights on NBC, where I took a job as a secretary, and soon joined the "Tomorrow" show as a production assistant helping to book celebrities. The requirement was not a television degree—just energy, eagerness, and a willingness to pay dues.

My career over the past 10 years has been based in both New York and L.A. as a writer for the "Today" show, reporter for ABC News, director for reality shows like "A Current Affair" and "Hard Copy," and most recently creator/producer of a new daytime syndicated program. During all this I covered the war in the Middle East, spoke with murderers and heroes, celebrities and ordinary people. I now hope to turn my goals toward filmmaking. And toward that end I have enhanced my technical knowledge with several courses in cinema. But I believe it is life experience that truly makes a filmmaker. As far as family background goes, it is both an inspiration and a responsibility, though I have not been comfortable "using it." At best it's a door opener—and I prefer to get in on my own. In the end, longevity and respect in this business are built on one's own talent and reputation. "Whom you know" can also be translated to "whom you have impressed along the way." People love to talk, but ultimately your work speaks for itself.

BAKER UNIVERSITY

7th and Dearborn,
Baldwin City, KS 66006
(913)594–6451

*Private four-year comprehensive
institution. Coed, rural location.
Enrollment: 800.*

DEPARTMENT OF COMMUNICATION

Chair/Contact: Dr. Rick Bayha
Calendar: Semesters
Degrees Offered: B.A., B.S., mass
communication (student may select
emphasis in TV-radio broadcasting)
Departmental Majors: Television: 80
students
Entrance Requirements: Minimum
2.2 grade-point average; ACT or
SAT scores, with a minimum of 18
on the ACT or 800 composite
on the SAT; interview; teachers'
recommendations; essay; interview
recommended for marginal
candidates. Application
deadline: rolling. Percent of
acceptances: 84%
Curricular Emphasis: Broadcast
production; documentary production;
broadcast continuity and scriptwriting;
cable communications; broadcast
programming and listener research;
stage lighting; broadcast news and
public affairs
Special Activities: Television/Radio:
program material produced for the
university's cable access television

channel and for KNBU-FM, the
university's radio station
Facilities: Television: studio; audio
bay; control room; video editing suites
Equipment: Television/Video:
complete ½" studio and location
Alumni: Eugene Pulliam, media
publisher; Harold Jackson, media
writer; Jerry Holley, TV/radio
executive; Jonni Rollins, radio disc
jockey

GUIDE POV: Undergraduates seeking a
practical course of studies covering all
aspects of broadcast and
nonbroadcast television production
may choose this degree program in
mass communications; study abroad
options; internship opportunities in
television production

BENEDICTINE COLLEGE

801 S. 8th St.,
Atchison, KS 66002
(913)367–5340

*Private four-year comprehensive
institution. Coed, urban location.
Enrollment: 1,000.*

JOURNALISM/MASS COMMUNICATIONS DEPARTMENT

Chair/Contact: Pat Marrin, Chair
Calendar: Semesters
Degrees Offered: B.A., journalism/
mass communications
Entrance Requirements: 2.0 grade-

point average; ACT or SAT scores. Application deadline: August 1. Percent of acceptances: 85%
Curricular Emphasis: Electronic media theory and culture; media writing; print journalism; video production
Special Activities: Television: program material produced for class projects and for local cable television
Facilities: Video: screening room
Equipment: Television/Video: ½" location equipment
Alumni: Coleen Mullen, media public relations; Stephen Pickman, media public relations

GUIDE POV: Students at this private liberal arts college are offered a journalism program providing training in print media with additional courses in video production; practicum opportunities

BETHEL COLLEGE

300 E. 27th St.,
North Newton, KS 67117
(316)283–2500

Private four-year comprehensive institution. Coed, suburban location. Enrollment: 610.

COMMUNICATION ARTS DEPARTMENT

Chair/Contact: John McCabe-Juhnke, Chair
Calendar: 4–1–4
Degrees Offered: B.A., communication arts
Departmental Majors:
Communication studies: 15 students
Entrance Requirements: 2.0 grade-point average; ACT or SAT scores; interview recommended. Application deadline: August 15. Percent of acceptances: 88%

Curricular Emphasis: Electronic media theory and culture; media writing; television and radio broadcast production; news journalism; media management
Special Activities: Television: program material produced for small industrial clients
Facilities: Television/Radio: studio; audio bay; control room; radio station KBCU
Equipment: Television/Video: complete ¾" studio; complete ¾" and ½" location
Alumni: Rachel Kasper, TV/film actress; Randy Schroeder, TV/film actor

GUIDE POV: Operated by the General Conference Mennonite Church, this small private liberal arts college offers a degree major in communication arts featuring studies in broadcast production, news journalism, and fiction writing; students may enroll concurrently in a peace studies program offered by the Kansas Institute for Peace and Conflict Resolution located on campus; required internships in television production

FORT HAYS STATE UNIVERSITY

600 Park St.,
Hays, KS 67601–4099
(913)628–4000

State four-year comprehensive institution. Coed, rural location. Undergraduate and graduate enrollment: 5,800.

COMMUNICATION DEPARTMENT

Chair/Contact: Dr. Willis M. Watt
Calendar: Semesters
Degrees Offered: B.A., M.S.,

communication (radio-television-film emphasis)

Departmental Majors: Undergraduate communication: 330 students. Graduate communication: 50 students

Entrance Requirements: Undergraduate: open-door policy; minimum 2.0 grade-point average; high school degree or GED certificate; ACT scores recommended; AP and CLEP credit accepted. Graduate: 3.0 grade-point average; GRE scores; transcripts; recommendations. Undergraduate application deadline: August 10. Graduate application deadline: January 15

Curricular Emphasis: Television production; news writing; broadcast management and sales; two courses in cinematography

Special Activities: Film: film series/festivals; participation in Kansas Film Institute. Television: program material produced for on-campus closed-circuit television, local commercial television station, and cable television; interactive television classroom

Facilities: Film: editing suite; screening room. Television: studio; control room; ¾" editing; Amiga computer graphics; Chyron VP-1 Titles; interactive television facilities

Equipment: Film: complete Super-8. Television/Video: ¾" studio

Alumni: Jon Burlew, TV general manager; Dave Moody, TV sales representative; Ed Smith, TV production supervisor

GUIDE POV: This state university offers hands-on broadcast and nonbroadcast training; students produce for a variety of network and cable outlets; emphasis on new technologies; interactive television; basic film training available; internship opportunities in television production

KANSAS STATE UNIVERSITY

Manhattan, KS 66506
(913)532–6011

State four-year comprehensive institution. Coed, suburban location. Undergraduate enrollment: 19,000. Graduate enrollment: 4,000.

A. Q. MILLER SCHOOL OF JOURNALISM AND MASS COMMUNICATION

Chair/Contact: Television: Paul Prince
Calendar: Semesters
Degrees Offered: B.A., B.S., M.S., journalism and mass communication
Departmental Majors: Undergraduate television: 120 students
Entrance Requirements: Undergraduate: 2.0 grade-point average; ACT or SAT scores; out-of-state applicants must have competitive ACT scores and class rank. Graduate: transcripts; GRE scores; recommendations. Undergraduate and graduate application deadline: rolling. Percent of acceptances: 83%
Curricular Emphasis: Broadcast journalism; electronic media theory and culture; media writing; television production; media management
Special Activities: Television: program material produced for cable television
Facilities: Television: studio; audio bay; control room
Equipment: Television/Video: complete ¾" studio; complete ¾" and ½" location
Alumni: Pat Meusberger, TV news anchor; Mitch Holthus, TV sports announcer; Susan Reid, video producer; Laverne Goering, TV production manager

GUIDE POV: This state university offers students a comprehensive program featuring mass media studies and television production; undergraduate emphasis on broadcast journalism; graduate emphasis on communication theory and media management; study abroad; internship opportunities in television production

KANSAS WESLEYAN UNIVERSITY

100 E. Claflin St.,
Salina, KS 67401
(913)827–5541

Private four-year comprehensive institution. Coed, small town location. Enrollment: 800.

SPEECH/THEATRE COMMUNICATIONS DEPARTMENT

Chair/Contact: Film: Dr. Eric R. Marshall
Calendar: Semesters (with micro-term in January)
Degrees Offered: B.A., communications (with emphasis in television, radio, or public relations)
Departmental Majors: 25 students
Entrance Requirements: 2.5 grade-point average; ACT or SAT scores; recommendations. Application deadline: August 31. Percent of acceptances: 57%
Curricular Emphasis: Film history; mass media theory; basic television production training; media management; creative writing
Special Activities: Film: film series/festivals. Television: program material produced for cable television and local public television station
Facilities: Students have use of well-equipped broadcast production facilities, including MidAmerica

Productions and local public access television
Equipment: Video: portable and broadcast quality cameras
Alumni: George Murdock, TV/film actor; Genard Burks, TV/theater actor

GUIDE POV: Undergraduates attending this small private university may choose a communications program that stresses a thorough liberal arts education along with the acquisition of basic production skills in either radio or television; senior year internship opportunities in television production at national affiliates in Wichita and Topeka as well as at area stations

SOUTHWESTERN COLLEGE

100 College St.,
Winfield, KS 67156
(316)221–4150

Private four-year comprehensive institution. Coed, small city location. Undergraduate enrollment: 550. Graduate enrollment: 43.

MASS COMMUNICATION AND FILM DEPARTMENT

Chair/Contact: Dr. Bill DeArmond
Calendar: Semesters
Degrees Offered: B.A., mass communications and film studies
Departmental Majors: Undergraduate mass communications and film studies: 30 students
Entrance Requirements: Undergraduate: 2.0 grade-point average; ACT or SAT scores; high school diploma or GED certificate; AP and CLEP credit accepted. Undergraduate application deadline: rolling
Curricular Emphasis: Video

production (short fiction/films); video art; television studio and fieldwork; corporate video production; critical studies in film (analysis and criticism)

Special Activities: Film: student publications. Television: program material produced for cable television includes weekly news show and original video features

Facilities: Television: studio; audio bay; control room; separate video editing lab

Equipment: Television/Video: complete VHS, S-VHS, and ½" studio and location; editing equipment

Alumni: Martin Mutti, radio sports director/announcer; Sheri Prochaska, production assistant; Steve Zendejas, TV switcher/production assistant

GUIDE POV: This small private college offers an innovative media program presenting students with the opportunity to explore the possibilities of dramatic storytelling in video as well as to train intensively in traditional broadcasting techniques; hands-on emphasis; critical studies in film; writing for film and television; internship opportunities in television production

---

UNIVERSITY OF KANSAS

Lawrence, KS 66045
(913)864–2700

State four-year comprehensive institution. Coed, suburban location. Undergraduate enrollment: 26,000. Graduate enrollment: 4,000.

DEPARTMENT OF THEATRE AND FILM

Chair/Contact: Charles E. Berg, critical studies; Edward Small

WILLIAM ALLEN WHITE SCHOOL OF JOURNALISM

Chair/Contact: John Katich, radio-television

Calendar: Semesters

Degrees Offered: Film: B.A., B.G.S., film, theatre and film; M.A., film; Ph.D., theatre and film. Television: B.S., M.S., journalism (students may select emphasis in broadcast news)

Departmental Majors: Undergraduate theatre and film: 150 students. Graduate theatre and film: 20 students. Undergraduate journalism: 139 students. Graduate journalism: 11 students

Entrance Requirements: Undergraduate: open admissions for KS high school graduates; ACT scores; 2.5 grade-point average for School of Journalism. Graduate: transcripts; GRE scores; 3.0 grade-point average; interview; teachers' recommendations; essay; and sometimes the following: portfolio; production credits; professional recommendations. Undergraduate and graduate application deadline: April 1 for KS state residents; February 1 for nonresidents; December 1 for spring entry for all students. Percent of acceptances: 85%

Curricular Emphasis: Theatre and film: film theory, history, and criticism; basic to advanced 16mm production; animation; VHS video production. Journalism: Broadcast news production, sales, and management

Special Activities: Film: film series/festivals; film societies; student publication. Television: program material produced for cable television and for local public television station; professional in-residence program

Facilities: Film: screening rooms; editing suites; sound stages; sound

mixing studios; on-line and off-line editing; animation stand; film library. Television: studio; audio bay; control room; computerized news room
Equipment: Film: complete 16mm. Television: complete ¾" studio and ½" location; portable cameras; time base corrector; switcher/special effects generators; VHS/S-VHS and ¾" cuts-only editors; S-VHS A/B computer editor
Alumni: Mike Robe, TV writer/director/producer; Bill Kurtis, TV news anchor; Bob Dotson, TV network reporter; Wendall Anschutz, TV news anchor; Gary Bender, TV sportscaster; Terry Shockley, TV executive

GUIDE POV: This public university offers separate, comprehensive degree programs in film and television; nonbroadcast/independent video production available through Department of Theatre and Film; modern facilities in film, video, and television; extensive internship opportunities in film, video, and television production

---

WICHITA STATE UNIVERSITY

1845 N. Fairmount Ave.,
Wichita, KS 67260–0031
(316)689–3456

State four-year comprehensive institution. Coed, urban location. Undergraduate enrollment: 14,000. Graduate enrollment: 3,600.

ELLIOTT SCHOOL OF COMMUNICATION

Chair/Contact: Dr. Vernon Keel, Chair
Calendar: Semesters
Degrees Offered: B.A., communications (students may select emphasis in electronic media/visual communications); M.A., mass communications
Departmental Majors:
Undergraduate: 400 students. Graduate: 90 students
Entrance Requirements:
Undergraduate: 2.5 grade-point average; ACT or SAT scores; application for admission; entrance examination. Graduate: 3.0 grade-point average; GRE scores; interview; teachers' recommendations. Undergraduate and graduate application deadline: rolling. Percent of acceptances: 80%
Curricular Emphasis: Electronic media theory and culture; media writing; video production; media management; research; new technologies; interactive multimedia
Special Activities: Film: film series/festivals. Television: program material produced for cable television
Facilities: Film: screening room; editing suite. Television: studio; audio bay; control room
Equipment: Film: complete Super-8. Television/Video: complete ¾" studio and location; editing in Hi-8, VHS, and ¾" formats; integrated media lab for digital audio and video production
Alumni: Ray Dorsett, TV executive; Denise Franklin, TV news anchor; Laurie Roberts, TV news anchor; Traci Weisen Gardener, TV news anchor; John Batten, video photographer; Richard Wood, video photographer; George Womack, TV/film production designer; Kevin Kiefer, TV news producer

GUIDE POV: This lively program offers an integrated curriculum in television and video production with a strong emphasis on new technologies and interactive multimedia; internship opportunities in television production

There are innumerable reasons why people decide to go to film school. Often they've failed in another creative endeavor and are not quite ready to face the world, but film school seems like a glamorous venture. Then there are those who just yearn for success. For them, film school is like business school, and they begin to act like producers and directors as soon as they've taken a course or two. Finally, there is a much smaller group: the committed artists who are determined that film school will help them discover their true voice.

In selecting a high-quality graduate program in cinema, you should realistically evaluate your motives. Don't be a dreamer. You may or may not consider yourself an artist—that's unimportant. But I am convinced the farther away you get from Hollywood, the greater the chance you will be able to maintain your creative integrity. On the other hand, you must also determine whether the school of your choice provides practical industry relationships.

As a final word, I've found that the technical craft of making films is like riding a motorcycle. You will easily learn the basics. The rest is a mental and intuitive process that usually takes a lifetime to master.

ASBURY COLLEGE

1 Macklem Dr.,
Wilmore, KY 40390–1198
(606)858–3511

Private four-year comprehensive institution. Coed, rural location. Enrollment: 1,100.

COMMUNICATION ARTS DEPARTMENT

Chair/Contact: Dr. Donald B. Simmons, Chair
Calendar: Semesters
Degrees Offered: B.A., broadcast communications (students may select emphasis in radio/television)
Departmental Majors: Radio/Television: 85 students
Entrance Requirements: 2.0 grade-point average; ACT or SAT scores; interview; recommendations; written statement of purpose. Application deadline: rolling. Percent of acceptances: 78%
Curricular Emphasis: Media management; performance; radio and television production; film studies
Special Activities: Television: program material produced for cable television as well as for local public and commercial television stations
Facilities: Film: sound stage; animation stand; film library. Television: studio; audio bay; control room
Equipment: Film: complete Super-8.

Television/Video: complete ¾" studio; complete ¾" and ½" location
Alumni: Lee Schissler, media executive; Kay Brown, cinematographer; James Taylor, TV technical director

GUIDE POV: Asbury College is a private liberal arts college that emphasizes Christian orthodoxy; small media program offers sequential television production training; focus on mass communications and ethics; studies in media ministries; internship opportunities in television production

EASTERN KENTUCKY UNIVERSITY

Richmond, KY 40475
(606)622–1000

State four-year comprehensive institution. Coed, small town location. Undergraduate enrollment: 11,500

DEPARTMENT OF MASS COMMUNICATIONS

Chair/Contact: Dr. Ron G. Wolfe, Chair
Calendar: Semesters
Degrees Offered: B.A.
Departmental Majors: Undergraduate: 325 students
Entrance Requirements: Undergraduate: ACT required; academic ranking in top 50% of graduating class. Undergraduate

application deadline: rolling. Percent of acceptances: 94%

Curricular Emphasis: Students receive hands-on experience in their area of specialization and may major in broadcasting and electronic media, journalism, or public relations; cooperative activities and internships stressed

Special Activities: Program material produced for cable news outlet located on campus; annually held Mass Communications Career Day

Facilities: Television: studio; audio bay; control room; video editing suites; Desktop Publishing Lab

Equipment: Television: complete ¾" production studio and ½" location

Alumni: Ferrell Wellman, TV writer/videographer; Rocky Pangallo, videographer; Suzanne Black, TV news reporter; Mindy Shannon, TV news anchor

GUIDE POV: Eastern Kentucky University offers comprehensive training in all aspects of broadcast production with an emphasis on both television and radio news; additional training in small systems video production and electronic cinema production; attention to new technologies; practical approach; hands-on philosophy complemented by a liberal arts core curriculum; internship opportunities in television and radio production; study abroad in Europe

---

MOREHEAD STATE UNIVERSITY

Morehead, KY 40351
(606)783–2221

State four-year comprehensive institution. Coed, small town location.

Undergraduate enrollment: 8,500. Graduate enrollment: 1,600.

COMMUNICATIONS DEPARTMENT

Chair/Contact: Dr. Lawrence Albert, Chair

Calendar: Semesters

Degrees Offered: A.B., A.A.A., M.A.

Departmental Majors:
Undergraduate: 375 students. Graduate: 25 students

Entrance Requirements:
Undergraduate: 2.0 grade-point average; ACT or SAT scores (ACT preferred, with a minimum test score of 14); interview recommended. Graduate: transcripts; 2.5 grade-point average; GRE scores; interview. Undergraduate and graduate application deadline: rolling. Percent of acceptances: 89%

Curricular Emphasis: Electronic media theory and culture; television and radio production; media management

Special Activities: Television: news and other program material produced for cable television

Facilities: Television: studio; audio bay; control room; digital recording studio; audio studios; video editing suites

Equipment: Television: complete ¾" production studio and location; ½" teaching studio; camcorders

Alumni: Vic Carter, TV reporter/anchor; Liz Everman, TV news anchor; Mark Pfeifer, TV news anchor; Mark Sok, TV sports anchor/reporter

GUIDE POV: Morehead State University offers comprehensive training in all aspects of broadcast production with an emphasis on news/documentary; practical approach; internship opportunities in television production

MURRAY STATE UNIVERSITY

Box 2456, University Station,
Murray, KY 42071–3303
(502)762–3011

*State four-year comprehensive
institution. Coed, rural location.
Undergraduate enrollment: 6,500.
Graduate enrollment: 2,000.*

DEPARTMENT OF JOURNALISM AND RADIO-TELEVISION

Chair/Contact: Dr. Robert H.
McGaughey III, Chair
Calendar: Semesters
Degrees Offered: B.A., B.S., M.A.,
M.S., communications (with emphasis
in radio-television or electronic
journalism)
Departmental Majors:
Undergraduate: 387 students. Graduate:
20 students
Entrance Requirements:
Undergraduate: 2.0 grade-point
average; ACT required with minimum
score of 18 in-state or 22 out-of-state;
teachers' recommendations. Graduate:
2.75 grade-point average; GRE scores;
recommendations; production credits.
Undergraduate and graduate
application deadline: six weeks prior
to start of term. Percent of
acceptances: 88%
Curricular Emphasis: Electronic
media theory and culture; broadcast
journalism; media writing; audio-video
production; media management
Special Activities: Film: film series/
festivals. Television: on-campus student
cablevision station MSU TV-11; AERho
chapter; PRSSA and SPJ membership;
ACBJMC accredited
Facilities: Television: two complete
full-color studios; audio bays; control
rooms

Equipment: Film: ENG equipment.
Television/Video: complete ¾" studio
and location
Alumni: Jackie Hays, TV news
anchor; John Mack Carter, media
publishing editor; Forrest Pogue,
author/historian; John Fetterman,
Pulitzer prize-winning journalist; Gene
Graham, Pulitzer prize-winning
journalist

GUIDE POV: Students here are
encouraged to participate in a variety
of daily programming activities;
undergraduate and graduate programs;
current broadcast facilities; overseas
study; internship opportunities in
television production

NORTHERN KENTUCKY UNIVERSITY

Highland Heights, KY 41076
(606)572–5100

*State four-year comprehensive
institution. Coed, suburban location.
Undergraduate enrollment: 9,200.
Graduate enrollment: 400.*

COMMUNICATIONS DEPARTMENT

Chair/Contact: Television: David S.
Thomson
Calendar: Semesters
Degrees Offered: B.A.,
communications (students may select
emphasis in radio-television)
Departmental Majors: Undergraduate
television: 220 students
Entrance Requirements:
Undergraduate: high school diploma
or GED certificate; ACT required with
a minimum score of 18.
Undergraduate application
deadline: May
Curricular Emphasis: The radio/

television major provides sequential courses in radio and television sales, production, and performance

Special Activities: Television: program material produced for cable television and for on-campus closed-circuit television

Facilities: Film: editing suite. Television: studio; audio bay; control room

Equipment: Film: complete Super-8. Television/Video: complete ¾" studio; complete ¾" and ½" location

Alumni: Thomas Feie, TV programming director; Michael Hoffbauer, TV news reporter; Lynn McGinty, TV assistant engineer; Mark Oliver, TV production director; Angelia Thomas, TV personality

GUIDE POV: Students majoring in radio/television gain career training for entry into the fields of media management (business sequence), performance and news (programming sequence), or production and engineering (engineering sequence); cross-registration with several colleges in nearby Cincinnati; selective admission to radio/television program, which has limited enrollment; internship opportunities in television production

---

THE SOUTHERN BAPTIST THEOLOGICAL SEMINARY

2825 Lexington Rd.,
Louisville, KY 40280
(502)897–4011

Private graduate-level institution. Coed, urban location. Graduate enrollment: 2,500.

SCHOOL OF CHRISTIAN EDUCATION

Chair/Contact: Dr. Robert Don Hughes, associate professor of communication, mass media and seminary director of professional studies

Calendar: Semesters

Degrees Offered: M.A., M.Div., Christian education (students may select vocational emphasis in media ministry)

Departmental Majors: Graduate television: 15–25 students

Entrance Requirements: Graduate admissions: B.A. degree; GRE scores. Graduate application deadline: June 30

Curricular Emphasis: Television/video production

Special Activities: Television: program material produced for on-campus closed-circuit television and for cable television

Facilities: Television: studio; audio bay; control room; audio-visual center; video editing suites

Equipment: Television/Video: complete ¾" studio; complete ¾" and ½" location

Alumni: Lonnie McNorrill, video producer; Julie Seckman, video producer; Mark Wyatt, newspaper editor

GUIDE POV: Both the master of arts and master of divinity programs in Christian education offer media ministry concentrations providing mass communication and religious journalism studies as well as audio/visual production training; courses in broadcast administration and marketing; internship opportunities in television production

UNIVERSITY OF KENTUCKY

Lexington, KY 40506
(606)257-9000

*State four-year comprehensive
institution. Coed, small town location.
Undergraduate enrollment: 11,500*

ENGLISH DEPARTMENT

Chair/Contact: David S. Durant, Chair

DEPARTMENT OF TELECOMMUNICATIONS

Chair/Contact: Douglas A. Boyd,
Dean
Calendar: Semesters
Degrees Offered: B.A., B.S., English
(emphasis in film studies). B.A., B.S.,
telecommunications
Departmental Majors:
Undergraduate: 325 students
Entrance Requirements:
Undergraduate: SAT or ACT required;
minimum grade-point average of 2.0.
Undergraduate application deadline:
June 1. Percent of acceptances: 80%
Curricular Emphasis: English:
students may choose a film studies
emphasis, which consists of five
courses exploring film history, theory,
and aesthetics. Telecommunications:
course work is offered in three areas:
programming and research;
communications technology; policy
and regulation of telecommunications
Special Activities: Film: series;
screenings; lectures. Television:
program material produced for variety
of outlets
Facilities: Television: studio; audio
bay; control room; video editing suites
Equipment: Television: complete ¾"
production studio and ½" location
Alumni: Mary Ann Carpenter, TV
producer/director; Kathy Black,
network TV associate producer; Jim
Host, media production executive

GUIDE POV: This selective state
university offers an emphasis in film
studies to those majoring in English;
special attention to film aesthetics and
criticism; English Department offers
diverse curriculum; comprehensive
training in television production is
available to those majoring in
telecommunications; media
professionals from the region regularly
teach special topics courses;
telecommunications majors may also
receive instruction in audio and video
production and performance;
internship opportunities; study abroad
in 36 countries

UNIVERSITY OF LOUISVILLE

Louisville, KY 40292
(502)588-5555

*State four-year comprehensive
institution. Coed, urban location.
Undergraduate enrollment: 18,000.
Graduate enrollment: 5,000.*

COMMUNICATION DEPARTMENT

Chair/Contact: Dr. Charles Willard,
Chair; John Ferre
Calendar: Semesters
Degrees Offered: B.A.,
Communication
Departmental Majors:
Undergraduate: 350 students
Entrance Requirements:
Undergraduate: SAT or ACT required,
with a minimum composite score of
20 on the ACT or 450 on each section
of the SAT. Undergraduate application
deadline: rolling. Percent of
acceptances: 64%
Curricular Emphasis: Broadcast news
journalism is studied within the
context of a broad communication
curriculum that covers radio and
television production, print journalism,

speech communication, mass media history, communication criticism, ethics, and public relations
Special Activities: Television: program material produced for class projects
Facilities: Television: studio; audio bay; control room; video editing suites
Equipment: Television: complete ¾" studio and ½" location
Alumni: Bob Edwards, National Public Radio broadcaster; Mary Ann Ott, TV sports broadcaster; Paul Zinner, TV cameraman

GUIDE POV: Founded in 1798, this state university offers communication majors solid instruction in broadcast news writing and reporting; basic techniques in television production; cross-registration with area schools; internship opportunities; study abroad

---

WESTERN KENTUCKY UNIVERSITY

1526 Russellville Rd.,
Bowling Green, KY 42101–3576
(502)745–2551

State four-year comprehensive institution. Coed, rural location. Undergraduate enrollment: 15,500. Graduate enrollment: 2,100.

DEPARTMENT OF COMMUNICATION AND BROADCASTING

Chair/Contact: Randall Capps, Chair
Calendar: Semesters
Degrees Offered: B.A., M.A., broadcasting, mass communication
Departmental Majors: Undergraduate: 600 students. Graduate: 200 students
Entrance Requirements: Undergraduate: 2.25 grade-point average; ACT required, with minimum score for in-state students being 14; interview recommended. Graduate: competitive undergraduate grade-point average; GRE scores. Undergraduate and graduate application deadline: August 1. Percent of acceptances: 76%
Curricular Emphasis: Film, video, radio, and television production including critical studies; documentary writing; mass communication law and ethics; broadcast and nonbroadcast production; broadcast news; computer graphics and electronic art, and cinematography
Special Activities: Television: program material produced for on-campus closed-circuit television, for cable television, and for local public television station
Facilities: Film: screening room; editing suite; animation stand. Television: two complete full-color studios; control rooms
Equipment: Film: complete 16mm. Television/Video: two complete ¾" studios and ¾" location; computer graphics; CMX editing with 1" videotape format
Alumni: Julian Goodman, former NBC/TV president; Kelly Sandefur, TV producer; Oliver Gillespie, TV sports anchor

GUIDE POV: Featuring an innovative program with a wide range of course listings in cinema, video, television, and radio production, this department offers professional degree studies including film production for television, broadcast news, film and computer animation, CMX editing, cinematography, and new cable technologies; graduate emphasis on corporate communications; internship opportunities in film and television production

Going to college intimidated me. I had been married, had a child, was now divorced and struggling, and hadn't taken a test or written a paper for over a decade. My fellow college students looked incredibly young, and I felt terribly old. But I went anyway, since I knew I couldn't send my own daughter through college unless I had a better career than working as a grocery checker.

So I returned to school with the intention of becoming a psychobiologist (my father had been a chemistry professor, and I figured there must be some scientific genes in me somewhere). Taking classes in physics, calculus, mathematics, and psychology, I also took the required general education courses and some other electives. The other electives, though, were film and television production.

Another part of me came to life; creativity and joy bubbled over while I worked in these film classes. So after my first year I decided to pursue a double major: psychobiology and film. I worked very hard and made my daughter and my mother proud by receiving straight A's. Pretty soon, although I knew I could become a psychobiologist or physicist, I became sure that my real love and joy would only be found in making movies. Dropping the double major, I concentrated on film.

I love every aspect of it: the organization required for preproduction, production, and postproduction, writing, directing, the production itself, sound, casting, working with actors, designing sets—all of it. Movie-making uses every skill and bit of knowledge I've ever acquired; to me, it's the arts and sciences rolled into one.

The experience of going to college as an "older student" eradicated much of my shyness. I've become much more confident. I believe I've already found my "voice" and have clarified exactly what it is I want to say with my films. Professionally, since I've been attending school, I have also been an art director, created storyboards, edited, written several screenplays, two books, and a one-act play—which won an award in a national theatre competition. During this same time I lost most of my belongings in the Santa Cruz earthquake and was forced to relocate.

Had I stayed with my original choice of becoming a psychobiologist, my career path would have been fairly predictable and my salary predictable also. With the film business, you never know where you might end up. And that still terrifies me. But I do know if I hadn't chosen to pursue filmmaking, I wouldn't be nearly as happy.

DELGADO COMMUNITY COLLEGE

615 City Park Ave.,
New Orleans, LA 70119–4399
(504)483–4114

State two-year comprehensive institution. Coed, urban location. Enrollment: 10,000.

TELEVISION PRODUCTION/ARTS AND HUMANITIES DIVISION

Chair/Contact: Television: Jeannette Snider
Calendar: Semesters
Degrees Offered: A.A.S., general studies (students may select emphasis in television)
Departmental Majors: Television: 75 students
Entrance Requirements: Official transcripts and recent ACT scores required; Delgado Community College placement tests in English, reading, and mathematics may be required. Application deadline: rolling
Curricular Emphasis: Double camera studio operation; single camera remote operation; lighting; editing; audio production; writing, producing, and directing live and taped programming
Special Activities: Television: program material produced for on-campus closed-circuit television including campus news show
Facilities: Television: studio; audio bay; control room
Equipment: Television/Video: complete ¾" studio; complete ¾" and ½" location; editing format (¾" and Beta I)
Alumni: Ralph Madison, TV editor; Richard Pecot, TV commercial producer; Jimmie Pennison, videographer; Chris Sunseri, TV teleprompter operator; Karen Costello, radio producer

GUIDE POV: Students wishing to explore different facets of broadcast and field video production may choose the television production emphasis at this professionally equipped two-year community college; practical approach; transfer program; varied internship opportunities in television production

LOUISIANA STATE UNIVERSITY

Baton Rouge, LA 70803
(504)388–3202

State four-year multi-campus institution. Coed, urban location. Undergraduate enrollment: 17,200.

SCHOOL OF MASS COMMUNICATION

Chair/Contact: Dr. John M. Hamilton, Director
Calendar: Semesters
Degrees Offered: B.A., mass communication
Departmental Majors: Undergraduate: 300 students
Entrance Requirements:

Undergraduate: SAT or ACT required; minimum grade-point average of 2.0. Undergraduate application deadline: July 1. Percent of acceptances: 79%
Curricular Emphasis: Mass communication: broadcasting curriculum emphasizes television production and news journalism; one course in film history
Special Activities: Television: program material produced for on-campus station LSU-TV
Facilities: Television: studio; audio bay; control room; video editing suites
Equipment: Television: complete ¾" studio and ½" location
Alumni: Stephanie Riegel, TV news reporter; Victor Howell, TV broadcaster; Jeff Duhe, TV news reporter

GUIDE POV: Communications majors learn to produce and direct programs, and to write and report for television, by selecting the broadcasting option; media internship opportunities; study abroad in seven countries

LOYOLA UNIVERSITY

6363 St. Charles Ave.,
New Orleans, LA 70118
(504)865–2011

Private four-year comprehensive institution. Coed, urban location. Enrollment: 5,000.

DEPARTMENT OF COMMUNICATIONS

Chair/Contact: Dr. William M. Hammel
Calendar: Semesters
Degrees Offered: B.A., communications (with emphasis in television production or broadcast journalism)
Departmental Majors: 175 students

Entrance Requirements: Transcripts; 2.2 grade-point average; recommendations; ACT or SAT scores; essay; three ATs recommended; interview recommended. Application deadline: March 1. Percent of acceptances: 83%
Curricular Emphasis: Film studies; screenwriting; television production; broadcast journalism
Special Activities: Television: program material produced for on-campus closed-circuit television, for cable television, and for local public television station
Facilities: Television: two studios; audio bays; control rooms
Equipment: Television: complete ¾" studio; complete ¾" and ½" location
Alumni: Manny Coto, film director; Mike Adams, cable TV executive; Al Coleman, film editor

GUIDE POV: This selective Jesuit liberal arts university offers courses in film theory and provides hands-on television broadcast training with an emphasis on news and documentary production; summer session in London; cross-registration with area universities; exchange programs with Tulane University; internship opportunities in television production

NICHOLLS STATE UNIVERSITY

Thibodaux, LA 70310
(504)446–8111

State four-year comprehensive institution. Coed, rural location. Undergraduate enrollment: 7,000. Graduate enrollment: 800.

DEPARTMENT OF MASS COMMUNICATION

Chair/Contact: Television: Bob Blazier
Calendar: Semesters

Degrees Offered: B.A., mass communication (students may select emphasis in broadcast journalism)
Departmental Majors: Undergraduate television: 26 students
Entrance Requirements: Undergraduate: ACT scores required; placement tests. Undergraduate application deadline: August 15. Percent of acceptances: 98%
Curricular Emphasis: Electronic media theory and culture; media writing; television/video production; media management
Special Activities: Television: program material produced for cable television
Facilities: Television: studio; audio bay; control room
Equipment: Film: 16mm editing equipment and projectors. Television/ Video: complete ¾" studio and location; computer graphics
Alumni: Margaret DuGuisson, TV news anchor; Martin Folse, TV executive; Lisa Roach Byrd, TV/film producer

GUIDE POV: Nicholls State University offers students participation in a variety of campus television production projects; practical emphasis; broad liberal arts curriculum; study abroad in nine countries; internship opportunities in television production

NORTHEAST LOUISIANA UNIVERSITY

Monroe, LA 71209
(318)342–1000

State four-year comprehensive institution. Coed, rural location. Undergraduate enrollment: 11,500. Graduate enrollment: 700.

RADIO, TELEVISION, AND FILM DEPARTMENT

Chair/Contact: Dr. Edwin H. Ryland
Calendar: Semesters
Degrees Offered: A.A., B.A., radio/ TV/film (with emphasis in filmmaking, television/radio production, performance, management, or broadcast news); M.A., communications (students may select emphasis in radio/TV/film)
Departmental Majors: Undergraduate: 163 students. Graduate: 16 students
Entrance Requirements: Undergraduate: high school diploma or GED certificate; ACT scores. Graduate: transcripts; 3.0 grade-point average; GRE scores; professional recommendations. Undergraduate and graduate application deadline: rolling. Percent of acceptances: Undergraduate: 99%. Graduate: 70%
Curricular Emphasis: Blend of theory and training in both film and television production; specializations in management, filmmaking, production, performance, and broadcast news
Special Activities: Film/Television/ Radio: students produce varied entries for regional and national AERho competition; television program material produced for on-campus closed-circuit television and for local commercial stations; video advertising assignments accepted from outside clients; two public radio stations licensed to university
Facilities: Film: screening room; editing suite; sound mixing room; two filmmaking labs. Television: two studios; three audio bays; two control rooms; editing suites and engineering room; video toaster
Equipment: Film: complete Super-8

and 16mm. Television: complete S-VHS studio; complete ¾" and S-VHS location

Alumni: Earl Casey, CNN newscaster; Barry DeCrane, TV producer; Chris Jasek, TV news producer

GUIDE POV: Northeast Louisiana University offers comprehensive training in both film and television production; students choose area of specialization; tuition waived for graduate assistants; practical student-faculty ratio; paid internship opportunities in broadcasting

NORTHWESTERN STATE UNIVERSITY

Natchitoches, LA 71497–9990
(318)357–6011

State four-year comprehensive institution. Coed, rural location. Undergraduate enrollment: 7,000. Graduate enrollment: 800.

DEPARTMENT OF LANGUAGE AND COMMUNICATION

Chair/Contact: Television: Tom Whitehead
Calendar: Semesters
Degrees Offered: B.A., journalism (with emphasis in broadcasting, news editorial, or public relations)
Departmental Majors: Undergraduate television: 60 students
Entrance Requirements: Undergraduate: official transcript; ACT required. Undergraduate application deadline: rolling. Percent of acceptances: 99%
Curricular Emphasis: Television/video production
Special Activities: Television: program material produced for cable television

Facilities: Television: studio; audio bay; control room
Equipment: Television/Video: complete ½" studio; Beta and S-VHS; complete ¾" and ½" location; KU-uplink
Alumni: Marlene Canfield, TV news anchor; David Goldstein, media executive; Mark Cottrell, location manager

GUIDE POV: This state university offers broadcasting students comprehensive degree studies with practical preparation for entry-level positions in the field; co-op programs; study abroad; internship opportunities in television production

SOUTHEASTERN LOUISIANA UNIVERSITY

Hammond, LA 70402
(504)549–2000

State four-year comprehensive institution. Coed, small city location. Undergraduate enrollment: 11,000. Graduate enrollment: 1,000.

COMMUNICATION AND THEATRE DEPARTMENT

Chair/Contact: Dr. Thomas Welford, Chair; John Wellman
Calendar: Semesters
Degrees Offered: B.A., communications
Departmental Majors: Undergraduate: 225 students
Entrance Requirements: Undergraduate: high school diploma or GED certificate; ACT or SAT scores. Undergraduate application deadline: July 15. Percent of acceptances: 95%
Curricular Emphasis: Electronic media theory and culture; critical studies in film; media writing;

television/video production; media management

Special Activities: Video material produced for various on- and off-campus groups

Facilities: Television: studio; audio bay; control room

Equipment: Television/Video: complete ¾" studio; complete ¾" and ½" location

Alumni: Robin Roberts, ESPN sports broadcaster; Todd Rossnagle, TV producer

GUIDE POV: Located 46 miles northwest of New Orleans, this public university offers a comprehensive degree in communication; internship opportunities available at various agencies and organizations

TULANE UNIVERSITY

New Orleans, LA 70118
(504)865–5000

Private four-year comprehensive institution. Coed, urban location. Undergraduate enrollment: 8,000. Graduate enrollment: 5,000.

COMMUNICATION DEPARTMENT

Chair/Contact: Ana M. Lopez
Calendar: Semesters
Degrees Offered: B.A., communication (concentration in mass media); film studies minor
Departmental Majors: Undergraduate communication: 120 students. Film minor: 20 students
Entrance Requirements: Undergraduate: academic rank within top third of graduating class; minimum B+ average; teachers' recommendations; ACT or SAT scores; three ATs recommended; written statement of purpose; interview

recommended. Undergraduate application deadline: January 15. Percent of acceptances: 70%

Curricular Emphasis: Film and mass media studies with course listings in theory, aesthetics, criticism, and history; television/video production

Special Activities: Film: film series/festivals; film societies; student publication

Facilities: Film: screening room; film library

Alumni: Bruce Paltrow, TV producer; Allison Migliore, filmmaker/videographer; Nicky Denick, media journalist; Tully Arminagna, broadcasting executive

GUIDE POV: This highly competitive university offers comprehensive critical studies in film and electronic media; basic production classes located off-campus; cross-registration with Loyola and Xavier universities; study abroad in England, Ireland, France, Germany, Italy, Spain, and Israel; internship opportunities in television production

UNIVERSITY OF NEW ORLEANS

Lakefront, New Orleans, LA 70148
(504)286–6000

State four-year comprehensive institution. Coed, urban location. Undergraduate enrollment: 9,000. Graduate enrollment: 4,000.

DEPARTMENT OF DRAMA AND COMMUNICATIONS

Chair/Contact: Dr. Kevin Graves, Chair; J. Steven Hank, television and film
Calendar: Semesters
Degrees Offered: B.A., drama; B.A., M.A., M.F.A., drama and communications

Departmental Majors:
Undergraduate: 625 students. Graduate: 50 students
Entrance Requirements:
Undergraduate: 2.0 grade-point average; ACT scores. Graduate: 2.5 grade-point average; GRE scores; recommendations; written statement of purpose. Undergraduate and graduate application deadline: July 1. Percent of acceptances: 93%
Curricular Emphasis: Electronic media theory and culture; critical studies in film; film and television production including news/documentary; fiction; experimental; media management
Special Activities: Film: film showcase. Television: program material produced for on-campus closed-circuit television, for local public television station, and for cable television
Facilities: Film: sound stage; screening room; editing suite; sound mixing room; film library. Television: studio; control room
Equipment: Film: complete Super-8 and 16mm. Television/Video: ¾" VTR; matched studio cameras; portable lighting packages; ¾" cassette recorders; sound recording equipment; monitors; audio mixers
Alumni: Mark Allen Williams, TV executive producer; Stephen Bellas, media teacher

GUIDE POV: Students choosing to major in drama and communications at this competitive state university are offered extensive undergraduate and graduate training in both film and television production; critical studies combined with exploration of both narrative and experimental forms; study abroad in Austria; cross-registration with Southern University of New Orleans; internship opportunities in film and television production

---

UNIVERSITY OF SOUTHWESTERN LOUISIANA

P.O. Box 43650,
Lafayette, LA 70504–3560
(318)231–6000

State four-year comprehensive institution. Coed, urban location. Undergraduate enrollment: 14,000. Graduate enrollment: 2,000.

DEPARTMENT OF COMMUNICATION

Chair/Contact: Dr. Robert E. Simmons, Chair
Calendar: Semesters
Degrees Offered: B.A., communication (mass communication emphasis in broadcasting or media advertising); M.S., communication (mass communication emphasis in radio-TV or print journalism)
Departmental Majors:
Undergraduate: 75 students. Graduate: 20 students
Entrance Requirements:
Undergraduate: 2.5 grade-point average; ACT or SAT scores. Graduate: 2.7 grade-point average; GRE scores, with a minimum verbal score of 470; recommended submission of writing sample such as a published work or undergraduate research paper. Undergraduate and graduate application deadline: March 31. Percent of acceptances: 85%
Curricular Emphasis: Television studio and field production; corporate video production; electronic field production and editing; producing short films for television; broadcast newswriting; news and public affairs broadcast journalism; documentary

production; separate concentrations in broadcast journalism and advertising
Special Activities: Film: film series/festivals. Television: program material produced for local cable access; broadcasting students have access to the campus radio station, television studios, and multiple lab facilities, as well as television field equipment for diverse practical experiences
Facilities: Television: studio; audio bay; control room; video editing suites
Equipment: Television/Video: complete ¾" studio and ½" location
Alumni: Christopher Allain, TV producer; John Ware, TV production director; Roger Weeder, TV news reporter; Roger Maier, TV news reporter; Stephen Foster, video production director

GUIDE POV: This public university offers both undergraduate and graduate media production programs; comprehensive course listings cover all aspects of writing and producing for television and video, emphasizing news, documentary, and public affairs programming; required core curriculum in communication theory; study abroad in Mexico, Canada, France, and Belgium; internship opportunities in television production

XAVIER UNIVERSITY OF LOUISIANA

7325 Palmetto St.,
New Orleans, LA 70125
(504)486–7411

Private four-year comprehensive institution. Coed, urban location. Undergraduate enrollment: 2,700. Graduate enrollment: 500.

COMMUNICATIONS DEPARTMENT

Chair/Contact: Dr. Joe Melcher, Chair; film: Dave Cardwell
Calendar: Semesters
Degrees Offered: B.A., mass communications (with emphasis in broadcast or print media)
Departmental Majors: Undergraduate television: 100 students
Entrance Requirements: Undergraduate: 2.0 grade-point average; ACT required. Undergraduate application deadline: March 1. Percent of acceptances: 80%
Curricular Emphasis: Electronic media theory and culture; media writing; television/video production; video art; media management; journalism, public relations
Special Activities: Television: program material produced by students for cable television
Facilities: Television: studio; audio bay; control room; electronic field production; news gathering; postproduction
Equipment: Television/Video: complete ¾" studio and location
Alumni: Kyle Claude, creative services producer; Keith Smith, cinematographer; Tarra Rhymes, public relations executive; Anthony Delfores, cinematographer; John Gibson, videographer

GUIDE POV: This small private university offers television and video production training within a liberal arts curriculum; studies include broadcast production, video art, and media management; students work on a variety of production projects that air locally; extensive co-op and cross-registration programs with area colleges and universities; internship opportunities in television production

You must be certain about your career choice before applying to film school. A prime ingredient of the Film Industry Survival Kit is your tenacity and talent. Make no mistake regarding directing or writing. It's a playing field of rejection and unanswered telephone calls.

Now that you're warned, I will tell you from personal experience: When you are watching your first film effort with a responsive audience, all the pain and effort is rewarded. Writing and directing—or other creative categories—for films can be the most exciting of all art forms.

A working knowledge of film directing and writing is obviously an important asset in propelling your career forward. Therefore my advice is to select the best film school available for your needs. Then learn the pro forma of the craft. The determined student will usually venture beyond the school curriculum and exploit the available facilities.

Practically speaking, writing requires a great deal of discipline in order to put your thoughts and ideas into an accepted industry form—namely the script. The more original and exciting your material, the greater the opportunity to have it read and hopefully produced. And directing requires equipment, personnel, and a facility to assemble components such as editing, sound effects, music, and opticals, etc. That translates into finance. And the one place those resources can be made available to the aspiring filmmaker is film school.

My own directing credits include *Cornbread, Earl and Me*, and *Beatlemania*. I have produced *Alice's Restaurant* and *A New Leaf*, among others. I have also been involved in a production capacity with *The Pawnbroker, The Swimmer*, and *West Side Story*. And over the years I have directed and produced many television film shows.

But I have often thought that my own career might have been helped had I graduated from film school. In the final analysis, of course, it's the content of one's efforts that matters. If you're good, your talent will eventually be recognized and given an opportunity to grow.

NEW ENGLAND SCHOOL OF BROADCASTING

One College Circle,
Bangor, ME 04401
(207)947–6083

*Private two-year institution. Coed,
suburban location. Enrollment: 60.
Tuition: $4,290 per academic year*

TV PRODUCTION

Chair/Contact: George Wildey; Ben
Haskell
Calendar: Semesters
Degrees Offered: A.S., broadcast
communications (administered by
Husson College); certificates
Entrance Requirements: High school
diploma or equivalent; interview;
recommendations. Application
deadline: August 1
Curricular Emphasis: Television
production; writing for media; sound
recording; news, sports, and weather
reporting; public service;
programming; broadcast sales;
promotion; business law
Special Activities: Television:
program material produced for cable
television includes half-hour weekly
series, "Mainely Speaking"
Facilities: Television: studio; audio
bay; control room
Equipment: Television/Video:
complete ¾" studio and location;
special effects generator

Alumni: Mark Nedeau, TV news
director; Bill Beale, media specialist;
Steve Carter, TV producer; Rod Verrill,
TV production director

GUIDE POV: Located on the campus
of Husson College, this private two-
year institution was established in 1981
to train students for entry-level
technical positions in the field of
broadcasting; faculty of working
professionals; hands-on emphasis;
internship opportunities

UNIVERSITY OF MAINE

Orono, ME 04469
(207)581–1110

*State four-year comprehensive
institution. Coed, rural location.
Undergraduate enrollment: 11,000.
Graduate: 2,000.*

JOURNALISM AND MASS COMMUNICATION DEPARTMENT

Chair/Contact: Stuart Bullion, Chair;
Steve Craig
Degrees Offered: B.A., broadcasting
(students may select emphasis in
radio/television); B.A., journalism
(students may select emphasis in
broadcast news)
Calendar: Semesters
Departmental Majors: Undergraduate
television broadcasting: 136 students

Entrance Requirements:
Undergraduate: 2.5 grade-point
average; ACT or SAT scores;
recommendations. Undergraduate
application deadline: February 1.
Percent of acceptances: 80%
Curricular Emphasis: Technical
aspects of radio/television production
with emphasis on broadcast news
Special Activities: Film: student
productions. Television: program
material produced for local public,
commercial, and cable television
Facilities: Television: studio; audio
studio; control room
Equipment: Film: 16mm cameras;
editing equipment; lighting; projectors.

Television: complete 1" and ¾" studio;
complete ¾" and ½" location
Alumni: Stephen King, writer/
screenwriter/director; Mark Cohen, TV
network executive; Jane Masserve, TV
news correspondent

GUIDE POV: This competitive, well-
equipped public university offers
students hands-on production training
in broadcast journalism; cross-
registration through the National
Student Exchange; study abroad in
more than 40 countries; varied
internship opportunities in television
production

The best film school is an old movie theatre, the kind that shows only one movie and has only one, gigantic screen. The kind that has intriguing architecture and displays its movie posters on a prominent marquee along with a series of black-and-white publicity stills. Growing up in Costa Rica, I had many theatres of this kind to choose from. You went there because you wanted to see and experience a film. In the multiplexes of today, such complete devotion is hardly possible.

Those old theatres made you love films, and if your career plans were already set in the movie industry, those theatres nurtured you. They literally became your school. For each movie showcased, you could analyze the advertising in its simplest form, then the film itself, then the advertising again to see how accurately the picture had been portrayed. That was the best course in filmmaking I ever took. I acquired a sense of not only how a movie should be made, but how it should be presented and shown.

Instead of dismissing a film as good or bad, I always tried to figure out exactly what made it so, often going back for a second or third viewing. This practice made me a keen observer of all the formal elements: the music, which I considered pivotal; the art direction; the cinematography—categories I was eventually able to refer to by name by studying the Academy Awards shows on TV.

After each movie I would board the bus and do my homework, which consisted basically of letting inspiration get the best of me. My task was simply to get ideas for movies of my own, and boy, was it easy. All I had to do was glance at the multicolored Costa Rican sunset, and ideas just started pouring in. The downside was, I often got too involved in my thoughts and missed my bus stop.

When I finally began studying film here in America, I never received quite as good a lesson. Film education is primarily good for one purpose: to teach you how to use the *tools of the trade*.

You can't find *inspiration* in a classroom, or even the right atmosphere to acquire it. You have to find it in your hometown, in your childhood, in your favorite park, beach, or mountain, or, as in my case, in a small Central American country 2,000 miles away.

ALLEGHENY COMMUNITY COLLEGE

Willow Brook Rd.,
Cumberland, MD 21502
(301)724–7700

State two-year comprehensive institution. Coed, rural location. Enrollment: 1,700.

COMMUNICATION MEDIA PROGRAM

Chair/Contact: Terry L. Feck; Bill Devlin, Director of instructional assistance
Calendar: Semesters
Degrees Offered: A.A., media arts
Departmental Majors: Film and television: 45 students
Entrance Requirements: Open-door policy; high school diploma or equivalent; interview. Application deadline: September 6. Percent of acceptances: 99%
Curricular Emphasis: Critical studies and production work in film, television, photography, radio, graphic design, and journalism
Special Activities: Film: student screenings. Television: program material produced for on-campus closed-circuit television and cable television
Facilities: Film: editing suite; sound mixing room; sound stage. Television: studio; control room; multimedia classroom; graphic production area; audio production facility

Equipment: Film: complete Super-8. Television/Video: complete ¾" studio; complete ¾" and ½" location
Alumni: Frankie Durst, radio disc jockey; Pat Sullivan, radio disc jockey

GUIDE POV: Utilizing a blend of lecture and laboratory experience, this two-year course of studies prepares specialists in the fields of television, film, graphic design, radio, photography, or journalism; practical career program designed for students seeking immediate employment upon graduation rather than transferring to four-year institution; internship opportunities in television production; 35-hour required practicum in final semester

ANNE ARUNDEL COMMUNITY COLLEGE

101 College Pkwy.,
Arnold, MD 21012
(410)647–7100

County two-year institution. Coed, suburban location. Enrollment: 7,000.

COMMUNICATION ARTS DEPARTMENT

Chair/Contact: James Privitera
Degrees Offered: A.A., communication arts technology; certificate in video production
Calendar: Semesters
Departmental Majors: Media production: 100 students

Entrance Requirements: High school diploma; ACT or SAT scores. Application deadline: September 1
Curricular Emphasis: Technical aspects of media production
Special Activities: Vocational placement service
Facilities: Film: sound stage; sound mixing room; animation stand. Television: studio; audio studio; control room
Equipment: Film: complete Super-8. Television: complete ½" location
Alumni: William Whiteford, TV producer; James Traavland, TV producer; Andrew Kirkey, video technician

GUIDE POV: This community college offers technical degrees in management as well as production, animation, and graphics; internship opportunities in television production

BOWIE STATE UNIVERSITY

Bowie, MD 20715
(301)464–3000

State four-year regional comprehensive institution. Coed, suburban location. Undergraduate enrollment: 2,500. Graduate enrollment: 1,800.

COMMUNICATIONS DEPARTMENT

Chair/Contact: Dr. Elaine Bourne-Heath, Chair
Calendar: Semesters
Degrees Offered: B.A., communications (students may select emphasis in broadcast journalism)
Entrance Requirements: Undergraduate: transcripts; minimum 2.0 grade-point average; SAT required with composite score of 700. Undergraduate application deadline: April 1

Curricular Emphasis: Television production training with emphasis on broadcast journalism
Special Activities: Television: program material produced for cable television; annual fine arts festival
Facilities: Television: studio; audio bay; control room; editing bays
Equipment: Television: complete ¾" studio and location
Alumni: Paula Tubman, TV news reporter; Nathaniel Herndon, TV news reporter; Michael Matthews, TV news reporter

GUIDE POV: This small, publicly funded liberal arts university offers undergraduates broadcast training covering all aspects of studio and field production; emphasis on news journalism; cross-registration with numerous area colleges and universities; internship opportunities in television production

CATONSVILLE COMMUNITY COLLEGE

800 S. Rolling Rd.,
Catonsville, MD 21228
(410)455–6050

County two-year comprehensive institution. Coed, suburban location. Enrollment: 2,200.

VIDEO PRODUCTION

Chair/Contact: Television: Jo-Ann Rasmussen
Calendar: Semesters
Degrees Offered: A.A., video production; certificate in corporate production
Departmental Majors: Video: 20 students
Entrance Requirements: Official transcripts; ACT/SAT scores, or college

placement tests. Application deadline: rolling. Percent of acceptances: 99%

Curricular Emphasis: Electronic media theory and culture; media writing; experiential learning in television/video production including fiction and news/documentary

Special Activities: Television: program material produced for cable television

Facilities: Television: studio; control room

Equipment: Television/Video: complete ¾" studio and location

Alumni: Ed Feurerherd, TV writer/producer; David Earnest, videographer; Gina Gilbert, film editor

GUIDE POV: Featuring small classes and production experience in both narrative and broadcast news forms, this two-year institution prepares students for technical support positions in the media industries; transfer program; innovative certificate program in corporate production designed for working technicians seeking to upgrade their skills; internship opportunities in television production

COLLEGE OF NOTRE DAME OF MARYLAND

4701 N. Charles St.,
Baltimore, MD 21210–2476
(410)435–0100

Private four-year comprehensive institution. Coed, urban location. Enrollment: 2,500.

COMMUNICATION ARTS DEPARTMENT

Chair/Contact: Karen Stoddard, Chair
Calendar: Semesters
Degrees Offered: B.A., communication arts

Departmental Majors: 40 students

Entrance Requirements: 2.5 grade-point average; interview; SAT required; written statement of purpose. Application deadline: February 15. Percent of acceptances: 70%

Curricular Emphasis: Electronic media theory and culture; critical studies in film; media writing; television/video production

Special Activities: Film: film series/festivals. Television: program material produced for local public television and for cable television

Facilities: Television: studio; audio bay; control room

Equipment: Television/Video: complete ¾" studio; complete ¾" and ½" location

Alumni: Eileen P. O'Neill, TV production manager; Ruth Cooper, video editor

GUIDE POV: This competitive private college features a small individualized program offering comprehensive television and video production training along with several courses in film criticism; cross-registration with several area colleges and universities including Johns Hopkins; study abroad may be arranged; weekend college program for working students; internship opportunities in television production

FROSTBURG STATE UNIVERSITY

Frostburg, MD 21532
(301)689–4000

State four-year comprehensive institution. Coed, rural location. Undergraduate enrollment: 4,400. Graduate enrollment: 600.

COMMUNICATION AND THEATRE ARTS DEPARTMENT

Chair/Contact: Howard Parnes
Calendar: Semesters
Degrees Offered: B.A., B.S., mass communication
Departmental Majors:
Undergraduate: 140 students
Entrance Requirements:
Undergraduate: 2.0 grade-point average; interview required; completion of CMAT 105.
Undergraduate application deadline: rolling. Percent of acceptances: 60%
Curricular Emphasis:
Interdisciplinary program; students specialize in writing, production/ performance, or management
Special Activities: Television: program material produced for cable television; teacher training
Facilities: Television: audio studio; control room
Equipment: Television/Video: complete ½" location
Alumni: Scott Paddack, media promotional director; Debra Monk, TV actress

GUIDE POV: This growing, affordable program offers television production training as part of a communication theory curriculum; new video facilities; required practicum; multimedia workshop; internship opportunities in television production

GOUCHER COLLEGE

Dulaney Valley Rd.,
Towson, MD 21204
(410)337–6000

Private four-year comprehensive institution. Coed; urban location. Undergraduate enrollment: 1,000. Graduate enrollment: 25.

COMMUNICATION DEPARTMENT

Chair/Contact: Dr. Gary Edgerton, Chair
Calendar: Semesters
Degrees Offered: B.A., communication (with emphasis in film or television)
Departmental Majors: Undergraduate film/television: 80 students combined
Entrance Requirements:
Undergraduate: 3.0 grade-point average; competitive ACT or SAT scores; teachers' recommendations; written statement of purpose.
Undergraduate application deadline: March 1. Percent of acceptances: 75%
Curricular Emphasis:
Communication theory and popular culture; critical studies in film; media writing; audio-film-video production; media management
Special Activities: Film: weekly film series; guest speakers; film festivals; film society. Television: program material produced for cable television
Facilities: Film: sound stage; screening room; editing suite; sound mixing room; film library. Television: studio; audio bay; control room; computer video laboratory
Equipment: Film: complete Super-8 and 16mm; complete photography. Television/Video: complete ¾" studio; complete ¾" and ½" location; satellite dish; projection video system
Alumni: Mildred Dunnock, film actress; Nancy Goldman Claster; Jean Reese Worthley

GUIDE POV: Formerly a women's college but coeducational since 1986, this selective, well-equipped private institution offers comprehensive studies and training in film, video, and television; junior year study abroad programs in Britain, Spain, France, and Russia; cross-registration at Johns

Hopkins and other area colleges; varied internship opportunities

positions; internship opportunities in television production

HAGERSTOWN JUNIOR COLLEGE

11400 Robinwood Dr.,
Hagerstown, MD 21742
(301)790–2800

County two-year institution. Coed, rural location. Enrollment: 3,000.

COMMUNICATIONS PROGRAM

Chair/Contact: Television: Ralph Chapin
Calendar: Semesters
Degrees Offered: A.A., communications
Departmental Majors: Television: 50 students
Entrance Requirements: 2.0 grade-point average; ACT or SAT scores. Application deadline: rolling. Percent of acceptances: 98%
Curricular Emphasis: Electronic media theory and culture; media writing; television/video production
Special Activities: Television: program material produced on campus
Facilities: Television: two studios; audio bay; control room
Equipment: Television/Video: complete ½" studios; complete ½" location and editing
Alumni: Michael Shank, radio disc jockey; Cynthia Garland, TV producer; Patricia Kinter, TV producer; David Dull, TV producer; William Lucas, TV technician

GUIDE POV: Comprehensive hands-on training in television production is offered at this affordable county institution; small classes; practical preparation for technical support

HARFORD COMMUNITY COLLEGE

401 Thomas Run Rd.,
Bel Air, MD 21015–1698
(410)836–4000

State and county two-year institution. Coed, suburban location. Enrollment: 7,000.

MASS COMMUNICATIONS DEPARTMENT

Chair/Contact: Television: John A. Davlin
Calendar: Semesters
Degrees Offered: A.A., mass communications (options in broadcast announcing/production; broadcast sales/advertising; and public relations/advertising); certificate programs
Departmental Majors: Television: 90 students
Entrance Requirements: Open-door policy; high school diploma or equivalent. Application deadline: rolling, but early registration deadlines are August 1 for fall semester and December 1 for spring semester. Percent of acceptances: 99%
Curricular Emphasis: All aspects of television/video production including news and video art
Special Activities: Television: program material produced for cable television
Facilities: Television: studio; audio bay; control room
Equipment: Television/Video: complete ¾" studio and ½" location
Alumni: Rob Tezai, video producer; Cynthia Miller, video executive; Christine Rice, TV producer/editor; Robert Brockmeyer, TV editor; Keith Williams, TV editor

GUIDE POV: Preparing students for entry-level employment in broadcast/ cable settings as well as for transfer to area universities, this program emphasizes writing, announcing, production, and news gathering; separate concentrations in media sales and public relations; internship opportunities in television production

GUIDE POV: This small private college offers its students an individualized course of studies in film and video production; areas explored include fiction, documentary, experimental, news, and video art; cross-registration with area colleges and universities; internship opportunities in film and television production

HOOD COLLEGE

Frederick, MD 21701
(301)663–3131

Private four-year comprehensive institution. Coed, small city location. Undergraduate enrollment: 1,000. Graduate enrollment: 900.

COMMUNICATION ARTS PROGRAM

Chair/Contact: Film: Harry St. Ours
Calendar: Semesters
Degrees Offered: B.A., communication arts
Departmental Majors: Undergraduate film: 12 students. Undergraduate television: 15 students
Entrance Requirements: Undergraduate: 2.5 grade-point average; SAT required; essay required; interview recommended. Undergraduate application deadline: March 15. Percent of acceptances: 90%
Curricular Emphasis: Critical studies in film and electronic media; film, video, and television production
Special Activities: Film: film series/ festivals; student publication
Facilities: Television: studio
Equipment: Television/Video: complete ¾" studio and location
Alumni: Susan Burke, TV news anchor; Donna Parker, TV news anchor; Betsy Widerman Hyle, director of TV news department

JOHNS HOPKINS UNIVERSITY

Charles and 34th St.,
Baltimore, MD 21218
(410)516–8000

Private four-year comprehensive institution. Coed, urban location. Undergraduate enrollment: 3,000. Graduate enrollment: 1,500.

WRITING SEMINARS PROGRAM

Chair/Contact: Film: Mark Crispin Miller; television: James Trone
Calendar: 4–1–4
Degrees Offered: B.A., writing seminars (with minor in film studies); M.A., nonfiction (film and media studies)
Departmental Majors: Undergraduate film minors: 5–15 students. Graduate film: 3–10 students
Entrance Requirements: Undergraduate: competitive grade-point average; ACT or SAT scores; three ATs including English composition required; personal essay required; interview recommended. Graduate: competitive undergraduate grade-point average and GRE scores; foreign language test; teachers' recommendations; written statement of purpose. Undergraduate and graduate application deadline: January 1. Percent of acceptances: 30%
Curricular Emphasis: Program places

strong emphasis on film and television criticism, history, theory/aesthetics; cultural studies and critiques; basic television production training
Special Activities: Film: film society; student publications
Facilities/Equipment: Television/Video: complete ¾" location
Alumni: Andrew Barth, TV news reporter; Frank Bond, TV news reporter

GUIDE POV: This highly competitive private university offers undergraduates a select writing program in which students choosing the film minor may elect to explore various critical, theoretical, and cultural concerns in the field of film and media scholarship; graduate nonfiction program tailored to student interests; basic video training available with emphasis on news/documentary; study abroad program includes enrollment at Johns Hopkins in Bologna, Italy; internship opportunities in television production

MORGAN STATE UNIVERSITY

Cold Spring Lane and Hillen Rd., Baltimore, MD 21239
(410)391–3333

State four-year comprehensive institution. Coed, urban location. Undergraduate enrollment: 26,000. Graduate enrollment: 3,000.

TELECOMMUNICATIONS DEPARTMENT

Chair/Contact: Dr. Gilbert Maddox, Chair
Calendar: Semesters
Degrees Offered: B.A., B.S., telecommunications
Departmental Majors: Undergraduate: 310 students

Entrance Requirements:
Undergraduate: minimum 2.0 grade-point average with combined 750 SAT or 17 ACT scores; essay recommended. Undergraduate application deadline: May 1. Percent of acceptances: 52%
Curricular Emphasis: Radio-TV production; broadcast journalism; communication theory and research
Special Activities: Television: program material produced for local PBS affiliate; AERho chapter; student telecommunications society
Facilities: Television: studio; audio bay; control room; video editing suites
Equipment: Television: complete ¾" studio; ¾" and ½" location including ¾" U-matic SP CMX editing with Ampex Vista switcher
Alumni: Gary Holland, TV producer; Jeffrey Grice, TV news editor; Kim Dickins, videotape editor; Harold Fisher, TV news reporter; Raymond Leftwich, videographer

GUIDE POV: Morgan State University features a comprehensive telecommunications program with tracks in radio-television production, broadcast journalism, and theory/research; internship opportunities in television production

TOWSON STATE UNIVERSITY

Towson, MD 21204
(410)830–2000

State four-year comprehensive institution. Coed, suburban location. Undergraduate enrollment: 14,000. Graduate enrollment: 1,290.

SPEECH AND MASS COMMUNICATION DEPARTMENT

Chair/Contact: Ronald J. Matlon
Degrees Offered: B.A.,

communication studies; B.A., M.A., mass communication

Calendar: Semesters

Departmental Majors: Undergraduate mass communication: 1,050 students; communication studies: 60 students. Graduate mass communication: 110 students

Entrance Requirements:
Undergraduate: priority admission granted to applicants with minimum 3.0 grade-point average and minimum SAT scores of 500 verbal and 500 math; regular admission granted with minimum 2.5 grade-point average and minimum SAT scores of 450 verbal and 450 math. Graduate: minimum 2.75 grade-point average; transcripts; production credits; professional recommendations. Application deadline: Undergraduate: April. Graduate: rolling

Curricular Emphasis: Students may receive general mass communication degree or specialize in film, television, radio, or broadcast journalism

Special Activities: Film: Film/Video Society sponsors annual festival; guest speakers. Television: program material produced for low-power station TSTV

Facilities: Film: 35mm screening facilities; sound mixing room; animation stand; computerization facilities; visual media library. Television: studio; audio bay; control room; video editing suites

Equipment: Film: complete Super-8 and 16mm; 35mm projectors. Television: two complete ¾" studios; complete ¾" and ½" location

Alumni: Donna Quante, director/producer/cinematographer; Lisa Torockio, TV producer; Katherine McQuay, media research coordinator

GUIDE POV: Students here may receive sequential training in film and television production; diverse curriculum includes courses in television production; broadcast journalism, narrative and experimental film production, video art; media management; internship opportunities in film and television production

---

UNIVERSITY OF MARYLAND

College Park, MD 20742
(301)405–1000

Public four-year comprehensive institution. Coed, suburban location. Undergraduate enrollment: 22,000. Graduate enrollment: 9,000

DEPARTMENT OF JOURNALISM

Chair/Contact: Dr. Cleghorn, Dean
Calendar: Semesters
Degrees Offered: B.A., M.A., Ph.D.
Entrance Requirements:
Undergraduate: competitive grade-point average; SAT required; essay required. Graduate: GRE scores; recommendations. Undergraduate and graduate application deadline: December 1. Percent of acceptances: 75% undergraduate; 61% graduate

Curricular Emphasis: There are sequences in broadcast news, advertising, public relations, and news-editorial; broadcast news sequence concentrates on news writing, editing, and management

Special Activities: Television: program material produced for class projects

Facilities: Television: studio; audio bay; control room; video editing suites

Equipment: Television: complete ¾" studio and ½" location

Alumni: Connie Chung, network TV broadcaster; Patrick Anastasi, radio news director; Lori Beecher, network

TV associate producer; Monica Pellegrini, TV sports reporter

GUIDE POV: The radio-television-film program has been closed; students may study broadcast writing and editing through the Journalism Department; film studies are pursued in the context of popular culture through the American Studies program; cross-registration with other colleges in the Consortium of Universities of the Washington Metropolitan Area; media internships

---

VILLA JULIE COLLEGE

Valley Rd.,
Stevenson, MD 21153
(410)486–7000

Private four-year comprehensive institution. Coed, suburban location. Enrollment: 2,000.

LIBERAL ARTS AND TECHNOLOGY: VIDEO PRODUCTION

Chair/Contact: Sally Harris
Calendar: Semesters
Degrees Offered: A.A., communication arts (students may select emphasis in television/theatre); B.S., humanities
Departmental Majors: 48 students

Entrance Requirements: High school diploma or GED certificate; SAT scores; interview; essay. Application deadline: rolling. Percent of acceptances: 60%
Curricular Emphasis: Interdisciplinary program emphasizing documentary production; multi-arts production; corporate production; writing for theatre and video
Special Activities: Video: broadcast advertising produced for local corporate clients; video/play presentations; screenings of student productions
Facilities: Television: studio; control room; theatre
Equipment: Television/Video: complete ½" studio and location; four editing suites; Amiga video toasters
Alumni: Amy Gottlieb, video producer; Kim Brooks, TV/film actress; Suzanne Griffith, producer/production assistant; Amy Weiczorek, TV/film actress; David Thompson, cinematographer

GUIDE POV: This commuter college offers students a small interdisciplinary program featuring video production training with studies in both the fine and liberal arts; diverse course listings; independent projects encouraged

When I was a young girl, my mother took me to see *Star Wars*, and my life changed forever. Not only did I become a big movie fan, but I became addicted to Milk Duds. I remember being completely transported into another realm of time, space, and emotion. The only word to describe what rushed into my head was *awe*. At a young age, that single movie made me appreciate the power of cinema.

George Lucas and Steven Spielberg became my heroes: They were the geniuses of my generation, worshiped filmmakers with an incredible grasp of the medium. They created an exciting new movie language. I wanted to be like them and was already focused on a future in the world of film and television.

Thanks to my wise mother, I grew up with a passion for the arts and humanities. I aspired to be a Renaissance Woman. This love of learning helped to form my choice in selecting a good liberal arts school, and I was accepted at Wesleyan University. In pursuing a liberal arts education there, I was exposed to ideas I would not have encountered at any undergraduate film school. I realized that great filmmakers are well-educated individuals—with or without formal schooling—able to reshape the history of film. Obviously, Coppola could not have made *Apocalypse Now* without a strong background in literature, music, and history, along with a profound understanding of humanity. And Chaplin could not have made people laugh so hard if he hadn't known what made them cry.

I strongly suggest that aspiring filmmakers pursue a liberal arts education and seek out a school where there is respect and love of the cinematic arts. As for myself, I have become extremely interested in children's television and animation. However, I still have an appreciation of live action and will forever be a student of movie-making. I attribute that commitment only to my diverse education.

BABSON COLLEGE

Babson Park,
Wellesley, MA 02157–0310
(617)235–1200

*Private four-year comprehensive
institution. Coed, suburban location.
Enrollment: 2,000.*

COMMUNICATION, DIVISION OF LIBERAL ARTS

Chair/Contact: Film: Julie Levinson;
television: Renee Hobbs
Calendar: Semesters
Degrees Offered: B.A.,
communication; minor, creative arts
Departmental Majors: Film and
television: 40 students
Entrance Requirements: Competitive
grade point average; ACT or SAT
scores; ATs in math and English
required; essay required; interview
recommended. Application
deadline: February 1. Percent of
acceptances: 57%
Curricular Emphasis: Critical studies
in film and electronic media including
theory, history, and aesthetics
Special Activities: Film: film series/
festivals
Facilities: Television: control room
Equipment: Television/Video: ½"
cassette recorders; portable cameras;
monitors; sound recording equipment;
audio mixers; editing equipment
Alumni: Arnold Chase, TV executive;
Michael Gwinn, TV sports director

GUIDE POV: This small private college
offers critical grounding for students
planning to pursue post-graduate
training; competitive entry; cross-
registration with Brandeis University,
Pine Manor College, Wellesley College,
and Regis College; study opportunities
in France and Italy

BOSTON UNIVERSITY

640 Commonwealth Ave.,
Boston, MA 02215
(617)353–2000

*Private four-year comprehensive
institution. Coed, urban location.
Undergraduate enrollment: 16,000.
Graduate enrollment: 11,000.*

COLLEGE OF COMMUNICATION/SCHOOL OF BROADCASTING AND FILM

Chair/Contact: Mel Howard, Chair,
School of Broadcasting and Film
Calendar: Semesters
Degrees Offered: B.S., broadcasting,
film; M.S., broadcasting, film studies,
film production, broadcast
administration
Departmental Majors: Undergraduate
film and television: 325 students.
Graduate film and television: 100
students
Entrance Requirements:
Undergraduate: transcripts; competitive
grade-point average; ACT or SAT
scores (SAT preferred); essay required.
Graduate: 3.0 grade-point average; GRE

or MAT scores; writing samples; three letters of recommendation. Undergraduate application deadline: January 15. Graduate application deadline: rolling. Percent of acceptances: 65%

Curricular Emphasis: Comprehensive training in all aspects of film, video, and television production; film emphasis on independent narrative/fictional productions; four-level writing sequence; advanced courses in cinematography; postproduction; directing; computer graphics; producing; both film and television programs have a studies/masterworks/critical analysis component; management studies

Special Activities: Film: speaker series/festivals; film unit accepts assignments from outside clients. Television/Video: program material produced for BUTV cable television and for off-campus clients

Facilities: Film: sound stage; 35mm screening facilities; screening room; editing suites; sound mixing room; animation stand; film library. Television/Video: two 45' × 30' studios; audio bay; control room; video editing suites

Equipment: Film: complete 16mm; 35mm projectors. Television/Video: two complete ¾" studios; complete ¾" and ½" location; on-line and off-line editing; EFP equipment; ¾" U-Matic SP and VHS formats available

Alumni: Don Segall, film director/producer; Joe Roth, film producer/director/executive; Jean Firstenberg, director, A.F.I.; Ted Harbert, president, ABC Entertainment; Seth Abraham, president, Time Warner Sports; David Kelley, TV writer/producer; Allan Wegman, supervising TV editor

GUIDE POV: Comprehensive undergraduate and graduate production, critical, and management studies are offered at this quality-oriented university, founded in 1839; separate tracks for film and television majors; film department is "director" oriented and encourages the development of independent narrative productions; sequential television program is "producer" oriented; admission to either program is highly selective; extensive internship opportunities in film and television production

---

BRIDGEWATER STATE COLLEGE

Bridgewater, MA 02325
(508)697–1200

State four-year comprehensive institution. Coed, suburban location. Undergraduate enrollment: 6,000. Graduate enrollment: 2,000.

DEPARTMENT OF HIGH SCHOOL, MIDDLE SCHOOL, AND ADULT EDUCATION/LIBRARY MEDIA PROGRAM

Chair/Contact: Richard Neubauer
Calendar: Semesters
Degrees Offered: M.Ed., instructional media; M.Ed., library media studies
Entrance Requirements: Undergraduate: 2.8 grade-point average; ACT or SAT scores; personal statement of purpose. Graduate: 3.0 grade-point average; GRE scores; recommendations. Undergraduate and graduate application deadline: March 31. Percent of acceptances: 54%
Curricular Emphasis: school library media certification
Special Activities: Video: off-campus projects
Facilities: Television: studio; control room; recently completed J. Joseph

Moakley Center for Technological Applications includes computer-generated interactive learning as well as satellite-transmitted video, voice, and data communication resources

Equipment: Film: editing; lighting; projectors. Television/Video: complete ¾" studio; ½" cassette recorders; portable cameras; interactive video; 10-meter video and data satellite dish

Alumni: Larry Dedian, media executive; Curtis Bailey, TV cameraman; Arthur Slotnick, video production assistant

GUIDE POV: Founded in 1840, this state-supported college offers practical studies in media as well as a special graduate concentration in educational/instructional production; new video facilities; special interest in new video technologies; cross-registration with several area colleges and universities; study abroad in Canada, England, Germany, and China; internship opportunities in television production

CAPE COD COMMUNITY COLLEGE

Route 132,
W. Barnstable, MA 02668
(508)362–2131

State two-year institution. Coed, suburban location. Enrollment: 2,000.

FINE AND PERFORMING ARTS DEPARTMENT

Chair/Contact: Dale B. Lumsden; Robert Kidd
Degrees Offered: A.A., media concentration
Calendar: semesters
Departmental Majors: 25–30 studying in this area (there are no designated majors for the A.A. degree)

Entrance Requirements: High school diploma. Application deadline: August 15
Curricular Emphasis: Film: critical studies; history; aesthetics. Television: production; critical studies; video art; audio production
Special Activities: Television/Radio: program material produced for local educational public access cable television; FM radio station
Facilities: Film: screening room; videotape library. Television/Radio: studio (tape or live cablecast); audio studio; control rooms; editing rooms; FM radio station
Equipment: Film: lighting; projectors. Television: complete S-VHS studio; ½" cassette recorders; S-VHS editing equipment; remote video equipment; audio production facility
Alumni: Thomas Lowell, TV news director; Douglas Horton, video producer/director; Andrew Titcomb, video producer/director

GUIDE POV: Comprehensive practical training in audio and video production is offered at this affordable community college; core curriculum in the liberal arts; students enjoy a high transfer record to four-year schools; internship opportunities in television and radio production

CLARK UNIVERSITY

950 Main St.,
Worcester, MA 01610
(508)793–7711

Private four-year comprehensive institution. Coed, urban location. Undergraduate enrollment: 2,500. Graduate enrollment: 500.

SCREEN STUDIES PROGRAM/VISUAL AND PERFORMING ARTS DEPARTMENT

Chair/Contact: Marvin D'Lugo; Marcia Butzel; Dana Benelli
Calendar: Semesters
Degrees Offered: B.A., screen studies; B.A./B.F.A., studio art; B.A., theatre; concentration in communications
Departmental Majors: Undergraduate film and television (screen studies): 15 students
Entrance Requirements: Undergraduate: competitive grade-point average; ACT or SAT scores (SAT preferred); essay required; AT in English composition; interview recommended. Undergraduate application deadline: February 15. Percent of acceptances: 70%
Curricular Emphasis: Electronic media theory and culture; critical studies in film; basic video production training includes fiction, news, and video art
Special Activities: Film: film series/ festivals; film society
Equipment: Television/Video: complete ½" location
Alumni: Walter Henritze, communication and production services executive; Charles Slatkin, communication and production services executive

GUIDE POV: Clark University offers undergraduates a small media program intended to sharpen critical skills while providing basic training in video production; selective admissions; emphasis on film and electronic media theory; cross-registration and study abroad programs available

DEAN JUNIOR COLLEGE

99 Main St.,
Franklin, MA 02038
(508)528–9100

Private two-year institution. Coed, suburban location. Enrollment: 1,100.

COMMUNICATION ARTS DEPARTMENT

Chair/Contact: Nancy Kerr
Calendar: Semesters
Degrees Offered: A.A., communication arts
Departmental Majors: Television, radio, and journalism: 120 students
Entrance Requirements: SAT or ACT scores; interview. Application deadline: April 1. Percent of acceptances: 90%
Curricular Emphasis: Electronic media theory and culture; media writing; audio and video production; broadcast journalism
Special Activities: Television/Radio: program material produced for cable television; WGAO-FM; campus newspaper
Facilities: Television/Radio: studio; audio studio; control room; ¾" and ½" editing suites; eight-track audio recording studio; on-air studio; news room; production room
Equipment: Television/Video: complete ¾" studio; complete ½" location; ¾" and ½" editing; Amiga graphics; Chyron; eight-track audio lab; three stereo audio labs
Alumni: Betty Jo Cugini, TV producer; Robert Crowley, TV production assistant

GUIDE POV: Sequential audio and video production studies are offered at this private junior college; practical training for technical support positions; transfer program; internship opportunities in television and radio production as well as journalism

EMERSON COLLEGE

100 Beacon St.,
Boston, MA 02116
(617)578–8500

Private four-year comprehensive institution. Coed, urban location. Undergraduate enrollment: 2,000. Graduate enrollment: 400.

MASS COMMUNICATION DIVISION

Chair/Contact: David Gordon, Chair
Calendar: Semesters
Degrees Offered: B.A., B.S., mass communication (concentration in film or television); B.F.A., film; M.A., video
Departmental Majors:
Undergraduate: 990 students. Graduate: 100 students
Entrance Requirements:
Undergraduate: competitive grade-point average; SAT preferred (median scores 950–1150); ACT accepted; interview recommended. Graduate: GRE scores; recommendations; written statement of purpose; portfolio. Undergraduate application deadline: March 1. Graduate application deadline: rolling. Percent of acceptances: 70%
Curricular Emphasis: Independent and commercial film and television production; communication studies
Special Activities: Film: independent film screenings; film societies; film publication; student production group. Television: program material produced for on-campus closed-circuit television, for cable television, and for local commercial television station; student production group
Facilities: Film: screening room; editing suite; animation stand; optical printer. Television: studios; audio bay; control room; editing suites
Equipment: Film: complete Super-8 and 16mm. Television/Video: complete ¾" studio; complete ¾" and ½" location; on-line and off-line editing
Alumni: Norman Lear, TV producer/writer; Henry Winkler, TV actor/producer/director; Vin Di Bona, TV producer/director

GUIDE POV: Specializing in communications and the performing arts, Emerson College has concentrations in both film and television production taught in conjunction with liberal arts courses, as well as courses in current communication theory and critical studies; student production societies in film and video; student-designed, interdisciplinary, and dual majors available; cross-registration through the Professional Arts Consortium and Suffolk University; internship opportunities in film and television production

FITCHBURG STATE COLLEGE

160 Pearl St.,
Fitchburg, MA 01420
(508)345–2151

State four-year comprehensive institution. Coed, small city location. Undergraduate enrollment: 4,000. Graduate enrollment: 800.

DEPARTMENT OF COMMUNICATIONS/MEDIA

Chair/Contact: Dr. Charles H. Sides, Chair
Calendar: Semesters
Degrees Offered: B.S., television, film, graphics, technical communication, photography, interactive

Departmental Majors:
Undergraduate: 400–440 students
Entrance Requirements:
Undergraduate: 2.0 grade-point
average; academic rank within top
half of graduating class;
recommendations. Undergraduate
application deadline: March 1 for
freshmen; April 1 for transfers. Percent
of acceptances: 65%
Curricular Emphasis: Comprehensive
training in media arts including
graphics, interactive communications,
public relations, and advertising
Special Activities: Film: film series/
festivals include VISIONS, an annual
juried exhibition of student work.
Television/Video: program material
produced for various outlets
Facilities: Film: sound stage;
screening room; editing suite; sound
mixing room; animation stand.
Television: two complete full-color
studios; audio bays; control rooms;
editing suites; computer graphics
multi-image suite; interactive suites;
desktop publishing lab
Equipment: Film: complete 16mm.
Television/Video: complete ¾" studio
and location
Alumni: Michael Bavarro, film
director; Bill Fairweather,
postproduction supervisor

GUIDE POV: Communication majors at
Fitchburg State College enjoy an
innovative program that makes full use
of its modern facilities; specializations
in interactive communications,
graphics, technical communications,
television, and film; 90% job
placement for graduates; required
senior internships

FRAMINGHAM STATE COLLEGE

100 State St.,
Framington, MA 01701
(508)620–1220

*State four-year comprehensive
institution. Coed, suburban location.
Enrollment: 3,500.*

COMMUNICATION ARTS DEPARTMENT

Chair/Contact: Donna Walcovy
Calendar: Semesters
Degrees Offered: B.A.,
communication arts
Departmental Majors: 160 students
Entrance Requirements: 2.5 grade-
point average; SAT scores; statement
of purpose; interview; teachers'
recommendations. Application
deadline: March 1. Percent of
acceptances: 56%
Curricular Emphasis: Television:
studio and electronic field production;
broadcast writing; documentary
Special Activities: Film: film series/
festivals; film societies. Television:
program material produced for cable
television; member of AERho
(National Broadcasting Society);
vocational placement service
Facilities: Film: screening room.
Television: studio; audio bay; control
room; two audio production studios
Equipment: Film: 16mm projectors.
Television/Video: complete ¾" studio;
complete ¾" and ½" location
Alumni: Carlo DiPersio, computer
animation executive; Paul Huckui, TV
set designer

GUIDE POV: Located 20 miles west of
Boston, this state college offers a
degree program in television
production that combines theoretical
studies with practical application;
study abroad in Canada, France, and

Spain; individualized major and experimental unstructured programs offered; internship opportunities in television production

GREENFIELD COMMUNITY COLLEGE

1 College Dr.,
Greenfield, MA 01301
(413)774–3131

State two-year institution. Coed, rural location. Enrollment: 3,000.

ART PROGRAM/MEDIA EMPHASIS

Chair/Contact: Tom Boisvert, Director of media division
Calendar: Semesters
Degrees Offered: A.S., art (media emphasis)
Departmental Majors: Media: 35 students
Entrance Requirements: Open-door policy; transcripts; ACT or SAT scores; possible placement testing. Application deadline: rolling. Percent of acceptances: 95%
Curricular Emphasis: Television studio and field production; electronic studio production training; graphic design
Special Activities: Television: program material produced for on-campus closed-circuit and cable television
Facilities: Television: studio; audio bay; control room
Equipment: Television/Video: complete ¾" studio; complete ¾" and ½" location
Alumni: Garry Longe, video technician; Keith Clark, videographer

GUIDE POV: Specializing in preparing students for entry-level technical support positions in television and video, this small, media program involves students in all aspects of studio and field production; internship opportunities in television production

HAMPSHIRE COLLEGE

Amherst, MA 01002
(413)549–4600

Private four-year comprehensive institution. Coed, rural location. Enrollment: 1,100.

FILM/PHOTOGRAPHY PROGRAM

Chair/Contact: A. Ravett
Calendar: Semesters
Degrees Offered: B.A., film/photography/video
Departmental Majors: 60 students
Entrance Requirements: Transcripts; personal statement; critical essay or academic paper; teachers' recommendations; interview recommended; portfolio optional. Application deadline: February 1. Percent of acceptances: 60%
Curricular Emphasis: Experimental, documentary, and narrative filmmaking and video production; photography
Special Activities: Film: film series/festivals. Television: program material produced for on-campus closed-circuit television and for cable television; vocational placement service
Facilities: Film: screening room; editing suite; animation stand; optical printer; film library. Television: studio; audio bay; control room; image processing workstation
Equipment: Film: complete Super-8 and 16mm. Television/Video: complete ¾", ½", and Hi-8 studio and location
Alumni: Kenneth Burns, film director/producer; Robert Epstein, film director/producer; Thomas Sigel,

cinematographer; Amy Burns, film editor; Karen Goodman, film director/producer; Ezra Swerdlow, film producer; Emily Hubley, animator

GUIDE POV: Students at this selective liberal arts college may attend film and video classes at Amherst College, Mt. Holyoke College, Smith College, and the University of Massachusetts; individualized program of study; students may complete their programs in fewer than four years; study abroad; internship opportunities

HARVARD UNIVERSITY

Cambridge, MA 02138
(617)495-1000

Private four-year comprehensive institution. Coed, urban location. Undergraduate enrollment: 7,000. Graduate enrollment: 12,000.

VISUAL AND ENVIRONMENTAL STUDIES

Chair/Contact: Kathleen Chaudhry
Calendar: Semesters
Degrees Offered: B.A., with concentration in visual and environmental studies
Departmental Majors: Undergraduate film: 15 students
Entrance Requirements: Undergraduate: competitive grade-point average; ACT or SAT scores; recommendations; interview; written statement of purpose. Undergraduate application deadline: January 1. Percent of acceptances: 18%
Curricular Emphasis: Film Production—documentary, animation
Special Activities: Film: film series/festivals; film societies
Facilities: Film: 35mm screening facilities; screening room; editing suite;

sound mixing room; animation stand; film library
Equipment: Film/Video: complete 16mm; small format video
Alumni: Phillip Kaufman, screenwriter/film director; Glenn Jordan, film/TV director; Reginald Hudlin, film director/producer; Allen Moore, film director/producer; Mira Nair, film director/producer

GUIDE POV: Harvard University offers an undergraduate visual arts program drawing upon the disciplines of architecture and anthropology; students in the program focus on structure and meaning in the visual arts and the environment through both theoretical and practical explorations; emphasis on nonfiction film and video making; study abroad; local area internship opportunities

MASSACHUSETTS COLLEGE OF ART

621 Huntington Ave.,
Boston, MA 02115
(617)232-1555

Public four-year comprehensive arts institution. Coed, urban location. Undergraduate enrollment: 1,000. Graduate enrollment: 90.

MEDIA AND PERFORMING ARTS DEPARTMENT

Chair/Contact: Abelardo Morell, Chair
Calendar: Semesters
Degrees Offered: B.F.A., M.F.A., fine arts (with concentrations in film, photography, and Studio for Interrelated Media, including video)
Departmental Majors: Undergraduates: 60 students. Graduates: 12 students

Entrance Requirements:
Undergraduate: portfolio; personal essay required; interview recommended. Graduate: portfolio; recommendations. Undergraduate and graduate application deadline: May 1. Percent of acceptances: 35%

Curricular Emphasis: Film students are offered courses in Super-8 and 16mm film production, including experimental animation; Studio for Interrelated Media students focus on expanded use of ¾" format production, including computer animation, while exploring interdisciplinary work in artistic media such as light, projection, movement, xerography, audio synthesizer, photography, filmmaking, or tools of their own design; separate critical studies program in film criticism

Special Activities: Film/Video: visiting artists program; student showcases; exhibitions

Facilities: Film: screening room; editing suites; sound mixing room; animation stand. Video: sound studio; computer graphics center; editing suites

Equipment: Film: complete Super-8 and 16mm. Video: complete ¾" format; computer graphics equipment including Apple IIGS, Macintosh, IBM, Amiga microcomputers

Alumni: Louis Bortone, TV executive art director; Dolly Cahill, TV producer

GUIDE POV: Founded in 1873, this was the first school of professional art education in the United States; concentrations in film or interrelated media (including video); students are encouraged to explore use of new technologies; multidimensional performance/eventworks; film and computer animation; selective admissions; varied internship opportunities

MASSACHUSETTS INSTITUTE OF TECHNOLOGY

20 Ames St.,
Cambridge, MA 02139
(617)253–1000

Private four-year comprehensive institution. Coed, urban location. Undergraduate enrollment: 6,000. Graduate enrollment: 6,000.

SCHOOL OF ARCHITECTURE/MEDIA ARTS AND SCIENCES

Chair/Contact: Stephen A. Benton, Chair

Calendar: 4–1–4

Degrees Offered: B.S., interdisciplinary major (students may select emphasis in media arts and sciences); M.S., visual studies; Ph.D., media arts and sciences

Departmental Majors:
Undergraduate: 200 students. Graduate: 200 students

Entrance Requirements:
Undergraduate: competitive grade-point average; ACT or SAT scores; three ATs (math level I, level II, or level IIC; English or history, and either physics, chemistry, or biology); essay and interview required. Graduate: GRE scores; recommendations; interview. Undergraduate and graduate application deadline: early action deadline: November 1; final deadline: January 1. Percent of acceptances: undergraduate and graduate: 20%

Curricular Emphasis: Research and active exploration of multimedia productions including generation of multimedia prototypes; interactive tools for makers and viewers; and descriptive structures of representing content and context; current advanced research includes experiments in elastic media; computational partnerships in video editing; new tools for directors; and context-based representation for video

Special Activities: Film: Interactive Cinema Group. Video: special projects in new technologies

Facilities: Video: state-of-the-art video center including experimental video workstations

Equipment: Video: state-of-the-art equipment including interactive video; video finger; MacGlib video library; elastic tools, etc., as well as various new equipment under development

Alumni: Alan Lasky, visual effects supervisor; Hans Peter Brondmo, media software developer

GUIDE POV: Students participating in this newly created program will explore the study, invention, and creative use of new information technologies; advanced research includes work in spatial imaging; graphics and design; interactive cinema; computer graphics and animation, holography; elastic media; television of the future, and advanced human interface; extensive media research opportunities; graduate research assistantships; highly selective admissions

MERRIMACK COLLEGE

North Andover, MA 01845
(508)683–7111

Private four-year comprehensive institution. Coed, suburban location. Enrollment: 3,500.

DEPARTMENT OF FINE ARTS

Chair/Contact: David E. Raymond, Chair
Calendar: Semesters

Degrees Offered: B.A., fine arts (minor in film/video)

Entrance Requirements: 2.0 grade-point average; ACT or SAT scores; interview recommended; written statement of purpose required. Application deadline: March 1. Percent of acceptances: 65%

Curricular Emphasis: Film studies including theory; history; aesthetics

Special Activities: Film: screenings; speakers. Television: program material produced for local public and cable television

Facilities: Television: studio

Equipment: Television/Video: ¾" studio and ½" location.

Alumni: Kelly Lange, TV newswoman; Albert Brenner, screenwriter; Mike Macklin, TV newsman; Andrew Wolfendon, screenwriter

GUIDE POV: Through its small fine arts program, students are offered a variety of courses in film history and criticism as well as basic video production training; individualized instruction; emphasis on a broad liberal arts education with core requirements in philosophy, theology, and mathematics/science, among others; cross-registration; study abroad

MOUNT WACHUSETT COMMUNITY COLLEGE

444 Green St.,
Gardner, MA 01440–1000
(508)632–6600

State two-year institution. Coed, suburban location. Enrollment: 2,000.

BROADCASTING AND TELECOMMUNICATIONS DEPARTMENT

Chair/Contact: Dr. Vincent S. Ialenti, Chair

Calendar: Semesters
Degrees Offered: A.S., broadcasting and telecommunications
Departmental Majors: Broadcasting and telecommunications: 110 students
Entrance Requirements: SAT or ACT scores; interview; teachers' recommendations. Application deadline: June 30. Percent of acceptances: 85%
Curricular Emphasis: Hands-on television production; broadcast writing; electronic media operations and management; photography; audio multitrack recording
Special Activities: Television: program material produced for on-campus closed-circuit television and cable television
Facilities: Television: two full-color studios; four audio bays; three editing suites; two control rooms; master control room; photo lab
Equipment: Television: two complete ¾" studios and ¾" location; mobile video remote van; multitrack audio recording suite; multisource video editing suite with computer graphics; edit decisionlist storage; digital video effects; EFP units
Alumni: Jeff Deiana, TV producer; Kevin A. Berg, TV producer; Mark Moran, cinematographer

GUIDE POV: This well-equipped two-year school offers career broadcast training; emphasis on new technologies; transfer program to four-year institutions; varied internship opportunities in television production

NORTH ADAMS STATE COLLEGE

Church St.,
North Adams, MA 01247
(413)664–4511

State four-year comprehensive institution. Coed, rural location. Enrollment: 1,700.

ENGLISH/COMMUNICATIONS DEPARTMENT

Chair/Contact: Harris Elder, Chair
Calendar: Semesters
Degrees Offered: B.A., English (concentration in broadcast media)
Departmental Majors: Television: 100 students
Entrance Requirements: Transcripts; ACT or SAT scores; interview; essay. Application deadline: May 1. Percent of acceptances: 48%
Curricular Emphasis: Television production and scripting
Special Activities: Television: program material produced for on-campus closed-circuit and cable television includes news, sports, and entertainment magazine shows; sponsored projects for nonprofit organizations; member National Broadcasting Society
Facilities: Film: screening room. Television: studio; control room; editing suite
Equipment: Television/Video: complete four-camera ¾" studio; complete ¾" editing
Alumni: David Steiner, video producer; Lori Carter, TV producer

GUIDE POV: Broadcast media students at this competitive college are offered a strong core curriculum that includes traditional literary studies as well as those in modern communications; students obtain studio and field production experience; cross-registration with area colleges; internship opportunities in television production

NORTHEASTERN UNIVERSITY

360 Huntington Ave.,
Boston, MA 02115
(617)372–2200

*Private four-year comprehensive
institution. Coed, urban location.
Undergraduate enrollment: 23,000.
Graduate enrollment: 5,300.*

PROGRAM IN CINEMA STUDIES

Chair/Contact: Dr. Inez Hedges, Chair
Calendar: Quarters
Degrees Offered: B.A. (with minor in
cinema studies)
Entrance Requirements:
Undergraduate: competitive grade-
point average; SAT (or ACT) scores;
essay required; interview
recommended. Undergraduate
application deadline: rolling. Percent
of acceptances: 75%
Curricular Emphasis: Film theory,
cultural studies; video production
Special Activities: Television:
program material produced for on-
campus closed-circuit television; ITFS/
satellite distribution.
Facilities: Television: studio; control
room; editing suites
Equipment: Television/Video:
complete ¾" studio and ½" location;
AVID computer editing system; ¾" A/B
roll editing with Paltex
Alumni: Matthew Herron, filmmaker;
Susan Brandon, filmmaker; Lorrie
Murray, video artist; Sasha Berman,
film archivist

GUIDE POV: Northeastern University
offers students an interdisciplinary
program of film studies for those
choosing a major in arts and sciences,
business, computer science, or
engineering; theoretical film studies
coupled with hands-on video
production training; study abroad in
Ireland, Northern Ireland, England,
and Russia; internship opportunities in
television production; university
committed to a cooperative education
plan for students seeking employment
to help finance their education

QUINSIGAMOND COMMUNITY COLLEGE

670 W. Boylston St.,
Worcester, MA 01606
(508)853–2300

*State two-year comprehensive
institution. Coed, urban location.
Enrollment: 2,500.*

HUMANITIES DEPARTMENT

Chair/Contact: Film: Carl Sundell
Calendar: Semesters
Degrees Offered: A.A., humanities
Entrance Requirements: Open-door
policy; high school diploma or
equivalent. Application deadline:
rolling. Percent of acceptances: 99%
Curricular Emphasis: Film criticism
Special Activities: Film: film series

GUIDE POV: Through its Humanities
Department, this small community
college offers several courses in film
history, theory, and criticism; transfer
program to area schools

SCHOOL OF THE MUSEUM OF FINE ARTS

230 The Fenway,
Boston, MA 02115
(617)267–6100

*Private four-year comprehensive arts
institution. Coed, urban location.
Undergraduate enrollment: 620.
Graduate enrollment: 50.*

Chair/Contact: Patricia Barsoumian
Calendar: Semesters
Degrees Offered: B.F.A., M.F.A., film, video, animation; B.F.A. with B.A. or B.S., combined five-year degree program; M.A.T.
Entrance Requirements:
Undergraduate: transcripts; portfolio. Graduate: transcripts; portfolio; three recommendations; statement of purpose. Undergraduate and graduate application deadline: February 15
Curricular Emphasis: Fine arts program with training in film, video, and animated production; combined five-year program leads to B.F.A. and either B.A. or B.S., depending on the second major field
Special Activities: Film: screenings; visiting artists; summer programs in Europe
Facilities: Film: screening room; editing suite; sound mixing room; animation stand; film library. Video: studio; editing bays
Equipment: Film: complete Super-8 and 16mm. Video: complete ¾" studio; ¾" and Hi-8/V-8 editing; special effects generator; digital visual effects unit
Alumni: Evans Brown, filmmaker; Kip Chinian, filmmaker; Flip Johnson, animator; Richard Lerman, film sound technician

GUIDE POV: A department of the Museum of Fine Arts, this private institution awards both undergraduate and graduate degrees in the visual arts; graduate programs offered in affiliation with Tufts University; faculty of practicing media artists; varied internship opportunities

SUFFOLK UNIVERSITY

Beacon Hill, 8 Ashburton Pl.,
Boston, MA 02108–2772
(617)573–8000

Private four-year comprehensive institution. Coed, urban location. Undergraduate enrollment: 2,200. Graduate enrollment: 2,500.

FILM/TV PROGRAM

Chair/Contact: Vicki Karns
Calendar: Semesters
Degrees Offered: B.A., B.S., communication (students may select emphasis in mass communications); B.A., B.S.J., journalism (students may select emphasis in broadcast journalism)
Entrance Requirements:
Undergraduate: academic rank within upper 60% of graduating class; ACT or SAT scores; recommendations and essay required; interview recommended. Undergraduate application deadline: July 1. Percent of acceptances: 82%
Curricular Emphasis:
Communications Department: mass communications track offers sequential course listings in radio, television, and cable production; popular culture track introduces students to critical perspectives on film, music, and popular culture. Journalism Department: broadcast journalism track offers emphasis in radio and television journalism
Special Activities: Television: program material produced for local commercial television station and for on-campus closed-circuit television
Facilities: Film: screening room. Television: studio; control room
Equipment: Television/Video: complete ¾" studio and location

Alumni: Dan Jaehnig, TV producer; Casey Carter, TV producer; George Comeau, TV producer

GUIDE POV: Students at Suffolk University are provided with technical career training in radio, television, and cable production; additional courses in film studies; broadcast journalism track includes sequential program in media writing; cross-registration with the New England School of Arts and Design; study abroad in 20 countries; numerous co-op and work-study programs available in Boston area; internship opportunities in television production and broadcast journalism

TUFTS UNIVERSITY

Medford, MA 02155
(617)628–5000

Private four-year comprehensive institution. Coed, urban location. Undergraduate enrollment: 4,300. Graduate and professional school enrollment: 1,700.

COMMUNICATIONS AND MEDIA STUDIES PROGRAM

Chair/Contact: Robyn Gittleman, Director, Experimental College
Calendar: Semesters
Degrees Offered: B.A., B.S.
Entrance Requirements:
Undergraduate: competitive grade-point average; ACT or SAT scores; three ATs required including English composition for all liberal arts applicants; personal essay required; recommendations. Undergraduate application deadline: January 1. Percent of acceptances: 40%
Curricular Emphasis: Electronic media theory and culture; critical studies in film
Special Activities: Film: film series/festivals. Television: program material produced for cable television and on-campus closed-circuit television
Facilities: Film: screening room; film/video library
Equipment: Television/Video: ¾" VTR; ½" cassette recorders; portable cameras; monitors
Alumni: William Hurt, film actor; Steven Tisch, TV/film producer; Jeffrey Greenstein, TV and film writer

GUIDE POV: This highly competitive private institution presents undergraduates with a critical foundation in film theory, aesthetics, and history including basic independent film/video production training; graduate programs in the visual arts are offered by the School of the Museum of Fine Arts affiliated with Tufts University; cross-registration with Boston College, Boston University, and Brandeis University; study abroad; internships available

UNIVERSITY OF MASSACHUSETTS AT AMHERST

101 S. College,
Amherst, MA 01003
(413)545–0111

State four-year comprehensive institution. Coed, rural location. Undergraduate enrollment: 17,000. Graduate enrollment: 6,000.

INTERDEPARTMENTAL PROGRAM IN FILM STUDIES

Chair/Contact: Catherine Portuges, Chair; Eva Rueschmann
Calendar: Semesters

Degrees Offered: Certificate in film studies

Entrance Requirements: Undergraduate: competitive grade-point average; ACT or SAT scores; written statement of purpose. Undergraduate application deadline: February 15. Percent of acceptances: 55%

Curricular Emphasis: Interdisciplinary humanities, fine arts, and social and behavioral sciences program offers courses in theory and history of film, genre, director, and national cinemas, screenwriting, film and television production

Special Activities: Film: visiting artists; screenings; festivals; Five-College film studies exchange; pilot exchange program with Springfield Technical Community College

Facilities: Film: screening room; editing room; animation stand. Television: studio; audio studio; control room

Equipment: Film: 16mm cameras; editing equipment; lighting; black-and-white film stock; projectors. Television/Video: complete ½" location

Alumni: Bill Cosby, film and TV actor/writer/producer; Richard Gere, film actor

GUIDE POV: This interdepartmental and intercollegial certificate program, instituted in 1991, provides an integrated course of studies in film and video as contemporary art forms; on-campus coordination of film/video equipment and facilities; students benefit from Five-College film studies exchange with Amherst College, Mt. Holyoke, Smith, Hampshire; study abroad in 20 countries; internship opportunities in film and video production

UNIVERSITY OF MASSACHUSETTS AT BOSTON

Harbor Campus, 100 Morrissey Blvd., Boston, MA 02125
(617)287–5000

State four-year comprehensive institution. Coed, urban location. Undergraduate enrollment: 11,000. Graduate enrollment: 3,000.

ART DEPARTMENT

Chair/Contact: John Gianvito; Ron Polito

Calendar: Semesters

Degrees Offered: B.A., art (film and video program)

Departmental Majors: Undergraduate: 180 students

Entrance Requirements: Undergraduate: 2.0 grade-point average; SAT scores (minimum 800 composite); submission of essay recommended; ACT may be substituted for the SAT. Undergraduate application deadline: June 15. Percent of acceptances: 60%

Curricular Emphasis: Film/Video studies and training with an emphasis on independent/experimental production

Special Activities: Film: Underground Film Society is student-run; visiting artists

Facilities: Film/Video: screening room; editing suites; film/video library

Equipment: Film/Video: Panasonic ½" video cameras; Sony Hi-8mm cameras; JVC ½" video editing decks; Super-8 cameras (Elmo, Minolta, and Bauer, among others); editing equipment; Lowell lighting equipment

Alumni: Betsy Conners, videographer/holographer; Anne Robertson, film/TV actress

GUIDE POV: Art Department majors choosing courses within the film and video program will be introduced to a variety of possible personal approaches to the film and video mediums; faculty of practicing media artists; study abroad; internship opportunities in film and video production

WORCESTER STATE COLLEGE

486 Chandler St.,
Worcester, MA 01602
(508)793–8000

State four-year comprehensive institution. Coed, urban location. Undergraduate enrollment: 4,000. Graduate enrollment: 1,600.

MEDIA, ARTS, AND PHILOSOPHY DEPARTMENT

Chair/Contact: Don Bullens, Chair
Calendar: Semesters
Degrees Offered: B.A., B.S., media (students may select emphasis in communication media); B.A., media (students may select emphasis in theatre)
Entrance Requirements: Undergraduate: competitive grade-point average; SAT scores required. Undergraduate application deadline: August 12. Percent of acceptances: 67%
Curricular Emphasis: Electronic media theory and culture; critical studies in film; media writing; film, video, and television production including film and computer animation; media management
Special Activities: Film: film series/festivals. Television: program material produced for on-campus closed-circuit television
Facilities: Film: editing suites; animation stand; film library. Television: studio; audio bay; control room; editing suites; computer animation equipment
Equipment: Film: complete Super-8. Television/Video: complete ¾" studio; complete ¾" and ½" location, including editing equipment
Alumni: Kelly McGee, TV news anchor; Bruce Chamberlain, public access executive

GUIDE POV: Established in 1874, this state college, located 40 miles west of Boston, offers students full training in both film and television production; diverse course listings; exploration of experimental, news, animation, narrative, and documentary forms; internship opportunities in film and television production

I completed my undergraduate film studies at Howard University in Washington, D.C. Fortunately, our class was blessed with an artistically sensitive group of instructors. I minored in playwriting, which led to my attending UCLA as a playwriting major. And while there I studied screenwriting.

I received a master's in stage directing from Catholic University of America, in Washington, D.C. And most recently I attended the American Film Institute as a directing fellow. Since then I have written on the staff of two television shows, "The New Odd Couple" and "227." In addition, I wrote my first feature, *A Rage in Harlem*, for Palace Productions.

Writer-director-producer is the hyphenate best expressing my aspirations. Indeed, it reflects both my film school studies and professional experience.

Having had the benefit of a formal film education, I cannot but feel it is an essential ingredient for success in this business. A formal education in any art form can't help but enlighten the aspirant. Santayana said: "Those who do not remember the past are condemned to repeat it." So it is with cinema. The pioneers of the film language have experimented with its grammar for many years. Mistakes have been made, innovations have emerged, and much has been learned from both the successes and failures of that art form. To ignore the value of what has been done is to doom ourselves to repeat past failures.

Every day the art form grows in technical sophistication. It's even tough for professionals to keep up. The film school environment provides an atmosphere in which learning and experimentation can take place without the overwhelming concerns of mainstream productions. This is not to say a student shoot is without its own brand of pressure. Indeed, when you've invested your last dime in your student film and when you haven't slept or eaten in four days, when the producer can't secure your most important location, and your lead actor is hired away on a "real film" for "real money," it's difficult to imagine a greater pressure cooker. However, this is all great preparation for the real movie-making world. You learn how to make monumental adjustments—how to cut corners and move mountains. In short, you learn how to overcome tremendous obstacles to finish your production.

My best advice to potential screenwriters and directors is to look for the truth in everything you write and in every moment you shoot. Be astute students of cinema, but be even more astute students of life. The medium is replete with examples of form without content. Too often students look to other films for ideas instead of looking to life. Live life and let it inform every frame of your work. All of the great films have done this.

ADRIAN COLLEGE

110 S. Madison St.,
Adrian, MI 49221
(517)265–5161

*Private four-year comprehensive
institution. Coed, urban location.
Enrollment: 1,600.*

DEPARTMENT OF COMMUNICATION ARTS AND SCIENCES

Chair/Contact: Sheri Bleam, Chair
Calendar: Semesters
Degrees Offered: B.A.,
communication arts and sciences
(students may select emphasis in
broadcasting)
Departmental Majors: Television: 50
students
Entrance Requirements: 2.8 grade-
point average; ACT or SAT scores;
written statement of purpose; interview
recommended. Application
deadline: August 15. Percent of
acceptances: 80%
Curricular Emphasis: Electronic
media theory and culture; media
writing; television/video production;
news/documentary; video art; media
management
Special Activities: Television:
program material produced for cable
television
Facilities: Television: studio; audio
bay; control room
Equipment: Television: matched
studio cameras; ¾" VTR; ¾" and ½"
cassette recorders; portable cameras;
sound recording equipment; monitors;
audio mixers; switcher/special effects
generator
Alumni: Wanda Doerner, TV news
editor; LuAnn Sharp, TV news director

GUIDE POV: This competitive liberal
arts college offers a media program
focusing on broadcast production;
journalism emphasis; cross-registration
with Siena Heights College; co-op
programs with American College,
London; study abroad in eight
countries; internship opportunities in
television production

CENTRAL MICHIGAN UNIVERSITY

Mount Pleasant, MI 48859
(517)774–4000

*State four-year comprehensive
institution. Coed, rural location.
Undergraduate enrollment: 17,000.
Graduate enrollment: 2,000.*

BROADCASTING AND CINEMATIC ARTS

Chair/Contact: B. R. Smith; J. Robert
Craig
Calendar: Semesters
Degrees Offered: B.A., B.A.A., B.F.A.,
B.S., M.A., broadcast and cinematic
arts
Departmental Majors:
Undergraduate: 400 students. Graduate:
15 students

Entrance Requirements:
Undergraduate: ACT or SAT scores.
Graduate: 2.7 grade-point average;
interview. Undergraduate and graduate
application deadline: rolling. Percent
of acceptances: 80%
Curricular Emphasis: Film: master's
program in critical studies. Television/
Video: production techniques; radio
and television news; electronic media
writing; media law and management
Special Activities: Television:
program material produced for cable
television
Facilities: Film: editing suites;
screening room. Television/Radio: two
three-camera color studios; audio
studio; control room; graphics facility;
300-watt stereo FM station; newsroom;
radio editing console lab
Equipment: Television: complete ¾"
studio; complete ¾" and ½" location
Alumni: Marilyn Doran, TV/film
producer; Phil Sgriccia, TV associate
producer; Sam Merrill, TV news
anchor; Sue Delia, TV sales manager

GUIDE POV: This competitive public
university offers critical film studies as
well as complete television production
training; emphasis on broadcast
journalism and media management;
study abroad in eight countries;
internships in television production

COLLEGE OF ART AND DESIGN

Center for Creative Studies,
201 E. Kirby,
Detroit, MI 48202
(313)872–3188

*Private four-year comprehensive arts
institution. Coed, urban location.
Enrollment: 1,000.*

VIDEO DEPARTMENT

Chair/Contact: Connie Bruner
Calendar: Semesters
Degrees Offered: B.F.A., video
Entrance Requirements: 2.5 grade-
point average; ACT scores; portfolio
and interview required. Application
deadline: March. Percent of
acceptances: 65%
Curricular Emphasis: Video and
8mm film production with an
emphasis on experimental,
documentary, and animation
Special Activities: Film/Video: film
series/showcases; visiting artists;
exhibitions; mixed-media installations
Facilities: Film: editing suites; sound
mixing room. Television: studio; audio
bay; control room; editing suites
Equipment: Film: complete Super-8.
Television/Video: complete ¾" studio;
complete ¾" and ½" location and
editing
Alumni: James Hood, TV sound
technician; John Schuchard, computer
animation specialist

GUIDE POV: Offering degrees in fine
arts, this small private college provides
separate, intensive one-year courses in
video production and 8mm film
production; emphasis on creative
expression; study abroad; some local
production internships available

DELTA COLLEGE

University Center, MI, 48710
(517)686–9000

*State two-year comprehensive
institution. Coed, rural location.
Enrollment: 14,000.*

BROADCASTING AND TELECOMMUNICATIONS DEPARTMENT

Chair/Contact: Television: Chris Lamar; Harold Briscoe
Calendar: Semesters
Degrees Offered: A.A., broadcasting and telecommunications
Departmental Majors: Television: 150 students
Entrance Requirements: Open-door policy; ACT or SAT scores; placement testing. Application deadline: rolling. Percent of acceptances: 99%
Curricular Emphasis: Television, video, and radio production including news; documentary; public affairs; features; sports; instructional/industrial
Special Activities: Film: hands-on experience at PBS production facility. Television: program material produced for local public television station
Facilities: Television: studio; audio bay; control room
Equipment: Television/Video: complete 1" studio; complete ¾" and ½" location
Alumni: Glen Groeschen, TV network news bureau chief; Paul Adler, corporate media director; Tony Ayala, CNN videotape editor

GUIDE POV: Featuring complete studio and remote production facilities, this two-year program prepares students for a variety of technical support positions in the broadcast, cable, and corporate media industries; seminar courses on topical issues; transfer program; internship opportunities in film and television production

EASTERN MICHIGAN UNIVERSITY

Ypsilanti, MI 48197
(313)487–1849

State four-year comprehensive institution. Coed, urban location. Undergraduate enrollment: 20,000. Graduate enrollment: 5,000.

TELECOMMUNICATIONS AND FILM DEPARTMENT

Chair/Contact: Dennis Beagen
Calendar: Semesters
Degrees Offered: B.A., B.S.
Departmental Majors: Undergraduate film: 50 students. Undergraduate television: 300 students
Entrance Requirements: Undergraduate: 2.5 grade-point average; ACT (minimum 17) or SAT (700 composite) scores; essay recommended. Undergraduate application deadline: March 1. Percent of acceptances: 65%
Curricular Emphasis: Electronic media including radio, television, cable, and film; program provides balance between theory and production
Special Activities: Television: program material produced for on-campus closed-circuit television and for cable television; corporate video projects
Facilities: Film: screening room; editing suite; 35mm screening facilities; animation stand; permanent film library. Television: studio; audio bay; control room
Equipment: Film: complete 16mm. Television/Video: complete ¾" studio; complete ¾" and ½" location
Alumni: Dann Florek, TV actor; Dennis Cockrum, TV actor; Suzanne Ogden, TV actress

GUIDE POV: The flexible liberal arts program at this competitive public university prepares students for graduate study or for entry-level positions in production and management; students work on a variety of projects; study abroad; cross-registration with the University of Michigan at Ann Arbor and Concordia and Washtenaw community colleges; required internships

FERRIS STATE UNIVERSITY

Big Rapids, MI 49307
(616)592–2000

State four-year comprehensive institution. Coed, small town location. Enrollment: 13,000.

TELEVISION PRODUCTION DEPARTMENT

Chair/Contact: Fred Wyman
Calendar: Quarters (until Fall 1993)
Degrees Offered: B.S., television production
Departmental Majors: Television (includes required film sequence): 200 students
Entrance Requirements: Open-door policy; high school graduate or equivalent; ACT (minimum 16) scores. Application deadline: rolling
Curricular Emphasis: Professional video production with an emphasis on nonbroadcast; basic 16mm production; developing multimedia
Special Activities: Television: program material produced for cable television; ITVA chapter
Facilities: Film: editing suite; sound mixing room. Television: studio; audio bay; control room
Equipment: Film: complete 16mm Bolex, Beaulieu. Television/Video: complete ¾" studio and location; A/B roll time code editing; U-matic SP; computer graphics; 8-Channel audio
Alumni: Kathy Buko, TV/film

producer; Pam Moore, TV producer; Sean Quinn, video producer/writer

GUIDE POV: Ferris State University, established in 1884, offers a full major in television production with a special focus on corporate video; faculty of working professionals; strong hands-on approach; study abroad; required six-month production internships at local corporate facilities

GRAND VALLEY STATE UNIVERSITY

Allendale, MI 49401
(616)895–6611

State four-year comprehensive institution. Coed, rural location. Undergraduate enrollment: 14,000; Graduate enrollment: 2,000.

SCHOOL OF COMMUNICATIONS

Chair/Contact: Dr. Alex Nesterenko
Calendar: Semesters
Degrees Offered: B.A., B.S., film and video production; B.A., B.S., broadcasting; M.S., communication
Departmental Majors:
Undergraduate: 600 students. Graduate: 50 students
Entrance Requirements:
Undergraduate: 2.7 grade-point average; ACT or SAT; AP and CLEP credit accepted. Graduate: 3.0 grade-point average; GRE scores; essay; professional recommendations. Undergraduate and graduate application deadline: rolling. Percent of acceptances: 72%
Curricular Emphasis: Film: history and aesthetics, 16mm production techniques, dramatic, documentary, animation, experimental, screenwriting, cinematography,

directing, lighting, postproduction, developing technologies, advanced workshops. Television/Video: critical studies; video production techniques; news/documentary; business and educational media; computer image making; video art; broadcast operations

Special Activities: Film: screenings; showcases. Television: program material produced for local public television station

Facilities: Film: screening room; editing room; animation stand. Television: studio; audio studio; control room; video editing suites

Equipment: Film: complete Super-8 and 16mm cameras. Television: complete ¾" studio; complete ¾" and ½" location

Alumni: Tim Wiles, property master; Chris Farley, production assistant

GUIDE POV: Featuring a small well-equipped program, this competitive state university offers studies in theory and aesthetics as well as professional production training in film, video art, and television; study abroad in Europe, Japan, and Mexico; local and national internship opportunities in film and television production

HENRY FORD COMMUNITY COLLEGE

5101 Evergreen Rd.,
Dearborn, MI 48128
(313)271–2750

State two-year institution. Coed, suburban location. Enrollment: 16,000.

PERFORMING ARTS/MASS COMMUNICATION

Chair/Contact: Jay B. Korinek, Chair
Calendar: Semesters

Degrees Offered: A.A., mass communication

Departmental Majors: 30 students

Entrance Requirements: High school diploma or GED certificate; 2.0 grade-point average; ACT or SAT scores. Application deadline: rolling. Percent of acceptances: 95%

Curricular Emphasis: Electronic media theory and culture; media writing; audio and video production

Special Activities: Film: film series/festivals. Television: program material produced for cable television

Facilities: Film: editing suite; sound stage; film library. Television: studio; audio bay; control room

Equipment: Film: 35mm SLR still cameras for composition and lighting exercises; video equipment. Television: complete ½" studio and location

Alumni: Michael McKenzie, radio program director/disc jockey; Susie Pepera, radio program director/disc jockey; Teri Richardson, radio disc jockey

GUIDE POV: The associate of arts program in mass communication provides students with core requirements for easy transfer to a four-year university program; training for technical support positions; broadcast journalism emphasis; internship opportunities in television production

HOPE COLLEGE

Holland, MI 49423–3698
(616)392–5111

Private four-year comprehensive institution. Coed, suburban location. Enrollment: 3,000.

COMMUNICATION DEPARTMENT

Chair/Contact: Television: Theodore L. Nielsen
Calendar: Semesters
Degrees Offered: B.A., communication
Departmental Majors: Television: 75 students
Entrance Requirements: Academic rank within top half of high school graduating class; recommendations; ACT or SAT scores; essay required; interview recommended. Application deadline: rolling. Percent of acceptances: 85%
Curricular Emphasis: Electronic media theory, history, and analysis; radio and television production; emphasis in nonfiction television
Special Activities: Film: film series/ festivals. Television: program material produced for on-campus closed-circuit television, cable television, and broadcast formats
Facilities: Television: studio; audio bay; control room; editing suite
Equipment: Television/Video: complete ¾" and Hi-8 studio and location
Alumni: Gary Kirchner, TV executive; Kevin Vanderkolk, location manager; Cathy Dannecker, video news editor

GUIDE POV: Founded by Dutch pioneers in 1866, this competitive private college offers a degree program emphasizing nonfiction television production; extensive study abroad program; national and regional internship opportunities in television and radio production

LANSING COMMUNITY COLLEGE

P.O. Box 40010,
Lansing, MI 48901–9963
(517)483–1957

State/city two-year comprehensive institution. Coed, urban location. Enrollment: 22,000.

MEDIA DEPARTMENT

Chair/Contact: Bill Blanchard
Calendar: Semesters
Degrees Offered: A.A.S., applied science (with emphasis in film or radio/TV/media); A.A.S., photographic technology
Departmental Majors: Film: 100; television: 100; still photo: 400; computer graphics: 250 students
Entrance Requirements: Open-door policy; placement tests; 18 years or older. Application deadline: rolling
Curricular Emphasis: Film: 16mm production techniques, dramatic, documentary, animation, experimental, story development, cinematography, directing, lighting, postproduction, developing technologies, advanced workshops. Television/Video: video production techniques, news and documentary, instructional and industrial, computer graphics, multi-image
Special Activities: Film: annual student film festival; FOCUS workshop on advancing technologies; film newsletter. Television: program material produced for cable television; vocational placement service
Facilities: Film: 16mm and electronic postproduction; animation stand. Television: studio; audio studio; control room
Equipment: Film: 16mm cameras; sound and editing for 16mm production; animation; sound

recording equipment; location lighting; projectors. Television: complete ¾" studio; complete ¾" and ½" location

Alumni: Wendy Stanzler, producer/editor; Larry Marshall, cinematographer/editor; Richard Poland, associate producer

GUIDE POV: Featuring an unusually diverse program for a two-year college, this school provides course listings that cover student interests ranging from new video technologies and multi-image workshops to experimental filmmaking; writing integrated at every level of program; separate concentrations in film and television; high transfer record to area schools; internship opportunities in film and television production

MADONNA UNIVERSITY

36600 Schoolcraft Rd.,
Livonia, MI 48150
(313)591–5000

Private four-year comprehensive institution. Coed, suburban location. Enrollment: 1,250.

VIDEO COMMUNICATION DEPARTMENT

Chair/Contact: Charles D. Derry
Calendar: Semesters
Degrees Offered: A.A., B.A., video communication
Departmental Majors: 10–50 students
Entrance Requirements: Transcripts; 2.5 grade-point average; ACT scores; interview recommended; GED accepted; AP and CLEP credit accepted. Application deadline: August 15. Percent of acceptances: 90%
Curricular Emphasis: All aspects of video production including hands-on work in single and multiple camera

production; editing; telecommunications; writing for media; media management and budgeting

Special Activities: Film: film series/festivals. Television: student-produced 30-minute interview program that is nationally distributed for cable television

Facilities: Television: studio; audio bay; control room; editing suites; cable origination

Equipment: Television/Video: complete ¾" studio and location with teleprompter, superscribe character generator and special effects generator; ¾", S-VHS, and VHS recording capability; cut and paste editing; CMX computerized editing

Alumni: Robert Ade, TV news reporter/cameraman; Denise McKeague, TV producer; Michelle Rust, TV producer; Brian Beleskey, audio engineer; Anne Sullivan, TV producer/writer

GUIDE POV: Affiliated with the Roman Catholic Church, this competitive liberal arts college offers a degree program designed to prepare students for entry into the video production field; flexible scheduling; diverse student body; cross-registration with Marygrove, Mercy, and St. Mary of Orchard Lake colleges, Sacred Heart Seminary, and the University of Detroit; study abroad in England and Taiwan; internship opportunities in television production

MICHIGAN STATE UNIVERSITY

East Lansing, MI 48824
(517)355–1855

State four-year comprehensive institution. Coed, urban location.

Undergraduate enrollment: 33,000.
Graduate enrollment: 9,000.

TELECOMMUNICATIONS DEPARTMENT

Chair/Contact: Barry Litman, Chair
Calendar: Semesters
Degrees Offered:
Telecommunications Department: B.A.,
M.A., telecommunication; Ph.D., mass
media. Film studies program:
certificate in film studies
Departmental Majors: Undergraduate
television: 250 students. Graduate
television: 10 students
Entrance Requirements:
Undergraduate: competitive ACT or
SAT scores; recommendations.
Undergraduate and graduate
application deadline: December 1.
Percent of acceptances: 70%
Curricular Emphasis: Electronic
media theory and culture, media
writing, television/video production;
graduate program focuses on media
management, communication theory;
film history and aesthetics
classes offered through film studies
program
Special Activities: Film: film series/
festivals presented by film studies
program. Television: program material
produced for on-campus closed-circuit
television, local public television
station, cable television, and
commercial television station in
Detroit
Facilities: Television: two studios; six
audio bays (including one 24-track
audio studio); control room; editing
suites
Equipment: Film: 16mm editing
equipment. Television/Video: complete
¾" studio; complete ¾" and ½"
location
Alumni: Frank Price, studio executive;
Jim Cash, screenwriter; Jack Epps, Jr.,
screenwriter

GUIDE POV: A pioneer land-grant
institution founded in 1855, this is one
of the largest universities in the
country; selective admissions;
Telecommunications Department
offers comprehensive course listings
with an emphasis on production;
graduate program stresses media
management and studies in
communication theory; separate,
theory-oriented film studies program
offers undergraduate certificate only;
study abroad in 15 countries;
internship opportunities in television
production

MUSKEGON COMMUNITY COLLEGE

221 S. Quarterline Rd.,
Muskegon, MI 49442
(616)773–9131

County two-year institution. Coed, urban
location. Enrollment: 6,000.

ENGLISH/COMMUNICATIONS DEPARTMENT

Chair/Contact: Film: Kent De Young;
television: Dave Mooney
Calendar: Semesters
Degrees Offered: A.A., media
Departmental Majors: Film: 5
students. Television: 15 students
Entrance Requirements: Open-door
policy; high school diploma or
equivalent; placement testing.
Application deadline: rolling. Percent
of acceptances: 99%
Curricular Emphasis: Film course
work concentrates on theoretical
studies; use of educational media;
documentary and instructional
production. Television course work
centers on television and video
production emphasizing broadcast
journalism
Special Activities: Film: film series/

festivals. Television: program material produced for cable television and for on-campus closed-circuit television
Facilities: Film: screening room; editing suite; sound mixing room; animation stand; film library. Television: studio; audio bay; control room
Equipment: Film: complete Super-8. Television/Video: complete S-VHS studio and location; Amiga graphics
Alumni: Dan Eley, CNN TV director; Julie Finnerman, TV producer/performer

GUIDE POV: Preparing students for entry-level career positions in video and television, this small two-year program focuses on studio and field broadcasting training; basic studies in 8mm film production; internship opportunities in television production

NORTHERN MICHIGAN UNIVERSITY

Marquette, MI 49885
(906)227–1000

State four-year comprehensive institution. Coed, urban location. Undergraduate enrollment: 7,500. Graduate enrollment: 1,000.

DEPARTMENT OF ART AND DESIGN

Chair/Contact: Michael Cinelli
Calendar: Semesters
Degrees Offered: B.A., B.S., B.F.A., M.A., M.A.E.
Departmental Majors: Undergraduate film and video: 16 students. Graduate: 2 students
Entrance Requirements:
Undergraduate: 2.25 grade-point average; ACT testing preferred, with a minimum score of 19, or SAT with a minimum composite score of 800.

Graduate: *B* average; GRE or MAT recommended; portfolio; recommendations. Undergraduate and graduate application deadline: August 1. Percent of acceptances: 85%
Curricular Emphasis: Electronic media theory and culture, critical studies in film, media writing, audio-film-video production, animation, video art, media management
Special Activities: Film: film series/festivals. Television: program material produced for local public television station and for cable television; video production for corporate clients
Facilities: Film: screening room; separate editing suites for juniors and seniors; sound mixing room; animation stand; film library. Television: studio; audio bay; control room
Equipment: Film: complete 16mm. Television/Video: ¾" VTR; ½" location; editing equipment
Alumni: John King, TV/film director; Jon Labby, film theatre owner; Russell Schaaf, film/video production executive; Michael Fornwald, media art director

GUIDE POV: This selective university offers a wide variety of course listings in film and television production and theory; study abroad in Latin America, Europe, and Japan; internship opportunities in film and television production

OAKLAND UNIVERSITY

Rochester, MI 48039–4401
(313)370–2100

State four-year comprehensive institution. Coed, suburban location. Undergraduate enrollment: 11,000. Graduate enrollment: 2,700.

HONORS COLLEGE

Chair/Contact: Brian F. Murphy, Chair

JOURNALISM PROGRAM

Chair/Contact: Jane Briggs-Bunting, Chair, Department of Rhetoric, Communications, and Journalism
Calendar: Semesters
Degrees Offered: Film: Interdepartmental program with concentration in film aesthetics and history. Journalism: B.A., broadcast journalism
Departmental Majors: Undergraduate television/video: 100 students
Entrance Requirements: Undergraduate: official transcripts; 2.5 grade-point average; ACT required. Undergraduate application deadline: July 15. Percent of acceptances: 70%
Curricular Emphasis: Film studies is an interdepartmental program emphasizing theoretical and historical studies in film; sponsored by departments of art and art history, the Center for International Programs, English, modern languages and literatures; rhetoric, communications and journalism, and sociology/anthropology. The journalism program within the Department of Rhetoric, Communications, and Journalism offers comprehensive course listings in radio-television news broadcasting; media management; advanced broadcasting; media writing; and producing video for public relations (corporate video), as well as formal studies in communication theory through the communication arts program.
Special Activities: Film: screenings; film society
Facilities: Television: studio; audio bay; control room

Equipment: Television/Video: complete ¾" studio and ½" location
Alumni: Gary Glaser, filmmaker; Richard Rothrock, filmmaker; June Schultz, TV production assistant

GUIDE POV: Students seeking career training in broadcast journalism and corporate video are offered comprehensive studies through the Department of Rhetoric, Communications, and Journalism; there is an interdepartmental honors program in film studies; very selective admissions; study abroad; internship opportunities in television/video production

OLIVET COLLEGE

Olivet, MI 49076
(616)749–7000

Private four-year comprehensive institution. Coed, rural location. Enrollment: 800.

LITERATURE, LANGUAGES, AND IDEAS

Chair/Contact: Film: Susan Gray; television: Stuart Blacklaw
Calendar: Semesters
Degrees Offered: B.A., American studies (concentration in film); B.A., journalism (concentration in broadcasting)
Departmental Majors: Film: 5 students. Television: 10 students
Entrance Requirements: 2.5 grade-point average; ACT or SAT scores. Application deadline: July 1. Percent of acceptances: 93%
Curricular Emphasis: The concentration in film is essentially theory and critically oriented; broadcast journalism covers all aspects of broadcast production including media writing

Special Activities: Film: series/ festivals; student publication. Television: program material produced for cable television, video sales, rentals and loans

Facilities: Film: sound mixing room; film library. Television: audio bay

Equipment: Film: 16mm sound recording equipment; lighting; projectors. Television/Video: ½" cassette recorders; portable cameras; monitors; sound recording equipment; audio mixers; ½" editing equipment format

Alumni: Robert Zahari, cable TV sports director; Liz Walker, TV news anchor; Steve Hoyt, cable TV producer; Phil Parsons, TV executive producer; Michelle Earl, TV production technician

GUIDE POV: Founded in 1844, this private college presents students with theoretical and critical studies in film within the context of a broader study of the humanities; the Journalism Department offers students practical career training in broadcast journalism; varied production internship opportunities

UNIVERSITY OF DETROIT MERCY

Box 19900
Detroit, MI 48219–0900
(313)993–1000

Private four-year comprehensive institution. Coed, urban location. Undergraduate enrollment: 4,000. Graduate enrollment: 2,000.

COMMUNICATION STUDIES

Chair/Contact: Dr. Vivian Dicks, Chair
Calendar: Semesters
Degrees Offered: B.A.

Departmental Majors:
Undergraduate: 130

Entrance Requirements:
Undergraduate: 3.0 grade-point average; upper 40% of high school graduating class; ACT or SAT scores; interview; teachers' recommendations; AP and CLEP credit accepted. Undergraduate application deadline: June. Percent of acceptances: 80%

Curricular Emphasis: Television/ Video: production; broadcast news; media management

Special Activities: Television: program material produced for various outlets

Facilities: Film: animation stand; film library. Television: studio; audio bay; control room

Equipment: Film: Super-8 cameras; 16mm editing; lighting; projectors. Television: complete ¾" studio and location

Alumni: Mort Meisner, TV news director; Allison Payne, TV news anchor

GUIDE POV: This competitive school offers communication students a curriculum featuring an interdisciplinary approach; concentration in television production; cross-registration available with a consortium of Catholic colleges in area; study abroad in England, Italy, Poland, Austria, Israel, and Africa; internship opportunities in television production

UNIVERSITY OF MICHIGAN

Ann Arbor, MI 48109
(313)764–1817

State four-year comprehensive institution. Coed, suburban location.

Undergraduate enrollment: 24,000.
Graduate enrollment: 14,000.

COLLEGE OF LITERATURE, SCIENCE, AND THE ARTS/PROGRAM IN FILM AND VIDEO STUDIES

Chair/Contact: Ira Konigsberg, film and video studies
Calendar: Semesters
Degrees Offered: B.A., film and video studies
Departmental Majors: Undergraduate film/video: 125 students
Entrance Requirements: Undergraduate: competitive grade-point average; ACT or SAT scores; essay required. Undergraduate application deadline: February 15. Percent of acceptances: 60%
Curricular Emphasis: Film history and theory with component in film and video production; separate communication degree that includes courses in film, television, and radio offered through Communication Department
Special Activities: Film/Video: series/festivals/showcases; societies. Television: program material produced for cable television and other outlets
Facilities: Film/Video: 35mm and 16mm screening facilities; film and video studio classroom; editing suites; film, video, and laserdisc library
Equipment: Film: complete Super-8 and 16mm. Television/Video: studio equipment; complete ½" location; computer animation
Alumni: Patricia Reich, film/TV director; Fred Adler, TV/film performer; Dwight D. Campbell, film gaffer

GUIDE POV: Founded in 1817, this is the main campus of the University of Michigan; the film and video studies program offers a multidisciplinary curriculum covering the history, aesthetics, theory, and techniques of film and video; emphasis on critical studies and theory, film and video art, computer animation, narrative, documentary, and varied experimental forms; program provides preparation for graduate film-video programs; separate course listings in broadcast television through Communication Department; highly selective admissions; media internship opportunities

---

WAYNE STATE UNIVERSITY

Detroit, MI 48202
(313)577-2424

State four-year comprehensive institution. Coed, urban location. Undergraduate enrollment: 20,000. Graduate enrollment: 10,000.

RADIO, TELEVISION, AND FILM DEPARTMENT

Chair/Contact: John Spalding
Calendar: Semesters
Degrees Offered: B.A., radio/television, film studies; M.A., Ph.D., communication (students may select emphasis in radio/TV/film)
Departmental Majors: Undergraduate film: 20 students. Undergraduate television: 300 students. Graduate film and television: 40 students
Entrance Requirements: Undergraduate: 2.75 grade-point average; ACT (minimum 21) or SAT (minimum composite 850) scores. Graduate: competitive grade-point average; GRE scores; recommendations. Undergraduate and graduate application deadline: rolling. Percent of acceptances: 75%

Curricular Emphasis: Critical studies in film; audio-video production; broadcast technology; media management

Special Activities: Film: film societies. Television: program material produced for cable television

Facilities: Film: screening room; editing suite; sound mixing room; film library. Television: studio; audio bay; control room

Equipment: Film: complete 16mm. Television/Video: complete ¾" studio; complete ¾" and ½" location

Alumni: Lily Tomlin, film/TV actress; Hugh Downs, TV personality/news anchor; Casey Kasem, TV and radio broadcaster

GUIDE POV: Students choosing the communications major at this state university receive practical training for careers within the television or corporate video industries; critical studies in film combined with basic 16mm production training; semester-long internship opportunities in television/video production

WESTERN MICHIGAN UNIVERSITY

Kalamazoo, MI 49008
(616)387–1000

State four-year comprehensive institution. Coed, suburban location. Undergraduate enrollment: 27,000. Graduate enrollment: 6,500.

DEPARTMENT OF COMMUNICATION

Chair/Contact: Dr. Richard Dieker, Chair

Calendar: Semesters

Degrees Offered: B.A., B.S., mass media; M.A., communication

Departmental Majors: Undergraduate film: 35 students. Undergraduate television: 200 students. Graduate communication: 100 students

Entrance Requirements: Undergraduate: 2.0 grade-point average; ACT scores; interview recommended; GED accepted. Graduate: transcripts; 3.0 grade-point average; GRE scores. Undergraduate and graduate application deadline: rolling. Percent of acceptances: 70%

Curricular Emphasis: Undergraduate: telecommunication management; broadcast and cable production; film production; media writing; media studies. Graduate: organizational communication; interpersonal communication

Special Activities: Television: program material produced for on-campus closed-circuit television

Facilities: Television: studios; audio bays; control rooms

Equipment: Film: complete Super-8; 16mm cameras. Television/Video: ¾" VTR; matched studio cameras; ½" location; switcher/special effects generators

Alumni: Jim Hickey, TV network news correspondent; Tim Allen, TV/film actor/comedian

GUIDE POV: This competitive public university offers students a mass media program with a strong emphasis on critical studies and practical broadcast training; cross-registration with three area colleges; study abroad in France, Germany, Spain, China, and Japan; internship opportunities in television production

Born with a natural love of the theatre and drama, I was fortunate enough to have studied acting with Stella Adler and Lee Strasberg. Then, as a professional stage director in New York and Los Angeles, I staged many new and classic plays, which allowed me to interpret and communicate various ideas and styles.

Subsequently I came to Los Angeles to coach the star of a television series, and although I continued to direct for the stage, I became interested in the art of filmmaking. I took a variety of extension courses, including practical courses in directing and producing.

I soon decided I wanted to be the kind of director who had knowledge of all the technical aspects of filmmaking. So I enrolled at Columbia College in L.A. and got hands-on training in editing, cinematography, and sound recording, as well as film directing and related areas of study. It turned out to be a fortuitous choice for me. I attended small classes taught by industry professionals, and there was easy access to equipment and studios, as well as a personal commitment of support from the administration.

It is still my firm belief, however, that for a young person fresh from high school, a strong liberal arts education is the most important preparation for a film career. In such an academic environment, the developing filmmaker is more likely to be provided with a full range of experiences. On the other hand, if a school is not giving you what you need—take your tuition money, buy a camera, and shoot your own film.

AUGSBURG COLLEGE

731 21st Ave. S.,
Minneapolis, MN 55454
(612)330–1000

Private four-year comprehensive institution. Coed, urban location. Enrollment: 2,600.

SPEECH, COMMUNICATION, AND THEATRE DEPARTMENT

Chair/Contact: David Lapakko, Chair
Calendar: Semesters
Degrees Offered: B.A., communication
Departmental Majors: Television: 30 students
Entrance Requirements: 2.5 grade-point average; ACT or SAT scores; essay required; interview recommended. Application deadline: August 1. Percent of acceptances: 80%
Curricular Emphasis: Electronic media theory and culture; broadcast production; documentary video; media law; journalism
Facilities: Television: studio; audio bay; control room; video editing suites
Equipment: Television/Video: complete S-VHS ½" studio and location; video toaster
Alumni: Kari Eklund Logan, TV writer/producer; Laurie Frattallone, TV newscaster

GUIDE POV: Established in 1869, this private college offers communication majors a liberal arts curriculum that emphasizes speaking and writing skills while providing basic video and television training; study abroad in Mexico, Norway, England, and Spain; internship opportunities in television production

CARLETON COLLEGE

One N. College St.,
Northfield, MN 55057–4099
(507)663–4000

Private four-year comprehensive institution. Coed, small town location. Enrollment: 2,000.

MEDIA STUDIES

Chair/Contact: Film: Vern D. Bailey; television: John Schott
Calendar: 3–3–3
Degrees Offered: B.A., liberal arts (concentration in media studies)
Departmental Majors: Film and television: 16 students
Entrance Requirements: Competitive grade-point average; competitive ACT or SAT scores; essay required; interview recommended. Application deadline: early decision November 15; January 15. Final deadline: February 1. Percent of acceptances: 20%
Curricular Emphasis: Film history, theory, and criticism; screenwriting; sequential video workshops; documentary production
Special Activities: Film: film

screenings; film society; student publication. Television: program material produced for local public television station

Facilities: Film: screening room; editing suite; sound mixing room. Television: studio; audio bay; control room; editing suites

Equipment: Film: complete Super-8; 16mm non-sync. Television/Video: complete ¾" studio and ½" location; S-VHS, VHS, and Beta editing

Alumni: Garrick Utley, TV network news anchor; Peter Scheldahl, film critic; John Schott, PBS executive; Robb Harriss, TV production executive; Bill Hinsman, video producer

GUIDE POV: This extremely selective private college offers a media concentration focusing especially on film theory, history, and criticism, along with sequential video production workshops; small classes; extensive study abroad program; cross-registration with St. Olaf College; internship opportunities in television production

COLLEGE OF ST. SCHOLASTICA

1200 Kenwood Ave., Duluth, MN 55811 (218)723-6000

Private four-year comprehensive institution. Coed, suburban location. Undergraduate enrollment: 1,800. Graduate enrollment: 100.

DEPARTMENT OF COMMUNICATION

Chair/Contact: Tammy Ostrander, Chair
Calendar: Quarters
Degrees Offered: B.A., communication

Departmental Majors:
Undergraduate: 50 students
Entrance Requirements:
Undergraduate: 2.5 grade-point average; ACT or SAT scores; students are individually considered. Undergraduate application deadline: rolling. Percent of acceptances: 60%

Curricular Emphasis: Broad-based communication program with specific tracks in production and writing; film equipment available for independent study

Special Activities: Film: film series/festivals. Television: program material produced for cable television; vocational placement service

Facilities: Television: studio; audio bay; control room; editing suite

Equipment: Film; complete Super-8 and 16mm. Television/Video: complete ¾" studio; complete ¾" and ½" location

Alumni: Craig Spellerberg, TV production manager; Nick Lansing, videographer; Mike Legarde, videographer

GUIDE POV: This private college provides students with a blend of practical video training and liberal arts studies; cross-registration available with the University of Minnesota at Duluth and the University of Wisconsin at Superior; internships available at local television and radio stations

FILM IN THE CITIES

2388 University Ave., St. Paul, MN 55114 (612)646-6104

State and privately supported four-year comprehensive institution. Coed, urban location. Enrollment: 600.

Chair/Contact: Cynthia Hanson, Director of Education
Calendar: Quarters
Degrees Offered: none; college credit as well as self-designed degree available through registration at Metropolitan State University, St. Paul
Departmental Majors: 600 students
Entrance Requirements: High school graduate or equivalent. Application deadline: rolling
Curricular Emphasis: Filmmaking; screenwriting; photography; audio and video production
Special Activities: Film; film series/festivals; weekend workshops with nationally recognized artists as part of "Lightworks" program; media access center; exhibition of independent work at movie theatre
Facilities: Film: 35mm screening facilities; screening room; editing suite; sound mixing room; film library. Television: audio studio
Equipment: Film: complete Super-8 and 16mm. Television/Video: portable cameras and lighting; ½" cassette recorders; monitors; sound recording equipment; audio mixers; editing equipment for VHS
Alumni: Joel Coen, screenwriter/director; Ethan Coen, screenwriter/director; Roger Schmitz, cinematographer; Sayer Frey, film editor

GUIDE POV: Film in the Cities is a non-degree granting media arts center with courses and weekend workshops taught by practicing filmmakers, video artists, and screenwriters; specialized training is offered for those considering a career change or wishing to design their own program of studies

GUSTAVUS ADOLPHUS COLLEGE

St. Peter, MN 56082
(507)933–8000

Private four-year comprehensive institution. Coed, small town location. Enrollment: 2,200.

DEPARTMENT OF ENGLISH/FILM AND MEDIA STUDIES

Chair/Contact: Film: Gregory Mason, Chair
Calendar: 4–1–4
Degrees Offered: B.A., communications
Departmental Majors: Communications: 75 students
Entrance Requirements: Transcripts; ACT or SAT scores (average ACT score 25; average SAT combined 1100); recommendations. Application deadline: April 1. Percent of acceptances: 75%
Curricular Emphasis: Electronic media theory and culture; film history and criticism; media writing; film and television production; video art
Special Activities: Film: series. Television: program material produced for on-campus closed-circuit television and for local public television station
Facilities: Television: studio; control room; two complete editing benches with Amiga toasters
Equipment: Television/Video: complete ¾" studio; character generator; ½" S-VHS Panasonic camcorders
Alumni: Cheryl Downey, film director; John Wirth, screenwriter; Jon Hyers, video production executive; Jeannie Baulere, TV news anchor; Dean Hyers, custom video executive

GUIDE POV: Students at this selective private college may pursue studies in media theory and criticism while learning basic film and video production; special emphasis on writing; student projects in news/documentary, narrative, and experimental forms; study abroad; cross-registration with Mankato State University

GUIDE POV: This private liberal arts university offers students a competitive media program stressing theoretical studies; selective admissions; cross-registration with the Associated Colleges of the Twin Cities Consortium; study abroad; internship opportunities in television production

HAMLINE UNIVERSITY

1536 Hewitt Ave.,
St. Paul, MN 55104–1284
(612)641–2800

Private four-year comprehensive institution. Coed, suburban location. Enrollment: 1,600.

THEATRE AND COMMUNICATION ARTS DEPARTMENT

Chair/Contact: Film: William Kimes; television: Patricia Palmerton
Calendar: 4–1–4
Degrees Offered: B.A., communication arts (with emphasis in television or mass communication); B.A., theatre
Departmental Majors: Film: 10 students. Television: 15 students
Entrance Requirements: 3.0 grade-point average; ACT or SAT scores; written statement of purpose; recommendations; interview recommended. Application deadline: March 1. Percent of acceptances: 80%
Curricular Emphasis: Electronic media theory and culture; film history
Special Activities: Film: film series
Facilities: Television: studio; audio bay; control room
Equipment: Film: complete Super-8. Television/Video: complete ¾" studio and ½" location
Alumni: Eugene Bunge, TV producer; Cyndi Hilger, TV news anchor

HENNEPIN TECHNICAL COLLEGE

9200 Flying Cloud Dr.,
Eden Prairie, MN 55347
(612)944–2222

9000 Brooklyn Blvd.,
Brooklyn Park, MN
(612)425–3800

State two-year comprehensive institution. Coed, suburban location. Enrollment: 13,000.

Chair/Contact: Eden Prairie campus: Susan Stromberg. Brooklyn Park campus: Melanie Siewert
Calendar: Quarters
Degrees Offered: A.A.S., television production
Departmental Majors: 50–100 students
Entrance Requirements: Open-door policy; high school graduate or equivalent; minimum age of 16 years to enroll; assessment testing for new students. Application deadline: rolling
Curricular Emphasis: Comprehensive training in television producing and directing includes writing and evaluating scripts, lighting, staging, control room equipment, electronic effects, graphics, and photography; location taping, postproduction techniques, and nonbroadcast video production
Special Activities: Television: program material, including documentary, news, promotional, and

children's programming, produced for various outlets; sponsored video projects

Facilities: Television: studio; audio bay; control room; remote van

Equipment: Television/Video: complete ¾" studio and location; editing equipment

Alumni: Debbie Enblom, TV news anchor; Garrett Fulton

GUIDE POV: Practical training for technical support positions in television and video may be acquired at this college; array of specialized courses; job counseling and placement center; internship opportunities

INTERMEDIA ARTS OF MINNESOTA

425 Ontario St. S.E.,
Minneapolis, MN 55414
(612)627–4444

Private nonprofit media arts center affiliated with the Department of Studio Arts, University of Minnesota. Coed, urban location. Enrollment: 300.

STUDIO ARTS DEPARTMENT

Chair/Contact: Holly Wright
Calendar: Quarters
Degrees Offered: B.A. and B.F.A. programs in video, computer, and audio arts accredited through the Studio Arts Department of the University of Minnesota
Departmental Majors: Television: 25 students
Entrance Requirements: Open-door policy; high school graduate or equivalent. Application deadline: rolling
Curricular Emphasis: Video and computer animation; video production
Special Activities: Video: material

produced for screening series; video installations; performance artists

Facilities: Television/Video: studio; video editing suites; computer graphics lab (all computer animation output to video)

Equipment: Television/Video: Ikegami ¾" and Sony Hi-8 production equipment; computer graphics and animation equipment including Newtek video toasters; MIDI sound station; ½" to ¾" and Hi-8 to ¾" editing stations

Alumni: Mark Frost, writer/director

GUIDE POV: Intermedia Arts is a nonprofit institution offering beginning to advanced studies in video technology; currently the only regional media arts center in the upper Midwest specializing in video and computer animation; degree programs through affiliation with University of Minnesota

LAKEWOOD COMMUNITY COLLEGE

3401 Century Ave.,
White Bear Lake, MN 55110
(612)779–3200

State two-year institution. Coed, suburban location. Enrollment: 6,000.

ENGLISH/HUMANITIES/SOCIAL SCIENCES DEPARTMENT

Chair/Contact: Lloyd Hackl; Richard Quinn; Patrick Gerster
Calendar: Quarters
Degrees Offered: A.A.
Departmental Majors: Film studies: 50 students
Entrance Requirements: Open-door policy; ACT or SAT scores. Application deadline: rolling. Percent of acceptances: 99%

Curricular Emphasis: Electronic media theory and culture; film theory, history, and criticism
Special Activities: Film: screenings
Facilities: Film: 35mm screening facilities; screening room; sound mixing room; film library
Equipment: Film: Super-8 and 16mm
Alumni: Steven Meyer, film/video production coordinator; Lori Creaver, TV floor manager

GUIDE POV: Students at this affordable two-year college study film and television theory, history, and criticism within the context of a liberal arts curriculum; transfer program to area universities

MINNEAPOLIS COLLEGE OF ART AND DESIGN

2501 Stevens Ave. S.,
Minneapolis, MN 55404
(612)341–7000

Private four-year comprehensive arts institution. Coed, urban location. Enrollment: 700.

MEDIA ARTS DEPARTMENT

Chair/Contact: Tom DeBiaso, Chair
Calendar: Semesters
Degrees Offered: B.F.A., media arts
Departmental Majors: 107 students
Entrance Requirements: Transcripts; 2.0 grade-point average; letter of recommendation; portfolio; personal statement of interest; ACT or SAT scores; interview recommended. Application deadline: March 1. Percent of acceptances: 81%
Curricular Emphasis: Media arts program in film, video, and photography; interactive media studies.
Special Activities: Film: film series/festivals. Television: program material

produced for cable television and for local public and commercial television stations; vocational placement service
Facilities: Film: screening room; editing suite; sound mixing room; animation stands and rotoscope tables; film library. Television: two studios; audio bay; control room; computer generated graphics station; computer center
Equipment: Film: complete Super-8 and 16mm. Television/Video: complete ¾" and Hi-8 studio and location
Alumni: Renee Kryon, TV/film director; Elizabeth Biron, cinematographer; Dan Lund, animator

GUIDE POV: Undergraduates attending this well-equipped fine arts school are encouraged to work in film, video, photography, and interactive media; state-of-the-art computer center; students may pursue one-semester studies at various art institutes in the United States as well as in Canada and Japan; varied internship opportunities; one-semester New York Studio Program

MINNEAPOLIS COMMUNITY COLLEGE

1501 Hennepin Ave.,
Minneapolis, MN 55403–1779
(612)341–7000

State two-year institution. Coed, urban location. Enrollment: 4,000.

FILM AND VIDEO PROGRAM

Chair/Contact: John Fillwalk, Program Coordinator
Calendar: Quarters
Degrees Offered: A.S., filmmaking, video production
Departmental Majors: Film and video program: 80 students

Entrance Requirements: Open-door policy; ACT or SAT scores. Application deadline: rolling. Percent of acceptances: 99%

Curricular Emphasis: Super-8 and 16mm filmmaking; screenwriting; video production and editing; computer graphics; theory courses include those in experimental and documentary cinema; video as an art form; financial management for film and video makers; MIDI (digital) recording

Special Activities: Film: student showcases; American Film Institute workshops. Television: program material produced for cable television

Facilities: Film: screening room; editing suite; sound mixing room; film library. Television/Video: studio; audio bay; control room; two four-track audio recording studios; editing suites; MIDI (digital) studio for designing sound tracks

Equipment: Film: complete Super-8 and 16mm. Television/Video: complete ¾" studio; complete ¾" and ½" location; audio recording equipment; MIDI studio equipment

Alumni: Steve Meyer, video executive; Gwyneth Gibby, film editor; Joe Mears, news videographer

GUIDE POV: Students enrolled in this well-equipped two-year film and video program may choose from diverse course listings in film and video production, theory, and writing; transfer program to area schools; varied internship opportunities in film and television production

MINNEAPOLIS TECHNICAL COLLEGE

1415 Hennepin Ave.,
Minneapolis, MN 55403
(612)370–9400

State two-year comprehensive institution. Coed, urban location. Enrollment: 2,000.

MEDIA PRODUCTION DEPARTMENT

Chair/Contact: Dennis C. Davies; Jack Mader

Calendar: Quarters

Degrees Offered: A.A.S., media production certificate

Departmental Majors: 50–100 students

Entrance Requirements: High school diploma or GED certificate with basic skills placement testing. Application deadline: six weeks prior to start of quarter

Curricular Emphasis: Video production (remote, studio, and editing); computer graphics and animation (desktop video); scripting and storyboarding

Special Activities: Television: sponsored projects for nonprofit clientele

Facilities: Television/Video: studio; audio bay; control room; editing suites; graphics studio

Equipment: Video: complete ¾" studio and location; ¾" A/B roll editing; toaster workstation; graphics station

Alumni: Tracey Kurilla, video editor

GUIDE POV: A professionally equipped two-year technical college, this institution offers training to prospective video technicians; emphasis on new technologies; focus on personal development as well as career training; extensive internship opportunities in local business and media

MOORHEAD STATE UNIVERSITY

Moorhead, MN 56560
(218)236–2011

State four-year comprehensive institution. Coed, suburban location. Enrollment: 8,000.

MASS COMMUNICATIONS DEPARTMENT

Chair/Contact: Martin Grindeland, Chair
Calendar: Quarters
Degrees Offered: B.A., mass communications (broadcast journalism concentration)
Departmental Majors: Radio and television: 125 students
Entrance Requirements: Academic rank within top half of high school graduating class or competitive ACT or SAT scores (ACT preferred). Application deadline: August 15. Percent of acceptances: 89%
Curricular Emphasis: Electronic media theory and culture; writing for film and television; television production; broadcast journalism; broadcast documentary; communications law; media management; mass media ethics; radio production
Special Activities: Television: program material produced for on-campus closed-circuit television and for cable television
Facilities: Television: studio; audio bay; control room
Equipment: Television/Video: complete ¾" studio and location
Alumni: Laurel Erickson, TV news reporter/anchor; Gerry Verdorn, TV producer/actor

GUIDE POV: This public university offers mass communications students a special concentration in broadcast journalism; aspects of radio and television writing, producing, editing, and performance are also focused; cross-registration with North Dakota State University and Concordia College; study abroad in more than 40 countries; varied internship opportunities in radio and television production

NATIONAL EDUCATION CENTER

2225 E. Lake St.,
Minneapolis, MN 55407
(612)721–2481

Private two-year special institution. Coed, urban location. Enrollment: 1,500.

RADIO, TELEVISION, AND FILM DEPARTMENT

Chair/Contact: Bonnie Hugeback
Calendar: Quarters
Degrees Offered: A.A.S., radio/television broadcasting; certificate in radio/television broadcasting
Departmental Majors: 100 students
Entrance Requirements: High school diploma or equivalent. Application deadline: rolling
Curricular Emphasis: Practical hands-on training in radio/television production
Special Activities: Television: vocational placement service
Facilities: Television: studio; audio bay; control room; editing rooms
Equipment: Television/Video: complete ¾" studio and location
Alumni: Bree Walker, TV news anchor; Pat Profit, screenwriter; George Moll, video producer

GUIDE POV: The Brown Institute campus of the National Education Center offers professional training for entry-level technical support positions in radio or television broadcasting; media internship opportunities

NORTHWESTERN COLLEGE

3003 N. Snelling Ave.,
St. Paul, MN 55113
(612)631-5100

Private four-year comprehensive institution. Coed, suburban location. Enrollment: 1,200.

DEPARTMENT OF BROADCASTING

Chair/Contact: Timothy Tomlinson
Calendar: Quarters
Degrees Offered: B.A., communication; B.S., broadcasting
Departmental Majors: 50 students
Entrance Requirements: Interview; ACT or SAT scores; essay; recommendations. Application deadline: September 1. Percent of acceptances: 90%
Curricular Emphasis: Broadcast journalism; production; media writing
Special Activities: Film: film series/ festivals. Television: weekly newscast and variety show produced for cable television
Facilities: Television: studio; control room; editing suite
Equipment: Television/Video: complete ¾" studio; A/B roll editing; two field production systems; portable lighting
Alumni: Scott Pelot, video producer; Timothy Swore, TV news anchor; Carlton Anderson, video producer/ executive

GUIDE POV: Northwestern College is a small private Christian institution providing departmental majors with practical broadcast training; the college offers co-op programs with the University of Minnesota and cross-registration with Bethel College, as well as a cooperative film studies/ internship program with the Los Angeles Film Study Center; internship opportunities in television production

SCHOOL OF COMMUNICATION ARTS IN MINNEAPOLIS

2526 27th Ave. S.,
Minneapolis, MN 55406
(612)721-5357

Private two-year institution. Coed, urban location. Enrollment: 400.

VIDEO ART DEPARTMENT

Chair/Contact: Kathy Dale
Calendar: Six-month courses
Degrees Offered: Certificates in video production and technology; professional video production; computer art and animation
Departmental Majors: 30–75 students
Entrance Requirements: Open-door policy; high school graduate or equivalent. Application deadline: January 15, September 15, March 15
Curricular Emphasis: Video animation (Macintosh, PC, and Silicon Graphics)
Special Activities: Television: program material produced for various outlets; vocational placement service; sister school in Raleigh, NC
Facilities and Equipment: Video: 58 workstations for computer graphics and animation; Betacam postproduction
Alumni: Neal Sopata, computer animator; Mark DeGallier, computer animator; Jace Hager;

graphic animator; John Slater, computer animator

GUIDE POV: Students here enroll in certificate programs that lead to entry-level broadcast positions in lighting, audio mixing, or television production; emphasis on video graphics and animation

---

ST. CLOUD STATE UNIVERSITY

St. Cloud, MN 56301
(612)255–0121

State four-year comprehensive institution. Coed, suburban location. Undergraduate enrollment: 17,000. Graduate enrollment: 1,500.

DEPARTMENT OF THEATRE AND FILM STUDIES

Chair/Contact: Dr. Ronald G. Perrier

DEPARTMENT OF MASS COMMUNICATIONS

Chair/Contact: Dr. Amde-Michael Habte, Chair
Calendar: Quarters
Degrees Offered: B.A., theatre; minor, theatre; minor, film studies; B.S., M.S., mass communication (students may select emphasis in television)
Departmental Majors: Undergraduate film: 50 students (film minors). Undergraduate television: 375 students. Graduate television: 12 students
Entrance Requirements: Undergraduate: academic rank within top half of graduating class; 2.5 grade-point average; college admission test; ACT scores. Graduate: 3.0 grade-point average; GRE scores. Undergraduate and graduate application deadline: August 10. Percent of acceptances: 83%
Curricular Emphasis: Theatre and

film studies: film history and criticism from a cultural studies perspective. Mass communications: television/video production
Special Activities: Film: film series/festivals; film societies. Television: program material produced for cable television and for local commercial television station; PRSSA; SPJ; WICI; AAF chapters
Facilities: Film: screening room; film library. Television: two studios; audio bay; control room; computer editing suites
Equipment: Television: complete 1" and ¾" studio; complete ¾" and ½" location; editing equipment
Alumni: Ty Ellingson, computer graphics designer; Susan Wiese, TV news reporter; Jeff Passolt, TV sportscaster; JoBeth Bender, TV meteorologist

GUIDE POV: Through a selective, well-equipped Department of Mass Communications, students at this state college acquire professional production experience in video and television; the Theatre and Film Studies Department offers a film minor concentrating on critical scholarship; cross-registration with Saint John's University and the College of Saint Benedict; study abroad; internship opportunities in television production

---

ST. OLAF COLLEGE

Northfield, MN 55057
(507)646–2222

Private four-year comprehensive institution. Coed, small town location. Enrollment: 3,000.

ART DEPARTMENT

Chair/Contact: Jan Shoger, Chair/
Judith Yourman
Calendar: 4–1–4
Degrees Offered: B.A., art (students
may select emphasis in film/video)
Departmental Majors: 40 students
Entrance Requirements: ACT or SAT
scores; recommendations; essay.
Application deadline: rolling. Percent
of acceptances: 67%
Curricular Emphasis: Film history;
film and video production within a
fine arts/liberal arts curriculum;
experimental; motion graphics
(animation); video art
Special Activities: Film: film series/
festivals; film societies. Video: program
material produced for cable television;
vocational placement service
Facilities: Film: animation studio;
audio studio; editing suite; sound
mixing room; animation stand
Equipment: Film: complete Super-8
and 16mm. Television/Video: complete
¾" studio and ½" location; Amiga and
Macintosh computers
Alumni: Barry Morrow, screenwriter;
Uttit Choomaung, Disney animator;
Joyce Knutson Salter, screenwriter;
Eric Berglund, puppeteer/director;
Stephanie Halleen, video producer

GUIDE POV: Founded a century ago
by Lutheran immigrants from Norway
and named after that country's patron
saint, this liberal arts college possesses
well-equipped postproduction facilities
for work in animation and video art;
competitive entrance standards; co-op
programs with Augsburg College;
cross-registration with Carleton
College; study abroad; internship
opportunities

UNIVERSITY OF MINNESOTA

Minneapolis, MN 55455
(612)625–5000

*State four-year comprehensive
institution. Coed, urban location.
Undergraduate enrollment: 38,000.
Graduate enrollment: 11,000.*

DEPARTMENT OF SPEECH-COMMUNICATION

Chair/Contact: Television: Donald
Browne, David Rarick; film: Rob
Silberman
Calendar: Quarters
Degrees Offered: B.A.,
interdepartmental film major; B.A.,
M.A., Ph.D., speech communication,
journalism
Departmental Majors: Undergraduate
film: 15 students. Undergraduate
television: 60 students. Graduate
television: 15 students
Entrance Requirements:
Undergraduate: 2.5 grade-point
average; ACT or SAT scores;
recommendations. Graduate: 3.3 grade-
point average; GRE scores;
recommendations; written statement of
purpose. Undergraduate application
deadline: January 31. Graduate
application deadline: July 15. Percent
of acceptances: 50%
Curricular Emphasis: Film:
interdepartmental film studies major;
off-campus production course work
through Intermedia Arts of Minnesota.
Television: electronic media theory
and culture; media writing; audio-
video production; broadcast
journalism; media management
Special Activities: Film: series/
festivals; film society. Television:
program material produced for on-
campus closed-circuit television and
for local cable television

Facilities: Television: studio; audio bay; control room; video editing suites
Equipment: Television/Video: complete ¾" studio and location
Alumni: Martin Bruestle, TV associate producer

GUIDE POV: This is the main campus of the University of Minnesota system; undergraduate emphasis on broadcast journalism and mass communication theory; honors program; graduate electronic media emphasis is research-oriented; internship opportunities in television production; study abroad; graduate research assistantships; film production courses are offered off-campus through Intermedia Arts of Minnesota

UNIVERSITY OF ST. THOMAS

2115 Summit Ave.,
St. Paul, MN 55105
(612)962–5000

Private four-year comprehensive institution. Coed, urban location. Enrollment: 6,000.

COMMUNICATION DEPARTMENT

Chair/Contact: Dr. Kevin Sauter, Chair; George Poletes (film minor)
Calendar: Semesters
Degrees Offered: B.A., communication (students may select emphasis in telecommunication), film minor
Departmental Majors: Telecommunications: 75 students
Entrance Requirements: Transcripts; ACT scores. Application deadline: rolling
Curricular Emphasis: Audio/video production; television criticism
Special Activities: Film: film series/festivals. Television/Video: program

material produced for cable television; summer dramatic video production workshop
Facilities: Television/Video: studio; multitrack audio studio; control room; editing suites; electronic music laboratory
Equipment: Film: complete Super-8. Television/Video: complete S-VHS studio and field location
Alumni: Brad Jacobson, TV director/producer; Paul David, TV news producer; Tom Waveham, video producer/executive

GUIDE POV: The communication program at this liberal arts college, affiliated with the Roman Catholic Church, offers a concentration in video production with emphases in broadcast journalism techniques and corporate video; some courses in basic film production and criticism; internship opportunities in television production

WINONA STATE UNIVERSITY

P.O. Box 5838,
Winona, MN 55987–5838
(507)457–5000

State four-year comprehensive institution. Coed, urban location. Undergraduate enrollment: 7,000. Graduate enrollment: 400.

MASS COMMUNICATION DEPARTMENT

Chair/Contact: Dennis Pack, Chair
Calendar: Quarters
Degrees Offered: B.A., mass communication (students may select emphasis in broadcasting)
Departmental Majors: Undergraduate broadcasting: 76 students
Entrance Requirements: Undergraduate: transcripts; academic

rank within top half of graduating class; 2.0 grade-point average; interview recommended; ACT (minimum score 21) or SAT (minimum composite score 900). Undergraduate application deadline: rolling. Percent of acceptances: 90%
Curricular Emphasis: Radio/Television writing, production, and management
Special Activities: Television: program material produced for local community access television
Facilities: Television: studio; audio bay; control room; editing labs

Equipment: Television: complete ¾" studio; complete ¾" and ½" location
Alumni: Jim Becher, TV news anchor; Randy Winter, assistant TV news director; John Fischer, TV news photographer; Sharon Rooney, TV promotions director

GUIDE POV: This competitive public university, part of the Minnesota state university system, offers practical training to students planning careers in television broadcasting; cross-registration with Saint Mary's College; study abroad in 25 countries; internship opportunities in television production

I came to America from Tokyo, Japan, in 1989. Shortly thereafter, I completed the Motion Picture Certificate Program at the UCLA Extension. I had been a television and movie actress in Japan but never attended acting or film school there.

In Japan, most acting schools are private and managed by agents. Tuition is very expensive. Several universities in Japan offer film studies, including Nihon Daigaku, Nihon Geijyutsu Daigaku, and Osaka Geijyutsu Daigaku. However, those who graduate from film school usually go into television rather than movies. There are several reasons for this. Making films in Japan is extremely difficult because of the many regulations regarding locations, as well as the high cost of production. And whether it is worth spending lots of money to study cinema in Japan is questionable, since the glamorous and lucrative movie industry, as it is known in Hollywood, certainly does not exist there.

Actually, Japanese professionals tend to discount one's having attended film school and instead tend to hire newcomers who wish to learn by working "in the field."

However, through the extension courses I attended in Los Angeles, I acquired numerous practical skills. The instructors were professionals in their various fields and had a lot of enthusiasm to share. They made us feel that we were part of the movie world. We had many lively discussions, and the classes were stimulating. I firmly believe attending film school in America is both inspirational and practical.

ALCORN STATE UNIVERSITY

Lorman, MS 39096
(601)877–6100

State four-year comprehensive institution. Coed, rural location. Enrollment: 3,000.

COMMUNICATIONS PROGRAM

Chair/Contact: Television: David Crosby
Calendar: Semesters
Degrees Offered: B.A., English/Communications (students may select emphasis in television)
Departmental Majors: Television: 110 students
Entrance Requirements: 2.0 grade-point average; ACT or SAT scores with minimum scores of 15 and 720, respectively; interview recommended. Application deadline: rolling. Percent of acceptances: 65%
Curricular Emphasis: Television and video production
Special Activities: Television: program material produced for class projects
Facilities: Television: studio; control room; TVRO; KV and C band satellite ground station
Equipment: Television/Video: complete ¾" studio; complete ¾" and ½" location
Alumni: Gwen Belton, TV news reporter; Melanie Jackson, TV news reporter

GUIDE POV: Students majoring in communications at this state university learn all aspects of television and video production in preparation for technical support positions in the entertainment industry; co-op and work-study programs available; internship opportunities in television production

HOLMES COMMUNITY COLLEGE

P.O. Box 409,
Goodman, MS 39079
(601)472–2312

State two-year institution. Coed, rural location. Enrollment: 1,300.

VOCATIONAL/TECHNICAL DEPARTMENT

Chair/Contact: Television: Michael D. Goodwin
Calendar: Semesters
Degrees Offered: A.A.S., broadcasting technology
Departmental Majors: Television: 15 students
Entrance Requirements: ACT or SAT scores. Application deadline: rolling. Percent of acceptances: 99%
Curricular Emphasis: Television/Video production; radio broadcasting
Special Activities: Television: program material produced for closed-circuit industrial instruction, public relations, and sales
Facilities: Television/Radio: studio;

control room; 20,000-watt FM radio station
Equipment: Television/Video: complete ¾" studio and location
Alumni: Devon Campbell, TV sports director; Patrick Hill, radio announcer; Doris Anderson, public relations specialist

GUIDE POV: Practical technical training in corporate video and broadcasting is offered to students at this small two-year vocational college

MISSISSIPPI COLLEGE

Clinton, MS 39058
(601)925–3000

Private four-year comprehensive institution. Coed, suburban location. Undergraduate enrollment: 3,000. Graduate enrollment: 1,000.

DEPARTMENT OF COMMUNICATION

Chair/Contact: Dr. Bill Lytal, Chair
Calendar: Semesters
Degrees Offered: B.A., communication; B.S., mass media; M.S., communication
Departmental Majors: Undergraduate: 134 students. Graduate: 23 students
Entrance Requirements: Undergraduate: transcripts; ACT scores (minimum 18); interview recommended. Undergraduate application deadline: rolling. Percent of acceptances: 80%
Curricular Emphasis: Television/ Video production and management
Special Activities: Television: program material produced for on-campus closed-circuit television
Facilities: Television: studio; audio bay; control room
Equipment: Film: 16mm cameras and

editing. Television/Video: complete ¾" studio and location; ¾" and ½" editing; character generator
Alumni: Don Moore, TV producer; Lindsey Fields, TV actress; Maggie Wade, TV news anchor; Dan Modisett, broadcast executive

GUIDE POV: Affiliated with the Southern Baptist Convention, this competitive liberal arts college offers its communication majors practical training in all aspects of television production; study abroad in Germany and England; internship opportunities in television production and public relations

UNIVERSITY OF MISSISSIPPI

University, MS 38677
(601)232–7211

State four-year comprehensive institution. Coed, rural location. Undergraduate enrollment: 8,500. Graduate enrollment: 2,000.

DEPARTMENT OF JOURNALISM

Chair/Contact: Don Sneed, Chair
Calendar: Semesters
Degrees Offered: B.A., B.S., M.A., journalism (students may select emphasis in television)
Departmental Majors: Undergraduate: 75 students. Graduate: six students
Entrance Requirements: Undergraduate: transcripts; 2.0 grade-point average; ACT (MS residents), with a minimum score of 15, or SAT, with a minimum score of 700. Graduate: transcripts; GRE general/ subject tests required; 3.0 grade-point average. Undergraduate application deadline: August 1. Graduate

application deadline: rolling. Percent of acceptances: 88%

Curricular Emphasis: Electronic media theory and culture; media writing; television production

Special Activities: Film/Television: program material produced for cable television

Facilities: Television: studio; audio bay; control room

Equipment: Television/Video: complete ¾" studio and location

Alumni: John Johnson, TV news director; Chris Berry, CBS Radio executive producer; Terry Ewert, NBC sports producer; Ron Franklin, ESPN announcer

GUIDE POV: Founded in 1844, this public university offers journalism majors a selective program with a concentration in broadcast journalism; comprehensive training in television production and writing; extensive study abroad program; internship opportunities in television production

---

UNIVERSITY OF SOUTHERN MISSISSIPPI

Box 5141, Southern Station, Hattiesburg, MS 39406–5141 (601)266–7011

State four-year comprehensive institution. Coed, suburban location. Undergraduate enrollment: 10,000. Graduate enrollment: 2,000.

SCHOOL OF COMMUNICATION/RADIO, TELEVISION, AND FILM DEPARTMENT

Chair/Contact: Dr. David H. Goff, Chair

Calendar: Semesters

Degrees Offered: B.A., B.S., radio, television, and film (with emphasis in broadcast journalism, film production, radio-television production, or broadcast management and sales)

Departmental Majors: Undergraduate film: 60 students. Undergraduate television: 170 students

Entrance Requirements: Undergraduate: 2.0 grade-point average; minimum 15 ACT score. Undergraduate application deadline: August 11. Percent of acceptances: 67%

Curricular Emphasis: The film production emphasis offers preparation for all phases of professional film production; the radio and television production emphasis is designed to prepare producers and directors for broadcasting, cable television, and corporate and other television production positions; the broadcast journalism emphasis prepares students for careers in radio and television news; the broadcast management and sales emphasis prepares students for the management of electronic media as well as advertising sales

Special Activities: Film: film series/festivals; film society. Television: program material produced for cable television

Facilities: Film: screening room; editing suite; sound mixing room; animation stand. Television: two full-color studios; audio bay; control room; broadcast newsroom

Equipment: Film: complete Super-8 and 16mm. Television/Video: matched studio cameras; ¾" VTR; portable cameras and lighting packages; ½" and ¾" recorders; monitors; time base corrector; switcher/special effects generators; sound recording equipment; audio mixers; VHS; U-matic; 1" C format; electronic graphics

Alumni: Chuck Scarborough, TV news

anchor; John Duffy, film/TV editor; Henry Price, broadcasting executive; Natalie Allen, TV news anchor

GUIDE POV: This public liberal arts institution offers comprehensive undergraduate studies in both film and television production; students choose area of emphasis along with a minor concentration; variety of course listings; admission to program is selective; study abroad in England, Austria, Germany, and Italy; nationwide senior-year internship opportunities in film and television production

When I was denied acceptance to USC the first time I applied, I decided to proceed with my training anyway. So I enrolled in a local community college for a year, submitted a second application, and was finally accepted.

Subsequently, the first piece of advice I got at USC was to say good-bye to my loved ones for the next three years. It was good advice. I learned more in a week at USC than I had learned in a year at any other school. It was like boot camp. There was more information thrown at us than most could digest, and the task of trying to digest it all proved overwhelming. The only ones who survived the rigorous curriculum were those completely committed to filmmaking, willing to throw themselves into it with everything they had. The rest, the relatives and idle wannabes, didn't stand a chance. They gave up and left, or were asked to leave.

It helps to start with talent. No school can give you that. The better schools foster your talent; they give it tools and practice. So does one need to go to film school to make it in Hollywood? No! But in a practical sense it helps to master techniques of the craft and to learn about the functioning of the industry as a whole, rather than to concentrate in one specialized field.

CENTRAL MISSOURI STATE UNIVERSITY

Warrensburg, MO 64093
(816)543–4111

*State four-year comprehensive
institution. Coed, small town location.
Undergraduate enrollment: 10,000.
Graduate enrollment: 1,600.*

COMMUNICATION DEPARTMENT

Chair/Contact: Dan Curtis, Chair
Calendar: Semesters
Degrees Offered: B.S., broadcasting and film
Departmental Majors: Undergraduate film, radio, and television: 170 students
Entrance Requirements: Undergraduate: academic rank within upper two-thirds of high school graduating class; 2.25 grade-point average; ACT scores. Undergraduate application deadline: rolling. Percent of acceptances: 95%
Curricular Emphasis: Electronic media theory and culture; critical studies in film; media writing; audio-film-video production; media management
Special Activities: Film: film series/festivals; guest speakers. Television: program material produced for local public television station KMOS-TV (housed on campus), and for local cable television
Facilities: Film: screening room; editing suite; sound mixing room; film library. Television: studio; audio bay; control room; video editing suites
Equipment: Film: complete 16mm. Television/Video: complete S-VHS studio and ½" location; satellite receiving dish
Alumni: Joey Ford, film and TV writer/director; Linda Vanneque, TV news reporter; Richard Stobaugh, sound recordist

GUIDE POV: This state university offers a mass communication program with a degree concentration in broadcasting and film; course listings in broadcast journalism, critical studies in mass media, film production/writing, and audio production; cross-registration with the Kansas City Regional Council for Higher Education; study abroad in Europe; internship opportunities in film and television production

DRURY COLLEGE

900 N. Benton Ave.,
Springfield, MO 65802
(417)865–8731

*Private four-year comprehensive
institution. Coed, urban location.
Undergraduate enrollment: 3,000.
Graduate enrollment: 300.*

DEPARTMENT OF COMMUNICATION

Chair/Contact: Dr. Joseph P. McAdoo, Chair

Calendar: Semesters
Degrees Offered: B.A., communication (with emphasis in broadcasting, sports communication, writing, speech communication, public relations, journalism, or mass communication); B.A., Art
Departmental Majors: Undergraduate television: 30 students
Entrance Requirements: Undergraduate: 2.5 grade-point average; ACT (minimum 18) or SAT scores; recommendations and essay required; interview recommended. Undergraduate application deadline: February 15. Percent of acceptances: 85%
Curricular Emphasis: Electronic media theory and culture; critical studies in film; radio and television broadcast production; media management
Special Activities: Television: program material produced for local public television station KOZK
Facilities: Television: studio; audio bay; control room; video editing suites
Equipment: Television/Video: ¾" VTR; ½" and ¾" cassette recorders; monitors; time base corrector; switcher/special effects generators; editing equipment (format ¾")
Alumni: Bob Barker, TV personality; Will Greer, TV actor; Betty Cole Dukert, TV producer

GUIDE POV: Communication majors seeking production experience at this selective private college may choose the radio/television broadcast track; department offers separate track in sports communication; small classes; cross-registration with Landowne College in London; co-op program with American University; study abroad in India and Europe; internship opportunities in television production

LINDENWOOD COLLEGE

209 S. Kings Hwy.,
St. Charles, MO 63301
(314)949–2000

Private four-year comprehensive institution. Coed, suburban location. Undergraduate enrollment: 1,200. Graduate enrollment: 300. Undergraduate tuition: $8,500 per academic year

MASS COMMUNICATION DEPARTMENT

Chair/Contact: Edie Barnard; Jim Wilson
Calendar: Semesters
Degrees Offered: B.A., mass communication (student may select emphasis in radio/television)
Departmental Majors: Undergraduate radio/television: 150 students
Entrance Requirements: Undergraduate: 2.0 grade-point average; ACT or SAT scores. Undergraduate application deadline: rolling. Percent of acceptances: 79%
Curricular Emphasis: Film: critical film studies. Television/Video: news/documentary; instructional; media law; media programming
Special Activities: Film: film series. Television: program material produced for cable television, including a daily newscast and coverage of local sporting events
Facilities: Television: studio; audio studio; control room
Equipment: Television: complete ¾" studio; complete ¾" and ½" location
Alumni: Betty Cole-Dukert, TV network news producer; Robin Smith, TV newscaster; Susan Shiller, TV news producer

GUIDE POV: Founded in 1827, this private college offers television production training combined with small classes and a supportive atmosphere; students engage in variety of programming from freshman year until graduation; recently expanded department is equipped with new studio facilities; college enjoys active association with local cable station; evening and weekend classes; study abroad; internship opportunities in television production

MISSOURI VALLEY COLLEGE

500 E. College St.,
Marshall, MO 65340
(816)886–6924

Private four-year comprehensive institution. Coed, rural location. Enrollment: 1,500.

ARTS AND HUMANITIES DEPARTMENT/ MASS COMMUNICATIONS PROGRAM

Chair/Contact: Karl Bean
Calendar: Semesters
Degrees Offered: B.A., B.S., mass communications (with emphasis in TV, radio, or journalism)
Departmental Majors: Broadcasting: 75 students
Entrance Requirements: 2.0 grade-point average; ACT or SAT recommended. Application deadline: August 15. Percent of acceptances: 95%
Curricular Emphasis: Television and radio production, writing, and management
Special Activities: Television/Radio: program material produced for on-campus stations MVC-TV and KNOS-FM
Facilities: Television: studio; audio bay; control room
Equipment: Television/Video: complete ¾" studio
Alumni: William Groner, radio sports

reporter; Tim Newman, mass communications executive

GUIDE POV: This private college offers broadcasting students a practical program featuring career training for announcers, news directors, copy writers, and program directors; students produce newscasts, music videos, and public service announcements; study abroad; internship opportunities in television production

ROCKHURST COLLEGE

1100 Rockhurst Rd.,
Kansas City, MO 64110–2508
(816)926–4000

Private four-year comprehensive institution. Coed, urban location. Enrollment: 1,900.

DEPARTMENT OF COMMUNICATION AND FINE ARTS

Chair/Contact: William Ryan
Calendar: Semesters
Degrees Offered: B.A., communication (students may select emphasis in mass media)
Departmental Majors: Television: 20 students
Entrance Requirements: ACT required, with a minimum score of 18; interview recommended. Application deadline: June 30. Percent of acceptances: 84%
Curricular Emphasis: Electronic media theory and culture; critical studies in film; media writing; television/video production; media management
Special Activities: Film: film series/ festivals. Television: program material produced for various outlets
Facilities: Film: 35mm screening

facilities. Television: studio; audio bay; control room
Equipment: Television/Video: complete ¾" studio and ½" location
Alumni: Joseph A. Flaherty, Jr., network TV executive; Patti Shine-DeWalt, TV news promotion director

GUIDE POV: This small Jesuit college offers studies in film theory and aesthetics as well as television production including news, fiction, and video art; selective admissions; study abroad in Italy, France, England, Spain, and Mexico; varied internship opportunities in television production

ST. LOUIS COMMUNITY COLLEGE —FLORISSANT VALLEY

3400 Pershall Rd.,
St. Louis, MO 63135
(314)595–4200

State two-year institution. Coed, suburban location. Enrollment: 34,000.

DEPARTMENT OF COMMUNICATIONS

Chair/Contact: Roger W. Carlson, Chair; John M. Balas, mass communications program
Calendar: Semesters
Degrees Offered: A.A., mass communications (with emphasis in broadcasting, creative writing [includes screenwriting], film studies, journalism, advertising, or public relations)
Departmental Majors: Film: 12 students. Television: 65 students
Entrance Requirements: Open-door policy; high school diploma or equivalent. Application deadline: rolling
Curricular Emphasis: Film history and aesthetics; media writing;

television/video production; media management
Special Activities: Television: program material produced for class projects and various outlets
Facilities: Television: studio; audio bay; control room
Equipment: Television/Video: complete ¾" studio and ½" location
Alumni: Donn Johnson, TV news anchor; Dan Gray, TV news anchor

GUIDE POV: Students choosing the Florissant Valley campus of St. Louis Community College may enter a degree program in communication arts that offers varied concentrations, including television/radio broadcasting, film studies, multimedia, and creative writing; core curriculum fulfills requirements for transfer to four-year schools; internship opportunities in television production

ST. LOUIS COMMUNITY COLLEGE —FOREST PARK

5600 Oakland Ave.,
St. Louis, MO 63110
(314)644–9100

District two-year institution. Coed, urban location. Enrollment: 6,500.

COMMUNICATIONS DEPARTMENT

Chair/Contact: Katherine Dunlop, mass communications
Calendar: Semesters
Degrees Offered: A.A.S., mass communications (with emphasis in broadcasting or print); certificate of proficiency in broadcast engineering
Departmental Majors: Television: 100 students
Entrance Requirements: Open-door policy; college assessment testing. Application deadline: rolling

Curricular Emphasis: Television/Video production with an emphasis in broadcast journalism; basic 8mm film production
Special Activities: Television: program material produced for on-campus closed-circuit television and for cable television
Facilities: Film: screening room; editing suite; sound mixing room; film library. Television: studio; audio bay; control room
Equipment: Film: complete Super-8. Television/Video: complete ¾" studio and location
Alumni: Donn Johnson, TV news anchor; Patrick McKee, assistant director

GUIDE POV: The Forest Park campus of St. Louis Community College offers communication students a broadcasting emphasis that provides practical training for careers in radio and television producing and writing; required internships in television production

ST. LOUIS COMMUNITY COLLEGE —MERAMEC

11333 Big Bend Blvd.,
St. Louis, MO 63122
(314)984-7500

State two-year comprehensive institution. Coed, suburban location. Enrollment: 15,000.

COMMUNICATIONS DEPARTMENT

Chair/Contact: Diane Carson
Calendar: Semesters
Degrees Offered: A.A., arts (with emphasis in film or broadcasting)
Departmental Majors: Film: 30 students. Television: 20 students
Entrance Requirements: Open-door

policy; high school diploma or GED certificate; college assessment tests. Application deadline: rolling
Curricular Emphasis: Film: history and aesthetics; screenwriting; Super-8 production. Television: broadcast production techniques; scriptwriting for television; cable television production
Special Activities: Film: film series. Television: program material produced for class projects and for local affiliates
Facilities: Film: sound mixing room; editing room; animation stand. Television: studio; audio studio; control room
Equipment: Film: complete Super-8. Television: complete ¾" studio and ½" location
Alumni: Jim Burcke, film/video director; Larry Boenzle, production assistant/stunt driver; Don Stovall, cinematographer; David Rutherford, video producer/lighting technician

GUIDE POV: The Meramec campus of St. Louis Community College offers students hands-on television and video production training along with film studies classes and basic Super-8 film production courses; students enjoy a high transfer rate to four-year schools; production internship opportunities

SOUTHWEST BAPTIST UNIVERSITY

1601 S. Springfield Rd.,
Bolivar, MO 65613
(417)326-5281

Denominational four-year comprehensive institution. Coed, suburban location. Enrollment: 1,700.

TELECOMMUNICATIONS DEPARTMENT

Chair/Contact: Jerry Jones
Calendar: 4–1–4
Degrees Offered: B.S.
Departmental Majors: 35 students
Entrance Requirements: Transcripts; academic rank within top half of graduating class; 2.0 grade-point average; ACT (preferred) or SAT scores; interview recommended; AP and CLEP credit accepted. Application deadline: rolling
Curricular Emphasis: Television production for corporate and religious markets
Special Activities: Television: on-campus practica
Facilities: Television: studio; audio bay; control room
Equipment: Television: complete ¾" studio and location
Alumni: Shawn Stone, TV director/editor; Susan Brock, cable TV director/switcher; Mike Royal, master control operator; Mark Fisher, TV equipment executive

GUIDE POV: This small liberal arts institution offers students a growing telecommunications program; study abroad in England; internship opportunities in television production

SOUTHWEST MISSOURI STATE UNIVERSITY

901 S. National Ave.,
Springfield, MO 65804
(417)836–5000

State four-year comprehensive institution. Coed, urban location. Undergraduate enrollment: 16,000. Graduate enrollment: 2,000.

DEPARTMENT OF COMMUNICATIONS, ELECTRONIC MEDIA

Chair/Contact: Dr. John I. Sisco, Chair
Calendar: Semesters
Degrees Offered: B.A., B.S., communication (with emphasis in production, media operations, or film studies); M.A., communication
Departmental Majors: Undergraduate: 972 students. Graduate: 65 students
Entrance Requirements: Undergraduate: 2.5 grade-point average; ACT or SAT scores. Graduate: 3.0 grade-point average; GRE scores (minimum 900). Undergraduate application deadline: August 15. Graduate application deadline: July 15. Percent of acceptances: 90%
Curricular Emphasis: Media production; broadcast operations; film studies; media management
Special Activities: Film: film series/festivals; guest speakers; film societies. Television: program material produced for local public and commercial television stations, and for cable television; IABC chapter
Facilities: Film: sound mixing room; film library. Television: studio; audio bay; students use postproduction facilities of local television station
Equipment: Film: complete Super-8; 16mm projectors. Television/Video: complete ¾" studio; complete ¾" and ½" location
Alumni: Jim Vickman, TV producer/director; Mark Kuhn, TV photographer; Chris Inman, radio sports director; Dan Nace, corporate media supervisor

GUIDE POV: This public, primarily commuter university offers communication students career training in television production and management coupled with a liberal arts emphasis; diverse course listings; variety of specialized programs; critical film studies for undergraduates; study abroad in London; internship opportunities in television production

UNIVERSITY OF MISSOURI— COLUMBIA

Columbia, MO 65211
(314)882–2121

State four-year comprehensive institution. Coed, urban location. Undergraduate enrollment: 18,000. Graduate enrollment: 6,000.

DEPARTMENT OF COMMUNICATION

Chair/Contact: Dr. Michael J. Porter, Director of graduate studies
Calendar: Semesters
Degrees Offered: B.A., M.A., Ph.D.
Departmental Majors:
Undergraduate: 200 students. Graduate: 50 students
Entrance Requirements:
Undergraduate: transcripts; 2.5 grade-point average; ACT or SAT scores. Graduate: transcripts; GRE scores; letters of recommendation; writing sample. Undergraduate and graduate application deadline: March 1. Percent of acceptances: 50%
Curricular Emphasis: Undergraduate: television production, criticism, and programming. Graduate: television criticism, theory, and history
Special Activities: Video: student video festival
Facilities: Television: studio; audio bay; control room
Equipment: Television/Video: complete ½" studio and location
Alumni: Brad Pitt, film actor; Susan Burchfield, TV network programming researcher; Jess Bushyhead, TV/film editor; Mark Stone, TV/film editor

GUIDE POV: Established in 1893, this is the largest of the four institutions in the University of Missouri system; selective program provides undergraduates with television production and management training; graduate program focuses on mass media studies; co-op and cross-registration programs available; study abroad; internships available in television production

UNIVERSITY OF MISSOURI— KANSAS CITY

5100 Rockhill Rd.,
Kansas City, MO 64110–2499
(816)235–1000

State four-year comprehensive institution. Coed, urban location. Enrollment: 11,500.

DEPARTMENT OF COMMUNICATION STUDIES

Chair/Contact: Gregory D. Black
Calendar: Semesters
Degrees Offered: B.A.
Departmental Majors: 100 students
Entrance Requirements: 2.5 grade-point average; ACT (preferred) or SAT scores. Application deadline: March 1. Percent of acceptances: 65%
Curricular Emphasis: Electronic media theory and culture; critical studies in film; video production
Special Activities: Television: program material produced for local commercial and public television stations and for cable television
Facilities: Television/Video: studio; audio bay; control room
Equipment: Television/Video: complete ¾" studio; complete ¾" and ½" location
Alumni: Art Salazar, TV director; Karen Foss, TV news anchor; Tom

Gilliland, TV/film actor; Anthony Knopp, TV newscaster; Mike Murphy; TV personality; Roberta Solomon, TV personality

GUIDE POV: Video production training along with critical studies in film and television are offered through this selective program; screenwriting classes through English Department; cross-registration with the Kansas City Regional Council for Higher Education; study abroad in Spain or China; internship opportunities in television production

UNIVERSITY OF MISSOURI—ROLLA

Rolla, MO 65401
(314)341–4111

State four-year comprehensive institution. Coed, small town location. Enrollment: 4,000.

PHILOSOPHY AND LIBERAL ARTS DEPARTMENT

Chair/Contact: Film: James Bogan
Calendar: Semesters
Degrees Offered: B.A. with an minor in communications
Entrance Requirements: Sum of applicant's class rank percentile and aptitude exam percentile must be 75 or higher; ACT or SAT scores. Application deadline: July 1. Percent of acceptances: 87%
Curricular Emphasis: Film theory, history, and criticism
Special Activities: Film: film series/festivals; guest speakers
Facilities: Film: library
Alumni: Steve Jankowski, TV news anchor; Eugene Jackson, TV executive

GUIDE POV: This selective public university is the oldest campus in the University of Missouri system; film minor emphasizes history and aesthetics; co-op programs with University of Missouri at Columbia and St. Louis; study abroad in London

WASHINGTON UNIVERSITY

One Brooking Drive
St. Louis, MO 63130-4899
(314)935–5000

Private four-year comprehensive institution. Coed, suburban location. Undergraduate enrollment: 5,000. Graduate enrollment: 5,000

DEPARTMENT OF PERFORMING ARTS

Chair/Contact: Dr. Henry I. Schvey, Chair
Calendar: Semesters
Degrees Offered: B.A., performing arts; B.A., drama (emphasis in acting, design, or literature and criticism)
Entrance Requirements: Undergraduate: competitive grade-point average; ACT or SAT scores; essay required. Undergraduate application deadline: February 1. Percent of acceptances: 75%
Curricular Emphasis: Undergraduates in the Performing Arts Department, while concentrating on various aspects of theatre studies and production, may explore national cinemas such as Japanese film; the history and theory of cinema as an art form; Super-8 filmmaking; basic video production with an emphasis on television as a dramatic medium
Special Activities: Film: series; lectures
Facilities: Film: screening room
Equipment: Film: Super-8 cameras and editing. Television/Video: video equipment

Alumni: Harold Ramis, film writer/
director; A.E. Hotchner, author/
screenwriter.

GUIDE POV: Drama majors attending
this selective university may study film
theory and aesthetics and receive
basic training in film and video
production within the context of a
comprehensive theatre arts curriculum

WEBSTER UNIVERSITY

470 E. Lockwood,
St. Louis, MO 63130–3194
(314)968–6900

*Private four-year comprehensive
institution. Coed, suburban location.
Undergraduate enrollment: 2,000.
Graduate enrollment: 1,500*

MEDIA COMMUNICATIONS DEPARTMENT

Chair/Contact: Barb Finan
Calendar: Semesters
Degrees Offered: B.A., M.A., media
communications (emphasis on video/
film)
Departmental Majors:
Undergraduate: 400 students. Graduate:
125 students
Entrance Requirements:
Undergraduate: transcripts; academic
rank within top half of graduating
class; 2.5 grade-point average; ACT or
SAT scores; ACT scores of 20 or better;
one-page autobiographical essay.
Graduate: B.A. degree; transcripts;
recommendations. Undergraduate and
graduate application deadline: March
1. Percent of acceptances: 80%
Curricular Emphasis: Film and video
production; applied media aesthetics;
interactive video; there is a separate
concentration in broadcast journalism;
combined B.A./M.A. accelerated

program option; certificate programs
in film theory and sports journalism
Special Activities: Film: Midwest
Center for Film Study; Webster Film
Series; visiting film and video artists;
film societies. Television: program
material produced for cable television;
interdisciplinary film production
projects
Facilities: Film: screening room;
editing suite; sound mixing room;
lighting studio; 16-track audio
recording studio; animation stand; film
library. Television/Video: studio; audio
bay; control room
Equipment: Film: complete Super-8
and 16mm cameras and editing
equipment. Television/Video: complete
¾" studio; complete ¾", ½", and
Super VHS location; editing in digital
D-3 format
Alumni: Scott Betz, cinematographer;
Terri Moore, film executive; Jeff
Ridgway, TV postproduction
supervisor; Michael Sandknop, film/TV
location manager

GUIDE POV: Students in this
innovative program are given
advanced training in both film and
video production; additional campuses
in England, Switzerland, Austria, and
the Netherlands; cross-registration with
several area colleges; internship
opportunities in television and film
production

WILLIAM WOODS COLLEGE

200 W. Twelfth St.,
Fulton, MO 65251
(314)642–2251

*Private four-year comprehensive
institution for women. Rural location.
Undergraduate enrollment: 750.*

PERFORMING ARTS AND COMMUNICATIONS

Chair/Contact: Christian West, Chair
Calendar: 5–4–1
Degrees Offered: B.A., B.F.A., radio-television; B.F.A., performing arts
Departmental Majors: 12 students
Entrance Requirements: Transcripts; academic rank within top half of graduating class; ACT or SAT scores; recommended composite score of 700 on SAT or 15 on ACT; interview recommended; essay required. Application deadline: rolling. Percent of acceptances: 90%
Curricular Emphasis: Television/Video production

Special Activities: Television: off-campus apprenticeships
Facilities: Television: audio and video production lab
Alumni: Matuschka Lindo, TV news anchor; Sally Sockwell, TV/film actress; Betty Sexton-Ball, TV news anchor.

GUIDE POV: Affiliated with the Disciples of Christ, this small college offers video production training and features a one-year internship at the Broadcast Center in St. Louis as well as a one-semester internship in Hollywood; practical approach; strong career placement program

What I am doing at Boston University is more or less what I did at NYU: transforming a school that had a documentary/industrial orientation to one having a narrative/fictional orientation. We work from the principle that if you learn to tell a story well—including studies in acting, directing, composition, script analysis, dramatic structure, resolution, and so on—then you can make any form of film more effectively. Toward that end, we have instituted some very good courses in writing, acting/directing, cinematography, editing, production, and postproduction. The film program is "director" oriented, while the television program is "producer" oriented. Both programs at BU have a studies/masterworks/critical analysis component so that students may have occasion to appreciate classic works and genres.

There are only a handful of schools—five or six at most—that attempt professional film or television training. The classic ones, UCLA, USC, NYU, and Columbia, are currently undergoing major changes. But I believe that BU has a healthy standing now. Our program is solid, and we keep adding exceptional faculty like Beda Batka, probably the world's greatest cinematographer/teacher, responsible for the NYU and Columbia programs. We've also added Ted Kazanoff, arguably the best teacher of acting and directing on the East Coast, having trained many notable actors and actresses both privately and as head of the program at Brandeis University.

We are a small school, so the faculty-to-student ratio is low, the equipment is—by university standards—more than adequate and plentiful, and we are situated in a beautiful and livable city. LA and NYC, as you know, have their problems as well as their advantages. Boston and San Francisco seem to be the two major cultural centers not yet overrun with urban problems. We have lots of theatre, television, film, dance, and music, so it is a stimulating place to come and study. We also have excellent contacts with the industry, and our students are winning prizes and getting jobs. The disadvantages are that we are somewhat expensive and don't offer many scholarships; but in contrast to industry-dominated film schools, we do encourage the independent filmmaker—which is only fitting for a school located in a city noted for its commitment to American independence and revolution.

MONTANA STATE UNIVERSITY

Bozeman, MT 59717
(406)994–0211

*State four-year comprehensive
institution. Coed, rural location.
Undergraduate enrollment: 9,000.
Graduate enrollment: 1,000.*

MEDIA AND THEATRE ARTS DEPARTMENT

Chair/Contact: Paul Monaco, Chair
Calendar: Semesters
Degrees Offered: B.A., media and
theatre arts (concentration in motion
picture/video production)
Departmental Majors:
Undergraduate: 320 students
Entrance Requirements:
Undergraduate: 2.5 grade-point
average; academic rank within top
half of high school graduating class;
ACT (18 minimum) or SAT (800
minimum composite) scores.
Undergraduate application deadline:
rolling
Curricular Emphasis: Learning
through experience all aspects of
motion picture and video production,
as well as television production,
photography, and theatre; students
study the basic elements of
production, including screenwriting,
directing, camera operation, editing,
and sound
Special Activities: Film: film series/
festivals. Television: program material

produced for PBS affiliate located on
campus; Yellowstone Media Arts
Summer Workshops in motion picture/
video production
Facilities: Film: screening room;
editing suite; sound mixing room;
animation stand; sound stage.
Television: studio; audio bay; control
room
Equipment: Film: complete Super-8
and 16mm. Television/Video: complete
1" and ¾" studio; complete ¾" and
½" location
Alumni: Ed Jones, special effects/
postproduction supervisor; Ken Slater,
cinematographer

GUIDE POV: The head of the Media
and Theatre Arts Department at this
well-equipped state university promises
that students who choose the motion
picture/video production option will
spend "many hundreds of hours"
engaged in hands-on production of
works-in-progress; study abroad with
formal relations to Germany, Estonia,
and Russia; media internship
opportunities

SALISH KOOTENAI COLLEGE

Box 117, Highway 93,
Pablo, MT 59855
(406)675–4800

*Tribal two-year comprehensive
institution. Coed, rural location.
Enrollment: 1,000.*

MEDIA/PUBLIC TELEVISION DEPARTMENT

Chair/Contact: Roy Bigcrane
Calendar: Quarters
Degrees Offered: B.A.
Departmental Majors: 10–50 students
Entrance Requirements: High school diploma or GED certificate; contact registrar for more information. Application deadline: rolling
Curricular Emphasis: Documentary television
Special Activities: Film: film series/ festivals. Television: program material produced for local public television station located on campus and for cable television
Facilities: Television: studio; audio bay; control room
Equipment: Film: 16mm cameras. Television/Video: complete ¾" studio; complete ¾" and ½" location
Alumni: Roy Bigcrane, documentary filmmaker

GUIDE POV: The second largest tribal college in the United States, Salish Kootenai offers its students professional video production training with special attention to the documentary form; internship opportunities in television production.

UNIVERSITY OF MONTANA

Missoula, MT 59812
(406)243–0211

State four-year comprehensive institution. Coed, urban location. Undergraduate enrollment: 8,300. Graduate enrollment: 1,700.

SCHOOL OF JOURNALISM

Chair/Contact: Joe Durso, Jr., Acting Dean

DEPARTMENT OF RADIO-TELEVISION

Chair/Contact: Greg MacDonald, Acting Chair
Calendar: Semesters
Degrees Offered: B.A., journalism (emphasis in print or broadcasting); B.A., radio-television; M.A., journalism (specialization in print or broadcasting)
Entrance Requirements:
Undergraduate: 2.5 grade-point average; academic rank within top half of high school graduating class; ACT (20 minimum) or SAT (800 minimum composite) scores.
Graduate: teachers' recommendations; GRE testing. Undergraduate application deadline: July 1. Graduate application deadline: March 1. Percent of acceptances: 83% undergraduate; 65% graduate
Curricular Emphasis: School of Journalism: Undergraduates and graduates may learn principles and techniques of television production within a comprehensive curriculum that emphasizes writing, reporting, editing, broadcasting, photojournalism, and news analysis. Department of Radio-Television: Students concentrate on acquisition of production skills in broadcasting for radio and television while fulfilling core requirements; emphasis on the production and direction of both studio and remote television programs; upperclassmen must engage in supervised production internships, complete at least 90 credits outside the major, and choose minor in another field of study
Special Activities: Television: program material produced for variety of outlets
Facilities: Television: studio; audio bay; control room
Equipment: Television/Video:

complete ¾" studio; complete ¾" and ½" location

Alumni: Solomon Levy, TV news producer; Shane Bishop, TV network producer; Denise Dowling, executive TV producer; Suzanne Lagoni, corporate communications director

GUIDE **POV:** Students in the School of Journalism examine the news media and receive solid instruction in those skills required for careers with print media as well as radio and television stations; undergraduates with a special interest in broadcast production may choose the major in radio-television, which blends practical experience with theoretical studies

To reflect on film school at the University of Michigan is to reflect on the film professor who was assigned to teach the introductory course. It was inside a large, comfortable lecture hall, where a hundred students focused on a big screen and lapsed in and out of being moviegoers and then students, that our instructor enlightened us to the beginnings of films and filmmakers—like Lumiere and his special effects of the moon, Dali and his unforgettable surrealistic images, Sergei Eisenstein and his montage theory. This particular professor was a solid disseminator of information, someone you could explore ideas with, and above all, someone who seemed truly to love the art of film. He also taught a practical filmmaking class that became the next step in my career. We students made one film on our own and then shared different functions on each other's shoots in groups of three or four, so we learned the technical aspects of movie-making as well as the art of collaboration. And upon graduation, our instructor provided names and numbers of alumni working in the industry to those students with the guts and drive to follow suit.

Later, as vice-president of creative affairs at various production companies, I would receive recent Michigan graduates referred to me as interns by that same teacher. In fact, his goodwill networking led to my meeting Larry Kasdan, another Michigan alumnus, who came on board as director of *I Love You to Death*, for which I was one of the producers. Now I am writing and producing my own material. I have also created the Hollywood Literary Retreat, a place for studio executives, producers, writers, and directors to return to the essentials of filmmaking; good storytelling. In fact, each year my former film professor sends a graduate student from the University of Michigan to attend. One day he promises to come himself. I look forward to the day when my academic hero meets the industry itself.

HASTINGS COLLEGE

7th and Turner Sts.,
Hastings, NE 68901
(402)463–2402

Private four-year comprehensive institution. Coed, small town location. Enrollment: 950.

COMMUNICATION ARTS DEPARTMENT

Chair/Contact: Dr. Ronald D. Davis
Calendar: 4–1–4
Degrees Offered: B.A., communication arts (students may select emphasis in broadcasting)
Departmental Majors: 30 students
Entrance Requirements: Transcripts; academic rank within top half of graduating class; ACT (minimum 19) scores; SAT accepted; recommendation from high school counselor. Application deadline: July 1
Curricular Emphasis: Television and radio production; broadcast journalism
Special Activities: Film: student publications. Television: live and taped news, sports and theatre program material produced for on-campus closed-circuit television, for cable television, and for local commercial television station
Facilities: Television: two full-color studios; three editing bays; control rooms; full-service electronic newsroom; remote van; Matrox computer postproduction suites

Equipment: Television/Video: complete ¾" or S-VHS studio and location including seven ENG units; Grass Valley switcher; teleprompter; computer graphics; A/B/C roll and cuts-only editing; DVE; three CGS
Alumni: John Walsh, TV sports anchor/field reporter; Kathy Toms, TV field reporter

GUIDE POV: Hastings College offers a competitive, lively communications program that stresses broadcast production; high placement rate for undergraduates in both industry and in graduate schools; study abroad; internship opportunities in television production

NORTHEAST COMMUNITY COLLEGE

801 E. Benjamin Ave.,
P.O. Box 469
Norfolk, NE 68702–0469
(402)371–2020

State/county two-year institution. Coed, small town location. Enrollment: 2,000.

BROADCASTING-RADIO-TV PROGRAM

Chair/Contact: John M. Skogstoe
Calendar: Semesters
Degrees Offered: A.A., A.A.S., radio/TV broadcasting
Departmental Majors: Television: 25 students

Entrance Requirements: Open-door policy; high school diploma or equivalent; student must be at least 16 years of age. Application deadline: rolling, but early application is advised for admission to the radio/TV program due to limited space

Curricular Emphasis: Radio/TV writing, announcing, and production; study of broadcasting history, regulations, and management

Special Activities: Television: program material produced for Channel 38 KHWK of the local cable system available to over 5,200 homes in the area

Facilities: Television: studio; audio bay; control room

Equipment: Television/Video: complete ¾" studio and location

Alumni: Dallas Michaels, media operations manager; Dan Feenstra, media account executive; Danielle Feenstra, creative services executive

GUIDE POV: Students entering this two-year broadcasting program receive practical career preparation in radio and television production and announcing, news writing/gathering, screenwriting, and broadcast programming and sales; high job placement record for graduates; career or transfer tracks offered; media internships available

---

UNIVERSITY OF NEBRASKA AT KEARNEY

Kearney, NE 68849–5230
(308)234–8441

State four-year comprehensive institution. Coed, rural location. Undergraduate enrollment: 10,000. Graduate enrollment: 2,000.

ENGLISH AND BROADCASTING DEPARTMENT

Chair/Contact: Samuel J. Umland, Film Chair; Tom Draper, Television Chair

Calendar: Semesters

Degrees Offered: B.A., telecommunications (with emphasis in production/reporting or sales/management)

Departmental Majors: Undergraduate television: 115 students

Entrance Requirements: Undergraduate: 2.0 grade-point average; ACT or SAT scores. Undergraduate application deadline: July 1. Percent of acceptances: 96%

Curricular Emphasis: Electronic media theory and culture; film history, theory, and criticism; screenwriting; media writing; film and video production; media management

Special Activities: Film: film series/festivals. Television: program material produced for on-campus closed-circuit television and for local public and commercial television station

Facilities: Film: sound stage; 35mm screening facilities; screening room; editing suite; animation stand. Television: studio; audio bay; control room

Equipment: Film: Super-8 projectors. Television/Video: studio cameras; portable lighting packages; ½" and ¾" cassette recorders; sound recording equipment

Alumni: Scott Sands, TV director; Jeri Snider, TV producer; Tim Martins, TV news anchor; Brad Fleck, TV technical director; Brian Vodennal, videographer

GUIDE POV: Founded in 1903 as part of the Nebraska state college system, the University of Nebraska at Kearney offers a competitive media arts program with studies in management, criticism, writing, and production; diverse course listings in documentary, news, and animated production; video students work on a variety of projects for local television markets; student-exchange programs in the U.S. and abroad; varied internships

UNIVERSITY OF NEBRASKA AT LINCOLN

Lincoln, NE 68588–0333
(402)472–7211

State four-year comprehensive institution. Coed, suburban location. Undergraduate enrollment: 19,755. Graduate enrollment: 3,821.

ENGLISH/FILM STUDIES PROGRAM

Chair/Contact: Film studies: Dr. Wheeler Winston Dixon, Chair, English Department; television: Dr. Larry L. Walkin, Journalism Department
Calendar: Semesters
Degrees Offered: B.A., M.A., Ph.D., English with a minor in film studies
Departmental Majors: No major offered in film or television
Entrance Requirements:
Undergraduate: 2.0 grade-point average; high school diploma or GED certificate; academic rank within top half of high school graduating class; ACT or SAT scores; AP credit accepted. Graduate: Two transcripts; GRE scores; interview; portfolio; essay. Undergraduate application deadline: August 1 for fall admission; December 1 for spring admission. Graduate application deadline: May 15 for fall admission; October 15 for spring admission; March 15 for summer admission. Percent of acceptances: Undergraduate: 95%. Graduate: 50%

Curricular Emphasis: Film: critical studies within context of liberal arts curriculum including philosophy and the arts; screenwriting. Television: mass media studies; broadcast journalism; documentary; cinematography and videography
Special Activities: Film: film series/festivals; film society; student publication. Television: program material produced for on-campus closed-circuit television and local cable television
Equipment: Film: 35mm and 16mm projection. Television: complete ¾" studio and ½" location
Facilities: Film: film theatre; film library. Television: studio; audio studio; control room
Alumni: Emmett Robinson, boom operator; Sarah Knight, production supervisor; Kent Nelson, assistant director; Michael Page, production supervisor

GUIDE POV: Part of the University of Nebraska system, this competitive school offers courses in film theory, history, and criticism through the English Department; television production and writing courses are offered through the Journalism Department; cross-registration and co-op programs; study abroad; internship opportunities in television and film production

UNIVERSITY OF NEBRASKA AT OMAHA

60th and Dodge St.,
Omaha, NE 68182–0112
(402)554–2800

State four-year comprehensive institution. Coed, urban location.

Undergraduate enrollment: 16,000.
Graduate enrollment: 2,500.

DEPARTMENT OF COMMUNICATION

Chair/Contact: Hugh P. Cowdin, Chair
Calendar: Semesters
Degrees Offered: B.A., B.S., M.A., communication (with emphasis in broadcast news, news-editorial, or public relations/advertising)
Departmental Majors: Undergraduate broadcasting: 174 students; journalism: 220 students; speech: 81 students. Graduate communication: 75 students
Entrance Requirements: Undergraduate: 2.25 grade-point average; ACT or SAT scores; transcripts or GED scores. Graduate: 3.25 grade point average; teachers' recommendations. Undergraduate application deadline: August 1, December 1, June 1. Graduate application deadline: July 15, December 1, April 15. Percent of acceptances: Undergraduate: 93%. Graduate: 75%
Curricular Emphasis: Sequential course work in television news and production; course listings in writing for mass media; electronic media management; mass media ethics and communication law
Special Activities: Television/Radio: program material produced for Cox Cable in Omaha, for local public radio station, and for campus public television station
Facilities: Television: three-camera studio; audio bay; control room
Equipment: Television: complete ¾" studio and location including Grass Valley switcher Chyron and three Sony editing bays
Alumni: John Clark, TV news director; Carrie Murphy, TV producer; Carol Shrader, TV news anchor; Stacie Hawkes, TV news reporter

GUIDE POV: This public commuter university offers a communications major featuring a curriculum covering all aspects of broadcast journalism; program promotes balance of conceptual and skills courses; co-op programs; study abroad; guaranteed media internships

Remember that when the Wizard of Oz wanted to grant the Scarecrow's wish for a brain, he offered him a diploma—but it didn't make him smarter? What the Scarecrow really wanted was a well-rounded education. For you, as a student of film, that education means a place to create, develop, and foster the exploration of new ideas—a place where education and creative thinking are more important than the piece of paper you get at the end. Every institution may state that is what their philosophy is, but that is not always the case.

I attended a very prominent film school. But my experience was more akin to an ostracized factory worker suggesting change than it was to an artist encouraged to develop her art. Generally, I found the professors to be passive recipients and transmitters of other people's views as opposed to active participants in the learning process. I expected the staff to teach, not indoctrinate; to educate rather than train; to explain their mode of thought instead of just reporting it. I felt the professors were paying so much attention to what it was going to be like when we "got out there" that they completely disregarded my education. Therefore, I left before getting my degree.

Film school should be an environment in which aspiring filmmakers can work together and experiment with the medium, where you are encouraged to take risks and make mistakes. The professors should provide encouragement and, together with the students, explore aesthetic and technical options. The atmosphere should be like a gathering place where participants are free to create new worlds in the expressive medium of film. Education can meet this need if innovative colleges with imaginative teachers—and they do exist—are sought out by students.

UNIVERSITY OF NEVADA— LAS VEGAS

4505 S. Marland Pkwy.,
Las Vegas, NV 89154–5015
(702)895–3011

State four-year comprehensive institution. Coed, urban location. Undergraduate enrollment: 20,000. Graduate enrollment: 1,500.

FILM STUDIES DEPARTMENT

Chair/Contact: Dr. Hart Wegner

COMMUNICATION STUDIES DEPARTMENT

Chair/Contact: Barbara Cloud
Calendar: Semesters
Degrees Offered: B.A., film studies, communication studies (students may select emphasis in television); M.A., film studies (projected), communication studies
Departmental Majors: Undergraduate film: 95 students. Undergraduate television: 90 students
Entrance Requirements: Undergraduate: 2.5 grade-point average; ACT or SAT scores. Graduate: transcripts; GRE scores. Undergraduate and graduate application deadline: April 1. Percent of acceptances: 80%
Curricular Emphasis: The film studies program offers both critical studies and production experience including screenwriting. The communication studies program offers both critical studies and production experience emphasizing news/documentary
Special Activities: Film: International Film Series/festivals
Facilities: Film: screening room; editing suite; sound mixing room. Television: studio; audio bay; control room
Equipment: Film: complete 16mm; four-track mixing system; flatbed and upright editing. Television/Video: complete ¾" studio; complete ¾" and ½" location
Alumni: Mimi Mayer, media talent agent

GUIDE POV: There are separate departments for film and television studies at this competitive state university; both programs offer hands-on comprehensive training as well as critical studies; film and television students share studio space; graduate program in film studies projected; accelerated degree programs; study abroad in Switzerland, Italy, Sweden, England, and Mexico; media internship opportunities

UNIVERSITY OF NEVADA—RENO

Reno, NV 89557
(702)784–1110

State four-year comprehensive institution. Coed, urban location. Undergraduate enrollment: 11,000. Graduate enrollment: 2,000.

DEPARTMENT OF ART, FILM STUDIES PROGRAM

Chair/Contact: Howard Rosenberg, Chair

Calendar: Semesters

Degrees Offered: B.A., art

Departmental Majors: Undergraduate art: 75 students

Entrance Requirements: Undergraduate: 2.3 grade-point average; ACT (preferred) or SAT scores; GED not accepted. Undergraduate application deadline: September 1. Percent of acceptances: 87%

Curricular Emphasis: Film/Video: electronic media theory and culture; film aesthetics and history; video art. Television: Journalism Department offers course listings in broadcast journalism including public affairs journalism, news production, and documentary production for broadcast; broadcast station operation; media management

Special Activities: Film: series. Television/Video: exhibitions

Facilities: Television: studio

Equipment: Television/Video: complete ¾" studio; ¾" and ½" location

Alumni: Craig Questa, screenwriter; Paul Basta, cinematographer

GUIDE POV: This campus of the University of Nevada system features a small, selective Art Department offering students a critical survey of film and video; production work emphasizes using both broadcast and nonbroadcast video as a means of creative expression; exploration of new media; course listings in television news, documentary, and public affairs broadcast production offered through Journalism Department; cross-registration available; accelerated degree program; study abroad; internship opportunities in television production

I do not believe a formal film education is essential for aspiring moviemakers. My own film training occurred while sitting in darkened chambers, occasionally enjoying a renewing snooze, but sometimes thrilled, very occasionally wonderfully thrilled and illuminated as to the human condition. But this has become increasingly difficult in a Hollywood controlled by technocrats and bureaucrats.

I had no particular plan that enabled me to become a professional writer save hard work. My advice to potential screenwriters and directors is to read voraciously, be aware of the world around, study human beings, and avoid at all costs film buffs.

As a playwright, I received the Stanely Drama Award for *The Club* and *The Little Gentleman*, and was awarded a Rockefeller Grant for *A Gun Play*. My screenplay *Bad Timing/A Sensual Obsession* was directed by Nicolas Roeg. For HBO, I wrote *Third Degree Burn*. And *Vera*, my adaptation of a Chekhov short story, won First Prize at the Houston Film Festival.

COLBY–SAWYER COLLEGE

Main St.,
New London, NH 03257
(603)526–2010

Private four-year comprehensive institution. Coed, small town location. Enrollment: 625.

HUMANITIES DEPARTMENT

Chair/Contact: Film: Patrick D. Anderson; video: Donald Coonley
Calendar: Semesters
Degrees Offered: B.S., communication arts (students may select emphasis in media communications)
Departmental Majors: Media communications: 45 students
Entrance Requirements: 2.5 grade-point average; ACT or SAT scores; recommendations. Application deadline: rolling. Percent of acceptances: 90%
Curricular Emphasis: Media criticism; special topics in communication theory; film aesthetics and history; creative writing; writing for the press and screen; electronic journalism; location video production
Special Activities: Film: film series/festivals. Television/Video: program material produced for cable television
Facilities: Video: editing bays
Equipment: Video: S-VHS camcorders and editing equipment
Alumni: Ethney McMahon, TV producer; Carla Gordon, TV producer; Jennifer Rogge, public relations producer

GUIDE POV: Established in 1837 as an independent women's college, this small institution has been coeducational since 1990; the interdisciplinary communication arts major draws upon the liberal arts while providing practical career training; track in media communications emphasizes broadcast journalism with special attention to location video production; study abroad in Switzerland, France, England, and Nova Scotia; media internship opportunities

DARTMOUTH COLLEGE

Hanover, NH 03755–3599
(603)646–1110

Private four-year comprehensive institution. Coed, small town location. Undergraduate enrollment: 4,500. Graduate enrollment: 300.

FILM STUDIES DEPARTMENT

Chair/Contact: Al LaValley, Chair
Calendar: Unique Dartmouth Plan divides academic calendar into four 10-week terms that coincide with the seasons
Degrees Offered: B.A., film studies (with emphasis in theory, history, and criticism, production, or screenwriting)

Departmental Majors: Undergraduate film and television/video: 25 students
Entrance Requirements: Undergraduate: competitive grade-point average; ACT or SAT scores; three ATs; AP credit accepted. Undergraduate application deadline: January 1. Percent of acceptances: 25%
Curricular Emphasis: Film theory/aesthetics, history, and criticism; screenwriting; film and video production
Special Activities: Film: film series/festivals; Dartmouth Film Society. Television: program material produced for on-campus closed-circuit television
Facilities: Film: 35mm screening facilities; screening room; editing suite; sound mixing room; animation stand; film library
Equipment: Film: complete Super-8 and 16mm. Television/Video: complete ½" studio and location
Alumni: Vincent Canby, film critic; Bram Towbin, filmmaker; Erica Stern, film producer/director; Mark Halliday, filmmaker; Will Rexer, cinematographer; Ciri Nottage, production assistant

GUIDE POV: Chartered in 1769, this highly selective private college is the smallest member of the Ivy League; small film studies program combines critical studies with hands-on production experience in 8mm, 16mm, VHS, and Super VHS; extensive study abroad program; cross-registration through the Twelve College Exchange Network that includes Amherst and Mount Holyoke; exchange programs with selected universities in California, Canada, Germany, Japan, and China; limited media internships available

FRANKLIN PIERCE COLLEGE

P.O. Box 0060
College Rd.,
Rindge, NH 03461–0060
(603)899–4000

Private four-year comprehensive institution. Coed, rural location. Enrollment: 1,200.

MASS COMMUNICATIONS

Chair/Contact: Phyllis Scrocco-Zrzavy; Ray Oakes
Calendar: Semesters
Degrees Offered: B.A.
Departmental Majors: 75 students
Entrance Requirements: Transcripts; recommendations; SAT scores; interview recommended. Application deadline: March. Percent of acceptances: 64%
Curricular Emphasis: Media theory and criticism, critical studies in film, film directing, media writing, broadcast studio and field production, broadcast journalism, print journalism, media management, broadcast sales
Special Activities: Film: annual communications seminar. Television/Radio: program material produced for on-campus closed-circuit television; student media clubs and publications; student-run radio station
Facilities: Television/Radio: studio; audio bay; control room; radio station WFPR
Equipment: Television/Video: complete ¾" studio and location
Alumni: James Breen, videographer; Robert Grossman, TV marketing manager

GUIDE POV: Focusing on video production and topics in media criticism, this program also provides students with an integrated core curriculum in the liberal arts; the college has an extensive continuing education program, offering bachelor's degrees from various New Hampshire locations; cross-registration offered through a consortium of area institutions; internship opportunities in television production

KEENE STATE COLLEGE

229 Main St.,
Keene, NH 03431
(603)352–1909

State four-year comprehensive institution. Coed, rural location. Undergraduate enrollment: 4,300. Graduate enrollment: 400.

THEATRE ARTS, SPEECH, AND FILM DEPARTMENT

Chair/Contact: Larry Benaquist, Chair; Carol Beck
Calendar: Semesters
Degrees Offered: B.A.
Departmental Majors: Undergraduate film program: 30 students
Entrance Requirements: Undergraduate: SAT scores; high school diploma. Graduate: GRE scores; transcripts; essay. Undergraduate and graduate application deadline: rolling
Curricular Emphasis: Film/Video: separate tracks in production and history/theory with attention to experimental, documentary, independent, and animated forms as well as the classical Hollywood narrative (e.g., courses on Hitchcock, Sam Fuller, etc.)
Special Activities: Film: visiting filmmakers; guest instructors; student film festivals; film society. Television: program material produced for on-campus closed-circuit television and for local cable

Facilities: Film: 35mm and 70mm projection with Dolby Surround Sound; editing suite; sound transfer facility; screening rooms; film library. Television: studio; audio studio; control room
Equipment: Film: complete Super-8 and 16mm including Arriflex B1, Eclair NPR, and Bolex 16mm; Nagra and Sennheiser sound; moviola 16mm flatbed editor; film to video transfer; Lowell lighting. Television/Video: complete ¾" and ½" location; video projection
Alumni: Geoff Miller, screenwriter; Hal Masonberg, filmmaker; Amanda Sherwin, film/TV production manager; Louis Gendron, music video production coordinator; Chris Peterson, film/TV property master

GUIDE POV: This small program features quality training in independent film and video production; cross-registration offered through the New Hampshire College and University Council; study abroad in Britain, Ireland, France, Japan, Ecuador, and Russia; individualized majors; internship opportunities with Ken Burns' production company Florentine Films, among others

UNIVERSITY OF NEW HAMPSHIRE

Durham, NH 03824
(603)862–1234

State four-year comprehensive institution. Coed, semirural location. Undergraduate enrollment: 9,300. Graduate enrollment: 1,200

DEPARTMENT OF COMMUNICATION

Chair/Contact: Sheila McNamee, Chair
Calendar: Semesters

Degrees Offered: B.A., B.S.
Entrance Requirements:
Undergraduate: SAT scores required with a minimum score of 1080; essay required; information interview recommended. Undergraduate application deadline: February 1. Percent of acceptances: 75%
Curricular Emphasis: Mass media: The Department of Communication offers a major that focuses attention on media studies as well as rhetorical and interpersonal/small group studies. Film: Elective course work in film studies may be chosen by students majoring in a variety of disciplines, including theatre, communication, and English
Special Activities: Film: film series/festivals
Facilities: Film/video: screening room

Alumni: Greg Kretchmar, TV/radio broadcaster, Kristan Bishop, media sales/promotion executive

GUIDE POV: Communication majors engage in media analysis and criticism; in addition, there is an introductory film course that constitutes part of the offering for students in the Communication Department; finally, students in various disciplines may elect advanced cinema studies; topics vary from year to year and may range from general exploration of film theory, criticism, and history, to genre studies or the analysis of particular directors or periods; the university offers an extensive cross-registration program as well as study abroad

I was born in London. As a youngster, I enjoyed making films with my father's cine camera. Unfortunately, for reasons only a skilled therapist could fathom, I sublimated my creative talent and chose to become a lawyer. I graduated from the College of Law in 1970, and I remained in that unhappy state until mid-life crisis plucked me from the dull world of financial and trade law and dropped me, as a willing conspirator, into the exciting business of making movies. Business? Well, it really *is* a business—but a much more creative one than law.

Although I had practiced the legal profession in Europe and the Middle East, I decided that the only place to gain an intimate knowledge of the many facets of the film industry was in the United States. But I did not know exactly what I wanted to do: produce, direct, write, or operate a camera. I had to learn as much as I could in the shortest possible time. At the age of forty-four, a job in the mail room was hardly the starting place from which I would rise to the giddy heights of fame and glory. Nor could I envisage any self-respecting financier furnishing me with the money to go off and direct a movie.

So I searched for and found a school where I could learn every aspect of the business—from loading raw stock into a camera to negotiating a complicated deal with a studio. In my case, it was the UCLA Continuing Education Program. Classes are usually held at night and on weekends, and frequently taught by industry professionals. There are many similar schools all over America where, after a relatively short period, students are able to gain a working knowledge of the industry which will enable them to choose which course to pursue.

Having spent twenty years as a lawyer, producing comes naturally, but I reserve the right to move on to directing. The grounding I received in film school should facilitate that, provided of course, I find the funds.

BROOKDALE COMMUNITY COLLEGE

Newman Spring Rd.,
Lincroft, NJ 07738
(908)842-1900

State/county two-year institution. Coed, suburban location. Enrollment: 10,600.

TELECOMMUNICATIONS DEPARTMENT

Chair/Contact: Paul Keating; Dr. Louis J. Pullano
Calendar: Semesters
Degrees Offered: A.A., humanities (students may select emphasis in media studies); A.A.S., communications media (students may select emphasis in television production)
Departmental Majors: A.A.: 45 students. A.A.S.: 32 students
Entrance Requirements: Open-door policy. Application deadline: rolling
Curricular Emphasis: Film: critical studies. Television: critical studies; production
Special Activities: Film: film series/festivals. Television: program material produced for on-campus closed-circuit television and local cable television
Facilities: Film: screening room. Television: studio; audio bay; control room
Equipment: Film: Super-8 cameras; editing equipment; projectors; lighting equipment. Television: complete ¾" studio; ½" and ¾" location

Alumni: Anthony Chiavolella, TV segment producer; Frank Farrell, videographer; Jim Matlosz, film special effects artist

GUIDE POV: A comprehensive television production training curriculum is offered at this two-year college; students either then transfer to four-year institutions or enter the work force, notably in cable television or corporate environments; varied internship opportunities in local media

CENTENARY COLLEGE

400 Jefferson St.,
Hackettstown, NJ 07840
(908)852-1400

Private four-year comprehensive institution. Coed, small town location. Enrollment: 600.

COMMUNICATIONS DEPARTMENT

Chair/Contact: Eric Slater
Calendar: Semesters
Degrees Offered: B.A., communications
Departmental Majors: 50 students
Entrance Requirements: ACT or SAT scores; interview recommended. Application deadline: rolling. Percent of acceptances: 80%
Curricular Emphasis: Electronic media theory and culture; media writing; audio-video production; media management

Special Activities: Television/Radio: program material produced for cable television; student-staffed WNTI-FM operates daily and is heard over portions of a three-state area
Facilities: Television: studio; audio bay; control room
Equipment: Television/Video: portable lighting packages; ¾" cassette recorders; monitors; switcher/special effects generators; sound recording equipment; audio mixers
Alumni: Chris Allen, video director; Dianna Schmitt, radio newscaster

GUIDE POV: This competitive private college offers a communications major that focuses on practical television and radio broadcast training; course listings in journalism, copywriting, mass communications law, and studio operations; required core curriculum in the liberal arts; junior semester abroad; summer study in England; internship opportunities in television and radio production

COUNTY COLLEGE OF MORRIS

214 Center Grove Rd.,
Randolph, NJ 07869–2086
(201)328–5000

County two-year comprehensive institution. Coed, suburban location. Enrollment: 10,000.

MEDIA STUDIES PROGRAM

Chair/Contact: E. Benintende
Calendar: Semesters
Degrees Offered: A.A., liberal arts and sciences (students may select emphasis in broadcasting)
Departmental Majors: Television: 150 students
Entrance Requirements: Open-door

policy. Application deadline: August 15. Percent of acceptances: 99%
Curricular Emphasis: Mass media studies; computer graphics for television; television production; audio production and radio broadcasting; co-op work experiences in television or radio; introduction to film theory
Special Activities: Film: film series/festivals. Television: program material produced for on-campus closed-circuit television
Facilities: Television: studio; audio bay; control room; editing suites; computer animation facilities
Equipment: Television/Video: complete ¾" studio; complete ¾" and ½" location; computer animation equipment
Alumni: Joann Young, TV producer/writer; Jerry Ketcham, film/TV assistant director

GUIDE POV: For students seeking careers in television or radio production, this two-year media studies program provides practical experience in all aspects of broadcast operations including training in digital video production technology; transfer program; internship and co-op work opportunities in television or radio production

ESSEX COUNTY COLLEGE

303 University Ave.,
Newark, NJ 07102
(201)877–3000

State two-year institution. Coed, urban location. Enrollment: 8,000.

MEDIA PRODUCTION AND TECHNOLOGY

Chair/Contact: Linda G. Corrin, Academic Coordinator
Calendar: Semesters

Degrees Offered: A.A.S., television production
Departmental Majors: 100 students
Entrance Requirements: Open-door policy with state placement examinations in math, English, and reading. Application deadline: rolling
Curricular Emphasis: History and theory of radio and television; studio and field production; cable television and broadcast technology; broadcast writing; media sales and technology; media management
Special Activities: Television: program material produced for cable television, on-campus closed-circuit television, and local cable educational access channel
Facilities: Television: studio; audio bay; control room; editing suites
Equipment: Television/Video: complete 1" and ¾" studio; complete ¾" and ½" location including graphics and special effects; Sony and Ikegami cameras; Grass Valley switcher; computerized editing
Alumni: Charlene Giles, TV production assistant; Gwen Meade, TV production assistant

GUIDE POV: Production students at this affordable community college enjoy practical training using modern television facilities; numerous volunteer crewing positions at on-campus cable station; separate track for broadcast engineering; internship opportunities in television production

FAIRLEIGH DICKINSON UNIVERSITY—MADISON

Florham-Madison Campus,
285 Madison Ave.,
Madison, NJ 07940
(201)593–8500

Private four-year comprehensive institution. Coed, suburban location. Undergraduate enrollment: 2,400. Graduate enrollment: 1,600.

ENGLISH/COMMUNICATIONS DEPARTMENT

Chair/Contact: Martin Green, Chair
Calendar: Semesters
Degrees Offered: B.A., M.A.
Departmental Majors: Undergraduate: 150 students. Graduate: 100 students
Entrance Requirements: Undergraduate: 2.5 grade-point average; ACT or SAT scores. Graduate: 3.0 grade-point average; GRE scores; writing sample. Undergraduate and graduate application deadline: rolling. Percent of acceptances: 73%
Curricular Emphasis: Video and television production training within a communications curriculum; graduate emphasis on corporate communications
Special Activities: Film: film series/festivals; film societies. Television: program material produced for various outlets
Facilities: Film: sound mixing room; screening room; editing room; sound stage; 35mm screening facilities; film library. Television: studio; audio studio; control room
Equipment: Film: complete Super-8 and 16mm. Television/Video: ¾" studio; ¾" and ½" location
Alumni: Colleen Neilson, video director/producer; Jeffrey Fisher, video director

GUIDE POV: Students here receive undergraduate preparation in communications with selected film and television courses; graduate program features course in audio-visual media for corporate communications professionals; study abroad in England; internship opportunities in New Jersey, New York, and Great Britain

FAIRLEIGH DICKINSON UNIVERSITY—TEANECK–HACKENSACK

1000 River Rd.,
Teaneck, NJ 07666
(201)692–2000

Private four-year comprehensive institution. Coed, urban location. Undergraduate enrollment: 11,000. Graduate enrollment: 2,000

DEPARTMENT OF COMMUNICATION AND SPEECH

Chair/Contact: Dr. Donald Jugenheimer, Chair
Calendar: Semesters
Degrees Offered: B.A., M.A., communication
Departmental Majors: Undergraduate film: 25; advertising/public relations: 100; broadcasting: 40; journalism: 30; theory: 5. Graduate corporate and organizational communication: 20
Entrance Requirements: Undergraduate: 2.0 grade-point average; ACT or SAT scores. Graduate: 3.0 grade-point average; GRE or GMAT scores; writing samples. Undergraduate and graduate application deadline: rolling. Percent of acceptances: 73%
Curricular Emphasis: Film and television production; broadcast journalism; media management
Special Activities: Film: film series/festivals; videos produced for cable television. Television: program material produced for on-campus closed-circuit television and cable television
Facilities: Film: 35mm screening facilities; film library. Television/Video:

two studios; audio bays; control rooms
Equipment: Film: complete Super-8; 16mm cameras; lighting; controls; editing; black-and-white film stock; color film stock; projectors. Television: complete ¾" studio; complete ¾" and ½" location
Alumni: "Chip" Berdinis, radio newscaster; Michael Perrone, TV sales executive; Duane Dickerson, videographer

GUIDE POV: This is a small, well-equipped program that offers comprehensive training in film and television production as well as national and international media sales and management; adult degree program; study abroad at campus in England; media internship opportunities in New Jersey, New York, and England

JERSEY CITY STATE COLLEGE

2039 Kennedy Blvd.,
Jersey City, NJ 07305
(201)200–2000

State four-year comprehensive institution. Coed, urban location. Undergraduate enrollment: 5,500. Graduate enrollment: 1,200.

MEDIA ARTS DEPARTMENT

Chair/Contact: Jane Steuerwald, Chair
Calendar: Semesters
Degrees Offered: B.A., media arts
Departmental Majors: Undergraduate: 227
Entrance Requirements: Undergraduate: 2.5 grade-point average; recommended SAT score 400 minimum for each part; interview; essay; teachers' recommendations. Undergraduate application deadline: June 1 for fall entry; December 1

for spring entry. Percent of acceptances: 53%

Curricular Emphasis: Film: critical studies; production; screenwriting; animation; experimental; computer graphics. Television/Video: critical studies; fiction; experimental; news/documentary; video art. Audio: critical studies; production; music engineering; radio production

Special Activities: Film: film societies. Television: program material produced for local, public, commercial, and cable television; vocational placement

Facilities: Film: sound mixing room; 16mm postproduction suite; screening room; five editing suites; black-and-white processing and printing laboratory; animation stand; film library. Television: four-camera color studio; audio bay; A and B roll ¾" editing suite; digital effects editing suite; three audio control rooms; computer graphics suite

Equipment: Film: complete 16mm. Television: complete ¾" studio; complete ¾" and ½" location

Alumni: Warren Schiff, TV network sports director; Tim Pankewicz, audio engineer; Kerry Mehan, TV producer

GUIDE POV: Hands-on film and video production training is offered at this fully equipped school; courses in film animation and video art; faculty of working professionals; most extensive cooperative education program in the state; study abroad in South America, Europe, and Africa; salaried internship opportunities locally and in New York.

MERCER COUNTY COMMUNITY COLLEGE

P.O. Box B,
Trenton, NJ 08690
(609)586–4800

County two-year comprehensive institution. Coed, suburban and urban locations. Enrollment: 8,500.

ARTS AND COMMUNICATIONS DEPARTMENT

Chair/Contact: Dr. David S. Levin, Chair

Calendar: Semesters

Degrees Offered: A.A., communications; A.A.S., television, radio, visual arts (students may select emphasis in computer graphics)

Departmental Majors: Communications: 80 students; television: 55 students; radio: 40 students

Entrance Requirements: Open-door policy; high school diploma or equivalent. Application deadline: rolling

Curricular Emphasis: Electronic media theory and culture; media writing; audio-video production; video art; media management

Special Activities: Television: program material produced for college county-wide cable television network

Facilities: Television: 40' by 50' studio; audio bay; control room; editing bays; audio studio; satellite teleconferencing

Equipment: Television/Video: complete ¾" studio with five color cameras; complete ¾" and ½" location including Chyron ACG; computerized prompter; Ampex switcher; five-meter TV satellite earth station; computer graphics

Alumni: John Maurer, film/TV executive; Bill Green, TV director/editor; Steve Mosley, video editor

GUIDE POV: This community college possesses the largest multi-use educational television and radio facility in New Jersey and features state-of-the-art equipment; separate concentration in computer graphics; practical approach; media internship opportunities

MONTCLAIR STATE COLLEGE

Upper Montclair, NJ 07043
(201)655–4000

State four-year comprehensive institution. Coed, suburban location. Undergraduate enrollment: 11,000. Graduate enrollment: 3,000.

CENTER FOR FILM STUDIES/FILM PRODUCTION

Chair/Contact: Dr. Janet K. Cutler, film studies; Michael S. Siporin, film production
Calendar: Semesters
Degrees Offered: B.A., with an interdisciplinary film minor (film studies and filmmaking)
Entrance Requirements:
Undergraduate: competitive grade-point average; SAT required; interview recommended. Undergraduate application deadline: March 1. Percent of acceptances: 47%
Curricular Emphasis: Film theory/aesthetics, history, and criticism; 8mm and 16mm film production including experimental, narrative, documentary, and animated
Special Activities: Film: film series/festivals
Facilities: Film: screening room; editing suite; sound mixing room; animation stand; film library
Equipment: Film: complete Super-8 and 16mm
Alumni: Eric Bross, film director/writer; Chriss Williams, film director/writer; Arish Fyzee, film producer/director

GUIDE POV: This selective state college is located 15 miles west of New York City; undergraduates choosing the film minor work in 8mm and 16mm production; attention to independent projects; small classes; study abroad in 13 countries; varied internship opportunities

PRINCETON UNIVERSITY

Princeton, NJ 08544–0430
(609)258–3000

Private four-year comprehensive institution. Coed, small town location. Undergraduate enrollment: 5,500. Graduate enrollment: 2,100

PROGRAM IN VISUAL ARTS

Chair/Contact: James Seawright, Director
Calendar: Semesters
Degrees Offered: B.A., visual arts
Entrance Requirements:
Undergraduate: SAT required; ACT accepted; essay required; interview recommended. Graduate: GRE scores; recommendations; essay required. Undergraduate application deadline: January 2. Percent of acceptances: 17%
Curricular Emphasis: Visual arts: course listings include Cinema and Modernism; Major Filmmakers; Problems of Film and Video Practice
Special Activities: Film: film series/screenings
Facilities/Equipment: Film/video: screening room; basic video equipment
Alumni: Ring Lardner, Jr., author/screenwriter

GUIDE POV: Students attending this Ivy League university, established in 1746, may receive basic video instruction as part of a visual arts curriculum that stresses film theory, aesthetics, and criticism; studio classes in photography, sculpture, and painting

RARITAN VALLEY COMMUNITY COLLEGE

P.O. Box 3300,
Somerville, NJ 08876
(908)526–1200

County two-year institution. Coed, suburban location. Enrollment: 6,000.

FINE AND PERFORMING ARTS DEPARTMENT

Chair/Contact: Ann Tsubota
Calendar: Semesters
Degrees Offered: A.A., studio arts, communications, commercial art with computers
Departmental Majors: Film and television/video: 25 students
Entrance Requirements: Open-door policy with placement testing. Application deadline: rolling. Percent of acceptances: 99%
Curricular Emphasis: Electronic media theory and culture; critical studies in film; media writing; basic video production including computer graphics; media management
Special Activities: Television: program material produced for on-campus closed-circuit television and for cable television
Facilities: Film: screening room; editing suite. Television: studio; control room
Equipment: Film: complete Super-8. Television/Video: studio equipment; complete ½" location; complete computer graphics/animation studio
Alumni: Cindy Burns, video

technician; Andrea Rosebrock, bio-medical video producer

GUIDE POV: Basic video production studies are offered at this affordable two-year county college; core curriculum fulfills transfer requirements to area universities; video students work on a variety of location projects for cable television; internship opportunities

RUTGERS UNIVERSITY AT CAMDEN

406 Penn Street
Camden, NJ 08102
(609)225–1766

Public multi-campus comprehensive institution. Coed, urban location. Undergraduate enrollment: 2,500

ENGLISH DEPARTMENT

Chair/Contact: Robert Ryan, Chair
Calendar: Semesters
Degrees Offered: B.A., English
Entrance Requirements:
Undergraduate: SAT or ACT required. Undergraduate application deadline: May 1. Percent of acceptances: 49%
Curricular Emphasis: English: option in film studies with areas of inquiry that include film history; literature and film; American film; world cinema; major filmmakers; special topics
Special Activities: Film: film series/screenings
Facilities: Film/Video: screening room
Alumni: Kevin DiNovis, film/TV writer; David L. Roehm, writer/cinematographer

GUIDE POV: The selective Rutgers Camden College of Arts and Sciences offers a full film studies option through the English Department; departmental honors program requires thesis completion; major requirements in

English can be completed either through daytime or evening attendance; study abroad throughout Europe, as well as in Israel and Mexico

---

SETON HALL UNIVERSITY

South Orange, NJ 07079
(201)761–9000

Private four-year comprehensive institution. Coed, suburban location. Undergraduate enrollment: 4,400. Graduate enrollment: 2,400

COMMUNICATION DEPARTMENT

Chair/Contact: Dr. Donald McKenna, Chair
Calendar: Semesters
Degrees Offered: B.A., communication
Departmental Majors: Undergraduate communication: 440 students
Entrance Requirements: Undergraduate: ACT or SAT scores; upper third of graduating class; teachers' recommendations. Undergraduate application deadline: March 1. Percent of acceptances: 65%
Curricular Emphasis: Film: critical studies; introductory and advanced film production; writing for film. Television/Video: electronic media theory and culture; four-course studio television production sequence; writing for television; news/documentary; video art; computer graphics for advertising, desktop publishing, and computer animation
Special Activities: Film: film series/festivals. Television: program material produced for on-campus cable television
Facilities: Film: editing suites; film library. Television: three-camera studio; audio bay; control room; postproduction; computer graphics laboratories
Equipment: Film: complete Super-8 and 16mm. Television/Video: complete ¾" studio; complete ¾" location; 16-station Macintosh desktop publishing laboratory; eight-station DOS-based computer graphics and animation laboratory featuring Paint, 3D animation, and image processing software, including Time Arts Lumena and Autodesk 3D Studio
Alumni: Robert A. Ley, ESPN TV sportscaster; James Hunter, CBS radio network sportscaster/producer

GUIDE POV: Affiliated with the Roman Catholic Church and founded by the first bishop of Newark, this well-equipped university offers intensive production training in both film and video; curriculum provides theoretical grounding; interest in new technologies; extensive media internship opportunities in South Orange and New York

---

WILLIAM PATERSON COLLEGE

300 Pompton Rd.,
Wayne, NJ 07470
(201)595–2000

State four-year comprehensive institution. Coed, suburban location. Undergraduate enrollment: 6,000. Graduate enrollment: 1,600

DEPARTMENT OF COMMUNICATION

Chair/Contact: Leandro Katz, film program
Calendar: Semesters
Degrees Offered: B.A., communication (with emphasis in broadcasting, film, journalism, interpersonal, or telecommunications); M.A., communication arts

Departmental Majors: Undergraduate film: 60 students. Undergraduate television: 80 students

Entrance Requirements: Undergraduate: academic rank within top half of graduating class; SAT (minimum 900 composite) scores. Graduate: transcripts; interview; 2.75 grade-point average; GRE (minimum 500 verbal) or MAT (minimum 42) scores; recommendations. Undergraduate and graduate application deadline: June 30. Percent of acceptances: 51%

Curricular Emphasis: Electronic media theory and culture; critical studies in film; media writing; audio-film-video production; media management

Special Activities: Film: film series/festivals; film production seminars. Television: program material produced for on-campus closed-circuit television and for cable television; teleconferencing seminars

Facilities: Film: sound stage; screening room; editing suite; sound mixing room; film library. Television: studio; audio bay; control room

Equipment: Film: complete Super-8 and 16mm. Television/Video: complete ¾" studio and location

Alumni: Mary Wardrop, TV director; Cora Ann Mihalik, TV news anchor; Kathy Millar, radio and TV disc jockey; Patti Ball, TV associate producer; Susan Liscovicz, TV correspondent

GUIDE POV: Communication majors at this competitive college may concentrate in either film or broadcast production; graduate program stresses communication theory with selected advanced production work in film or television; study abroad in five countries; media internship opportunities

There is an underlying absurdity to the basic concept of film school. You can't teach anyone how to make good films. But you can learn by doing and seeing what other people are doing or what other people have done. Film school has certainly provided the resources for me to do that.

Now at the end of my second year of a three-year M.F.A. program, I have directed eight short films. And it has been both stressful and exhilarating. A friend of mine in medical school dropped by recently to see what I was doing. "This is much more intense than med school, Marty. Of course, you're making movies. We're just saving lives."

You have to hit the ground running at most graduate film schools. Sometimes you'd swear you were given an assignment the day after it's due. Everyone's scared, but there's no time to get caught up in your fears. Somehow just by doing you find out what you've got and what you want to say.

I feel fortunate to have found myself amid a group of students who are exceptionally talented, motivated, and generous. You form deep bonds based on mutual respect, sleep deprivation, and stress.

As a former actor with professional experience, I am acquainted with the harsh realities of the industry. I realize that the film school degree is by itself virtually meaningless. Only those born to the business know how they'll get their first job.

Yet with all that said, I feel infinitely better prepared to make my way into the world. Quite simply, film school has been the most rewarding time of my life. But there is one tangible thing grad school has taught me: Story is everything. And casting is everything. And the images and soundtrack, they're everything too. Yeah, that much I've learned.

COLLEGE OF SANTA FE

1600 St. Michael's Dr.,
Santa Fe, NM 87501–5634
(505)473–6000

Private four-year comprehensive institution. Coed, urban location. Undergraduate enrollment: 700. Graduate enrollment: 60.

DEPARTMENT OF MOVING IMAGE ARTS

Chair/Contact: Joseph Dispenza, Chair
Calendar: Semesters
Degrees Offered: B.A.
Departmental Majors:
Undergraduate: 200 students
Entrance Requirements:
Undergraduate: minimum scores ACT 19 or SAT verbal 410/SAT math 370; 2.5 grade-point average; teachers' recommendations. Undergraduate application deadline: rolling. Percent of acceptances: 60%
Curricular Emphasis: Film/Video: integrated curriculum of production, screenwriting, and critical studies
Special Activities: Film: guest artist program; screenings; film club; departmental student council
Facilities: Film: 16mm editing room; two screening rooms equipped to screen works in Hi-8, U-matic, standard and super VHS, and Laserdisc through video projection, as well as 16mm prints; larger screening room also equipped for Betacam-SP. Video: six cuts-only editing suites; two A/B roll suites; audio production studio; three-camera studio with master and audio control rooms; single-camera production studio; duplication room for format-to-format transfers; video formats in Hi-8, U-matic; Betacam-SP; small private viewing room equipped with U-matic, VHS, and Laserdisc
Equipment: Film: complete 16mm. Video: complete studio; complete location including Hi-8 camcorders, light kits, audio recorders and mixers, microphones, portable monitors, and tripods
Alumni: Carmalee McGuinnis, TV producer/executive; Guy Thomas Koepp, production assistant; Charles Montoya, production assistant

GUIDE POV: Founded by the Christian Brothers, this competitive liberal arts college offers courses in film and video theory and production, along with core requirements in philosophy, especially ethics; emphasis on independent filmmaking; professional internship opportunities

EASTERN NEW MEXICO UNIVERSITY

Station #3,
Portales, NM 88130
(505)562–1011

State four-year comprehensive institution. Coed, rural location.

Undergraduate enrollment: 4,000.
Graduate enrollment: 600.

DEPARTMENT OF COMMUNICATIVE ARTS AND SCIENCES

Chair/Contact: Dr. Anthony B. Schroeder, Chair
Calendar: Semesters
Degrees Offered: B.A., B.S., M.A.
Departmental Majors:
Undergraduate: 50–100 students.
Graduate: 10–25 students
Entrance Requirements:
Undergraduate: 2.0 grade-point average; ACT required (minimum score 18). Graduate: 3.0 grade-point average; writing sample; recommendations. Undergraduate and graduate application deadline: April 15. Percent of acceptances: 70%
Curricular Emphasis: Broadcast journalism; broadcast production
Special Activities: Television: program material, including nightly news show, produced for local PBS affiliate as well as on-campus television
Facilities: Television: studio; audio bay; control room; VHS editing bay
Equipment: Television/Video: complete ¾" studio and location; camcorders; VHS editing
Alumni: Michael Anthony, TV news director/reporter; Jeffrey Nielsen, TV producer/anchor/reporter; Timothy Dill, broadcasting executive; Theresa Rodriguez, TV news reporter

GUIDE POV: Students attending this state university gain technical experience in all phases of broadcast production; graduates have good employment ratio, especially in commercial production houses, television stations, and radio stations in New Mexico and neighboring states; study abroad through the International Students Exchange Program; varied internship opportunities

NEW MEXICO STATE UNIVERSITY

Box 30001,
Las Cruces, NM 88003–0001
(505)646–0111

State four-year comprehensive institution. Coed, suburban location. Undergraduate enrollment: 12,000. Graduate enrollment: 2,000.

DEPARTMENT OF JOURNALISM AND MASS COMMUNICATIONS

Chair/Contact: Dr. Sean McCleneghan, Chair
Calendar: Semesters
Degrees Offered: B.A.
Departmental Majors: Undergraduate television: 60 students
Entrance Requirements:
Undergraduate: students must meet one of three requirements: 2.0 grade-point average with an ACT score of at least 18; 2.5 grade-point average; score of 20 or above on the ACT. Undergraduate application deadline: August 1. Percent of acceptances: 91%
Curricular Emphasis: Mass communications theory; media writing; television and radio production; broadcast journalism; studio and field production; broadcast studio operations
Special Activities: Television: program material produced for PBS station KRWG-TV, housed on campus, which reaches a population of 300,000 in southern New Mexico and west Texas area; department newsletter
Facilities: Television: studio; audio bay; control room; editing suites
Equipment: Television/Video: complete ¾" studio and location
Alumni: Carla Aragon, TV news

anchor; Roberta Romero, TV news reporter; Tommy Downs, TV meteorologist; Scott Davis, TV news reporter; Pat Monacelli, TV news reporter; Ev Avara, TV assignments editor; Ward Matthews, TV news reporter

GUIDE POV: This competitive state university offers students mass communication studies with a strong emphasis on broadcast journalism; cross-registration with the Doña Ana Branch Community College; internship opportunities in television production

UNIVERSITY OF NEW MEXICO— ALBUQUERQUE

Albuquerque, NM 87131
(505)277–2440

State four-year comprehensive institution. Coed, urban location. Undergraduate enrollment: 24,000. Graduate enrollment: 2,000.

FILM/TELEVISION PROGRAM IN THE MEDIA ARTS

Chair/Contact: Film: Ira S. Jaffe; television: Maryjo Cochran
Calendar: Semesters
Degrees Offered: B.A., with a minor in film or television
Entrance Requirements: Undergraduate: 2.0 grade-point average; ACT required; SAT recommended; GED accepted. Undergraduate application deadline: August 15. Percent of acceptances: 83%
Curricular Emphasis: Electronic media theory and culture; critical studies in film; media writing; film and video production
Special Activities: Film: International Cinema Lecture Series; Southwest Film

Center. Television: program material produced for on-campus closed-circuit television, for local public television station, and for cable television
Facilities: Television: studio; control room
Equipment: Film: complete Super-8 and 16mm. Television/Video: complete ¾" studio; complete ¾" and ½" location
Alumni: Brian Levant, film director; Steve Anderson, film director; Christine Williams, film editor

GUIDE POV: This selective public university offers students a comprehensive minor in either film or television criticism and production; film production classes focus on independent projects; television production is news/documentary oriented; study abroad; internship opportunities in film and television production

UNIVERSITY OF NEW MEXICO— GALLUP

200 College Rd.,
Gallup, NM 87301
(505)863–7500

State two-year comprehensive institution. Coed, small town location. Enrollment: 3,000

FINE ARTS DEPARTMENT

Chair/Contact: Robert Bell
Calendar: Semesters
Degrees Offered: A.A.
Departmental Majors: Fine arts: 20 students
Entrance Requirements: 2.0 grade-point average; teachers' recommendations. Application deadline: rolling. Percent of acceptances: 99%

Curricular Emphasis: Electronic media theory and culture; critical studies in film; media writing; basic documentary film production; news/documentary video production
Special Activities: Film: film series/festivals. Television: program material produced for cable television
Facilities: Television: students have access to area broadcast facilities
Equipment: Film: Super-8 and 16mm projectors. Television/Video: complete ½" location; ¾" editing equipment; computer graphics equipment
Alumni: Deenise Becenti, TV cameraperson

GUIDE POV: Students at this two-year community college study film/video theory and basic production as part of a fine arts curriculum; transfer program to area schools

Having written and directed ten features, including *A Safe Place, Tracks, Sitting Ducks, Can She Bake a Cherry Pie? Always, But Not Forever, Someone to Love, New Year's Day*, and *Eating*, I can unequivocally say that a formal film education is not essential for aspiring filmmakers. I had none. Anything, anyplace, or anybody that gets you to see films and enables you to make films—of any kind, any length, or any format—is where your education lies.

Personally, I went to movies, thought about movies, got to see people make movies, and made movies. I was determined just to find the way in to get to the point where someone was crazy enough to let me make my first film. An 8mm home movie I made in Israel on the Six Day War got me a job to help edit *Easy Rider*, which turned out to be the magic key for me.

My advice to potential screenwriters and directors is: Tell the truth. Don't listen to anybody but yourself. And know that you can do it.

ADELPHI UNIVERSITY

South Ave.,
Garden City, NY 11530
(516)877–3000

*Private four-year comprehensive
institution. Coed, suburban location.
Undergraduate enrollment: 7,000.
Graduate enrollment: 2,500.*

DEPARTMENT OF COMMUNICATIONS

Chair/Contact: Leonard Price, Chair;
Louise Leonard
Calendar: Semesters
Degrees Offered: B.A.
Departmental Majors:
Undergraduate: 150 students
Entrance Requirements:
Undergraduate: 2.5 grade-point
average; ACT or SAT scores;
interview; written statement of
purpose; recommendations.
Undergraduate application deadline:
rolling
Curricular Emphasis: Film and
electronic media studies; film and
television production
Special Activities: Film: film series/
annual student film and video festival.
Video: program material produced for
sponsored projects
Facilities: Film: screening room;
editing suite; sound mixing room;
animation stand; film library. Video:
studio; audio bay; control room;
editing facilities
Equipment: Film: complete 16mm.

Video: complete ¾" studio; complete
¾" and ½" location
Alumni: Scott James, TV news
director; Tom Cammisa, TV producer;
Ken Bornstein, TV editor

GUIDE POV: Located 20 miles east of
New York City, Adelphi University
offers students a Communications
Department that provides sequential
production training in both film and
video along with studies in aesthetics;
liberal arts curriculum; professional
internships in all areas of the media,
in New York City and surrounding
areas

ADIRONDACK COMMUNITY COLLEGE

Bay Rd.,
Queensbury, NY 12804–1498
(518)793–4491

*State two-year comprehensive
institution. Coed, rural location.
Enrollment: 3,700.*

BROADCAST COMMUNICATIONS TECHNOLOGY

Chair/Contact: Ronald Pesha
Calendar: Semesters
Degrees Offered: A.A.S., broadcast
communications
Departmental Majors: Television:
40 students
Entrance Requirements: High school

diploma, GED scores, or one year past normal high school graduation date. Application deadline: August 15. Percent of acceptances: 100%
Curricular Emphasis: Video production
Special Activities: Television: program material produced for cable and commercial television stations
Facilities: Television: studio; audio studio; control room
Equipment: Television: VHS cameras and S-VHS editing suite; SEG, waveform and vectorscope monitors, ¾" VCRs; ¾" location
Alumni: Mark Mulholland, TV sports anchor; Mark Bradway, TV graphics designer; Scott Valentine, film/TV actor

GUIDE POV: This two-year school offers hands-on video production training; internship opportunities in television production

---

BARD COLLEGE

Annandale-on-Hudson, NY 12504
(914)758–6822

Private four-year comprehensive institution. Coed, rural location. Undergraduate enrollment: 920. Graduate enrollment: 60.

FILM DEPARTMENT

Chair/Contact: Adolfas Mekas; Arthur Gibbons
Calendar: Semesters
Degrees Offered: B.A., M.F.A.
Departmental Majors: Undergraduate: 75 students. Graduate: 10 students
Entrance Requirements: Undergraduate: high school diploma or GED certificate; interview; essay; strong academic record. Graduate: transcripts; 16mm completed film,

videotape, or script(s); graduate transfer credit accepted with grade of *B* or better; brief history of professional activity; two letters of recommendation; essay. Undergraduate application deadline: February 15 for fall entry; January 1 for spring entry. Graduate application deadline: December 15 for early admission; March 1 deadline. Percent of acceptances: 55%
Curricular Emphasis: Film: 16mm production and editing; screenwriting; aesthetics; experimental and documentary forms
Special Activities: Film: film series/festivals; student publication
Facilities: Film/Video: film editing suites; screening room; optical printer; ½" video editing rooms; film library
Equipment: Film/Video: complete 16mm production and postproduction; upright and flatbed editing; sound transfer equipment; film-to-video transfer; optical printer; JVC and S-VHS cameras and editing units; Amiga computers; time coder/reader, etc.
Alumni: Chevy Chase, film/TV actor; Thom Mount, film producer/executive; Larry Gross, TV writer; Robert Avrech, film/TV writer

GUIDE POV: This selective private college offers a small program emphasizing aesthetics, experimental film production, and postproduction techniques; classes taught by working media artists; study abroad; internship opportunities

---

BOROUGH OF MANHATTAN COMMUNITY COLLEGE

City University of New York,
199 Chambers St.,
New York, NY 10007
(212)346–8000

City two-year institution. Coed, urban location. Enrollment: 12,000.

CORPORATE AND CABLE COMMUNICATIONS PROGRAM

Chair/Contact: Dr. George W. Fleck, Program Director
Calendar: Semesters
Degrees Offered: A.A.S., nonbroadcast television
Departmental Majors: 390 students
Entrance Requirements: ACT or SAT scores; interview. Application deadline: rolling
Curricular Emphasis: Corporate television production
Special Activities: Television: program material produced for on-campus closed-circuit and cable television; electronic news gathering club
Facilities: Television: studios; audio bays; control rooms; video graphics
Equipment: Television/Video: complete 1" and ¾" studio; complete ¾" and ½" location
Alumni: Greg Wright, TV producer; Robert Von Rhyn, TV production assistant; Brenda Rivera, TV production assistant; Dante Pagano, TV production assistant; Donna Farnum, TV sound engineer; Marlon Bickford, TV camera operator

GUIDE POV: This community college offers a two-year program featuring specialized training in video production with a nonbroadcast emphasis; internship opportunities in corporate video production

BRONX COMMUNITY COLLEGE

University Ave. and W. 181 St.,
Bronx, NY 10453
(718)220–6456

City two-year comprehensive institution. Coed, urban location. Enrollment: 7,000.

AUDIOVISUAL TECHNOLOGY

Chair/Contact: Donald J. Canty, Chair
Calendar: Semesters
Degrees Offered: A.A.S.
Departmental Majors: 80 students
Entrance Requirements: Open-door policy; high school diploma or equivalent. Application deadline: rolling
Curricular Emphasis: Video production emphasizing corporate and cable markets
Special Activities: Film: film series/festivals. Television: program material produced for New York City cable network
Facilities: Television: studio; audio bay; control room; editing suites
Equipment: Video: complete ¾" studio and location including MII mastering; Grass Valley 200 switcher; A/B roll editing; VHS, Hi-8, and ¾" off-line editing
Alumni: Ana Moreno, lighting technician; Albert Stewart, video technician; Fitzroy Francis, video technician

GUIDE POV: This community college offers its students a nonbroadcast video program specializing in corporate and cable video production; core curriculum with practical training prepares students for technical support positions as well as for transfer to four-year schools; varied internship opportunities

BROOME COMMUNITY COLLEGE

P.O. Box 1017,
Binghamton, NY 13902
(607)778–5000

State two-year comprehensive institution, coed, urban location. Enrollment: 6,500.

COMMUNICATION AND MEDIA ARTS DEPARTMENT

Chair/Contact: John T. Butchko
Calendar: Semesters
Departmental Majors: Film and television: 90 students
Degrees Offered: A.S., communication and media arts
Entrance Requirements: High school diploma or GED; placement tests in math and English. Application deadline: rolling
Curricular Emphasis: Film/Video: sequential production training in both film (8mm and 16mm) and video; writing for the media; studies in media and culture; journalism; theatre; image theory; audio production; photography
Special Activities: Film/Video: art/video/photography shows; field trips to Manhattan related to theatre and television production
Facilities: Film: film/photo studio; sound mixing room; screening room; editing room. Television: studios; audio production studios; control room
Equipment: Film: complete Super-8 and 16mm. Television: complete ¾" and ½" color studios and ½" location; ¾" and ½" editing systems
Alumni: Mike Sterling, TV director; Dave Kenney, TV director; Vince Burns, film actor/production assistant; Michele Haun, TV news producer; Stan Sherwood, actor/Disney tour guide

GUIDE POV: Supervised by SUNY, Broome Community College offers a highly professional two-year technical production program in film and video that prepares students for transfer to upper division colleges as well as for immediate employment; excellent transfer and career placement records for graduates; varied media internship opportunities

CAYUGA COMMUNITY COLLEGE

197 Franklin St.,
Auburn, NY 13021
(315)255–1743

State two-year comprehensive institution. Coed, suburban location. Enrollment: 2,000.

TELECOMMUNICATIONS DEPARTMENT

Chair/Contact: Steven R. Keeler
Calendar: Semesters
Degrees Offered: A.A.S., radio/TV broadcasting, broadcasting technology
Departmental Majors: 90 students
Entrance Requirements: High school diploma or GED; ACT or SAT scores; high school transcript. Application deadline: rolling
Curricular Emphasis: Hands-on TV and radio production
Special Activities: Program material produced for cable television; vocational placement service
Facilities: Television: studio; control room; master control room; editing suites
Equipment: Television: complete ¾" TV studio; S-VHS and Hi-8 remote postproduction; videotoaster workstation
Alumni: Craig Braden, videographer; James Marco, TV engineer

GUIDE POV: This well-equipped community college offers a production-oriented two-year program in telecommunications; travel-study course in London offers comprehensive view of broadcasting industry in Great Britain; varied internship opportunities in television production

CITY UNIVERSITY OF NEW YORK— BROOKLYN COLLEGE

Bedford Ave. & Ave. H.,
Brooklyn, NY 11230
(718)951–5000

State four-year comprehensive institution. Coed, urban location. Undergraduate enrollment: 14,000. Graduate enrollment: 3,000.

DEPARTMENT OF TELEVISION AND RADIO

Chair/Contact: Robert C. Williams

FILM DEPARTMENT

Chair/Contact: Lindley P. Hanlon
Degrees Offered: B.A., with a concentration in film production and film studies; certificate in film production; B.A., M.A., television/radio; B.S., broadcast journalism; M.S., television/radio; M.F.A., television production
Calendar: Semesters
Departmental Majors: Undergraduate radio/television: 400 students. Undergraduate film: 100 students. Graduate radio/television: 70 students
Entrance Requirements:
Undergraduate: 2.0 grade-point average; SAT score 900 minimum; passing grade on CUNY English and math placement tests. Graduate: transcripts; two letters of reference; interview; GRE scores. Undergraduate

application deadline: rolling. Graduate application deadline: March 1 for fall entry; November 1 for spring entry. Percent of acceptances: 60%
Curricular Emphasis: Film: theory, criticism, history; fiction and nonfiction production; screenwriting; editing; directing; sound; cinematography; animation. Television/Video: critical studies; production and postproduction; broadcast journalism; media management
Special Activities: Film: film series/festivals; film societies. Television: program material produced for on-campus closed-circuit television, local public and commercial television stations, and cable television
Equipment: Film: complete Super-8 and 16mm. Television/Video: complete 1" and ¾" full-color studios and postproduction facilities; complete ¾" and ½" location
Facilities: Film: sound mixing room; screening room; editing room; 35mm screening facilities; animation stand; film library. Television: studios; audio bays; control rooms
Alumni: Michael Kochman, TV/film archivist; Tamara Rawitt, TV/film producer; Tracy Nalevanko, TV/film producer

GUIDE POV: This competitive university offers comprehensive, separate programs in film and television production and criticism; highly diverse curriculum; graduate program in television production; faculty of working film and television professionals; numerous media internship opportunities in New York City

CITY UNIVERSITY OF NEW YORK— CITY COLLEGE

Convent Ave. at 138th St.,
New York, NY 10031
(212)650–7000

*State four-year comprehensive
institution. Coed, urban location.
Undergraduate enrollment: 14,000.
Graduate enrollment: 3,200*

COMMUNICATIONS, FILM, AND VIDEO DEPARTMENT

Chair/Contact: Dennis DeNitto, Chair;
David Davidson, Deputy Chair and
Adviser, film and video production
specialization
Calendar: Semesters
Degrees Offered: B.A.,
communications (with concentrations
in film and video production,
communication studies, journalism, or
advertising and public relations);
B.F.A., M.F.A., film and video
production
Departmental Majors: Undergraduate
film and video: 150 students
Entrance Requirements:
Undergraduate: academic rank within
top third of high school graduating
class or 900 minimum combined SAT
scores; GED accepted with minimum
score 270; recommendations.
Undergraduate and graduate
application deadline: January 15.
Percent of acceptances: 60%
Curricular Emphasis: Film and video
production including screenwriting,
directing for film and video, television
studio and location production;
graduate production program; history
and theory of film
Special Activities: Film: film series/
festivals. Television: program material
produced for local PBS affiliates, Arts
& Entertainment network, and various
cable outlets; students participate in
festivals, including the Global Village
Documentary Festival, the AFI/A&E
Video Competition, and student
festivals sponsored by the Academy of
Motion Picture Arts and Sciences
Facilities: Film/Video: sound stage;
two screening rooms; film, video, and
nonlinear postproduction suites; digital
audio post and mixing suite;
Macintosh video graphics lab;
Macintosh writing lab with
screenwriting and budgeting software;
film library. Television: studio; audio
bay; control room; video editing suites
Equipment: Film: complete Super-8
and 16mm including three Arriflex 16
SR with Zeiss Super Speed lenses and
video tap; four Cinema Productions
CP-16 with Angenieux zoom lenses;
Sachtler tripods; dollies; Mole
Richardson location and studio
lighting packages; Nagra 4.2 and
Stelladat synch sound recorders; four,
six, and eight plate Steenbeck flatbed
editors; sound transfer equipment;
digital nonlinear postproduction for
film and video including four AVID
Media Composer; negative transfer
system; Otari ProDisk sound editing
and mixing system. Television/Video:
complete ¾" studio including four
Sony M-7 cameras, Sony 3200 switcher,
Quanta character generator, Pinnacle
digital effects; complete location
including Betacam SP, S-VHS, and Hi-8
field cameras with Sachtler tripods,
location lighting packages, and
portable monitors; six S-VHS off-line
editing systems; Interformat on-line
room (Betacam and S-VHS) with Sony
9100 controller; Soundcraft Delta
mixing board
Alumni: Julie Dash, film director;
Joseph Vasquez, film director; Robert
Gardner, film director; Bianca Miller,
videographer; Lloyd Goldfine,

cinematographer; Dominick Tauella, sound mixer

GUIDE POV: Students enrolled in this expanding, highly competitive department are provided with a wide range of skills, concentrating in the areas of dramatic narrative filmmaking and nonfiction video production, as well as in the operation of a multi-camera television studio; emphasis on independent film/video thesis project; cross-registration with other City University colleges; accelerated degree programs; study abroad; junior-senior year Manhattan internship opportunities in film and television production

CITY UNIVERSITY OF NEW YORK— COLLEGE OF STATEN ISLAND

130 Stuyvesant Place,
Staten Island, NY 10301
(718)982–2000

State four-year comprehensive institution. Coed, urban location. Undergraduate enrollment: 16,000. Graduate enrollment: 1,000.

CINEMA STUDIES PROGRAM

Chair/Contact: Dr. Ella Shohat
Calendar: Semesters
Degrees Offered: B.A., M.A.
Departmental Majors:
Undergraduate: 30 students. Graduate: 20 students
Entrance Requirements:
Undergraduate: academic rank within top third of high school graduating class; transfer students must pass CUNY proficiency examinations. Graduate: undergraduate *B* average; GRE scores; critical or historical essay on film. Undergraduate application

deadline: rolling. Percent of acceptances: 95%
Curricular Emphasis: Program emphasizes critical studies in film, with some basic production training in film/video
Special Activities: Film: film series/festivals. Television: program material, including "Cinema Then, Cinema Now," produced for CUNY/TV, the public service cable station of CUNY and marketed nationally
Facilities: Film: film laboratory; extensive film archives. Television: studio
Equipment: Film: complete Super-8 and 16mm. Television/Video: matched studio cameras; portable lighting packages; ½" cassette recorders; portable cameras; monitors; switcher; ½" VHS editing
Alumni: Kent Green, film researcher; William Beck, media journalist; Jeff Heinle, film/TV archivist

GUIDE POV: For those pursuing careers as film historians or critics, this young program offers undergraduate and graduate critical studies combined with basic production courses in film; study abroad in Italy, Greece, Spain, Israel, and Ecuador; internship opportunities in Manhattan

CITY UNIVERSITY OF NEW YORK— HUNTER COLLEGE

695 Park Ave.,
New York, NY 10021
(212)772–4000

Four-year liberal arts college. Coed, urban location. Undergraduate enrollment: 10,000. Graduate enrollment: 5,000.

THEATRE AND FILM DEPARTMENT

Chair/Contact: Mira Felner, Chair
Calendar: Semesters
Degrees Offered: B.A., film
production, film studies
Departmental Majors:
Undergraduate: 120 film majors
Entrance Requirements:
Undergraduate: academic rank within
top third of graduating class;
composite score of 900 on SAT; GED
accepted (minimum score 270).
Undergraduate application deadline:
January 15
Curricular Emphasis: Film and video
production emphasizing narrative,
documentary, experimental, and
animation
Special Activities: Film: student
publications
Facilities: Film: screening room;
editing suite; animation stand; film
library. Television: studio; control
room
Equipment: Film: complete 16mm.
Television/Video: complete ¾"
telecine; portable lighting packages;
½" and ¾" cassette recorders; portable
cameras; monitors; sound recording
equipment
Alumni: Judith Crist, film/drama critic;
Nancy Lane, CNN TV executive
producer; Robyn Wheeler, CNN
assignment editor; Jeri Perrone, film
editor

GUIDE POV: Students who select the
production major will participate in
film and video production projects
while refining screenwriting
techniques; substantial work in fiction;
film studies majors may contribute to
the school's creative and critical
publications as well as participate in
local film/video festivals; varied
internship opportunities in film and
television production

CITY UNIVERSITY OF NEW YORK— LAGUARDIA COMMUNITY COLLEGE

31–10 Thomson Ave.,
Long Island City, NY 11101
(718)482-7200

*City two-year institution. Coed, urban
location. Enrollment: 9,000.*

DEPARTMENT OF HUMANITIES

Chair/Contact: Joyce Rheuban
Calendar: Quarters
Degrees Offered: A.A., A.S.,
communication arts
Departmental Majors: 15–20 students
Entrance Requirements: Open-door
policy; high school diploma or GED
certificate. Application deadline:
rolling
Curricular Emphasis: Film and
media studies; video production
Special Activities: Vocational
placement office
Facilities: Film: screening rooms;
16mm projectors. Television: studio;
control room
Equipment: Television/Video:
complete 1" and ¾" studio; VHS
location
Alumni: Clay Walker, filmmaker;
Edward Garcia, industrial video writer/
producer/director

GUIDE POV: Students enrolled in the
Humanities Department and
specializing in visual arts are offered
basic video production workshops as
well as theoretical courses in film and
media studies; practical emphasis;
transfer program; three required media
internships

CITY UNIVERSITY OF NEW YORK— QUEENS COLLEGE

65–30 Kissena Blvd.,
Flushing, NY 11367
(718)997-5000

State four-year comprehensive institution. Coed, urban location. Undergraduate enrollment: 16,500. Graduate enrollment: 3,000.

COMMUNICATION ARTS AND SCIENCES

Chair/Contact: Jonathan Buchsbaum
Calendar: Semesters
Degrees Offered: B.A., film (interdisciplinary major); B.A., M.A., communications/media studies
Departmental Majors:
Undergraduate: communications 350 students; film 30 students. Graduate: communications 25 students
Entrance Requirements:
Undergraduate: combined SAT score of 900, or academic rank within top third of graduating class; recommendations. Graduate: recommendations; written statement of purpose; GRE scores; TOEFL scores of 550 or more for foreign students. Undergraduate application deadline: March 15. Graduate application deadline: April 1. Percent of acceptances: 60%
Curricular Emphasis: Film: critical studies; theory and history; Super-8 and 16mm production. Television: electronic media theory and culture; media writing; production; news/documentary; video art; media management
Special Activities: Film: series/festivals. Television: program material produced for cable television; vocational placement service
Facilities: Film: 35mm screening facilities; editing suite; sound mixing rooms; screening rooms; study center. Television: studios; audio bays; control rooms
Equipment: Film: complete Super-8 and 16mm cameras and editing; sound recording equipment; lighting. Television/Video: complete 1" and ¾" studio; complete ¾" and ½" location
Alumni: Jerry Seinfeld, TV actor/comedian; Eileen Starger, casting director

GUIDE POV: Queens College is a very competitive, well-equipped commuter institution offering a solid film, television, and video studies program within a liberal arts context; 8mm and 16mm film production training; diverse courses in film history, theory, and criticism; studio and portable video production; varied internship opportunities in Manhattan

CITY UNIVERSITY OF NEW YORK— YORK COLLEGE

94–20 Guy R. Brewer Blvd.,
Jamaica, NY 11451
(718)262-2000

State four-year comprehensive institution. Coed, urban location. Enrollment: 5,000.

DEPARTMENT OF FINE AND PERFORMING ARTS

Chair/Contact: James T. Como, Chair
Calendar: Semesters
Degrees Offered: None in film or television
Entrance Requirements: Open-door policy, but York prefers that applicants be in the upper two-thirds of their high school graduating class with a minimum grade-point average of 2.0; SAT recommended. Undergraduate application deadline: March 1

Curricular Emphasis: Film history, theory, and criticism; electronic media history and culture; basic video production

Special Activities: Television: program material produced for cable television

Facilities: Film: editing suite. Television: studio; audio bay; control room

Equipment: Film: Super-8 editing equipment. Television/Video: complete 1" studio

Alumni: Tony Carpenter, radio producer; Jeannette Gyles, TV production assistant

GUIDE POV: This public commuter college offers production training in both film and video within a strong fine arts context; experimental approaches explore cinematic and video experiences in relation to image, light, sound, time, and motion; study of film history as aesthetic medium; studies in mass media and culture; cross-registration permitted with all schools in the City University system; study abroad in Paris

COLLEGE OF NEW ROCHELLE

Castle Place,
New Rochelle, NY 10801
(914)654–5000

Private four-year comprehensive institution. Women's college, suburban location. Undergraduate enrollment: 500. Graduate enrollment: 1,000.

DEPARTMENT OF COMMUNICATION ARTS

Chair/Contact: Dr. James O'Brien
Calendar: Semesters
Degrees Offered: B.A.
Departmental Majors:
Undergraduate: 80 students

Entrance Requirements:
Undergraduate: academic rank within top 40% of graduating class; SAT required, with minimum composite scores of 800; essay recommended; interview recommended.
Undergraduate application deadline: rolling. Percent of acceptances: 75%

Curricular Emphasis: Film aesthetics, criticism, and history. Television production and management

Special Activities: Television: program material produced for on-campus closed-circuit television

Facilities: Television: four-camera color studio; audio bay; control room

Equipment: Television/Video: complete ¾" studio; complete ¾" and ½" location

Alumni: Mercedes Ruehl, film actress; Claire Chiavetta, TV associate producer

GUIDE POV: This small, competitive women's college offers a communication major stressing hands-on television production; good student-faculty ratio; cross-registration with Iona, Marymount, and Concordia colleges; study abroad in nine countries; varied internship opportunities in Manhattan

COLLEGE OF SAINT ROSE

432 Western Ave.,
Box 79,
Albany, NY 12203
(518)454–5111

Private four-year comprehensive institution. Coed, urban location. Undergraduate enrollment: 2,400. Graduate enrollment: 1,200.

PUBLIC COMMUNICATIONS DEPARTMENT

Chair/Contact: Mary Alice Molgard, Chair
Calendar: Semesters
Degrees Offered: B.A.
Departmental Majors: Undergraduate film, radio, and television: 135 students
Entrance Requirements: Undergraduate: academic rank within top 30% of high school graduating class; essay required; ACT or SAT scores. Undergraduate application deadline: rolling. Percent of acceptances: 72%
Curricular Emphasis: Electronic media theory and culture; film appreciation; industrial-grade television production; radio production; journalism; advertising; public relations
Special Activities: Television: program material produced for class projects and local outlets
Facilities: Film: screening room; film library. Television: studio; audio bay; control room
Equipment: Television/Video: complete ¾" studio and ½" location including graphics system; Macintosh and IBM computer access
Alumni: Thom Gonyeau, documentary film producer; William Duffy, Jr., TV news producer; Joni Sabatino, videographer

GUIDE POV: Affiliated with the Roman Catholic Church, this private liberal arts college offers a comprehensive communication major with emphases on both print and broadcast journalism; selective admissions; study abroad program; nine-credit media internships recommended

COLUMBIA UNIVERSITY

New York, NY 10027
(212)854-1754

Private four-year comprehensive institution. Coed, urban location. Undergraduate enrollment: 5,600. Graduate enrollment: 13,000.

FILM DIVISION

Chair/Contact: Annette Insdorf, Chair
Calendar: Semesters
Degrees Offered: B.A., film studies; M.F.A., film
Departmental Majors: Undergraduate film: 30 students. Graduate film: 175 students
Entrance Requirements: Undergraduate: transcripts; SAT scores; three AT scores; essay required; interview recommended. Graduate: transcripts; written statement of purpose; writing samples; recommendations. Undergraduate and graduate application deadline: January 8 for film and writing programs. Percent of acceptances: 15%
Curricular Emphasis: Undergraduate: film history, theory, and criticism. Graduate: producing, screenwriting, directing, acting, history, and theory, culminating in thesis project
Special Activities: Film: weekly guest speaker series; student screenings; student publication
Facilities: Film: sound stage; 35mm screening facilities; screening room; editing suite; sound mixing room; animation stand; film library
Equipment: Film: 35mm cameras; complete 16mm; Super-8 projectors; sound recording equipment; lighting. Television/Video: complete ¾" studio and location
Alumni: David Brown, film producer; Kathryn Bigelow, TV/film director;

Malia Scotch-Marmo, screenwriter; Joe Minion, screenwriter

GUIDE POV: Undergraduates at this highly selective Ivy League university, founded in 1754, focus on film theory and criticism; the graduate program is production-oriented; video production facilities available to film students; comprehensive broadcast training through Department of Journalism; co-op programs with Oxford and Cambridge universities, and with the university's own facility in Paris; extensive internship opportunities

CORNELL UNIVERSITY

Ithaca, NY 14850
(607)255–2000

Private/state four-year comprehensive institution. Coed, rural location. Undergraduate enrollment: 13,000. Graduate enrollment: 5,000.

THEATRE ARTS PROGRAM

Chair/Contact: Don Fredericksen

COMMUNICATION ARTS DEPARTMENT

Chair/Contact: Royal Colle
Calendar: Semesters
Degrees Offered: B.A., theatre arts (concentration in film); B.A., film (independent major); B.A., communication arts
Departmental Majors: Undergraduate film: 20 students. Undergraduate television: 75 students
Entrance Requirements: Undergraduate: ACT or SAT scores; essay required. Undergraduate application deadline: January 1. Percent of acceptances: 30%
Curricular Emphasis: Film: the Theatre Arts Department offers film production training with special

interest in documentary and experimental/avant-garde cinema. Television/Video: the Communication Arts Department offers a full range of television and video studies
Special Activities: Film: film series/ festivals; film societies. Television: program material produced for cable television
Facilities: Film: 35mm screening room; editing suite; film library. Television: studio; audio bay; control room; video editing suites
Equipment: Film: complete 16mm. Television/Video: complete ¾" studio and location
Alumni: Jan Kravitz, documentary filmmaker; Michael Miller, film editor; Jon Gartenberg, film archivist

GUIDE POV: Chartered in 1865 and a member of the Ivy League, Cornell University offers separate majors for those wishing to work in film or television/video; both programs offer comprehensive production training within a liberal arts curriculum; film program emphasizes independent cinema; admission to the university is highly selective; students may cross-register with Ithaca College; study abroad in 13 countries; varied internship opportunities

FIVE TOWNS COLLEGE

305 N. Service Rd.,
Dix Hills, NY 11746–6055
(516)424–7000

Private four-year institution. Coed, suburban location. Enrollment: 700.

VIDEO ARTS/VIDEO MUSIC

Chair/Contact: Dr. Edwin Schultneis, Chair; James Lambriola, video arts
Calendar: Semesters

Degrees Offered: B.M., music (concentration in video music); A.A.S., business management (concentration in video arts)

Departmental Majors: Video: 35 students

Entrance Requirements: 2.0 grade-point average; SAT recommended; evidence of creative ability. Application deadline: rolling. Percent of acceptances: 92%

Curricular Emphasis: Producing, writing, directing, shooting, and editing television commercials, music video, documentary video, and television talk shows

Special Activities: Television/Video: program material produced for local commercial and cable television includes documentaries, music videos, celebrity interviews, and instructional videos

Facilities: Television/Video: studio; audio bay; control room; video editing suites; screening room. Audio: 48-track recording studio with MIDI and special effects for music videos; 600-seat "acoustically perfect" theatre

Equipment: Television/Video: complete ¾" studio and location

Alumni: Phillip Falcone, video engineer; Paul Huston, media producer; Thor Thorstein, media sales executive

GUIDE POV: Five Towns College offers comprehensive video production training with a strong emphasis on music video and documentary production; professional audio and video facilities; concentration in media management; core curriculum in the liberal arts; cross-registration with schools in the Long Island Regional Advisory Council on Higher Education; media internships available in Manhattan with music industry-related firms as well as television networks

---

FORDHAM UNIVERSITY—COLLEGE AT LINCOLN CENTER

113 W. 60th St.,
New York, NY 10023
(212)870–2535

Private four-year comprehensive institution. Coed, urban location. Enrollment: 1,800.

MEDIA STUDIES PROGRAM

Chair/Contact: Eva M. Stadler

Calendar: Semesters

Degrees Offered: B.A., media studies (emphasis on film)

Departmental Majors: Film: 30 students

Entrance Requirements: Interview required; ACT or SAT scores; written statement of purpose. Application deadline: February 1. Percent of acceptances: 70%

Curricular Emphasis: Film production; film studies; television production; broadcast news; television criticism; video art

Special Activities: Film: Contemporary Filmmakers Series offered in conjunction with the New York Film Festival at neighboring Lincoln Center. Television: program material produced for various independent outlets

Facilities: Film: screening room; editing suite; film library. Television: studio; control room

Equipment: Film: complete Super-8 and 16 mm. Television/Video: complete ¾" and ½" studio and location

Alumni: Denzel Washington, film actor; Dan Stillman, second unit film director; Bruce Nachbar, TV network producer; Andy Struse, TV producer

GUIDE POV: Offering a liberal arts program in the Jesuit tradition, this competitive private college provides sequential training in both film and television production; individualized and interdisciplinary majors available; study abroad; career-oriented internship opportunities offered to qualified students in their junior or senior years

FORDHAM UNIVERSITY— FORDHAM COLLEGE

441 E. Fordham Rd.,
Bronx, New York 10458
(718)817–1000

Private four-year comprehensive institution. Coed, urban location. Enrollment: 2,700.

FILM ARTS DEPARTMENT

Chair/Contact: Dr. Edward Wachtel, Chair; Dr. Ron Jacobson
Calendar: Semesters
Degrees Offered: B.A.
Departmental Majors: Film: 75 students. Television: 250 students
Entrance Requirements: ACT or SAT scores; essay; interview. Application deadline: February 1. Percent of acceptances: 77%
Curricular Emphasis: Electronic media theory and culture; critical studies in film; media writing; audio-film-video production; media management
Special Activities: Film: film series/ festivals. Television: program material produced for cable television
Facilities: Film: screening room; editing suite; sound mixing room.

Television/Video: studio; audio bay; control room; video editing suites
Equipment: Film: complete Super-8 and 16mm. Television/Video: complete ¾" studio; ¾" and ½" location
Alumni: Alan Alda, TV/film actor/ director; Vince Scully, sportscaster; Pat Harrington, TV actor

GUIDE POV: Comprehensive production training is available in both film and television at this private Jesuit college; selective admissions; study abroad; honors program; extensive junior-senior year internship opportunities in film and television

GENESEE COMMUNITY COLLEGE

One College Rd.,
Batavia, NY 14020–9704
(716)343–0055

State and county two-year institution. Coed, small town location. Enrollment: 3,500.

COMMUNICATIONS AND MEDIA ARTS DEPARTMENT, RADIO-TELEVISION PROGRAM

Chair/Contact: Television: Chuck Platt
Calendar: Semesters
Degrees Offered: A.S., communications and media arts (with a concentration in radio/TV)
Departmental Majors: Radio-Television: 50 students
Entrance Requirements: ACT or SAT scores; interview; teachers' recommendations. Application deadline: rolling. Percent of acceptances: 95%
Curricular Emphasis: Electronic media theory and culture; television/ video production; media management
Special Activities: Television:

program material produced for on-campus closed-circuit television and for cable television
Facilities: Television: studio; audio bay; control room
Equipment: Television/Video: complete ¾" full-color studio and ½" location including DXC-327 Sony Chip cameras; computerized graphics; video toaster; FCC-licensed radio station WGCC-FM; educational band
Alumni: Robert Stuhura, TV director; Matt Locker, radio personality

GUIDE POV: Intensive television and radio production training is offered to students at this two-year community college; core requirements in journalism, graphic design, black-and-white photography, and mass media; internship opportunities in television production

HOFSTRA UNIVERSITY

1000 Fulton Ave.,
Hempstead, NY 11550
(516)463–6600

Private four-year comprehensive institution. Coed, suburban location. Undergraduate enrollment: 7,000. Graduate enrollment: 5,500.

COMMUNICATION ARTS DEPARTMENT

Chair/Contact: Peter Haratonik, Chair of the Communication Arts Department and Director of the Television Institute
Calendar: Semesters
Degrees Offered: B.A., communication arts (with concentrations in broadcasting, film, and journalism); B.S., communication arts (with concentrations in television production, television production with a minor in management/marketing, and television and film production)
Departmental Majors: Undergraduate film: 70 students. Undergraduate broadcasting: 450 students. Undergraduate journalism: 100 students
Entrance Requirements: Undergraduate: ACT or SAT scores; essay and interview recommended. Undergraduate application deadline: February 15. Percent of acceptances: 65%
Curricular Emphasis: Electronic media theory and culture; critical studies in film; media writing; film and television production; media management
Special Activities: Film: film series/festivals. Television: program material produced for on-campus closed-circuit television, local public television station, and cable television
Facilities: Film: screening room; editing suite; sound mixing room. Television: three studios; audio bays; control rooms; video editing suites
Equipment: Film: complete Super-8 and 16mm. Television/Video: complete ½" and ¾" studio and location
Alumni: Charles Bangort, film/TV producer; Wayne Jaffe, TV producer; Patricia Falese, Cablevision executive

GUIDE POV: Featuring a choice of six media concentrations, this Communication Arts Department offers a full range of studies in film and television production, management, and criticism; selective admissions; study abroad in France, Italy, Spain, and Jamaica; internship opportunities in film and television production

IONA COLLEGE

715 North Ave.,
New Rochelle, NY 10801–1890
(914)633–2000

*Independent four-year commuter
college. Coed, suburban location.
Undergraduate enrollment: 4,000.
Graduate enrollment: 1,500.*

COMMUNICATION ARTS DEPARTMENT

Chair/Contact: Dr. John Darretta,
Chair
Calendar: Semesters
Degrees Offered: B.A., B.S., M.S.,
communication arts
Departmental Majors: Undergraduate
communication arts: 310 students.
Graduate communication arts: 70
students
Entrance Requirements:
Undergraduate: ACT or SAT scores;
upper half of graduating class; 2.5
grade-point average; teachers'
recommendations; interview; essay.
Graduate: 3.0 grade-point average; GRE
scores. Undergraduate application
deadline: rolling. Percent of
acceptances: 70%
Curricular Emphasis: Film: critical
studies; screenwriting. Television/
Video: studio television production;
portable video production; broadcast
journalism; media programming
Special Activities: Film: film series/
festivals. Television: program material
produced for cable television
Facilities: Film: 80-seat film theater.
Television/Video: complete three-
camera studio; audio bay; control
room; screening room; editing suite
Equipment: Film: complete Super-8
and 16mm projection. Television/
Video: complete 1" and ¾" studio;
complete ¾" location; ENG/EFP
cameras

Alumni: John Casale, film/TV director/
producer/executive; Kim Kennedy, TV
producer; Effie Samios, TV
commercials producer; Peter Barossi,
film/TV lighting engineer

GUIDE POV: Film theory, video
production, and broadcast journalism
training are offered at this competitive
commuter college; co-op programs
with Concordia and Marymount
colleges and the College of New
Rochelle; cross-registration with three
consortiums; study abroad in Belgium,
Great Britain, Italy, Spain, and Central
America; varied internship
opportunities

ITHACA COLLEGE

Ithaca, NY 11850
(607)274–3011

*Private four-year comprehensive
institution. Coed, rural location.
Undergraduate enrollment: 6,000.
Graduate enrollment: 150.*

ROY H. PARK SCHOOL OF COMMUNICATIONS

Chair/Contact: Thomas W. Bohn,
Dean; cinema and photography: Peter
Klinge, Chair; television and radio:
Wenmouth Williams, Jr., Chair;
corporate communications: Steven
Seidman, Chair
Calendar: Semesters
Degrees Offered: B.S., B.A., B.F.A.,
communications
Departmental Majors:
Undergraduate: B.S., cinema and
photography: 200; B.F.A., film,
photography, and visual arts: 80; B.S.,
television and radio: 540; B.A., media
studies: 20; B.S., corporate
communication: 160; B.A., journalism:

60; B.S. telecommunications
management: 20
Entrance Requirements:
Undergraduate: academic rank within
top 20% high school class; 1100 SAT;
transcripts; written statement of
purpose; recommendations.
Undergraduate application deadline:
March 1. Percent of acceptances: 60%
Curricular Emphasis: Film and video
production combined with theory and
criticism within liberal arts curriculum
Special Activities: Film: film series/
festivals. Television: program material
produced for on-campus closed-circuit
television and local cable television;
Professional Production Unit
Facilities: Film: sound mixing room;
screening room; editing rooms;
animation lab; sound stage. Television:
studios; multitrack sound studios;
editing suites
Equipment: Film: complete 16mm.
Television/Video: complete ¾" studio
and location
Alumni: Bob Kur, TV network
journalist; Robert Iger, TV network
executive; Michael Nathanson, studio
executive; Chet Curtis, TV news
anchor; Judy Girard, TV executive

GUIDE POV: This very competitive
private college offers students a lively
program in interdisciplinary media
studies; hands-on film and video
training coupled with studies in theory
and criticism; cross-registration with
Cornell University; study abroad in
London; internship opportunities;
extensive radio, television, journalism,
and film co-curricular facilities

LONG ISLAND UNIVERSITY— BROOKLYN

One University Plaza,
Brooklyn, NY 11201
(718)488–1000

*Private four-year comprehensive
institution. Coed, urban location.
Undergraduate enrollment: 5,000.
Graduate enrollment: 4,000.*

MEDIA ARTS DEPARTMENT

Chair/Contact: Kevin Lauth; Claire
Goodman; Stuart Fishelson
Calendar: Semesters
Degrees Offered: B.A., media arts
(students may select emphasis in
television)
Departmental Majors:
Undergraduate: 100 students
Entrance Requirements:
Undergraduate: academic rank within
top half of high school graduating
class, or *B* average; ACT or SAT scores,
with a minimum composite of 950 on
SAT. Undergraduate application
deadline: rolling. Percent of
acceptances: 95%
Curricular Emphasis: Television
production; film history; media writing;
audio production; broadcast
management
Special Activities: Film: university
annually co-sponsors the Spike Lee
Film Workshop; film series; festivals.
Television: program material produced
for contract cable television; industrial
video projects
Facilities: Film: 35mm screening
facilities; screening room; editing suite;
sound mixing room; animation stand.
Television: studio; two audio bays;
control room; graphics studio
Equipment: Film: complete Super-8
and 16mm. Television/Video: complete
¾" three-camera 30' × 50' studio with

18' ceilings; computer graphics; A/B roll editing suites
Alumni: Robert Bedford, TV/film producer; Neil Blake, assistant TV director

GUIDE POV: Part of the Long Island University system, this university offers a media arts program designed for students seeking professional training in television and audio production, multimedia, and mass communications; practical student-teacher ratio; accelerated degrees; cross-registration with other Long Island University campuses; study abroad; credit internship opportunities in television and audio production

LONG ISLAND UNIVERSITY— C.W. POST CAMPUS

Brookville, NY 11548
(516)299–0200

Private four-year comprehensive institution. Coed, suburban location. Undergraduate enrollment: 5,000. Graduate enrollment: 3,000.

DEPARTMENT OF THEATRE AND FILM

Chair/Contact: Norman R. Seider, Director of Film

COMMUNICATION ARTS DEPARTMENT

Chair/Contact: Dr. Barbara Fowles
Calendar: Semesters
Degrees Offered: B.F.A., film, communication arts (concentration in broadcasting); B.S., broadcasting
Departmental Majors: Undergraduate film: 45 students. Undergraduate television: 200 students
Entrance Requirements:
Undergraduate: transcripts or GED test results; academic rank within top 40% of graduating class; 2.5 grade-point average. SAT combined score 900 minimum; ACT combined score 22; interview; essay. Undergraduate application deadline: rolling. Percent of acceptances: 70%
Curricular Emphasis: Film: critical studies; production; directing; screenwriting; video art. Television: broadcast journalism; general programming
Special Activities: Film: film series/festivals; film societies. Television: visiting instructors and lecturers in television broadcasting; program material produced for various outlets
Facilities: Film: sound stage; sound mixing room; screening rooms; editing bays; film archive; film library. Television: studio; audio bay; control room
Equipment: Film: complete 16mm. Television: complete ¾" studio; complete ¾" and ½" location
Alumni: Michael Stone, cinematographer; Mitchell Goldman, corporate film executive; Dan Turret, cinematographer; Steve James, film/TV actor; Tony Sanelli, cinematographer

GUIDE POV: Separate, comprehensive degree programs are available to students in both film and television production; cross-registration available with other Long Island University campuses; small production classes; study abroad; varied media internship opportunities

LONG ISLAND UNIVERSITY— SOUTHAMPTON CAMPUS

Montauk Highway,
Southampton, NY 11968
(516)283–4000

Private four-year comprehensive institution. Coed, rural location. Enrollment: 1,100.

COMMUNICATION ARTS

Chair/Contact: Jon Fraser
Calendar: Semesters
Degrees Offered: B.F.A., communication arts; B.A., film and video (in association with Friends World Program)
Departmental Majors: Film and television: 65 students
Entrance Requirements: Combined SAT scores 900 minimum; essay; recommendations. Application deadline: rolling. Percent of acceptances: 85%
Curricular Emphasis: Film: critical studies. Television/Video: critical studies; production; news/documentary; video art
Special Activities: Film: film series/festivals; film societies. Television: program material produced for cable television
Facilities: Television: studio; audio studio; control room
Equipment: Television/Video: complete ¾" studio
Alumni: Don Wall, TV news reporter; Alexandra McCarty, radio executive

GUIDE POV: Small television production classes within a liberal arts context are offered at this competitive school; blend of hands-on instruction and theory; cross-registration with other university campuses; Friends World Program headquartered here offers a separate film and video concentration with studies in New York, Costa Rica, England, Israel, Kenya, India, Japan, and China; internship opportunities in film and television production in Long Island and Manhattan; international media internship opportunities for those enrolled in Friends World Program

---

MARIST COLLEGE

North Rd.,
Poughkeepsie, NY 12601
(914)575-3000

Private four-year comprehensive institution. Coed, suburban location. Undergraduate enrollment: 3,000. Graduate enrollment: 100.

COMMUNICATION ARTS DEPARTMENT

Chair/Contact: Dr. Sarah King, Chair
Calendar: Semesters
Degrees Offered: B.A., communication arts (concentration in film, television, radio)
Departmental Majors: Undergraduate: 236 students
Entrance Requirements: Undergraduate: academic rank with top 40% of graduating class; ACT or SAT scores recommended; essay recommended; interview recommended; AP or CLEP credit accepted. Undergraduate application deadline: March 1. Percent of acceptances: 60%
Curricular Emphasis: Balance of theory and practice in film, television, and radio
Special Activities: Film: film series/festivals. Television: program material produced for on-campus closed-circuit television
Facilities: Film: screening room; editing suites. Television: studio; audio bay; control room
Equipment: Film: complete Super-8 and 16mm; film to tape transfer. Television/Video: complete ¾" studio and location including Grass Valley switcher; three ENG portable units
Alumni: Joseph L. Podesta, Jr., TV

producer; Bill O'Reilly, TV news anchor; Marilyn Papa, TV production assistant

GUIDE POV: This private liberal arts college offers theoretical studies combined with basic production training in film and video; selective admissions; small classes; study abroad in Africa, Latin and Central America, Europe, and the Far East; internship opportunities

NEW SCHOOL FOR SOCIAL RESEARCH

66 W. 12th St.,
Room 401,
New York, NY 10011
(212)229–5600

Four-year comprehensive institution emphasizing adult education. Coed, urban location. Undergraduate enrollment: 6,000. Graduate enrollment: 2,000.

DEPARTMENT OF COMMUNICATION

Chair/Contact: Mark Schulman, Chair
Calendar: Semesters
Degrees Offered: Undergraduate: B.A., humanities (emphasis in film); certificate in film production. Graduate: M.A., media studies
Departmental Majors: Graduate: about 200 students
Entrance Requirements: Graduate: transcripts; 3.0 grade-point average; written statement of purpose; recommendations. Graduate application deadline: June 1 for fall entry; December 1 for spring entry. Percent of acceptances: 80%
Curricular Emphasis: Graduate: communication theory with emphasis on media concepts and practice through production leading to an M.A.

degree with advanced course listings in audio, video, and film production
Special Activities: Film: film series; screenings; guest speakers; Annual Film Festival sponsored by the New School; students also participate in a number of other festivals. Video: program material produced for festivals, as well as for local public and cable television
Facilities: Film: screening room; editing suite; sound mixing room; animation stand; film library. Television/Video: audio, video, and computer graphics production facilities
Equipment: Film: complete 16mm. Television/Video: audio, video, and computer graphics equipment; personal computers
Alumni: Indu Krishnan, filmmaker; Joy Ciarcia-Levy, TV news producer; Louis Giansante, radio producer

GUIDE POV: Conceived as an alternative school for working adults, the New School offers a variety of options for students interested in the media arts; an individually tailored graduate program offers studies in communication theory as well as production work in both 16mm film and video; most communication courses may also be chosen as part of a flexible curriculum leading to a B.A. degree in humanities and social science; certificate program in film production; accelerated B.A./M.A. option; study abroad; extensive media internship opportunities in Manhattan

NEW YORK FILM ACADEMY

Tribeca Film Center,
375 Greenwich St.,
New York, NY 10013
(212)941–4007

Coed, urban location.

CHAIR/CONTACT: Jerry Sherlock,
Director
Calendar: Basic non sync sound
course is eight weeks long; advanced
sync sound course is 10 weeks long
Degrees Offered: B.F.A. available
through affiliated institutions
Entrance Requirements: Enrollment
in the basic course requires little or no
experience. Enrollment in the
advanced course requires completion
of the basic course or equivalent.
Basic courses begin April 7; May 3;
May 25; July 12; September 13.
Advanced courses begin April 12; June
7; September 14
Curricular Emphasis: Hands-on film
production
Special Activities: Guest lectures
Facilities/Equipment: Film: field
including Arriflex S cameras; Arriflex
BL and SR cameras; Lowell and Arri
light kits; Steenbeck editing equipment
Alumni: Linwood Neverson, music
video director; Joe Napoli, filmmaker;
Wendy Cohen, documentary
filmmaker; Robert Mckenna,
experimental filmmaker

GUIDE POV: This relatively new
academy, in which students are able
to make films immediately in a hands-
on environment, provides an
alternative to a traditional film school
education

NEW YORK INSTITUTE OF TECHNOLOGY

Old Westbury Campus,
Old Westbury, NY 11568
(516)686–7516

*Private four-year comprehensive
institution. Coed, suburban location.*

*Undergraduate enrollment: 8,000.
Graduate enrollment: 4,000.*

**SCHOOL OF LIBERAL ARTS, SCIENCES,
AND COMMUNICATION/COMMUNICATION
ARTS**

Chair/Contact: Dr. Bob Schuessler,
Chair, communication arts
Calendar: Semesters
Degrees Offered: B.F.A.,
communication arts (students may
select emphasis in film/television);
B.S., advertising (with emphasis in
computing and newer digital
technologies); M.A., communication
arts (with emphasis in film, television,
or computer graphics)
Departmental Majors: Undergraduate
film: 150+ students; undergraduate
television: 150+ students. Graduate
film: 20+ students; graduate television:
20+ students
Entrance Requirements:
Undergraduate: high school transcripts
or GED certificate; specific college
preparatory course requirements; SAT
score. Graduate: 3.0 grade-point
average; GRE scores; interview;
teachers' and professional
recommendations. Undergraduate and
graduate application deadline: rolling.
Percent of acceptances: 50%
Curricular Emphasis: Human
communication/electronic media
theory; media writing; film and
television production; media
management; critical studies in media
and culture
Special Activities: Film: film series/
festivals. Television: program material
produced for cable television
Facilities: Film: screening room;
editing suite; sound mixing room;
animation stand; film library.
Television: studio; audio bay; control
room; video editing suites
Equipment: Film: complete Super-8

and 16mm. Television/Video: complete
¾" studio and location
Alumni: Babaloo Mandel,
screenwriter; Ray Lambiase, video
editor; Vicky Metz, ABC TV bureau
chief

GUIDE POV: Comprehensive
undergraduate and graduate training
in film and television production is
offered at this private institute; special
graduate concentration in computer
graphics; cross-registration with the
C.W. Post campus of Long Island
University; study abroad in Paris and
Rome; internship opportunities in film
and television production

NEW YORK UNIVERSITY

Tisch School of the Arts,
721 Broadway,
New York, NY 10003
(212)998–1820

*Private four-year comprehensive
institution. Coed, urban location.
Undergraduate enrollment: 2,200.
Graduate enrollment: 800.*

FILM AND TELEVISION DEPARTMENT

Chair/Contact: Eavonka Ettinger,
Portfolio Co-ordinator
Calendar: Semesters
Degrees Offered: B.F.A., film, video,
television, radio; M.F.A., film; B.F.A.,
M.A., Ph.D., cinema studies; B.F.A.,
M.F.A., dramatic writing
Departmental Majors:
Undergraduate: 980 students. Graduate:
140 students
Entrance Requirements:
Undergraduate: transcripts; 3.0 grade-
point average; ACT or SAT scores;
recommendations; written statement of
purpose; department requires one-page
résumé highlighting creative work

accomplished as well as a
nonreturnable portfolio; contact
department for further details.
Graduate: transcripts; 3.0 grade-point
average; portfolio; teachers' and
professional recommendations; written
statement of purpose. Undergraduate
application deadline: February 1;
December 15 for early decision.
Graduate application deadline:
January 15. Percent of undergraduate
and graduate acceptances: 50%
Curricular Emphasis: Students are
offered concentrations in production
(film, television, or radio), and in
writing, video, sound, photography,
and animation. Double majors
combining liberal and professional
emphases are also available;
producing tracks in both film and
television
Special Activities: Film/Video:
Directors' Series; First Run Film
Festival; Haig P. Manoogian Screenings
in L.A.; student showcases; video
festival; animation festival; student
publications. Television/Radio:
program material produced for local
public and commercial television
stations, and for cable television;
licensed student-run AM/FM radio
station
Facilities: Film: 35mm screening
facilities; animation stand; three sound
mixing rooms; recording studio; digital
sound postproduction facility;
screening rooms; 26 editing suites; one
Todman sound stage plus two
teaching sound stages; film library/
archive. Television: studios; audio
bays; control rooms; video editing
suites; computer graphics studio
Equipment: Film: complete Super-8
and 16mm; complete 35mm available
for graduate students. Television/
Video: two complete ¾" studios and
locations

Alumni: Spike Lee, film director/ producer; Martin Scorsese, film director/producer; Oliver Stone, screenwriter/director; Joel Coen, film director; Bill Duke, film director; Martin Brest, film director; Allan Arkush, TV director; Susan Seidelman, film director; Joel Silver, film producer/studio executive; Amy Heckerling, film director; Chris Columbus, film director; Alan Landsburg, TV director/producer; Billy Crystal, film/TV actor/director

GUIDE POV: This highly selective professional school offers undergraduates comprehensive, quality-oriented training in film and television production combined with studies in the liberal arts; undergraduates may begin 35mm production in freshman year and full film/video production program in sophomore year; separate graduate programs in critical studies, film/ dramatic television production, and dramatic writing; double majors; London summer program; West Coast Alumni Group job bank matches listings and graduates; over 900 local and national internships available in film, television, corporate video, and radio production at Disney Studios, MTV, HBO, and NPR, among others

---

NIAGARA UNIVERSITY

Niagara, NY 14109
(716)285-1212

Private four-year comprehensive institution. Coed, suburban location. Undergraduate enrollment: 2,450. Graduate enrollment: 650.

COMMUNICATION STUDIES PROGRAM

Chair/Contact: Robert F. Crawford
Calendar: Semesters
Degrees Offered: B.A.
Departmental Majors:
Undergraduate: 61 students
Entrance Requirements:
Undergraduate: SAT or ACT scores; interview; essay; GED accepted; AP or CLEP credit accepted. Undergraduate application deadline: August 15. Percent of acceptances: 80%
Curricular Emphasis: Film: interdisciplinary study of media; screenwriting; basic filmmaking; experimental. Television: interdisciplinary study of media; two-semester television production workshops; news/documentary; electronic media management
Facilities: Film: film library. Television/Video: studio; control room
Equipment: Film: Super-8 cameras and editing; projectors. Television/ Video: complete ¾" studio and ½" location
Alumni: Norm E. Eick, advertising producer; Greg Conillin, media researcher

GUIDE POV: Founded by the Vincentian fathers and brothers in 1856 and today a private nonsectarian university, Niagara offers its students comprehensive television production training; basic film training; selective admissions; cross-registration through the Western New York Consortium; study abroad in England, France, Switzerland, and Spain; local and national media internship opportunities

ONONDAGA COMMUNITY COLLEGE

Syracuse, NY 13215–7901
(315)469–7741

*County two-year institution. Coed,
suburban location. Enrollment: 7,954.*

RADIO/TELEVISION DEPARTMENT

Chair/Contact: Catherine Hawkins,
Chair
Calendar: Semesters
Degrees Offered: A.A.S., radio-
television (concentrations in cinema
and journalism)
Departmental Majors: Television:
175 students
Entrance Requirements: Open-door
policy; interview and placement
testing required. Application deadline:
rolling. Percent of acceptances: 99%
Curricular Emphasis: Electronic
media theory and culture; critical
studies in film (for cinema
concentration only); media writing;
audio and video production;
sportscasting
Special Activities: Film: film series/
festivals. Television: program material
produced for on-campus closed-circuit
television and for cable television.
Radio: on-campus radio station
Facilities: Film: film library.
Television: studio; audio bay; control
room; video editing bays; four audio
studios
Equipment: Television/Video:
complete ¾" studio and location
Alumni: John Faratzis, TV network
sports producer; John Haygood, TV
sports producer; Bill Bonnell, TV
network sports producer; Karen Pirli,
TV production assistant

GUIDE POV: Students enrolled in this
practical two-year program gain career
skills that prepare them to enter the
field of broadcasting as well as cable,
institutional, corporate, and
educational television; focus on
creating, writing, producing, and
directing television and radio
programs; separate concentration in
film theory offered through English
Department; transfer program for those
wishing to enter four-year university;
faculty of working professionals;
extensive internship opportunities in
television and radio production

PRATT INSTITUTE

200 Willoughby Ave.,
Brooklyn, NY 11205
(718)636–3600

*Private four-year comprehensive
institution. Coed, urban location.
Undergraduate enrollment: 3,000.
Graduate enrollment: 750.*

MEDIA ARTS

Chair/Contact: Donald Pitkoff, Chair
Calendar: Semesters
Degrees Offered: B.F.A.
Departmental Majors:
Undergraduate: 50 students
Entrance Requirements:
Undergraduate: ACT or SAT scores;
transcripts; film, video, fine art, or
photography portfolio. Undergraduate
application deadline: May 15. Percent
of acceptances: 60%
Curricular Emphasis: Half film and
half video study; minor in animation.
Film: history; production; cel and
computer animation; screenwriting.
Television/Video: production; cel and
computer animation; computer
graphics
Special Activities: Film: film series/
festivals. Television: program material

produced for local commercial television station

Facilities: Film: sound mixing room; screening room; editing suites; sound stage; two animation stands; film library. Video: three-camera studio; audio bays; control room; computer graphics suites; viewing suites

Equipment: Film: complete Super-8 and 16mm; editing. Video: complete ¾" studio; complete ¾" and ½" location; complete broadcast quality Chyron center; electronic editing ¾" and ½"; Quantel Paint Box

Alumni: Bob Giraldi, film/TV director/producer; Steve Horn, film/TV director/producer; Jordan Levine, film editor; Adam DeFelice, special effects artist/computer graphics designer

GUIDE POV: This highly ranked, well-equipped arts school offers 24-hour access to facilities; special attention to postproduction and computer video graphics; small classes taught by active professionals; students participate in a variety of film/video festivals and competitions; film and video internship opportunities

---

ROCHESTER INSTITUTE OF TECHNOLOGY

P.O. Box 9887,
Rochester, NY 14623–0887
(716)475–2411

Private four-year comprehensive institution. Coed, suburban location. Undergraduate enrollment: 11,000. Graduate enrollment: 1,500.

FILM AND VIDEO DEPARTMENT

Chair/Contact: Malcom Spaull, Chair
Calendar: Quarters
Degrees Offered: A.A.S., B.F.A., film

and video; M.F.A., imaging arts (concentration in computer animation)

Departmental Majors:
Undergraduate: 140 students. Graduate: 20 students

Entrance Requirements:
Undergraduate: required writing sample; SAT scores (minimum 1100 composite); ACT scores accepted; academic rank within top quarter of graduating class. Graduate: transcripts; letters of recommendations; GRE scores; portfolio. Undergraduate and graduate application deadline: rolling. Percent of acceptances: 30–50%

Curricular Emphasis: Film and video animation; writing; directing; producing

Special Activities: Film: visiting filmmakers program; film festivals; film societies. Video: program material produced for on-campus closed-circuit television, local commercial television, and cable television

Facilities: Film: sound stage; 35mm screening facilities; 16mm postproduction room; 16mm machine room; 16mm/video sound mix room; screening rooms; animation stands; film library. Video: ¾" and ½" editing; on-line and off-line rooms; computer graphics generators; microcomputer animation room with MAC II microcomputers and hi-res TOPAZ 3-D animation systems

Equipment: Film: complete Super-8 and 16mm. Video: complete ¾" and ½" location; editing including Grass Valley 110 component switch; Amiga toaster; computer and cel animation

Alumni: Fred Elmes, cinematographer; Peter Burell, film producer; John Dowdell, postproduction executive; Francis Aliwalas, film editor; Ron Mix, documentary filmmaker

GUIDE POV: Students enrolled in this lively hands-on program work in both film and video and must produce animation, fiction narrative, and documentary work before choosing a concentration in animation, writing, directing, or production; innovative graduate major in computer animation; students participate in national film/video festivals; 24-hour equipment checkout; required senior thesis project; required crew assignments; faculty of working professionals; numerous internship opportunities in film and television production

SAINT JOHN FISHER COLLEGE

3690 East Ave.,
Rochester, NY 14618
(716)385–8000

Private four-year comprehensive institution. Coed, suburban location. Enrollment: 2,000.

COMMUNICATION DEPARTMENT

Chair/Contact: James E. Seward, Chair
Calendar: Semesters
Degrees Offered: B.A., communication (students may select emphasis in television/radio)
Departmental Majors: Television: 30 students
Entrance Requirements: ACT or SAT scores; essay required; interview recommended. Application deadline: rolling. Percent of acceptances: 75%
Curricular Emphasis: Electronic media theory and culture; media management; programming; technology
Special Activities: Film: film series/

festivals. Television: program material produced for on-campus closed-circuit television, for local commercial television station, and for cable television
Facilities: Television: studio; audio bay; control room
Equipment: Television/Video: complete ¾" studio and ½" location
Alumni: Wanda Miller, TV news anchor; Donna Dede, TV news anchor; Patricia Johnson, TV news reporter; John Turner, TV assignment editor

GUIDE POV: Communication majors at this private college may choose a concentration in television/radio with an emphasis on broadcast journalism; management training; cross-registration with Rochester-area colleges and universities; study abroad in eight European countries; internship opportunities in television production

SAINT JOHN'S UNIVERSITY

Grand Central and Utopia Pkwys.,
Jamaica, NY 11439
(718)990–6161

Private four-year comprehensive institution. Coed, urban location. Undergraduate enrollment: 16,000. Graduate enrollment: 5,000.

DIVISION OF COMMUNICATIONS, MEDIA, AND PROFESSIONAL STUDIES AT ST. VINCENT'S COLLEGE

Chair/Contact: Alan Seeger, Chair
Calendar: Semesters
Degrees Offered: B.S., communication arts (with a choice of concentrations in film history, aesthetics, and criticism; film and video production; television production; sports in the mass media;

dramatic writing; radio production; business communications; advertising/public relations)

Departmental Majors:
Undergraduate: 600 students

Entrance Requirements:
Undergraduate: transcripts; ACT or SAT scores; GED accepted; interview recommended. Undergraduate application deadline: rolling, but applicants are encouraged to apply before March 1 for admission to the fall semester, and before November 1 for admission to the spring semester. Percent of acceptances: 68%

Curricular Emphasis: Electronic media history, theory, and culture; film theory/aesthetics, history, and criticism; media writing; film, television, and radio production; media management

Special Activities: Film: film series/festivals; film club. Television/Video: program material produced for local commercial television station and for cable television; television club; video competition

Facilities: Film: screening room; editing suite; film library. Television/Radio: studio; audio bay; control room; video editing suites; television and radio complex with full recording facilities

Equipment: Film: complete 16mm. Television/Video: complete 1" and ¾" studio; complete ¾" and ½" location

Alumni: Nicholas Davatzes, broadcasting executive; Mike Francesca, TV sportscaster; Donald Taffner, broadcasting executive; Bob Sheppard, TV announcer

GUIDE POV: This selective private college offers communication students a comprehensive major with a choice of eight media concentrations; diverse course listings cover all aspects of radio, film/video, and television production, criticism, writing, and management; study abroad in Europe; internship opportunities in film and television production

---

SAINT THOMAS AQUINAS COLLEGE

Rte. 340,
Sparkill, NY 10976
(914)359–9500

Private four-year comprehensive institution. Coed, small town location. Enrollment: 1,500.

COMMUNICATION ARTS DEPARTMENT

Chair/Contact: Dr. James Vendetti, Chair of the Humanities Division

Calendar: Semesters

Degrees Offered: B.A., communication arts (concentration in journalism or general studies)

Departmental Majors: 86 students

Entrance Requirements: High school diploma or GED certificate; SAT scores; interview required; writing and math samples required. Application deadline: rolling. Percent of acceptances: 85%

Curricular Emphasis: Film theory; mass media theory and culture; media writing; television and radio production; media management

Special Activities: General: lecture series with invited speakers from NYC film, video, and radio communities. Television: program material produced for cable television

Facilities: Television/Radio: studio; control room; video editing suite; WSTK college radio station

Equipment: Video/Radio: complete ¾" studio and ½" location; ENG equipment; closed-carrier radio station

Alumni: Mary Duffy, TV producer;

Catherine Donovan, radio production manager

GUIDE POV: Located just north of NYC, this private college offers radio and television production studies within a liberal arts curriculum; small enrollment provides every student with ample hands-on experience; concentration in broadcast journalism; study abroad; extensive NYC internship opportunities in television and radio production

---

SARAH LAWRENCE COLLEGE

1 Mead Way,
Bronxville, NY 10708
(914)337–0700

Private four-year comprehensive institution. Coed, suburban location. Undergraduate enrollment: 1,000. Graduate enrollment: 150.

FILMMAKING AND FILM STUDIES PROGRAM

Chair/Contact: Admissions office
Calendar: Semesters
Degrees Offered: B.A.
Departmental Majors:
Undergraduate: 25–50 students
Entrance Requirements:
Undergraduate: transcripts; competitive grade-point average; ACT or SAT scores; two teachers' recommendations; essay required; interview strongly recommended; portfolio recommended.
Undergraduate application deadline: November 15 early decision I; January 1 early decision II; February 1 final deadline. Percent of acceptances: 48%
Curricular Emphasis: Independent film production
Special Activities: Film: film series/festivals; guest speakers.

Facilities: Film: screening room; editing suite; sound mixing room. Video: editing facilities
Equipment: Film: complete Super-8 and 16mm. Video: camera and editing equipment
Alumni: Brian DePalma, film director/writer; Yoko Ono, filmmaker/videographer; Robin Givens, TV/film actress

GUIDE POV: Students enrolled at this selective private college participate in biweekly tutorials and small seminars; program encourages student to creatively explore varied styles; cross-registration available with the American Collegiate Consortium and the Universities of Wisconsin and Michigan; study abroad in Oxford, London, Florence, Paris, St. Croix, and Russia; extensive internship opportunities in Manhattan including ABC's "Nightline."

SCHOOL OF VISUAL ARTS

209 E. 23rd St.,
New York, NY 10010
(212)592–2000

Private four-year comprehensive arts institution. Coed, urban location. Undergraduate enrollment: 2,200. Graduate enrollment: 160.

FILM/VIDEO/ANIMATION DEPARTMENT

Chair/Contact: Reeves Lehmann, Chair
Calendar: Semesters
Degrees Offered: B.F.A.; M.F.A. as of September 1994
Departmental Majors:
Undergraduate: 275 students
Entrance Requirements:
Undergraduate: SAT verbal 450 minimum; 3.0 grade-point average;

interview; essay; portfolio.
Undergraduate application deadline:
rolling. Percent of acceptances:
35–40%
Curricular Emphasis: Film: directing;
screenwriting; cinematography; editing;
animation. Television/Video: video art;
studio and field production with ENG
Special Activities: Film and
television/video: industry seminars;
vocational placement
Facilities: Film: editing suites;
screening room; animation stands;
production studios; film/video library.
Television/Video: two complete ¾"
studios; audio bay; control room; ¾"
editing suites; film to tape transfer;
audio transfer; audio mixing;
permanent video disc library
Equipment: Film: 75 Bolex and
Arriflex 16mm cameras including Arri
S, BL, and SR. Television/Video:
complete ¾" studio; complete ¾" and
½" location; 50 Hi-8 video cameras;
two Oxberry animation cameras;
optical bench for film; two video
animation systems; on-line and off-line
editing; moviola dollies
Alumni: Tom Sito, animator; James
Muro, Stedicam operator; Michael
Attanassio, TV producer; Bettiann
Fishman, TV/film assistant director

GUIDE POV: This quality-oriented, well-
equipped school offers complete
production training in all aspects of
film and video, including animation;
faculty of working professionals;
selective admissions; study abroad in
Italy, France, England, Spain, and
Portugal; extensive Manhattan
internship opportunities in film and
video production

STATE UNIVERSITY OF NEW YORK —BINGHAMTON

P.O. Box 6000,
Vestal Pkwy. E.,
Binghamton, NY 13902–6000
(607)777–2000

*State four-year comprehensive
institution. Coed, urban location.
Enrollment: 8,315.*

CINEMA DEPARTMENT

Chair/Contact: Ralph Hocking, Chair
Calendar: Semesters
Degrees Offered: B.A.
Departmental Majors: 51 students
Entrance Requirements: 90+ grade-
point average; ACT or SAT scores;
interview; portfolio; written statement
of purpose; teachers' and professional
recommendations. Application
deadline: January 15. Percent of
acceptances: 35%
Curricular Emphasis: Beginning to
advanced film; digital electronic art
making; topical studies in cinema
Special Activities: Film: film societies
Facilities: Film/Video: screening
room; editing suites; sound stage;
sound mixing room; animation stand;
optical printers; projection
rooms; video art-making studio;
film to video transfer suite; film
library
Equipment: Film: complete Super-8
and 16mm. Video: telecine; portable
lighting packages; ½" and ¾" cassette
recorders; portable cameras; monitors;
sound recording equipment; audio
mixers; lighting; switcher/special
effects generators; VHS editing
equipment
Alumni: Stephanie Black, filmmaker;
Phil Solomon, filmmaker; Dan
Eisenberg, filmmaker; Mark Lapore,
filmmaker; Steve Anker, filmmaker;

Alan Berliner, filmmaker; Ken Ross, filmmaker

GUIDE POV: This selective school offers professional production training with an emphasis on film and video art; exploration of new media; experimental forms; good student-faculty ratio in production classes; faculty of working professionals; cross-registration with Broome Community and Empire State colleges; attention to individual projects; internship opportunities in film and television production

STATE UNIVERSITY OF NEW YORK —BUFFALO

3435 Main St.,
Buffalo, NY 14214
(716)645–2000

State four-year comprehensive institution. Coed, urban location. Undergraduate enrollment: 18,831. Graduate enrollment: 8,812.

DEPARTMENT OF MEDIA STUDY

Chair/Contact: Dr. Brian Henderson, Chair
Calendar: Semesters
Degrees Offered: B.A., M.A., humanities
Departmental Majors: Undergraduate media studies: 51 students. Graduate media studies: 26 students
Entrance Requirements:
Undergraduate: 3.0 grade-point average; ACT or SAT scores; interview. Graduate: 3.0 grade-point undergraduate average; interview. Undergraduate and graduate application deadline: rolling
Curricular Emphasis: Independent production in film, video, and digital arts; narrative, ethnographic, and

documentary forms; film theory, history, and analysis
Special Activities: Student shows; visiting artists
Facilities: Film: sound stage; screening, editing, and sound mixing rooms; animation stand; film library. Television/Video: studio; audio bay; control room
Equipment: Film: Super-8 and 16mm. Video: ¾" and ½" studio and location
Alumni: Vibeke Sorenson, film/video/electronic music artist/teacher; F. Scott Sweeney, video editor/filmmaker; Chris Hill, video artist/curator; Julie Zando, video artist/teacher

GUIDE POV: Both undergraduate and graduate media programs are provided to students at this selective state university; emphasis on independent film and video production with special interest in the integration of media technologies; diverse course listings; cross-registration with the Western New York Consortium; study abroad in Germany, Spain, and France; media internship opportunities

STATE UNIVERSITY OF NEW YORK —COLLEGE OF AGRICULTURE AND TECHNOLOGY

Cobleskill, NY 12043
(518)234–5011

State four-year comprehensive institution. Coed, small town location. Enrollment: 3,000.

HUMANITIES DEPARTMENT

Chair/Contact: Michael Vandow
Calendar: Semesters
Degrees Offered: A.A., humanities
Departmental Majors: Humanities: 75 students
Entrance Requirements: Completion

of college preparatory courses; ACT or SAT strongly recommended; interview required. Application deadline: rolling. Percent of acceptances: 62%

Curricular Emphasis: General studies in the humanities with one course listing in single camera video production

Special Activities: Film: film series/ festivals

Equipment: Television/Video: portable lighting packages; ½" cassette recorders; portable cameras; sound recording equipment; ½" VHS editing equipment

Alumni: Steven Ginsburg, TV producer; Patricia Bourke Randazzo, system support technician

GUIDE POV: A two-year degree program in telecommunications with an emphasis on computer science and telephony is offered to students at this state university; one course offered in video production; internship opportunities

---

STATE UNIVERSITY OF NEW YORK —FREDONIA

Fredonia, NY 14063
(716)673-3110

State four-year comprehensive institution. Coed, small town location. Enrollment: 5,000.

DEPARTMENT OF COMMUNICATION

Chair/Contact: Television and radio: Ted Schwalbe, Chair
Calendar: Semesters
Degrees Offered: B.S., communication (with emphasis in video design and production, audio/ radio production, media management, or human communication)

Departmental Majors: Television: 300 students

Entrance Requirements: 2.80 grade-point average; ACT or SAT scores. Application deadline: March 1. Percent of acceptances: 41%

Curricular Emphasis: Electronic media theory and culture; critical studies in film; media writing; audio-film-video production; media management

Special Activities: Film: film series/ festivals. Television: program material produced for on-campus closed-circuit television and for cable television; AERho member

Facilities: Film: screening room; film library. Television: studio; audio bay; control room

Equipment: Television/Video: complete ¾" studio; complete ¾" and ½" location

Alumni: Louis Adler, broadcasting executive; Tom Skinner, TV producer/ executive; Mary McDonnell, film actress; Peter Michael Goetz, film/TV actor

GUIDE POV: Established in 1826, this public university offers comprehensive studies in video production through its selective Communication Department; diverse course listings; students receive training in video documentary, video drama, video art, corporate video, and television news; studies in film history, theory, and criticism offered through English Department; cooperative programs and cross-registration available with many institutions; study abroad in more than 90 countries; internship opportunities in television production

STATE UNIVERSITY OF NEW YORK —NEW PALTZ

New Paltz, NY 12561–2499
(914)257–2121

State four-year comprehensive institution. Coed, suburban location. Undergraduate enrollment: 7,000. Graduate enrollment: 1,700.

DEPARTMENT OF COMMUNICATION MEDIA

Chair/Contact: Television: Lynn Spangler; Adelaide Haas
Calendar: Semesters
Degrees Offered: B.A., B.S., communication media (with emphasis in production or management)
Departmental Majors: Undergraduate television: 250 students
Entrance Requirements: Undergraduate: 2.5 grade-point average; ACT or SAT scores. Undergraduate application deadline: rolling. Percent of acceptances: 39%
Curricular Emphasis: Electronic media theory and culture; media writing; television/video production; media management
Special Activities: Television: program material produced for on-campus closed-circuit television and for local cable television
Facilities: Television: studio; audio bay; control room; video editing suites
Equipment: Television/Video: complete ¾" studio with Sony three-chip cameras and Grass Valley switcher; complete ¾" location; editing equipment
Alumni: Carl Gurmsen, TV producer; Rebecca Martin, MTV graphics assistant; Dave Michel, TV production assistant

GUIDE POV: Founded in 1828, this competitive state university offers a communication media program with options in either radio/television production or management; production sequence includes hands-on experience as well as writing, performance, and theory; faculty of working professionals; study abroad in Russia, England, Italy, Jamaica, and Spain; internship opportunities in television production locally and in Manhattan

STATE UNIVERSITY OF NEW YORK —OSWEGO

Oswego, NY 13126
(315)341–2500

State four-year comprehensive institution. Coed, suburban location. Enrollment: 8,000.

COMMUNICATION STUDIES DEPARTMENT

Chair/Contact: Brian R. Betz, Chair; Fritz Messere, Program Coordinator of broadcasting/mass communications
Calendar: Semesters
Degrees Offered: B.A., studies in broadcasting and mass communications; communication studies
Departmental Majors: Television: 150 students
Entrance Requirements: 3.0 grade-point average; ACT or SAT scores. Application deadline: March 15. Percent of acceptances: 40%
Curricular Emphasis: Electronic media theory and culture; media writing; television/video production; media management
Special Activities: Film: film series/festivals. Television/Radio: program material produced for on-campus closed-circuit television, cable

television, and corporate television; student radio station WNYO-FM and NPR affiliate WRVO-FM located on campus

Facilities: Television/Radio: studio; audio bay; control room; video editing suites; Amiga graphics computers; radio production center

Equipment: Television/Video: complete ¾" studio and location

Alumni: Al Roker, TV meteorologist/personality; Jeff Carr, TV program executive; Kathy Quinn, TV network sales executive

GUIDE POV: Within the comprehensive broadcasting and mass communications major, students receive a core curriculum covering American broadcasting history, sales, regulation, and management, and are offered diverse electives in television or radio production, cable television, computer graphics, international broadcasting, media performance, and broadcast journalism; cross-registration with SUNY-Visiting Student Program; selective admissions; internship opportunities in television production

STATE UNIVERSITY OF NEW YORK —PLATTSBURGH

Plattsburgh, NY 12901
(518)564-2000

State four-year comprehensive institution. Coed, small town location. Enrollment: 6,000.

DEPARTMENT OF COMMUNICATION

Chair/Contact: Television journalism: A. R. Montanaro, Jr.
Calendar: Semesters
Degrees Offered: B.A., B.S.
Departmental Majors: 350 students

Entrance Requirements: SAT score (1100 minimum); essay and portfolio required; 2.5 grade-point average for transfer students. Application deadline: March 15 for fall entry; November 15 for spring entry. Percent of acceptances: 45%

Curricular Emphasis: Film: critical studies. Television/Video: studio and field production; broadcast journalism; documentary

Special Activities: Television/Video: program material produced for on-campus closed-circuit television and cable television; Intra-SUNY distribution

Facilities: Television/Video: two complete ¾" studios; audio bays; control rooms; six editing suites including one ½", two ¾", and three Hi-8; nonbroadcast studio

Equipment: Television/Video: complete ¾" studio and location

Alumni: Dawn Fratangelo, TV co-anchor/journalist; Raghida Dergham, U.N. TV news correspondent; Tim Singer, TV sportscaster; Adam Marx, videographer

GUIDE POV: This selective Communication Department offers hands-on television production training; emphasis on broadcast journalism; study abroad in 24 countries through the SUNY Study Abroad Program; cross-registration with Clinton Community College; varied internship opportunities in television production and journalism

STATE UNIVERSITY OF NEW YORK —PURCHASE

35 Anderson Hill Rd.,
Purchase, NY 10577
(914)251-6000

State four-year comprehensive institution. Coed, suburban location. Enrollment: 4,000.

FILM DEPARTMENT

Chair/Contact: Jon Rubin, Chair
Calendar: Semesters
Degrees Offered: B.F.A., film; professional training program
Departmental Majors: Film: 70 students
Entrance Requirements: ACT or SAT scores; written statement of purpose; portfolio. Application deadline: August 1. Percent of acceptances: 65%
Curricular Emphasis: Critical studies in film; film production including cinematography, sound, animation, screenwriting, video, and directing
Special Activities: Film: film series/festivals
Facilities: Film: sound stage; two screening rooms; editing suites; 10-track mixing studio; animation stand; film library
Equipment: Film/Video: complete Super-8 and 16mm; ½" and ¾" video cameras; studio and portable lights, location and studio audio recorders, mixers, editing equipment
Alumni: Charles Lane, film director; Hal Hartley, film director

GUIDE POV: Aspiring filmmakers at SUNY Purchase produce, write, direct, and edit their own work, completing at least one original film per academic year; professional program leads to degree in motion picture directing; separate concentrations in narrative, documentary, and experimental film; students participate in national film/video festivals; 80% of graduates now work in industry as screenwriters, directors, cinematographers, or editors; cross-registration with area colleges

and universities; study abroad; internship opportunities in film production

---

STATE UNIVERSITY OF NEW YORK AT STONY BROOK

Stony Brook, NY 11794–1901
(516)689–6000

State four-year comprehensive institution. Coed, suburban location. Undergraduate enrollment: 12,000. Graduate enrollment: 6,000.

HUMANITIES INSTITUTE

Chair/Contact: Dr. E. Ann Kaplan
Calendar: Semesters
Degrees Offered: B.A., humanities (interdisciplinary major with minor in film or media arts)
Entrance Requirements: Undergraduate: high school academic average of approximately 85; SAT composite score of approximately 1000 or ACT composite score of approximately 25; teachers' recommendations. Undergraduate application deadline: rolling. Percent of acceptances: 75%
Curricular Emphasis: Major in humanities with offerings in film history, theory, and criticism; electronic media studies; basic video production
Special Activities: Film: film series/festivals. Television: program material produced for on-campus closed-circuit television
Facilities: Film: screening room; sound stage; film library
Equipment: Film: 16mm projectors. Television/Video: complete ¾" studio
Alumni: Craig Allen Weiner, TV meteorologist; Teddy Chu, cinematographer; Ben Oshman, film/

TV property master; Scott Kincaid, TV/ film lighting technician

GUIDE POV: Students at this competitive state university may choose a broad-based interdisciplinary major in the humanities with a minor in film or media arts; emphasis on film/electronic media theory, history, and criticism; video production; diversified liberal arts curriculum; research internship opportunities

SUFFOLK COUNTY COMMUNITY COLLEGE

533 College Rd.,
Selden, NY 11784
(516)451–4110

State and county two-year institution. Coed, suburban location. Enrollment: 19,000.

DEPARTMENT OF COMMUNICATIONS

Chair/Contact: Richard Britten, Chair
Calendar: Semesters
Degrees Offered: A.A.S.
Departmental Majors: 100 students
Entrance Requirements: High school diploma or equivalent. Application deadline: August 21
Curricular Emphasis: Broadcast/ corporate audio-video production and management
Special Activities: Film: film series/ festivals. Television: program material produced for on-campus closed-circuit television and for cable television; member AERho; ITVA
Facilities: Film: 35mm screening facilities; screening room; editing suite; animation stand; film library.
Television: studio; audio bay; control room; ¾" A-B editing suites; ½" editing suites
Equipment: Film: complete Super-8.

Television/Video: complete 1,200 sq. ft. ¾" studio; complete ¾" and ½" location including Tascam audio switcher; Echolab switcher; Abner controller; five complete ¾" ENG field packages
Alumni: Denise Cavanaugh, TV promotions coordinator

GUIDE POV: Students planning careers as television/video production technicians or managers receive professional two-year training through this program; media internship opportunities

SYRACUSE UNIVERSITY

Syracuse, NY 13244
(315)443–1870

Private comprehensive institution. Coed, urban location. Undergraduate enrollment: 11,000. Graduate enrollment: 4,000.

ART MEDIA STUDIES

Chair/Contact: Owen Shapiro
Calendar: Semesters
Degrees Offered: B.F.A., M.F.A.
Departmental Majors:
Undergraduate: 71 film; 10 video; 60 computer graphics; 70 photography.
Graduate: 15 film; 3 video; 3 computer graphics; 4 photography
Entrance Requirements:
Undergraduate: SAT scores; written statement of purpose; portfolio; interview; teachers' recommendations. Graduate: 3.0 grade-point average; interview; teachers' recommendations; essay; portfolio. Undergraduate application deadline: December 1. Graduate application deadline: February 1. Percent of acceptances: Undergraduate: 60%. Graduate: 20%
Curricular Emphasis: Film: critical

studies; animation; experimental and narrative production; screenwriting. Video: video art; computer graphics; postproduction techniques

Special Activities: Film/Video: film societies; film/video program material produced for on-campus closed-circuit television and cable television; student films screened annually at local theatre

Facilities: Film: complete 16mm production and postproduction; sound stage; sound transfer studio; lighting studio; screening rooms; sound mixing studios; flatbed editing suites; bench editing stations; 16mm screening; 16mm Oxberry animation studio; optical printer studio; film library. Video: two large studios; audio bay; control room; editing suites; video postproduction sound studio; screening rooms; Shafer Art Building and S. I. Newhouse School of Public Communications

Equipment: Film: complete 16mm. Video: complete ¾" studio; complete ¾", ½", and Hi-8 location; Amiga toaster and special effects video equipment

Alumni: Peter Guber, studio executive/producer; Peter Hyams, film director; Rob Edwards, TV writer; Bob Dishy, film/TV actor; Suzanne Pleshette, TV/film actress; Tom Oliphant, film/TV producer/director; Leighton Pierce, filmmaker/videographer; Gil Cates, film/TV director/producer/educator

GUIDE POV: This well-equipped private university offers students a quality program in film and video in the Art Media Studies Department; synthesis of production and theory; small faculty-student ratio; emphasis on experimental and narrative filmmaking and theory; selective

admissions; separate comprehensive degree program in communications focusing on broadcast journalism; study abroad; varied internship opportunities

---

TOMPKINS CORTLAND COMMUNITY COLLEGE

170 North St.,
Dryden, NY 13053
(607)844–8211

County two-year institution. Coed, rural location. Enrollment: 2,000.

TELEVISION/RADIO BROADCASTING

Chair/Contact: R. Brooks Sanders
Calendar: Semesters
Degrees Offered: A.A.S., television and radio; A.S., radio-television broadcasting, advertising and communications
Departmental Majors: Television: 70 students
Entrance Requirements: Open-door policy with placement testing; ACT or SAT testing recommended. Application deadline: August 15 for fall entry. Percent of acceptances: 98%
Curricular Emphasis: Electronic media theory and culture; broadcast production; media sales and management
Special Activities: Television: program material produced for local commercial and cable television
Facilities: Television: studio; audio bay; control room
Equipment: Television/Video: complete ½" location
Alumni: Kim Niles, radio news reporter; John Davison, radio program director; Matt Steele, radio personality

GUIDE POV: This two-year community college of SUNY offers students interested in television and radio broadcast communications three separate degree programs; studies in broadcast writing, production, and sales/marketing; practical approach; core curriculum fulfills transfer requirements to four-year universities; special tuition awards for Vietnam veterans and New York state Native Americans; internship opportunities in television production

UNIVERSITY OF ROCHESTER

College of Arts and Sciences,
River Campus Station,
Rochester, NY 14627
(716)275–2121

Private four-year comprehensive institution. Coed, suburban location. Undergraduate enrollment: 5,000. Graduate enrollment: 3,000.

FILM STUDIES PROGRAM

Chair/Contact: George Grella
Calendar: Semesters
Degrees Offered: B.A., M.A., Ph.D.
Departmental Majors:
Undergraduate: 30 students. Graduate: 10 students
Entrance Requirements:
Undergraduate: ACT or SAT scores; essay required; ATs recommended; interview recommended. Graduate: transcripts; GRE scores; recommendations. Undergraduate and graduate application deadline: January 15. Percent of acceptances: Undergraduate: 50%. Graduate: 30%
Curricular Emphasis: Critical studies in film; film production
Special Activities: Film: film series/festivals; film societies; student publication
Facilities: Film: screening room;

editing suite; extensive film archives. Television: control room
Equipment: Film: complete Super-8; 16mm editing equipment and projectors. Television/Video: portable lighting packages; ½" cassette recorders; portable cameras; monitors; switcher/special effects generators; sound recording equipment
Alumni: Peter Barg, commercials director; Sidney Rosenzweig, filmmaker/critic/lecturer; Premier Maldonado, commercials director

GUIDE POV: This private multicampus institution provides undergraduate and graduate critical studies in film through a small interdepartmental program; there are course listings in production; selective admissions; film internship opportunities locally and abroad

UTICA COLLEGE

1600 Burrstone Rd.,
Utica, NY 13502–4892
(315)792–3111

Private four-year comprehensive institution. Coed, urban location. Enrollment: 1,500.

HUMANITIES DIVISION

Chair/Contact: Scott MacDonald, Professor of English and Film Coordinator
Calendar: Semesters
Degrees Offered: B.A., with a minor in film studies
Entrance Requirements: SAT, essay, and interview recommended. Application deadline: rolling. Percent of acceptances: 66%
Curricular Emphasis: Film theory/aesthetics, history, and criticism; studies in mass media culture

Special Activities: Film: film series/ festivals; guest speakers
Alumni: Linda Randulfe, TV producer/ director; James Bradley, TV news anchor

GUIDE POV: Students in the humanities division who choose the film minor will approach the medium from both artistic and sociocultural viewpoints; theoretical foundation for graduate-level film production or scholarship; study abroad in eight countries

VASSAR COLLEGE

Poughkeepsie, NY 12601
(914)437-7000

Private four-year comprehensive institution. Coed, suburban location. Undergraduate enrollment: 2,250. Graduate enrollment: 10.

DRAMA/FILM PROGRAM AND FILM WORKSHOP

Chair/Contact: James B. Steerman
Calendar: Semesters
Degrees Offered: B.A., drama (students may select emphasis in film)
Departmental Majors:
Undergraduate: 50 students
Entrance Requirements:
Undergraduate: academic rank within top 10% of graduating class; ACT or SAT scores; essay required; interview recommended. Undergraduate application deadline: January 15. Percent of acceptances: 40%
Curricular Emphasis: Balance of film theory and production courses within liberal arts curriculum; basic video production training
Special Activities: Film: film series/ festivals; film societies. Television: program material produced for cable television
Facilities: Film: screening room; editing suite; sound mixing room; film library
Equipment: Film: complete 16mm. Television/Video: complete ¾" and ½" location
Alumni: Meryl Streep, film actress; Mary Anne Page, film producer; Hart Getzen, film producer/director/special effects artist

GUIDE POV: A division of the drama program, the media concentration at this highly selective college is designed to give students intensive training in all aspects of film production, including writing for the cinema; there are courses in basic video production; small, seminar-style classes; study abroad in Scotland, Ireland, England, Germany, and Spain; internship opportunities

Ironically, I'd always been dubious about film schools, just as I've always been down on journalism schools—except for graduate-level specialization in urban affairs, or the law or science, and so on.

The danger of film schools—by no means vanished—is that they often encourage students to become sedulous apes, eager to make *Nightmare XV* and earn big bucks before they have even tried to create a film as a vehicle of personal expression and urgent communication for themselves.

A related danger is furthering the myth of the director as filmmaker who does it all, with insufficient stress on the collaborative nature of the medium. Perhaps unintentionally, the schools hide the pragmatic truth that the percentage of film school graduates with even a prayer of becoming an auteur is absolutely minimal, certainly in the theatrical film area and only a little less so in television.

The gulf between the dream and reality is probably wider in film school than anywhere else on campus. The creative writing major may not get to do the great American novel, or find a publisher if he or she does. But you can always write in a garret. The minicam gives the film student more hope than he has had before, more chance to make a video as a calling card. But it remains delusive to say that getting work is going to be easy.

The University of Southern California, the school where I teach, seems to me to be coping more and more with reality. During Frank Daniel's brief tenure as head of the school, he put fresh emphasis on writing as the key to a successful film. The school makes abundant use of professionals in the community: producers to give seminars on producing, writers to work almost one-on-one with writers, editors, cinematographers, and so on. Nina Foch lectures on working with actors, a long neglected area, as a look at most student films confirms all too quickly.

The facilities here are, as noted elsewhere, first-rate and probably unmatched. I think the technical competence and knowledge of the graduates is probably second to none, and the student work excels in animation and documentary as well as live-action fiction. The documentary work that I have seen is particularly outstanding.

The school also stresses the collaborative nature of filmmaking. This is partly out of necessity, since only a relative handful of all the students are granted the resources to make a film. In his remarkable generation in the mid-sixties, George Lucas would show up as the editor on one film, the camera on another, and, of course, the director on his own *THX 1138 XEB*. He was everywhere, and my impression is that this tradition continues. A student's dream of eventually directing is intact, but it is made clear that entry-level is likely where you'll begin. A signal advantage here is that student work is widely seen by agents, particularly, and studio people in Los Angeles.

My contact with students is largely limited to the graduate papers I read and to the questions asked at the sessions after the Thursday screenings. But I'm impressed by their intelligence, energy, and commitment to the medium, i.e., the visual medium embracing film and television. Film studies students are like a campus within a campus, close-knit and quite indifferent to the usual university enthusiasms. So it seems at USC.

BARTON COLLEGE

600 W. Lee St.,
Wilson, NC 27893
(919)399–6300

Private four-year comprehensive institution. Coed, urban location. Enrollment: 1,300.

DEPARTMENT OF COMMUNICATION, PERFORMING, AND VISUAL ARTS

Chair/Contact: John A. Hancock, Chair
Calendar: Semesters
Degrees Offered: B.A., B.S., communications (with a focus in film/video, broadcast, business, journalism, or international communications)
Departmental Majors: Film: 10 students. Television: 45 students
Entrance Requirements: 2.0 grade-point average; ACT (20 recommended) or SAT (420 verbal and 380 math) scores; essay and interview recommended. Application deadline: July 15. Percent of acceptances: 78%
Curricular Emphasis: Electronic media theory and culture; critical studies in film; media writing; film, video, and broadcast television production; media management
Special Activities: Film: student publication. Television: program material produced for on-campus closed-circuit television, local commercial television station, and cable television
Facilities: Film: sound mixing room; animation stand. Television: studio; audio bay; control room
Equipment: Film: complete Super-8 and 16mm; 35mm sound recording equipment; lighting; film stock; projectors. Television/Video: complete ¾" studio; complete ¾" and ½" location
Alumni: Robert Marshall, radio news reporter; Brian Stembridge, TV producer

GUIDE POV: This nonprofit college offers undergraduates a choice between a film/video major, centering on studio and on-site production, and a broadcast major, concentrating on news journalism; separate degree in business covers all aspects of media management; internship opportunities in television production

DAVIDSON COLLEGE

Davidson, NC 28036
(704)892–2000

Private four-year comprehensive institution. Coed, small town location. Enrollment: 1,550.

DEPARTMENT OF ENGLISH

Chair/Contact: Zoran Kuzmanovich
Calendar: Semesters

Degrees Offered: B.A., English
Entrance Requirements: Competitive grade-point average; ACT or SAT scores; 3 ATs recommended (English composition with essay, mathematics II, and another); five essays required; interview recommended. Application deadline: February 1. Percent of acceptances: 34%
Curricular Emphasis: Film/Video studies and basic video production
Special Activities: Film: film series/festivals; film society. Television: program material produced for college television station
Facilities: Film: screening room. Television: studio; control room
Equipment: Film: Super-8 cameras; sound recording equipment; lighting; projectors. Television/Video: complete ½" studio; access to ¾" studio
Alumni: Lester F. Strong, TV news anchor/reporter; Bob Faw, Jr., TV network correspondent; Lawrence H. Wilkinson, TV managing director; Robert C. Allen, cinema/TV/radio teacher

GUIDE POV: Davidson College is a small, selective private institution founded in 1837; courses in film history, theory, and criticism as well as basic video production training are offered through the English Department and the Center for Special Studies; study abroad semesters in Russia, England, France, Germany, Italy, and India; accelerated degree program; cross-registration with members of the Charlotte Area Education Consortium

---

DUKE UNIVERSITY

Durham, NC 27708
(919)684–8111

Private four-year comprehensive institution. Coed, urban location. Undergraduate enrollment: 6,500. Graduate enrollment: 4,500.

FILM AND VIDEO PROGRAM

Chair/Contact: Jane Gaines, Director; Tom Whiteside
Calendar: Semesters
Degrees Offered: certificate in film and video
Departmental Majors: Undergraduate: 85 students. Graduate: 10 students
Entrance Requirements: Undergraduate: ACT or SAT scores; three ATs; two essays. Graduate: GRE scores; recommendations; statement of purpose. Undergraduate and graduate application deadline: January 1. Undergraduate and graduate percent of acceptances: 30%
Curricular Emphasis: Independent film and video production; theory, history, and cultural criticism
Special Activities: Film/Video: Screen/Society film series; Freewater Productions, student filmmaking collective; student showcases; visiting film and video artists. Television: program material produced for on-campus closed-circuit Cable 13 television. Radio: full broadcast quality recording studio available to film and video students
Facilities: Film: 35mm and 16mm screening facilities; screening room; editing suite; sound mixing room; animation stand. Television: studio; audio bay
Equipment: Film: complete Super-8 and 16mm. Television/Video: ¾" and ½" Beta SP on-line and off-line editing
Alumni: William Styron, author; Carl Kurlander, screenwriter; Harvey

Bullock, TV/film writer; Charlie Rose, TV journalist

GUIDE POV: Students at Duke University enjoy fine facilities for independent work in both film and video; highly selective admissions; good student-faculty ratio; lively student filmmaking collective; cross-registration with the University of North Carolina/Chapel Hill, North Carolina State and North Carolina Central universities; study abroad programs; internship opportunities in film and television production

EAST CAROLINA UNIVERSITY

Greenville, NC 27834
(919)757–6131

State four-year comprehensive institution. Coed, small town location. Enrollment: 17,700.

DEPARTMENT OF COMMUNICATION

Chair/Contact: Television: Carlton Benz
Calendar: Semesters
Degrees Offered: B.A., B.S., communication
Departmental Majors: Television: 250 students
Entrance Requirements: 2.0 grade-point average; ACT or SAT scores; AP and CLEP credit accepted; GED accepted. Application deadline: March 15 for fall entry; November 1 for spring entry. Percent of acceptances: 75%
Curricular Emphasis: Electronic media theory and culture; media writing; television production; media management
Special Activities: Film: film series/festivals. Television: program material produced for on-campus closed-circuit television
Facilities: Television: studio; audio bay; control room
Equipment: Film: 16mm cameras, lighting, and projectors. Television/Video: complete ¾" studio and location
Alumni: Kevin Dill, TV producer/director; John Beard, TV news anchor; Maureen O'Boyle, TV news anchor

GUIDE POV: This competitive state-supported university offers a comprehensive major in communication for students seeking career preparation in television/video production or management; study abroad and work-study programs; varied internship opportunities in television production

NORTH CAROLINA STATE UNIVERSITY

Raleigh, NC 27695–8104
(919)515–2011

State four-year comprehensive institution. Coed, suburban location. Undergraduate enrollment: 21,000. Graduate enrollment: 4,000.

DEPARTMENT OF COMMUNICATION

Chair/Contacts: Ed Funkhouser; Jim Alchediak; Terry Kauffman

FILM STUDIES MINOR

Chair/Contact: Joseph Gomez, Department of English
Calendar: Semesters
Degrees Offered: B.A., communication (concentration in mass communication); film minor offered by departments of English, Communication, and Multidisciplinary Studies

Departmental Majors: Undergraduate mass communication: 200 students
Entrance Requirements: Undergraduate: academic rank within top 30% of graduating class; SAT or ACT scores; minimum 3.0 grade-point average. Undergraduate application deadline: February 1. Percent of acceptances: 48%
Curricular Emphasis: Film: critical studies; experimental and animated production. Television: criticism; television and video production; broadcast journalism
Special Activities: Television: program material produced for cable television
Facilities: Film: sound mixing room; editing room; animation stand. Television/Video: studio; audio bays; control room; editing suites
Equipment: Film: complete Super-8. Television/Video: complete ¾" studio and ½" location
Alumni: Jeff Eagle, TV director; Davy Nethercutt, video editor; John Ward, assistant producer

GUIDE POV: This competitive university offers comprehensive, professional television and video training as well as critical studies in media through the Department of Communication; the film studies minor offers students a blend of criticism, theory, and basic film production training, including animation; cross-registration within the Cooperating Raleigh Colleges Network; study abroad in the Netherlands, Germany, Spain, Austria, England, Mexico, and France; internship opportunities in television production

PEMBROKE STATE UNIVERSITY

Pembroke, NC 28372
(919)521–6000

State four-year comprehensive institution. Coed, small town location. Undergraduate enrollment: 3,000. Graduate enrollment: 200.

TELECOMMUNICATIONS

Chair/Contact: Oscar Patterson, III
Calendar: Semesters
Degrees Offered: B.A., mass communications (with emphasis in broadcasting, journalism, or public relations)
Departmental Majors: Undergraduate mass communications: 65 students
Entrance Requirements: Undergraduate: SAT or ACT scores; 2.0 grade-point average; essay and interview recommended. Undergraduate application deadline: July 15
Curricular Emphasis: Broadcast training including production, news journalism, and media management
Special Activities: Television: student-staffed TV facility serving over 500,000 homes telecasts 24 hours daily over microwave interconnect system linked to cable companies in five communities; student-produced live news program as well as an entertainment program
Facilities: Television/Video: studio; production control; editing suites; master control
Equipment: Television/Video: A/B roll editing; control track and time code; animation and graphics; computers; S-VHS and ¾" cameras; C band; microwave
Alumni: Dean Sheets, TV news producer; Jeff Gilmore, public TV

program director/producer; Eric Walters, videographer/editor

GUIDE POV: Pembroke State University, part of the University of North Carolina system, offers complete broadcast training along with theoretical studies in mass communication; hands-on acquisition of skills; cross-registration; internship opportunities in television production

SCHOOL OF COMMUNICATION ARTS IN RALEIGH

3220 Spring Forest Rd.,
Raleigh, NC 27604
(919)981–0972

Private two-year institution. Coed, urban location. Enrollment: 500.

VIDEO ART DEPARTMENT

Chair/Contact: Debra Hooper
Calendar: Six-month courses
Degrees Offered: Certificates in video production and technology, professional video production, computer art and animation
Departmental Majors: 30–75 students
Entrance Requirements: Open-door policy; high school graduate or equivalent. Application deadline: January 15, September 15, March 15
Curricular Emphasis: Video production and technology; computer animation (Macintosh, PC, and Silicon Graphics)
Special Activities: Television: program material produced for various outlets; vocational placement service; sister school in Minneapolis, MN
Facilities and Equipment: Video: 58 workstations for computer graphics and animation; Betacam postproduction

Alumni: Paul Kaufman, videographer; David Powell, videographer

GUIDE POV: Students enrolled in this private institution enter certificate programs that provide training for entry-level broadcast positions in lighting, audio mixing, and television production; the school places special emphasis on video graphics and animation

SOUTHWESTERN COMMUNITY COLLEGE

275 Webster Rd.,
Sylva, NC 28779
(704)586–4091

State two-year comprehensive institution. Coed, rural location. Enrollment: 1,400.

RADIO AND TELEVISION BROADCAST TECHNOLOGY

Chair/Contact: Roy Burnette
Calendar: Quarters
Degrees Offered: A.A.S.
Departmental Majors: Television: 12 students
Entrance Requirements: Open-door policy with placement testing; high school graduate or equivalent. Application deadline: rolling
Curricular Emphasis: Broadcast journalism; audio-video production; media management; programming; media law
Special Activities: Television: sponsored projects in corporate video programs, public service videos, and advertising
Facilities: Film: sound mixing room. Television/Radio: television studio; audio bay; control room; two ½" editing suites; video toaster system; three radio stations

Equipment: Film: complete Super-8. Television/Video: complete S-VHS studio; complete ¾" and ½" location
Alumni: Jim Schumacher, TV news editor; John Hendon, TV news videographer; Brad Simmons, TV/film production assistant

GUIDE POV: Students attending this small community college learn all aspects of broadcast operations, including management and technical troubleshooting as well as media writing, production, and broadcast performance; individual attention to projects; internship opportunities in television production

UNIVERSITY OF NORTH CAROLINA AT CHAPEL HILL

Chapel Hill, NC 27599–6235
(919)962–2211

State four-year comprehensive institution. Coed, urban location. Undergraduate enrollment: 16,000. Graduate enrollment: 8,000.

RADIO, TELEVISION, AND MOTION PICTURES DEPARTMENT

Chair/Contact: Gorham Kindem, Chair
Calendar: Semesters
Degrees Offered: B.A., M.A.
Departmental Majors: Undergraduate: 291 students. Graduate: 18 students
Entrance Requirements: Undergraduate: SAT scores; competitive grade-point average. Graduate: GRE scores; written statement of purpose; recommendations. Undergraduate and graduate application deadline: January 15. Percent of acceptances: 27%
Curricular Emphasis: This liberal arts major emphasizes writing, practice, and film and media theory
Special Activities: Film: film series/festivals; film production company. Television: student television production unit produces program material for on-campus closed-circuit television, local public television station, and cable television; television production company
Facilities: Film: screening room; editing suite; sound mixing room; animation stand. Television: studio; audio bay; control room
Equipment: Film: complete 16mm. Television/Video: complete ¾" studio; complete ¾" and ½" location
Alumni: Leon Capetanos, screenwriter; Paul Edwards, screenwriter; Michael Piller, TV executive producer

GUIDE POV: Founded in 1795, this highly regarded state university offers both undergraduate and graduate training in all aspects of film and television production and criticism; diverse course listings; students may participate in joint programs with Duke University and North Carolina State University; study abroad; local and national internship opportunities in film and television production

UNIVERSITY OF NORTH CAROLINA —GREENSBORO

Greensboro, NC 27412
(919)334–5000

State four-year comprehensive institution. Coed, urban location. Undergraduate enrollment: 8,000. Graduate enrollment: 2,500.

DEPARTMENT OF COMMUNICATION AND THEATRE/BROADCASTING AND CINEMA DIVISION

Chair/Contact: David R. Batcheller, Director
Calendar: Semesters
Degrees Offered: B.A., media studies; M.F.A., film and video production
Departmental Majors: Undergraduate broadcasting and cinema:
160 students. Graduate film and video:
25 students
Entrance Requirements:
Undergraduate: 2.5 grade-point average; SAT or ACT scores. Graduate: strong undergraduate record with a grade-point average of 3.0 or better; portfolio; recommendations; essay. Undergraduate application deadline: August 1. Graduate application deadline: March 15. Percent of acceptances: Undergraduate: 50%. Graduate: 85%
Curricular Emphasis: Undergraduate: media production; broadcast journalism. Graduate: film and video production
Special Activities: Film: Carolina Film and Video Festival (national competition)
Facilities: Film: sound mixing room; screening room; 16mm editing suite; animation stand. Television/Video: complete 40' × 40' studio; control room; ½" editing bays; ¾" editing bay; audio production suite (16 channel mixer)
Equipment: Film: complete Super-8 and 16mm. Television: complete ½" studio; complete ¾" and ½" VHS location
Alumni: Richard Griffiths, TV producer; John O'Donnell, assistant cinematographer; Danny Hall, special effects producer; Rod Thomas, video

production executive; Lee Kinard, TV news anchor

GUIDE POV: Limited enrollment at this selective university promotes individual attention and support to serious undergraduate and graduate projects in film, video, and television; strong emphasis on developing creative potential; cross-registration with several area colleges; university sponsors semester in Madrid; internship opportunities in film and television production for qualified students; practicum required for graduate students

---

WAKE FOREST UNIVERSITY

P.O. Box 7347
Winston-Salem, NC 27109
(919)759–5000

Private four-year comprehensive institution. Coed, suburban location. Enrollment: 3,500.

DEPARTMENT OF SPEECH COMMUNICATION

Chair/Contact: Michael David Hazen
Calendar: Semesters
Degrees Offered: B.A., speech communication
Departmental Majors: Speech communication: 150 students
Entrance Requirements: Competitive grade-point average; SAT required; 3 ATs, including English composition and math, are recommended; essay required. Application deadline: January 15. Percent of acceptances: 30%
Curricular Emphasis: Electronic media theory and culture; critical studies in film; media writing; audio-film-video production; media management

Special Activities: Film: film series/ festivals; student publication. Television: program material produced for local commercial television station and cable television
Facilities: Film: sound mixing room; screening room; editing room; sound stage; animation stand; film library. Television: studio; audio bay; control room
Equipment: Film: complete Super-8 and 16mm. Television/Video: complete ¾" studio; complete ¾" and ½" location
Alumni: Cameron Kent, screenwriter; Robert Cosner, TV news director; Jennifer Mills, TV broadcaster

GUIDE POV: Established in 1834, this highly selective private university offers students an intensive degree program in film, video, television, and radio production and criticism; diverse course listings; cross-registration with Salem College; study abroad in China, Germany, Austria, Spain, France, Italy, Japan, Russia, and England; varied internship opportunities in film and television production

Entrance Requirements:
Recommendations; ACT or SAT scores. Application deadline: April 5. Percent of acceptances: 79%
Curricular Emphasis: Media arts; broadcast journalism; speech communications
Special Activities: Film: film series/ festivals. Television: three weekly half-hour programs produced for on-campus closed-circuit television and for cable television
Facilities: Television: studio; audio bay; control room; remote van
Equipment: Film: complete Super-8. Television/Video: complete ¾" studio; complete ¾" and ½" location with ¾" editing; EFP ¾"
Alumni: Emilia Pastina, TV producer/ writer; Brad Cartner, TV producer

GUIDE POV: This private liberal arts institution offers a communications major that emphasizes hands-on television production, including video art; attention to individual projects; cross-registration available with area colleges; study abroad in London; internship opportunities in Charlotte and other cities

WINGATE COLLEGE

Wingate, NC 28174
(704)233–8000

Private four-year comprehensive institution. Coed, suburban location. Enrollment: 1,700.

COMMUNICATIONS DEPARTMENT

Chair/Contact: Leon Smith
Calendar: Semesters
Degrees Offered: B.A., B.S., communications (students may select emphasis in television)
Departmental Majors: 140 students

WINSTON-SALEM STATE UNIVERSITY

601 Martin Luther King Dr.
Winston-Salem, NC 27110
(919)750–2000

State four-year comprehensive institution. Coed, urban location. Enrollment: 2,700.

MASS COMMUNICATIONS DEPARTMENT

Chair/Contact: Dr. Brian Blount, Chair
Calendar: Semesters
Degrees Offered: B.A.

Departmental Majors: 256 students
Entrance Requirements: 2.5 grade-point average; ACT or SAT scores; recommendations. Application deadline: rolling. Percent of acceptances: 56%
Curricular Emphasis: Television: radio-television sequence prepares students for careers in performance, production, management, and sales
Special Activities: Film: student publication. Television: program material produced for cable television and for local commercial television station; AERho chapter
Facilities: Film: 35mm screening facilities; animation stand. Television: studio; audio bay; control room

Equipment: Film: 35mm cameras and projectors. Television/Video: complete custom-designed ¾" studio including wireless lavaliere microphone system, state-of-the-art control room and postproduction equipment; complete ¾" and ½" location including ENG cameras and related remote accessories
Alumni: Maurice Rouse, TV assignment editor

GUIDE POV: This state-supported liberal arts university offers a sequential program in radio-television production; students receive hands-on training utilizing professional studio facilities; required media internships

I was an English major at college who had the chance to make several films before actually going to film school. My specific goal was to improve my technical understanding of the craft. While some of the ideas in my early films were good, I found the execution lacking. Film school helped me fill in those gaps.

One of my disappointments, however, was how little time we spent discussing the content of our films. Too often lighting, camera work, and focus seemed to rate a higher priority than character, theme, or story. One reason this occurred was that production schedules were often very tight, and when you had to find locations or gather props, there usually wasn't enough time to work on the script. As a result, the films often looked slick but lacked substance.

My advice to anyone considering film school is think carefully about what kind of films you want to make. If you want to be an avant-garde filmmaker, an industry-oriented school is not the place for you. But if you want to be a Hollywood cinematographer, it might be exactly right. Each school has its strengths and weaknesses, and the best way to figure out what they are is to talk with the students. And don't buy into the myth some film schools promote—that they can give you immediate access to the film business. They can't.

Also, students should consider how they will respond to a competitive environment, because film school is a *very* competitive place. Some schools allow everyone to make their own films, while other schools—usually those that provide funding—have you compete with your colleagues to get an advanced project. Either way there are a lot of late nights involved in finishing any project, and the pressure to meet deadlines can get very intense.

Last, I would advise against going to film school as an undergraduate. Study something besides filmmaking so that you have some basis and inspiration for your work. Travel, work, do whatever you have to do to learn more about yourself and the world *before* you have to run a set surrounded by strange people, pretending you know what you're doing. Obviously you don't have to attend film school to be a success in the movie business. What it can do for you, though, is give you greater confidence about your skills as a filmmaker, give you a chance to study some great films, and hopefully help you find a group of new friends who can come up with better answers to the question your parents and old friends will eventually ask: "When are you going to get a real job!"

NORTH DAKOTA STATE UNIVERSITY

Fargo, ND 58105
(701)237–8011

State four-year comprehensive institution. Coed, urban location. Undergraduate enrollment: 10,000. Graduate enrollment: 10,000.

MASS COMMUNICATION DEPARTMENT

Chair/Contact: C. W. Chandler, Program Coordinator
Calendar: Semesters
Degrees Offered: B.A., M.A., mass communication
Departmental Majors:
Undergraduate: 33 students. Graduate: 2–5 students
Entrance Requirements:
Undergraduate: transcripts; ACT (preferred), SAT, or PSAT scores. Graduate: GRE scores; teachers' recommendations; transcripts; 600 minimum score on TOEFL for foreign students. Undergraduate and graduate application deadline: rolling. Percent of acceptances: 80%
Curricular Emphasis: Electronic media theory and culture; broadcast journalism; broadcast production; media management
Special Activities: Television: program material produced for cable television; member PRSSA
Facilities: Television: studio; audio bay; control room; video editing suites

Equipment: Television/Video: complete ¾" studio; complete ¾" and VHS location; computer writing lab
Alumni: Michael Laliberti, TV news assistant producer; Milo Smith, videographer/reporter; Brad Oakey, videographer; Shawn Moyer, engineering technician; Alf Claussen, TV/film composer

GUIDE POV: This state university offers a strong regional program in mass communication; emphasis on broadcast journalism; small production classes; cross-registration with area colleges and universities; internship opportunities in television production

UNIVERSITY OF NORTH DAKOTA

P.O. Box 8118,
Grand Forks, ND 58202
(701)777–2011

State four-year comprehensive institution. Coed, urban location. Undergraduate enrollment: 10,000. Graduate enrollment: 1,100.

SCHOOL OF COMMUNICATION

Chair/Contact: Neil J. McCutchan
Calendar: Semesters
Degrees Offered: B.A., M.A.
Departmental Majors:
Undergraduate: 70–80 students. Graduate: 70–80 students
Entrance Requirements:
Undergraduate: transcripts; 2.5 grade-

point average; ACT (preferred), SAT, or PSAT scores; English composition test. Graduate: GRE scores; transcripts; teachers' recommendations. Undergraduate application deadline: July 15. Graduate application deadline: contact admissions. Percent of acceptances: 85%

Curricular Emphasis: Electronic media theory and culture; media writing; broadcast production; media management

Special Activities: Television: program material produced for on-campus closed-circuit television and for cable television; their "Studio One" has been rated best college-produced news program by National College Broadcast Association

Facilities: Television: studio; audio bay; control room; video editing suites

Equipment: Television: complete ¾" studio; complete ¾" and ½" location, including Hatachi Z-31 cameras, Intergroup 9600 switcher, Pinnacle Prism DVE; Laird CG; two ¾" editing suites; one ½" editing suite

Alumni: Micky Ford, news producer; Fabrice Mousses, international news photographer; Robert Cary, news photographer; Nathan Kvinge, TV photographer; Brad Nygaard, TV photographer

GUIDE POV: This state university offers a comprehensive broadcasting arts program; students work in television and radio production by second or third semester; study abroad in over 40 countries; media internship opportunities

Perhaps the most important lesson of film school was that it taught me how to focus. I now visualize each new experience, thinking of how best to communicate in images in order to reach an audience. At first I found that the rigorous schedule at film school tended to isolate me from the real world. But good films cannot be made inside a vacuum. My advice is to always remember that your films are for an audience, and to draw upon the entire world for inspiration.

After film school I found employment making television commercials, and soon developed an interest in the business aspects of film. Currently I am attending law school at Georgetown University so that I can better deal with the all-important financial side of the industry as an independent producer and filmmaker.

ANTIOCH COLLEGE

795 Livermore,
Yellow Springs, OH 45387
(513)767–7331

Private four-year comprehensive institution. Coed, small town location. Enrollment: 550.

COMMUNICATIONS AND MEDIA ARTS

Chair/Contact: Robert Devine
Calendar: Quarters
Degrees Offered: B.A., communication and media arts (with emphasis in film, video, documentary arts, journalism, or photography)
Departmental Majors: 60 students
Entrance Requirements: Written statement of purpose and life aims; portfolio; interview advised; teachers' recommendations; high school diploma or GED; SAT recommended. Application deadline: rolling. Percent of acceptances: 75%
Curricular Emphasis: Separate concentrations in film, video, and documentary arts production, as well as in journalism and photography; experimental and independent forms; cultural criticism; studies in media and social change
Special Activities: Film: film societies. Television: program material produced for public access cable television; apprenticeships; independent study; cooperative education program in which students alternate quarters of work/internship and study
Facilities: Film: screening room; editing suite; sound mixing room; animation stand. Television: studio; audio bay; control room
Equipment: Film: complete 16mm. Television/Video: complete ½" location
Alumni: John Korty, film/TV director; Jack Sholder, film/TV director; Jim Klein, documentary filmmaker; Dee Dee Walleck, media producer/activist; Peter Adair, documentary filmmaker

GUIDE POV: This private college offers an individualized program of study emphasizing independent film and video production; course work balances theory and practical training; curriculum grounded in socially responsible media practice; 24-hour access to postproduction facilities; job placement opportunities through extensive cooperative education program

BOWLING GREEN STATE UNIVERSITY

Bowling Green, OH 43403
(419)372–2531

State four-year comprehensive institution. Coed, suburban location. Undergraduate enrollment: 16,000. Graduate enrollment: 2,600.

FILM STUDIES PROGRAM

Chair/Contact: Giacchino Balducci

SCHOOL OF MASS COMMUNICATION, DEPARTMENT OF TELECOMMUNICATIONS

Chair/Contact: Bruce Klopfenstein, Chair
Calendar: Semesters
Degrees Offered: B.A., film studies (interdisciplinary major); B.A., M.A., Ph.D., mass communication
Departmental Majors: Undergraduate film: 30 students. Undergraduate television: 150 students. Graduate mass communication: 30 students
Entrance Requirements: Undergraduate: ACT or SAT scores; academic rank within upper 40% of graduating class. Undergraduate application deadline: February 15. Percent of acceptances: 65%
Curricular Emphasis: Film: major has core, then two tracks: creative (production) and critical (history/theory/criticism); students may pursue graduate critical study of film through the American Culture Studies Program, which offers M.A. and Ph.D. degrees. Television: School of Mass Communication offers undergraduate and graduate studies in electronic media theory and culture; media writing; broadcast production; corporate video; media management
Special Activities: Film: film series/festivals; international film week. Television: program material produced for carrier-current and cable station WFAL as well as for local public television station WBGU-TV; annual Broadcasting Day features special workshops
Facilities: Film: screening room; editing suite; sound mixing room; sound stage; archives. Television: studio; audio bay; control room

Equipment: Film: complete Super-8; some 16mm; students also work in video. Television/Video: complete ¾" studio; complete ¾" and ½" location
Alumni: Lillian Gish, film actress; Christine Wasserman, corporate video director

GUIDE POV: Students at Bowling Green are offered a professional telecommunications program with tracks in television and radio production and management; separate film studies program with tracks in theory and basic film/video production; co-op programs offered through the National Student Exchange; study abroad; local and national internship opportunities in film and television production

---

CAPITAL UNIVERSITY

Columbus, OH 43209–2394
(614)236–6011

Private four-year comprehensive institution. Coed, suburban location. Undergraduate enrollment: 2,400. Graduate enrollment: 1,150.

SPEECH AND COMMUNICATION ARTS

Chair/Contact: Armin Langholz, Chair
Calendar: Semesters
Degrees Offered: B.A., speech and communication arts (students may select an emphasis in radio/TV)
Departmental Majors: Undergraduate television: 35 students
Entrance Requirements: Undergraduate: 2.0 grade-point average; ACT or SAT scores; interview recommended. Undergraduate application deadline: rolling. Percent of acceptances: 75%
Curricular Emphasis: Electronic media theory and culture; media

writing; television/video production; media management

Special Activities: Television: program material produced for cable television

Facilities: Television: studio; audio bay; control room

Equipment: Television/Video: complete ¾" studio; ½" editing equipment

Alumni: Betty Anne Petitt, TV production coordinator; Angela Pace, TV news anchor; Steve Holzaphel, TV newscaster/technical director

GUIDE POV: Capital University, established in 1830, is the oldest four-year comprehensive liberal arts institution in central Ohio; degree program in television/video production emphasizes professional training in broadcast journalism; cross-registration with the Higher Education Council of Columbus; study abroad in 21 countries; adult degree program; internship opportunities in television production

CASE WESTERN RESERVE UNIVERSITY

University Circle, Cleveland, OH 44106
(216)368–2000

Private four-year comprehensive institution. Coed, urban location. Undergraduate enrollment: 3,000. Graduate enrollment: 5,000.

ENGLISH DEPARTMENT

Chair/Contact: Louis Giannetti
Calendar: Semesters
Degrees Offered: B.A., M.A., Ph.D., English (students may select emphasis in film)
Departmental Majors: Undergraduate: 60–70 students.

Graduate: 60–70 students

Entrance Requirements: Undergraduate: ACT or SAT scores; recommendations. Graduate: transcripts; GRE scores; writing sample. Undergraduate and graduate application deadline: February 15. Percent of acceptances: 85%

Curricular Emphasis: Film theory, history, and criticism

Special Activities: Film: film series/festivals; film societies

Facilities: Film/Video: small library of student films and videos

Equipment: Film: 16mm, 35mm, and 70mm projectors

Alumni: Stefan Czapsky, cinematographer; Jon Forman, theatre chain executive; David Wittkowsky, film festival executive

GUIDE POV: Through the English Department, students at this selective private university, may undertake both undergraduate and graduate critical studies in film; study abroad; cross-registration with nine colleges in the Cleveland area; local media research internship opportunities

CLEVELAND STATE UNIVERSITY

Cleveland, OH 44115
(216)687–2000

State four-year comprehensive institution. Coed, urban location. Undergraduate enrollment: 19,000. Graduate enrollment: 5,000

DEPARTMENT OF COMMUNICATION

Chair/Contacts: Vic Wall, Chair; Austin Allen
Calendar: Quarters
Degrees Offered: B.A., communication (with emphasis in film

or broadcasting); M.A., applied communication, theory, and methodology
Departmental Majors: Undergraduate film: 25 students. Undergraduate television: 55 students
Entrance Requirements: Undergraduate: ACT or SAT scores. Undergraduate application deadline: rolling. Percent of acceptances: 99%
Curricular Emphasis: Electronic media theory and culture; film theory/aesthetics, history, and criticism; television production and postproduction; audio production
Special Activities: Film: film series/festivals. Television: program material produced for class projects as well as various Cleveland-area cable systems
Facilities: Film: screening room; editing suite. Television: studio; control room
Equipment: Film: complete Super-8 and 16mm. Television/Video: complete ½" studio
Alumni: Mary Deme, filmmaker; Joe Benny, TV producer

GUIDE POV: Focusing on mass communication studies together with film history and theory, this communication program develops writing and reasoning skills in the context of a liberal arts curriculum; comprehensive television production training offers emphasis on news/feature direction, writing, editing, and programming; cross-registration available with other Cleveland area colleges; study abroad program; media internships available

COLLEGE OF MOUNT SAINT JOSEPH

5701 Delhi Rd.
Cincinnati, OH 45233–1670
(513)244–4200

Private four-year comprehensive institution. Coed, urban location. Undergraduate enrollment: 2,500. Graduate enrollment: 300.

HUMANITIES DEPARTMENT

Chair/Contact: William Schutzius
Calendar: Semesters
Degrees Offered: B.A., communication arts (students may select emphasis in visual media)
Departmental Majors: Undergraduate visual media: 50 students
Entrance Requirements: Undergraduate: ACT or SAT scores required; essay and interview recommended. Undergraduate application deadline: rolling. Percent of acceptances: 70%
Curricular Emphasis: Electronic media theory and culture; critical studies in film; media writing; film and television production including animation
Special Activities: Film: film series/festivals. Television: program material produced for cable television
Facilities: Film: screening room; editing suite; sound mixing room; animation stand. Television: studio; control room
Equipment: Film: complete Super-8 and 16mm. Television/Video: complete ¾" studio; complete ¾" and ½" location
Alumni: Michael Schlomer, TV program director

GUIDE POV: This private college offers an emphasis in visual media that includes production training in film, corporate video, and broadcast television; documentary, news, and animated production; small classes; cross-registration with seven Cincinnati-area colleges; study abroad in England, Germany, and Spain; internship opportunities in television production

GUIDE POV: This selective private college offers pre-graduate training in communication theory as well as basic film and video production; cross-registration possible with the Great Lakes Colleges Association; all students participate in a one-term senior project; study abroad; internship opportunities in television production

THE COLLEGE OF WOOSTER

Beall Ave.,
Wooster, OH 44691
(216)263-2000

Private four-year comprehensive institution. Coed, suburban location. Enrollment: 1,800.

COMMUNICATION DEPARTMENT

Chair/Contact: Dr. Rod Korba
Calendar: Semesters
Degrees Offered: B.A.
Departmental Majors: 43 students
Entrance Requirements: 2.5 grade-point average; ACT (minimum 20) or SAT (minimum composite 900) scores; average SAT score 1090; essay required; interview recommended. Application deadline: February 15. Percent of acceptances: 60%
Curricular Emphasis: Visual literacy; basic production
Facilities: Film: screening room; editing suite. Television: studio; control room
Equipment: Film: Super-8 cameras; editing equipment; lighting; black-and-white film stock; projectors; 16mm cameras; editing equipment; lighting; projectors. Television/Video: complete ½" location
Alumni: Vince Cellini, CNN sports anchor

DENISON UNIVERSITY

Granville, OH 43023
(614)587-0810

Private four-year comprehensive institution. Coed, small town location. Enrollment: 1,950.

DEPARTMENT OF THEATRE AND CINEMA

Chair/Contacts: David Bussan; R. Elliott Stout
Calendar: Semesters
Degrees Offered: B.A., cinema
Departmental Majors: Film: 35 students
Entrance Requirements: Competitive grade-point average; ACT and/or SAT scores; portfolio materials on video are accepted but not required; recommendations; consideration is also given to course load and extra curricular activities both at school and in the community. Application deadline: February 1. Percent of acceptances: 75%
Curricular Emphasis: Cinema at Denison is taught in a liberal arts setting; cinema majors evenly balance production and film studies course load; all production in 16mm or S-VHS video
Special Activities: Film: student-run Denison Film Society schedules screenings of two films per week during the school year; annual Denison Film Festival screens student

and faculty work; artist-in-residence program

Facilities: Film/Video: sound stage; screening room; editing suite; sound mixing room; Oxberry animation stand; J-K optical printer; 52" video monitor; film/video library

Equipment: Film: complete 16mm; cameras include an Arri S, two Auricon 600s and one 200, two Beaulieus, eight Bolex RXs, seven Canon Scoopics, an Eclair NPR, and a Traid (200 f.p.s.); editing equipment includes seven benches with rewinds, Moviescopes and squawk boxes, three upright moviolas, an eight-plate Steenbeck flatbed, and a six-plate KEM flatbed; sound equipment includes a Nagra III, a Nagra IV, two Tandbergs, one Uher, one Magnasync, and an RCA fullcoat mixing system. Video: two Panasonic AG 450s and two 460 S-VHS camcorders; one S-VHS editing system that allows for A/B rolling; laserdisc player

Alumni: Michael Eisner, Disney CEO; David Irving, film director; Jane Martin, film producer; Ann Magnuson, film/TV actress

GUIDE POV: The small but quality-oriented cinema program is for the motivated film/video student who wishes to explore the possibilities of cinematic art; students produce narrative, animated, documentary, and avant-garde works; additional course listings in cinema history and theory, screenwriting, and film analysis; study abroad programs geared toward cinema students; film students may participate in the Great Lakes College Association's New York Arts Semester in which they are paired with artists in NYC; local and national media internships available

FRANCISCAN UNIVERSITY OF STEUBENVILLE

100 Franciscan Way,
P.O. Box 7200,
Steubenville, OH 43952–6701
(614)283–3771

Private four-year comprehensive institution. Coed, urban location. Undergraduate enrollment: 2,000. Graduate enrollment: 200.

MASS COMMUNICATION DEPARTMENT

Chair/Contact: James E. Coyle, Jr., Chair

Calendar: Semesters

Degrees Offered: B.A., mass communications (concentration in radio/television or journalism)

Departmental Majors: Undergraduate radio and television: 75 students

Entrance Requirements: Undergraduate: 2.0 grade-point average; ACT or SAT scores; essay and interview recommended; AP or CLEP credit accepted. Undergraduate application deadline: August 1. Percent of acceptances: 80%

Curricular Emphasis: Electronic media theory and culture; media writing; audio-video production; media management

Special Activities: Television: program material produced for on-campus closed-circuit television and for national Catholic cable networks

Facilities: Television/Radio: matched camera studio; audio bay; control room; radio station

Equipment: Television/Video: complete ¾" studio; complete ¾"; S-VHS recording and editing

Alumni: Charles Beaudry, TV director; Wendy Wilmowski, TV producer; Jeanmarie Ahern, TV director/technical director

GUIDE POV: Students intending to pursue either professional careers in the broadcast and recording industries or graduate study in radio/television may choose this comprehensive degree program that emphasizes both theoretical understanding and practical application of mass media skills; course listings in radio/television writing, production, editing, management, and media ethics; study abroad in England; internship opportunities in television and radio production

FRANKLIN UNIVERSITY

201 S. Grant Ave.,
Columbus, OH 43215–5399
(614)341–0237

Private four-year comprehensive institution. Coed, urban location. Undergraduate enrollment: 26,000. Graduate enrollment: 7,000.

APPLIED COMMUNICATION

Chair/Contact: Janice Gratz, Program Director
Calendar: Semesters
Degrees Offered: B.S., applied communication (concentration in video production)
Departmental Majors: Undergraduate video: 50 students
Entrance Requirements: Undergraduate: 2.0 grade-point average; ACT or SAT scores. Undergraduate application deadline: rolling. Percent of acceptances: 99%
Curricular Emphasis: Electronic media theory and culture; media writing; television, radio, video, and audio-visual production; media management
Special Activities: Television: program material produced for local

public television station; student newsletter
Facilities: Television: studio; audio bay; control room
Equipment: Television/Video: complete ¾" studio; complete ½" location; VHS format video editing equipment
Alumni: Steffanie Bennett, radio/TV producer; Marilyn Musick-Dennis, media buyer

GUIDE POV: This private university offers a practical program in communications focusing on the acquisition of electronic media production skills; core requirements in financial accounting, marketing, and media management; students in the major acquire an extensive media portfolio in preparation for future employment; cross-registration with area colleges; study abroad at Richmond College in London; internship opportunities in television/video and radio production

KENT STATE UNIVERSITY

Kent, OH 44242
(216)672–3000

State four-year comprehensive institution. Coed, small town location. Undergraduate enrollment: 22,000. Graduate enrollment: 4,300.

SCHOOL OF JOURNALISM AND MASS COMMUNICATION

Chair/Contact: Dr. Gene Stebbins, Coordinator, radio-television
Calendar: Semesters
Degrees Offered: B.A., B.S., journalism and mass communication (with emphasis in news, broadcast news, advertising, photo journalism and illustration, radio-television

production, corporate video, or media sales and management); M.A., journalism and mass communication (with emphasis in news, radio-television, or public relations)
Departmental Majors: Undergraduate broadcast news: 50; radio/TV production: 75; broadcast management: 35; corporate video: 15. Graduate television: 15 students; media management: 8
Entrance Requirements: Undergraduate: 2.5 grade-point average; ACT or SAT scores. Graduate: 3.0 grade-point average; GRE scores; portfolio; interview; teachers' recommendations; written statement of purpose; professional recommendations. Undergraduate and graduate application deadline: April 1. Percent of acceptances: Undergraduates: 100% state residents; 70% nonresidents. Graduates: 60%
Curricular Emphasis: Professional preparation for careers in broadcast station and corporate video settings
Special Activities: Television: program material produced for on-campus closed-circuit television TV-2 includes nightly newscast and other student-produced programs
Facilities: Television: two color-equipped studios; four video editing suites; three audio production/editing areas
Equipment: Television/Video: VHS; ¾" portable video units
Alumni: Ted Henry, TV news anchor; Mally McCoy, CNN news anchor; Jack Marschall, TV news anchor; John Zaccardelli, videographer

GUIDE POV: This state university offers students professional media training with particular attention to television and radio news broadcasting and corporate video production; cross-registration and co-op programs; study abroad; honors college; internship opportunities in television, corporate video, and radio production

---

LORAIN COUNTY COMMUNITY COLLEGE

1005 N. Abbe Rd.,
Elyria, OH 44035–1691
(216)365–5222

State two-year comprehensive institution. Coed, suburban location. Enrollment: 6,000.

LANGUAGE AND HUMANITIES DIVISION, COMMUNICATION AND PERFORMING ARTS

Chair/Contact: Dee Gross
Calendar: Quarters
Degrees Offered: A.A., communication and performing arts (concentration in drama, radio, speech, or television)
Departmental Majors: Radio and television: 60 students
Entrance Requirements: Open-door policy. Application deadline: rolling. Percent of acceptances: 99%
Curricular Emphasis: Electronic media theory and culture; television production; broadcast speaking; videotape editing; small format television production
Special Activities: Film: film series. Television: program material produced for local commercial television station includes news show
Facilities: Television: studio; audio bay; control room; editing station
Equipment: Television/Video: complete ¾" studio and location including switcher and character generator; A/B roll and VHS ½" editing equipment
Alumni: Matt Lundy, media

consultant; Ron Jantz, TV sportscaster; Rebecca O'Hare, TV floor manager

GUIDE POV: The pre-professional media production option at this community college offers a two-year intensive program that prepares students for technical support positions in broadcasting and corporate video; internship opportunities in television, corporate video, and radio production

MARIETTA COLLEGE

Marietta, OH 45750–3031
(614)374–4600

Private four-year comprehensive institution. Coed, small town location. Enrollment: 1,200.

DEPARTMENT OF MASS MEDIA

Chair/Contact: Dr. Joseph H. Berman, Chair
Calendar: Semesters
Degrees Offered: B.A., mass media (concentration in radio/TV, journalism, advertising, public relations, or political journalism)
Departmental Majors: Television: 50 students
Entrance Requirements: Competitive grade-point average; ACT or SAT scores; ATs in English and mathematics recommended; AP and CLEP credit accepted; teachers' recommendations. Application deadline: May 1. Percent of acceptances: 75%
Curricular Emphasis: Electronic media theory and culture; media writing; television broadcast and field production; one film theory course offered through the English Department
Special Activities: Film: film series/

festivals. Television: program material produced for WCMO-TV cable television
Facilities: Television: studio; audio bay; control room; editing stations on campus; students also operate Channel 2, WCMO-TV, a local cable station
Equipment: Television/Video: complete ¾" studio and location including CCD camera equipment; ¾" editing
Alumni: Laura Baudo, screenwriter; David Anthony, TV personality; Jennifer Burdell, media executive

GUIDE POV: Students attending this competitive private college, chartered in 1835, are offered a small media program that emphasizes television broadcast and field journalism; co-op programs; study abroad; internship opportunities in television production

MIAMI UNIVERSITY

Oxford, OH 45056
(513)529–1809

State four-year comprehensive institution. Coed, rural location. Undergraduate enrollment: 14,000. Graduate enrollment: 2,000.

COMMUNICATION DEPARTMENT

Chair/Contact: Jack L. Rhodes, Chair
Calendar: Semesters
Degrees Offered: B.A., M.A., M.S., mass communication
Departmental Majors: Undergraduate: 940 students. Graduate: 65 students
Entrance Requirements: Undergraduate: 2.5 grade-point average; ACT or SAT scores; recommendations; community activities. Graduate: 3.0 grade-point average (for mass communication

program); interview; three letters of recommendation; writing sample; portfolio. Undergraduate and graduate application deadline: January 31. Percent of acceptances: Undergraduate: 71%. Graduate: 40%

Curricular Emphasis: Undergraduate: broadcast journalism; media management. Graduate: self-directed video studies and production in consultation with adviser

Special Activities: Film: film series/festivals. Television: program material produced for local public television station and for MUTV, curricular and noncurricular university cable television; AERho broadcasting honorary; PRSSA; WICI

Facilities: Television: three introductory and one advanced audio suites; two video studios; viewing rooms; two introductory editing and two advanced editing suites; remote van

Equipment: Television/Video: complete ¾" studio; complete ¾" and ½" location

Alumni: Rick Ludwin, TV network executive; Janet Davies, TV new anchor

GUIDE POV: Miami University, founded in 1809, offers students a strong liberal arts program combined with practical training in broadcast journalism; cross-registration with Cincinnati-area colleges; admission is highly competitive; study abroad in Luxembourg; honors program; internship opportunities in television production

---

NOTRE DAME COLLEGE OF OHIO

4545 College Rd.,
South Euclid, OH 44121
(216)381–1680

Private four-year comprehensive institution. Women, suburban location. Enrollment: 900.

DEPARTMENT OF ENGLISH COMMUNICATIONS

Chair/Contact: Tony Zupancic
Calendar: Semesters
Degrees Offered: B.A., English communications (with emphasis in media, writing, or theatre)
Departmental Majors: Film and television: 40 students
Entrance Requirements: 2.5 grade-point average; ACT or SAT scores; teachers' recommendations. Application deadline: August 1. Percent of acceptances: 78%
Curricular Emphasis: Electronic media theory and culture; critical studies in film; basic film and video production
Special Activities: Film: student publication. Television: program material produced for cable television
Facilities: Film: film/video library
Equipment: Film: Super-8 cameras, projectors, and editing; 16mm projectors. Television/Video: ½" cassette recorders; portable cameras; monitors; sound recording equipment
Alumni: Patricia Choby, media producer; Marge Banks, broadcast journalist; Mary Strassmeyer, media columnist

GUIDE POV: Affiliated with the Roman Catholic Church, this small women's college offers courses in film and video with an emphasis on theory and criticism; strong liberal arts curriculum; basic film and video production training; competitive entry; cross-registration available; internships in film and television production

OBERLIN COLLEGE

173 W. College St.,
Oberlin, OH 44074–1191
(216)775–8121

*Private four-year comprehensive
institution. Coed, rural location.
Enrollment: 3,000.*

THEATRE AND DANCE PROGRAM

Chair/Contact: Daniel J. Goulding,
Chair
Calendar: Semesters
Degrees Offered: B.A., theatre
(concentration in film studies)
Entrance Requirements: Competitive
grade-point average; ACT or SAT
scores; interview recommended; essay
required; three ATs, including English,
recommended. Application
deadline: January 15. Percent of
acceptances: 55%
Curricular Emphasis: Film theory/
aesthetics, history, and criticism;
television production
Special Activities: Film: film series/
festivals; film society
Facilities: Film: screening room;
editing suite; film library. Television:
studio; audio bay; control room
Equipment: Television/Video:
complete ¾" studio; complete ¾" and
½" location
Alumni: William Goldman, writer/
screenwriter; Eric Bogosian, writer/
screenwriter; Richard Orloff, TV writer

GUIDE POV: This highly competitive
private college offers a concentration
in film studies through the Theatre
Department; emphasis on theoretical
studies along with basic television
production training; attention to
individual projects; study abroad;
internship opportunities in film and
television production

OHIO NORTHERN UNIVERSITY

Ada, OH 45810
(419)772–2000

*Private four-year comprehensive
institution. Coed, small town location.
Enrollment: 3,000.*

DEPARTMENT OF COMMUNICATION ARTS

Chair/Contacts: Nils Riess, Chair
Calendar: Quarters
Degrees Offered: B.A.,
communication arts (concentrations in
broadcasting, speech communication,
theatre, public relations, and musical
theatre)
Departmental Majors: Radio and
television: 20 students
Entrance Requirements: Academic
rank within top half of graduating
class; interview recommended; ACT or
SAT scores. Application deadline:
rolling. Percent of acceptances: 85%
Curricular Emphasis: Electronic
media theory and culture; media
writing; audio-video production; media
management
Special Activities: Television/Radio:
program material produced for ONU
Cable, the university's on-campus
cable system; noncommercial radio
station WONB-FM is student-run
Facilities: Television: video editing
stations; audio studio
Equipment: Television/Video:
complete ¾" and ½" location; ¾"
editing format
Alumni: Ron McGreavy, video
producer; Julie Buchan, TV sales
executive; Michael Smith, video
producer; Kyle McPeck, television
editor

GUIDE POV: Students majoring in
communication arts at this private
liberal arts university may choose a

broadcasting concentration emphasizing radio and television production, writing, and management; summer study tours to Europe and Japan; competitive admissions; internship opportunities in television and radio production

---

OHIO STATE UNIVERSITY

Oval Mall,
Columbus, OH 43210
(614)292–6446

State four-year comprehensive institution. Coed, urban location. Undergraduate enrollment: 50,000. Graduate enrollment: 10,000.

THEATRE DEPARTMENT

Chair/Contact: Dr. Kathleen F. Conlin

SCHOOL OF JOURNALISM

Chair/Contact: Dr. Pamela Shoemaker, Chair; Conrad Smith
Calendar: Quarters
Degrees Offered: Theatre Department: B.A., B.F.A., M.A., (with emphasis in film/video production, television production, or history); M.F.A., directing program in cinema; Ph.D., interdepartmental (emphasis available in cinema). Journalism: B.A., journalism (sequences in broadcasting, advertising, public relations, and news-editorial); M.A., journalism
Departmental Majors: Undergraduate film/video: 100 students. Graduate film/video: 20 students. Undergraduate broadcast journalism: 125 students. Graduate television: 10 students
Entrance Requirements: Undergraduate: 2.0 grade-point average; ACT or SAT scores; written statement of purpose; portfolio. Graduate: 3.0 grade-point average; GRE scores; teachers' recommendations;

written statement of purpose; portfolio. Undergraduate and graduate application deadline: February 15. Percent of acceptances: Undergraduate: 80%. Graduate: 73%
Curricular Emphasis: Theatre Department: undergraduate and graduate course work in electronic media theory and culture; critical studies in film; screenwriting; film/video production; directing program. School of Journalism, broadcast sequence: course work in telecommunication production; reporting and newswriting for broadcast, as well as core requirements in the fields of political science, sociology, history, and economics. Graduate: advanced work concentrates on sharpening reporting and writing skills
Special Activities: Film: film series/festivals; film society. Television: program material produced for local public television station, cable television, and video festivals, including "Metro Beat," a regularly aired television magazine program produced by journalism majors
Facilities: Film: 35mm screening facilities; screening room; editing suite; sound mixing room; animation stand; film library. Television: studio; audio bay; control room
Equipment: Film: Super-8, 16mm, and 35mm cameras; sound recording equipment; lighting; projectors; nitrate restoration printer. Television/Video: complete ¾" studio; complete ¾" and ½" location
Alumni: Jerome Lawrence, film/TV writer; Richard Lewis, TV/film actor/comedian; Eileen Heckert, film/TV actress; Jean Peters, film actress; James C. Katz, film producer

GUIDE POV: This large, competitive public university offers professional undergraduate and graduate training in film and video through the Department of Photography and Cinema; separate tracks for critical studies and production; well-equipped facilities open to students at all levels; diverse course listings; quality-oriented School of Journalism offers comprehensive broadcast sequence; cross-registration with all central Ohio colleges; extensive study abroad program; local and national internship opportunities in film and television production

---

OHIO UNIVERSITY AT ATHENS

Athens, OH 45701
(614)593–1000

State four-year comprehensive institution. Coed, small town location. Undergraduate enrollment: 14,000. Graduate: 2,500.

SCHOOL OF FILM

Chair/Contact: Dr. David O. Thomas, Director

SCHOOL OF TELECOMMUNICATIONS

Chair/Contact: Dr. David Mould, Associate Director
Calendar: Quarters
Degrees Offered: B.F.A. with an emphasis in film; minor in film; honors tutorial M.F.A., film; M.A., film. B.S.C., M.A., Ph.D., telecommunications
Departmental Majors: Undergraduate film: 6. Graduate film: 40. Undergraduate telecommunications: 750. Graduate telecommunications: 30
Entrance Requirements:
Undergraduate: academic rank within upper half of high school graduating class for telecommunication majors

and within top 10% for applicants to honors tutorial program in film; SAT or ACT scores; portfolio. Graduate: transcripts; three letters of recommendation; sample of written work; interview recommended; 500-word personal essay; in addition, M.F.A. applicants in film should have accumulated an undergraduate 3.0 grade-point average and are required to submit portfolio of creative work. Undergraduate and graduate application deadline: February 1. Percent of acceptances: Film: 20%. Telecommunications: 65%
Curricular Emphasis: Film: independent narrative, experimental, and documentary film production; international cinema history, theory, and criticism. Television: management; criticism; news/documentary; video art
Special Activities: Film: *Wide Angle*, a student quarterly journal of film; annual film conference. Television: program material produced for on-campus closed-circuit television and for local public television station
Facilities: Film: sound mixing studio; screening room; flatbed editing; video editing. Television: studio; audio bay; control room
Equipment: Film: complete 16mm film and S-VHS video; production and editing equipment; 35mm editing equipment; sound recording equipment; projectors. Television: complete ¾" studio; complete ¾" and ½" location
Alumni: Tony Buba, filmmaker; Ann Alter, filmmaker; Ed Lachman, cinematographer; Paul Glabicki, teacher/animator; Rick Hancock, filmmaker/teacher

GUIDE POV: Training in film production, arts administration, and university teaching is available to students through the Film Department; School of Telecommunications offers separate sequences in professional management/administration and video production; accelerated degree program available through honors tutorial college; competitive admissions; study abroad; internship opportunities in film and television production

OHIO UNIVERSITY AT ZANESVILLE

11425 Newark Rd.,
Zanesville, OH 43701
(614)453–0762

State two-year comprehensive institution. Coed, suburban location. Enrollment: 1,300.

RADIO/TELEVISION DEPARTMENT

Chair/Contact: Reed Smith
Calendar: Quarters
Degrees Offered: A.A.S.
Departmental Majors: 40 students
Entrance Requirements: Recommendations; ACT or SAT scores; portfolio. Application deadline: September 1
Curricular Emphasis: Radio/TV production
Special Activities: Television: program material produced for local commercial television station and for cable television
Facilities: Television: studio; audio bay; control room
Equipment: Television/Video: complete ¾" studio and S-VHS location; ¾" and S-VHS editing
Alumni: Brent Greene, TV producer; David Briggs, video editor; Doug Mathias, TV production assistant

GUIDE POV: Featuring thorough television production training this community college has a high success rate placing graduates in technical support positions; core program enables students to transfer to four-year university; internship opportunities in television and radio production

UNIVERSITY OF CINCINNATI

Clifton Ave.,
Cincinnati, OH 45221–0091
(513)556–6000

State four-year comprehensive institution. Coed, urban location. Undergraduate enrollment: 31,000. Graduate enrollment: 5,200.

SCHOOL OF ART

Chair/Contact: Derrick Woodham

COLLEGE-CONSERVATORY OF MUSIC, DIVISION OF ELECTRONIC MEDIA

Chair/Contact: Dr. Manfred K. Wolfram, Head
Calendar: Quarters
Degrees Offered: B.F.A., art, electronic media. M.F.A., art
Departmental Majors: Undergraduate art: 160 students. Graduate art: 44 students. Undergraduate electronic media: 35 students
Entrance Requirements: Undergraduate: 2.0 grade-point average; 20–22 ACT or 900 composite SAT scores; academic rank within upper third of graduating class; letters of recommendation; essay and interview recommended for all students and required for electronic media majors. Graduate: transcripts; portfolio. Undergraduate application deadline: December 15 recommended; February 15 for electronic media applicants; July 15 final deadline for all other departments. Graduate

application deadline: February 15.
Percent of acceptances:
Undergraduate art: 50%. Graduate art:
10–15%. Undergraduate electronic
media: 10–15%

Curricular Emphasis: Art: electronic
art stressing computer-based
applications that either output to
videotape or are interactive; live
action production; experimental
animation. Electronic media: study of
radio, sound recording, television,
video production, and other forms of
electronic media communication;
broadcast journalism and corporate
video emphasis

Special Activities: Film/Video: series/
festivals; societies; visiting artists.
Television: program material produced
for on-campus closed-circuit television
and cable television

Facilities: Film: screening room;
editing suite; sound mixing room;
animation stand; film/video library.
Television: studio; audio bay; control
room; ¾" SMPTE editing suite includes
Videographics and special video
effects; additional ¾" and ½" off-line
editing bays; and ¾" and ½"
videotape editing suites; 16-track, 24-
channel audio production control
room and studio; radio production
control room and studio

Equipment: Film: complete 16mm.
Television/Video: complete ¾" studio;
complete ¾" and ½" location

Alumni: Willie Moore, animator; John
Erhardt, cinematographer; David
Bastian, animator

Guide POV: An innovative film and
video program is offered through the
Art Department, emphasizing
interactive media, electronic arts, and
animation; emphases on both artistic
and technical merit; separate, well-
equipped electronic media program

offers professional career training in
television and radio broadcasting with
a news/documentary sequence; study
abroad in Spain, France, and
Germany; freshman honors program;
electronic media program offers
extensive internship opportunities in
television and radio production

UNIVERSITY OF DAYTON

300 College Pk.,
Dayton, OH 45469
(513)229–1000

*Private four-year comprehensive
institution. Coed, urban location.
Undergraduate enrollment: 7,000.
Graduate enrollment: 2,000.*

DEPARTMENT OF COMMUNICATION

Chair/Contact: Dr. Don Morlan, Chair;
Alan Hueth

Calendar: Semesters

Degrees Offered: B.A.,
communication (concentration in
electronic media); M.A.,
communication

Departmental Majors: Undergraduate
television: 100 students

Entrance Requirements:
Undergraduate: competitive grade-
point average; ACT or SAT scores and
interview recommended; essay
required; letter of recommendation
required. Graduate: GRE scores;
recommendations; statement of
purpose. Undergraduate and graduate
application deadline: rolling. Percent
of acceptances: 77%

Curricular Emphasis: Electronic
media theory and culture; media
writing; television production; media
management

Special Activities: Television:
program material produced for cable
television

Facilities: Television: studio; audio bay; control room
Equipment: Television/Video: complete ¾" studio and location
Alumni: Dave Long, TV sportswriter; Jeff Morlan, TV production manager; Geoff Vargo, broadcasting executive

GUIDE POV: This selective private university offers undergraduate communication majors a concentration in electronic media production; grounding in contemporary mass media studies; graduate program is theory-oriented; cross-registration with the Miami Valley Consortium; study abroad; media internship opportunities for students maintaining 3.0 grade-point average in the major

UNIVERSITY OF TOLEDO

2801 W. Bancroft St.,
Toledo, OH 43606
(419)537–2072

State four-year comprehensive institution. Coed, suburban location. Undergraduate enrollment: 17,000. Graduate enrollment: 5,000.

THEATRE, FILM, AND DANCE

Chair/Contact: Bob Arnold
Calendar: Quarters
Degrees Offered: B.A., film; B.F.A., film/video
Departmental Majors: Undergraduate film: 33 students
Entrance Requirements: Undergraduate: SAT or ACT scores; 2.0 minimum grade-point average; high school diploma or GED. Undergraduate application deadline: rolling. Percent of acceptances: 85%
Curricular Emphasis: Film: theory; production; narrative; experimental

forms. Video: theory; production; documentary; experimental forms; video art
Special Activities: Film: annual film showcase; visiting filmmakers and lecturers; student-run film screening series. Television: program material produced for on-campus closed-circuit television
Facilities: Film: screening room; 16mm editing suites; animation stand; film library. Video: editing suite; screening room
Equipment: Film: 16mm (Bolex and Arriflex); Steenbeck six-plate editor. Video: ½" portable VHS cameras and editing; monitors; Amiga graphics; sound recording equipment; audio mixers; JK optical printer
Alumni: Brett Leonard, film director; Tim Jones, filmmaker; Randy Bahnsen, animator; Dana Jill Meaux, TV/film editor

GUIDE POV: The film production courses taught in this visual arts program include training in video and promote exploration of narrative, animated, and experimental forms; cross-registration with Bowling Green State University; study abroad; film/video workshops; media internship opportunities

WRIGHT STATE UNIVERSITY

Dayton, OH 45435
(513)873–3333

State four-year comprehensive institution. Coed, suburban location. Undergraduate enrollment: 13,000. Graduate enrollment: 4,000.

DEPARTMENT OF THEATRE ARTS

Chair/Contact: Dr. William Lafferty, Chair

Calendar: Quarters
Degrees Offered: B.A., film studies;
B.F.A., film production
Departmental Majors: Undergraduate
film/video: 86 students
Entrance Requirements:
Undergraduate: Open-door policy for
OH state residents; higher standards
for nonresidents; ACT or SAT scores;
interview required for admittance
to B.F.A. program; portfolio review
and evaluation before junior year;
3.0 GPA in film/video courses for
major status. Undergraduate
application deadline: rolling. Percent
of acceptances: 95%
Curricular Emphasis: Production and
history/theory treated equally;
narrative/documentary/experimental
treated equally
Special Activities: Film: university-
subsidized filmmaking grants for
students; university filmmakers
association; commercial theatre
screenings of student films; workshops
and master classes with industry
professionals. Television/Video:
program material produced for cable
television
Facilities: Film: screening room;
editing suites; conforming room; sound
mixing room; audio postproduction
facility; mixing theatre;
animation stand. Video: screening
rooms; extensive videotape
library
Equipment: Film: complete Super-8
and 16mm; Nagra sound recorders;
Steenbeck and moviola editing tables.
Television/Video: ¾" video cameras;
portable lighting packages; ½" VHS
cassette recorders and editing;
portable cameras; monitors; sound
recording equipment; audio mixers
Alumni: Heidi Kling, TV/film actress;
Brad Sherwood, film/TV actor; James
Baldridge, TV news anchor

GUIDE POV: Undergraduates choosing
a motion picture concentration within
the Department of Theatre Arts are
offered a program stressing practical
training in film and video in addition
to extensive study of media theory;
separate production-oriented B.F.A.
program; diverse course listings; study
abroad; cross-registration with area
colleges; internship opportunities in
film and video production

XAVIER UNIVERSITY

3800 Victory Pkwy.,
Cincinnati, OH 45207–5171
(513)745–3000

*Private four-year comprehensive
institution. Coed, urban location.
Undergraduate enrollment: 4,100.
Graduate enrollment: 2,300.*

COMMUNICATION ARTS DEPARTMENT

Chair/Contact: Dr. William Daily,
Chair; Bill Hagerty
Calendar: Semesters
Degrees Offered: B.A.,
communication arts (students may
select emphasis in electronic media)
Departmental Majors: Electronic
media: 100 students
Entrance Requirements: SAT or ACT
scores; high school C+ average;
transcripts; recommendations.
Undergraduate application deadline:
rolling. Percent of acceptances: 90%
Curricular Emphasis: Electronic
media concentration offers courses in
video production, television directing,
postproduction, video graphics,
broadcast news and sports production,
broadcast performance, media
management, and film history
Special Activities: Television/Video:
program material produced for cable

television; TV club; advertising club; PRSSA chapter

Facilities: Television: studio; control room; editing areas; conference/ viewing rooms

Equipment: Television/Video: ¾" recorders; editing; field equipment

Alumni: Linda Finnell, associate TV director; John Thai, TV producer; Jeannie Jacobs, corporate video producer

GUIDE POV: Founded in 1831, this private university offers television and video production and management training with an emphasis on broadcast journalism; co-op programs with the University of Cincinnati and Duke University; cross-registration through the Greater Cincinnati Consortium; study abroad in Argentina, France, Spain, or Germany; internship opportunities in television production

YOUNGSTOWN STATE UNIVERSITY

410 Wick Ave.,
Youngstown, OH 44555–3150
(216)742–3000

State four-year comprehensive institution. Coed, urban location. Undergraduate enrollment: 14,179. Graduate enrollment: 1,275.

SPEECH COMMUNICATION AND THEATRE DEPARTMENT, TELECOMMUNICATIONS STUDIES

Chair/Contact: Dr. Alfred W. Owens, Chair

Calendar: Quarters

Degrees Offered: B.A., telecommunications studies

Departmental Majors: Undergraduate television: 250 students

Entrance Requirements: Undergraduate: open-door policy for OH residents; 2.0 grade-point average; GED accepted; ACT or SAT scores are required if the applicant has been out of high school for less than two years; out-of-state applicants must meet higher requirements. Undergraduate application deadline: August 15. Percent of acceptances: 99%

Curricular Emphasis: Electronic media theory and culture; media writing; television production; media management

Special Activities: Film: film series/ festivals. Television: program material produced for cable television

Facilities: Television: four-camera color studio; audio bay; control room; electronic teleprompting; color film island; color switching

Equipment: Television/Video: complete ¾" studio and ½" location

GUIDE POV: Offering a practical program with a strong career orientation, this public commuter university provides telecommunications students with professional skills to enter the corporate communication, cable, and television industries; management training; internship opportunities in television and radio production

After high school I attended Columbia University in NYC.

There was no film major at the time, so I majored in comparative literature. I took some film theory courses, but I was eager to make films, not just talk about them. Transferring to USC in my junior year, I immediately jumped into production. But my problem with film school was money. And since I had very little, I had to take a year off to drive a cab back in New York. When I returned to USC, I discovered I had won the Nissan Focus award as best student editor for the year.

After graduating, I wrote and edited a feature documentary, edited several shorts, and wrote a half-hour film for Universal Television that won the 1990 Gold Hugo at the Chicago Film Festival. Then I enrolled as a Directing Fellow at the AFI, where I made three video shorts in the space of a year. While there, I was recommended for a directing internship on a television pilot that turned out to be the best learning experience of all.

The reality of the business is that you need a directing reel and a property. Going to school merely delays the inevitable: going out and getting a job, schmoozing, writing, or finding a property. On the other hand, film school affords the luxury of creating a demo reel, making contacts, and making mistakes that won't be costly. My advice to prospective students: Any school that stresses story rather than theory or even technique is the place to go.

CAMERON UNIVERSITY

2800 W. Gore Blvd.,
Lawton, OK 73505
(405)581–2200

*State four-year comprehensive
institution. Coed, urban location.
Undergraduate enrollment: 6,000.
Graduate enrollment: 600.*

DEPARTMENT OF COMMUNICATIONS

Chair/Contact: Tony Allison
Calendar: Semesters
Degrees Offered: B.A.,
communications (radio/TV
concentration)
Departmental Majors: Undergraduate
radio/TV: 80 students
Entrance Requirements:
Undergraduate: 2.7 grade-point
average; ACT scores (minimum 18).
Undergraduate application deadline:
rolling. Percent of acceptances: 85%
Curricular Emphasis: Electronic
media theory and culture; media
writing; audio-video production; media
management
Special Activities: Television:
program material produced for on-
campus closed-circuit television and
cable television; broadcast industry
guest speakers; broadcast student
showcases
Facilities: Television/Radio: studio;
audio bay; control room; video editing
bay; FM radio NPR affiliate on
campus; two radio labs

Equipment: Television/Video:
complete ¾" and ½" S-VHS studio; ¾"
location
Alumni: Jeff Hagy, video director; Jeff
Bridges, video associate director;
David McCracken, video technician;
Ellis Meeks, broadcasting teacher

GUIDE POV: This public university
affords immediate exposure to all
aspects of broadcast radio-television
and corporate video production;
practical career training offered along
with courses in management and mass
communications theory; internship
opportunities in television and
corporate video production

EAST CENTRAL UNIVERSITY

200 S. Stadium Dr.,
Ada, OK 74820–6899
(405)332–8000

*State four-year comprehensive
institution. Coed, small town location.
Undergraduate enrollment: 4,000.
Graduate enrollment: 500.*

COMMUNICATION DEPARTMENT

Chair/Contact: Dr. Bob Payne, Chair
Calendar: Semesters
Degrees Offered: B.S., mass
communications
Departmental Majors:
Undergraduate: 80 students
Entrance Requirements:
Undergraduate: 2.75 grade-point

average; ACT or SAT scores (ACT preferred), with a minimum enhanced score of 19 on the ACT. Undergraduate application deadline: August 22. Percent of acceptances: 89%

Curricular Emphasis: Electronic media theory and culture; media writing; audio-video production; media management; media advertising

Special Activities: Television: program material produced for both broadcast and cable television. Radio: news program produced regularly for local broadcast

Facilities: Television: studio; audio bay; control room

Equipment: Television/Video: complete ¾" studio and location

Alumni: Regina Moon, TV programming director; Steve Myers, TV news anchor; Jim Spencer, TV meteorologist

GUIDE POV: East Central University provides professional training to communications students in both broadcast and nonbroadcast technologies; co-op programs with Westfield (Massachusetts) State College and the Ardmore (Oklahoma) Higher Education Center; internship opportunities in television and radio production

---

LANGSTON UNIVERSITY

Langston, OK 73050
(405)272–0431

State land-grant four-year comprehensive institution. Coed, small town location with two urban bases for upper-division study. Enrollment: 3,200.

DEPARTMENT OF ARTS AND SCIENCES, COMMUNICATION PROGRAM

Chair/Contact: Dr. Clyde Montgomery, Division Director; Karen Clark, Coordinator, Communication Department

Calendar: Semesters

Degrees Offered: B.A., broadcast journalism

Departmental Majors: Broadcast journalism: 75 students

Entrance Requirements: 2.7 grade-point average; ACT testing required, with a score placing student among the top 60% of OK high school seniors. Application deadline: rolling. Percent of acceptances: 90%

Curricular Emphasis: Mass media studies; broadcast writing; radio and television production; field production; announcing; broadcast law, libel, and ethics

Special Activities: Television: program material produced for cable television

Facilities: Television: studio; audio bay; control room; video editing suites; telecommunication network interface

Equipment: Television/Video: complete ¾" studio; complete ¾" studio and ½" location

Alumni: Terrel Harris, TV news anchor; Kim Hudson, TV news anchor; Willie Reeves, TV producer; George Smith, TV camera operator; Ernest L. Holloway, Jr., broadcasting executive

GUIDE POV: Undergraduates majoring in broadcast journalism at this land-grant university are offered sequential training in television and radio writing and production; required media internship in junior or senior year

NORTHEASTERN OKLAHOMA A&M COLLEGE

Second and I St. NE,
Miami, OK 74354–0001
(918)542–8441

State two-year institution. Coed, small city location. Enrollment: 2,000.

RADIO/TV/FILM DEPARTMENT

Chair/Contact: Brian Inbody; Rodney Clark; Jimmy Brown
Calendar: Semesters
Degrees Offered: A.S., A.A., radio-TV-film; two-year certificate
Departmental Majors: Film, TV, and radio: 30 students
Entrance Requirements: ACT required; high school diploma or acceptable GED score; students may be required to undergo placement testing. Application deadline: rolling. Percent of acceptances: 98%
Curricular Emphasis: Technical knowledge of equipment in a working situation with an emphasis on training for immediate employment in the media industries
Special Activities: Television/Video: program material produced for college channel includes nightly news broadcast; department annually sponsors high school video contest; college students participate in national video festivals and competitions, such as the Hometown Video Festival and the Chicago International Festival
Facilities: Television: studio (state-of-the-art chip cameras); audio bay; control room; two editing suites; digital graphics laboratory; full audio facility for radio
Equipment: Television/Video: complete ¾" studio; complete ¾" and ½" location and postproduction

Alumni: Brandon Terrell, TV news writer; Tim Garrison, TV assistant producer; Grant Williams, TV production assistant

GUIDE POV: Faculty at this two-year college describe their program as "comprehensive, student-friendly, and responsive to the needs and demands of the students and the job market that will employ them"; emphasis on practical training for technical support positions in television and radio; writing for media; news journalism; several courses in film theory; internship opportunities in television and radio production

NORTHWESTERN OKLAHOMA STATE UNIVERSITY

Alva, OK 73717
(405)327–1700

State four-year comprehensive institution. Coed, small town location. Enrollment: 2,000.

SCHOOL OF HUMANITIES, FINE ARTS, AND LANGUAGES/MASS COMMUNICATIONS DEPARTMENT

Chair/Contact: School of Humanities, Fine Arts, and Languages: Dr. John Barton. Mass Communications Department: Robert L. Martin; Terry D. Winn
Calendar: Semesters
Degrees Offered: B.A., mass communications (with emphasis in radio-television-journalism or public relations)
Departmental Majors: Radio and television production: 50 students
Entrance Requirements: 2.7 grade-point average; ACT, with a minimum score of 19, is required. Application

deadline: rolling. Percent of acceptances: 71%

Curricular Emphasis: Electronic media theory and culture; media writing; audio-video production; advanced broadcasting

Special Activities: Television/Radio: program material produced for on-campus cable channel and radio station

Facilities: Television: studio; audio bay; control room; video editing suites

Equipment: Television/Video: complete ¾" studio; ½" location

Alumni: Mark Norman, university media director; Rick Betzen, media consultant; Charlotte Brockus, radio news director; Tamara Van Meter, TV spokesperson

GUIDE POV: This state university offers a comprehensive degree program featuring courses in television and radio announcing, writing, and production; media internship opportunities

OKLAHOMA BAPTIST UNIVERSITY

Shawnee, OK 74801
(405)275–2850

Private four-year comprehensive institution. Coed, small town location. Enrollment: 2,000.

TELECOMMUNICATION DEPARTMENT

Chair/Contact: Dr. Roger Hadley, Chair

Calendar: 4–1–4

Degrees Offered: B.A., telecommunication

Departmental Majors: Radio and television: 75 students

Entrance Requirements: 2.0 grade-point average; ACT or SAT required,

with a minimum composite score of 720 on the SAT or 20 on the ACT. Application deadline: rolling. Percent of acceptances: 97%

Curricular Emphasis: Electronic media theory and culture; media writing; audio-video production; media management; broadcast news

Special Activities: Television/Video: program material produced for on-campus cable television; student screenings

Facilities: Film: screening room; editing rooms. Television: studio; control room; audio production suite; video editing suites

Equipment: Television/Video: complete ¾" studio and location

Alumni: Amy Austin, TV news reporter; John Holcomb, TV sportscaster; Kirsten McIntire, TV news reporter

GUIDE POV: This private university offers students a practical degree program in broadcast production with an emphasis on news journalism; cross-registration with St. Gregory's College; interdisciplinary degrees available; study abroad in Hungary, Japan, and China; internship opportunities in television and radio production

OKLAHOMA CHRISTIAN UNIVERSITY OF SCIENCE AND ARTS

2501 E. Memorial Rd.,
Box 11000,
Oklahoma City, OK 73136–1100
(405)425–5000

Private four-year comprehensive institution. Coed, suburban location. Enrollment: 1,700.

Mass Communication Department

Chair/Contact: Dr. Philip Patterson, Chair; Dr. Larry Jurney
Calendar: Trimesters
Degrees Offered: B.S., mass communication (students may select emphasis in radio and television, journalism, or public relations-advertising)
Departmental Majors: Radio and television: 50 students
Entrance Requirements: ACT or SAT scores (ACT preferred). Application deadline: rolling. Percent of acceptances: 55%
Curricular Emphasis: Mass communication theory; news and feature writing and gathering; film criticism; television production; radio production; media administration; media marketing and sales; mass communication ethics
Special Activities: Television: program material produced for on-campus cable television KOCC
Facilities: Television/Video: studio; audio bay; control room; video editing suites
Equipment: Television/Video: complete ¾" studio and location
Alumni: Greg Lee, PBS TV broadcaster; Tom Burkhard, TV writer; Tamara Pratt, TV newscaster

GUIDE POV: Mass communication majors at this small private university who select the emphasis in radio and television study all aspects of broadcast production and management; cross-registration with Central State University; study abroad in Japan and Austria; internship and practicum opportunities in television and radio production

OKLAHOMA CITY COMMUNITY COLLEGE

7777 S. May Ave.,
Oklahoma City, OK 73159
(405)682–1611

State two-year comprehensive institution. Coed, urban location. Enrollment: 22,500.

School of Arts and Humanities/ Journalism and Broadcasting Department

Chair/Contact: Gwin C. Faulconer
Calendar: Semesters
Degrees Offered: A.A., journalism and broadcasting (students may select emphasis in broadcasting)
Departmental Majors: Broadcasting: 125 students
Entrance Requirements: High school diploma; ACT testing required; college assessment testing required. Application deadline: August 24. Percent of acceptances: 95%
Curricular Emphasis: Mass communication theory; news writing; media technology; public relations; basic and small format video production; still photography
Special Activities: Television/Video: program material produced for class projects and for local cable television
Facilities: Television/Video: studio; audio bay; control room; video editing suites
Equipment: Television/Video: complete ¾" studio; complete ½" location
Alumni: Sadie Tomlin, TV camera operator; Paul Tomlin, TV camera operator

GUIDE POV: This large, affordable community college offers a comprehensive degree program in broadcasting; emphasis on practical training for varied entry-level positions in the television, corporate video, and radio industries; program also provides core requirements for those planning transfer to four-year universities; flexible program allows for independent film projects; honors program; internship opportunities in television and radio production

OKLAHOMA CITY UNIVERSITY

Oklahoma City, OK 73106
(405)521–5000

Private four-year comprehensive institution. Coed, urban location. Enrollment: 1,500.

MASS COMMUNICATIONS DEPARTMENT

Chair/Contact: Karlie Harmon, Chair
Calendar: Semesters
Degrees Offered: B.A., mass communications (students may select emphasis in radio-TV-film, public relations, advertising, news-editorial, magazine, or media management)
Departmental Majors: Television: 50 students
Entrance Requirements: 2.0 grade-point average; ACT (minimum 18) or SAT (minimum composite 920) scores. Application deadline: one week before start of semester. Percent of acceptances: 78%
Curricular Emphasis: Electronic media theory and culture; media writing; audio-video production; mass media management; mass media law and ethics
Special Activities: Television: program material produced for cable television
Facilities: Television: studio; audio bay; control room; video editing suites

Equipment: Television/Video: complete ¾" studio and ½" location
Alumni: Mark Talla, TV/radio producer; Elizabeth Walker, media teacher

GUIDE POV: Students attending this competitive private university may choose a mass communications major that offers a blend of critical theory and practical technical training in the media arts; study abroad in Taiwan, China, Singapore, England, Germany, and Russia; internship opportunities in television and radio production

OKLAHOMA STATE UNIVERSITY

Stillwater, OK 74078–0195
(405)744–5000

State four-year comprehensive institution. Coed, small town location. Undergraduate enrollment: 21,000. Graduate enrollment: 4,000.

SCHOOL OF JOURNALISM AND BROADCASTING

Chair/Contact: Dr. Marlan Nelson, Director
Calendar: Semesters
Degrees Offered: B.A., B.S., journalism and broadcasting (concentrations in production and performance; broadcast journalism; news-editorial; journalism-advertising-public relations; broadcast sales and management; public relations); M.S., mass communications
Departmental Majors: Undergraduate television: 300 students. Graduate mass communications: 45 students
Entrance Requirements: Undergraduate: academic rank within top 40% of high school graduating class; 3.0 grade-point average; ACT required, with a minimum score of 19.

Graduate: master's program requires 3.0 grade-point average, competitive GRE scores, and two teachers' recommendations. Undergraduate and graduate application deadline: rolling. Percent of acceptances: Undergraduate: 88%. Graduate: 45%

Curricular Emphasis: Electronic media theory and culture; media writing; television and radio production; public relations; media sales and management

Special Activities: Film: screenings. Television: program material produced for cable television; member AERho

Facilities: Film: screening room; editing suites; sound mixing room; animation stand; film library; special effects library. Television/Video: studio; audio bay; control room; video editing suites

Equipment: Film: complete 16mm. Television/Video: complete ¾" studio and location; ½" Betacam and complete editor; displacement recorder

Alumni: Karen Keith, TV news anchor; Jack Willis, media journalist; Evan Todd, film executive assistant; David Renfro, media journalist; Marianne Miller, TV executive producer assistant

GUIDE POV: This very competitive state university offers comprehensive undergraduate and graduate degree programs for those interested in broadcast television production; Semester at Sea program; study abroad in seven countries; internships in television and radio production

---

ORAL ROBERTS UNIVERSITY

7777 S. Lewis St.,
Tulsa, OK 74171
(918)495–6161

Private four-year comprehensive institution. Coed, suburban location. Undergraduate enrollment: 3,500. Graduate enrollment: 600.

FILM AND VIDEO STUDIES

Chair/Contact: Film: Gary Noggle; Video: Dr. Evan A. Culp

Calendar: Semesters

Degrees Offered: B.A., B.S.

Departmental Majors: Undergraduate film and video: 100 students

Entrance Requirements: Undergraduate: 2.5 grade-point average; written statement of purpose; portfolio; production credits; ACT (minimum score 23) or SAT (minimum composite 950) scores. Undergraduate application deadline: August 15. Percent of acceptances: 80%

Curricular Emphasis: Film: motion picture production and criticism; emphasis on Christian drama. Video: writing for mass media; broadcast news; television directing and production; video art; ENG field production; administration and management; broadcast electronics

Special Activities: Film: film series/festivals. Television: program material produced for on-campus closed-circuit television; educational video material produced for corporate clients; daily nationally televised live broadcast of religious programming

Facilities: Film: screening room; editing suite; sound mixing room; sound stage. Television: three studios; six audio bays; three control rooms

Equipment: Film: complete Super-8 and 16mm. Television/Video: complete 1", Beta, and ¾" studio at Mabee Center; complete S-VHS and ¾" studio at Educational Television Studios; ¾" and ½" student facilities; S-VHS and Beta location

Alumni: R. Stacy Ratliff, cinematographer/videographer; Melany Secrist, corporate film executive; Jan Moody, script supervisor

GUIDE POV: Students choosing film and video studies at Oral Roberts University enjoy professional studio facilities and equipment, particularly in television; strong emphasis on programming for religious markets; campus internship opportunities in broadcast production may lead to permanent career positions

PANHANDLE STATE UNIVERSITY

P.O. Box 430,
Goodwell, OK 73939
(405)349–2611

State four-year comprehensive institution. Coed, small town location. Enrollment: 1,500.

SPEECH COMMUNICATION/RADIO-TELEVISION

Chair/Contact: Russell Allen Guthrie
Calendar: Semesters
Degrees Offered: B.A., mass communication studies; B.A., speech and drama studies
Departmental Majors: Radio and television: 50 students
Entrance Requirements: High school transcripts; ACT scores. Application deadline: September 15. Percent of acceptances: 97%
Curricular Emphasis: Electronic media theory and culture; media writing; audio-video production; news/sports journalism
Special Activities: Television/Radio: program material produced for class projects, local cable television, and campus radio station
Facilities: Television/Radio: classroom

studio; control room; video editing suites; KPSU-FM campus radio station
Equipment: Television/Video: complete ¾" studio and ½" location
Alumni: Neal Weaver, TV sports reporter; Bill Weldon, TV program director; Pamela Sartain, media teacher

GUIDE POV: Designed to prepare graduates for careers in radio/television production, this mass communication program offers writing seminars and broadcast workshops; internship opportunities in television and radio production

ROGERS STATE COLLEGE

Will Rogers and College Hill,
Claremore, OK 74017–2099
(918)341–7510, x300

State two-year comprehensive institution. Coed, small town location. Enrollment: 4,000.

BROADCASTING PROGRAM

Chair/Contact: Larry Filkins
Calendar: Semesters
Degrees Offered: A.A., broadcasting (radio option; TV option); A.A.S., broadcasting; certificate in broadcasting
Departmental Majors: Radio and television: 60 students
Entrance Requirements: High school transcripts; ACT scores. Application deadline: rolling. Percent of acceptances: 98%
Curricular Emphasis: Media writing; audio-video production; radio and television sales; voice and diction
Special Activities: Television/Radio: program material produced for KXON TV-35 and for campus radio station
Facilities: Television/Radio: studio;

audio bay; control room; video editing suites; campus radio station
Equipment: Television/Video: complete ¾" studio and ½" location
Alumni: Sumner Douglas, programming specialist; Troy Cook, video engineer; Tom Needham, video engineer

GUIDE POV: Named for humorist Will Rogers, this two-year community college offers a broadcasting program with separate options in television or radio; both options offer hands-on training with an emphasis on liberal arts studies, writing, producing, and announcing; core curriculum fulfills requirements for transfer to four-year institutions; those seeking immediate employment are offered a separate degree program emphasizing announcing, sales, and studio practice

ROSE STATE COLLEGE

6420 SE 15th St.,
Midwest City, OK 73110–2799
(405)733–7311

State two-year institution. Coed, small town location. Enrollment: 1,300.

HUMANITIES DIVISION/BROADCAST PRODUCTION AND TECHNOLOGY

Chair/Contact: Skip Leckness
Calendar: Semesters
Degrees Offered: A.A.S., broadcasting (option in production or technology)
Departmental Majors: Radio and television production: 40 students
Entrance Requirements: High school transcripts; ACT scores. Application deadline: rolling. Percent of acceptances: 98%
Curricular Emphasis: Production option includes intensive radio and television broadcast writing, production, announcing, and ENG/video editing training
Special Activities: Television: program material produced for campus eight-channel, closed-circuit television system; multipurpose television studio is designed for producing instructional videotapes
Facilities: Television/Video: studio; audio bay; control room; video editing suites
Equipment: Television/Video: complete ¾" studio and ½" location
Alumni: Valerie Lasater, TV news director; Chuck Musgrove, TV news photographer; Dawn Fitzgerald, corporate video producer

GUIDE POV: For students seeking to enter the fields of radio and television production, this two-year degree program provides comprehensive training with an emphasis on broadcast journalism and instructional video projects; additional writing courses offered through the Journalism Department; media internships available

UNIVERSITY OF CENTRAL OKLAHOMA

Edmond, OK 73034
(405)341–2980

State four-year comprehensive institution. Coed, suburban location. Undergraduate enrollment: 10,500. Graduate enrollment: 4,000.

DEPARTMENT OF ORAL COMMUNICATION

Chair/Contact: Dr. Barbara Norman, Chair; Television: Jack W. Deskin
Calendar: Semesters

Degrees Offered: B.A., oral communication/broadcasting
Departmental Majors: Undergraduate television: 175 students
Entrance Requirements: Undergraduate: 2.7 grade-point average; ACT required, with a minimum score of 16 or an enhanced score of 19. Undergraduate application deadline: August 15. Percent of acceptances: 90%
Curricular Emphasis: Electronic media theory and culture; media writing; television production; news journalism; corporate video; media management
Special Activities: Television: program material produced for cable television
Facilities: Television: studio; audio bay; control room; video editing suites; electronic news room
Equipment: Television/Video: complete ¾" studio; complete ¾" and ½" field units
Alumni: Rick Kirkham, TV news reporter; Lim Peacock, TV producer; Laura Shepard, TV production manager

GUIDE POV: A practical degree program covering all aspects of television broadcast production is offered at this competitive state university; emphasis on news journalism; internship opportunities in television production

---

UNIVERSITY OF OKLAHOMA

520 Parrington Oval,
Norman, OK 73019
(405)325–0311

State four-year comprehensive institution. Coed, urban location.

Undergraduate enrollment: 20,000.
Graduate enrollment: 2,000.

SCHOOL OF ART, VIDEO/FILM PROGRAM

Chair/Contact: John Alberty; Jackie Frost

SCHOOL OF JOURNALISM/MASS COMMUNICATION

Chair/Contact: Jerry Allen White
Calendar: Semesters
Degrees Offered: B.A., M.F.A., film/video; B.A., radio/TV/film; M.A., journalism/mass communication
Departmental Majors: Video/Film: 90 undergraduate students; 7 graduate students. Journalism/Mass Communication: 25 undergraduate students in film; 350 undergraduate students in television; 20 graduate students in television
Entrance Requirements: Undergraduate: 2.5 grade-point average; ACT or SAT scores; teachers' recommendations. Graduate: 3.0 grade-point average; portfolio. Undergraduate and graduate application deadline: rolling
Curricular Emphasis: Video/Film: production and theory taught as part of fine arts curriculum; experimental; narrative; documentary; film and video art. Journalism/Mass Communication: emphasis on film and video production; television news/broadcast journalism
Special Activities: Film: film and video series/festivals; film societies; media art produced for cable television. Television: program material produced for cable television
Facilities: Film: screening room; editing suite; sound mixing room; animation stand; film library. Television: studio; audio bay; control room

Equipment: Film: complete Super-8 and 16mm. Television/Video: complete ¾" studio; complete ¾" and ½" location
Alumni: Alan Berliner, filmmaker; Chris Burke, production assistant; Dan Brown, production assistant

GUIDE POV: Both the School of Art and the School of Journalism at this competitive university offer comprehensive studies in film and video production; study abroad in 21 countries; internship opportunities in television production

UNIVERSITY OF SCIENCE AND ARTS OF OKLAHOMA

Box 82345,
Chickasha, OK 73018–0001
(405)224–3140

State four-year comprehensive institution. Coed, urban location. Enrollment: 12,000.

ARTS AND HUMANITIES

Chair/Contact: Film/Television: Dr. Alan Todd; Dr. Ann Frankland, Chair, Arts and Humanities
Calendar: Trimesters
Degrees Offered: B.A., English (film concentration)
Entrance Requirements: Minimum 2.7 grade-point average; ACT required with minimum composite score of 15. Application deadline: rolling. Percent of acceptances: 80%
Curricular Emphasis: Film theory/ aesthetics, history, and criticism; basic film production; basic television production
Special Activities: Film: film series/ festivals. Television: program material produced for cable television
Facilities: Film: sound stage;

screening room; editing suite. Television: studio; audio bay; control room; video editing suite
Equipment: Film: complete 16mm. Television: complete ¾" studio and ½" location
Alumni: John Marshall, TV producer

GUIDE POV: English majors here may choose a concentration in film theory; communication program emphasizes mass media theory; accelerated degree programs; independent study European tours; internship opportunities in television production

UNIVERSITY OF TULSA

600 S. College Ave.,
Tulsa, OK 74104
(918)631–2000

Private four-year comprehensive institution. Coed, urban location. Undergraduate enrollment: 4,000. Graduate enrollment: 1,000.

COMMUNICATION DEPARTMENT

Chair/Contact: Robert J. Doolittle, Chair
Calendar: Semesters
Degrees Offered: B.A., B.S.
Departmental Majors:
Undergraduate: 185 students
Entrance Requirements:
Undergraduate: open-door policy; however, admission to the major is selective. Undergraduate application deadline: September 4. Percent of acceptances: 90%
Curricular Emphasis: Organization communication, political com-munication, and mass communication (including television and video production training with an emphasis on news/documentary and video art)
Special Activities: Television: student-

run TUTV produces weekly program material for cable television; current projects include a documentary video series focusing on Native American culture, history, and contemporary concerns

Facilities: Television: studio; audio bay; control room; remote van; computer graphics laboratory

Equipment: Television/Video: complete ¾" studio; complete ¾" and ½" location

Alumni: Bob Losure, CNN reporter/anchor; Julie Payne, TV director; Julia Carpenter, TV/radio announcer

GUIDE POV: This private university offers competitive mass communication studies in video and television; undergraduates have high success rate entering major graduate cinema/television programs; extensive study abroad program; internship opportunities in television production

In addition to practical experience, one of the most meaningful and satisfying areas for me has been playing around with the 8mm movies I've done simply for my own enjoyment.

My first eight years as an animation writer were spent at the Walt Disney Studios, where I wrote *Lady and the Tramp* and worked on Mickey Mouse, Donald Duck, and Pluto. Later at UPA, I wrote *Mr. Magoo's Arabian Nights*. Then the opportunity to work with John Hubley enabled me to write *Finian's Rainbow*.

Regarding schools, I attended Hollywood High and that's about it. But I heartily urge aspiring writers—whether in live-action or animation—to read, read, and read, until your eyes hurt. After all, look what happened to Mr. Magoo.

GEORGE FOX COLLEGE

Newberg, OR 97132
(503)538–8383

*Private four-year comprehensive
institution. Coed, suburban location.
Enrollment: 900.*

COMMUNICATION ARTS DEPARTMENT

Chair/Contact: Dr. Craig Johnson,
Chair
Calendar: Semesters
Degrees Offered: B.A.,
communication/video production
Departmental Majors: Television:
19 students
Entrance Requirements: High school
transcripts; ACT or SAT scores;
recommendations. Application
deadline: August 1. Percent of
acceptances: 87%
Curricular Emphasis:
Communication and rhetorical theory;
technical and production-oriented
courses in video
Special Activities: Television:
program material produced for cable
television BCN includes videotaping of
local sporting events; occasional
sponsored projects for outside clients
Facilities: Television: Video
Communication Center, including
studio, audio bay, control room, and
video editing suites, is used for the
technical aspects of the major and is
also used by the college for
contracted work

Equipment: Television/Video:
complete ¾" studio with two Hitachi
SK-70 cameras and full cyc and
lighting grid; EFP video equipment
includes two three-tube cameras, two
single-tube cameras, one S-VHS
dockable camera, and two ¾"
portable VTRs; editing equipment
includes two ¾" cuts-only; one S-VHS
A/B roll with Amiga computer
including CG software and video
toaster; Mac II with graphics software
Alumni: Tom Stram, TV production
grip; Curt Hadley, media services
specialist

GUIDE POV: Founded in 1891 by
Oregon Quakers, this well-equipped
private college offers students a major
in communication arts that integrates
the areas of speech communication,
drama, journalism, and media;
students may also choose the
communication/video production
major, which combines a strong
production and theory core with
extensive electives; approximately half
the graduates enter broadcasting field
while half enter corporate/industrial
market; study abroad; required
internships in television production

LANE COMMUNITY COLLEGE

4000 E. 30th Ave.,
Eugene, OR 97405
(503)747–4501

State two-year institution. Coed, urban location. Enrollment: 9,000.

MEDIA ARTS AND TECHNOLOGY DEPARTMENT

Chair/Contact: Nanci LaVelle; Bob Prokop
Calendar: 10-week terms
Degrees Offered: A.A.S., broadcasting/visual design and production; radio production; certificates
Departmental Majors: Film, radio, and television: 125 students
Entrance Requirements: Open-door policy. Application deadline: rolling. Percent of acceptances: 98%
Curricular Emphasis: Diverse course listings in film, television, and radio production and postproduction; writing for film/television/radio; mass media studies; corporate media; film theory; still photography
Special Activities: Film: film series/festivals. Television: program material produced for cable television
Facilities: Film: screening room; editing suites; sound mixing room. Television/Video: two complete studios; audio bays; control rooms; switchers; character generators; video editing suites; multitrack audio production/sweetening room
Equipment: Film: complete 16mm. Television/Video: complete ¾" studio and location; postproduction
Alumni: Roger Thompson, TV producer/director/executive; Paul Machu, creative director/executive

GUIDE POV: Lane Community College offers students a diverse program with training in film, television, radio, and photography, along with several courses in film and electronic media theory and criticism; 25% of graduates enter four-year college programs; most others enter local television-radio market; extensive internship opportunities in film and television

LINFIELD COLLEGE

McMinnville, OR 97128–6894
(503)472–4121

Private four-year comprehensive institution. Coed, small town location. Enrollment: 1,432.

DEPARTMENT OF COMMUNICATIONS

Chair/Contact: Craig Singletary
Calendar: Semesters
Degrees Offered: B.A., mass communications (broadcast sequence)
Departmental Majors: Television: 40 students
Entrance Requirements: 2.5 grade-point average; ACT or SAT scores; essay required; interview recommended. Application deadline: rolling. Percent of acceptances: 80%
Curricular Emphasis: Broadcast sequence includes course listings in video production (VHS and S-VHS formats), mass communication theory, and mass media history, law, and ethics; other courses include media writing and editing, broadcast newswriting, nonbroadcast video production, audio production, and film appreciation
Special Activities: Television/Radio: program material produced for cable television; KSLC-FM college station
Facilities: Television/Video: studio; audio bay; control room; video editing suites
Equipment: Television/Video: two studio and three field video cameras; VHS/S-VHS editing system; two audio field mixers
Alumni: Marcia Coffey, TV news anchor/reporter; Ron Callan, TV news

anchor/reporter; Gary Walker, executive news producer; Nancy Bolton, TV executive producer

GUIDE POV: Founded in 1849, this small private liberal arts institution offers a growing mass communications program with a comprehensive broadcast sequence; students are encouraged to create a variety of television and radio programming; study abroad in six countries; selective admissions; internship opportunities in television and radio production; some media internships may be arranged in New York during January term

MT. HOOD COMMUNITY COLLEGE

26000 S.E. Stark St.,
Gresham, OR 97030
(503)667–6422

District two-year institution. Coed, suburban location. Undergraduate enrollment: 1,200.

COMMUNICATION ARTS

Chair/Contact: Ralph E. Ahseln, television
Calendar: Quarters
Degrees Offered: A.A.S., television production technology or community television
Departmental Majors: Communication arts: 75 students
Entrance Requirements: Open-door policy; placement test given to determine reading, writing, and math skills
Curricular Emphasis: Shared first-year curriculum emphasizes fundamental skills with hands-on training; TV production technology takes a video generalist's approach covering areas from directing to closed-circuit systems design; the

program in community television deals specifically with community communication, centering on documentary style production techniques
Special Activities: Television: students produce programming for local cable access channel
Facilities: Television/Video: three-camera video production studio
Equipment: Television/Video: 12 field production units in three formats; A/B roll editing suite; three cuts-only editing positions; audio and video production equipment
Alumni: Laura Schuller, production services executive; Perry Loveridge, TV production executive; Bruce Moore, TV/film producer/lighting director

GUIDE POV: Hands-on broadcast training is offered at this community college; students have choice of separate degree options with sequences in television production or community television; internship opportunities in television production

NORTHWEST FILM CENTER

Portland Art Museum,
219 S.W. Park Ave.,
Portland, OR 97205
(503)221–1156

Regional media arts center. Coed, urban location. Enrollment: 1,000.

CHAIR/CONTACT: Bill Foster, Director; Ellen Thomas, Education Director
Calendar: Three 15-week terms per year as well as separate semester program
Degrees Offered: B.F.A., filmmaking and animation (co-offered with the Pacific Northwest College of Art); certificate program in film and video studies

Departmental Majors: 20–25 (attending the Pacific Northwest College of Art)
Entrance Requirements: Enrollment operates on a first-come basis. Application deadline: rolling
Curricular Emphasis: Hands-on production classes with professional film/video makers; short seminars and workshops conducted by visiting artists
Special Activities: Film/Video: Northwest Film Center annually sponsors three major film festivals: Northwest Film and Video Festival (for independent producers); Young People's Film and Video Festival (for K-college, held in November); Portland International Film Festival (invitational festival, held in February); touring film programs; year-round exhibition program of foreign, classic, independent, and experimental films in 480-seat Berg Swann Auditorium; video/filmmaker-in-residence program; video art installations; circulating library of films including major works of regional artists. Television: program material produced for local public and commercial television stations and for cable television
Facilities: Film: 35mm screening facilities; screening room; editing suite; sound mixing room; animation stand; film library. Television/Video: studio; audio bay; control room; video editing suites
Equipment: Film: complete Super-8 and 16mm. Television/Video: complete ¾" studio; complete ¾" and ½" location; access to computer graphics lab through Pacific Northwest College of Art
Alumni: Gus Van Sant, film director; Joanna Priestley, animator; John Stewart, filmmaker/director

GUIDE POV: Classes at this media arts center are primarily designed for the working professional who is either already in film/video or wishing to make a career transition; through an affiliation with the Pacific Northwest College of Art, the Film Center offers accredited semester-long courses in filmmaking and animation toward the B.F.A. degree; a significant number of students take classes for undergraduate credit through Maryhurst College, Reed College, Lewis and Clark College, Pacific University, and Portland State University; various internship and grant opportunities in film, video, and television production

OREGON STATE UNIVERSITY

Corvallis, OR 97331
(503)737–0123

State four-year comprehensive institution. Coed, small town location. Undergraduate enrollment: 13,000. Graduate enrollment: 3,000.

DEPARTMENT OF SPEECH COMMUNICATION

Chair/Contact: Cleon V. Bennett, Chair
Calendar: Quarters
Degrees Offered: B.A., B.S., speech communication; M.A.I.S., interdisciplinary studies
Departmental Majors: Undergraduate film studies: 5–10 students
Entrance Requirements: Undergraduate: high school transcripts; ACT or SAT scores. Undergraduate application deadline: March 1. Graduate application deadline: February 1. Percent of acceptances: 93% undergraduate; 65% graduate
Curricular Emphasis: Film theory,

history, and aesthetics; recent course listings include Image and Myth in Film; Film Rhetoric; Advanced Research
Special Activities: Film: film series/screenings; lectures
Facilities: Film: screening room
Alumni: Dave Basinski, film/TV director; Boyd Levet, media affairs manager; Frank Taylor, film/video production manager

GUIDE POV: A variety of topics in film aesthetics, history, and criticism, along with mass media studies, may be explored within the Speech Communication Department; the graduate program in film studies is interdisciplinary; students may cross-register at any college in the Oregon state system; study abroad in 13 countries

PACIFIC UNIVERSITY

Forest Grove, OR 97116
(503)357–6151

Private four-year comprehensive institution. Coed, small town location. Enrollment: 1,000.

DEPARTMENT OF COMMUNICATION

Chair/Contact: Dr. Dave Cassady
Calendar: Semesters
Degrees Offered: B.A., B.S., communication (sequences in television, journalism, and mass communications)
Departmental Majors: 60 students
Entrance Requirements: 3.0 minimum grade-point average; competitive ACT or SAT scores; personal essay required; interview recommended. Application deadline: rolling. Percent of acceptances: 80%

Curricular Emphasis: Pre-professional audio-video production training
Special Activities: Television/Radio: student-run Pacific Productions, an audio/video production company, produces program material for various outlets; KPUR-FM on-campus radio station
Facilities: Television: studio; audio bay; control room; video editing suites; remote van; graphics system
Equipment: Television/Video: complete ¾" studio; ¾" and S-VHS location; off-line and on-line editing systems
Alumni: James Jarman, TV news anchor/producer/writer; Ray Nelson, TV producer/writer; Brad Grove, TV producer; Bruce Fleskes, lighting director; Kris Leichner, advertising writer/producer; Kathy Rommerdahl, TV production assistant

GUIDE POV: This quality-oriented private university offers a competitive telecommunications program within a liberal arts framework; study abroad in Europe, Asia, and Central America; co-op programs with Washington University, Oregon Graduate Center, and Oregon Art Institute; cross-registration with Lewis and Clark University; internship opportunities in television production

SOUTHERN OREGON STATE COLLEGE

Ashland, OR 97520
(503)552–7672

State four-year comprehensive institution. Coed, small town location. Undergraduate enrollment: 5,000.

HUMANITIES AND ENGLISH DEPARTMENT

Chair/Contact: Professors Karen Hamer; Peter Belcastro

COMMUNICATIONS DEPARTMENT, BROADCASTING

Chair/Contact: Karen Shafer, Chair; Mark Chilcoat; Timothy Shove, Director, Media Center
Calendar: Quarters
Degrees Offered: B.A., B.S., M.A., M.S., humanities (concentration in English); B.A., B.S., communication (concentrations in broadcasting, human communication, and journalism)
Departmental Majors: Undergraduate film studies: no major. Undergraduate television: 50 students
Entrance Requirements: Undergraduate: high school transcripts; 3.0 grade-point average; ACT or SAT scores, with a minimum score of 21 or a combined score of 890, respectively; GED accepted, with a minimum score of 58. Graduate: transcripts; GRE scores; recommendations. Undergraduate application deadline: August 30. Graduate application deadline: at least 30 days prior to the quarter in which one is planning to enroll. Percent of acceptances: 86%
Curricular Emphasis: Through the Department of Humanities and English, students may take courses on such topics as film genres, masterpieces of film, and major film directors. The communication major offers broadcasting students diverse course listings emphasizing announcing or production techniques; news/sports writing; special attention to contemporary electronic media and international mass media
Special Activities: Film: film series/festivals. Television: program material produced for Ashland Cable Access Channel broadcast from the Media Center on campus
Facilities: Film: screening room. Television/Video: studio; audio bay; control room; video editing suites; computer graphics system
Equipment: Film: Super-8 camera. Television/Video: complete ¾" studio and location; three editors, one with A/B roll
Alumni: Aaron Townsend, video producer; Mary Lichtenwalner, TV news anchor; Rene Knott, TV sportscaster

GUIDE POV: Several courses in film history, theory, and criticism are offered through the Humanities and English Department; students who wish to emphasize film studies must design their own program with the help of an instructor; the Department of Communication offers a full concentration in broadcasting with emphases in radio and television, production techniques, and announcing; diverse course listings; cross-registration through the National Student Exchange; study abroad in Europe, Asia, or Mexico; internship opportunities in television and radio production

---

UNIVERSITY OF OREGON

Eugene, OR 97403–1206
(503)346–3111

State four-year comprehensive institution. Coed, urban location. Undergraduate enrollment: 15,000. Graduate enrollment: 4,000.

FINE AND APPLIED ARTS DEPARTMENT

Chair/Contact: Kenneth O'Connell; Mike Holcomb

SCHOOL OF JOURNALISM/ TELECOMMUNICATIONS PROGRAM

Chair/Contact: Bill Willingham
Calendar: Quarters
Degrees Offered: B.A., B.S., B.F.A., M.F.A.
Departmental Majors: Undergraduate film: 375 students. Undergraduate television: 200. Graduate film: 47
Entrance Requirements: Undergraduate: transcripts; ACT or SAT scores; letters of reference; portfolio for film students; interview recommended; fine art applicants should write directly to department for specific application requirements and deadlines. Graduate: GRE/GMAT/MAT; three letters of recommendation; transcripts; portfolio including prior motion-graphic work for film students; statement of interest; fine art applicants should write directly to department for specific application requirements and deadlines. Undergraduate application deadline: August 1. Graduate application deadline: rolling. Percent of acceptances: Undergraduate: 60%. Graduate: 50%
Curricular Emphasis: Fine and Applied Art Department: film/video production with an experimental arts and animation approach; developing an understanding of time as a design consideration; investigation of continuity, movement, and communication in time-based media. School of Journalism: hands-on broadcast production and postproduction training. Film studies: courses in film theory and history are offered through the English Department
Special Activities: Film: visiting artists; field trips; client projects; film societies. Television: program material produced for cable television
Facilities: Film: screening room; editing suite; sound mixing room; animation compounds and stands; computer lab. Television: studio; control room
Equipment: Film: Super-8 and 16mm cameras; editing equipment; sound recording equipment; lighting. Television/Video: matched studio cameras; ½" VTRS; portable lighting; ½" cassette recorders; portable cameras; switcher/special effects generators; sound recording equipment; audio mixers; computers
Alumni: Stephen Cannell, TV writer/producer; Craig Henderson, commercials director; Rod McCall, TV director/producer; Don New, graphic media executive; John Ripper, TV director/producer; Uli Kretzschmar, cinematographer; Gregg Maffei, multimedia designer; Todd Kesterson, computer animator

GUIDE POV: Through this innovative Fine and Applied Art Department, experimental, animated, and documentary film production training is offered with an emphasis on individual projects; the School of Journalism provides professional telecommunications training with an emphasis on news/documentary production; the English Department offers several courses on film theory; study abroad; internships in film and television production

Like many other screen and television writers, I got into writing through acting. After graduating from Fairleigh Dickinson University with a B.A. in English literature, I worked in summer stock and studied acting in New York. During that time I became interested in producing as well. I decided to move to Hollywood, where I entered Cal State and got an M.A. in drama.

I have discovered that the crux of getting employment in this business is really "who you know"—a very important crux. After graduating, it took me two years to find a job in the entertainment business. While waiting, I was able to get on a set and "observe," or to watch how they put together a television sitcom. One thing I did observe was that all the jobs I wanted to do involved writing. If I wanted to produce, I would have to write. So I began to take screenwriting classes, from which I learned a great deal.

My big break came when I finally landed a job with a production company. I was a secretary, but it was there that I got the chance to meet other writers who were already established. I wrote a spec script with one of them, and his agent took me on. And my career started.

I do not believe a formal film school education is essential for aspiring professionals. But it helps, because you have to learn the basics of the creative craft you are entering. Also, there is a certain camaraderie that exists among those who have shared a similar experience—or there can be. So fellow alumni can help you meet people and get into the job market.

Regarding my professional credits: I have written, in collaboration with my husband, Michael, several episodes of "Murder She Wrote," "Hotel," "Spies," "Matlock," and "Shadow Chasers." Michael and I also brought *Topper* back to television in an ABC Movie of the Week. Currently, I am a member of Women in Film, where I formerly served as Chairperson for the Writers' Workshop.

ALBRIGHT COLLEGE

P.O. Box 15234,
Reading, PA 19612–5234
(215)921–2381

*Private four-year comprehensive
institution. Coed, suburban location.
Enrollment: 1,300.*

ART DEPARTMENT

Chair/Contact: Bert Brouwer
Calendar: Semesters and interim
Degrees Offered: B.A., B.S.
Departmental Majors: 25 students
Entrance Requirements: Competitive
grade-point average; ACT or SAT
scores; ATs in English composition,
mathematics, and a foreign language
are recommended; written statement
of purpose; portfolio recommended;
interview recommended. Application
deadline: March 15. Percent of
acceptances: 55%
Curricular Emphasis: Film/video
experimental and animated
production; critical theory explored in
context of modern visual/fine arts
media
Special Activities: Film: monthly
visits by American and foreign
experimental film and video artists;
film series/festivals; film societies;
cooperative relationship with Berks
Filmmakers
Facilities: Film: screening room;
editing suite; animation stand; film
library of avant-garde/experimental
films and videotapes
Equipment: Film: complete Super-8
and 16mm. Video: 8mm and VHS
cameras and editing
Alumni: Jerry Tartaglia, experimental
filmmaker; Anthony Portantino, film
writer/producer; Albert Kilchesty, film
executive

GUIDE POV: Albright College offers a
fine arts program that focuses on the
production of innovative
noncommercial/experimental film and
video; strong visiting artist series;
highly selective admissions; faculty of
working media artists; study abroad;
production internships

ALLEGHENY COLLEGE

Meadville, PA 16335
(814)332–3100

*Private four-year comprehensive
institution. Coed, rural location.
Enrollment: 1,800.*

COMMUNICATION ARTS/THEATRE DEPARTMENT

Chair/Contact: Film: Lloyd Michaels;
television: Beth Watkins
Calendar: Semesters
Degrees Offered: B.A.,
communication arts (students may
select emphasis in video studies)

Departmental Majors: Film: 5 students. Television: 30 students
Entrance Requirements: Competitive grade-point average and ACT or SAT scores; ATs recommended in English composition and subjects relevant to student's major; interview recommended; essay required. Application deadline: February 15. Percent of acceptances: 70%
Curricular Emphasis: Electronic media theory and culture; critical studies in film; media writing; video production
Special Activities: Film: film series/festivals; international film journal. Television: program material produced for cable television
Facilities: Television/Video: studio; audio bay; control room; video editing suites
Equipment: Film: moviola; videotape collection. Television/Video: complete ½" studio and location
Alumni: Ted Shaker, TV network sports producer; Rick Weaver, TV producer; Suzanne Hoffman, children's TV producer

GUIDE POV: Founded in 1815, this small, competitive college offers video students an individualized program of instruction within a liberal arts curriculum; cross-registration with Chatham College; study abroad; internship opportunities in television production

---

BUCKS COUNTY COMMUNITY COLLEGE

Swamp Rd.,
Newtown, PA 18940
(215)968–8000

County two-year institution. Coed, rural location. Enrollment: 10,000.

COMMUNICATIONS DEPARTMENT

Chair/Contact: Film: Art Landry; television: Dan Hauser
Calendar: Semesters
Degrees Offered: A.A., cinema program of study; telecommunications program of study
Departmental Majors: Film: 40 students. Television: 110 students
Entrance Requirements: Open-door policy. Application deadline: August 1; January 15. Percent of acceptances: 98%
Curricular Emphasis: Film production including narrative, documentary, and experimental filmmaking; film studies including history, theory/aesthetics, and criticism; television/video production including instructional/industrial, news/documentary, and fiction
Special Activities: Film: student film/video festivals twice yearly. Television: program material produced for on-campus closed-circuit television and cable television
Facilities: Film: screening room; editing suites; sound mixing room; animation stand; film library. Television/Video: studio; audio bay; control room; video editing suites; computer graphics laboratory
Equipment: Film: complete 16mm. Television/Video: VHS/S-VHS and broadcast Betacam studio/field equipment; computerized graphics and editing; digital audio and multitrack recording
Alumni: Hank Capshaw, TV writer; Aaron Landy, screenwriter; Joe Candrella, assistant director; Eileen Candrella, TV technical director; Joan Rivera, media specialist; Jim Schumann, animator; Eve Schultz, TV writer/producer; Peter Wood, TV producer; Bruce Hepler, TV editor

GUIDE POV: Featuring strong programs in both film and television, this affordable community college offers a blend of theory and training in animation, fiction, documentary, experimental, and news production; supportive atmosphere; liberal laboratory hours; small production classes; study abroad; internships in film, television/video, and radio production available locally and in nearby Philadelphia

CARLOW COLLEGE

3333 Fifth Ave.,
Pittsburgh, PA 15213
(412)578–6000

Private four-year comprehensive institution. Coed, urban location. Enrollment: 1,600.

COMMUNICATION ARTS DEPARTMENT/ SOCIAL SERVICE DIVISION

Chair/Contact: Chrys Gabrich
Calendar: Semesters
Degrees Offered: B.A., communications; minor, media
Entrance Requirements: *B* grade-point average; academic class rank within top two-fifths of high school graduating class; ACT or SAT scores (SAT preferred); interview recommended. Application deadline: rolling. Percent of acceptances: 84%
Curricular Emphasis: Communication theory with emphasis on applications in mass media, organizations, and print
Facilities: Television/Video: studio; audio bay; control room; video editing suites
Equipment: Television/Video: complete ¾" and ½" studio and location

Alumni: Lynn Duleba, media center director

GUIDE POV: This Roman Catholic, primarily women's liberal arts college offers students a major in communications and a minor in media; cross-registration with area schools; accelerated degree programs; weekend college for working adults; internship opportunities in television and radio production

CARNEGIE MELLON UNIVERSITY

5000 Forbes Avenue
Pittsburgh, PA 15213
(412)268–2000

Private four-year comprehensive institution. Coed, urban location. Undergraduate enrollment: 4,500. Graduate enrollment: 3,000.

DRAMA DEPARTMENT

Chair/Contact: Elizabeth Orion, Head
Calendar: Semesters
Degrees Offered: B.A., drama; M.A., design and production; directing; playwriting
Entrance Requirements: Undergraduate: SAT or ACT required; ATs in English composition and mathematics; essay required; interview recommended; audition and/or portfolio review for aspiring drama majors. Graduate: portfolio review; GRE scores; recommendations. Undergraduate application deadline: January 1. Graduate application deadline: February 1. Percent of acceptances: 69% undergraduate; 42% graduate
Curricular Emphasis: Department of Drama: sequential, intensive studies in all aspects of theatrical production, including film and television studies.

The College of Humanities and Social Sciences: interdisciplinary minor in film studies; courses provide techniques for analyzing and criticizing film, for exploring and assessing its value in terms of historical, social, scientific, and anthropological data, and for understanding aesthetic and philosophical premises of varied film genres; in addition, interested students may undertake sequential film production training through the nonprofit media arts center Pittsburgh Filmmakers
Special Activities: Film: film screenings; lectures; workshops. Television: annual project; workshops
Facilities: Film/video: studio; screening room; film library
Equipment: Film/video: complete production and postproduction
Alumni: Steven Bochco, TV producer/writer; Bud Yorkin, film/TV director; Bob Finkel, TV director/producer; John Wells, TV/film producer; Holly Hunter, TV/film actress; Ted Danson, TV/film actor; Jack Klugman, TV/film actor

GUIDE POV: This selective private university, formed by the merger of the Carnegie Institute of Technology and the research-oriented Mellon Institute, was the first post-secondary school to have offered a degree in drama; program provides hands-on experience in the creation and production of stage, film, and video performances; graduate program emphasizes theatrical production; there is a separate interdisciplinary minor in film studies; students may pursue additional production training in film through special arrangement with the Pittsburgh Filmmakers; study abroad in Switzerland, France, and Japan

---

COMMUNITY COLLEGE OF BEAVER COUNTY

One Campus Dr.,
Monaca, PA 15061–2588
(412)775–8561

County two-year institution. Coed, suburban location. Enrollment: 2,869.

HIGH TECHNOLOGY COMMUNICATIONS

Chair/Contact: Television: Jan C. Jacobsen; Dr. John Shaver
Calendar: Semesters
Degrees Offered: A.A.S., high technology communications
Departmental Majors: Television: 50 students
Entrance Requirements: Open-door policy. Application deadline: August 25. Percent of acceptances: 98%
Curricular Emphasis: Electronic media theory and culture; broadcast and nonbroadcast video production including news, fiction, and local commercial advertising; media management; film appreciation courses offered through the Liberal Arts Department
Special Activities: Television: program material produced for cable television and local commercial television station; nonbroadcast work for nonprofit groups
Facilities: Television/Video: location studio; audio bay; multiformat on-line and off-line video editing suites (Hi-8, VHS, S-VHS, and ¾"); computer lab for video graphics
Equipment: Television/Video: complete video studio; complete Hi-8, VHS, and S-VHS location; computer graphics for video; video photography;

desktop audio workstation; MIDI; desktop publishing
Alumni: Jeff Ginther, video editor; JoAnne McBride, media public relations director; Fritz Hartman, computer graphics animator

GUIDE POV: Designed for students seeking immediate employment upon graduation, this practical two-year video program covers both broadcast and nonbroadcast production; computer graphics training; internship opportunities in television/video production

COMMUNITY COLLEGE OF PHILADELPHIA

17th and Spring Garden St., Philadelphia, PA 19130
(215)751–8000

County two-year institution. Coed, urban location. Enrollment: 40,000.

PHOTOGRAPHY DEPARTMENT

Chair/Contact: Loring F. Hill, Chair
Calendar: Semesters
Degrees Offered: A.A., A.S.
Departmental Majors: 20 students
Entrance Requirements: Open-door policy; high school diploma or equivalent. Application deadline: rolling
Curricular Emphasis: Film and television production
Special Activities: Television: program material produced for on-campus closed-circuit television and cable television
Facilities: Film: sound stage; screening room; editing suite; sound mixing room; film library. Television: studio; audio bay; control room; editing suite

Equipment: Film: complete 16mm. Television/Video: complete ¾" studio and location; cuts-only editing
Alumni: Vince DiPersio, film/TV writer/producer/director; David Zito, film/TV writer/producer/director; Karol Silverstein, production assistant; Tom Razzano, location scout

GUIDE POV: Intensive career-oriented training for both film and television industries is offered at this urban community college; curriculum favors production over theory; faculty of working professionals; extensive internship opportunities in television production

DREXEL UNIVERSITY

Philadelphia, PA 19104
(215)895–2000

Private four-year comprehensive institution. Coed, urban location. Undergraduate enrollment: 10,000. Graduate enrollment: 3,000.

FILM AND VIDEO PRODUCTION, NESBITT COLLEGE OF DESIGN ARTS

Chair/Contact: Yvonne D. Leach, Director
Calendar: Quarters
Degrees Offered: B.S., film and video production
Departmental Majors: Undergraduate film and television: 50 students
Entrance Requirements: Undergraduate: ACT or SAT scores; essay required; interview recommended. Undergraduate application deadline: March 1. Percent of acceptances: 83%
Curricular Emphasis: Culture; critical studies in film and video; film and

video production; audio production; writing for the visual media

Special Activities: Film: film series/festivals. Cable television: DUTV

Facilities: Film: 16 and super 8mm screening facilities; screening room; editing suite. Television/Video: studio; audio bay; control room; video editing suites

Equipment: Film: complete 16 and super 8mm. Television/Video: complete ¾" studio S-VHS video for location; postproduction

Alumni: Susan Seidelman, film director; Francine Douwes, film producer; Chuck Barris, TV writer/producer/personality

GUIDE POV: Undergraduates attending this competitive private university are offered a liberal arts education and practical training in film and video production; required creative or analytical project in senior year; cross-registration with Eastern Mennonite College, Indiana University of Pennsylvania, and Lincoln University; study abroad; extensive internship opportunities in film and television production

---

DUQUESNE UNIVERSITY

600 Forbes Ave.,
Pittsburgh, PA 15282
(412)396–6000

Private four-year comprehensive institution. Coed, urban location. Undergraduate enrollment: 7,000. Graduate enrollment: 1,500.

DEPARTMENT OF COMMUNICATION

Chair/Contact: Dr. Paul Traudt, Acting Chair
Calendar: Semesters
Degrees Offered: B.A.,

communication (concentrations in media production, media management/operations, media performance, broadcast journalism, advertising, communication [academic preparation], organizational communication, print journalism, and public relations); M.A., corporate communication

Departmental Majors: Undergraduate television: 25 students

Entrance Requirements: Undergraduate: academic rank within upper three-fifths of high school graduating class; SAT required; essay and interview recommended. Graduate: GRE scores; transcripts; recommendations; statement of purpose. Undergraduate and graduate application deadline: July 1. Percent of acceptances: 62%

Curricular Emphasis: Electronic media theory and culture; media writing; broadcast journalism; television production; corporate communication; media management

Special Activities: Television: program material produced for on-campus closed-circuit television

Facilities: Television/Video: studio; audio bay; control room; video editing suites

Equipment: Television/Video: complete ¾" studio; complete ¾" and S-VHS ½" location

Alumni: Joe DeNardo, TV meteorologist; Glenn Huffman, radio/TV production consultant; Janice Stefko, corporate graphic designer

GUIDE POV: This private liberal arts university offers students a variety of course listings in the communications field; media-related concentrations include those in video production, performance, management/operations, broadcast journalism, and corporate communication; accelerated degree program; study abroad in five countries; internship opportunities in television production

EAST STROUDSBURG UNIVERSITY

Prospect St.,
East Stroudsburg, PA 18301
(717)424–3600

State four-year comprehensive institution. Coed, small town location. Undergraduate enrollment: 5,000. Graduate enrollment: 500.

DEPARTMENT OF MEDIA, COMMUNICATION, AND TECHNOLOGY

Chair/Contact: David Campbell, Chair
Calendar: Semesters
Degrees Offered: B.S., media; communication and technology
Departmental Majors:
Undergraduate: 130 students
Entrance Requirements:
Undergraduate: high school diploma; competitive grade-point average. Undergraduate application deadline: January 2. Percent of acceptances: 45%
Curricular Emphasis: Television production; basic film production; microcomputer applications
Special Activities: Film: film series/ festivals. Television: program material produced for on-campus closed-circuit television and cable television
Facilities: Film: editing suites; sound mixing room; animation stand. Television: two three-camera studios; audio bays; control rooms; three off-line editing suites
Equipment: Film: complete Super-8; 16mm cameras and lighting.

Television/Video: complete ¾" studio and ½" location; three off-line editing systems including A/B roll editing; Amiga toaster; special effects
Alumni: Grey Seamans, NBC TV account executive

GUIDE POV: Undergraduates at this state university located in the Pocono Mountains are offered a competitive communications program cross-registration through the National Student Exchange; study abroad; nearby semester-long internships available in television production

EDINBORO UNIVERSITY OF PENNSYLVANIA

Edinboro, PA 16444
(814)732–2000

State four-year comprehensive institution. Coed, small town location. Undergraduate enrollment: 6,339. Graduate enrollment: 665.

ART DEPARTMENT

Chair/Contact: Dr. George Shoemaker
Calendar: Semesters
Degrees Offered: B.F.A., applied/ media arts (cinema)
Departmental Majors:
Undergraduate: 30–50 students
Entrance Requirements:
Undergraduate: ACT or SAT scores; transcripts; interview; portfolio; teachers' recommendations. Undergraduate application deadline: rolling. Percent of acceptances: 50%
Curricular Emphasis: Film: character animation, computer animation, documentary, narrative, fiction, experimental, film history, theory, aesthetics, criticism

Special Activities: Film: regular visits by guest animators and filmmakers; film series; Alternative Film Festival; film society

Facilities: Film: computerized digital sound mixing room with 16-track analog tape; screening rooms; editing suites; sound stage; animation stands; film/video library

Equipment: Film: complete Super-8 and 16mm; computer animation; rotoscope unit; film transfer unit; Amiga computers; black-and-white film processor

Alumni: Tony Buba, filmmaker; Bill Waldman, animator; David Ruggiero, CNN news crew

GUIDE POV: This small, selective university, founded in 1857, offers an individually planned cinema program featuring both live-action and animation training in Super-8 and 16mm within a media arts context; courses in cinema history; electronic cinematography; minors program offers television production training; cross-registration with Gannon University and Mercyhurst College; study abroad in eight countries; media internship opportunities at regional production studios

GWYNEDD-MERCY COLLEGE

Sumneytown Pike,
Gwynedd Valley, PA 19437
(215)646–7300

State four-year comprehensive institution. Coed, suburban location. Enrollment: 700.

LANGUAGE, LITERATURE, AND FINE ARTS DIVISION, MEDIA DEPARTMENT

Chair/Contact: Dr. Jules Tasca, Chair
Calendar: Semesters

Degrees Offered: B.A., media component

Departmental Majors: English with media component: 10–15 students

Entrance Requirements: Competitive grade-point average; ACT or SAT scores; interview recommended. Application deadline: rolling. Percent of acceptances: 75%

Curricular Emphasis: Small program emphasizing journalism, basic television production, film theory, and mass media critical studies

Special Activities: Television: program material produced for class projects

Facilities: Film: screening room; editing suite. Television/Video: studio; video editing suites

Equipment: Film: complete Super-8 and 16mm. Television/Video: complete ½" location

Alumni: Jeff Hill, TV director; Marilyn Lewis, TV technical director; Jeff Miller, media consultant

GUIDE POV: This program emphasizes critical studies in film and television; production work focuses on the creation of radio and television commercials and the development of group video projects; competitive entry; senior internship opportunities in television production and print journalism

KING'S COLLEGE

133 N. River St.,
Wilkes-Barre, PA 18711
(717)826–5900

Private four-year comprehensive institution. Coed, urban location. Enrollment: 1,750.

MASS COMMUNICATIONS DEPARTMENT

Chair/Contact: Dr. Anthony J. Mussari
Calendar: Semesters
Degrees Offered: B.A.
Departmental Majors: 160 students
Entrance Requirements: Average SAT 950; academic rank within top 40% of high school graduating class; 3.0 grade-point average; interview; recommendations. Application deadline: rolling. Percent of acceptances: 68%
Curricular Emphasis: Mass communications; radio and television broadcast news production; computer graphics
Special Activities: Film: film series/festivals. Television: program material produced for cable television
Facilities: Film: editing suite; sound mixing room. Television/Video: studio; audio bay; control room; ¾" SP video editing suite with computer graphics; ½" editing suite
Equipment: Film: complete Super-8. Television/Video: complete ¾" studio; complete ¾" and ½" location
Alumni: Jim Sweeney, cable TV producer; Pat Romano, videographer

GUIDE POV: Offering a well-equipped, hands-on television/video program, this private liberal arts college provides seminar-style training; faculty of working professionals; selective admissions; study abroad in three countries; extensive local and national media internship and practicum opportunities through the school's Experiential Learning Program

KUTZTOWN UNIVERSITY

P.O. Box 730,
Kutztown, PA 19530–0730
(215)683–4000

State four-year comprehensive institution. Coed, small town location. Undergraduate enrollment: 7,500. Graduate enrollment: 635.

TELECOMMUNICATIONS DEPARTMENT

Chair/Contact: Helen E. Clinton, Chair
Calendar: Semesters
Degrees Offered: B.S., M.S.
Departmental Majors:
Undergraduate: 360 students. Graduate: 30 students
Entrance Requirements:
Undergraduate: academic rank within top 40% of high school graduating class; minimum 900 combined SAT scores. Graduate: transcripts; GRE scores; three letters of recommendation. Undergraduate application deadline: January 1 for fall; October 1 for spring. Graduate application deadline: February 1 for fall admission; July 1 for spring admission. Percent of acceptances: 54%
Curricular Emphasis: Television/Video: all aspects of electronic communication including television broadcast and nonbroadcast production, media management, and microwave and satellite distribution of programming
Special Activities: Television: program material produced for on-campus closed-circuit television and local cable television
Facilities: Television: studio; audio bay; control room; remote production truck
Equipment: Television: two complete full-color ¾" studios; complete ¾" and ½" location; on-line and off-line video editing systems; multichannel audio production system
Alumni: J. R. Aquila, film/TV director/

production manager; David Durso, TV writer; Jane Rudolph, TV personality

GUIDE POV: Students choosing the telecommunications major at this well-equipped, competitive university are offered extensive hands-on training through a variety of student productions; accelerated degree program; media internship opportunities

LA SALLE UNIVERSITY

1900 W. Olney Ave.,
Philadelphia, PA 19141
(215)951–1000

Private four-year comprehensive institution. Coed, urban location. Undergraduate enrollment: 3,400. Graduate enrollment: 1,065.

COMMUNICATION DEPARTMENT

Chair/Contact: Gerard Molyneaux, F.S.C.
Calendar: Semesters
Degrees Offered: B.A., communication
Departmental Majors: Undergraduate communication: 340 students
Entrance Requirements: Undergraduate: SAT required; ATs in English composition and math recommended. Undergraduate application deadline: August 15. Percentage of applicants accepted: 60%
Curricular Emphasis: Film studies: theory, criticism, history; narrative and animated production. Television: history, theory/aesthetics, and criticism; production work emphasizes fiction, news/documentary, and instructional/industrial
Special Activities: Film: film series and biannual student film festivals;

film societies; student publications. Television: program material produced for local cable television Channel 56
Facilities: Film: sound mixing room; editing and screening rooms; animation stand. Television: studio; audio studio; control room
Equipment: Film: complete Super-8 production featuring 12 cameras. Television: complete ½" studio and location featuring 12 camcorders and 3 studio cameras
Alumni: Peter Boyle, film actor; Ilia Labunka, associate film producer; Ralph Garman, film/TV actor

GUIDE POV: La Salle University offers comprehensive career training as well as preparation for graduate study in cinema and television production and acting; balance of theory and production courses; competitive entry; cross-registration with Chestnut Hill College; study abroad in Switzerland and Spain; accelerated degree program; internship opportunities in film and television production

LOCK HAVEN UNIVERSITY

Lock Haven, PA 17745
(717)893–2011

State four-year comprehensive institution. Coed, small town location. Enrollment: 3,500.

ENGLISH, JOURNALISM, AND PHILOSOPHY

Chair/Contact: Douglas S. Campbell, Chair
Calendar: Semesters
Degrees Offered: B.A. journalism and mass communications (students may select emphasis in television); minor in film

Departmental Majors: Television: 70 students
Entrance Requirements: 3.0 grade-point average; SAT scores; interview. Application deadline: June 1. Percent of acceptances: 44%
Curricular Emphasis: Film: critical studies within liberal arts curriculum. Television/Video: critical studies; news/documentary production; video art; fiction
Special Activities: Film: student publication. Television: newscast produced for on-campus closed-circuit television and cable television
Facilities: Film: screening room; editing suite. Television: studio; editing rooms
Equipment: Television/Video: complete ¾" studio; complete ¾" and ½" location
Alumni: Debora Pinkerton, TV meteorologist; Gary Jones, TV announcer; Maureen Campbell, TV/ film actress

GUIDE POV: Lock Haven University offers a competitive media program emphasizing broadcast news production; good student-faculty ratio; selective admissions; accelerated degree program for honor students; study abroad in 18 countries; media internship opportunities

LYCOMING COLLEGE

Academy St.,
Williamsport, PA 17701
(717)321–4000

Private four-year comprehensive institution. Coed, rural location. Enrollment: 1,250.

MASS COMMUNICATION DEPARTMENT

Chair/Contact: Brad Nason, Chair
Calendar: Semesters

Degrees Offered: B.A.
Departmental Majors: 23 students
Entrance Requirements: 2.0 grade-point average; ACT or SAT scores; written statement of purpose. Application deadline: rolling. Percent of acceptances: 77%
Curricular Emphasis: Mass communication degree with tracks in journalism and persuasive media
Special Activities: Film: film societies; special inter-media arts program with Theatre Department in acting and design related to film. Television: program material produced for on-campus cable television
Facilities: Film: screening room; film library; laser discs. Television: studio; audio bay; control room; editing room
Equipment: Film: 16mm projectors. Television/Video: complete ¾" studio and location
Alumni: Tom Woodruff, film special effects artist; Peter Ornati, TV actor; Alison Rupert, TV performer

GUIDE POV: Established in 1812, Lycoming College features a nontechnical communications major; program focuses on writing, theory, and production within a liberal arts framework; cooperative programs with Pennsylvania State and Duke universities; study abroad in four countries; media internship opportunities

MANSFIELD UNIVERSITY

Mansfield, PA 16933
(717)662–4000

State four-year comprehensive institution. Coed, rural location. Undergraduate enrollment: 3,000. Graduate enrollment: 200.

DEPARTMENT OF COMMUNICATION AND THEATRE

Chair/Contact: A. Vernon Lapps, Chair; Dr. Howard Travis
Calendar: Semesters
Degrees Offered: B.A., B.S., mass communication
Departmental Majors: Undergraduate television: 70 students
Entrance Requirements: Undergraduate: ACT (minimum 19) or SAT (minimum composite 800) scores; interview recommended. Undergraduate application deadline: July 15 for fall semester; January 2 for spring semester. Percent of acceptances: 75%
Curricular Emphasis: Electronic media theory and culture; broadcast journalism; audio-video production; media management
Special Activities: Television: program material produced for on-campus closed-circuit television, for cable television, for nonprofit community agencies, and for university special programming; Electronic Media Association; student affiliation with all professional organizations
Facilities: Television: studio; audio bay; control room; four editing suites
Equipment: Television/Video: complete ½" studio; complete ¾" and ½" location
Alumni: Marvin Schlenker, TV director; Stuart Jay Weiss, TV network creative services executive; Sean Fox, assistant road manager

GUIDE POV: Founded in 1857, Mansfield University has a small communication program that combines a strong academic emphasis with an active production schedule; graduates have high professional placement record; study abroad in England, Germany, Russia, Canada, Australia, and Spain; media internship opportunities for seniors throughout the country

---

MARYWOOD COLLEGE

2300 Adams Ave.,
Scranton, PA 18509
(717)348–6211

Private four-year comprehensive institution. Coed, urban location. Undergraduate enrollment: 2,500. Graduate enrollment: 1,000.

DEPARTMENT OF COMMUNICATION ARTS

Chair/Contact: Television: Dr. George F. Perry, Chair
Calendar: Semesters
Degrees Offered: B.A., radio and television, theatre, advertising, and public relations
Departmental Majors: Undergraduate radio and television, theatre, advertising, and public relations: 125 students
Entrance Requirements: Undergraduate: academic rank within top half of high school graduating class; 2.5 grade-point average; ACT or SAT scores; recommendations. Undergraduate application deadline: July 1. Percent of acceptances: 78%
Curricular Emphasis: Electronic media theory and culture; media writing; video production; media management
Special Activities: Television: program material produced for on-campus closed-circuit TV-MARYWOOD and local cable television; member PRSSA and ITVA
Facilities: Television/Video: studio; audio bay; control room; video editing suites; news room; multimedia theatre; computer graphics lab

Equipment: Television/Video: complete ¾" studio and ½" location
Alumni: Mary Ellen Keating, media public relations executive; Carolyn Hailey, TV producer; Brian Francis, TV news anchor

GUIDE POV: This private liberal arts college offers students a comprehensive, sequential media studies program that includes courses in radio and television writing and production, media programming, and computer graphics; study abroad in five countries; internship opportunities in television and radio production

MERCYHURST COLLEGE

Glenwood Hills,
Erie, PA 16546
(814)824–2000

Private four-year comprehensive institution. Coed, urban location. Enrollment: 2,400.

COMMUNICATIONS DEPARTMENT

Chair/Contact: Richard Ragan
Calendar: Three terms
Degrees Offered: B.A.
Departmental Majors: 60 students
Entrance Requirements: ACT or SAT scores; interview. Application deadline: rolling. Percent of acceptances: 80%
Curricular Emphasis: Public relations; journalism; radio/television production
Special Activities: Television: program material produced for Erie Cablevision, the college television channel
Facilities: Television: studio; control room; editing suite. Radio: college-operated FM station

Equipment: Television: ¾" studio; editing equipment
Alumni: Allen Carpenter, radio personality; Debbie D'Allesio, TV news reporter; Chris Kovski, TV editor; Matt Clark, media copy editor

GUIDE POV: This Catholic liberal arts college offers a flexible communications department emphasizing production work coupled with writing and academics; cross-registration with Gannon University; study abroad in Dublin and London; media internships available

PENNSYLVANIA COLLEGE OF TECHNOLOGY

One College Ave.,
Williamsport, PA 17701
(717)326–3760

City-state two-year comprehensive institution. Coed, urban location. Enrollment: 4,000.

COMMUNICATION ARTS DEPARTMENT

Chair/Contact: Professor G. Joseph Loehr, Head
Calendar: Semesters
Degrees Offered: A.S., mass communications (students may select emphasis in electronic media)
Departmental Majors: Electronic media: 50 students
Entrance Requirements: 2.0 grade-point average. Application deadline: rolling. Percent of acceptances: 95%
Curricular Emphasis: Film theory, video production, and media management
Special Activities: Film: film series/festivals. Television: program material produced for cable television
Facilities: Film: screening room; editing suite. Television/Video: studio;

audio bay; control room; video editing suites

Equipment: Film: complete 16mm; 35mm cameras. Television/Video: complete 1" and ¾" studio; complete ¾" and ½" location

Alumni: James Crouse, radio broadcaster; Steven Brutzman, radio broadcaster

GUIDE POV: Students seeking a practical degree program in video production may choose this two-year college; emphasis on news, public affairs, and documentary forms; media management training; communication majors are expected to undertake related studies in political science, sociology, psychology, and language; internship opportunities in television and corporate video production

---

PENNSYLVANIA STATE UNIVERSITY

University Park, PA 16802
(814)865–4700

State four-year comprehensive institution. Coed, small town location. Undergraduate enrollment: 31,000. Graduate enrollment: 600.

FILM AND VIDEO/SCHOOL OF COMMUNICATIONS

Chair/Contact: Tom Keiter
Calendar: Semesters
Degrees Offered: B.A., M.F.A.
Departmental Majors:
Undergraduate: 80 students maximum. Graduate: 10 students maximum
Entrance Requirements:
Undergraduate: transcripts; ACT or SAT scores; special attention given to advanced placement or honors courses. Graduate: transcripts; GRE scores; minimum 3.0 grade-point average; writing or production portfolio. Undergraduate application deadline: rolling, but university recommends filing by November 30. Graduate application deadline: all materials must be received at least one month prior to registration. Percent of acceptances: 44%

Curricular Emphasis: Film as a storytelling medium; strong project/process orientation; program integrates writing, directing, and production crafts

Special Activities: Film: film series/festivals; Film Exhibition/Theatre Management Project. Television: program material produced for cable television

Facilities: Film: 35mm screening facilities; screening room; editing suite; sound mixing room; demo studio; animation stand; film library. Television: studio; audio bay; control room

Equipment: Film: complete 16mm. Television/Video: complete ¾" studio; ¾" SP, ½", and Hi-8 location

Alumni: Andrew Walker, screenwriter; Gerald Abrams, media executive; Carmen Finestra, executive producer/writer

GUIDE POV: Founded in 1855, this competitive state university offers a four-year program featuring comprehensive studies and production training in film and video; students work in narrative, documentary, and experimental forms; limited enrollment in all production classes; study abroad in Australia, Africa, South America, the Middle and Far East, and Europe; local and national media internship opportunities

PITTSBURGH FILMMAKERS

3712 Forbes Ave., 2nd Floor,
Pittsburgh, PA 15213
(412)681–5449

*Private four-year comprehensive
institution. Coed, urban location.
Enrollment: 1,200.*

FILM AND VIDEO PRODUCTION

Chair/Contact: Brady Lewis, Director
of Education
Calendar: Semesters
Degrees Offered: B.F.A., film
and video production (offered
in conjunction with Point Park
College)
Departmental Majors: 70 students
Entrance Requirements: Determined
by individual colleges and universities.
Application deadline: determined by
individual colleges and universities
Curricular Emphasis: Narrative,
documentary, experimental, and
animated film/video productions; still
photography
Special Activities: Film: Pittsburgh
Filmmakers operates a first-run 35mm
movie theatre; special screenings;
showcases. Television/Video: program
material produced for cable television,
and for local public and commercial
television stations; major grant funding
available for students in film, video,
and television
Facilities: Film: 35mm screening
facilities; 16mm screening room;
bench and flatbed editing suites;
interlock sound mixing studio; Oxberry
animation stand; film/video library.
Television/Video: editing suites; access
to complete television studio at local
cable station
Equipment: Film: complete Super-8
and 16mm. Television/Video: complete
¾" studio and ½" location

Alumni: John Bick, assistant film
editor; Greg Funk, special effects
makeup artist; Paula Connelly, TV/film
producer; Michael Trcic, model
builder/special effects artist

GUIDE POV: Pittsburgh Filmmakers is
an innovative, independent media arts
center that works in cooperation with
other area schools; Point Park College
offers a four-year B.F.A. in film and
video production through this
institution; Carnegie Mellon University
and Carlow College offer the art
center's complete course listings for
elective credit; the University of
Pittsburgh offers all Pittsburgh
Filmmakers' production courses as a
complement to its own major in film
studies; courses also available on a
noncredit basis to independent
students; encouragement of individual
creative expression; internship
opportunities in film, video, and
television production

POINT PARK COLLEGE

201 Wood St.,
Pittsburgh, PA 15222–1984
(412)391–4100

*Private four-year comprehensive
institution. Coed, urban location.
Undergraduate enrollment: 2,500.
Graduate enrollment: 100.*

FILM AND VIDEO PRODUCTION

Chair/Contact: Carole Berger,
Department of Fine, Applied, and
Performing Arts

JOURNALISM AND COMMUNICATIONS DEPARTMENT

Chair/Contact: Dr. Nancy C. Jones,
Chair
Calendar: Semesters

Degrees Offered: B.F.A., film and video production (in conjunction with Pittsburgh Filmmakers); B.A., M.A., journalism and communications (emphasis on television and radio)
Departmental Majors: Undergraduate journalism and communications: 250 students. Graduate: 50 students
Entrance Requirements:
Undergraduate: 2.0 grade-point average; ACT or SAT scores; interview required. Graduate: 3.0 grade-point average; written statement of purpose; recommendations; competitive GRE scores. Undergraduate and graduate application deadlines: August 1 and November 15. Percent of acceptances: 83%
Curricular Emphasis: Film and video production: comprehensive production training in all aspects of film and video given at Pittsburgh Filmmakers facilities; for more details, see listing under "Pittsburgh Filmmakers." Journalism and communications: electronic media theory and culture; broadcast journalism; screenwriting; audio-video production; media management
Special Activities: Film: film series/festivals. Television: program material produced for cable television; multimedia activities with college-operated Pittsburgh Playhouse; student broadcasting clubs
Facilities: Film/Video: see listing under "Pittsburgh Filmmakers." Television: studio; audio bay; control room; video editing suites; news room
Equipment: Film/Video: see listing under "Pittsburgh Filmmakers." Television: complete ¾" studio and location with ENG capability
Alumni: Dennis Miller, TV comedian/actor; Bob Pompeani, TV sports producer; Carrie Minot, TV news producer; Tim Estiloy, TV news anchor

GUIDE POV: Point Park College offers separate programs for students planning careers in film/video production, television and radio production, or media management; communications students receive pre-professional training in all aspects of television and radio production; graduate communications program stresses advanced production and writing; comprehensive, B.F.A. program in film/video offered through Pittsburgh Filmmakers located off-campus; cross-registration with the Pittsburgh Council of Higher Education; co-op program with the Art Institute of Pittsburgh; internship opportunities in film and television production

ROBERT MORRIS COLLEGE

Narrows Run Rd.,
Coraopolis, PA 15108–1189
(412)262–8206

Private four-year comprehensive institution. Coed, urban and rural locations. Undergraduate enrollment: 4,500. Graduate enrollment: 1,000.

COMMUNICATIONS DEPARTMENT

Chair/Contact: Dr. John D. O'Banion; Dr. Lutz Bacher
Calendar: Semesters
Degrees Offered: B.A., communication; B.A., B.S., communication management
Departmental Majors:
Undergraduate: 250 students
Entrance Requirements:
Undergraduate: 2.0 grade-point average; ACT or SAT scores. Undergraduate application deadline: rolling. Percent of acceptances: 90%
Curricular Emphasis: Film and video production; media management

Special Activities: Film: film society. Television: program material produced for on-campus closed-circuit television, local cable television, and the Pittsburgh Cable Television system; PBS/RMC-TV teleconferences; live satellite broadcasts; corporation projects

Facilities: Film: editing suite; sound mixing room. Television: studio; audio bay; control room; video editing suites

Equipment: Film: complete Super-8 and 16mm. Television/Video: complete ¾" studio; complete ¾" and ½" location

Alumni: Andrew Taylor, film production/best boy; Bart Flaherty, film production/best boy; Cheryl Tkach, production office coordinator

GUIDE POV: Robert Morris College provides opportunities for student participation in corporate video, studio television, and 16mm film production; cross-registration through the Pittsburgh Council of Higher Education; film and television production internships available

---

ROSEMONT COLLEGE

Montgomery Ave.,
Rosemont, PA 19010
(215)527–0200

Private four-year comprehensive institution. Women, suburban location. Undergraduate enrollment: 650. Graduate enrollment: 50.

ARTS DIVISION

Chair/Contact: Michael Willse, Chair
Calendar: Semesters
Degrees Offered: B.A., B.S., B.F.A.
Departmental Majors: Undergraduate film and video studies: 100 students

Entrance Requirements:
Undergraduate: 2.5 grade-point average; SAT required, with a minimum composite score of 800; two recommendations. Undergraduate application deadline: rolling. Percent of acceptances: 70%

Curricular Emphasis: Film and video theory/aesthetics, criticism, and history

Special Activities: Film: student publications

Facilities: Film/Video: screening rooms; computer laboratories

Equipment: Film/Video: video cameras; audio recorders; film projectors

Alumni: Pat Ciarrocchi, TV news anchor

GUIDE POV: Art history majors at this small, selective college for women may include formal studies in film/video history, theory, and criticism as part of their undergraduate arts curriculum; examination of film and video from varied political, psychological, and literary perspectives; basic video production training available; cross-registration with Villanova University, Cabrini College, and the Eastern Art Institute; dual and student-designed majors; study abroad; extensive media internship opportunities

---

SUSQUEHANNA UNIVERSITY

Selinsgrove, PA 17870
(717)374–0101

Private four-year comprehensive institution. Coed, small town location. Enrollment: 1,400.

COMMUNICATIONS AND THEATRE ARTS DEPARTMENT

Chair/Contact: Dr. James Sodt, Chair; television: Robert Gross; Larry Augustine
Calendar: Semesters
Degrees Offered: B.A., communication and theatre arts (students may select emphasis in broadcasting, mass communication, public relations, journalism, speech communication, or theatre)
Departmental Majors: 140 students
Entrance Requirements: ACT or SAT scores (SAT preferred); transcripts; recommendations; ATs in English composition and math are recommended. Application deadline: December 15 for early decision; final deadline is March 15. Percent of acceptances: 68%
Curricular Emphasis: Radio broadcasting; video production; media management
Special Activities: Radio: program material produced for student-operated radio station serving community year round
Facilities: Television/Video: studio; audio bay; control room; video editing suite; computer laboratories
Equipment: Television/Radio: complete S-VHS studio; eight-track audio production suite; radio broadcasting facilities
Alumni: Linda Davis, TV assistant producer; John Theillon, radio marketing consultant; John Bell, TV production executive

GUIDE POV: This competitive private university offers comprehensive training in television and radio production with an emphasis on news and documentary programming; special interest in new digital technologies; cross-registration with Bucknell University; extensive study abroad program; local practicum and internship opportunities in television and radio production

---

SWARTHMORE COLLEGE

500 College Ave.,
Swarthmore, PA 19081–1397
(215)328–8000

Private four-year comprehensive institution. Coed, suburban location. Undergraduate enrollment: 1,400. Graduate enrollment: 5.

ART DEPARTMENT

Chair/Contact: Dr. Michael Cothren, Chair; Dr. T. Kaori Kitao, film

ENGLISH DEPARTMENT

Chair/Contact: Dr. Craig Williamson, Chair; Dr. Alex Juhasz, film
Calendar: Semesters
Degrees Offered: B.A., art history, English literature
Departmental Majors: Undergraduate art history: 35 students. Undergraduate English: 200 students
Entrance Requirements: Undergraduate: SAT required; three ATs required; competitive grade-point average. Undergraduate application deadline: December 1. Percent of acceptances: 30%
Curricular Emphasis: Critical study of film as medium and visual image; discourse in context of art history, feminism, and literary studies
Special Activities: Film: film series; film societies
Facilities: Film/Video: screening room; film and video editing suites
Equipment: Video: ½" location
Alumni: Jeff Schon, filmmaker/producer; John Siceloff, network TV

producer; Thomas Drescher, film editor

GUIDE POV: Undergraduates at this selective private college study film as a visual and narrative art as well as in its historical context as part of a major in art history, English, or modern languages; genre studies encompass variety of critical perspectives, such as semiotics; cross-registration with Haverford and Bryn Mawr colleges and the University of Pennsylvania; study opportunities in Russia, Spain, France, and Thailand

---

TEMPLE UNIVERSITY

Broad and Montgomery Sts., Philadelphia, PA 19122–1803 (215)204–7000

State four-year comprehensive institution. Coed, urban location. Undergraduate enrollment: 24,000. Graduate enrollment: 10,000.

RADIO, TELEVISION, AND FILM DEPARTMENT

Chair/Contact: Dr. Howard Myrick, Chair
Calendar: Semesters
Degrees Offered: B.A., M.F.A., radio/television/film; M.A., Ph.D., communications
Departmental Majors: Undergraduate film and television: 650 students. Graduate film and television: 75 students. Graduate communication studies: 180 students
Entrance Requirements: Undergraduate: 2.5 grade-point average; ACT or SAT scores; recommendations. Graduate: 3.0 grade-point average; written statement of purpose; GRE scores; portfolio required for M.F.A. applicants.

Undergraduate application deadline: June 15. Graduate application deadline: M.F.A., February 1; Ph.D., March 1. Percent of acceptances: Undergraduate: 69%. Graduate: 48%
Curricular Emphasis: After taking a required number of courses, undergraduates may choose a production emphasis in film, television, and media studies; M.F.A. program emphasizes independent production work; M.A.-Ph.D. program is theory-oriented
Special Activities: Film: film series/festivals; film societies. Television: program material produced for on-campus closed-circuit television, cable television, and local public television stations
Facilities: Film: cine studio; screening room; editing suite; sound mixing room; animation stand; film library. Television/Video: three complete television studios; audio bays; control rooms; video editing suites
Equipment: Film: complete 16mm and processing laboratory; 35mm editing and sound recording equipment. Television/Video: complete ¾" and Super-VHS studios; complete ¾" and ½" location; Betacam and 1" available in local production houses for advanced graduate projects
Alumni: Noam Pitlik, TV director; David Brenner, TV director/producer/comedian; Robert Saget, TV writer/producer/comedian

GUIDE POV: Undergraduates at this competitive university may select a communications majors with an emphasis in film, television, and media studies that combines production training with core requirements in theory and criticism; the M.F.A. program is production-oriented with an emphasis on socially aware independent film and video production; the graduate communication program trains scholars in the field of media studies; study abroad; extensive internship opportunities in film, television, and radio production

UNIVERSITY OF THE ARTS

Broad and Pine Sts.,
Philadelphia, PA 19102
(215)875–4800

Private four-year liberal arts institution. Coed, urban location. Enrollment: 1,400.

PHOTO/FILM/ANIMATION DEPARTMENT

Chair/Contact: Peter Rose
Calendar: Semesters
Degrees Offered: B.F.A., film and/or animation
Departmental Majors: Film/Video: 30 students. Animation: 45 students
Entrance Requirements: ACT or SAT scores; interview; portfolio; essay; recommendations. Undergraduate application deadline: April 1. Percent of acceptances: 70%
Curricular Emphasis: Independent experimental work exploring the creative possibilities of media; secondary emphasis on history and theory; department encourages interaction among schools of dance, music, and theatre
Special Activities: Film: Black Maria Film Festival; visiting artists series/ screenings; collaborative projects in experimental media
Facilities: Film/Video: screening room; ½" video editing suite; sound mixing and recording room; Steenbeck editing room; Oxberry animation stand; JK optical printer; computer animation and processing facilities; film and video library
Equipment: Film/Video: complete 16mm film production; complete ½" video; Amiga and MacIntosh computer labs
Alumni: Tim Young, playwright; Francis Quinn, media executive; David Mortlock, paintbox animator; Gary Schwartz, animator

GUIDE POV: This small nonprofit university encourages the exploration of film, video, animation, and multimedia techniques; faculty of working media artists; cross-registration with the 10-member Consortium of East Coast Art Schools as well as with the Pennsylvania Academy of Fine Arts; extensive summer programs; study abroad; media internship opportunities

UNIVERSITY OF PENNSYLVANIA

1 College Hall,
Philadelphia, PA 19104–6376
(215)898–5000

Private four-year comprehensive institution. Coed, urban location. Undergraduate enrollment: 10,000. Graduate enrollment: 12,000.

DEPARTMENT OF COMMUNICATIONS

Chair/Contact: Joseph Turow, Associate Dean
Calendar: Semesters
Degrees Offered: B.A., B.S., M.A., M.S., Ph.D.
Entrance Requirements: Undergraduate: competitive grade-point average; SAT required; ACT accepted; ATs in English composition, mathematics, and a foreign language are required; essay required; interview recommended. Graduate: GRE scores;

essay required; recommendations.
Undergraduate and graduate
application deadline: January 1.
Percent of acceptances: 47%,
undergraduate and graduate
Curricular Emphasis:
Communications Department: Students
study the history and theory of social
and mass communication, explore the
relationship between public policy
and popular culture, and examine
media in terms of semiotics,
communications structures, and other
areas. General: Theoretical and critical
film/media studies are also offered
through several other venues,
including the Comparative Literature
and Literary Theory Department, as
well as through the American
Civilization Department; such courses
vary and are presented in the context
of the major and its thrust of inquiry.
Special Activities: Film: film
screenings; lectures
Facilities: Film: screening room; film
library
Equipment: Video: basic video
equipment; interactive video
Alumni: Stanley Jaffe, film executive/
producer; Josephine Holz, TV network
executive; Edward Keller, TV executive

GUIDE POV: Founded in 1740, this
highly selective private university offers
the communications major a critical
examination of electronic media,
advertising, and film; areas of inquiry
include cinema as cultural
construction; art and visual
manipulation; semiotics; there is a
video lab course, which acquaints
students with experimental video
processes including interactive video;
various other departments include
courses examining film and other
media primarily from social and
cultural perspectives; there is no film

minor; cross-registration with
Haverford, Swarthmore, and Bryn
Mawr Colleges; study abroad in 14
countries

UNIVERSITY OF PITTSBURGH

526 Cathedral of Learning,
Pittsburgh, PA 15260
(412)624–4141

*State-related four-year comprehensive
institution. Coed, urban location.
Undergraduate enrollment: 19,000.
Graduate enrollment: 10,000.*

FILM STUDIES PROGRAM

Chair/Contact: Dr. Lucy Fischer,
Director
Calendar: Semesters
Degrees Offered: B.A., film studies;
Ph.D., English (students may select
emphasis in film)
Departmental Majors: Undergraduate
film studies: 100 students. Graduate
English (film emphasis): 15 students
Entrance Requirements:
Undergraduate: 2.5 grade-point
average; ACT or SAT scores;
recommendations. Graduate: 3.0 grade-
point average; GRE scores;
recommendations. Undergraduate and
graduate application deadline: rolling.
Percent of acceptances: 81%
Curricular Emphasis: Film history,
theory/aesthetics, and criticism; film,
video, and still photography
production through Pittsburgh
Filmmakers
Special Activities: Film: film series/
festivals; special relationship with
Carnegie Museum of Art. Television:
program material produced for on-
campus closed-circuit television, local
public and commercial television
stations, and cable television
Facilities: Film: 35mm screening

facilities; screening room; editing suite; sound mixing room; animation stand; film and videotape library. Television/Video: studio; audio bay; control room; video editing suites
Equipment: Film: complete Super-8 and 16mm. Television/Video: complete ¾" studio and location
Alumni: Tom Nicholson, filmmaker; Marylynn Uricchio, film critic; Betsy Callomon, media executive; Matt Yocobowski, media curator

GUIDE POV: The interdisciplinary film studies program at this selective university, founded in 1787, provides a theoretical foundation for graduate production work; the program is also appropriate for students who wish to pursue careers in film teaching, journalism, museum curatorial, or library/archival professions; by special arrangement with Pittsburgh Filmmakers, film and video production courses are made available for credit; the English Department offers a graduate film studies program that integrates work in the areas of literature and film; cross-registration available through the Pittsburgh Council on Higher Education Consortium; study abroad; Semester at Sea; extensive internship opportunities in film and television production

---

UNIVERSITY OF PITTSBURGH AT BRADFORD

300 Campus Dr.,
Bradford, PA 16701
(814)362–7500

State-related four-year comprehensive institution. Coed, small town location. Enrollment: 1,200.

COMMUNICATION ARTS

Chair/Contact: Jeffrey Guterman, Chair
Calendar: Semesters
Degrees Offered: B.A., communication (emphasis in radio and television)
Departmental Majors: Communication: 50 students
Entrance Requirements: Competitive high school records; SAT or ACT scores. Application deadline: rolling
Curricular Emphasis: Television production and programming; radio production
Special Activities: Media-related trips to NYC and Buffalo; sponsored video productions for independent clients
Facilities: Television: television studio; audio studio; control room; video editing suite
Equipment: Television/Video: ½" and ¾" (both standard and SP) with A/B roll; four editing bays; seven field cameras; two three-tube studio cameras; digital effects; Grass Valley switcher
Alumni: Douglas Major, TV news videographer; Terry Rensel, TV master control technician; Chris MacKowski, radio news anchor; Lori Maze, radio news director

GUIDE POV: Featuring practical training in broadcast journalism as well as corporate video production, this small competitive program prepares students for career industry positions; cross-registration available with other colleges in the University of Pittsburgh system; study abroad; some paying internships available locally

UNIVERSITY OF SCRANTON

Scranton, PA 18510–4592
(717)941–7400

*Private four-year comprehensive
institution. Coed, urban location.
Undergraduate enrollment: 4,500.
Graduate enrollment: 700.*

COMMUNICATION DEPARTMENT

Chair/Contact: Dr. Robert P.
Sadowski, Chair
Calendar: 4–1–4
Degrees Offered: B.A.,
communication (with emphasis in
broadcasting/film, radio/TV
production, journalism,
communication studies, or advertising/
public relations)
Departmental Majors: Undergraduate
broadcasting/film: 40 students.
Undergraduate radio/TV production:
60 students
Entrance Requirements:
Undergraduate: ACT or SAT
scores; essay and interview
recommended. Undergraduate
application deadline: March 1. Percent
of acceptances: 59%
Curricular Emphasis:
Communication theory; critical studies
in film; media writing; audio-film-video
production; media management; radio
and television journalism; cable
television; mass media management;
communication law; advertising;
public relations; print journalism
Special Activities: Film: film series/
festivals. Television: program material
produced for cable television
Facilities: Film: screening room;
editing suite; sound mixing room;
animation stand. Television/Video:
studio; audio bay; control room; video
editing suites

Equipment: Film: Super-8 and 16mm.
Television/Video: complete ¾" studio
and location
Alumni: Susan Swain, C-SPAN TV
executive; John A. Walsh, ESPN TV
executive director

GUIDE POV: Operated by the Jesuit
order, this competitive private
university offers diverse course listings
in the field of communication with
core requirements in the liberal arts;
students may then choose an
emphasis in broadcasting/film that
blends theory and production training;
separate radio/TV production
emphasis involves the student in a
variety of hands-on projects; study
abroad; media internship opportunities

VILLANOVA UNIVERSITY

Villanova, PA 19085–1699
(215)645–4500

*Private four-year comprehensive
institution. Coed, suburban location.
Undergraduate enrollment: 6,500.
Graduate enrollment: 3,500.*

COMMUNICATION ARTS DEPARTMENT

Chair/Contact: Dr. Joan D. Lynch
Calendar: Semesters
Degrees Offered: B.S.
Departmental Majors:
Undergraduate: 200 students
Entrance Requirements:
Undergraduate: transcripts; competitive
SAT scores; recommendations.
Undergraduate application
deadline: January 15. Percent of
acceptances: 75%
Curricular Emphasis: Film: critical
studies. Television: media writing;
production; programming; media
management
Special Activities: Film: film series/

festivals; student publications.
Television: program material produced
for local cable television
Facilities: Television: studio; audio
bay; control room
Equipment: Television/Video:
complete ¾" studio and ½" location
Alumni: David Rabe, screenwriter/
playwright; Peter Mattaliano,
playwright; Bill Garrity, producer/
assistant director; Bill Mann, film
editor

GUIDE POV: Founded in 1842, this
Catholic liberal arts university offers
media studies and practical video
production training; selective entry;
study abroad in Russia, the Caribbean,
the Pacific Rim, East Africa, and Great
Britain; media internship opportunities
available in Philadelphia, New York,
and Washington, D.C.

WEST CHESTER UNIVERSITY

West Chester, PA 19383
(215)436–1000

*State four-year comprehensive
institution. Coed, small town location.
Undergraduate enrollment: 6,000.
Graduate enrollment: 3,000.*

ENGLISH DEPARTMENT

Chair/Contact: John Kelly
Calendar: Semesters
Degrees Offered: B.A., English (minor
in film criticism)
Departmental Majors: Undergraduate
English: 300 students
Entrance Requirements:
Undergraduate: 2.0 grade-point
average; SAT required (minimum 900
composite); essay required.
Undergraduate application deadline:
April. Percent of acceptances: 65%
Curricular Emphasis: Critical studies
in film
Special Activities: Film: film series/
festivals
Facilities: screening room; film library
Equipment: Film: 16mm projectors
Alumni: Warren Trent, TV news
editor; Robert Momyer, video
executive

GUIDE POV: West Chester University
offers critical studies in film through
the English Department; selective
admissions; study abroad in Wales,
France, and Austria; cross-registration
with Cheyney University

I first became interested in show business at a rather tender age. My parents met in an acting class at college in the early 1960s, and my mother tells stories of crawling around the auditorium for a repertory company audition while pregnant with me. When I was a child, there was always a lot of drama around the house. My sister and I would present our own "plays" in the backyard, inviting the neighborhood kids in to see us smash up fake furniture as cowboys or pirates, and toss pies in each other's face. My father, with acting work scarce and a young family to raise, took up private investigation by day and did plays at night. Sixteen-millimeter camera in hand, he'd take me on surveillance scouts—disability insurance cases and domestic disputes mostly—but sneaky-fun nonetheless. He taught me how to operate an 8mm camera, and during summer vacations I would work in his office, logging and splicing together scratchy, shaky long shots of the injured, the nefarious, and the illegitimate.

At the age of ten I directed my first movie, a five-minute silent monster epic, edited in the camera. My mother taught high school English and also performed. As described by my dad, she was "absolutely brilliant" in local productions of *A Little Night Music* and *Hamlet.* Throughout my years in high school, college theatre, and film courses, my parents never pushed me onto the stage or into filmmaking as a profession. They were well aware of the risks and disappointments to be found there. But their support was constant, and the high standards they set for the art they both loved were passed on to me as I struggle to find my place in both the business and the art of filmmaking.

As a director starting my own production company, I have found that the variety of courses and flexible scheduling offered through continuing education programs best suit my needs. And those courses have proven most beneficial to me.

BROWN UNIVERSITY

Providence, RI 02912
(401)863–1000

Private four-year comprehensive institution. Coed, urban location. Undergraduate enrollment: 5,000. Graduate enrollment: 1,500.

CENTER FOR MODERN CULTURE AND MEDIA

Chair/Contact: Mary Ann Doane, Chair
Calendar: Semesters
Degrees Offered: B.A., semiotics (students may select emphasis in film); modern culture (students may select emphasis in video)
Departmental Majors: Undergraduate: 30 students
Entrance Requirements: Undergraduate: ACT or SAT scores; three AT scores; personal essay; teachers' recommendations; AP credit accepted. Percent of acceptances: 23%
Curricular Emphasis: Theory and analysis of the media; film and video production
Special Activities: Film: film series/festivals; film society; student publications. Television: program material produced for on-campus closed-circuit television
Facilities: Film: screening room; editing suites; film library. Video: studio; editing suites
Equipment: Film: complete Super-8 and 16mm. Television/Video: complete ¾" studio; complete Hi-8 and ¾" location
Alumni: Robert Evans, film producer/executive; Richard Fleischer, film director; Todd Haynes, filmmaker; Christine Vachon, TV/film producer; Sollaca Mitchell, director/screenwriter; Jane Rosenthal, TV/film producer

GUIDE POV: This small, highly selective program offers an intensive critical studies curriculum in film and video that focuses on semiotic theory and readings in modern culture; 24-hour access to production facilities; exchange program with Howard University Communication Department; cross-registration with Rhode Island School of Design; study abroad in 18 countries; media internship opportunities

RHODE ISLAND COLLEGE

600 Mt. Pleasant Ave.,
Providence, RI 02908
(401)456–8000

State four-year comprehensive institution. Coed, urban location. Undergraduate enrollment: 8,000. Graduate enrollment: 2,500.

FILM STUDIES PROGRAM

Chair/Contact: Kathryn Kalinak, Chair
Calendar: Semesters

Degrees Offered: B.A., film studies; film studies minor
Departmental Majors:
Undergraduate: 35 students
Entrance Requirements:
Undergraduate: ACT or SAT scores; recommendations; interview optional; written statement of purpose. Undergraduate application deadline: May 1. Percent of acceptances: 70%
Curricular Emphasis: Film criticism; theory; history
Special Activities: Film: film series/festivals; film societies
Facilities: Film: screening room; film library. Television: studio
Equipment: Film: complete Super-8. Television/Video: complete ½" and ¾" production and editing equipment
Alumni: Sally Mendzela, filmmaker/TV producer; Lisa Cruz, TV producer

GUIDE POV: Students majoring in film studies at this state-supported liberal arts college are encouraged to select optional courses within related arts and humanities areas; independent production projects supplement critical studies; cross-registration permitted with other Rhode Island schools; internship opportunities in film, video, and television production

RHODE ISLAND SCHOOL OF DESIGN

Two College St.,
Providence, RI 02903
(401)454–6100

Private four-year comprehensive arts institution. Coed, urban location. Undergraduate enrollment: 2,000. Graduate enrollment: 100.

FILM/VIDEO PROGRAM

Chair/Contact: Dennis Hlynsky, Chair
Calendar: Semesters and winter session
Degrees Offered: B.F.A.
Departmental Majors:
Undergraduate: 85 students
Entrance Requirements:
Undergraduate: transcripts; SAT scores; personal statement of purpose; portfolio. Undergraduate application deadline: February 15. Percent of acceptances: 45%
Curricular Emphasis: Production-based curriculum for young artists in film, video, and animation
Special Activities: Film/Video: film and video series/festivals; visiting film/video artists
Facilities: Film/Video: two large shooting studios; numerous smaller studios; audio bay; editing rooms; computer workstation; two Filmmaker and one Master Series animation stand
Equipment: Film: complete 16mm; full-coat audio mixing; Steenbeck 16mm editing tables. Video: Hi-8 field recording with Hi-8 to ¾" off-line editing and ¾" to ¾" A/B roll editing; IBM RS-6000 computer workstation running Wavefront 3D animation software; eight-track mixing studio with MIDI/video/tape chase
Alumni: Martha Coolidge, film director; Gus Van Sant, film producer/director; Robert Richardson, cinematographer

GUIDE POV: A highly regarded fine arts college, Rhode Island School of Design offers visual arts students opportunities to work in film, video, and animation while refining conceptual and aesthetic skills; cross-registration with Brown University and the East Coast Art Schools Consortium; various three-to-six week travel courses available; extensive local and national internships available in film and video during six-week mid-year winter session

ROGER WILLIAMS UNIVERSITY

Ferry Rd., Bristol, RI 02809–2921
(401)253–1040

Private four-year comprehensive institution. Coed, suburban location. Enrollment: 2,200.

SCHOOL OF HUMANITIES

Chair/Contact: Film: Janet Gilmore
Calendar: Semesters
Degrees Offered: Individualized minor in film studies
Entrance Requirements: ACT or SAT scores; recommendations. Application deadline: rolling. Percent of acceptances: 80%
Curricular Emphasis: Film history, theory/aesthetics, and criticism; basic Super-8 film production including narrative, animated, and experimental
Special Activities: Film: film series/festivals
Facilities: Film: screening room; animation stand; film/video library
Equipment: Film: complete Super-8
Alumni: Kerryanne Kelly, media communications coordinator; Delores Del Padre, media communications coordinator

GUIDE POV: Roger Williams University offers students an opportunity to construct an individually planned program of studies leading to an independent film minor; blend of theory and criticism classes taught along with basic Super-8 production training; core curriculum in the liberal arts; study abroad in Europe; internship opportunities in film and television production

Attending film school is expensive, so I've taken several jobs to help pay for tuition. Among the things I do is work in the university's administration department, where I see countless students with all kinds of problems. It can be very frustrating. Sometimes I actually believe that film school is the biggest mistake in the world, that only a foolhardy person would pursue such a tenuous degree as film and television production. Then in a moment of reflection, I think film school is the next best thing to chocolate chip Häagen-Dazs. In reality, it is neither a one-way ticket to the industry nor an esoteric trip leading nowhere.

Film school should be a place to make mistakes, to fall flat on your face, to fulfill your dreams. Most students won't get this opportunity in the professional world, where mistakes or "interesting" approaches often mean never eating lunch again at Morton's. Film school is a place to meet bright and talented people, some of whom may become industry luminaries. If you want to write screenplays, you get to meet future producers. If you want to be a cinematographer, you get to meet future directors.

Film school is also a place to experience criticism and use it wisely. I have learned that the best film schools dole out praise and analysis equally and encourage dialogue between faculty and students.

ANDERSON COLLEGE

Anderson, SC 29621
(803)231–2000

*Private four-year comprehensive
institution. Coed, urban location.
Enrollment: 1,100.*

JOURNALISM DEPARTMENT

Chair/Contact: Lawrence Webb
Calendar: Semesters
Degrees Offered: B.A.
Departmental Majors: 35 students
Entrance Requirements: 2.0 grade-
point average; ACT or SAT scores.
Application deadline: August 1.
Percent of acceptances: 90%
Curricular Emphasis: Electronic
media theory and culture; broadcast
journalism; media management
Special Activities: Television:
program material produced for
campus-based cable television station
Facilities: Television: studio; control
room; editing bays; on-campus news
bureau for local CBS affiliate
Equipment: Television/Video:
complete ¾" studio and location;
character generator
Alumni: Joe Edwards, TV sports
announcer; David Acker, videographer

GUIDE POV: Anderson College offers
hands-on television broadcast training
with a strong emphasis on news
journalism; opportunities to work with
campus-based CBS-affiliate staff; media
internships available

BOB JONES UNIVERSITY

Greenville, SC 29614
(803)242–5100

*Private four-year comprehensive
institution. Coed, urban location.
Undergraduate enrollment: 5,000.
Graduate enrollment: 300.*

DIVISION OF CINEMA AND VIDEO PRODUCTION

Chair/Contact: Tim Rogers, Chair
Calendar: Semesters
Degrees Offered: B.S., M.A., cinema
and video production; B.S., radio and
television broadcasting, broadcast
engineering
Departmental Majors:
Undergraduate: 70–80 students.
Graduate: 8–10 students
Entrance Requirements:
Undergraduate: ACT or SAT scores.
Graduate: recommendations.
Undergraduate and graduate
application deadline: July 1
Curricular Emphasis: Film, television,
and video production
Special Activities: Film: film series/
festivals; university production unit
(Unusual Films). Television: program
material produced for cable television
Facilities: Film: sound stage;
screening room; editing suite; sound
mixing room; animation stand.
Television: studio; audio bay; control
room; editing suites
Equipment: Film: complete 16mm.
Television/Video: complete ¾" studio

and ½" location; on-line editing equipment

Alumni: John Ridley, film/video producer; Larry Jackson, corporate communications executive

GUIDE POV: Bob Jones University is a well-equipped non-denominational Protestant institution offering comprehensive training in film, television, and video along with evangelical religious studies; program director actively seeks to attract students who identify with college's "strong conservative Christian orientation"; media internship opportunities

CLEMSON UNIVERSITY

Strode Tower,
Clemson, SC 29634–1503
(803)656–3311

State four-year comprehensive institution. Coed, rural location. Undergraduate enrollment: 9,400. Graduate enrollment: 3,000.

ENGLISH DEPARTMENT

Chair/Contact: Mark Charney; Carol Ward
Calendar: Semesters
Degrees Offered: B.A., M.A., M.A.P.C. (master of professional communications)
Departmental Majors: Undergraduate English: 260 students. Graduate: 50 students
Entrance Requirements:
Undergraduate: minimum composite of 800 on SAT scores; academic rank in top 25% of class; 2.0 minimum grade-point average; AP credit accepted. Graduate: GRE scores; recommendations. Undergraduate application deadline: rolling, but

students are advised to apply by March 15. Graduate deadline: February 15.
Curricular Emphasis: Studies in literature and film theory
Special Activities: Film: member of Southern Circuit Film Series, which brings independent film/video makers to campus to discuss and screen work
Equipment: Film: five projection rooms
Alumni: Stephen Lomas, screenwriter; Matthew Ferreira, production assistant

GUIDE POV: Clemson University offers several undergraduate and graduate film theory courses through its English Department; comprehensive writing program; admission is competitive; co-op programs; study abroad in five countries

UNIVERSITY OF SOUTH CAROLINA

Columbia, SC 29208
(803)777–7000

State four-year comprehensive institution. Coed, urban location. Undergraduate enrollment: 20,000. Graduate enrollment: 3,000.

DEPARTMENT OF MEDIA ARTS

Chair/Contact: Dr. Sandra Wertz
Calendar: Semesters
Degrees Offered: B.M.A., M.M.A.
Departmental Majors: Undergraduate media arts: 230. Graduate media arts: 250
Entrance Requirements:
Undergraduate: high school diploma; minimum 900 composite SAT score. Graduate: GRE; portfolio; interview. Undergraduate application deadline: December 31. Graduate application deadline: May 15. Percent of

acceptances: Undergraduates: 83%. Graduates: 75%

Curricular Emphasis: Screenwriting; film, audio, and video production; photography

Special Activities: Film: Carolina Cinematographers Association; media institute. Television: program material produced for on-campus closed-circuit television, local public television, and cable television

Facilities: Film: editing room; animation stand; film library

Equipment: Film: complete Super-8 and 16mm. Television: complete ¾" studio; complete ¾" and ½" location

Alumni: Paul Bernard, film director; Kim McDonald, TV producer; Dan Kneece, cinematographer

GUIDE POV: The stated goal of this lively department is to educate the media production generalist with training in film, audio, video, television, photography, and screenwriting; course listings cover areas of aesthetics, production processes, and administrative functions; innovative system of interactive television instruction transmitted statewide; study-abroad programs through the Byrnes International Center; cross-registration offered through the National Student Exchange; internship opportunities

---

WINTHROP UNIVERSITY

Rock Hill, SC 29733–0001
(803)323–2211

State four-year comprehensive institution. Coed, suburban location. Undergraduate enrollment: 5,000. Graduate enrollment: 1,000.

DEPARTMENT OF MASS COMMUNICATION

Chair/Contact: Dr. J. William Click, Chair

Calendar: Semesters

Degrees Offered: B.A., mass communication with major in broadcast journalism/production or broadcast writing/management

Departmental Majors: Undergraduate television broadcasting: 100 students

Entrance Requirements: Undergraduate: competitive grade-point average; ACT or SAT scores; recommendations. Undergraduate application deadline: April 1. Percent of acceptances: 74%

Curricular Emphasis: Professional broadcasting studies with emphasis on news and television production

Special Activities: Television: students produce programming for cable television; AERho member

Facilities: Television: studio; audio bay; control room

Equipment: Television/Video: matched studio cameras; ¾" VTR and cassette recorders; monitors; portable cameras; time base corrector; switcher/special effects generators; audio mixers

Alumni: Cecily Truett, media executive; Maryanne G. Genus, media sales executive; Pamela S. Gladman, production assistant; Joe H. Ligon, TV producer

GUIDE POV: Mass communication students at Winthrop University receive pre-professional broadcast training within a liberal arts curriculum; admission to program is competitive; cross-registration through the Charlotte Area Educational Consortium; study abroad in eight countries; internship opportunities

Over the years I have been asked the same question by aspiring writers, producers, and directors: "Is it really necessary to acquire a formal education to succeed in the entertainment business?" The answer, of course, is no. Ours is a business driven by commercial goals, but fueled by creative talent. And raw, natural creativity cannot be taught in any school.

So does it follow that a formal academic education in the film and television field is without value? The answer is an equally resounding no. As colleges and universities become more and more sophisticated in their approach to the entertainment field, the opportunity increases to enhance whatever natural ability one has. And, for every "natural" talent, there are many others who will succeed through sheer hard work, initiative, and desire. Both types of individuals benefit by learning the basics, then honing their skills and testing their creative abilities in the protective womb of an academic environment. What a valuable opportunity!

Still, academia can be a trap. The "ivory tower" syndrome can destroy a career before it begins. Movies and television are not, unfortunately, made for the sake of art. The school you choose must be able to maintain this balance between the artistic and practical approach.

BLACK HILLS STATE UNIVERSITY

Box 9003,
1200 University,
Spearfish, SD 57799–9003
(605)642–6011

State four-year comprehensive institution. Coed, rural location. Enrollment: 2,800.

COLLEGE OF ARTS AND HUMANITIES

Chair/Contact: Television: John Walsh
Calendar: Semesters
Degrees Offered: A.S., radio and television; B.S., speech/mass communication
Departmental Majors: Television: 70 students
Entrance Requirements: Academic rank within upper two-thirds of graduating class; 2.0 grade-point average; ACT or SAT scores. Application deadline: May 15. Percent of acceptances: 99%
Curricular Emphasis: Electronic media theory and culture; media writing; television production; broadcast journalism; corporate video; video art
Special Activities: Television: program material produced for local cable television
Facilities: Television: studio; audio bay; control room
Equipment: Television/Video: complete ¾" studio and ½" location
Alumni: Mary Burkholtz, media consultant; Kim Hubbard, assistant sales radio executive

GUIDE POV: This state-supported institution offers communications students a special concentration in radio and television journalism; practical experience in both broadcast television and corporate video production; internship opportunities in television, video, and radio production

SIOUX FALLS COLLEGE

1501 S. Prairie,
Sioux Falls, SD 57105–1699
(605)331–5000

Private four-year comprehensive institution. Coed, suburban location. Enrollment: 1,000.

DEPARTMENT OF MASS COMMUNICATIONS

Chair/Contact: Gerry Schlenker; Terry Harris
Calendar: 4–1–4
Degrees Offered: B.A., communications
Departmental Majors: Radio and television: 35 students
Entrance Requirements: 2.5 grade-point average; ACT or SAT testing, with a minimum score of 19 or a composite score of 800, respectively. Application deadline: rolling. Percent of acceptances: 87%
Curricular Emphasis: Electronic

media theory and culture; media writing; audio-video production; media management
Special Activities: Television: program material produced for on-campus closed-circuit television and local cable television
Facilities: Television/Video: studio; audio bay; control room; video editing suites
Equipment: Television/Video: complete ¾" studio and location
Alumni: Rebecca Shaw Gumina, TV news anchor; Jan Peterson, TV news producer

GUIDE POV: This selective private college offers a comprehensive communications program with course listings in radio and television production, communication theory, and media management; small production classes; co-op programs with Augustana College and the North American Baptist Seminary; study abroad in Central America, Japan, and China; internship opportunities in television and radio production

SOUTH DAKOTA STATE UNIVERSITY

Brookings, SD 57007–0649
(605)688–4151

State four-year comprehensive institution. Coed, small town location. Undergraduate enrollment: 6,500. Graduate enrollment: 1,500.

DEPARTMENT OF JOURNALISM AND MASS COMMUNICATION

Chair/Contact: Dr. Richard W. Lee, Head
Calendar: Semesters
Degrees Offered: B.A., B.S., journalism and mass communication

(with sequences in broadcast journalism, news-editorial, advertising, journalism, science and technical writing, agricultural journalism, home economics journalism, or printing and journalism); M.S., journalism
Departmental Majors: Undergraduate radio and television: 55 students. Graduate journalism: 40 students
Entrance Requirements: Undergraduate: acceptable grades in college preparatory classes or academic rank within top half of high school graduating class; ACT required with a minimum score of 22 for in-state, Minnesota or Wyoming residents or 23 for nonresidents; recommendations; AP and CLEP credits accepted. Graduate: GRE scores; transcripts; recommendations; personal statement of purpose. Undergraduate and graduate application deadline: August 30. Percent of acceptances: Undergraduate: 90%. Graduate: 80%
Curricular Emphasis: Undergraduate broadcast journalism sequence: radio and television news production, writing, direction, and reporting. Graduate journalism: emphasis on media studies and print journalism
Special Activities: Television: program material produced for cable television and local public broadcasting station
Facilities: Television/Video: studio; audio bay; control room; video editing suites
Equipment: Television/Video: complete ¾" studio and location
Alumni: Sandra Johnson, assistant A.P. bureau chief; Mark Millage, TV news director; Deborah McDermott, TV station manager

GUIDE POV: This is South Dakota's largest state university; undergraduates wishing to pursue careers in radio or television news broadcasting are offered a broad liberal arts curriculum combined with professional training in broadcast journalism; graduate program emphasizes educational broadcasting as well as media administration and management; competitive entry; required media internships for upper-level students

UNIVERSITY OF SOUTH DAKOTA

Vermillion, SD 57069
(605)677–5011

State four-year comprehensive institution. Coed, small town location. Undergraduate enrollment: 6,000. Graduate enrollment: 1,500.

DEPARTMENT OF MASS COMMUNICATION

Chair/Contact: Dr. William Nevious, Chair; Charles Cranston
Calendar: Semesters
Degrees Offered: B.A., B.S., M.A., mass communication
Departmental Majors: Undergraduate television: 215 students. Graduate television: 10 students
Entrance Requirements: Undergraduate: 2.0 grade-point average; ACT required. Graduate: GRE scores; recommendations. Undergraduate and graduate application deadline: rolling. Percent of acceptances: Undergraduate: 88%. Graduate: 75%
Curricular Emphasis: Undergraduate: electronic media theory and culture; media writing; television production; news journalism; media management. Graduate: mass media studies and management training
Special Activities: Television: program material, including daily live newscasts and news briefs, produced for KYOT-TV, which telecasts over two channels of the Vermillion cable system, as well as over a university channel and a city public-access channel. Radio: student-operated fully equipped KAOR-FM
Facilities: Television/Video: studio; audio bay; control room; computer assisted newsroom; electronic editing bays
Equipment: Television/Video: complete ¾" studio and location including ENG equipment
Alumni: Tom Brokaw, NBC TV news anchor; Pat O'Brien, TV network sports broadcaster

GUIDE POV: This competitive public university presents students with diverse course listings in communication theory, television production, and media management; graduate program offers media theory and management studies; study abroad in France and Germany; internship opportunities in television production at CNN and CBS News, among others; required management-level practica for graduate students pursuing careers in the mass communication industry

The only formal course I took in writing was one taught in continuing education by Tom Gaddis, who wrote *Birdman of Alcatraz*. On my thirtieth birthday, married with two nestlings to care for, I decided with trepidation to abandon a successful career as an advertising copywriter and take a crack at free-lancing. And I have never regretted that decision, because eventually I got the opportunity to write for "Columbo," "The Bill Cosby Show," and "All in the Family," among others.

I broke into the business as a performer. When an agent heard a comedy album I'd written and recorded, he introduced me to some people at American International Pictures, where I began rewriting *Beach Party* films. Then I met Howie Horwitz, who was producing a new TV series called "Batman." Horwitz liked my work and gave me a chance with a "batscript." I went on to write more than thirty episodes, and the doors to writing zapped open.

I believe that a formal film education can be valuable but only if taught by active professionals in the field. And I would strongly advise aspiring writers and directors to practice their craft as much as possible. The more you do it, the better you become. Never give up. Each script you send out is a balloon you've blown up and put in the air, and each rejection is a bullet they've fired at your balloon. Be sure in your heart that they will run out of bullets before you run out of breath.

CARSON-NEWMAN COLLEGE

Jefferson City, TN 37760
(615)475–9061

*Private four-year comprehensive
institution. Coed, small town location.
Undergraduate enrollment: 2,000.
Graduate enrollment: 100.*

HUMANITIES DIVISION

Chair/Contact: Film studies: Dr.
Gerald C. Wood, Chair, English
Department. Communication Arts
Department: Dr. Jerry Harvill, Chair;
Glenn Cragwall, broadcasting program
Calendar: Semesters
Degrees Offered: B.A.,
communication arts (students may
choose emphasis in broadcasting);
B.A., English (students may choose
emphasis in film studies)
Departmental Majors: Undergraduate
film studies: 5–10 students.
Undergraduate television: 50 students
Entrance Requirements:
Undergraduate: 2.0 grade-point
average; ACT required, with a
minimum score of 10; SAT may be
substituted, with a minimum
composite score of 800. Undergraduate
application deadline: May 1. Percent
of acceptances: 90%
Curricular Emphasis: Electronic
media theory and culture; critical
studies in film; media writing;
television production
Special Activities: Film: film series/
festivals. Television: program material
produced for cable television
Facilities: Film: screening room; film
library. Television/Video: studio; audio
bay; control room; video editing suites
Equipment: Film: Super-8 and 16mm
projectors. Television/Video: complete
¾" studio and location
Alumni: Ben Vanaman, TV/film story
editor; Jana Rhinehart, TV producer;
Jamey Tucker, broadcast journalist

GUIDE POV: English majors attending
this small private college may
concentrate in film studies and choose
from a variety of course listings in film
history, criticism, and theory/
aesthetics; comprehensive television
broadcasting curriculum is offered
through the Communication Arts
Department; study abroad in England,
France, and Spain; internship
opportunities in television production

EAST TENNESSEE STATE UNIVERSITY

Johnson City, TN 37614
(615)929–4112

*State four-year comprehensive
institution. Coed, urban location.
Undergraduate enrollment: 11,000.
Graduate enrollment: 1,600.*

DEPARTMENT OF COMMUNICATION

Chair/Contact: Charles Roberts
Calendar: Semesters

Degrees Offered: B.A., B.S., broadcasting
Departmental Majors: Undergraduate broadcasting: 185
Entrance Requirements: Undergraduate: 2.3 grade-point average; ACT score of 19. Undergraduate application deadline: July 15. Percent of acceptances: 83%
Curricular Emphasis: Broadcast journalism
Special Activities: Television: program material produced for on-campus closed-circuit television and local PBS affiliate; ACEJMC accreditation
Facilities: Television: sound mixing room; production studio; newsroom with AP feed; control room
Equipment: Television/Video: complete ¾" studio and location
Alumni: Larry Harding, TV/film producer/director; Doug Harrington, video production manager; Jim Cline, TV sports director; Mike Williams, cable program manager; Will McDonald, video producer; Steve Hawkins, TV news director

GUIDE POV: This competitive state university features a practical curriculum emphasizing hands-on television broadcast training; high career placement ratio for program graduates; cross-registration with Milligan College; study abroad in Scotland, England, France, and Spain; internship opportunities in radio and television production

JOHNSON BIBLE COLLEGE

7900 Johnson Dr.,
Knoxville, TN 37998
(615)573–4517

Private four-year comprehensive institution. Coed, suburban location. Enrollment: 450.

DEPARTMENT OF TELECOMMUNICATIONS

Chair/Contact: Professor Richard Phillips, Chair
Calendar: Semesters
Degrees Offered: B.A., telecommunications
Departmental Majors: Radio and television: 40 students
Entrance Requirements: Official transcripts; ACT scores; commitment to specialized Christian service. Application deadline: August 15. Percent of acceptances: 95%
Curricular Emphasis: Mass media studies; media writing; audio-video production including news/documentary and fiction; broadcast management and advertising; performing
Special Activities: Television: program material produced for on-campus JBC television station, local public and commercial television stations, and cable television; student work includes documentary and fiction projects
Facilities: Television/Video: studio; audio bay; control room; video editing suites
Equipment: Television/Video: complete ¾" studio and location
Alumni: Rich Cambell, radio announcer/programmer; Karla Filsinger, recording engineer; Jeff Marshall, industrial communications producer

GUIDE POV: Specializing in training Christian evangelists for the preaching ministry, this small private college offers comprehensive training in broadcast telecommunications; studies in media management and advertising;

internship opportunities in radio and television production

MEMPHIS STATE UNIVERSITY

Memphis, TN 38152
(901)678–2041

State four-year comprehensive institution. Coed, suburban location. Undergraduate enrollment: 16,000. Graduate enrollment: 3,600.

THEATRE AND COMMUNICATION ARTS

Chair/Contact: David Appleby; Steven Ross; Roxana Gee
Calendar: Semesters
Degrees Offered: B.A., M.A.
Departmental Majors:
Undergraduate: 311 students. Graduate: 45 students
Entrance Requirements:
Undergraduate: 2.0 grade-point average; ACT or SAT scores. Graduate: 3.0 grade-point average; GRE scores. Undergraduate and graduate application deadline: August 1. Percent of acceptances: 65%
Curricular Emphasis: Audio-film-video production; electronic media theory and culture; critical studies in film and television; media writing; media management
Special Activities: Film: film series; film societies. Television: program material produced for local public and commercial television stations and cable television
Facilities: Film: screening rooms; editing suites. Television: studios; audio bays; control rooms; video editing suites
Equipment: Film: complete 16mm. Television/Video: complete 1" studio; complete VHS and S-VHS location
Alumni: Jay Russell, film writer/

director; Craig Leake, TV producer/cameraman

GUIDE POV: Narrative and documentary film/video as well as television studio production training are part of a diverse curriculum with additional courses in directing, screenwriting, and aesthetics; interrelated training in theatre, music, and art available; competitive admissions; cross-registration with area colleges and universities; study abroad in England and Spain; media internship opportunities

MIDDLE TENNESSEE STATE UNIVERSITY

E. Main St.,
Murfreesboro, TN 37132
(615)898–2300

State four-year comprehensive institution. Coed, small town location. Undergraduate enrollment: 17,000. Graduate enrollment: 1,500.

DEPARTMENT OF RADIO-TELEVISION/ PHOTOGRAPHY

Chair/Contact: Elliott A. Pood, Chair
Calendar: Semesters
Degrees Offered: B.S., mass communications (with emphasis in radio-television or photography); M.S., mass communications
Departmental Majors: Undergraduate radio and television: 400 students
Entrance Requirements:
Undergraduate: 2.0 grade-point average; ACT required, with a minimum score of 19; recommendations. Undergraduate application deadline: July 1. 88% of those who apply
Curricular Emphasis: Radio-television majors may select a specialty area in

broadcast journalism, broadcast production, or broadcast management; digital imaging/animation
Special Activities: Television: program material produced for cable television
Facilities: Television/Video: three studios; audio bays; control rooms; video editing suites; 39-ft. mobile production lab. Radio: two FM radio stations
Equipment: Television/Video: three complete Beta, D2, Hi-8 studios and location
Alumni: Diane Crabtree, TV producer; David Ivy, TV master control engineer; Tracy Moore, TV assignment editor

GUIDE POV: Separate tracks in broadcast production, journalism, and management are available to undergraduates at this state university; program offers a blend of mass media studies and extensive hands-on television and radio broadcast training; practical emphasis; graduate studies in media management, law, and regulation; cross-registration with Tennessee State University; internship opportunities in television and radio production

NASHVILLE STATE TECHNICAL INSTITUTE

120 White Bridge Rd.,
Nashville, TN 37209
(615)353–3333

State two-year comprehensive institution. Coed, suburban location. Enrollment: 6,000.

AUDIO VISUAL TECHNOLOGY

Chair/Contact: John Chastain
Calendar: Semesters
Degrees Offered: A.A., visual communication; photography certificate
Departmental Majors: 200 students
Entrance Requirements: High school diploma or equivalent. Application deadline: rolling
Curricular Emphasis: Television/ Video production
Facilities: Television: studio; audio bay; control room; editing room; film processing laboratory
Equipment: Television/Video: complete six-camera ¾" studio; complete ¾" and ½" location
Alumni: Robert Deaton, cinematographer; Catherine O'Bryant, photography teacher; Chris Amacher, audio visual specialist

GUIDE POV: Accessible to all high school graduates, this technical college offers a two-year practical program in video/television production; hands-on training by working professionals; internship opportunities in television production

TENNESSEE WESLEYAN COLLEGE

Box 281TWC, Athens, TN 37303
(615)745–7504

Private four-year comprehensive institution. Coed, urban location. Undergraduate enrollment: 2,600. Graduate enrollment: 500.

MASS COMMUNICATIONS DEPARTMENT

Chair/Contact: Tom King, Chair
Calendar: Semesters
Degrees Offered: B.A., mass communications
Departmental Majors: Undergraduate television: 20 students
Entrance Requirements: Undergraduate: 2.0 grade-point average; ACT or SAT scores;

recommendations. Undergraduate application deadline: rolling. Percent of acceptances: 83%

Curricular Emphasis: Electronic media theory and culture; basic video production including news and instructional programming; public relations and advertising

Special Activities: Film: film series. Television: program material produced for local cable television

Facilities: Film: screening room

Equipment: Television/Video: complete ½" location

Alumni: Lance Linsell, CNN TV news producer; Debbie Dunbar, radio news producer

GUIDE POV: Students attending this small nonprofit college may choose a major in mass communications that emphasizes broadcast history, performance, writing, and management; video production curriculum emphasizes news reporting on location; study abroad in Japan, France, and England; internship opportunities in television production

---

UNION UNIVERSITY

Highway 45 Bypass,
Jackson, TN 38305
(901)668–1818

Private four-year comprehensive institution. Coed, suburban location. Enrollment: 2,000.

COMMUNICATION ARTS DEPARTMENT

Chair/Contact: Dr. Kina Mallard, Chair

Calendar: 4–1–4

Degrees Offered: B.A., communication arts (students may select emphasis in journalism,

broadcasting, speech-theatre, or public relations-advertising)

Departmental Majors: Television: 80 students

Entrance Requirements: 2.5 grade-point average; ACT (preferred) or SAT testing, with minimum scores of 20 or a composite score of 820, respectively. Application deadline: rolling. Percent of acceptances: 70%

Curricular Emphasis: Electronic media theory and culture; critical studies in film; media writing; television production; media management

Special Activities: Television: program material produced for cable television

Facilities: Film: screening room; editing suite. Television/Video: studio; audio bay; control room; video editing suites

Equipment: Film: projectors; lighting. Television/Video: complete ¾" studio; complete ¾" and ½" location

Alumni: John Dancy, NBC TV news correspondent

GUIDE POV: Undergraduates attending this small, competitive private university are offered an emphasis in broadcast television production within a broad communication arts curriculum; emphasis on writing for mass media, broadcast management, and television production; cross-registration with Lambuth and Free-Hardeman colleges; internship opportunities in television production

---

UNIVERSITY OF TENNESSEE AT CHATTANOOGA

615 McCallie Ave.,
Chattanooga, TN 37403–2598
(615)755–4111

State four-year comprehensive institution. Coed, urban location. Undergraduate enrollment: 6,300. Graduate enrollment: 1,400.

DEPARTMENT OF COMMUNICATION

Chair/Contact: Dr. Kittrell Rushing, Chair
Calendar: Semesters
Degrees Offered: B.A., communication (students may select emphasis in broadcasting and electronic media or broadcast journalism)
Departmental Majors: Undergraduate television: 125 students
Entrance Requirements: Undergraduate: 2.75 grade-point average; ACT or SAT scores. Undergraduate application deadline: August 15. Percent of acceptances: 59%
Curricular Emphasis: Electronic media theory and culture; media writing; television/video production
Special Activities: Television: program material produced for cable television includes newscasts, commercials, and public service/promotional announcements
Facilities: Television/Video: studio; audio bay; control room; video editing suites
Equipment: Television/Video: complete ¾" studio; complete ¾" and ½" location
Alumni: Mark Peace, TV sports director; Elbert Tucker, TV news producer; Jamarva McKinley, TV broadcast engineer

GUIDE POV: Part of the state university system, the University of Tennessee at Chattanooga offers comprehensive training to students pursuing careers in broadcast journalism; strong liberal arts curriculum; competitive entry; all communication majors must complete a minor in one department outside the program; study abroad in England; internship opportunities in television production

UNIVERSITY OF TENNESSEE AT KNOXVILLE

Knoxville, TN 37996–0220
(615)974–1000

State four-year comprehensive institution. Coed, urban location. Undergraduate enrollment: 22,000. Graduate enrollment: 7,000.

COLLEGE OF COMMUNICATIONS, DEPARTMENT OF BROADCASTING

Chair/Contact: Broadcasting: Dhyana Ziegler
Calendar: Semesters
Degrees Offered: B.A., broadcasting, journalism, advertising; M.S., Ph.D., communications
Departmental Majors: Undergraduate television: 400 students. Graduate television: 40 students
Entrance Requirements: Undergraduate: 2.3 grade-point average; ACT or SAT scores. Graduate: 3.2 grade-point average; GRE scores; recommendations; statement of purpose. Undergraduate and graduate application deadline: July 1. Percent of acceptances: Undergraduate: 72%. Graduate: 65%
Curricular Emphasis: Undergraduate: electronic media theory and culture; news writing; television production; media management; advertising and public relations; radio broadcasting. Graduate: emphasis on broadcast production, management, programming, and research
Special Activities: Television: program material produced for local

public and commercial television stations as well as for cable television **Facilities:** Television/Video: studio; audio bay; control room; video editing suites; Communications Research Center

Equipment: Film: 16mm lighting; projectors. Television/Video: complete 1" and ¾" studio; complete ¾" and ½" location

Alumni: Melissa Carter, TV administrative assistant; Tony Hudson, TV news anchor/reporter; Cassandra McGee, TV news reporter

GUIDE POV: The original campus of the state university system founded in 1794 has been offering communication courses since 1923; a separate College of Communications was organized in 1969; the broadcasting major provides practical production training with core requirements in the liberal arts, as well as required courses in broadcast regulations, management, and history; emphasis on news journalism; cross-registration available through the Academic Common Market, a southern 14-state consortium of colleges and universities; study abroad in Europe; accelerated study; internship opportunities in television and radio production

UNIVERSITY OF TENNESSEE AT MARTIN

University St., Martin, TN 38238–5099
(901)587–7000

State four-year comprehensive institution. Coed, rural location. Undergraduate enrollment: 5,400. Graduate enrollment: 200.

COMMUNICATION DEPARTMENT

Chair/Contact: Ralph R. Donald, Chair
Calendar: Semesters
Degrees Offered: B.A., B.S., communications
Departmental Majors: Undergraduate television: 100 students
Entrance Requirements: Undergraduate: 2.0 grade-point average; ACT or SAT scores; interview; portfolio. Undergraduate application deadline: April 1. Percent of acceptances: 82%
Curricular Emphasis: Broadcasting, print journalism, and public relations
Special Activities: Television: students produce programming for on-campus public television station and for local cable television; Media Day brings students together with 60–70 media professionals every year to discuss career goals and opportunities
Facilities: Television/Radio: three studios; audio studios; control rooms; editing suites; two radio stations; film/video library
Equipment: Television/Video: three complete ¾" studios and locations; transportation van
Alumni: Terry Goulder, TV producer; Mark Gray, TV executive; Terry Hailey, broadcasting executive

GUIDE POV: This well-equipped state-supported university offers comprehensive studies in broadcast journalism within a liberal arts context; early exposure to hands-on production training; study abroad; honors program; internship opportunities in television and radio production

VANDERBILT UNIVERSITY

Nashville, TN 37240–2701
(615)322–7311

Private four-year comprehensive institution. Coed, urban location. Undergraduate enrollment: 5,200. Graduate enrollment: 4,000.

COMMUNICATION STUDIES AND THEATRE DEPARTMENT

Chair/Contact: Kassian A. Kovalcheck, Jr., Chair; film: Robert A. Baldwin
Calendar: Semesters
Degrees Offered: B.A., B.S.
Departmental Majors: There is no major in film or television
Entrance Requirements: Undergraduate: ACT or SAT scores; ATs are required in English composition, math level I, II or IIc, and one other area. Undergraduate application deadline: January 15. Percent of acceptances: 54%
Curricular Emphasis: Film history, theory/aesthetics, and criticism
Special Activities: Film/Video: summer film and video festival
Facilities: Film: film/video library
Equipment: Film: Super-8 cameras
Alumni: Delbert Mann, film/TV director/producer; Dinah Shore, TV/film performer/actress; Tom Schulman, screenwriter; Bradley Wigor, film/TV writer/producer

GUIDE POV: Vanderbilt University offers undergraduates an interdepartmental, individually structured program in the liberal arts, with a possible emphasis on film history, theory/aesthetics, and criticism; selective admissions; study abroad in five countries; cross-registration offered with Fisk and Howard universities

Opportunity. For me, that's what film school is all about. Having access to equipment and facilities, not to mention the talents, insights, and personalities of fellow students and faculty, means endless resources. The charged atmosphere will help you mature both as an individual and as a team player. Plus, you'll make friends for life.

It's important to find a quality school that allows you the creative freedom to experiment, whether by giving you leeway to make original artistic statements, providing access to new technologies such as high definition television and interactive media, or simply presenting the opportunity to pitch your personal story ideas to visiting industry executives.

Reflecting on my own experiences, I'd have this advice to offer anyone seriously considering a career in film or video: 1. Be realistic about the sacrifices and workload. 2. Expect to keep learning for the rest of your life. And 3. Don't quit.

ABILENE CHRISTIAN UNIVERSITY

1600 Campus Ct., Abilene, TX 79699
(915)674–2000

*Private four-year comprehensive
institution. Coed, urban location.
Undergraduate enrollment: 4,000.
Graduate enrollment: 550.*

DEPARTMENT OF JOURNALISM AND
MASS COMMUNICATION, DIVISION OF
TELECOMMUNICATIONS

Chair/Contact: Professor Dutch
Hoggatt, Director
Calendar: Semesters
Degrees Offered: B.A., B.S.
Departmental Majors: Undergraduate
television: 60 students
Entrance Requirements:
Undergraduate: transcripts; 2.0 grade-
point average; ACT required, with
minimum score of 19; ATs in English
composition and essay, math level II,
and a foreign language are required;
letters of reference; interview
recommended; GED accepted.
Undergraduate application deadline:
rolling. Percent of acceptances: 99%
Curricular Emphasis: Electronic
media theory and culture; media
writing; television production; religious
programming; media management;
corporate video production; broadcast
journalism
Special Activities: Television:
program material produced for on-
campus closed-circuit television station
KLGP as well as KUF-TV7, a low-power
television station; ACU-Video produces
video cassettes, especially for the
Christian market
Facilities: Television/Video: studio;
audio bay; control room; video editing
suites
Equipment: Television/Video:
complete ¾" studio; complete ¾" and
½" location
Alumni: Ed Bailey, broadcasting
executive; Mike Blanton, media
executive; Regina Gilmore Burns,
broadcasting journalist; Nelson Coates,
TV art director

GUIDE POV: Journalism and mass
communication majors at this private
nonprofit university may choose from
several concentrations, including
corporate video production, religious
broadcasting, broadcast production,
and broadcast journalism; students
receive extensive hands-on
telecommunications training coupled
with courses in media writing and
mass communication theory; cross-
registration with Hardin-Simmons,
McMurry, and Texas Tech universities;
study abroad in England, France, and
Spain; internship opportunities in
television and radio production

AMARILLO COLLEGE

P.O. Box 447,
Amarillo, TX 79178–0001
(806)371–5000

District two-year comprehensive institution. Coed, suburban location. Enrollment: 5,300.

RADIO-TELEVISION PRODUCTION

Chair/Contact: Danita McAnally, Chair
Calendar: Semesters
Degrees Offered: A.A.S., radio-television production; A.A., mass communication with concentration in radio-television
Departmental Majors: Television: 70 students
Entrance Requirements: Open-door policy; high school graduate or equivalent. Application deadline: rolling. Percent of acceptances: 99%
Curricular Emphasis: Television and radio broadcast production with an emphasis on news/documentary
Special Activities: Television: program material produced for on-campus closed-circuit television and KACV-TV, the Texas Panhandle's public television station located on campus
Facilities: Television/Video: studio; audio bay; control room; video editing suites
Equipment: Television/Video: complete 1" and ¾" studio; complete ¾" location
Alumni: Royce Ellis, TV production manager; James Bearden, TV newscast director; Elisa Harrison, TV producer/corporate executive

GUIDE POV: Designed to prepare students for entry positions at television and radio stations and in the field of advertising, this two-year degree program emphasizes practical television/video and radio production training; separate degree program provides students with core requirements for transfer to four-year schools; all production students participate in a variety of studio and remote projects; internship opportunities in television and radio production

BAYLOR UNIVERSITY

Waco, TX 76798–7368
(817)755–1011

Private four-year comprehensive institution. Coed, urban location. Undergraduate enrollment: 11,000. Graduate enrollment: 1,000.

COMMUNICATION STUDIES DEPARTMENT

Chair/Contact: Dr. Corey Carbonara
Calendar: Semesters
Degrees Offered: B.A., M.A.
Departmental Majors: Undergraduate: 240 students. Graduate: eight students
Entrance Requirements: Undergraduate: academic rank within top half of graduating class; ACT (minimum 25) or SAT (minimum composite 1000) scores. Graduate: 3.0 grade-point average. Undergraduate and graduate application deadline: May 1. Percent of acceptances: 88%
Curricular Emphasis: Film, video, and television production; new communication technologies; media processes and effects
Special Activities: Film and video: research in new media technologies
Facilities: Television/Video: studio; audio bay; control room; video editing suites
Equipment: Film: complete Super-8 and 16mm. Television/Video: 1" studio; complete ¾" and ½" location
Alumni: Brian Greene, video producer/director; Frank Patterson, film/TV teacher; Walt Wilkins, film

coordinator for the state of Texas; Tim Bird, TV executive

GUIDE POV: This private university offers a competitive communications program that emphasizes advanced research in new media technologies; study abroad in Russia, Germany, Spain, Israel, and Great Britain; student and faculty exchange programs with universities in the Far East; research and internship opportunities in film and video

CONCORDIA LUTHERAN COLLEGE

3400 Interstate 35 N.,
Austin, TX 78705
(512)452–7661

Private four-year comprehensive institution. Coed, urban location. Enrollment: 700.

COMMUNICATION DEPARTMENT

Chair/Contact: Dr. John H. Frahm
Calendar: Semesters
Degrees Offered: B.A., communication (students may select emphasis in television)
Departmental Majors: Television: 90 students
Entrance Requirements: 2.5 grade-point average; ACT (minimum 14) or SAT (minimum composite 750) scores; interview; recommendations; written statement of purpose. Application deadline: May 30. Percent of acceptances: 75%
Curricular Emphasis: Electronic media theory and culture; media writing; television production; media management
Special Activities: Film: film series/festivals. Television: program material produced for local public television

station; college-operated ITFS broadcast center
Facilities: Television: studio; audio bay; control room
Equipment: Television/Video: complete ¾" studio and ½" location; ENG editing; Beta equipment; some conversion to S-VHS
Alumni: Diane Kerns, TV network news producer; Michael Broyles, TV producer; Linda Nabors, computer support specialist

GUIDE POV: This well-equipped, selective communications program encourages student participation at all levels in a variety of studio and ENG field projects; attention to individual interests; study abroad in Mexico; media internships available

CORPUS CHRISTI STATE UNIVERSITY

6300 Ocean Dr., ·
Corpus Christi, TX 78412
(512)991–6810

State junior and senior level institution. Coed, urban location. Undergraduate enrollment: 2,400. Graduate: 2,000.

CENTER FOR THE ARTS

Chair/Contact: TV/Film: William O. Huie, Jr., Chair
Calendar: Semesters
Degrees Offered: B.A., communication arts (student may select emphasis in television-film); M.A., interdisciplinary study (component in television-film)
Departmental Majors: Undergraduate TV-film: 35 students. Graduate interdisciplinary studies major with TV-film component: five students
Entrance Requirements: Undergraduate: all entering students

must have completed 60 semester credit hours of academic course work at a regionally accredited junior college, senior college, or university other than CCSU in order to be considered for admission.
Graduate: GRE scores of 1000 or adequate combination of GRE and GPA for last 60 hours of undergraduate study; written statement of purpose; recommendations. Undergraduate and graduate application deadline: rolling. Percent of acceptances: 90%
Curricular Emphasis: Undergraduate: electronic media theory and culture; film history, theory/aesthetics, and criticism; broadcast news writing and performance; Super-8 and television/video production. Graduate: communication theory
Special Activities: Film: film series/festivals. Television: program material produced for cable television
Facilities: Film: editing suite. Television/Video: studio; control room; video editing suites
Equipment: Film: complete Super-8. Television/Video: complete ¾" studio and ½" location; switcher/special effects generator
Alumni: Frank Van Heugten, TV/film director/production manager; T. C. Smith, screenwriter; Sonya Lopez, video producer

GUIDE POV: Corpus Christi State University is designed for the undergraduate who has already completed the freshman and sophomore years of college; students selecting the TV-film concentration develop basic production skills while receiving formal training in film/television history and criticism; production emphasis on broadcast journalism and the documentary form; internship opportunities in television production

HOUSTON BAPTIST UNIVERSITY

7502 Fondren, Houston, TX 77074
(713)774-7661

Private four-year comprehensive institution. Coed, suburban location. Enrollment: 2,500.

COMMUNICATIONS DEPARTMENT

Chair/Contact: Dr. James S. Taylor
Calendar: Quarters
Degrees Offered: B.A., B.S.
Departmental Majors: Speech, 60 students; mass media, 70 students
Entrance Requirements: Transcripts; 900 minimum composite SAT scores. Application deadline: rolling. Percent of acceptances: 50%
Curricular Emphasis: Media major with print and electronic concentrations
Special Activities: Television: program material produced for microwave ITFS system
Facilities: Film: 35mm screening facilities; screening room. Television: studio; control room; editing suite
Equipment: Television/Video: complete ¾" studio; complete ¾" and ½" location
Alumni: Maria Barron, film producer; Leslie Hill, TV news anchor/reporter; Doug Harris, TV marketing executive

GUIDE POV: A small program in media studies with hands-on broadcast and nonbroadcast video production training is offered at this competitive private university; print and electronic concentrations; individual attention to student projects; extensive media internship opportunities

NAVARRO COLLEGE

3200 W. 7th Ave.,
Corsicana, TX 75110
(903)874–6501

State and county supported two-year institution. Coed, rural location. Enrollment: 2,000.

RADIO AND TELEVISION BROADCASTING

Chair/Contact: Jerry V. Zumwalt, Director
Calendar: Semesters
Degrees Offered: A.A., radio/television broadcasting; A.A.S., radio/television production
Departmental Majors: 45 students
Entrance Requirements: Open-door policy. Application deadline: rolling
Curricular Emphasis: Radio and television production and technology
Special Activities: Film: film series/festivals. Television: students produce various programs for broadcast at college-operated television station (low-power Channel 30) with satellite uplink
Facilities: Television: two full-color studios; audio bays; control rooms; teleconference center; four-track recording studio; satellite uplink
Equipment: Television: complete ¾" studios; complete ¾" and ½" location
Alumni: Annette Gonzales, TV news anchor; Stephen Chudej, TV costume designer

GUIDE POV: This small, program offers hands-on broadcast production training in radio and television, and has provided an avenue to broadcast careers for low-income students; transfer program for students planning transfer to four-year institutions; media internship opportunities

PRAIRIE VIEW A&M UNIVERSITY

P.O. Box 8156,
Prairie View, TX 77446–0156
(409)857–3311

State four-year comprehensive institution. Coed, rural location. Undergraduate enrollment: 5,000. Graduate enrollment: 1,000.

DEPARTMENT OF COMMUNICATIONS

Chair/Contact: Dr. Millard F. Eiland; Carol Means
Calendar: Semesters
Degrees Offered: B.A.
Departmental Majors:
Undergraduate: 235 students
Entrance Requirements:
Undergraduate: 2.0 grade-point average; ACT (minimum 15) or SAT (minimum composite 700) scores. Undergraduate application deadline: August 1. Percent of acceptances: 65%
Curricular Emphasis: Mass communications; media writing; audio-video production; media management
Special Activities: Television: program material produced for media art exhibit; industrial training
Facilities: Television: studio; audio bay; control room
Equipment: Television/Video: complete ¾" studio and location
Alumni: Charles Williams, TV editor; Janet Campbell, TV production assistant; Shawn Wade, TV production assistant

GUIDE POV: Practical professional training for commercial media employment is offered to communications students at this state university; internship opportunities in television production

RICE UNIVERSITY

Houston, TX 77251
(713)527–8101

*Private four-year comprehensive
institution. Coed, urban location.
Undergraduate enrollment: 3,000.
Graduate enrollment: 1,000.*

THE MEDIA CENTER

Chair/Contact: Brian Huberman
Calendar: Semesters
Degrees Offered: B.A., B.F.A., art and
art history (emphasis in film)
Departmental Majors: Undergraduate
film: seven students
Entrance Requirements:
Undergraduate: official transcripts;
competitive grade-point average; the
SAT is required; three ATs, including
English composition, are required;
interview recommended; personal
essay required. Undergraduate
application deadline: January 2.
Percent of acceptances: 20%
Curricular Emphasis: Electronic
media theory and culture; film theory/
aesthetics, history, and criticism; film
and video production within a visual/
media arts context
Special Activities: Film: film series/
festivals. Television: program material
produced for local public television
station
Facilities: Film/Video: 35mm
screening facilities; screening room;
editing suite; sound mixing room;
animation stand; film/video library
Equipment: Film: complete Super-8
and 16mm; 35mm projectors.
Television/Video: complete ¾" and ½"
location
Alumni: Mark Brice, cinematographer;
Brad Walker, video engineer/designer;
Amy Hobby, assistant cinematographer

GUIDE POV: Rice University offers
comprehensive film and video studies
within a visual/media arts context;
students produce experimental,
narrative, documentary, and animated
works; highly selective admissions;
cross-registration with a variety of area
colleges and universities; extensive
study abroad program; limited number
of internships available in film and
video production

SAM HOUSTON STATE UNIVERSITY

Box 2207, Huntsville, TX 77341
(409)294–1111

*State four-year comprehensive
institution. Coed, suburban location.
Undergraduate enrollment: 11,000.
Graduate enrollment: 1,000.*

RADIO-TELEVISION-FILM DEPARTMENT

Chair/Contact: Dr. Robert E. Eubanks,
Program Coordinator
Calendar: Semesters
Degrees Offered: B.A., B.F.A., radio-
television-film (students may choose
emphasis in production, broadcast
journalism, advertising, marketing and
management, or promotion and public
relations)
Departmental Majors: Undergraduate
film-radio-television: 400 students
Entrance Requirements:
Undergraduate: ACT or SAT testing,
with a minimum score of 21 or
composite score of 900, respectively;
interview recommended.
Undergraduate application deadline:
rolling. Percent of acceptances: 68%
Curricular Emphasis: Electronic
media theory and culture; critical
studies in film; media writing; audio-
film-video production; media
management; public relations

Special Activities: Film: screenings; film societies. Television: program material produced for student-operated Cable Channel 7
Facilities: Film: screening room; sound stage. Television/Video: three studios; two audio bays; three control rooms; video editing suites
Equipment: Film: Super-8 and 16mm cameras and lighting; no editing equipment available on campus. Television/Video: complete ¾" studio and ½" location; editing formats in ¾", VHS, and S-VHS
Alumni: Dan Rather, CBS TV news anchor; Dana Andrews; film actor

GUIDE POV: Since 1975, this competitive media program has offered concentrations in production and broadcast journalism; film courses are theory-oriented; diverse electronic media course listings include training in sports and special events coverage; various program material produced for campus television and radio stations; media management studies; internship opportunities in film, television, and radio production

SAN ANTONIO COLLEGE

1300 San Pedro,
San Antonio, TX 78212
(210)733–2000

District two-year institution. Coed, urban location. Enrollment: 22,000.

RADIO-TV-FILM DEPARTMENT

Chair/Contact: Tiana Spivey, Program Coordinator
Calendar: Semesters
Degrees Offered: A.A., A.A.S., radio-TV-film

Departmental Majors: Radio-TV-film: 300 students
Entrance Requirements: Open-door policy; high school diploma or equivalent. Application deadline: rolling. Percent of acceptances: 99%
Curricular Emphasis: Electronic media theory and hands-on production; media writing; film production; news writing and production; television production; audio production
Special Activities: Video: on-campus production company for special student projects. Radio: on-campus, licensed KSYM-FM radio station
Facilities: Film: editing suites. Television/Video: studio; control room; video editing suites; audio production rooms and multitrack recording room
Equipment: Film: complete Super-8. Television/Video: complete ½" studio and location
Alumni: David Przybylski, film/TV producer/director; Fred Chappa, media specialist/teacher; Diane De Los Santos, media editor

GUIDE POV: Students attending this community college may produce works in film as well as video; all film production courses taught with Super-8 equipment; both career and transfer tracks available; good record of placing graduates in local media market; internship opportunities in television and radio production

SOUTH PLAINS COLLEGE

1401 College Ave.,
Levelland, TX 79336
(806)894–9611

District two-year institution. Coed, suburban location. Enrollment: 4,000.

TELECOMMUNICATIONS DEPARTMENT

Chair/Contact: Television: John Sparks
Calendar: Semesters
Degrees Offered: A.A., A.A.S., telecommunications
Departmental Majors: Radio and television: 60 students
Entrance Requirements: Open-door policy; high school diploma or equivalent. Application deadline: rolling. Percent of acceptances: 99%
Curricular Emphasis: Television/Video production with an emphasis on broadcast journalism and corporate video
Special Activities: Television: program material produced for on-campus closed-circuit television
Facilities: Television/Video: studio; audio bay; control room; video editing suites
Equipment: Television/Video: complete ¾" studio and location
Alumni: Robin Grevelle, TV news director; Kevin Smith, TV investigative reporter; Elaine Quezada, TV producer

GUIDE POV: South Plains College offers telecommunications students a practical two-year program preparing them for technical support positions in the media industry; strong emphasis on radio-television news production, writing, and announcing; TV practicum in documentary production; internship opportunities in television and radio production

SOUTHERN METHODIST UNIVERSITY

Dallas, TX 75275
(214)768–2000

Private four-year comprehensive institution. Coed, suburban location.

Undergraduate enrollment: 6,000.
Graduate enrollment: 4,000.

CENTER FOR COMMUNICATION ARTS

Chair/Contact: Film: Donald Pasquella; television: Lynn Gartley
Calendar: Semesters
Degrees Offered: B.F.A., cinema; B.A., TV/radio; M.A., communication
Departmental Majors: Undergraduate film: 60 students. Undergraduate television: 75 students. Graduate television: 15 students
Entrance Requirements: Undergraduate: 2.5 grade-point average; ACT or SAT scores; interview; written statement of purpose. Graduate: 3.0 grade-point average; GRE scores; written statement of purpose; recommendations. Undergraduate application deadline: January 15. Graduate application deadline: rolling. Percent of acceptances: undergraduate: 65%. Graduate: 50%
Curricular Emphasis: Electronic media theory and culture; critical studies in film; media writing; audio-film-video production; media management
Special Activities: Film: film series/festivals; Southwest Film Archive. Television: program material produced for on-campus closed-circuit television
Facilities: Film: 35mm screening facilities; screening room; sound mixing room; six editing suites; film archive; film projection hall. Video/Radio: studio; audio bay; control room; video editing suites; two video logging rooms; seven basic video/audio modules; graphics lab; teaching radio studio; 16-track audio sweetening rooms; production classrooms; three off-line editing rooms; window dubbing
Equipment: Film: complete Super-8 and 16mm. Television/Video: complete

1" and ¾" studio; complete ¾" and ½" location

Alumni: Maryann Razzouk, TV news reporter; Dina Steele, PBS news reporter

GUIDE POV: This private university offers degree programs in both film and video production that combine technical, creative, historical, and economic studies; graduate program in media management; very selective admissions; study abroad in Japan, Italy, Denmark, Spain, Russia, France, and Austria; summer SMU-in-London Communications Program; extensive internship opportunities for pay and/or credit in film, television, and radio production

---

SOUTHWESTERN ADVENTIST COLLEGE

Keene, TX 76059
(817)645–3921

Private four-year comprehensive institution. Coed, small town location. Enrollment: 1,000.

COMMUNICATION DEPARTMENT

Chair/Contact: Herbert J. Roth, Chair; John D. Williams
Calendar: Semesters
Degrees Offered: B.A., B.S., communication (students may select emphasis in broadcasting, corporate communication, journalism, or speech)
Departmental Majors: Television: 50 students
Entrance Requirements: Open-door policy; ACT or SAT scores. Application deadline: rolling. Percent of acceptances: 99%
Curricular Emphasis: Electronic media theory and culture; critical studies in film; media writing; audio-film-video production; media management
Special Activities: Film: film series/festivals. Television: program material produced for cable television
Facilities: Film: editing suite. Television/Video: audio studio; video laboratory
Equipment: Film: complete 16mm (silent). Television/Video: complete ½" location
Alumni: Sheridan Adams, associate TV producer; Kevin Emerson, associate TV producer; Tim Hines, TV editor; Donna Webb, assistant director of TV development

GUIDE POV: Located near Fort Worth, this Seventh-Day Adventist college offers students basic television/video production training along with course listings in mass media history, theory, and management; emphasis on broadcast journalism and documentary production; college enjoys special ties to local cable station; basic film production training available; high placement record for graduates within area media industries; study abroad may be arranged in Spain, France, or Germany through the Adventist Colleges Abroad Program; internship opportunities in television and radio production

---

TARRANT COUNTY JUNIOR COLLEGE

Northeast Campus,
828 Harwood Rd.,
Hurst, TX 76054
(817)281–7860

County two-year institution. Coed, urban location. Enrollment: 26,000.

COMMUNICATION ARTS DEPARTMENT/ MEDIA COMMUNICATIONS PROGRAM

Chair/Contact: Lawrence Baker, Coordinator of media communications program
Calendar: Semesters
Degrees Offered: A.A.S., media communications (students may select emphasis in television)
Departmental Majors: Television: 90 students
Entrance Requirements: Open-door policy; official transcripts; TASP (Texas Academic Skills Program) testing used to determine placement. Application deadline: rolling. Percent of acceptances: 99%
Curricular Emphasis: Electronic media theory and culture; critical studies in film; media writing; film and television/video production
Special Activities: Film: film series/ student screenings. Television: program material produced for cable television; district-wide ITFS station
Facilities: Film: screening room; editing suite; sound mixing room; animation stand; film library. Television/Video: studio; audio bay; control room; video editing suites
Equipment: Film: complete Super-8. Television/Video: complete ¾", ½", Beta, and Hi-8mm studio and location
Alumni: Gerald Albrecht, TV production specialist; Kristin Rister, TV production assistant

GUIDE POV: Tarrant County Junior College is a large, comprehensive community college with locations at three urban campuses; the media communications program is designed to train students in all aspects of television production; emphasis in training for corporate/industrial market; some film production training available; diverse course listings include those in film animation and video art; internship opportunities in television production

---

TEXAS CHRISTIAN UNIVERSITY

Box 30793, Fort Worth, TX 76129
(817)921-7000

Private four-year comprehensive institution. Coed, urban location. Undergraduate enrollment: 6,000. Graduate enrollment: 1,000.

DEPARTMENT OF RADIO/TV/FILM

Chair/Contact: John Freeman, Chair
Calendar: Semesters
Degrees Offered: B.S., radio/TV/film, broadcast journalism; M.S., media studies
Departmental Majors:
Undergraduate: 240 students. Graduate: 16 students
Entrance Requirements:
Undergraduate: 3.0 grade-point average; ACT or SAT scores; essay required; interview recommended. Graduate: 3.0 grade-point average; GRE scores (minimum 1000 cumulative); recommendations; written statement of purpose. Undergraduate and graduate application deadline: February 15. Percent of acceptances: 80%
Curricular Emphasis: Electronic media theory and culture; critical studies in film; broadcast journalism; audio-video production; broadcast management
Special Activities: Film: film series/ festivals. Television: program material produced for cable television and local commercial television station; AERho chapter
Facilities: Film: screening room; editing suite; sound mixing room;

animation stand; 6,000-film library. Television: two studios; audio bays; control rooms; editing suites; multimedia studio; multitrack studio
Equipment: Film: complete Super-8 and 16mm. Television/Video: complete ¾" studio; complete ¾" and ½" location including EFP/ENG; multimedia equipment
Alumni: Scott Tobin, film producer; Scott Wilson, cinematographer

GUIDE POV: Affiliated with the Disciples of Christ, Texas Christian University is a private teaching and research institution offering a selective communications program; stress on broadcast production and critical/cultural studies; study abroad in eight European cities as well as in Singapore and Japan; various research opportunities and a Disney media internship program available for qualified majors

TEXAS SOUTHERN UNIVERSITY

3100 Cleburne, Houston, TX 77004
(713)527–7011

State four-year comprehensive institution. Coed, urban location. Undergraduate enrollment: 7,500. Graduate enrollment: 1,000.

DEPARTMENT OF COMMUNICATIONS

Chair/Contact: Television: Dr. James W. Ward, Chair; Samuel Andrews
Calendar: Semesters
Degrees Offered: B.A., B.S., B.F.A., communications (students may select emphasis in telecommunications, theatre/cinema, speech communication, or journalism); M.A., communications
Departmental Majors: Undergraduate

film studies: 10 students. Undergraduate television: 300 students. Graduate television: 50 students
Entrance Requirements:
Undergraduate: open-door policy; high school diploma or equivalent; 2.0 grade-point average; ACT or SAT recommended. Graduate: GRE scores; teachers' recommendations. Undergraduate application deadline: August 21. Graduate application deadline: rolling. Percent of acceptances: Undergraduate: 99%. Graduate: 80%
Curricular Emphasis: Electronic media theory and culture; television production; critical film studies; media management
Special Activities: Television: program material produced for on-campus closed-circuit television
Facilities: Film: screening room. Television/Video: studio; audio bay; control room; video editing suites
Equipment: Television/Video: complete ¾" studio and ½" location
Alumni: Vivian Isom, TV news director; Frederic W. Strond, film producer; Steven James, TV production manager

GUIDE POV: Offering a comprehensive media program, this state university provides students with hands-on experience producing news and documentary television programming; film studies emphasis; graduate studies in media management and communication theory; study abroad in Africa; internship opportunities in television production

TEXAS TECH UNIVERSITY

Box 43082, Lubbock, TX 79409
(806)742–2011

State four-year comprehensive institution. Coed, urban location. Undergraduate enrollment: 24,000. Graduate enrollment: 4,000.

TELECOMMUNICATIONS DIVISION, SCHOOL OF MASS COMMUNICATIONS

Chair/Contact: Dennis A. Harp
Calendar: Semesters
Degrees Offered: B.A., telecommunications; M.A., mass communications
Departmental Majors: Undergraduate corporate video: 20 students. Undergraduate television: 100 students. Graduate communications: 30 students
Entrance Requirements: Undergraduate: 2.5 grade-point average; ACT or SAT scores. Graduate: combination GRE scores and grade-point average; average GRE score 1000–1200; TOEFL score 550 minimum for international students. Undergraduate application deadline: rolling; entrance exams should be taken before July 1. Graduate application deadline: rolling. Percent of acceptances: 80%
Curricular Emphasis: Media sales, management, and promotion; corporate telecommunications; broadcast journalism
Special Activities: Television: program material produced for local public television station; Mass Communications Week
Facilities: Television: two studios, 40' × 60' and 30' × 40'; audio bays; control rooms; five editing bays; multi-image lab
Equipment: Television/Video: complete ¾" studio and location; ¾", super-Beta, S-VHS editing equipment; Grass Valley switcher; stereo audio including DAT; Laird CG
Alumni: David Dea, cable TV executive; Barry Propes, network radio production director; Dusty Rector, multimedia executive; Keith Sommer, TV station general manager

GUIDE POV: Students attending this large public university are offered a communications major with both undergraduate and graduate specializations in television/video production and management; degree programs are AEJMC accredited; accelerated degree program; local and state internship opportunities in television, corporate video, and radio production

---

TEXAS WESLEYAN UNIVERSITY

1201 Wesleyan St.,
Fort Worth, TX 76105
(817)531–4444

Private four-year comprehensive institution. Coed, urban location. Enrollment: 1,500.

DEPARTMENT OF MASS COMMUNICATION

Chair/Contact: Dr. Michael Sewell, Chair
Calendar: Semesters
Degrees Offered: B.S.
Departmental Majors: 91 students
Entrance Requirements: 2.0 grade-point average; ACT (minimum 19) or SAT (minimum composite 800) scores. Application deadline: Rolling. Percent of acceptances: 95%
Curricular Emphasis: Broadcast and nonbroadcast television and video; audio production; audience analysis; advertising
Special Activities: Film: student publication. Television/Video: sponsored projects
Facilities: Television: studio; audio bay; control room
Equipment: Television/Video:

complete ¾" studio; complete ¾" and ½" location
Alumni: Ken "Hubcap" Carter, radio/TV personality; Amanda Warren, TV traffic director

GUIDE POV: This private liberal arts university offers students a career-oriented program with emphasis on management training; study abroad programs; internship opportunities in television/video production; growing internship opportunities in film production

---

TRINITY UNIVERSITY

715 Stadium Dr.,
San Antonio, TX 78212
(210)736–7011

Private four-year comprehensive institution. Coed, urban location. Undergraduate enrollment: 2,300. Graduate enrollment: 300.

DEPARTMENT OF COMMUNICATION

Chair/Contact: Dr. Robert O. Blanchard, Chair
Calendar: Semesters
Degrees Offered: B.A.
Departmental Majors:
Undergraduate: 100 students
Entrance Requirements:
Undergraduate: 2.0 grade-point average; ACT (minimum 20) or SAT (minimum 1000) scores; average SAT scores of admitted freshmen is 1207; essay required. Undergraduate application deadline: February 1. Percent of acceptances: 75%
Curricular Emphasis: Media studies, media writing and production, and media management
Special Activities: Television: program material produced for cable television

Facilities: Television: studio; audio bay; control room; 40' remote unit
Equipment: Television/Video: complete 1" and ¾" studio; complete ¾" and ½" location
Alumni: Victoria Sterling, TV network story editor; Sean Stratton, animation postproduction coordinator; Jill Graham Collins, media public affairs executive

GUIDE POV: Balancing conceptually oriented studies with production training, this competitive communications department assists students in polishing their writing and media skills, developing production portfolios, and preparing for leadership positions in media management; study abroad in Mexico, Africa, Japan, China, Israel, and Europe; internship opportunities in television and radio production

---

UNIVERSITY OF HOUSTON

4800 Calhoun,
Houston, TX 77204–3786
(713)743–1000

State four-year comprehensive institution. Coed, urban location. Undergraduate enrollment: 22,000. Graduate enrollment: 11,000.

SCHOOL OF COMMUNICATION/RADIO-TV-FILM PROGRAM

Chair/Contact: Robert Musburger
Calendar: Semesters
Degrees Offered: B.A., M.A.
Departmental Majors: Undergraduate radio/TV/film: 500 students. Graduate mass communications: 85 students
Entrance Requirements:
Undergraduate: 2.0 grade-point average; ACT (minimum 19) or SAT (minimum composite 800) scores.

Graduate: GRE scores; competitive undergraduate grade-point average; personal statement. Undergraduate and graduate application deadline: June 15. Percent of acceptances: 70%

Curricular Emphasis: Undergraduate: broadcasting, film production, writing, performance, management, corporate communication, telecommunication. Graduate: mass communication research and advanced studies

Special Activities: Film: film series. Television: program material produced for on-campus closed-circuit television, local public television station, and cable television

Facilities: Film: complete 16mm studio and location; six-channel full-coat mixing theatre. Television: studio; audio bay; control room; video editing suites

Equipment: Film: complete 16mm. Television/Video: complete ¾", Hi-8, and Betacam studio and location; film to video conversion

Alumni: Walter Coblenz, film producer; John Tracy, TV sitcom director; Art Maulsby, TV/film writer; Robert Leake, TV sports producer; Jim Nantz, TV news editor; Bill Worrell, TV sports director; Deborah Wrigley, TV news reporter

GUIDE POV: Communication students at this well-equipped research university may develop professional skills in both film and television production; graduate studies in communication theory, research, and management; cross-registration with the University of Texas and Texas Wesleyan University; study abroad in England; internship opportunities in film and television production

UNIVERSITY OF HOUSTON— CLEAR LAKE

2700 Bay Area Blvd.,
Houston, TX 77058
(713)283–7600

State junior and senior level comprehensive institution. Coed, suburban location. Undergraduate enrollment: 7,500.

MEDIA STUDIES PROGRAM

Chair/Contact: Film: Edward T. Hugetz; television: R. B. Fowles
Calendar: Semesters
Degrees Offered: B.A., media studies
Departmental Majors: Undergraduate film: 30 students. Graduate film: 10 students
Entrance Requirements: Undergraduate: associate degree from accredited institution or minimum of 54 semester hours of college credit with grades of *C* or better; proof of exemption from TASP (Texas Academic Skills Program) or test results indicating passing scores in all areas of test. Undergraduate application deadline: July 1. Percent of acceptances: 98%
Curricular Emphasis: Electronic media theory and culture; critical studies in film; media writing; film-video production; computer graphics
Special Activities: Film: film series/festivals. Television: program material produced for cable television
Facilities: Film: 35mm screening facilities; screening room; editing suite; sound mixing room; film library. Television/Video: studio; audio bay; control room; video editing suites; computer graphics lab
Equipment: Film: complete Super-8. Television/Video: complete ¾" studio;

complete ¾" and ½" location; computer graphics equipment
Alumni: Kimberly Crabb, video teacher

GUIDE POV: Upper-division students accepted into the media studies program at this state-supported university will have occasion to produce works in both film and video; diverse course listings; program emphasizes corporate communications; internships are encouraged

UNIVERSITY OF NORTH TEXAS

P.O. Box 13108,
Denton, TX 76203–3108
(817)565–2000

State four-year comprehensive institution. Coed, urban location. Undergraduate enrollment: 27,500. Graduate enrollment: 3,500.

RADIO, TELEVISION, AND FILM DEPARTMENT

Chair/Contact: Dr. John B. Kuiper, Chair
Calendar: Semesters
Degrees Offered: B.A., M.A., M.S.
Departmental Majors:
Undergraduate: 720 students. Graduate: 53 students
Entrance Requirements:
Undergraduate: transcripts; ACT or SAT scores; minimum scores depend on high school class rank; AP and CLEP credits accepted. Graduate: transcripts; minimum composite score of 900 on GRE. Undergraduate application deadline: June 15. Graduate application deadline: at least six weeks prior to registration. Percent of acceptances: Undergraduate: 62%. Graduate: 38%

Curricular Emphasis: Film: critical studies; short narrative/documentary/experimental film production; media management. Television: broadcast production; broadcast copy writing; corporate film/video
Special Activities: Film: film series/festivals; visiting filmmakers; student publications. Television: program material produced for local public television station and for access cable television; AERho chapter, ITVF chapter
Facilities: Film: screening room; editing suites; sound mixing room; sound stage; animation stand; film/television archives. Television: studio; audio bay; control room; video editing labs; satellite downlink
Equipment: Film: complete 16mm. Television/Video: complete S-VHS studio and location
Alumni: Bill Moyers, TV journalist/author; Peter Weller, film actor/director; Doug Adams, TV executive

GUIDE POV: Undergraduates at this competitive public university may concentrate on the production of documentaries and short narratives; department also places emphasis on film research and media management; graduate program stresses research as well as documentary and corporate video production; co-op programs; study abroad in Mexico, Australia, France, Germany, and Great Britain; internship opportunities in television/video production

UNIVERSITY OF ST. THOMAS

3800 Montrose Blvd.,
Houston, TX 77006
(713)522–7911

Private four-year comprehensive institution. Coed, urban location. Enrollment: 900. Tuition: $5,660 per academic year.

DEPARTMENT OF COMMUNICATION

Chair/Contact: Dr. Robin Williamson, Chair
Calendar: Semesters
Degrees Offered: B.A.
Departmental Majors: Department of Communication: 100 students
Entrance Requirements: Academic rank in upper half of graduating class; ACT or SAT scores; interview; recommendations. Application deadline: rolling. Percent of acceptances: 75%
Curricular Emphasis: Radio and TV production
Special Activities: Television: program material produced for cable television
Facilities: Television: studio; editing bay; control room; video editing suites; comprehensive audio studio
Equipment: Television: studio and field production capabilities for video; audio broadcasting setup
Alumni: Samantha Mohr, TV news anchor; Darrell Maness, TV producer; Liz Latta, radio promotions director; David Pfeiffer, TV audio operator

GUIDE POV: Students may pursue an individually planned program of studies at this selective private university; production training in audio, video, and broadcast television; cross-registration with the universities of Houston and Notre Dame, as well as Rice and Texas Southern universities; study abroad in 10 countries; media internship opportunities

UNIVERSITY OF TEXAS AT AUSTIN

Austin, TX 78712
(512)471–3434

State four-year comprehensive institution. Coed, urban location. Undergraduate enrollment: 38,000. Graduate enrollment: 12,000.

RADIO-TELEVISION-FILM DEPARTMENT

Chair/Contact: Paul Johnson; Kathryn Burger
Calendar: Semesters
Degrees Offered: B.S., M.A., radio/television/film; M.F.A., film/video production; M.A., screenwriting; M.A., joint degree with Latin America studies; Ph.D., communication (students may select emphasis in radio/television/film); M.A./M.B.A., joint degree with business administration
Departmental Majors: Undergraduate: 600 students. Graduate: 175 students
Entrance Requirements: Undergraduate: 2.25 grade-point average; SAT scores. Graduate: 3.0 grade-point average; GRE scores. Undergraduate application deadline: March 1. Graduate application deadline: February 1. Percent of acceptances: 70%
Curricular Emphasis: Media studies (film and TV; international; technology and policy; ethnic minorities; mass communication research). Production studies (16mm and video; screenwriting)
Special Activities: Film: film series/festivals; film societies. Television: program material produced for local cable television
Facilities: Film: 35mm screening facilities; screening room; editing suites; sound mixing room; film

library. Television: four color studios; audio bays; control rooms; 24 video and film editing stations
Equipment: Film: complete 16mm; full editing. Television/Video: complete ¾" studio; complete ¾" and ½" location; full editing
Alumni: Michael Zinberg, TV/film producer; Cary White, set designer; Allison Gibson, writer/script editor; Wayne Lemon, writer/script editor

GUIDE POV: Rigorous programs are offered both in production and media studies at this selective state university; writing is emphasized; strong international and critical dimensions in media studies program; small, diverse graduate production program requires combined film and video instruction; study abroad; extensive local and national internship opportunities in film and television production

UNIVERSITY OF TEXAS—EL PASO

El Paso, TX 79968–0599
(915)747–5000

State four-year comprehensive institution. Coed, urban location. Undergraduate enrollment: 14,000. Graduate enrollment: 2,500.

COMMUNICATION DEPARTMENT

Chair/Contact: Samuel C. Riccillo, Chair
Calendar: Semesters
Degrees Offered: B.A., communication, speech; M.A., communication
Departmental Majors: Undergraduate television: 50 students
Entrance Requirements: Undergraduate: 2.0 grade-point average; ACT or SAT scores. Graduate:

3.0 grade-point average; GRE scores. Undergraduate and graduate application deadline: rolling. Percent of acceptances: Undergraduates: 95%. Graduate: 75%
Curricular Emphasis: Undergraduate: mass media theory; writing for mass media; television production; audio production; news reporting; broadcast news; media management; mass communication law and ethics. Graduate: advanced studies in mass communication; media management
Special Activities: Television: program material produced for cable television
Facilities: Television/Video: studio; audio bay; control room; video editing suites
Equipment: Television/Video: complete ¾" studio; complete ¾" and ½" location and editing
Alumni: Susan Johnson, radio development director; Alfredo Corchado, media journalist; Sieto Negrone, media journalist

GUIDE POV: Students attending this state university are offered a professional program blending mass communication studies with practical training in audio and video production; emphasis on news journalism; study abroad in England and Germany; internships available for qualified juniors and seniors

UNIVERSITY OF TEXAS—TYLER

3900 University Blvd.,
Tyler, TX 75799
(903)556–7200

State upper-division comprehensive institution. Coed, rural location. Undergraduate enrollment: 2,300. Graduate enrollment: 700.

DEPARTMENT OF THEATRE AND COMMUNICATION

Chair/Contact: Kenneth R. Casstevens
Calendar: Semesters
Degrees Offered: B.A., B.S., journalism; M.A., M.S., interdisciplinary degrees
Entrance Requirements: Undergraduate: associate degree from accredited institution or minimum of 54 semester hours of college credit with grades of *C* or better; proof of exemption from TASP (Texas Academic Skills Program) or test results indicating passing scores in all areas of test. Graduate: GRE scores; 3.0 grade-point average. Undergraduate and graduate application deadline: rolling. Percent of acceptances: Undergraduate: 95%. Graduate: 75%
Curricular Emphasis: Undergraduate: news journalism with an emphasis on writing and announcing. Graduate: communication theory; topics in mass media and popular culture
Special Activities: Film: screenings. Television: program material produced for class assignments
Facilities: Film: screening room; editing suite. Television/Video: studio; control room
Equipment: Film: complete Super-8. Television/Video: matched studio cameras; portable lighting packages; ½" cassette recorders; portable cameras; monitors
Alumni: Robert Hilliard, TV producer; Kingsley Smith, TV news producer; Sandra Strait, TV news writer; Jimmy Miller, TV cameraman

GUIDE POV: Students attending this state university are offered a choice of degree programs stressing print journalism; limited television and radio course listings emphasize news writing and performance; interdepartmental graduate program is theory-oriented; some media internships available

---

WILEY COLLEGE

711 Wiley Ave.,
Marshall, TX 75670
(903)927-3300

Private four-year comprehensive institution. Coed, urban location. Enrollment: 535.

MASS COMMUNICATIONS DEPARTMENT

Chair/Contact: Alex Mwakikoti
Calendar: Semesters
Degrees Offered: B.A., mass communications
Departmental Majors: Television: 15 students
Entrance Requirements: ACT or SAT scores; written statement of purpose; letter of recommendation required; GED accepted with minimum score of 40. Application deadline: June 1. Percent of acceptances: 99%
Curricular Emphasis: Mass media history and theory; television production; broadcast and print journalism; media research
Special Activities: Film: student publications
Alumni: Joan Faith Robinson, TV marketing director; Kimberly D. Gilkey, optical technician

GUIDE POV: Media majors attending this small private college are provided with preparation for graduate school or a career position in the media industry; course listings in mass media history, theory, writing, production, and research; hands-on training; concurrent registration program with East Texas Baptist College

I grew up in a small farm community in central Illinois. Like many Americans growing up in the sixties, I was a child of television. Films, television shows— I gobbled them up like candy. In junior high, my friends and I made Super-8 films in which demons battled each other for control of the world—or at least for part of our backyard.

We are all products of diverse, sometimes contradictory influences. Science has its own special magic of explaining how and why things work, with a stricter sense of rules than those of the arts—but with its own rewards. Pursuing my early interest in the sciences, I attended and eventually graduated from Illinois College with a B.A. in biology and chemistry.

In a way, the practice of medicine, with its interdisciplinary approach, was a natural progression for me. So I went to the University of Illinois Medical School, then graduated to a family practice residency program in Kenosha, Wisconsin. While there, I borrowed a camcorder and proceeded to make a series of videotapes about my fellow residents. This led me to consider a career that would encompass my interests in both medicine and film.

After school, I spent a year traveling throughout the country as a substitute doctor, taking over other physicians' practices for a week or so because of a sudden vacancy or vacation. I worked in a small town in the California redwoods, lived alongside the Amish in northern Indiana, and roamed over the South Carolina mountains. Being a doctor gave me the unique opportunity to arrive in a community and become instantly engaged in the lives of its people.

Finally settling in California, I entered film school and have completed an M.F.A. in production. While there, I worked on a variety of projects—among them two documentaries: one researching the German Expressionist films of the twenties, the other exploring the ethics of lobotomies.

A major theme that speaks to me in reviewing my experiences is that I continually feel the need to explore different methods of communication. Filmmaking and much of medicine are both about the art of expressing information or emotions about which you feel strongly. Your passion about what you want to communicate will often make up for deficiencies in style or training. If you can understand and use that passion, film school will be a valuable place to hone your skills. If this passion is undeveloped or pursued in an indifferent manner, film school simply becomes an expensive way station in life. School will not give you anything to say that does not already come from within, but it will help you articulate and focus your message.

BRIGHAM YOUNG UNIVERSITY

Provo, UT 84602
(801)378–4636

*Private four-year comprehensive
institution. Coed, urban location.
Undergraduate enrollment: 26,000.
Graduate enrollment: 2,500.*

DEPARTMENT OF THEATRE AND FILM

Chair/Contact: Harold R. Oaks, Chair

DEPARTMENT OF COMMUNICATIONS

Chair/Contact: Television: Norman C.
Tarbox; Larrie Gale
Calendar: Semesters
Degrees Offered: B.A., B.F.A., film;
Ph.D., theatre and film; B.A., broadcast
communication; M.A.,
communications
Departmental Majors: Undergraduate
film: 75 students. Graduate film: 15
students. Undergraduate radio and
television: 225 students. Graduate
television: 10 students
Entrance Requirements:
Undergraduate: competitive grade-
point average; ACT scores and
teachers' recommendations required.
Graduate: GRE scores; written
statement of purpose;
recommendations; 3.0 grade-point
average. Undergraduate and graduate
application deadline: February 15.
Percent of acceptances:
Undergraduate: 77%. Graduate: 70%
Curricular Emphasis: Film: separate

degree programs for students pursuing
film studies or film production/writing;
Ph.D. program for film scholars.
Television: comprehensive training in
all aspects of broadcast
communication including
management, production, and news
writing; graduate program is
management- and theory-oriented, with
additional broadcast production
training in the documentary form
Special Activities: Film: film series/
festivals; student screenings.
Television: program material produced
for on-campus closed-circuit television,
local public television station, cable
television, and off-campus clients
Facilities: Film: screening rooms;
editing suites; sound mixing room;
animation stand. Television/Video:
studio; audio bay; control room; CMX
editing suites; computer graphics lab;
multisplit feed remote facility
Equipment: Film: complete Super-8
and 16mm. Television/Video: complete
1" and ¾" studio; complete ¾" and
½" location
Alumni: Keith Merrill, film producer/
director; Reed Smoot, film director/
cinematographer; Sterling
Vanwagenen, film producer

GUIDE POV: Comprehensive film and
television training is provided at this
selective private university; film
department offers separate degree
programs in production/writing or
critical studies; broadcast

communication majors receive extensive television production training; diverse course listings in both film and television; study abroad in eight countries; internship opportunities in film and television production

SOUTHERN UTAH UNIVERSITY

350 W. Center St.,
Cedar City, UT 84720
(801)586–7700

State four-year comprehensive institution. Coed, small town location. Undergraduate enrollment: 4,000. Graduate enrollment: 200.

COMMUNICATION DEPARTMENT

Chair/Contact: Jon Smith
Calendar: Quarters
Degrees Offered: B.A., B.S.
Departmental Majors:
Undergraduate: 250 students
Entrance Requirements:
Undergraduate: combination of high school grade-point average and ACT scores determine admissibility. Undergraduate application deadline: June 15. Percent of acceptances: 90%
Curricular Emphasis: Electronic media theory and culture; broadcast news production; media writing; directing; technical broadcasting; media sales and management; communication graphics; communication law
Special Activities: Television: program material produced for local commercial station and for entire schedule of local cable channel; program material includes news shows, local sports coverage, interview and information shows, and feature coverage
Facilities: Television: studio; audio

bays; master, video, and audio control rooms; computer graphics; full-service multicamera; multisplit feed remote facility
Equipment: Television/Video: complete ¾" studio; ¾" and ½" location
Alumni: Brad Steinke, TV sports anchor; Dan Matheson, media sales executive; Dan Brienholt, TV news anchor

GUIDE POV: A small program featuring hands-on training in broadcast television production is offered at this state university; co-op programs with Weber State College; internships in television production are strongly encouraged

UNIVERSITY OF UTAH

206 Performing Arts Bldg.,
Salt Lake City, UT 84112
(801)581–7200

State four-year comprehensive institution. Coed, urban location. Undergraduate enrollment: 19,000. Graduate enrollment: 5,000.

THEATRE AND FILM DEPARTMENT

Chair/Contact: Brian Patrick, Director; Lillian Cahoy
Calendar: Quarters
Degrees Offered: B.A., M.F.A.
Departmental Majors: Undergraduate film: 85 students. Graduate film: 12 students
Entrance Requirements:
Undergraduate: minimum 2.5 grade-point average. Graduate: transcripts; minimum 3.0 grade-point average; portfolio of work in film or video; written statement of purpose; recommendations. Undergraduate application deadline: rolling. Graduate

application deadline: February 1.
Percent of acceptances:
Undergraduate: 95%. Graduate: 20%
Curricular Emphasis: Undergraduate:
broad-based liberal arts degree with 50
credits in film required, 25 optional;
production training. Graduate:
emphasis in film and video production
and screenwriting; film history and
theory
Special Activities: Film:
volunteerships at Sundance Film
Festival; student organization sponsors
yearly international student film
festival, the University Film Front,
which features seminars and visits by
guest artists; Utah Film and Video
Festival co-sponsors several activities
with the Theatre and Film Department
and holds its festival every spring
Facilities: Film: 35mm screening
facilities; screening room; sound
mixing room; animation stand; video
and film editing rooms; permanent
library. Video: ½" and ¾" location
Equipment: Film: Super-8 and 16mm.
Video: ½" and ¾" editing suites
Alumni: Trent Harris, TV film director;
Rhea Gavry, documentary filmmaker;
Mel Halbach, documentary filmmaker;
Bryan Clifton, TV/film corporate
executive

GUIDE POV: This innovative program
emphasizes narrative screenwriting
and the production of socially relevant
documentaries; entry to program is
competitive; cross-registration with
area colleges; study abroad on several
continents; local and national
internship opportunities in film and
video production

UTAH STATE UNIVERSITY

Logan, UT 84322–4605
(801)750–1000

*State four-year comprehensive
institution. Coed, urban location.
Undergraduate enrollment: 12,000.
Graduate enrollment: 2,500.*

COMMUNICATION DEPARTMENT

Chair/Contact: Penny M. Byrne
Calendar: Quarters
Degrees Offered: B.A., B.S.,
journalism; M.A., M.S., communication
(with emphasis in broadcasting or
media management)
Departmental Majors:
Undergraduate: 150 students. Graduate:
10 students
Entrance Requirements:
Undergraduate: 2.0 grade-point
average; ACT or SAT scores. Graduate:
3.0 grade-point average; GRE scores;
recommendations. Undergraduate and
graduate application deadline:
September 1. Percent of
acceptances: 85%
Curricular Emphasis:
Communication theory; writing for the
mass media; television production;
mass media management
Special Activities: Television:
program material includes daily
newscast inserted on CNN Headline
News in local viewing area
Facilities: Television: studio; audio
bay; control room; editing suites
Equipment: Television/Video:
complete 1" and ¾" studio; complete
¾" location; video toaster
Alumni: Hal Ashby, film director;
Merlin Olsen, TV actor/spokesman;
Paul Norton, PBS TV executive

GUIDE POV: Following a sequential
program, communication students at
Utah State University learn all aspects
of mass media production and
management; special emphasis on
broadcast journalism; cross-registration
with area colleges and universities

through the National Student Exchange Program; competitive entry; study abroad; internship opportunities in television production

WEBER STATE UNIVERSITY

Ogden, UT 84408–1903
(801)626–6000

State four-year comprehensive institution. Coed, urban location. Enrollment: 12,000.

DEPARTMENT OF COMMUNICATION

Chair/Contact: Dr. Randolph J. Scott, Chair; Dr. Raj Kumar, Broadcasting Coordinator
Calendar: Quarters
Degrees Offered: B.A., B.S., communication (student may select broadcasting emphasis)
Departmental Majors: Television: 75 students
Entrance Requirements: 2.0 grade-point average; ACT required for students 22 and under. Application deadline: rolling. Percent of acceptances: 97%
Curricular Emphasis: Electronic media theory and culture; media writing; television/video news and documentary production; media management; radio news production
Special Activities: Television: program material produced for on-campus closed-circuit television and for cable television
Facilities: Television/Video: studio; audio bay; control room; video editing suites. Radio: KWCR-FM on-campus radio station
Equipment: Television/Video: complete ¾" studio; complete ¾" and ½" location; 1" VTR
Alumni: Jim Alvey, commercials producer; Ron Kirby, TV program manager; Jon Foster, TV associate producer

GUIDE POV: This public commuter university offers undergraduates an emphasis in broadcasting within the Department of Communication; emphasis on broadcast journalism; management training; department offers honors program; study abroad in England and Mexico; internships available in television and radio production

The film and entertainment world is always changing from one day to the next, and that's how I like it—with all its surprises.

I started as a gofer, and when I decided to pursue a full-time career in the film business, I was unable to afford the tuition for school. Seven years and hundreds of days later, I had finally earned enough money to attend a few classes at both the UCLA Extension Program and the AFI. I was thrilled, though I soon discovered there was very little difference between what these schools were offering. In fact, the only differences were the faculty credits. Each catalog boasted of its most successful graduates, with a list of their awards and accomplishments. To the student eager to get into the glamorous movie business, that can be very seductive. What remained unsaid, however, was that many of those alumni became successful many years after they started. So, I quickly became frustrated and angry at not getting what I had come to school for.

I realize I probably sound too critical, and there are a lot of things I've learned at school: mainly, research is the key; meet your instructors and pick their brains; don't just be taken in by their credits or overwhelmed by the hype. And if you don't know what direction you want to take, talk to students who attended the classes you are interested in. Employers mostly want to hire grounded, honest students. Any opportunity you have to work on a real movie set—do it. Money or no money. Nothing in this business is more valuable than experience. In the beginning, keep your eyes and ears open, and your mouth shut. Nobody really cares about your formal film education. Just be sure the coffee is hot!

CASTLETON STATE COLLEGE

Castleton, VT 05735
(802)468–5611

State four-year comprehensive institution. Coed, rural location. Undergraduate enrollment: 1,500. Graduate enrollment: 300.

THEATRE ARTS DEPARTMENT

Chair/Contact: Roy Vestrich, Coordinator of film studies program

COMMUNICATIONS PROGRAM

Chair/Contact: Robert Gershon
Calendar: Semesters
Degrees Offered: B.S., communication (concentration in mass media, journalism, or corporate communications); A.S., communication; film minor (through Theatre Arts Department)
Departmental Majors: Undergraduate television: 75 students
Entrance Requirements: Undergraduate: competitive grade-point average; ACT or SAT scores; essay required; interview recommended. Undergraduate application deadline: rolling. Percent of acceptances: 78%
Curricular Emphasis: Electronic media theory and culture; critical studies in film; media writing; television/video production; radio production
Special Activities: Film: film series/ festivals. Television/Video: program material produced for on-campus closed-circuit television, local public television station, and cable television. Radio: student-operated
Facilities: Film: screening room. Television/Video: studio; audio bay; control room; video editing suites
Equipment: Film: Super-8 and 16mm projectors and lighting. Television/ Video: complete ¾" studio; complete ¾" and ½" location
Alumni: Peter Willett, TV producer/ director; Jeffrey Andrews, TV program director; Elza Hammer, TV director of operations; Don Wells, video editor

GUIDE POV: Founded in 1787, Castleton State College is the oldest institution of higher learning in Vermont; students planning to pursue careers in broadcasting are offered a professional program blending mass media studies with ample studio and field experience; production training in television news, documentary, and fiction; a minor in film studies, offered through the Theatre Arts Department, emphasizing genre studies, film aesthetics, experimental and documentary video production, and media writing; competitive entry; cooperative program with Clarkson University; study abroad in 14 countries; honors programs; local and national internship opportunities in film and television production

LYNDON STATE COLLEGE

Lyndonville, VT 05851
(802)626–9371

*State four-year comprehensive
institution. Coed, small town location.
Undergraduate enrollment: 1,000.
Graduate enrollment: 100.*

COMMUNICATION ARTS AND SCIENCES

Chair/Contact: Darlene R. Bolduc;
Keith C. Borgstrom
Calendar: Semesters
Degrees Offered: A.S.,
communication arts and sciences;
B.A., communication arts and sciences
(concentration in graphic design);
B.S., communication arts and sciences
(concentration in video performance
and scriptwriting, video production
and videography, or radio
performance and writing)
Departmental Majors:
Undergraduate: 30–50 students
Entrance Requirements:
Undergraduate: SAT scores (minimum
900 composite); essay required;
interview recommended.
Undergraduate application
deadline: rolling. Percent of
acceptances: 90%
Curricular Emphasis: Electronic
media theory and culture; media
writing; audio-video production; media
management; visual design; on-line
video graphics
Special Activities: Television: live
and taped program material produced
for local cable television includes
daily news and weather reporting,
panel discussions, and dramatic
presentations; video projects for local
clients
Facilities: Television: studio; audio
bay; control room; black/white and
color photo laboratories; editing suites;
graphics studio; satellite downlink
programming and teleconferencing
Equipment: Television/Video:
complete ¾" studio and location;
multibay editing; computer graphics
Alumni: Christopher Boden, TV
cameraman; Evelyn Cramer, TV
newscaster

GUIDE POV: Lyndon State College
offers a well-equipped media program
integrating oral and visual
communication with writing and
dramatic arts; aesthetics and practical
training in video technologies;
extensive internship opportunities in
television production through LINC
program

MARLBORO COLLEGE

P.O. Box A, Marlboro, VT 05344
(802)257–4333

*Private four-year comprehensive
institution. Coed, rural location.
Enrollment: 250.*

DEPARTMENT OF FILM AND VIDEO

Chair/Contact: Geoffrey Brown
Calendar: Semesters
Degrees Offered: B.A.
Departmental Majors: Five students
Entrance Requirements: Transcripts;
ACT or SAT scores; teachers'
recommendations; writing sample;
autobiographical statement; interview.
Application deadline: August 1.
Percent of acceptances: 60%
Curricular Emphasis: Film aesthetics;
hands-on process of structuring the
story, organizing and directing the
shoot, and editing
Special Activities: Film: film series/
festivals. Television: program material
produced for local public television
station

Facilities: Film: 16mm screening facilities. Television/Video: studio; control room

Equipment: Television/Video: ½" cassette recorder; portable cameras; editing equipment

Alumni: Alonzo Lamont, Jr., film director; Madeleine Potter, TV writer; Chris North, TV/film actor

GUIDE POV: Marlboro College offers its students a small, selective video and film program that emphasizes theory, screenwriting, and story structure; tutorial-style classes; all production work accomplished on video equipment; students individually design own major with the aid of a faculty advisor; cross-registration with School for International Training

MIDDLEBURY COLLEGE

Middlebury, VT 05753
(802)388–3711

Private four-year comprehensive institution. Coed, rural location. Enrollment: 1,900.

PROGRAM IN FILM/VIDEO

Chair/Contact: Ted Perry, Director
Calendar: 4–1–4
Degrees Offered: B.A.
Departmental Majors: 20 students
Entrance Requirements: ACT or SAT scores; interview; teachers' recommendations; essay. Application deadline: December 15; early decision November 15. Percent of acceptances: 25%
Curricular Emphasis: Film/video/television study and production within liberal arts context
Special Activities: Film/Video: extensive film/video screening program (four to eight programs per week); frequent visits by media artists and scholars

Facilities: Film: 16 and 35mm screening; film/video library. Television/Video: editing bays; video projection

Equipment: Film: projectors. Television/Video: complete VHS, Hi-8, and ¾" video shooting and editing (control track and time code)

Alumni: Michael Tolkin, screenwriter/director; Charles Frank, TV actor; Dan Curry, special effects supervisor; Susan Moore, postproduction supervisor; Barbara Ottinger, media executive/editor; Plummy Tucker, film editor

GUIDE POV: Middlebury College, founded in 1800, offers students a small, flexible program in film/video with a strong emphasis on individual projects; intimate atmosphere; highly selective admissions; extensive study abroad program offered through Middlebury campuses in other countries; junior-year abroad; exchange programs with Berea, St. Mary's, and Swarthmore colleges; independent scholar program; internship opportunities

UNIVERSITY OF VERMONT

Burlington, VT 05405
(802)656–3131

State four-year comprehensive institution. Coed, large town location. Undergraduate enrollment: 9,000. Graduate enrollment: 1,000.

ART DEPARTMENT

Chair/Contact: Dr. Christie Fengler-Stephany, Chair

ENGLISH MINOR

Chair/Contact: Dr. Frank Manchel, English Department
Calendar: Semesters
Degrees Offered: B.A., art
Entrance Requirements:
Undergraduate: SAT or ACT required; 2.0 minimum grade-point average. Undergraduate application deadline: February 1. Percent of acceptances: 73%
Curricular Emphasis: Art Department: students may elect production training in film, video, animation, and computer art; there is also a course in film/video/ photography history. Film Minor: Courses include Development of the Motion Picture I and II; Special Topics I and II; Film Criticism; History of the Optical Media as Art; Contemporary Cinema; American Film Genres; Survey of Mass Communication; Seminar in Film

Special Activities: Film/video: screenings; lectures
Facilities: Film/video: screening room; video studio
Equipment: Film/video: cameras; editing, lighting, and sound equipment
Alumni: Jon Kilik, film producer; Marlo Nussbaum, television production assistant; Yudi Bennett, film/TV assistant director

GUIDE POV: Established in 1791, this selective state university offers art majors an opportunity to explore techniques of both film and video; students pursue individual and class film projects; live-action studio and location video projects; single-frame film animation; computer imagery techniques; interdepartmental film studies minor is offered with courses culled from the English, art, psychology, sociology, and theatre departments

Continuing education in film can be a double-edged sword. Its strengths can create its weaknesses. Intended for adults, the courses often have no requirements and are taught by working professionals. Before completing a certificate program in film, I had earned my B.F.A. in literature and both an M.F.A. and a Ph.D. in theatre, so I had been expecting both a more rigorous curriculum and higher teaching standards.

Since the quality of continuing education programs varies, it's a good idea to research all such programs before investing any money. Scan the course listings to see if the program concentrates on general instruction, or if it meets any needs you have for specialized, in-depth training in areas such as directing, editing, or writing. Look for a designed progression of courses leading from basic to advanced work in your field of interest. Some programs, such as the one I entered, leave it all up to the student to determine which courses to take, and it is usually difficult to make decisions about this, for some courses appear and disappear each quarter or semester. In general, I've found that short courses tend to have minimal value. As a last note, check to see if your program offers any permanent facilities and equipment for production. Mine didn't.

As a trained theatre director, I found the film directing courses that I took as a continuing education student much too brief and insubstantial. There was no master plan for the subject area. In my experience, the situation seemed to be an inversion of normal university education. Instead of courses being designed and instructors hired to teach them, it seemed as if an instructor was hired—based on his or her specialty—and then a course designed around the person. And the instructors—most of whom were not career teachers—were a mixed lot. Generally, the first two classes revealed the strengths and weaknesses of both the course and its instructor. For me, the good courses were very exciting and challenging, and I learned a great deal from those. If you do the research first, you can indeed choose an extension program providing a structured formal film education.

COLLEGE OF WILLIAM AND MARY

Williamsburg, VA 23187
(804)221–4000

*State four-year comprehensive
institution. Coed, small town location.
Undergraduate enrollment: 6,000.
Graduate enrollment: 2,300.*

AMERICAN STUDIES PROGRAM

Chair/Contact: Dr. Alan Wallach,
acting director
Calendar: Semesters
Degrees Offered: B.A.
Entrance Requirements:
Undergraduate: SAT or ACT required;
three ATs recommended, in English,
mathematics, and a foreign language;
essay required. Undergraduate
application deadline: January 15.
Percent of acceptances: 40%
Curricular Emphasis: The American
Studies program offers an
interdisciplinary course of studies that
includes exploration of the film
medium especially as it relates to
American culture and history
Special Activities: Film/video:
screenings; lectures
Facilities: Film/video: screening room
Alumni: Roger Mudd, NBC
congressional correspondent; Glenn
Close, film actress; Linda Lavin, TV/
film actress

GUIDE POV: Founded in 1693, this
selective college offers an American
Studies program that examines film
studies in the context of a broad
exploration of American culture,
values, and history; required courses
in history, social sciences, English, and
the fine arts; independent studies/
honors project; the college offers
programs with the University of
Virginia, Rensselaer Polytechnic
Institute, Columbia University, Case
Western Reserve University, and
Washington University in St. Louis;
study abroad in ten countries

GEORGE MASON UNIVERSITY

Fairfax, VA 22030–4444
(703)993–1000

*State four-year comprehensive
institution. Coed, suburban location.
Undergraduate enrollment: 10,000.
Graduate enrollment: 8,000.*

COMMUNICATION DEPARTMENT

Chair/Contact: Undergraduate: Dr.
Don M. Boileau, Chair; graduate: Dr.
Deborah Boehm-Davis, Assistant Dean
Calendar: Semesters
Degrees Offered: B.A.,
communication; M.A.,
telecommunication
Departmental Majors: Undergraduate
radio and television: 700 students.
Graduate communication: 20 students
Entrance Requirements:
Undergraduate: SAT required, with a
minimum composite score of 1000;

three ATs required in English, math, and either a foreign language or a science; ACT accepted. Graduate: GRE scores; recommendations. Undergraduate and graduate application deadline: February 1. Percent of acceptances: undergraduate: 85%. Graduate: 70%
Curricular Emphasis: Undergraduate: electronic media theory and culture; media writing; audio-video production; media management. Graduate: telecommunication theory and research
Special Activities: Television: program material produced for cable television; video yearbook produced annually
Facilities: Television/Video: studio; audio bay; control room; video editing suites
Equipment: Television/Video: complete ¾" studio and location
Alumni: Lyndell Core, TV program director; Don Sargent, video technical writer; Julia Mapelli, TV operations manager

GUIDE POV: This state university offers comprehensive broadcast television-radio and corporate video production training in the context of a strong liberal arts curriculum; the English Department offers film theory and history studies; co-op programs with Shenandoah College and Conservatory, Virginia Polytechnic Institute and State University, Old Dominion University, and the University of Virginia; cross-registration with the Washington Consortium of Universities; study abroad in nine countries; media internship opportunities in Fairfax and Washington, D.C.

HAMPTON UNIVERSITY

Hampton, VA 23668
(804)727–5000

Private four-year comprehensive institution. Coed, urban location. Undergraduate enrollment: 5,000. Graduate enrollment: 400.

DEPARTMENT OF MASS MEDIA ARTS

Chair/Contact: Vanessa Coombs, Chair
Calendar: Semesters
Degrees Offered: B.A., mass media arts
Departmental Majors: Undergraduate television: 225 students
Entrance Requirements: Undergraduate: 2.0 grade-point average; ACT or SAT testing, with minimum composite score of 800 required on the SAT; interview recommended. Undergraduate application deadline: February 15. Percent of acceptances: 45%
Curricular Emphasis: Electronic media theory and culture; media writing; television/video production; media management
Special Activities: Film: student publications. Television: program material produced for cable television and for class projects
Facilities: Television/Video: studio; audio bay; control room; video editing suites
Equipment: Television/Video: complete ¾" studio and ½" location
Alumni: Kirk Johnson, media production executive; Fitzhugh Houston, TV/film actor

GUIDE POV: Hampton University offers mass media studies with a strong emphasis on television news and documentary production; management training; cross-registration with area colleges and universities; limited media internships available

HOLLINS COLLEGE

Roanoke, VA 24020
(703)362–6000

Private four-year comprehensive women's institution, suburban location. Enrollment: 800.

THEATRE ARTS DEPARTMENT

Chair/Contact: Klaus Phillips; Carl Plantinga
Calendar: 4–1–4
Degrees Offered: B.A., theatre arts (film concentration)
Departmental Majors: Eight majors, 25 minors
Entrance Requirements: ACT or SAT scores; essay; interview recommended. Application deadline: February 15. Percent of acceptances: 70%
Curricular Emphasis: Film history, criticism, and theory; strong emphasis on writing program; film/video production
Special Activities: Film: visiting filmmakers series; film festivals; strong national film internship program
Facilities: Film: screening room; editing suite; sound mixing room; animation stand; film library. Television: audio studio
Equipment: Film: complete Super-8 and 16mm. Television/Video: complete ½" location and editing
Alumni: Sandra Brice, TV/film producer

GUIDE POV: Critical film studies, creative writing, and independent production techniques are emphasized at this competitive private college; study abroad in Paris, London, and Kobe, Japan; cross-registration with Seven Colleges Exchange as well as Mills College in California; accelerated degree program; local and national film production internship opportunities

JAMES MADISON UNIVERSITY

Harrisonburg, VA 22807
(703)568–6211

State four-year comprehensive institution. Coed, small town location. Undergraduate enrollment: 9,946. Graduate enrollment: 766.

DEPARTMENT OF MASS COMMUNICATION

Chair/Contact: Dr. George Wead, Chair
Calendar: Semesters
Degrees Offered: B.A., B.S., mass communication (students may select emphasis in corporate media, journalism, telecommunication, or visual communication)
Departmental Majors: Undergraduate radio and television: 250 students
Entrance Requirements: Undergraduate: competitive grade-point average; SAT required; personal statement. Undergraduate application deadline: February 1. Percent of acceptances: 35%
Curricular Emphasis: Electronic media theory and culture; critical studies in film; media writing; audio-video and multimedia production
Special Activities: Film: screenings. Television: program material produced for cable television
Facilities: Film: screening room. Television/Video: studio; audio bay; control room; video editing suites
Equipment: Television/Video: complete ¾" studio and location
Alumni: Phoeff Sutton, TV writer/

producer; Christopher Hulich, video editor; Cheryl Carson, TV news producer

GUIDE POV: This highly competitive university offers professional training in television/video with emphasis in broadcast journalism and corporate media; diverse course listings; study abroad in four countries; optional May session; 28 national honor societies on campus; departmental honors program; internship opportunities in radio and television production

LIBERTY UNIVERSITY

Box 2000, Lynchburg, VA 24506
(804)582-2000

Private four-year comprehensive institution. Coed, suburban location. Enrollment: 4,800.

TELECOMMUNICATIONS DEPARTMENT

Chair/Contact: Dr. Carl Windsor, Chair
Calendar: Semesters
Degrees Offered: B.S., telecommunications (concentration in video production)
Departmental Majors: Video production: 100 students
Entrance Requirements: Minimum 2.35 grade-point average; written statement of purpose; teachers' recommendations. Application deadline: August 1. Percent of acceptances: 95%
Curricular Emphasis: Production of religious/family television programming
Special Activities: Television: program material produced for on-campus closed-circuit television as well as for public access and cable

television; major weekly national telecast
Facilities: Television: studio; control room
Equipment: Television/Video: complete ¾" studio; complete 1", ¾", and ½" location
Alumni: Jon Daggett, TV network executive; Dan Bathurst, videographer; Chuck Boscaljon, TV producer; Steve Van Dusen, audio producer; Shari Brown-Ahrens, video producer

GUIDE POV: Affiliated with the Independent Baptist Church, Liberty University offers a full concentration in television/video production; emphasis on programming for religious media; worldwide internship opportunities

MARY BALDWIN COLLEGE

Staunton, VA 24401
(703)887-7000

Private four-year comprehensive institution. Women, small town location. Enrollment: 1,000.

COMMUNICATIONS DEPARTMENT

Chair/Contact: Dr. William DeLeeuw, Head
Calendar: 4-4-1
Degrees Offered: B.A., communication (concentrations in media writing, broadcasting, advertising/public relations, and instructional)
Departmental Majors: Radio and television: 35 students
Entrance Requirements: ACT or SAT scores; ATs recommended; essay required; interview recommended. Application deadline: April 15. Percent of acceptances: 90%

Curricular Emphasis: Mass media theory; critical studies in film; media writing; audio-video production; mass media research; mass media law and ethics

Special Activities: Film: film series. Television: program material produced for MBC Community TV

Facilities: Film: screening room. Television/Video: studio; audio bay; control room; video editing suites

Equipment: Film: complete Super-8. Television/Video: complete ¾" and ½" VHS studio and location

Alumni: Virginia Munce Bertholet, film producer; Elizabeth Dawson, TV broadcaster; Margaret Moore, TV newscaster

GUIDE POV: This private college for women offers an individualized media arts program featuring ample hands-on broadcast experience; emphasis on news and documentary writing and production; cooperative programs with Randolph-Macon, Sweet Briar, and Hampden-Sydney colleges as well as Washington and Lee University; May term abroad programs in Spain, France, England, and Italy; summer study at Oxford University; school year abroad in Japan; honors program; internship opportunities

---

RADFORD UNIVERSITY

E. Norwood St., Radford, VA 24142
(703)831–5000

State four-year comprehensive institution. Coed, suburban location. Undergraduate enrollment: 9,500. Graduate enrollment: 800.

TELECOMMUNICATIONS PROGRAM

Chair/Contact: William Yerrick, Director

Calendar: Semesters

Degrees Offered: B.A., B.S., speech (communication studies track offers concentration in radio and television communication or broadcast journalism). B.A., B.S., journalism (concentration in news/editorial)

Departmental Majors: Undergraduate radio and television: 115 students

Entrance Requirements: Undergraduate: 2.0 grade-point average; ACT or SAT scores; AP and CLEP credits accepted. Undergraduate application deadline: rolling. Percent of acceptances: 84%

Curricular Emphasis: Mass communication theory; broadcast writing; radio and television broadcast production; news journalism; corporate/industrial video production; media management

Special Activities: Film: film series. Television: Radford University Network, Channel 9, operating on the Simmons Cable System transmits programming via satellite from the National College Cable Network; Channel 9 also generates university and public affairs programs

Facilities: Film: screening room. Television/Video: studio; audio bay; control room; video editing suites

Equipment: Film: complete Super-8. Television/Video: complete ¾" studio and location

Alumni: Dave Parker, TV news anchor/meteorologist; Dave Mattingly, TV news producer; Marjorie O'Brian, TV producer; Stacey Gieb, TV producer; Roger Bell, TV production specialist

GUIDE POV: Radford University offers students a communication major featuring professional training in all aspects of radio and television production, including broadcast news; corporate and industrial video production; study abroad; internship opportunities in radio and television production

REGENT UNIVERSITY

Virginia Beach, VA 23464
(804)523–7400

Private four-year comprehensive institution. Coed, suburban location. Graduate enrollment: 1,000.

RADIO, TELEVISION, AND FILM DEPARTMENT

Chair/Contact: Dr. Robert Schihl; Dr. Terry Lindvall
Calendar: Quarters
Degrees Offered: M.A., Ph.D.
Departmental Majors: Film and television production: 62 graduate students
Entrance Requirements: Graduate: B.A. degree from accredited institution; official transcripts; GRE scores; interview recommended
Curricular Emphasis: Television production and writing, film aesthetics, film production, animation screenwriting, and media management
Special Activities: Film/Television: grants for summer film projects; airing of student films through the Family Channel, HBO, Cinemax, Showtime, and other cable networks; students may premiere films at Virginia Festival of American Films; coordinated Speakers' Series with Friends of Virginia Beach Library; nationally broadcast religious news program airs weekly
Facilities: Family Channel TV network on campus

Equipment: Network TV studio; video editing room; ADR suite; 16mm cameras; Steenbeck editing bay
Alumni: Frank Schroeder, film director/producer; Sam Ebersole, TV director/producer; Chris Aver, TV writer/executive producer; Cindy Glaser, TV producer; Chip Fortier, broadcasting executive

GUIDE POV: Film and television production combined with critical studies are taught from an evangelical Christian perspective at this well-equipped university; fiction and nonfiction projects; departmental grants awarded; extensive local and national media internship opportunities

UNIVERSITY OF VIRGINIA

Charlottesville, VA 22906
(804)982–3200

State four-year comprehensive institution. Coed, suburban location. Undergraduate enrollment: 13,000. Graduate enrollment: 7,000.

DRAMA DEPARTMENT

Chair/Contact: Robert C. Chapel, Chair

DEPARTMENT OF RHETORIC AND COMMUNICATION STUDIES

Chair/Contact: Bernard Mayes
Calendar: Semesters
Degrees Offered: B.A., drama; B.A., M.A., Ph.D., rhetoric and communication studies
Entrance Requirements: Undergraduate: The SAT is required; three ATs required, in English, mathematics, and either a foreign language, science, or history; essay required. Graduate: GRE scores;

recommendations; statement of purpose. Undergraduate and graduate application deadline: January 2. Percent of acceptances: 34%, undergraduate and graduate

Curricular Emphasis: The Drama Department offers courses in film criticism and history within the context of a strong theatre arts curriculum. The Department of Rhetoric and Communications Studies offers a concentration in mass media and culture, which explores both electronic media and film from a variety of theoretical and cultural perspectives

Special Activities: Film/video: screenings

Facilities: Film/video: screening room

Alumni: Lewis Allen, film producer; Andrew Scheinman, film producer; Katherine Couric, TV network co-anchor

GUIDE POV: Within the Drama Department of this highly selective university, students explore various topics in film history and criticism; course work requires weekly screenings; through the Department of Rhetoric and Communication Studies, students critically explore mass media from a variety of theoretical perspectives; curriculum includes an examination of American mass-produced culture, special studies in documentary form and content, and a comparative study of broadcast television policies and their expression in America and other countries

---

VIRGINIA COMMONWEALTH UNIVERSITY

325 N. Harrison St.,
Richmond, VA 23284–2519
(804)367–0100

State four-year comprehensive institution. Coed, urban location. Undergraduate enrollment: 12,000. Graduate enrollment: 6,000.

PHOTOGRAPHY AND FILM DEPARTMENT

Chair/Contact: George Nan, Chair; Clifton Dixon; Joan Strommer

Calendar: Semesters

Degrees Offered: B.F.A., communication arts and design (students may select emphasis in film or media); M.F.A., film

Departmental Majors: Undergraduate film: 12 students. Graduate film: two to five students

Entrance Requirements: Undergraduate: 2.25 grade-point average; ACT or SAT scores. Graduate: 3.0 grade-point average; GRE scores; interview; recommendations. Undergraduate application deadline: February 1. Graduate application deadline: April 15. Percent of acceptances: undergraduate: 71%. Graduate: 65%

Curricular Emphasis: Film production; film history and aesthetics

Special Activities: Film: film series/festivals; film societies; student screenings

Facilities: Film: screening room; editing suite; animation stand; film library

Equipment: Film: complete Super-8 and 16mm

Alumni: David Williams, filmmaker; Tom Carson, filmmaker/production assistant; Teri Berrie, film historian

GUIDE POV: A full major in film production is offered here, with an emphasis on experimental, animated, and documentary forms; competitive entry; study abroad in six countries; local and national internship opportunities in film production

VIRGINIA INTERMONT COLLEGE

1013 Moore St.,
Bristol, VA 24201–4298
(703)669–6101

*Private four-year comprehensive
institution. Coed, rural location.
Enrollment: 500.*

PHOTOGRAPHY DEPARTMENT

Chair/Contact: Jay Phyfer, Chair
Calendar: Semesters
Degrees Offered: B.A., B.S.,
photography (concentration in
computer imaging)
Departmental Majors: Film/Video: 40
students
Entrance Requirements: 2.0 grade-
point average; ACT or SAT scores, with
a minimum score of 15 or a combined
score of 650, respectively; essay
required; interview recommended.
Application deadline: August 15.
Percent of acceptances: 95%
Curricular Emphasis: Critical studies
in film; basic video production;
computer imaging
Special Activities: Film/Video:
student screenings; film series/festivals
Facilities: Film: screening room.
Video: editing suites; computer
imaging lab
Equipment: Video: ½" location;
switcher/special effects generator
Alumni: Craig Young, video producer;
Melissa Villafana, TV production
assistant; Michael Hensdill, video artist

GUIDE POV: Students attending this
small private college are offered
course listings in film history, theory/
aesthetics, and criticism; video
production work includes computer
imaging and video art; cross-
registration with King College; study
abroad in two countries

VIRGINIA POLYTECHNIC INSTITUTE AND STATE UNIVERSITY

Blacksburg, VA 24061–0311
(703)231–6000

*State four-year comprehensive
institution. Coed, rural location.
Enrollment: 20,000.*

DEPARTMENT OF COMMUNICATION STUDIES

Chair/Contact: Robert Denton, Jr.,
Head
Calendar: Semesters
Degrees Offered: B.A.,
communication studies (student may
select emphasis in film, journalism,
broadcasting, public relations, or
speech communication)
Departmental Majors:
Communication studies: 650 students
Entrance Requirements: ACT or SAT
scores; ATs in English and math;
recommendations; AP credits
accepted. Application deadline:
February 1. Percent of acceptances:
70%
Curricular Emphasis: Media theory
and criticism; television production;
broadcast journalism; basic film
production
Special Activities: Television/Radio:
VTTV, student-run television
station; VTNews, a weekly
departmental news program; WUVT-
AM/FM, student-run radio station;
student organizations include WICI
and PRSSA
Facilities/Equipment: Film/Television:
television studio; video editing studio;
some film production facilities;
darkroom
Alumni: Robert E. Denton, Jr., TV
political news analyst; Steven
Anderson, TV meteorologist

GUIDE POV: Located 40 miles southwest of Roanoke, this school offers a telecommunications program offering television and radio production training along with critical studies in mass media; basic film production training available; media internship opportunities

VIRGINIA WESTERN COMMUNITY COLLEGE

3095 Colonial Ave., SW,
Roanoke, VA 24015
(703)857–7231

State two-year comprehensive institution. Coed, urban location. Enrollment: 6,500.

RADIO/TELEVISION PRODUCTION TECHNOLOGY

Chair/Contact: Tom Finton
Calendar: Semesters
Degrees Offered: A.A.S.
Departmental Majors: Television: 45 students
Entrance Requirements: Open-door policy. Application deadline: first day of class
Curricular Emphasis: Electronic media history; copywriting; introductory and advanced radio/ television production; broadcast speech; television design and videography; varied seminar studies on film genres, popular culture, photography, and other areas; media management
Special Activities: Television: program material produced for various nonprofit outlets
Facilities: Television: studio; multitrack audio bay; control room
Equipment: Television/Video: complete four-camera full-color ¾" studio and location; 12-input switcher;

Laird CG with paint graphics and camera capture; U-matic control track and timecode editing; U-matic EFP equipment
Alumni: Les Atkins, TV public affairs host; Chad Widdifield, video switcher

GUIDE POV: This small community college offers a quality training program in broadcast media; studio is a teaching facility; strong hands-on approach; graduates may enter market as television directors, videographers, copywriters, audio and video commercial producers, disc jockeys, or news anchors; core program fulfills transfer requirements to four-year programs that are generally pursued by those students seeking upper-level media management positions; required internships

WASHINGTON AND LEE UNIVERSITY

Lexington, VA 24450
(703)463–8400

Private four-year comprehensive institution. Coed, small town location. Enrollment: 1,650.

DEPARTMENT OF JOURNALISM AND MASS COMMUNICATIONS

Chair/Contact: John Kelley Jennings; Robert Joseph de Maria
Calendar: 12–12–6
Degrees Offered: B.A., journalism (broadcast journalism sequence)
Departmental Majors: Television: 75 students
Entrance Requirements: SAT required; three ATs or the ACT required; essay required; interview recommended. Application deadline: January 15. Percent of acceptances: 30%

Curricular Emphasis: Electronic media theory and culture; critical studies in film; media writing; audio-film-video production; media management

Special Activities: Film: film series/festivals; film society. Television/Radio: student-operated Cable 9 presents daily news and public affairs programming through the Lexington cable television system; WLUR-FM campus radio station

Facilities: Film: screening room; editing suite. Television/Video: studio; audio bay; control room; video editing suites

Equipment: Film: complete Super-8 and 16mm. Television/Video: complete ¾" studio and location

Alumni: Fielder Cook, film director; Jeb Rosebrook, screenwriter; Michael Norell, screenwriter

GUIDE POV: Established in 1749 by Scots-Irish pioneers, this highly selective private university offers professional training in television production with an emphasis on news and documentary forms; courses in film theory and basic production; study abroad; extensive internship opportunities in film and television production

In the year 1898, Salvador Toscano Barragan (1872–1947) created Mexico's first fiction film: *Don Juan Tenorio*. In 1963, the National Autonomous University of Mexico (UNAM) established a cinema department, CUEC, the first of its kind in the country. And it wasn't until the early seventies that the only bona-fide filmmaking school in Mexico opened: el Centro de Capacitación Cinematográfica (CCC). Until that time, during more than seven decades, the Mexican film industry grew, flourished, declined, developed again, went through social, economic, and political crises, and most notably, managed to survive without the support of one serious film school in the country. All the filmmakers that became well-known around the world because of features created in Mexico (Luis Buñuel, Emilio Fernandez, Gabriel Figueroa, etc.) either had learned the craft formally in other countries or through years of intense work in the film industry.

The massive cinematographic movement in Mexico since the late eighties has come mostly from CUEC or CCC graduates. Mexican films have begun to reappear at international film festivals (obtaining some awards along the way). Independent productions of both shorts and features were actually shot and completed, and the music video industry has gained recognition locally, in the United States, and in Europe.

To have an idea and make it come alive. Humans have always been fascinated by this process. Perhaps cinema is the expression wherein form and content interact the most. One needs the other to exist.

Do we really need film schools? Of course we do. They teach us about form. Can creativity be taught or learned? Of course not. Content is the world inside of us that we bring to our studies. Form and content create an equilibrium, and therein art is born.

As for my personal history, I am the son of a film producer. And it was my father and mother who encouraged me to study music in Mexico and then film at the UCLA Extension Program. I began editing in 1990 and directed my first music video soon after. Some of my works have received MTV, Grammy, and "Billboard" magazine recognition.

BELLEVUE COMMUNITY COLLEGE

3000 Landerholm Circle S.E.,
Bellevue, WA 98007
(206)641–0111

*State two-year institution. Coed,
suburban location. Enrollment: 14,000.*

MEDIA COMMUNICATION AND TECHNOLOGY

Chair/Contact: Christopher James
Calendar: Quarters
Degrees Offered: A.A., media
communication and technology;
certificate programs in video media
and computer media
Departmental Majors: Video
media and computer media: 25
students
Entrance Requirements: Open-door
policy; high school diploma or
equivalent; minimum 18 years of age;
eight-semester high school transcript
required; Washington Pre-College Test
recommended. Undergraduate
application deadline: June 1. Percent
of acceptances: 100%
Curricular Emphasis: Electronic
media theory and culture; television/
video production; media management;
new digital technologies; interactive
multimedia design and application
Special Activities: Television:
program material produced for on-
campus closed-circuit television and
cable television
Facilities: Television/Video: studio;
audio bay; control room; video editing
suites; interactive multimedia lab
Equipment: Television/Video:
complete ¾" studio and ½" location.
Interactive multimedia: 15 interactive
multimedia workstations with
Macintosh and PC
Alumni: Ellen Lockert, TV/film
producer; Scott Munro, media arts
producer/teacher; Tim Kennedy,
media specialist/teacher

GUIDE POV: Located in a suburban
area east of Seattle, this community
college features diverse and innovative
course listings; video production
training includes interactive
multimedia; advanced students create
special projects; core curriculum
fulfills transfer requirements to some
four-year universities; internship
opportunities in television production

CENTRAL WASHINGTON UNIVERSITY

Ellensburg, WA 98926
(509)963–1111

*State four-year comprehensive
institution. Coed, rural location.
Undergraduate enrollment: 6,000.
Graduate enrollment: 400.*

DEPARTMENT OF COMMUNICATION

Chair/Contact: Phil Backlund, Chair;
Robert Fordan, video communication
studies

Calendar: Quarters
Degrees Offered: B.A., communication (students may select emphasis in video communication)
Departmental Majors: Undergraduate: 100 students
Entrance Requirements: Undergraduate: 2.25 grade-point average; ACT or SAT scores. Undergraduate application deadline: rolling. Percent of acceptances: 75%
Curricular Emphasis: Broadcast and nonbroadcast video production; preparation in writing, producing, and directing in variety of media settings, including corporate, industrial, and organizational video operations
Special Activities: Television/Video: program material produced for on-campus closed-circuit television and local commercial and cable television; departmental awards for excellence
Facilities: Television: studio; audio bay; control room; four editing suites (two S-VHS, two ¾")
Equipment: Television/Video: complete ¾" studio and ½" location
Alumni: Rich Carr, broadcasting executive; Jim Bach, broadcaster; Wendy Warren, broadcasting executive

GUIDE POV: Central Washington University offers students a diversified communications major that has recently shifted emphasis from broadcast news to nonbroadcast video production; study abroad in seven countries; cooperative and accelerated degree programs; cross-registration; internship opportunities in television/video production

---

EASTERN WASHINGTON UNIVERSITY

Cheney, WA 99004
(509)359–6200

State four-year comprehensive institution. Coed, suburban location. Undergraduate enrollment: 9,000. Graduate enrollment: 300.

DEPARTMENT OF RADIO-TELEVISION

Chair/Contact: Marvin Smith, Chair; David Terwische
Calendar: Quarters
Degrees Offered: B.A., radio/television (students may choose emphasis in electronic media journalism, sales/management, or production/performance); M.S., communication
Departmental Majors: Undergraduate television: 90 students. Graduate television: three to five students
Entrance Requirements: Undergraduate: 2.2 grade-point average; ACT or SAT scores. Graduate: 3.0 grade-point average. Undergraduate and graduate application deadline: rolling. Percent of acceptances: undergraduate: 87%. Graduate: 75%
Curricular Emphasis: Electronic media theory and culture; critical studies in film; media writing; audio-video production; media management
Special Activities: Television: program material produced for on-campus closed-circuit television and cable television including news, features, and sports
Facilities: Television/Video: studio; audio bay; control room; video editing suites
Equipment: Television/Video: complete 1" and ¾" studio; complete ¾" and ½" location; ENG location equipment
Alumni: Scott Schaefer, TV director/producer; Tim Kelleher, TV writer; Beth Loucks, technical services manager; Pat Hughes, production coordinator

GUIDE POV: Undergraduates attending this public university are offered a comprehensive major in radio-television with emphases in production/performance, electronic media journalism, and sales/management; graduate studies include management training and communication theory; cooperative programs with Whitworth College and Washington State University; study abroad in 12 countries; internship opportunities in radio and television production

GONZAGA UNIVERSITY

Spokane, WA 99258–0001
(509)328–4420

Private four-year comprehensive institution. Coed, urban location. Enrollment: 3,000.

COMMUNICATION ARTS DEPARTMENT

Chair/Contact: Colleen A. McMahon, Chair; Robert V. Lyons, Director, broadcast studies
Calendar: Semesters
Degrees Offered: B.A., broadcasting, journalism, public relations, speech, theatre
Departmental Majors: Broadcasting: 40 students
Entrance Requirements: competitive grade-point average; ACT or SAT scores; essay and letters of recommendation required; interview recommended. Application deadline: August 15. Percent of acceptances: 86%
Curricular Emphasis: Electronic media theory and culture; media writing; audio-video production with an emphasis on commercial, educational, public, and cable

television/radio production; media management
Special Activities: Television: program material produced for cable television
Facilities: Television/Video: studio; audio bay; control room; video editing suites
Equipment: Television/Video: complete ¾" studio and location
Alumni: Mark Benchiedt, TV executive; Sanjiv More, TV executive; Robin Briley, TV news programmer

GUIDE POV: This small, selective Jesuit university offers students a major in broadcast studies with the purpose of preparing students for career work in radio and television; junior year/semester abroad programs in Japan, Italy, England, France, and Spain; involvement with the university FM radio station and cable television channel is required for broadcast studies majors; internships available

PACIFIC LUTHERAN UNIVERSITY

Tacoma, WA 98447
(206)531–6900

Private four-year comprehensive institution. Coed, suburban location. Enrollment: 3,500.

DEPARTMENT OF COMMUNICATION AND THEATRE

Chair/Contact: Dr. Michael Bartanen, Chair
Calendar: Semesters
Degrees Offered: B.A., B.F.A., communication (emphasis in broadcasting)
Departmental Majors: Radio and television: 225 students
Entrance Requirements: Academic rank within top half of high school

graduating class; SAT required; ACT recommended; essay required. Application deadline: March 1. Percent of acceptances: 80%

Curricular Emphasis: Electronic media theory and culture; media writing; audio-video production; broadcast journalism; media law; media ethics; media management

Special Activities: Film: film series/ festivals. Television/Radio: program material produced for on-campus closed-circuit television and local cable television; student-operated on-campus radio station

Facilities: Film: screening room. Television/Video: studio; audio bay; control room; video editing suites

Equipment: Television/Video: complete ¾" studio and location

Alumni: Tom Glasgow, TV sports director; Michael Marcotti, TV news director; Tom McArthur, TV news anchor

GUIDE POV: This independent private university provides undergraduates with media management training and studies in communication theory along with extensive production experience in radio and television; accelerated degree program; extensive study abroad program in 40 countries; internship opportunities in television and radio production

SEATTLE CENTRAL COMMUNITY COLLEGE

1700 Broadway Ave.,
Seattle, WA 98122
(206)587–3800

State two-year institution. Coed, urban location.

APPLIED VIDEO COMMUNICATIONS PROGRAM

Chair/Contact: Bob Ormbrek
Calendar: Quarters
Degrees Offered: A.A.S.
Departmental Majors: 40 students
Entrance Requirements: ASSET test and writing sample; assessment testing may be required in math or English. Application deadline: June 1

Curricular Emphasis: Direction, production, editing, scriptwriting, media law, computer graphics, talent development

Special Activities: Television/Video: program material produced for video festivals, on-campus closed-circuit and cable television, and local public and commercial television stations

Facilities: Television: studio; audio bay; control room; four editing suites (two ½"; two ¾")

Equipment: Television/Video: complete 1" and ¾" studio; complete ¾" and ½" location; Amiga toaster; Amiga 500; ENG equipment; audio sweetening equipment; Hi-8 dubbing

Alumni: Derik Loso, cinematographer; Kate Whitney-Blyth, video technician; Matt Quinn, grip

GUIDE POV: Offering communication students a varied two-year curriculum, this community college provides a fundamental technical core as well as course listings in written and oral communication, critical thinking and analysis, human relations, and computations; professional video facilities; internship opportunities in television production

THE EVERGREEN STATE COLLEGE

Olympia, WA 98505
(206)866–6000

*State four-year comprehensive
institution. Coed, rural location.
Enrollment: 3,000.*

**EXPRESSIVE ARTS: FILM/VIDEO
PROGRAM**

Chair/Contact: Sally Cloninger; Ann
Fischel; Laurie Meeker
Calendar: Quarters
Degrees Offered: B.A.
Departmental Majors: 36 students
Entrance Requirements: Interview;
recommendations; portfolio.
Application deadline: March 1. Percent
of acceptances: undergraduates: 64%;
expressive arts: 20%
Curricular Emphasis: History, theory,
and production of nonfiction media
stressing experimental and
documentary forms
Special Activities: Film: film series/
festivals. Television: program material
produced for on-campus closed-circuit
television and cable television
Facilities: Film: screening room;
editing suite; sound mixing room;
Oxberry animation stand; JK optical
printer; film library. Television: studio;
audio bay; control room
Equipment: Film: complete Super-8
and 16mm. Television/Video: complete
1" and ¾" studio; complete ¾" and
½" location
Alumni: Matt Groening, animator/
designer/writer; Rhyena Halpern, film
director; Michael Solinger, film editor;
Lisa Farnham, film/TV producer;
Stephen Thomas, TV personality

GUIDE POV: This versatile state college
offers students an intensive,
interdisciplinary media arts program
featuring nonfiction image making;
program encourages development of
personal forms of expression; intimate
atmosphere; entry to program is
competitive; all majors are

student-designed; study abroad in
three countries; internship
opportunities in film and television
production

UNIVERSITY OF WASHINGTON

Seattle, WA 98195
(206)543–2100

*State four-year comprehensive
institution. Coed, urban location.
Undergraduate enrollment: 22,000.
Graduate enrollment: 9,500.*

SCHOOL OF COMMUNICATIONS

Chair/Contact: Dr. Edward P. Bassett,
Director
Calendar: Quarters
Degrees Offered: B.A., M.A., Ph.D.,
communications
Departmental Majors: Undergraduate
television: 100 students. Graduate
communications: 35 students
Entrance Requirements:
Undergraduate: 2.0 grade-point
average; recommendations; ACT or
SAT scores; admission is based on an
indexing system. Graduate: GRE
scores; personal statement of purpose;
recommendations. Undergraduate
application deadline: February 1.
Graduate application deadline: April 1.
Percent of acceptances: 67%
Curricular Emphasis: Broadcast
journalism with a strong emphasis on
reporting and scripting
Special Activities: Television:
program material produced for on-
campus closed-circuit television
Facilities: Film: screening room.
Television/Video: studio; audio bay;
control room; video editing suites
Equipment: Television/Video:
complete ¾" studio; complete ½"
location
Alumni: Sharon Warsinske, TV/

multimedia producer; Bruce Carlson, TV producer

GUIDE POV: The University of Washington offers students highly competitive degree programs through its School of Communications; undergraduate concentration in broadcast journalism; graduate program focuses on problems in communication theory; study abroad in 21 countries; accelerated degree program; extensive internship opportunities in television and corporate video production

WASHINGTON STATE UNIVERSITY

Pullman, WA 99164–2520
(509)335–3564

State four-year comprehensive institution. Coed, rural location. Undergraduate enrollment: 16,000. Graduate enrollment: 2,000.

EDWARD R. MURROW SCHOOL OF COMMUNICATION

Chair/Contact: Val E. Limburg, Broadcast Sequence Head
Calendar: Semesters
Degrees Offered: B.A., M.A.
Departmental Majors:
Undergraduate: 668 students. Graduate: 77 students
Entrance Requirements:
Undergraduate: 2.5 grade-point average; ACT or SAT scores. Graduate: transcripts; GRE scores; 3.0 grade-point average; personal statement of purpose; recommendations. Undergraduate and graduate application deadline: May 1; December 15. Percent of acceptances: undergraduate: 75%. Graduate: 80%
Curricular Emphasis: Broadcast

news; broadcast production; media management; media law and ethics
Special Activities: Television: program material, including nightly newscasts, produced for cable television and for public television station located on campus; five television shows syndicated for National College Television Network
Facilities: Television: two complete full-color studios; audio bay; control room; video editing suites; interlinking telecommunications system
Equipment: Television/Video: complete ¾" and ½" studio and location including three ¾" field units
Alumni: Edward R. Murrow, radio/TV journalist; Keith Jackson, TV network sports announcer; Barry Serafin, TV network news correspondent; Peter Van Sant, TV network news correspondent; Kathi Goertzen, TV news anchor/reporter

GUIDE POV: Students choosing the broadcast sequence at this state university will find a program emphasizing news writing and production; special attention to media law and ethics; program enjoys strong ties to professional broadcast industry; study abroad in more than 80 countries; co-op program with the University of Idaho; extensive internship opportunities through university's Professional Experience Program

WESTERN WASHINGTON UNIVERSITY

Bellingham, WA 98225
(206)650–3000

State four-year comprehensive institution. Coed, urban location.

Undergraduate enrollment: 10,000.
Graduate enrollment: 800.

DEPARTMENT OF COMMUNICATION

Chair/Contact: Broadcast media:
Alden C. Smith
Calendar: Quarters
Degrees Offered: B.A.,
communication (concentration in
broadcast media studies)
Departmental Majors: Undergraduate
broadcast: 50 students
Entrance Requirements:
Undergraduate: 2.75 grade-point
average; ACT or SAT scores; freshman
applicants meeting minimum GPA and
subject requirements are ranked by an
index combining GPA and a
standardized test score.
Undergraduate application deadline:
March 1. Percent of acceptances:
undergraduate: 85%
Curricular Emphasis: Electronic
media theory and culture; media
writing; television/video production;
media management
Special Activities: Film: film series/
festivals. Television: program material
produced for cable television includes
news and documentary, fiction, and
video art

Facilities: Film: screening room;
editing suite; sound mixing room;
animation stand. Television/Video:
studio; audio bay; control room;
video editing suites; computer graphics
lab
Equipment: Film: complete 16mm.
Television/Video: complete ¾" studio;
complete ¾" and ½" location
Alumni: Janice Moore, TV producer/
director; Joyce Taylor, TV news
anchor; Marianne McClary, TV news
anchor/reporter; Jack Underwood, TV
producer

GUIDE POV: The broadcast media
program at this innovative and well-
regarded university offers students
professional video production training;
competitive entry; study abroad in
over 60 countries; student-designed
majors available through the College
of Arts and Sciences as well as
through Fairhaven College, which
offers video and photographic
documentary; honors program; cross-
registration through the National
Student Exchange; internship
opportunities in television production

Having started college at the University of North Carolina at Greensboro, I obtained my B.A. from USC in cinema and television.

One of my professors at USC always met individually with each student to go over post-school job possibilities. And we would discuss the three basic ways of contacting prospective employers: phoning, dropping by, or writing a letter. For me, writing a letter proved both the best and least obtrusive way. Fortunately, I landed a job as director Mark Rydell's personal assistant.

When writing a résumé and cover letter, there are a few things to keep in mind: First, you are now a member of a very large club—ex-film students looking for work. One assistant at a studio told me that her office received as many as forty résumés a day. A smaller studio receives anywhere from five to ten a week. So it's a good idea to be creative when presenting yourself. Try to demonstrate that you are interesting, talented, and tireless. It is a fine line to walk between keeping in good taste and being outrageous. But almost anything is better than ending up in the wastepaper basket. Think of your letter as a movie trailer. And present the best parts of yourself as quickly and entertainingly as possible.

ALDERSON-BROADDUS COLLEGE

Box 1428, Philippi, WV 26416
(304)457-1700

Private four-year comprehensive institution. Coed, small town location. Enrollment: 800.

DEPARTMENT OF SPEECH COMMUNICATION

Chair/Contact: Robert Powell, Director of broadcast services
Calendar: Semesters
Degrees Offered: B.A., humanities
Departmental Majors: Radio and television: 35 students
Entrance Requirements: 2.0 grade-point average; ACT or SAT testing, with recommended minimum scores of 18 or 800 composite, respectively. Application deadline: rolling. Percent of acceptances: 86%
Curricular Emphasis: Electronic media theory and culture; critical studies in film; media writing; audio-video production; media management
Special Activities: Film: film series/festivals. Television/Radio: program material produced for local public access television; student-operated FM radio station
Facilities: Film: screening room; editing suite. Television/Video: studio; audio bay; control room; video editing suites
Equipment: Film: complete Super-8.

Television/Video: complete ¾" studio and ½" location
Alumni: Alex Bain, TV master control engineer; Ricardo Madison, educational public relations specialist; Anita Payne, media advertising executive; Eddie Morris, radio announcer

GUIDE POV: Alderson-Broaddus College offers broadcasting majors a small program with the aim of promoting creative, artistic, critical, and abstract thinking; solid liberal arts foundation within a Christian tradition; cross-registration with the Mountain State Association of Colleges; study abroad through the college's programs in Austria and England or through the junior year abroad program; internship opportunities in radio and television production

BETHANY COLLEGE

Bethany, WV 26032
(304)829-7000

Private four-year comprehensive institution. Coed, small town location. Enrollment: 900.

COMMUNICATIONS DEPARTMENT

Chair/Contact: James Keegan, Head
Calendar: 4-1-4
Degrees Offered: B.A., communications

Departmental Majors: Radio and television: 55 students
Entrance Requirements: ACT or SAT scores; essay required; interview recommended. Application deadline: August 15. Percent of acceptances: 90%
Curricular Emphasis: Media theory and practice; media writing; audio-video production; international communication; organizational communication
Special Activities: Film: film series/festivals. Television: program material produced for cable television. Radio: student-operated FM radio station
Facilities: Film: screening room; editing suite. Television/Video: studio; audio bay; control room; video editing suites; computer graphics lab
Equipment: Film: complete Super-8. Television/Video: complete ¾" studio and ½" location
Alumni: Faith Daniels, national TV news reporter; Jane Barnett Leonard, White House political correspondent; Yvonne Zanos, consumer affairs reporter; Rick Clancy, corporate communications executive

GUIDE POV: Students at Bethany College may study television and radio production, writing, and management training; co-op programs with Columbia, Washington, and Case Western Reserve universities; cross-registration with West Liberty State and Wheeling Jesuit colleges; study abroad in France, Spain, England, and Germany; January term is voluntary and experimental; required internships for upper-division students

CONCORD COLLEGE

Box 33, Athens, WV 24712
(304)384–3115

State four-year comprehensive institution. Coed, small town location. Enrollment: 2,000.

COMMUNICATION ARTS DEPARTMENT

Chair/Contact: Larry E. Smith
Calendar: Semesters
Degrees Offered: B.A.
Departmental Majors: 100–200 students
Entrance Requirements: 2.0 grade-point average; minimum ACT score of 17. Application deadline: rolling. Percent of acceptances: 98%
Curricular Emphasis: Broadcast journalism and production; media management
Special Activities: Television: all programming on campus cable television is produced by students
Facilities: Television: three-camera full-color studio; audio bay; control room; three editing bays (S-VHS)
Equipment: Television/Video: complete ¾" studio and location including ENG
Alumni: Rich Cisney, TV cameraman

GUIDE POV: Concord College instituted a broadcasting program in 1985, which has rapidly expanded; emphasis on practical approach; variety of student programming produced regularly; cross-registration with Bluefield State College; internship opportunities in television production

MARSHALL UNIVERSITY

Huntington, WV 25755
(304)696–3170

State four-year comprehensive institution. Coed, urban location. Undergraduate enrollment: 10,000. Graduate enrollment: 2,300.

SCHOOL OF JOURNALISM AND MASS COMMUNICATION

Chair/Contact: Dr. Harold Shaver, Director
Calendar: Semesters
Degrees Offered: B.A., journalism; M.A.J.
Departmental Majors:
Undergraduate: 368 students. Graduate: 49 students
Entrance Requirements:
Undergraduate: 2.0 grade-point average; ACT (minimum 14) or SAT (minimum composite 670) scores. Graduate: transcripts; GRE scores. Undergraduate and graduate application deadline: two weeks prior to start of term. Percent of acceptances: 99%
Curricular Emphasis: Broadcasting sequence covers all aspects of broadcast production
Special Activities: Television: program material produced for noncommercial cable television WPBY located on campus; PRSSA and SPJ membership
Facilities: Television: studio; audio bay; control room; ¾" and Hi-8 editing suites; Macintosh and IBM computer labs
Equipment: Television/Video: complete ¾" studio and location
Alumni: Soupy Sales, TV personality; Marvin L. Stone, media journalist

GUIDE POV: Founded in 1837, Marshall University offers broadcasting students a carefully planned curriculum providing a balanced mixture of practical and theoretical studies; faculty of active scholars and working professionals; study abroad in 20 countries; internship opportunities in television production

SALEM-TEIKYO COLLEGE

Valley of Learning,
Salem, WV 26426
(304)782-5011

Private four-year comprehensive institution. Coed, rural location. Enrollment: 600.

BROADCASTING/TELECOMMUNICATIONS DEPARTMENT

Chair/Contact: Television: Venita F. Zinn
Calendar: Semesters
Degrees Offered: A.A., B.S., broadcast/telecommunications; B.S., communications
Departmental Majors: Television: 35 students
Entrance Requirements: 2.0 grade-point average; ACT or SAT scores; interview recommended. Application deadline: rolling. Percent of acceptances: 99%
Curricular Emphasis: Electronic media theory and culture; television production with special attention to news/documentary and instructional/industrial production
Special Activities: Film: student publications. Television: program material produced for on-campus closed-circuit television
Facilities: Television/Video: studio; audio bay; control room; video editing suites
Equipment: Television/Video: complete ¾" studio and ½" location
Alumni: Valerie Black, TV director/editor; Jay Randolf, TV sports announcer; Mark Venarelli, TV news anchor; Tracey Moore, TV production specialist

GUIDE POV: Geared for students seeking practical career training, this comprehensive broadcasting program provides production and management training; broad liberal arts curriculum features international studies and topics in theology; small, seminar-style classes; cross-registration through the Mountain State Association of Colleges; study abroad in Japan, the Netherlands, and Germany; internship opportunities available in radio and television production

WEST LIBERTY STATE COLLEGE

West Liberty, WV 26074
(304)336–5000

State four-year comprehensive institution. Coed, rural location. Enrollment: 2,800.

DEPARTMENT OF COMMUNICATION

Chair/Contact: Dr. Gary Williamson, Chair
Calendar: Semesters
Degrees Offered: B.S., communications (concentration in radio and television, journalism, theatre, or public relations)
Departmental Majors: Television: 50 students
Entrance Requirements: 2.0 grade-point average; composite score of at least 17 on the enhanced ACT or a combined score of 680 on the SAT. Application deadline: August 1. Percent of acceptances: 88%
Curricular Emphasis: Electronic media theory and culture; critical studies in film; media writing; audio-video production; basic film production; video art
Special Activities: Television: program material produced for on-campus closed-circuit television includes news/documentary, fiction, and video art projects

Facilities: Film: sound stage. Television/Video: studio; audio bay; control room; video editing suites; computer graphics lab. Radio: student-operated WGLZ-FM
Equipment: Film: complete Super-8. Television/Video: complete ¾" studio and ½" location
Alumni: Ed Ross, TV news anchor; George Kellas, TV news anchor; Paige Beck, TV news journalist

GUIDE POV: With a comprehensive concentration in radio and television production, this state college offers communication students an opportunity to create projects in fiction and nonfiction; cross-registration with the Four-College Consortium; internship opportunities in radio and television production

WEST VIRGINIA STATE COLLEGE

Institute, WV 25112
(304)768–9842

State four-year comprehensive institution. Coed, suburban location. Enrollment: 4,500.

DEPARTMENT OF COMMUNICATIONS

Chair/Contact: Dr. David Wohl, Chair
Calendar: Semesters
Degrees Offered: A.A.S., B.S., communications (with concentrations in filmmaking, broadcasting, theatre, and public relations)
Departmental Majors: Film: 25 students. Television: 65 students
Entrance Requirements: 2.0 grade-point average; ACT required, with a minimum score of 14.3; GED accepted. Application deadline: August 11. Percent of acceptances: 91%
Curricular Emphasis: Electronic media theory and culture; critical

studies in film; screenwriting; film animation; writing for television; audio-film-video production; video art; media management

Special Activities: Film: film series/festivals; full-length features produced and distributed by students and faculty. Television: program material produced for on-campus closed-circuit television and cable television

Facilities: Film: 35mm screening facilities; screening room; editing suite; sound mixing room; animation stand; film library. Television/Video: studio; audio bay; control room; video editing suites; satellite uplink; computer animation lab

Equipment: Film: complete Super-8 and 16mm. Television/Video: complete 1" and ¾" studio; complete ½" location

Alumni: Steve Boyd, film/video editor; Lou Myers, TV actor; Rhea Blakley, TV newscaster

GUIDE POV: West Virginia State College is the only institute of higher learning in the state offering comprehensive training in filmmaking, film animation, and screenwriting; faculty and students produce and internationally distribute full-length feature films; separate concentration in broadcast production; students are encouraged to explore personal creativity while mastering production techniques; diverse course listings; management training; required media internships

---

WEST VIRGINIA UNIVERSITY

Morgantown, WV 26506–6001
(304)293–0111

State four-year comprehensive institution. Coed, small town location.

Undergraduate enrollment: 16,000. Graduate enrollment: 6,000.

THE PERLEY ISAAC REED SCHOOL OF JOURNALISM

Chair/Contact: Dr. Lynn Hinds, Head of broadcast news sequence

Calendar: Semesters

Degrees Offered: B.S.J., M.S.J.

Departmental Majors: Undergraduate radio and television: 100 students. Graduate communication: 42 students

Entrance Requirements:
Undergraduate: 2.0 grade-point average for WV residents; 2.25 for nonresidents; minimum composite score of 720 on the SAT or 19 on the ACT for in-state students; minimum of 800 or 20, respectively, for out-of-state students. Graduate: GRE scores; recommendations. Undergraduate and graduate application deadline: rolling. Percent of acceptances: undergraduate and graduate: 83%

Curricular Emphasis: Broadcast journalism; audio-video production; graduate program is research-oriented

Special Activities: Film: film series/festivals. Television: program material produced for on-campus closed-circuit television and for cable television; ACEJMC accreditation; member Radio-Television News Directors Association

Facilities: Television/Video: studio; audio bay; control room; video and audio tape assembly areas; video editing suites

Equipment: Television/Video: complete studio and ½" location

Alumni: Natalie Tennant, TV news anchor; Mark Casey, TV news director; Jeff Hertrick, TV news director; John McPherson, TV news director

GUIDE POV: West Virginia University provides full training in broadcast production with an emphasis on news journalism; competitive entry; graduate-level studies in communication theory and research; cross-registration with schools in the Southern Regional Education Board and the Academic Common Market; study abroad in seven countries; internship opportunities in television production

Though now a director, I started as an actor. So instead of attending film or TV school, I hung out with directors, camera operators, and editors. Passionately interested, I watched them all and sought the best advice from the best people. Then I started shooting on 8mm film. What I learned from those professionals is that it's vital to develop both your own style and an ever-evolving sense of formal criticism.

After many trials and errors, I went on to direct television programs like "The Bob Newhart Show," "Mary Tyler Moore," and "Murphy Brown."

Obviously, I do not believe that a formal film education is essential for aspiring professionals—although it can't hurt, and it may help. But what you really need is a vital interest in the craft that you choose.

BELOIT COLLEGE

700 College St., Beloit, WI 53511
(608)363–2000

*Private four-year comprehensive
institution. Coed, small town location.
Enrollment: 1,162.*

THEATRE ARTS DEPARTMENT

Chair/Contact: Rod Umles, Chair; Carl
G. Balson
Calendar: Semesters
Degrees Offered: B.A.
Departmental Majors: Television: five
to ten students
Entrance Requirements: ACT or SAT
scores; ATs recommended; essay
required; interview recommended.
Application deadline: March 15;
December 15 early admission. Percent
of acceptances: 85%
Curricular Emphasis: Electronic
media theory and culture; media
writing; video production
Special Activities: Television:
program material produced for cable
television
Facilities: Television/Video: studio;
audio bay; control room; video editing
suites; computer graphics lab
Equipment: Television/Video:
complete ¾" studio; complete ¾" and
½" location
Alumni: John Pasquin, TV director;
Taggart Seigel, filmmaker; Margaret
Robinson, TV producer

GUIDE POV: Intensive television
production studies at Beloit College
are offered through the Theatre Arts
Department; emphasis on scriptwriting
and analysis as well as broadcast
performance, producing, directing, and
editing; competitive admissions; cross-
registration with the University of
Wisconsin/Madison; study abroad in
30 countries; dual, student-designed,
and interdisciplinary majors;
departmental honors program;
internship opportunities in television
and radio production

MARQUETTE UNIVERSITY

1131 W. Wisconsin Ave.,
Milwaukee, WI 53233
(414)288–7700

*Private four-year comprehensive
institution. Coed, urban location.
Undergraduate enrollment: 9,200.
Graduate enrollment: 2,000.*

DEPARTMENT OF BROADCAST AND ELECTRONIC COMMUNICATION

Chair/Contact: Dr. Judine Mayerle,
O.S.B., Chair
Calendar: Semesters
Degrees Offered: B.A., broadcast and
electronic communication (students
may select minor in film); M.A.,
communication
Departmental Majors: Undergraduate

television: 250 students. Graduate
television: 50 students
Entrance Requirements:
Undergraduate: 2.5 grade-point
average; minimum score of 21 on
enhanced ACT or composite score of
800 on SAT; interview recommended.
Graduate: GRE of at least 1000
combined; personal statement of
purpose; recommendations.
Undergraduate application deadline:
May 1. Graduate application deadline:
February 15. Percent of acceptances:
undergraduate: 81%. Graduate: 75%
Curricular Emphasis: Broadcast
news; production; management/
corporate communication;
entertainment television; media writing
Special Activities: Television:
program material produced for
student-run MUTV on-campus closed-
circuit television; Women in
Communication, Marquette chapter.
Radio: student-run WMUR-FM on-
campus radio station
Facilities: Film: screening room.
Television/Video: two fully equipped
color studios; three audio studios;
control room; nine video editing
suites; extensive computer graphics
platforms including facilities for
animation; digital video effects;
television mobile unit; audio and
video field equipment
Equipment: Television/Video:
complete ¾" studio; complete ¾" and
½" location
Alumni: Tom Snyder, TV personality;
John C. Schwartz, ABC-TV executive;
Maryann Lazarsky, TV news director

GUIDE POV: Comprehensive training
in television studio and field
production is offered at this
competitive Jesuit university; emphasis
on news, entertainment, and corporate

media production; diverse course
listings in media performance,
management, law, history, and ethics;
film minor is theory-oriented;
departmental honors program;
extensive study abroad program;
internship opportunities in television
and radio production

MILWAUKEE AREA TECHNICAL COLLEGE

700 W. State St.,
Milwaukee, WI 53233
(414)278–6600

*State two-year institution. Coed, urban
location. Enrollment: 4,600.*

TELEVISION AND VIDEO PRODUCTION DEPARTMENT

Chair/Contact: David Baule
Calendar: Semesters
Degrees Offered: A.A., television and
video production
Departmental Majors: Television and
video production: 95 students
Entrance Requirements: High
school diploma. Application
deadline: September 1. Percent of
acceptances: 75%
Curricular Emphasis: Television/
Video production
Special Activities: Course work
offered through facilities at WMVS/
WMVT-TV; students produce a variety
of programming
Equipment: Three studios, two 40' ×
60' and one 20' × 16'; computer,
lighting control, and prompter; Sony
306 cameras, audio and switching;
Postproduction—D2 with Betacam SP
capture; electronic graphics including
ArtStar and WaveFront; Digital audio
(stereo and surround); analog
switching; four Betacam SP chip

cameras; three camera remote unit and microwave vans with Hitachi 350s and D2 record/playback; C Band uplink with KU; Digital video effects; High Definition and Beta Test for broadcast; Ampex Alex character generators; Sony 9000 edit controllers
Alumni: Allen Kuskowski, operations executive; Tom Rozek, videographer; Tom Endres, broadcasting assistant director

GUIDE POV: Students attending this two-year college enjoy extensive television/video production experience in professional facilities; media internship opportunities

SAINT NORBERT COLLEGE

100 Grant St.,
De Pere, WI 54115–2099
(414)337–3181

Private four-year comprehensive institution. Coed, suburban location. Enrollment: 2,000.

DEPARTMENT OF COMMUNICATION, MEDIA, AND THEATRE

Chair/Contact: Dr. Kelly Collum, Chair
Calendar: Semesters
Degrees Offered: B.A., communication
Departmental Majors: Television: 65 students
Entrance Requirements: 2.5 grade-point average; ACT (minimum 19) or SAT (minimum 900) scores; essay and recommendations required; interview recommended. Application deadline: rolling. Percent of acceptances: 85%
Curricular Emphasis: Media history and ethics; media writing; directing; basic audio-video production
Special Activities: Television/Radio:

program material produced for student-run WSNC-TV and WSNC-Radio, which distribute satellite feeds and locally produced programs to the community; student broadcasts include academic, educational, sports, entertainment, and promotional programs about campus events
Facilities: Television/Video: studio; audio bay; control room; video editing suites
Equipment: Television/Video: complete ¾" studio and location
Alumni: Alison Ebert, TV producer/director; Gretchen Mattingley, TV producer; Eric Brown, TV sportscaster

GUIDE POV: This small college offers students a major that emphasizes writing, directing, and acting; strong liberal arts curriculum; honors program; study abroad in 12 countries; internship opportunities in radio and television production

UNIVERSITY OF WISCONSIN— EAU CLAIRE

Eau Claire, WI 54701
(715)836–2637

State four-year comprehensive institution. Coed, urban location. Enrollment: 9,000.

DEPARTMENT OF COMMUNICATION AND THEATRE ARTS

Chair/Contact: W. Robert Sampson, Chair; Daniel J. Perkins
Calendar: Semesters
Degrees Offered: B.A., communication arts (students may select emphasis in telecommunications, communication studies, public communication, organizational communication, or organizational public relations)

Departmental Majors: Television: 75 students

Entrance Requirements: ACT or combined SAT score of 22 or 1000, respectively, or academic rank within top half of graduating class. Application deadline: December 1 for early admission; April 1 for regular admission. Percent of acceptances: 79%

Curricular Emphasis: Electronic media theory and culture; critical studies in film; radio-television writing and production; programming for radio-television-cable; media management

Special Activities: Film: film series. Television: program material produced for on-campus closed-circuit television is broadcast to students on Campus Cable and to the city of Eau Claire on WIS CATV; program material produced for local commercial television station and cable television

Facilities: Film: screening room. Television/Video: studio; audio bay; control room; video editing suites; computer graphics lab

Equipment: Television/Video: complete ¾" studio and ½" location

Alumni: Laila Robbins, theatre/film/TV actress; Rick Fuller, director of music videos; Scott Miller, video editor

GUIDE POV: This member of the University of Wisconsin system offers students a variety of production opportunities in the context of a solid liberal arts curriculum; emphasis on news, sports, and public affairs broadcast production as well as media programming and management; study abroad in 14 countries; competitive entry; internship opportunities in radio and corporate television production

UNIVERSITY OF WISCONSIN— GREEN BAY

Green Bay, WI 54302
(414)465–2000

State four-year comprehensive institution. Coed, rural location. Undergraduate enrollment: 6,000. Graduate enrollment: 400.

COMMUNICATION PROCESSES

Chair/Contact: Jerry Dell, Chair; Roger Vanderperren, Director of Media Resources

Calendar: 4–1–4

Degrees Offered: B.A., M.A., communication

Departmental Majors: Undergraduate television: 115 students. Graduate communication: 20 students

Entrance Requirements: Undergraduate: 2.0 grade-point average; ACT or SAT scores. Graduate: GRE scores; recommendations. Undergraduate application deadline: November 30. Graduate application deadline: rolling. Percent of acceptances: undergraduate: 81%. Graduate: 70%

Curricular Emphasis: Electronic media theory and culture; critical studies in film; media writing; audio-video production; broadcast journalism; media management; communication law

Special Activities: Film: film series. Television: program material produced for local cable television

Facilities/Equipment: Television/Video: complete television field production equipment and video editing capabilities; lighting studio; electronic photography computer studio

Alumni: Roger Downey, TV producer; James Gordon Douglas, TV news reporter/videographer; Mary Thuermer, film actress; Gordon Hempstead, audio recordist

GUIDE POV: Communication students at this large rural campus of the University of Wisconsin may study video production and writing as part of a major in Communication Processes; interdisciplinary media studies, including film history and aesthetics, offered through communication and the arts program; cross-registration with the universities of Wisconsin at Milwaukee and Oshkosh and through other members of the National Student Exchange; study abroad in Mexico, Denmark, Sweden, and Germany, as well as through the ISEP Exchange Program; internship opportunities

UNIVERSITY OF WISCONSIN— LA CROSSE

La Crosse, WI 54601
(608)785–8000

State four-year comprehensive institution. Coed, small city location. Enrollment: 9,000.

DEPARTMENT OF MASS COMMUNICATIONS

Chair/Contact: Dr. John D. Jenks, Chair
Calendar: Semesters
Degrees Offered: B.A., mass communication
Departmental Majors: Television: 75 students
Entrance Requirements: Academic rank within top half of graduating class; ACT required, with a minimum score of 22. Application deadline: September 15. Percent of acceptances: 89%

Curricular Emphasis: Electronic media theory and culture; critical studies in film; media writing; audio-video production; media management
Special Activities: Television: program material produced for cable television
Facilities: Film: screening room. Television/Video: studio; audio bay; control room; video editing suites
Equipment: Television/Video: complete ¾" studio and ½" location
Alumni: Gene Purcell, radio director of operations; Laura Littel, director of communications

GUIDE POV: This public university offers video production training with an emphasis on nonfiction television programming; diverse course listings; cooperative programs and cross-registration available with Viterbo College; study abroad in eight countries; internship opportunities in television and radio production

UNIVERSITY OF WISCONSIN— MADISON

821 University Ave.,
Madison, WI 53706
(608)262–1234

State four-year comprehensive institution. Coed, urban location. Undergraduate enrollment: 30,000. Graduate enrollment: 11,000.

DEPARTMENT OF COMMUNICATION ARTS

Chair/Contact: Lea Jacobs, film and television studies
Calendar: Semesters
Degrees Offered: B.A., M.A., Ph.D.
Departmental Majors: Undergraduate: 477 students. Graduate: 27 film; 17 television

Entrance Requirements:
Undergraduate: 2.5 grade-point average; teachers' recommendations. Graduate: 3.25 grade-point average; GRE scores; teachers' recommendations; written statement of purpose. Undergraduate application deadline: February 1 for fall entry; November 15 for spring entry. Graduate application deadline: March 1 for fall entry; October 1 for spring entry. Percent of acceptances: undergraduate: 89%. Graduate: 60–80%
Curricular Emphasis: Film history, theory, and criticism; some courses in film and video production
Special Activities: Film: film series/festivals; film societies; student publications; extensive archives collection at Wisconsin Center for Film and Theater Research. Television: program material produced for on-campus closed-circuit television; local public television station; cable television
Facilities: Film: screening room; editing suite; sound stage; sound mixing room; animation stand; film library; research facilities; archives. Television: studio; audio bay; control room
Equipment: Film: complete 16mm. Television/Video: complete ½" studio and location
Alumni: Bette Gordon, film director; Jim Benning, animator; Steven Starr, film director; Maria Benfield, videographer

GUIDE POV: This competitive public university emphasizes the formal study of film and television history, theory, and criticism; extensive archives collection on campus; program is intended to provide training for serious scholars as well as for undergraduates seeking a strong

theoretical background for graduate work in production; study abroad in Asia, South America, and Europe; internship opportunities in film/mass media research and to a lesser degree in film/video production

UNIVERSITY OF WISCONSIN—MILWAUKEE

3203 N. Downer Ave.,
MIT B-69, Milwaukee, WI 53211
(414)229-1122

State four-year comprehensive institution. Coed, urban location. Undergraduate enrollment: 25,000. Graduate enrollment: 4,500.

DEPARTMENT OF FILM AND VIDEO

Chair/Contact: Dick Blau, Chair
Calendar: Semesters
Degrees Offered: B.F.A., M.F.A.
Departmental Majors: Undergraduate film and video: 80 students. Graduate film and video: 12 students
Entrance Requirements:
Undergraduate: ACT scores; portfolio. Graduate: written statement of purpose; portfolio. Undergraduate application deadline: June 30. Graduate application deadline: March 15. Percent of acceptances: Undergraduate: 73%. Graduate: 30%
Curricular Emphasis:
Interdisciplinary fine arts production program in film and video stressing imaginative exploration of personal and cultural questions through experimental forms
Special Activities: Film: film series/festivals; international conferences through the Center for Twentieth Century Studies on varied topics relating to media and culture. Television: program material produced for cable television

Facilities: Film: studio; screening room; editing suite; three multitrack audio transfer and sound mixing studios; animation stands; Mag film to optical sound recording; film archives. Video: studio; three editing suites; computer animation lab

Equipment: Film: complete 16mm including Arri, Bolex, Bell & Howell, among others. Video: complete ¾" studio; complete Hi-8 and ½" location

Alumni: Dawn Wiedermann, filmmaker; Chris Bratton, videographer/teacher; Cathy Cook, filmmaker; Michael Collins, video artist

GUIDE POV: Students at this highly competitive state university are offered an interdisciplinary program emphasizing avant-garde and experimental production as part of a fine arts curriculum; exposure to a variety of cinematic styles; faculty includes figures in the American and European avant-garde; study abroad in Europe and Asia; accelerated degree program; internship opportunities

UNIVERSITY OF WISCONSIN— OSHKOSH

800 Algoma Blvd.,
Oshkosh, WI 54901–8601
(414)424–1234

State four-year comprehensive institution. Coed, urban location. Undergraduate enrollment: 9,600. Graduate enrollment: 1,600.

DEPARTMENT OF COMMUNICATION

Chair/Contact: Douglas Heil, Coordinator of radio-TV-film
Calendar: Semesters
Degrees Offered: B.A., B.S., communication (students may select emphasis in radio-TV-film)

Departmental Majors: Undergraduate radio-TV-film: 240 students
Entrance Requirements:
Undergraduate: academic rank within top half of graduating class; 2.5 grade-point average; ACT or SAT scores. Undergraduate application deadline: rolling. Percent of acceptances: 77%
Curricular Emphasis: Dramatic film and animation; corporate video and advertising; industrial video; broadcast news; independent film and video; documentary film and video; solid background in creative aesthetics
Special Activities: Film: international film series; film society. Television: eight weekly programs produced by and for students for Titan Television; program material also produced for Oshkosh Public Access Television and run out of department; advanced students are chosen for paid assignments producing corporate videos for outside clients
Facilities: Film: screening room; editing suites; sound stage; Oxberry animation stand; film library. Television: two studios; audio bays; control rooms; remote trailer; video editing suites
Equipment: Film: complete 16mm and 8mm. Television/Video: complete 1" and ¾" studio and complete ¾" location including Ikegami studio cameras and JVC ENG units with ¾" Sony VCRs; 1" video special effects; portable lighting kits; Nagra recorders; Superscope recorders; Grass Valley 200-2 switcher
Alumni: Larry Klein, TV producer; Ralph Berge, TV network production manager

GUIDE POV: This highly professional school offers students a quality program with advanced production training in both film and video;

Oshkosh Film Society receives allocation for 16mm student projects; students actively participate in national and regional festivals; internship opportunities in film, video, and television production

UNIVERSITY OF WISCONSIN— PLATTEVILLE

Platteville, WI 53818–3099
(608)342–1194

State four-year comprehensive institution. Coed, small town location. Enrollment: 5,000.

DEPARTMENT OF COMMUNICATION

Chair/Contact: Virgil Pufahl, Chair
Calendar: Semesters
Degrees Offered: B.A., B.S., communication (major in broadcast technology management)
Departmental Majors: Radio and television: 130 students
Entrance Requirements: ACT of 22 or class rank within upper 40% of high school graduating class. Application deadline: rolling. Percent of acceptances: 87%
Curricular Emphasis: Electronic media theory and culture; audio-video production; broadcast technology management
Special Activities: Television: program material produced for on-campus closed-circuit television and for cable television
Facilities: Television/Video: studio; audio bay; control room; video editing suites
Equipment: Television/Video: complete ¾" studio and ½" location
Alumni: Kevin Peckham, media sales executive; Don Byrne, TV operations manager; Tom Koser, media executive

GUIDE POV: The University of Wisconsin at Platteville offers comprehensive undergraduate broadcast studies covering both technical and creative aspects; separate emphasis in media management; study abroad in 12 countries; internship opportunities in television and radio production

UNIVERSITY OF WISCONSIN— RIVER FALLS

River Falls, WI 54022
(715)425–3911

State four-year comprehensive institution. Coed, suburban location. Enrollment: 6,000.

DEPARTMENT OF JOURNALISM

Chair/Contact: Ray Niekamp; Michael Norman

SPEECH, COMMUNICATION, AND THEATRE ARTS

Chair/Contact: Jim Zimmerman
Calendar: Semesters
Degrees Offered: B.A., B.S., journalism, speech (emphasis in mass communication)
Departmental Majors: Television: 141 students (Department of Journalism). Film and television: 50 students (Speech, Communication, and Theatre Arts Department)
Entrance Requirements: Academic rank within top half of graduating class; ACT scores (minimum 22). Application deadline: December 1. Percent of acceptances: 78%
Curricular Emphasis: Television/Video production
Special Activities: Television: program material produced for student-run cable television channel; accredited by ACEJMC

Facilities: Television: studio; audio bay; control room

Equipment: Television/Video: two complete ¾" studios; complete ¾" and ½" location including ENG

Alumni: Roland Rosenkranz, TV scenic artist; Felix DeNeau, TV/film actor; Boyd Huppert, TV news reporter; Cathy Wurzer, radio news anchor/reporter

GUIDE POV: Students majoring in journalism at this state university receive intensive studio production training and broadcast writing instruction; in addition, basic film and video production training is offered through the Speech, Communication, and Theatre Arts Department; study abroad; internship opportunities in television production

UNIVERSITY OF WISCONSIN— SUPERIOR

Superior, WI 54880
(715)394–8101

State four-year comprehensive institution. Coed, small town location. Enrollment: 6,000.

COMMUNICATING ARTS DEPARTMENT

Chair/Contact: Paul J. Kending; Thomas J. Notton; Joseph Tarantowski

Calendar: Semesters

Degrees Offered: B.A., communicating arts

Departmental Majors: Radio and television: 75 students

Entrance Requirements: Academic rank within top half of high school graduating class; ACT required; SAT accepted from out-of-state students; recommendations. Application

deadline: rolling. Percent of acceptances: 84%

Curricular Emphasis: Electronic media theory and culture; media writing; audio-video production

Special Activities: Television: program material produced for on-campus closed-circuit television UWS and for cable television. Radio: student-run radio station FUWS-FM affiliated with Wisconsin Public Radio network

Facilities: Television/Video: studio; audio bay; control room; video editing suites

Equipment: Television/Video: complete ¾" studio and location including computerized video editing system; video switcher; eight-channel stereo audio console; character generator; teleprompters; Sony M7 CCD cameras

Alumni: Dan Woods, filmmaker; Peter G. Blank, video corporate executive; Cliff Dodge, media supervisor; Wendy Jean Fabbri, TV/film actress

GUIDE POV: The expanding television production curriculum at this competitive state university offers students professional writing and production experience emphasizing broadcast journalism; diverse course listings in film and electronic media theory and criticism; cross-registration with the University of Minnesota at Duluth, the College of St. Scholastica, and Northland College; internship opportunities in radio and television production

UNIVERSITY OF WISCONSIN— WHITEWATER

800 Main St., Whitewater, WI 53190
(414)472–1234

State four-year comprehensive institution. Coed, small town location. Undergraduate enrollment: 9,300. Graduate enrollment: 1,300.

COLLEGE OF LETTERS AND SCIENCES

Chair/Contact: Mary Quinlivan, Dean

COMMUNICATION DEPARTMENT

Chair/Contact: Peter Conover
Calendar: Semesters
Degrees Offered: B.A., B.S., speech communication (students may select emphasis in radio-TV); M.S., communication
Departmental Majors: Undergraduate radio-television: 70 students. Graduate mass communication: five students
Entrance Requirements: Undergraduate: class rank within top half of high school graduating class; ACT or SAT scores (ACT is preferred); 2.0 grade-point average. Graduate: 2.75 grade-point average; GRE score; recommendations. Undergraduate and graduate application deadline: rolling. Percent of acceptances: undergraduate: 84%. Graduate: 77%
Curricular Emphasis: Electronic media theory and culture; media writing; audio-video production; media management
Special Activities: Television/Radio: program material produced for the university and community cable television; university licensed FM radio station
Facilities: Television/Radio: studio; audio bay; control room; video editing suites; remote van; FM radio station and digital audio laboratory
Equipment: Television/Radio: complete SP ¾" and S-VHS studio; SP ¾" and S-VHS ½" field production and editing; advanced graphics; digital audio studio; fully equipped audio broadcast FM station
Alumni: Craig Coshun, TV sports anchor; Jim Socha, TV sports anchor; Scott Durand, cable TV executive

GUIDE POV: The University of Wisconsin—Whitewater, located between Milwaukee and Chicago, offers a dynamic and growing radio and television program with production emphasis; internships apply audio and video communication in a variety of broadcast, corporate, industrial, and new technology settings

I had always been obsessed with movies. Since I was a boy in Panama—where my father was a federal engineer—I watched everything the matinees of the 1950s had to offer, knowing nothing of the genre, but particularly fascinated by films involving elements of science fiction, horror, and fantasy. In college, studying religion and art, I saw the great foreign films of the late sixties and was blown away by the depth of experience provided by many of them. I never tried hard to get into the overcrowded film criticism classes—it didn't even seem like school—a class in "viewing films." Movie theaters were more my style. Much later, after I started making movies, I finally began to seriously analyze the films of the past. That wasn't until my midthirties, when, after years of carpentry, small businesses, painting pictures, and itinerant hippiedom, I began to goof around with a 16mm Bolex camera along with a friend, who had gone to film school at the University of North Carolina and who knew something about F-stops and editing. It marked a significant change in my life, and movies rose to the top of the list of things I wanted to do. Until then I had never known enough about filmmaking to seriously consider it as a possible occupation. But I borrowed some money and risked everything to produce my first and successful horror movie, called *Re-Animator*.

As I learned more and more about the art and business of film, I came to appreciate the professionalism and collaboration that a good movie celebrates. For someone who loves to work with creative people as I do, filmmaking provides unlimited opportunities.

If ever I had known that I would end up in the film industry, I would probably have fought to get into the best film school available. Instead, I learned from doing, with people who did study in the field. Film is a myth-making medium, storytelling to entertain, inspire, educate, or subvert. The value of film school, I expect, is providing an environment of like-minded individuals determined to explore and master an evolving art and technology, with the freedom that comes from being more or less separate from the immediate forces of commerce. Although it still becomes necessary to finally go out and "do it in the real world," I can't help but believe that studying filmmaking in school can be a decided advantage. But it is having a rich life outside of film and school that is essential to having anything to say once you have the opportunity.

The greatest thrill for me is seeing my subjective work become an objective experience for an audience, an image that takes on a life of its own: for example, the kids on the bee and the ant in *Honey, I Shrunk the Kids*, which I created, or the finger-eye creature in *Bride of Re-Animator*. I also wrote and produced *From Beyond* and directed and produced *Society*, *Return of the Living Dead 3*, and *Necronomicon*.

CASPER COLLEGE

125 College Dr., Casper, WY 82601
(307)268–2110

*State two-year comprehensive
institution. Coed, urban location.
Enrollment: 3,000.*

LANGUAGE AND LITERATURE DEPARTMENT

Chair/Contact: Paul Wolz, Chair
Calendar: Semesters
Degrees Offered: A.A., English and
literature (students may select
emphasis in film studies), journalism,
communication
Departmental Majors: Film: 10
students
Entrance Requirements: 2.0 grade-
point average; ACT scores. Application
deadline: rolling. Percent of
acceptances: 99%
Curricular Emphasis: Film history,
theory/aesthetics, and criticism; mass
media theory; corporate and
educational single-camera video
production
Special Activities: Film: film series.
Video: students create private and
institutional videotapes for class
projects
Facilities: Film: screening
room
Equipment: Film: Super-8 and 16mm
projectors. Television/Video: complete
¾" location
Alumni: Kent Hughes, assistant

cameraman; Trenda Bothel, TV
production manager

GUIDE POV: Providing a thorough
background for students intending to
transfer to a four-year institution, this
liberal arts college offers mass media
studies through its Communication
Department, film theory through the
English and Literature Department as
well as corporate and educational
single-camera video production
through the Journalism Department;
media internship opportunities

UNIVERSITY OF WYOMING

P.O. Box 3904,
Laramie, WY 82071
(307)266–1121

*State four-year comprehensive
institution. Coed, urban location.
Undergraduate enrollment: 9,300.
Graduate enrollment: 1,700.*

COMMUNICATION AND MASS MEDIA

Chair/Contact: Dr. Frank Millar, Chair
Calendar: Semesters
Degrees Offered: B.A., B.S.,
journalism, broadcasting, and
communication; M.A., communication
Departmental Majors:
Undergraduate: 250 students. Graduate:
20 students
Entrance Requirements:
Undergraduate: high school diploma
or GED; nonresidents must have

minimum 2.5 grade-point average; ACT or SAT scores; interview recommended. Graduate: transcripts; 900 composite GRE scores; 3.0 undergraduate grade-point average. Undergraduate application deadline: August 10. Percent of acceptances: undergraduate: 80%. Graduate: 40%

Curricular Emphasis: Electronic media theory and culture; media writing; broadcast journalism; audio-video production; media management

Special Activities: Television: program material produced for community access television located on campus

Facilities: Television: studio; audio bay; control room

Equipment: Television/Video: complete ¾" studio and ½" location

Alumni: Gene Levitt, screenwriter

GUIDE POV: Professional production training in radio and television is offered at this public multicampus school; competitive entry; cross-registration with area community colleges; study abroad; internship opportunities in television and radio production

Years ago when I attended New York University as a journalism major, I was lucky enough to take a number of cinema courses at the School of the Arts. It was an eye-opening experience: my first encounter with film instructors—and with film students.

Most of the students then were filmmakers; there was no major in film studies. The prevailing attitude among those budding Truffauts was one of arrogance; they had little to learn from watching films of the past. And after listening to some of the teachers who presented these films, I couldn't really blame the students for their indifference. Without having any social or historical context for these films from the 1920s, '30s, '40s, or '50s, how was any young person supposed to appreciate a film's strengths or innovations?

I once sat in on a course at City College of New York taught by a noted film historian, who proceeded to talk right over the heads of his young and rowdy class. He showed them the classic British documentary *The Granton Trawler*. It had no meaning for anyone in the room, because the professor's condescending introduction fell on deaf and hostile ears.

It was then I decided that knowledge is not the most important ingredient in the teaching of film history and appreciation: A more important quality is passion. Film is an exciting, emotional medium. To present it in any other way is to kill it.

By the time a student enrolls in a film appreciation or film history course, he or she has probably already experienced the visceral power of movies. To ignore that fact and proceed to examine film in a cold, clinical manner is to say, tacitly if not explicitly, "The films we're going to study are not like the ones you've grown up watching and enjoying. Consider these more as laboratory animals." In other words, dead.

It's tough enough that most teachers are obliged to show movies in less than perfect circumstances: in classrooms instead of theatres, stripped of the accoutrements that average moviegoers are accustomed to. Light may be streaming into the room, the projection and sound may not be the best. Silent films may not have adequate music tracks, and there may not even be time enough to view an entire film in one session. This isn't the way moviegoers first experienced Chaplin, Griffith, Eisenstein, or Hitchcock. But it's often the way students see their work for the first time.

Considering these enormous handicaps, if a teacher cannot communicate a sense of excitement about a great film or filmmaker, there is no point in screening the film at all. We can learn so much from films of the past—socially and aesthetically—without relying solely on that laboratory-animal approach.

If we produce good film teachers who can inspire their students, perhaps we will develop a more film-savvy audience that will one day demand better movies from Hollywood—and not be willing to settle for mediocrity.

American College Testing (ACT) Program: The ACT Assessment is a multiple-choice examination required for admission to many colleges. It takes 2 hours and 55 minutes to complete. Although the ACT is based on subjects studied in high school, it emphasizes thinking and reasoning skills. An interesting component is the hour-long personal questionnaire that makes up part of the registration form for this test. Questions posed involve your prospective career plans, personal interests, and high school academic background. Your answers, along with the results of your ACT, make up the ACT Assessment Student Report, which is furnished to your high school and to any college, university, or scholarship source upon your written instructions. The ACT Assessment Student Report is used by college and scholarship officials to determine acceptance and awards.

The test is divided into four parts. The English section consists of a 45-minute, 75-item multiple-choice test measuring one's knowledge of English grammar, usage, punctuation, sentence structure, vocabulary, and spelling. The mathematics section is composed of a 60-question, 60-minute multiple-choice test measuring quantitative reasoning skills in the areas of basic mathematics (decimals, fractions, integers, etc.), algebra, coordinate and plane geometry, and, to a lesser extent, trigonometry. The reading section is a 40-item, 35-minute multiple-choice test measuring reading comprehension, with topics in prose fiction/humanities, social studies, and the pure sciences. The science reasoning section consists of a 40-item, 35-minute multiple-choice test presupposing scientific reasoning skills rather than an advanced scientific or mathematical background. Test content is drawn from all spheres of science including astronomy, biology, chemistry, geology, meteorology, and physics. Information is presented through description of experiments, through tables, graphs, and other schematic forms, or through the expression of conflicting scientific viewpoints.

When taking the ACT, you are advised to answer all questions, since there is no penalty for guessing. One's score is based solely upon the number of questions answered correctly.

To obtain an ACT application form, visit your high school guidance counselor or contact ACT Registration, P.O. Box 414, Iowa City, Iowa 52243, (319)337–1270.

Advanced Placement (AP) Examinations: These subject tests administered by the College Board measure knowledge of a specific subject, and are given to high school students who have completed advanced or honors courses and wish to obtain college credit. Colleges also use such tests to determine placement. In addition, foreign language tests may be used to determine exemption from a foreign language requirement. Whether or not required to do so, many students take these tests to demonstrate mastery of a subject.

Tests are given in most college preparatory subjects, including writing, literature, history, foreign languages, mathematics, and the sciences. There is also a proficiency test in English as a second language. One may take up to three tests on any one test date.

For more information, visit your guidance counselor or contact the College Board, Box 6200, Princeton, New Jersey 08451, or Box 1025, Berkeley, California 94701.

College Level Examination Program (CLEP): The CLEP General Examinations, administered by the College Entrance Examination Board (CEEB), cover the material taught in many introductory college courses. Sufficient performance on the CLEP may exempt a student from taking introductory college courses. As well, CLEP subject examinations are given in these areas: English composition; humanities (literature and fine arts); mathematics; natural sciences; social sciences; history. These tests may be taken by students seeking to obtain college credit and/or to waive introductory course requirements in one or more particular subjects.

The main purpose of this program is to provide adults who have decided to enter college after several years with an opportunity to receive college credit for knowledge gained through self-study, work experience, etc. However, some high school students take these tests on their own initiative, and have received college credit or placement accordingly. Students transferring from community colleges also take advantage of these tests for credit or placement purposes.

It is not generally advisable to take more than two subject examinations on any one day. For more information, consult your guidance counselor or contact the Educational Testing Service, Princeton, New Jersey 08541.

General Educational Development Tests (GED): The General Educational Development Tests, also known as the High School Equivalency Examinations, are a series of five separately timed tests designed to determine if the person taking them possesses the educational background equivalent to the upper two-thirds of American high school graduates. The tests are sponsored by the American Council on Education and designed by the Educational Testing Service of Princeton, N.J., the same agency that produces the Scholastic Aptitude Tests. The five test areas covered in the GED are: writing skills, social science, literature and the arts, natural science, and mathematics. Through taking these examinations, one may earn an equivalency diploma. Many colleges and junior colleges accept GED test results in lieu of a high school degree. For more information, contact your GED testing program state administrator.

Graduate Record Examination (GRE): The GRE General Test is a 3½ hour multiple-choice examination designed to measure the verbal, quantitative, and reasoning skills one has developed in the course of an undergraduate academic career. It is used by most graduate schools to help determine eligibility, since it has been established that there exists a marked correlation between GRE scores and ability to successfully pursue graduate-level work. As such, most graduate programs require GRE testing. The examination consists of seven sections: two verbal sections consisting of 38 questions each, which measure vocabulary and reading skills; two 30-question sections in math; and two 25-question word-problem and reading-interpretation sections that test analytical abilities. In addition, one experimental section is included in one of the three test areas. The experimental test result is not counted in the scoring. Students may also take specific subject tests in one or more of 17 fields. For more information, consult your undergraduate adviser or contact the Educational Testing Service, Princeton, New Jersey 08541.

Miller Analogies Test (MAT): The Miller Analogies Test is a high-level test of mental ability required by many graduate schools for admission to a master's or doctoral program, or as a basis for granting graduate grants and scholarships. The test consists of 100 analogies (mostly verbal) that are to be answered in 50 minutes. Questions are arranged in order of difficulty. Although considered an aptitude test, the MAT presupposes an extensive vocabulary as well as a solid grounding in literature, social studies, mathematics, and the pure sciences. For an information bulletin, check with your undergraduate guidance counselor or write to: The Psychological Corporation, 555 Academic Court, San Antonio, Texas 78204–2498.

Scholastic Aptitude Test (SAT): This standardized test measuring verbal and mathematical skills is offered by the Admissions Testing Program of the College Board, and is used to help determine one's aptitude for college work. The three-hour multiple-choice examination is divided into six parts of 30 minutes each. The first two sections test reading comprehension and vocabulary skills. The second two sections, consisting of the mathematical reasoning portion of the test, deal with general number concepts. Calculators are permitted in the test room. One's performance on these four parts determines the scores that colleges will use in evaluating your application. The Test of Standard Written English, making up the fifth part of the test, is scored separately. It is used to determine one's placement in college English courses. The sixth section of the examination is experimental, and the score obtained is not counted in your final result. However, as the order of the examinations is not fixed, it is not possible to determine which section is experimental; therefore, one should answer all questions to the best of one's ability.

Scoring is based on the number of questions answered correctly minus points for those answered incorrectly. It is advisable to make educated guesses by eliminating wrong answers, while avoiding blind guesswork, since it may lower one's score.

To obtain a registration form for the SAT, visit your guidance counselor or write directly to the College Entrance Examination Board, Box 6200, Princeton, New Jersey 08451, (609)771–7600, or Box 1025, Berkeley, California 94701.

A and B Roll Editing: A postproduction term referring to two rolls of film, arbitrarily A and B, containing alternating segments of the original film that overlap each other when dissolves are needed. The A and B technique permits dissolves and fades to be made without going through another processing generation.

A and B Roll Printing: Printing that is done with two or more rolls of film, conformed and matching, with alternate scenes intercut with black leader. This process allows for checkerboard cutting, which eliminates visual film splices on the screen. It also permits single or double exposures, multiple exposure, and hands-on re-editing by the frame.

Animation Camera: Camera used for filming animation. It is usually mounted on an animation stand with its optical axis vertical so that it looks down on the objects being photographed. The camera-drive meter allows the film to move forward one frame at a time.

Animation Stand or Crane: A precise, customized camera mount for animation usage. This mount is capable of accurate gradations of movement above the art work, pegboard, or platen. The unit has various capabilities for subtle and complex moves.

Animation Table: A flat table with a circular rotary inset to allow the cel to be turned to any angle for observations, matching, inking, or painting.

Arri: The industry designation for an Arriflex camera. The 16mm versions are used for news gathering, industrials, commercials, and documentaries. 35mm models are also used for commercials, high-budget documentaries and industrials, as well as for feature motion pictures. Features or parts of features are also shot on 16mm models and blown up into 35mm.

Beaulieu: A lightweight professional motion picture camera that is used extensively for news and documentary coverage.

Bell and Howell: An early motion picture equipment manufacturer of cameras, projectors, and accessories. A pioneer, leader, and competitor with Eastman Kodak in the development of the 8mm and 16mm markers.

Cel: A sheet of transparent plastic in width and height accommodating screen ratios in size. These sheets are used to paint, ink, or draw on directly and are used mainly for animation and titling. The cels have pre-measured, pre-punched holes, customized to the particular film ratio and animation-camera system. Cels are put into proper registration by slipping the camera-ready cels over matching pegs on the device that holds these cels while they are being filmed.

Cel Animation: Film made with drawings, full art work, graphics, or abstract designs photographed or video-recorded on standardized cellulose acetate or triacetate sheets.

Computer-Generated Animation: Images created by computers and their scanning lines as well as utilization of pattern-forming devices. Final images are then fed into a holding videotape or master, or else transferred to motion picture film.

Computer Graphics: Used as a synonym for computer-generated animation, this term also refers to specific special effects wherein computer-generated animation is mixed with live action.

Control Room: The soundproofed enclosure within a radio or TV studio, wherein the director, producer, and technicians supervise the logistics of taping or live broadcasting.

Cuts-Only Editing: Refers to video editing with basic "cut" transitions between shots, i.e. no dissolves, wipes, or fades.

Digital Video Effects: Special graphics and special effects produced by a programmed computer control unit based on a numerical system.

Dub (Dubbing): Synchronization to on-camera lip movement that replaces the existing voice, whether his or her own, or that of another actor. Umbrella term for re-recording, electronic line replacement, and looping.

Eclair: Initially, the prime camera for shooting synch sound documentaries in the new lightweight portable style. Its design was such that it made hand-held shots easier and smoother. It was almost silent-running, and its magazines could be changed in about ten seconds as opposed to several minutes it would take to change the Arriflex magazine. Today, however, the Arriflex, Aaton, and Frezzolini magazines can be changed rapidly as well.

Edit: To arrange and assemble film or tape, prepare it for TV playback or projection, and set it up for final sound mix.

Electronic Field Production (EFP): Location production that utilizes lightweight, portable video gear.

Electronic News Gathering (ENG): On-the-spot news coverage, employing highly portable videotaping systems in place of motion pictures cameras. Standard practice for television stations.

Field Camera: General location camera used by second units. Also the name for easily portable, lightweight cameras used in news coverage and documentaries.

Flatbed Editing: An editing machine with a horizontal bed instead of an upright working area, consisting of matching pairs of circular plates—one for feed-out and one for take-up. There are at least two sets of these plates—one pair for picture, one for sound.

Mixer: Sound recording or reproducing system or device, capable of handling two or more inputs in conjunction with a common output. Also used to describe the senior member of a sound-recording crew in charge of balance control of all dialogue, music, and/or sound effects to be recorded.

Moviola: The trade name of a portable motor-driven film-viewing machine, upright or table variety, with the latter replacing the former. It is used for viewing but primarily for editing. Although there are now numerous flatbed editing units manufactured by numerous companies, they are still often referred to as "moviolas."

Nagra: Standard state-of-the-art portable tape recorder, using ¼" reel-to-reel magnetic tape.

Off-Line: The first step in video editing used to make decisions about all edits in a production; the next process usually is on-line editing, or the final editing stage.

On-Line: All pre-edited tapes tied into the tape-mastering units for the full mix. Also, the state of doing the final tape edit, utilizing audio and video components prepared in the off-line sessions.

Optical Effects: Modifications of the photographic image, filmed in a motion picture camera of normal type, produced in an optical printer. Many of the new optical effects are now, initially, or in final form, computer-generated.

Optical Printer: This is an apparatus with an internal camera/projector interlink, designed to make the final optical negative that can also be used for superimpositions, titling, and special effects.

Resolution: Ability of a lens or emulsion to render fine detail in a photographic image. In TV, resolution is the maximum number of discernible lines of a TV image.

Switcher: In TV, the control room technician in charge of electronically switching from one camera to another.

Synchronizer: A device in cutting rooms for maintaining synchronism between picture and sound elements. It consists of two or more sprockets rigidly mounted on a revolving shaft or drum. The tracks are placed on the sprockets and accurately positioned by their perforations so that they can be wound along by rewinds while maintaining a proper synchronous interlocking.

Synch Sound: Sound that matches frame to frame with the picture, especially critical in close shots. The frame-to-frame marriage of sound and picture.

Telecine: This is a device used originally to send out motion pictures over the TV channel(s). Now it is also used to convert original film to video "prints."

Time Coding: The numerical synchronization of sound and film elements, encoded with matching numbers (frame to frame) to ensure synchronicity.

Transfer: To copy picture or sound being transmitted by one recorder onto another. Or, to make a tape copy from film.

FOR THE BEST IN PAPERBACKS, LOOK FOR THE

In every corner of the world, on every subject under the sun, Penguin represents quality and variety—the very best in publishing today.

For complete information about books available from Penguin—including Pelicans, Puffins, Peregrines, and Penguin Classics—and how to order them, write to us at the appropriate address below. Please note that for copyright reasons the selection of books varies from country to country.

In the United Kingdom: For a complete list of books available from Penguin in the U.K., please write to *Dept E.P., Penguin Books Ltd, Harmondsworth, Middlesex, UB7 0DA.*

In the United States: For a complete list of books available from Penguin in the U.S., please write to *Consumer Sales, Penguin USA, P.O. Box 999— Dept. 17109, Bergenfield, New Jersey 07621-0120.* Visa and MasterCard holders call 1-800-253-6476 to order all Penguin titles.

In Canada: For a complete list of books available from Penguin in Canada, please write to *Penguin Books Canada Ltd, 10 Alcorn Avenue, Suite 300, Toronto, Ontario, Canada M4V 3B2.*

In Australia: For a complete list of books available from Penguin in Australia, please write to the *Marketing Department, Penguin Books Ltd, P.O. Box 257, Ringwood, Victoria 3134.*

In New Zealand: For a complete list of books available from Penguin in New Zealand, please write to the *Marketing Department, Penguin Books (NZ) Ltd, Private Bag, Takapuna, Auckland 9.*

In India: For a complete list of books available from Penguin, please write to *Penguin Overseas Ltd, 706 Eros Apartments, 56 Nehru Place, New Delhi, 110019.*

In Holland: For a complete list of books available from Penguin in Holland, please write to *Penguin Books Nederland B.V., Postbus 195, NL-1380AD Weesp, Netherlands.*

In Germany: For a complete list of books available from Penguin, please write to *Penguin Books Ltd, Friedrichstrasse 10-12, D-6000 Frankfurt Main 1, Federal Republic of Germany.*

In Spain: For a complete list of books available from Penguin in Spain, please write to *Longman, Penguin España, Calle San Nicolas 15, E-28013 Madrid, Spain.*

In Japan: For a complete list of books available from Penguin in Japan, please write to *Longman Penguin Japan Co Ltd, Yamaguchi Building, 2-12-9 Kanda Jimbocho, Chiyoda-Ku, Tokyo 101, Japan.*